C000071153

1 MONTH OF
FREE
READING

at

www.ForgottenBooks.com

By purchasing this book you are eligible for one month membership to ForgottenBooks.com, giving you unlimited access to our entire collection of over 1,000,000 titles via our web site and mobile apps.

To claim your free month visit:

www.forgottenbooks.com/free918756

ISBN 978-0-265-97983-9
PIBN 10918756

PROBATE REPORTS ANNOTATED:

CONTAINING

RECENT CASES OF GENERAL VALUE DECIDED IN
THE COURTS OF THE SEVERAL STATES
ON POINTS OF PROBATE LAW.

WITH NOTES AND REFERENCES.

BY

GEORGE A. CLEMENT,

OF THE NEW YORK BAR.

AUTHOR OF CLEMENT'S DIGEST OF FIRE INSURANCE DECISIONS.

VOL. V.

NEW YORK:
BAKER, VOORHIS & COMPANY,
1 01.

TABLE OF CASES REPORTED

IN THIS VOLUME.

iii

VOL. V—B

TABLE OF CASES CITED

IN THE OPINIONS IN THIS VOLUME.

LIST OF EDITORIAL NOTES.

IN VOLUME I.

LIST OF EDITORIAL NOTES.

IN VOLUME II.

LIST OF EDITORIAL NOTES.

.

IN VOLUME III.

EDITORIAL NOTES, Vol. IV.

EDITORIAL NOTES, Vol. V.

PROBATE REPORTS ANNOTATED

Probate Reports Annotated.

Field *vs.* Peeples *et al.*

[Supreme Court of Illinois, June 19, 1899; 180 Illinois, 376; 54 N. E. Rep. 304.]

Wills— Construction— Life estates— Conveyance— Merger—Remainders—Limitations—Sale of infant's land—Jurisdiction—Collateral attack—Approval.

1. In a will creating a remainder in case a life tenant "dies without issue" the words "dies without issue" mean if the life tenant dies without having had issue.

2. A child of a devisee of a life estate with remainder to his children has a vested remainder, if he is *in esse* when testator dies, and, if other children are born afterwards, the estate will open for their benefit.

3. A life estate becomes merged in the fee, where the life tenant conveys to one having a vested remainder.

4. Infant remainder-men who are grantees of the life tenant may recover the land, against persons in adverse possession, within two years after becoming of age, under Hurd's Rev. St. 1897, p. 1048, though, before the conveyance to them, the statute of limitations would have barred the life tenant's right of recovery, as the statute does not transfer the title, but merely bars a right to recover the land.

5. On a collateral attack of a decree of the County Court ordering a sale of a minor's land, jurisdiction to make the decree will be presumed, where the record does not show a want of it.

6. A decree of the County Court, ordering a sale of a minor's land will be sustained when collaterally assailed, though the petition has been destroyed and the decree does not show that the land was to be sold for the minor's support or education or for investment in other land, and such facts were essential to give jurisdiction under the statute in force when the decree was made.

7. The approval by the court of a report of a sale of a minor's land, indorsed on the report, is valid, though the better practice would be to require an order of the court to be duly entered on the records of the court, approving the sale.

APPEAL from Circuit Court, Pulaski county.

Ejectment by Clarence M. Peeples and another against Curtis Field. Judgment for plaintiffs, and defendant appeals. Reversed.

James C. Courtney and *Boyd & Wall,* for appellant.

Lansden & Leek and *C. L. V. Mulkey,* for appellees.

CRAIG, J.—This was an action of ejectment brought by Clarence M. and Cornelia Peeples against Curtis Field to recover the N. W. ¼ of the S. W. ¼ of the S. W. ¼ of the S. W. ¼, and the S. E. ¼ of the S. E. ¼, of section 34, township 14, range 2, in Pulaski county. On a trial in the Circuit Court the issues were found in favor of the plaintiffs,—that the plaintiffs were seized in fee simple of the lands described in the declaration,—and judgment was entered on the finding. The defendant, Curtis Field, appealed.

It is first claimed that plaintiffs failed to show a fee-simple title to the premises and hence the judgment was erroneous. The parties claim from a common source, Orville Pool, who died testate June 30, 1871. On the trial plaintiffs read in evidence a certified copy of the will of said Orville Pool, the fifth clause of which is as follows: " Fifth. I hereby devise, will, and bequeath to my daughter, Ellen Poole Peeples, all the real estate of which I shall die seized in the counties of Pulaski, Johnson, and Alexander, in the state of Illinois, to have and to hold the same for and during her natural life, and at her death to descend to her children, and, in case she dies without issue, the said lands in the said counties of Pulaski, Johnson, and Alexander to descend to the said Marshall M. Pool and Augusta M. Pool Townsend and their heirs, equally, in fee simple." A deed was also introduced, dated February 1, 1893, from Ellen P. Peeples and husband to Clarence M. Peeples and Cornelia Peeples, purporting to convey the land in controversy and other lands. Plaintiffs also read in evidence a deposition of Ellen P. Peeples, in which she, among other things, testified as follows: Interrogatory fifth: " If you have any child or children, give the name or names thereof, and the date or dates of their birth, respectively. A. I have two children. Their names are Clarence M. Peeples and Cornelia Peeples. Clarence M. Peeples was born July 30, 1871, and Cornelia Peeples November 11, 1874." Interrogatory sixth: " If you have had any other child or children, give dates of birth and death thereof. A. I never had any other children." It will be observed that the last part of clause 5 of the will provides that, in case the life tenant dies without issue, the property shall descend to Marshall Pool and Augusta Townsend. The birth of a child to the life tenant, Ellen P. Peeples, settled any controversy that might arise in regard to the land ever passing as a contingent remainder to Marshall Pool and Augusta Townsend. The words, " in case she dies without issue," have been construed by this court to mean without having had issue,—not without surviving issue. (*Voris* v. *Sloan,* 68 Ill. 588; *Smith* v. *Kimbell,* 153 id. 368; 38 N. E. 1029.) No further attention will therefore be given to that clause in the will. It is, however, claimed that, under the fifth clause of the will, the fee of the lands therein devised would not pass to the children of Ellen P. Peeples until her death, and, as she was living when the action was brought, the plaintiffs could not recover. Clarence Peeples was *in esse* at the time of the death of the testator, and we are of opinion that the only construction that can be placed upon the fifth clause of the will, under the authorities, is that he took a vested remainder. In *Doe* v. *Provoost* (4 Johns. 61), where P. devised lands to his daughter C. during the term of her life, and upon her death unto all children C. shall have lawfully begotten at the time of her death, it was held that the four children of C. who were living at the time of the devise and at the death of the testator took a vested remainder in fee, and, in case there had been any children born afterwards. the estate would have opened for their benefit. In *Doe* v. *Considine* (6 Wall. 458), it was held that, if A. devises to B. for life, with remainder to his children, and B. marries and has a child, the remainder becomes a vested remainder in fee in the child as soon as the child is born, and, if the child dies in the lifetime of the parent, the vested estate in remainder descends to his heirs. See, also, *Doe* v. *Perryn* (3 Term R. 484). Here the remainder was limited to a class some of whom were *in esse,* and the rule in such cases, as we understand it, is that the fee vests in those who are *in esse*, subject to be opened and let in those who may afterwards be born during the continuance of the life estate. Under the rule indicated, upon the death of the testator Orville Pool, the fee went to Clarence Peeples, and when Cornelia Peeples was born the two children of the life tenant held as tenants in common. The fact that another child may be born to the life tenant and may come in and share with the two children of the life tenant who were in existence at the time the suit was brought, does not militate against the rule indicated. There is no controversy here with after-born children claiming a portion of the fee. The question is, in whom was the fee vested at the time the action was brought? If the fee was in Clarence and Cornelia Peeples, as we are satisfied it was, they, so far as the question under consideration is concerned, would be entitled to recover. It may be conceded that appellees could not have maintained an action of ejectment, if the life estate had remained in the life tenant; but, when she conveyed all her interest in the life estate to appellees, the life estate became merged in the fee and became extinct. (4 Kent Comm. 100.) There was, then, after the execution of the deed by the life tenant, nothing to prevent appellees from bringing their action of ejectment.

On the trial the appellant read in evidence a deed for the land in controversy from John M. Peeples, guardian of Clarence M. Peeples to Ezekiel Field. This deed was made on a sale of the land at public vendue, under a decree of the County Court of Gallatin county; also a deed from Field to Summers, a deed from Summers to Brooks, a deed from Brooks to Todd, and a deed from Todd to himself. The appellant also proved actual residence on the land, by himself and his predecessors in title, for more than seven years before the bringing of the action. This evidence was introduced for the purpose of claiming under the Limitation Act of 1835. Appellant also proved actual possession under color of title, together with payment of all taxes on the land for each successive year from 1883 to 1894, inclusive, as a compliance with the Limitation Act of 1839. It is claimed, as we understand the argument, that the evidence thus introduced is a bar to a recovery on the part of the life tenant, Ellen Pool Peeples, and that, as she was barred by the statute, appellant, by force of the statute, became the owner of the life estate possessed by her, and thus, being the owner of the life estate, appellant, regardless of other questions, was entitled to possession of the land, as against appellees, who held as remainder-men. In support of the position that where the owner of the paramount title is barred by the statute such title is transferred to the party holding under the limitation law, we are referred to *Jacobs* v. *Rice* (33 Ill. 370), and *Hale* v. *Gladfelder* (52 id. 91). As to the first case mentioned, it is said by the court, in substance, that, where a bar has been established under the statute, the effect is to transfer the title. The expression, however, was not necessary to a decision of the case, and may be regarded as obiter. The other case, as we understand it, holds a directly opposite view. Indeed, before and since the decision in *Jacobs* v. *Rice,* this court has expressly held that the operation of sections 6 and 7 of chapter 83 (Starr & C. Ann. St.), entitled "Limitations," is not to transfer the title of the former owner to the person claiming under those sections, but the effect merely is to bar or extinguish the former owner's right of recovery. Such is the doctrine of the following cases: *Newland* v. *Marsh* (19 Ill. 376); *Hinchman* v. *Whetstone* (23 id. 185); *McCagg* v. *Heacock* (42 id. 153); *Hale* v. *Gladfelder* (*supra*). The fact that the statute of limitations might have been successfully interposed as a defense, had the action been brought by Ellen Pool Peeples, has no special bearing on this case. Here appellees are claiming to recover as owners of the fee, and it is not claimed, as we understand the argument, that they are barred by the Statute of Limitations. Nor could such claim be successfully made, as the record shows that when the land was sold under decree by the guardian, and at the time possession was taken under that title, Clarence and Cornelia Peeples were minors, and that they became of age, respectively, on July 30, 1892, and November 11, 1892. They commenced this action in the Circuit Court on January 17, 1894. Having brought their action within two years after they became of age, they are therefore taken out of the operation of the Statute of Limitations by the express provision of the ninth section of the act. (Hurd's Rev. St. 1897, p. 1048.)

On the trial the appellant claimed that appellees were not entitled to recover, because the land had been sold by a guardian under a decree of court, and, for the purpose of establishing this defense, appellant introduced a decree of the County Court of Gallatin county, authorizing John M. Peeples, as the guardian of Clarence M. Peeples, to sell the land in question. A sale of the land was made under this decree, a report of the sale was presented to the court and was approved, and a deed made to the purchaser. The decree, report, and alleged approval of sale and deed were all put in evidence; but the petition upon which the decree was rendered, having been lost or destroyed during the high water in Shawnee-town, was not in evidence. Many technical objections are urged to the proceedings. It is claimed, in the absence of a petition, there is nothing to show that the court had jurisdiction of the subject-matter, and hence the decree and deed are void. In 1873, when the decree was rendered, the statute authorized County Courts to order the sale of real estate belonging to minors for their support and ed-ucation, or to invest the proceeds in other real estate, on the petition of the guardian, in the county where the ward resided, or if the ward did not reside in the state, on filing petition in the county where the real estate or some part of it was situated. The statute required the petition to set forth the condition of the estate and the facts and circumstances on which the petition was founded; that it should be signed by the guardian and verified by his affidavit, and be filed at least ten days before the commencement of the term of court at which application was made; that "notice of such ap-plication shall be given to all persons concerned, by publication in some newspaper published in the county where the application is made, at least once in each week for three successive weeks, or by setting up written or printed notices in three of the most public places in the county, at least three weeks before the session of the court at which such application shall be made. The ward shall be served with a copy of such notice at least ten days before the hearing of the application."

The decree rendered by the court was, in substance as follows: "State of Illinois, Gallatin county—ss.: At a County Court in and for said county judicially sitting to be holden at the Court House in the city of Shawneetown, Monday, the 21st day of April, 1873. Present, Hon. Milton Bartley, Judge; Joseph B. Boyer, Clerk; and Joel Cook, Sheriff. Court opened by proclamation by Sher-iff Cook. In the matter of the petition of John M. Peeples, guardian of Clarence M. Peeples. Petition to sell real estate. And now, on this 21st day of April, 1873, being the first day of the term

of said court, comes the said John M. Peeples, guardian, etc., and
it appearing to the court that due notice of this application has been
made and published according to the provision of the statute in that
behalf, and that the said Clarence M. Peeples, a ward of the said
guardian, has been personally served with said notice, by delivering
to him a true copy thereof more than ten days before the present
term of this court: It is therefore ordered by the court that Ed.
Youngblood, attorney and solicitor in chancery, be and is hereby
appointed guardian *ad litem* for said ward to inquire into and make
answer to said petition, and otherwise protect and guard the interest of said ward in the matter of the petition of John M. Peeples,
guardian, etc. And now, on this 21st day of April, it being the first
day of the present term of court, as aforesaid, comes again the said
petitioner, and it appearing that said guardian *ad litem* has filed his
answer to said petition, and the same having been examined and
approved by the court, and the said petition coming on to be heard
upon the proofs and evidence in this cause, and the court, after having duly considered the proof and evidence aforesaid, finds, therefore, that said petition, and the matters and things therein stated,
are true in substance and in fact, and that full and satisfactory proof
thereof has been made: It is therefore ordered, adjudged, and decreed that said petitioner proceed without delay, as guardian aforesaid, to sell lands in said petition mentioned and described, viz.:
The south half of section 34, township 14 S., range 2 east, and
north half of section 3, township 15 S., range 2 east, situated in the
county of Pulaski, state of Illinois; also the south half of section 2,
township 11 S., range 2 east, situated in the county of Johnson and
state of Illinois, in manner and upon the following terms: (Then
follow terms of sale, provision for notice, etc.)"

It is insisted, as the decree fails to show the existence of the
facts required by the statute to authorize a court to order the sale
of the minors' lands, the decree and sale are void.   There may be
errors in the proceeding to sell the minors' lands which might lead
to a reversal of the decree on a writ or error; but where the decree
is attacked collaterally, as is the case here, it cannot be defeated or
impeached for mere errors.   It is a rule of uniform application
that in relation to courts of general jurisdiction nothing is presumed to be out of their jurisdiction but that which specially appears to be so; but, on the contrary, nothing shall be intended to

be within the jurisdiction of an inferior court but that which is expressly alleged. This rule is limited to collateral proceedings, and, where the record of a judgment or decree is relied on collaterally, jurisdiction must be presumed in favor of a court of general jurisdiction, although it be not alleged or fails to appear in the record. (*Swearengen* v. *Gulick,* 67 Ill. 208.) In *Matthews* v. *Hoff* (113 Ill. 90), where the jurisdiction of a County Court was called in question collaterally, it was said (page 96) : " Every presumption will be indulged in favor of the jurisdiction of a court of general jurisdiction, and County Courts in this state are courts of general jurisdiction with respect to all matters coming within the provision of their jurisdiction as given by law." In *Osgood* v. *Blackmore* (59 Ill. 261), in discussing the question of jurisdiction, it was said (page 267) : " Where a court of superior general jurisdiction has proceeded to adjudicate and to decree in a matter before it, all reasonable intendments will be indulged in favor of its jurisdiction. * * * The presumption which the law indulges in favor of its jurisdiction can only be overcome, in a collateral proceeding, where the record itself shows there was no jurisdiction." See, also, *Harris* v. *Lester* (80 Ill. 307) ; *Spring* v. *Kane,* (86 id. 580) ; *Kenney* v. *Greer* (13 id. 432) ; *Peacock* v. *Bell* (1 Saund. 74). Under the rule announced in the cases cited, can the decree in question be held void? We think not. It appears from the face of the decree that a petition of John M. Peeples, guardian of Clarence M. Peeples, for leave to sell real estate, was presented to the court on the first day of the April term of court, 1873 ; that notice of the application, as required by law, was given ; that the ward was personally served with notice, as required by the statute ; that an answer to the petition was put in by the guardian *ad litem,* which was approved by the court ; that a hearing on the petition was had and evidence was introduced before the court ; that upon the hearing the court found the petition and matters and things therein stated to be true. Now, under the rule declared in the *Swearengen Case, supra,* that nothing shall be intended to be out of the jurisdiction of a Superior Court or court of general jurisdiction but that which specially appears to be so, the decree in question will have to be sustained. The record contains nothing whatever tending to show that the County Court in which the decree was rendered had no jurisdiction. Moreover, it would be a dangerous precedent to hold that a decree rendered twenty-five years ago, as was the case here, could be impeached in a collateral proceeding, because the petition upon which it was predicated had been lost or destroyed and could not be produced, and we are not inclined to establish a rule of that character.

One other question remains to be considered. It is contended that the report of sale was not approved. Where land belonging to a minor is sold under decree of court by a guardian, it is essential to the validity of the sale that the report of sale should be approved. Here the guardian made a report of sale, which was signed and sworn to by him, as required by the statute. On the back of the report of sale is the following: " Approved and recorded in Journal F. p. 429, August 27, 1879." On the margin of the report is the following indorsement by the court: " Now, on this day, comes John M. Peeples, guardian, by Silas Rhodes, attorney, and files his report of sale, which is now approved and filed and ordered spread of record, to wit." The report of sale is marked: " Filed in the County Court, this 22d day of August, A. D. 1879. Jo B. Byers, Clerk." On the 17th day of January, 1880, the following order appears of record: " Amended report of sale filed by leave of the court." The amended report of sale is like the original, except that it contains a tract of land not embraced in the original report. In *Young* v. *Lorain* (11 Ill. 624), where the approval was indorsed on the report, as here, it was held that the order made on the return was a substantial and sufficient confirmation. So in *Smith* v. *Race* (27 Ill. 387), where the confirmation or approval of the sale was indorsed on the report, it was sustained, although the question is not discussed. In a case of this character, while we think the better practice would be to require an order of court entered upon its records approving the report of sale, yet we are not prepared to hold that the approval of the report in question is invalid. There was here a substantial compliance with the law, and that is all that can be required. From what has been said it follows that Clarence M. Peeples was not entitled to recover. As to the other plaintiff, Cornelia Peeples, her interest in the land was not affected by the sale under the decree. The judgment of the Circuit Court will be reversed, and the cause will be remanded.

Reversed and remanded.

Subsequently, upon considering this case on rehearing, the following additional opinion was filed:

PER CURIAM.—This rehearing was asked and allowed on the single ground that the right of possession in the life tenant, Ellen Pool Peeples, had become vested in appellant by the running of the statute of limitations, and consequently appellees could not maintain ejectment against him until after her death. The right of possession, under color of title, to the life estate, is not involved in the case. Plaintiffs below, by their declaration, claimed the premises in fee, and the defendant, both by virtue of the guardian's sale and deed and possession under that deed as claim and color of title and payment of taxes for more than seven years, also claimed the title in fee simple. He does not claim color of title to the life estate, and counsel are therefore mistaken in the assertion that the opinion heretofore filed overruled cases cited, to the effect that when the bar of the statute is complete the holder of the title, by limitation, may assert it against all others; that his right of possession is as perfect as though he were invested with a paramount title; and that his title is as available for attack as defense. The petition and argument in support of it assume a state of case not shown by this record. If appellant had set up and shown color of title to the life estate, and relied upon that title under the Statute of Limitations, then the position here contended for would have been tenable. In that case the remainder-men would undoubtedly have been postponed in their right of action until after the death of the life tenant; but, under the issues in this case, they were bound to bring their action within the time limited by the statute after they became of age, and if they had delayed their action until the death of their mother, and that event had occurred more than two years after they became of age, they would have been barred.

We held in *Nelson* v. *Davidson* (160 Ill. 254; 43 N. E. 361), following *Enos* v. *Buckley* (94 Ill. 458), that possession for the statutory period, under claim of title, to an estate in fee, sufficient to constitute color of title, with payment of taxes for the same period, would bar the estate in remainder, notwithstanding the existence of the outstanding life estate, where the remainder-man claiming title was under no disability. The outstanding estate for life in their mother formed no impediment to the payment of taxes any time after the plaintiffs below reached their majority. It was said in the *Enos Case* (id. 464): " The taxes should have been kept paid, not on any one's particular interest in the land, but on the whole land. As between the owner of the life estate and the reversioner, it is undoubtedly the duty of the former to pay the taxes. But the statute requires the payment of the taxes on the entire interest in the land, no matter how it may be divided and owned; and, if they be not kept paid, the whole estate in the land may become barred, as against the owners, under the statute." It will scarcely be claimed that the position of appellant can be maintained consistently with the foregoing decisions; that is to say, it cannot be held that plaintiffs below were bound to bring their action within two years after they became of age, and, at the same time, that they had no right to do so until after the death of the life tenant. Upon a reconsideration of the case, we are satisfied that the conclusion reached in the above opinion is fully sustained by the decisions of this court, and it will accordingly be readopted.

KAENDERS *et al. vs.* MONTAGUE *et al.*

[Supreme Court of Illinois, June 19, 1899; 180 Illinois, 300; 54 N. E. Rep. 321.]

WILLS—MENTAL CAPACITY—REASONABLENESS OF PROVISIONS—
DECLARATIONS OF TESTATOR.

1. The reasonableness of the provisions of a will may be considered by the jury only as a circumstance tending to show unsoundness of mind or undue influence, in connection with all the other facts and circumstances in the case.
2. Prior declarations and statements of a testator, whether oral or contained in previous wills, are admissible, where in harmony with the provisions of the last will, to rebut the claim of undue influence.

APPEAL from Circuit Court, Madison county.

Bill in equity by Mary Montague and another against Peter Kaenders and others. From a decree for complainants, defendants appeal.

Reversed.

This is·a bill filed by the appellees, Mary Montague and Ella Cody, against the appellants, to set aside the will of Annie Squire, deceased.   Answers were filed to the bill by the executors, Kaenders and McNulty, who were also devisees under the will, and by Adelaide F. Beattie, another devisee under the will.   The will sought to be set aside bore date September 19, 1896.   The question of the validity of the will was submitted to the jury, who returned a verdict finding that the writing produced, executed on September 19, 1896, purporting to be the will of Annie Squire, was not her will.   Motion for new trial was overruled, and a decree was entered by the Circuit Court in accordance with the verdict, and adjudging the costs of the suit against the defendants.   The present appeal is prosecuted from the decree so entered.

Annie Squire, who lived at Venice, in Madison county, died on October 3, 1896, leaving the will aforesaid, dated September 19, 1896, and leaving no husband, and no child or descendant of a child, surviving her, but leaving, as her only heirs at law, four nieces, children of a deceased brother and of two deceased sisters; said nieces being the appellees, Mary Montague, Ella Cody, Annie Montague, and Julia Slighton.   The will is as follows: " In the name of God, Amen: I, Annie Squire, of Venice, Madison county, Illinois, being of sound and disposing mind and memory, do make, publish, and declare this my last will and testament; hereby revoking and making void all former wills by me at any time heretofore made.   First. I desire all my just debts and funeral expenses to be paid as soon after my death as possible.   Second.   I leave to George F. McNulty, as trustee, five hundred dollars ($500), to be invested in United States bonds or in St. Louis city bonds, and the interest to be annually expended to keep in good order and repair the lot my husband, children, and myself will be interred in; provided, however, if the Calvary Cemetery Association shall agree to keep said lot in repair forever, said trustee may, at his option, give said five hundred dollars ($500) to said cemetery association or its trustees.   Third.   In case I have not purchased·another lot in said Calvary Cemetery before my death, and removed the bodies of my husband and children there, then it is my will that my executors hereinafter named purchase a lot in said cemetery costing not more than two thousand dollars ($2,000) and remove the bodies of my husband and children there, and see that I am buried there. Fourth. I give to the Catholic priest who is the pastor of St. Mark's Catholic church at Venice, Illinois, at the time of my death, the sum of eleven hundred dollars; he to hold the same in trust, and apply it for the following purposes, namely: One hundred dollars ($100) is to be used in having masses said for the repose of my soul; one thousand dollars is to be used for the Roman Catholic parish school in the parish of St. Mark's, at Venice, Madison county, state of Illinois. Fifth. I have made a contract with George H. Norman to make for me a marble monument, for which he is to be paid, when it is finished and erected in the cemetery, the sum of eight hundred and seventy-nine dollars ($879). It is my will that said monument be placed in the cemetery as soon as my executors, hereinafter named, shall have purchased another lot in Calvary Cemetery, and have removed to it the bodies of my husband and children. Sixth. I give to my nieces, Julia Slighton, Ella Cody, Mary Montague, and Annie Montague, the sum of one dollar each. It is my will that none of my relatives or my husband's relatives shall have or take any of my property, except the sum of one dollar, as above given to each of my said nieces. Seventh. I give to Adelaide Frances Beattie, of St. Louis, Missouri, who is my dearest and kindest friend, all my clothing, and such of my household furniture and effects as she may desire. Eighth. I give to George F. McNulty the sum of one thousand dollars. Ninth. After the payment of the above legacies and bequests, which, if the personal property I leave is not sufficient to pay them, they are to be a charge upon my real estate until paid, then the rest and residue of my property, of whatsoever name or nature, and wheresoever situated, I devise and bequeath to my dearest friend, Adelaide Frances Beattie, of St. Louis, state of Missouri, she to own the same absolutely. My friend, the said Adelaide Frances Beattie, has during all her life been a kind, dear friend to me, and since the death of my husband and daughter Mary she has been very kind, in every way, to me, and during my illness she has been constant in her kindness and attention to me; and to reward her as well as I can is the reason I make the said Adelaide Frances Beattie my residuary legatee in this my last will and testament. Tenth. I constitute and appoint Rev. Peter Kaenders, of Venice, Madison county, Illinois, and George F. McNulty, executors of this my last will and testament, and I do not wish them to give any bond or security as such executors. I give to my said executors full power to sell and convey any real or personal property I may own at my death. In witness whereof, I have hereunto set my hand and seal this 19th day of September, A. D. 1896. Annie Squire. (Seal.)"

Hadley & Burton, for appellants.

John G. Irwin and *J. P. Vastine,* for appellees.

MAGRUDER, J. (after stating the facts).—It is sought to set aside the will attacked by the bill in this case upon the ground of want of testamentary capacity in the testatrix, and upon the ground of the exercise of undue influence over her. It is assigned as error by the counsel for the appellants that the verdict of the jury is not sustained by the evidence. At the close of all the testimony the defendants below asked the court to instruct the jury "that under the evidence in this case, they must find that the instrument in writing dated September 19, 1896, purporting to be the last will and testament of Annie Squire, is the last will and testament of Annie Squire." This instruction was refused, and it is claimed that its refusal by the court below was error. The case is exceedingly close upon the facts. The three subscribing witnesses to the execution of the will, and seven other witnesses acquainted with the deceased, swear that she was of sound mind and memory at the time of the execution of the will. Indeed, the proof shows that when the testatrix made her will she was of sufficiently sound mind and memory to remember the amount and nature of her property, the various relatives and friends to whom she might desire to distribute the same by will, and to enable her to make an intelligent disposition of her estate among them at the time the will was signed. At that time, although she was feeble in body and mind from sickness, she had sufficient capacity to understand the particular business in which she was then engaged. It is claimed, however, that while she was at that time capable of transacting the ordinary business affairs of life, such as settling accounts and collecting and paying out money, etc., yet that she was subject to a morbid or insane delusion upon subjects connected with the disposition of her property by will, and as to the natural objects of her bounty. It is contended that this insane delusion was in reference to her nieces and the relatives of her husband. By the sixth clause of her will she gives to her four nieces the sum of one dollar each, and then says: " It is my will that none of my relatives or my husband's relatives shall have or take any of my property, except the sum of one dollar as above given to each of my said nieces." The will gave all her property away from her relatives and from the relatives of her husband. This ignoring of such relatives by her will is attributed by the appellees to the existence of the insane delusion above referred to. It has been said by this court " that there may be insanity without the general business capacity of the individual being affected thereby." (*Society* v. *Price,* 115 Ill. 623; 5 N. E. 126). Where there is insane delusion in regard to those who are the objects of the testator's bounty, and in regard to his duty or moral obligation to make a will in favor of a particular individual, corporation, or society, and a will is made as the result of that delusion, it cannot be sustained. (*Society* v. *Price, supra.*) The evidence to establish the insane delusion contended for is slight in the present case, although it may be sufficient to have justified the trial court in submitting the question to the jury. It is true that Mrs. Squire made bequests in her will to her lawyer, to her priest, and to her intimate friend who was with her in her last sickness. But it is well settled that the owner of property, who has capacity to attend to his ordinary business, has the lawful right to dispose of such property, either by deed or by will, as he may choose; and the reasonableness or justice or propriety of the will are not questions for the jury to pass upon, although the unreasonableness of a testamentary disposition of property may be considered as a mere circumstance tending to show unsoundness of mind or undue influence, in connection with all the other facts and circumstances proven in the case. (*Taylor* v. *Pegram,* 151 Ill. 106; 37 N. E. 837; *Nicewander* v. *Nicewander,* 151 Ill. 156; 37 N. E. 698.)

In view of the fact that the evidence in this case upon the questions of unsoundness of mind and of the exercise of undue influence is close, it was important that the jury should be correctly instructed. The eleventh instruction given by the court for the contestants below, who are the appellees here, is as follows: " The court further instructs the jury that the declarations and statements of Annie Squire were admitted in evidence for the purpose of illustrating and showing her mental condition, and are not to be considered as having any legitimate bearing upon any question involved in the case, except as to her soundness or unsoundness of mind and memory at the time of making the instrument which purports to be her will." We regard this instruction as erroneous, under the facts developed by the testimony in the case. It is broad enough to include two wills which were made by Mrs. Squire before the execution of her last will, dated September 19, 1896. It is also broad enough to include certain declarations and statements made by her prior to the execution of her last will, which were in conformity with the provisions of the will itself. She made a will on July 25, 1896, and another on August 13, 1896. These wills were canceled and supplanted by the will of September 19, 1896, but they were both introduced in evidence without objection. As they had been canceled, they amounted to mere declarations of the testatrix as to her intentions at the respective times of their execution in regard to the disposition of her property. Several of the provisions contained in these prior wills were the same as provisions contained in the will finally executed by her. These prior wills it was proper for the jury to consider, inasmuch as they furnished some evidence to rebut the idea of undue influence having been exercised to procure the execution of the last will. When a testator, being of sound mind and free from the control of any undue influence, disposes of his property by a prior will, and the disposition which he thereby makes of his property approximates very nearly to the provisions of the will which is contested, such circumstance tends to rebut the idea that undue influence has been exercised to procure the execution of the last will. (*Roe* v. *Taylor*, 45 Ill. 485; *Taylor* v. *Pegram*, 151 id. 106; 37 N. E. 837.) We have also held that, where a will is charged to have been executed through undue influence, the declarations of the testator made before its execution are admissible by way of rebuttal to show his intention as to the disposition of his property, upon the ground that a will made in conformity with such declarations is more likely to have been executed without undue influence than if its terms are contrary to such declarations. (*Harp* v. *Parr*, 168 Ill. 459; 48 N. E. 113; *Goodbar* v. *Lidikey*, 136 Ind. 1; 35 N. E. 691). The rule, as above stated, in regard to prior declarations which are in harmony with the provisions of a contested will, in no way conflicts with the well-settled rule that statements made by the testator either before or after the execution of a contested will, which are in conflict with the provisions thereof, do not invalidate or modify such will in any manner. Parties making wills cannot invalidate them by their own parol declarations made previously or subsequently. (*Taylor* v. *Pegram, supra; Dickie* v. *Carter,* 42 Ill. 376.) The eleventh instruction given by the court evidently had the effect of excluding from the consideration of the jury all the declarations of the testatrix in harmony with the provisions of her last will which were made by her prior to the execution thereof, whether such declarations were made orally or were embodied in the previous wills. As the declarations thus excluded had a tendency to rebut the proof of the contestants, which tended to show the exercise of undue influence in the making of the last will, the giving of the eleventh instruction was unfair to the appellants. For the error above indicated, the decree of the Circuit Court is reversed, and the cause is remanded to that court for further proceedings in accordance with the views herein expressed.

Reversed and remanded.

Subsequently, upon considering this case on rehearing, the following additional opinion was filed:

PER CURIAM.—Since granting the rehearing in this cause, we have given it further consideration, and have reached the same conclusion announced in the opinion heretofore filed. The contention that *Harp* v. *Parr* (168 Ill. 459; 48 N. E. 113), cited in support of the holding that the eleventh instruction was erroneous, is in conflict with former decisions of this court, ignores a clear distinction pointed out in the *Harp Case* and in the above opinion. The authorities are not harmonious on the subject, but the general rule recognized by this court is that prior declarations of a testator are not admissible to prove undue influence. That rule, however, is applicable only in cases where the declarations and statements are offered for the purpose of varying or controlling the operation of the contested will, and not to those in which the will is in harmony with the declared intentions of the testator. The reason for the distinction is pointed out in the above opinion and the cases there cited. It is also clearly stated in *Hill* v. *Bahrns,* (158 Ill. 314; 41 N. E. 912), where we said (page 318, 158 Ill.

and page 913, 41 N. E.) : "And it is held that a prior will, and
statements and declarations of the testator, made at a time when his
mental capacity was undisputed, as to the manner in which he had
disposed of his property by a prior will which has been destroyed,
are admissible in evidence, where it appears that such disposition
of his property by such prior will is approximately the same as
that made by the contested will, as tending to rebut the idea of undue influence." The cases cited by counsel for appellees in support
of their petition are all cases in which the declarations and statements were sought to be introduced to vary the terms of the will
being contested, and the general rule above indicated was strictly
applicable. Keeping in mind the proper distinction between the
two classes of cases, there is no conflict or want of harmony in our
decisions. The foregoing opinion will be readopted, and the decree below reversed, and the cause remanded, as there directed.

Reversed and remanded.

Note.—DECLARATIONS OF TESTATOR AS EVIDENCE.

(a) Revocation.
(b) Undue influence.
(c) Mental capacity.
(d) Issue of execution.
(e) Latent ambiguity in will.
(f) Issue of fraud or duress.
(g) Lost or missing will.
(h) Illustrative cases—Admitting evidence.
(i) Illustrative cases—Excluding evidence.

(a) **Revocation.**—Where the statute clearly provides a method of revocation by destruction or by a subsequent testamentary writing, a declaration by the testator to the effect that he had revoked a will, in any one of
the modes prescribed is not receivable where its sole purpose is to prove
that fact. But the general rule of evidence that oral statements are competent when the mental state of the person who utters them is material,
should not be lost sight of. If, therefore, the testator is proved to have
performed any act which would have constituted a revocation of the will
if it was accompanied by an intention to revoke, his statements accompanying that act are admissible as part of the *res gestæ* to show his intention to revoke, or the absence of such intention. (1 Underhill, Wills,
§ 234 [ed. 1900] ; and see 1 Greenleaf Evid. 162e [ed. 1899].)

Upon an issue of revocation only admissible when they accompany the
alleged act of revocation. (Waterman v. Whitney, 11 N. Y. 157; Will of

Ladd, 60 Wis. 187; 18 N. W. Rep. 734; and see Clark v. Smith, 34 Barb. 140; Williams v. Williams, 142 Mass. 515; 8 N. E. Rep. 424; Eighmy v. The People, 79 N. Y. 547, 558.)

Admissible on issue as to revocation or cancellation. (Boyle v. Boyle, 158 Ill. 229; 42 N. E. Rep. 140; Collagan v. Burns, 57 Me. 449; Law v. Law, 83 Ala. 432; 3 So. Rep. 752.)

Not admissible. (Hoitt v. Hoitt, 63 N. H. 475; 3 Atl. Rep. 604; Kirkpatrick v. Jenkins, 96 Tenn. 85; 33 S. W. Rep. 819; Atkinson v. Morris, L. R. [1897] P. D. 40.)

But where statute prescribes requisites of a revocation, there must be evidence of act required before declarations of deceased admissible as to intention. (Gay v. Gay, 60 Iowa, 415; 14 N. W. Rep. 238; and see Hargroves v. Redd, 43 Ga. 143.)

Admitted to effect "that he was leaving a will" for purpose of showing a lost will not revoked. (Re Johnson's Will, 40 Conn. 587.)

And so presumption of a revocation is rebutted by evidence of deceased declarations. (Re Steinke's Will, 95 Wis. 121.)

In Tucker v. Whitehead (59 Miss. 594), will was found among papers of deceased perfect with exception that the name had been torn from it. Upon an issue of *devisavit vel non*, there being doubt whether the testator or a spoliator mutilated the will, declarations of the deceased relative to the fact of his having made a will and of his affection, testamentary intentions and desires, and of what he had done, were held admissible. These declarations extended from date of will to within four days of testator's death, a period of eighteen months.

This case is interesting as commenting on difference of opinion and in reviewing the authorities.

Upon an issue of revocation as to *intention* of testator in omission to provide for a child in a will, under a state statute, evidence of declarations of testator is admissible, on the question of such intention created by the statute. (Coulam v. Doull, 133 U. S. 216; 10 Sup. Ct. Rep. 253; and see 1 Underhill on Wills, § 243 [ed. 1900], wherein the author comments on the decisions as being "hopelessly at variance." The statutes vary in the different states. See in support of above, Whittemore v. Russell, 80 Me. 297; 14 Atl. Rep. 197; Miller v. Phillips, 9 R. I. 141; Buckley v. Girard, 123 Mass. 8, and compare where extrinsic evidence not admissible, under different statutes, Re Stevens, 83 Cal. 322; 23 Pac. Rep. 379; Thomas v. Black, 113 Mo. 66; 20 S. W. Rep. 657; Bresee v. Stiles, 22 Wis. 120; Rhodes v. Weldy, 46 Ohio St. 234; 20 N. E. Rep. 461; Lurie v. Radnitzer, 166 Ill. 609; 46 N. E. Rep. 1116.)

(b) **Undue influence.**—Schouler says: " In short, a testator's declarations, whether made before or after the execution of the will, aside from the time of execution itself, are admissible chiefly to show his mental condition, or the real state of his affections; and they are received rather as his own external manifestations than as evidence of the truth or untruth of facts relative to the exertion of undue influence upon him; they may corroborate but the issue calls for its own proof from the living; and the more remote such declarations from the time will was executed, the less their value. There should be independent testimony indicating undue influence before the decedent's declarations are considered, and then they are chiefly pertinent to show a susceptible condition of mind." (Schouler Wills, § 243 [ed. 1900]. And see to same effect, 1 Underhill on Wills, § 126 [ed. 1900]; and see 1 Greenleaf Evid. § 162e [ed. 1899]; Bush v. Bush, 87 Mo. 480; Herster v. Herster, 122 Pa. St. 239; 16 Atl. Rep. 342.)

Underhill in his recent work says: "There must be some evidence other than the declarations of the testator, for it is settled that his declarations are not admissible as direct evidence of undue influence, or to show that the will was procured thereby. Thus, for example, it cannot be proved as *direct evidence of coercion* that the testator after he executed his will, stated that it had been procured by fraud, force or coercion, that the instrument was not his will voluntarily framed or that in some particular respect it did not contain his intention." (1 Underhill on Wills, § 161 [ed. 1900]; and see 1 Greenleaf Evid. § 162e [ed. 1899].)

Admissible on issue of undue influence. (Bever v. Spangler, 93 Iowa, 579; Re Langford, 108 Cal. 609; 41 Pac. Rep. 701; Hill v. Bahns, 158 Ill. 314, 319; 41 N. E. Rep. 912; Estate of Lefevre, 102 Mich. 569; 61 N. W. Rep. 3; Taylor v. Pegram, 151 Ill. 107; 37 N. E. Rep. 837; Roberts v. Trawick, 17 Ala. 55; May v. Bradley, 127 Mass. 414.)

Not as evidence of the fact but as tending to show state of testator's mind. (Herster v. Herster, 122 Pa. St. 239; 16 Atl. Rep. 342; McConnell v. Wildes, 153 Mass. 487; 26 N. E. Rep. 1114; Kirkpatrick v. Jenkins, 96 Tenn. 85; 33 S. W. Rep. 819; Marx v. McGlynn, 4 Redf. 455; Waterman v. Whitney, 11 N. Y. 157; Cudney v. Cudney, 68 id. 148; Coghill v. Kennedy, 119 Ala. 641; 24 So. Rep. 459.)

Not admissible to prove undue influence. (Middleditch v. Williams, 45 N. J. Eq. 727; Bush v. Bush, 87 Mo. 480; Doherty v. Gilmore, 136 id. 414; 37 S. W. Rep. 1127; Conway v. Vizzard, 122 Ind. 266, 268; 23 N. E. Rep. 771; Gordon v. Burris, 141 Mo. 602; 43 S. W. Rep. 642.)

May be too remote to establish mental incapacity, but not so upon an issue of undue influence. (Taylor v. Pegram, 151 Ill. 107; 37 N. E. Rep. 837.)

In Ormsby v. Webb (134 U. S. 47; 10 Sup. Ct. Rep. 478), the declarations of deceased held not admissible on issue of undue influence related to the manner in which decedent had acquired his property. The court said the evidence was wholly immaterial. (P. 65.)

As to declarations of executor bearing on an issue of undue influence, see Re Yorke's Estate (185 Pa. St. 61; 39 Atl. Rep. 1119).

(c) **Mental capacity.**—Upon the question of mental capacity to make a will, declarations of testator made at or about the time of its execution, and his conduct are admissible as part of the *res gestæ*. But made long after the will was executed for instance two years, are too remote to be admissible. (Schouler on Wills, § 193 [ed. 1900]; and to same effect, 1 Underhill on Wills, § 106 [ed. 1900]; and see 1 Greenleaf Evid. § 162e [ed. 1899].)

Admissible on issue of mental capacity or condition of mind. (Boylan v. Meeker, 28 N. J. L. 274; Colvin v. Worford, 20 Md. 358; Middleditch v. Williams, 45 N. J. Eq. 727; 17 Atl. Rep. 826; Re Langford, 108 Cal. 609; 41 Pac. Rep. 701; Hill v. Bahrns, 158 Ill. 315, 318; 41 N. E. Rep. 912; Estate of Lefevre, 102 Mich. 569; 61 N. W. Rep. 3; Taylor v. Pegram, 151 Ill. 107; 37 N. E. Rep. 837; Conway v. Vizzard, 122 Ind. 266; 23 N. E. Rep. 771; Re Burns' Will, 121 N. C. 336; 28 S. E. Rep. 519; Manatt v. Scott, 106 Iowa, 203; 76 N. W. Rep. 717; Waterman v. Whitney, 11 N. Y. 157; May v. Bradlee, 127 Mass. 414.)

Not admissible when made subsequently to execution of will, when of sound mind, to show mental condition when will was executed. (Crocker v. Chase, 57 Vt. 413.)

Upon an issue of mental capacity and undue influence declarations of deceased, *thirteen* years prior to making of the will as to his intention, *held* not too remote, in absence of other evidence. The remoteness affected the weight and not the admissibility of the testimony. (Estate of Lefevre, 102 Mich. 568; 61 N. W. Rep. 3.)

" If the judge can see that the evidence offered cannot justly reflect any light upon the mental condition of the testator at the time of making the will, he has an undoubted right to exclude it." SELDEN, J. (Waterman v. Whitney, 11 N. Y. 157.)

(d) **Issue of execution.**—The declarations of a testator before or after making a will, are inadmissible on the issue of its execution. And evidence of one's statement of his intentions made long before making his will, or under remote circumstances, is properly excluded. (Schouler Wills, § 317a [ed. 1900]; and see 1 Greenleaf Evid. § 162e [ed. 1899].)

Not admissible on an issue as to execution of the will. (Kennedy v. Uphow, 64 Tex. 411; Walton v. Kendrick, 122 Mo. 504; 27 S. W. Rep. 872; Atkinson v. Morris, L. R. [1897] P. D. 40; Re Ripley, 1 Sw. & T. 68.)

Declarations after making of will not competent to show that testator never made will in question. (Boylan v. Meeker, 28 N. J. L. 274.)

(e) **Latent ambiguity in will.**—Admissible in case of latent ambiguity as to thing or object. (Morgan v. Burrows, 45 Wis. 211; Cotton v. Southwick, 66 Me. 360.)

As bearing on intention not expressed in will not admissible, unless language of the bequest is equally applicable to two persons or two things. (Charter v. Charter, L. R. 7 H. L. 364.) And then such evidence is competent for purpose of identifying legatee. (Matter of Wheeler, 32 App. Div. 183, aff'd on opinion below, 161 N. Y. 652.)

Testimony of scrivener as to declarations of testator not admissible to explain conflicting provisions in will. (Lewis v. Douglass, 14 R. I. 604.)

Declarations of testator may be admissible in evidence of facts upon which the will is to operate, as would be any other competent testimony to the same effect, and to fit the words of the will to their appropriate and intended objects. But no evidence of the kind will be heard to show an intent modified and different from that expressed in the will. (Thomas v.

Lines, 83 N. C. 191; and see note on "Extrinsic Evidence as applied to Wills," 4 Prob. Rep. Ann. 467.)

(f) **Issue of fraud or duress.**—Execution of will being established, not admissible on an issue of fraud, duress or forgery, or to disprove the execution; but if made at time instrument was executed may be admissible as part of the *res gestæ*. (Boylan v. Meeker, 28 N. J. L. 274.)

Where issue is on fraud, duress or imposition, not drawing in question testator's mental capacity—not admissible. (Waterman v. Whitney, 11 N. Y. 157; Gordan's Case, 50 N. J. Eq. 397; 26 Atl. Rep. 268.)

(g) **Lost or missing will.**—As to lost or missing will, the cases English and American are in irreconcilable contradiction. It is admitted by all cases that where the will is proved to have been executed, and where it was last seen in the possession of the testator, but cannot be found at his death, or is found mutilated, his declarations accompanying an act of destruction or cancellation, are admissible to show with what intent the act was done. But his declarations to the effect that he has or has not made a will uttered subsequently to the act of execution or destruction, stand on a different footing. Statutory requirements as to execution applied to lost or destroyed wills as well as to those which are produced. Hence, ordinarily the *fact of the execution* of a will which is lost, cannot be proved by showing that the testator subsequent to the date it is alleged to have been executed, asserted that he had made such will. If valid execution is otherwise shown and the will was last seen in the possession of the testator, his declarations tending to show that he has or has not destroyed it, or which show it was in existence at his death, are received to strengthen or rebut the presumption of revocation which arises from its disappearance. (1 Underhill, §§ 274, 277; and see 1 Greenleaf Evid. § 162e [ed. 1899].)

In proceeding to establish and prove lost or destroyed will, where the will is proved to have been duly executed and cannot be found after death, declarations of deceased may be competent as bearing upon question of intent. (Matter of Marsh, 45 Hun, 107.)

But must accompany an act of the testator so as to characterize it and make them a part of the *res gestæ*. (Matter of Kennedy, 53 App. Div. 105; 65 N. Y. Supp. 879.)

There was an able dissenting opinion. While this is a recent case subject to appeal, both opinions are exceptionally valuable as reviewing the authorities, both English and American, and pointing out conflict in the cases.

(h) **Illustrative cases—Admitting evidence.**—Admissible to establish meaning and application of the word "indebtedness" in a will. (Scott v. Neeves, 77 Wis. 305; 45 N. W. Rep. 421.)

Admissible for purpose of showing intent with which testator's act was done in canceling a will as bearing on revival of an earlier will. (Pickens v. Davis, 134 Mass. 252.)

Admissible on issue as to contents of a lost will, and of revocation, as bearing on right of a contestant of another will to maintain action. (McDonald v. McDonald, 142 Ind. 56; 41 N. E. Rep. 336.)

When contemporaneous with making of the will, admissible on an accounting by the executor to show testator's intent upon an issue as to how or from ,what source they should receive payment for services. (Matter of Thompson, 5 Dem. 117; and see Daggett v. Simonds, 175 Mass. 340; 53 N. E. Rep. 907.)

To rebut evidence bearing on condition of testator's mind. (Re Barney's Will, 71 Vt. 217; 44 Atl. Rep. 75.)

Admissibility of declarations of deceased as against interest. See McDonald v. Wesendonck (30 Misc. 601; 62 N. Y. Supp. 764).

(i) **Illustrative cases—Excluding evidence.**—Not admissible to show mistake in a will. (Pocock v. Redinger, 108 Ind. 573; 9 N. E. Rep. 473.)

Declarations of testator not admissible to control language of a devise. (Turner v. Hallowell Savings Inst., 76 Me. 527.)

Not admissible to contradict or explain intention expressed in will. (Williams v. Freeman, 83 N. Y. 562.)

Not admissible to show intention to charge legacies upon land. (Massaker v. Massaker, 13 N. J. Eq. 264.)

Not admissible to show intention to execute a power. (Hogle v. Hogle, 49 Hun, 313; 2 N. Y. Supp. 172; White v. Hicks, 33 N. Y. 383.)

In an action of ejectment, title depending on will, instructions by testator to person who drew the will not admissible. (Choppel v. Avery, 6 Conn. 31.)

A valid will duly executed cannot be made invalid by testator's parol declarations made previously or subsequently. (Dickie v. Carter, 42 Ill. 376.)

In action for construction of a will, evidence of declarations of testator as to wishes and intentions is not admissible. (Re Denfield, 156 Mass. 265; 30 N. E. Rep. 1018.)

In action by heir to recover on ground that will was inoperative as a devise, declarations of testator as to intent not admissible. (Heidenheimer v. Bauman, 84 Tex. 174; 19 S. W. Rep. 382.)

In action against estate to recover for services, declarations of testator to person who drew the will, that a legacy therein was intended as payment —not admissible. (Reynolds v. Robinson, 82 N. Y. 103.)

Taft *vs.* Stow.

[Supreme Judicial Court of Massachusetts, July 11, 1899; 174 Mass. 171; 54 N. E. Rep. 506.]

Trusts—Accounting—Remedy at law—Money received— Executors—Limitation of actions—Costs—Executions.

1. Where money is received to be invested and held in trust, and after investment the trustee withdraws the money without the beneficiary's knowledge, and mingles it with his own funds, an accounting is necessary to enforce the beneficiary's rights, and, since a trust is involved, it can be obtained only in equity.

2. The beneficiary cannot sue at law as for money had and received, nor has he any remedy at law that is plain and adequate. .

3. Where a demurrer to a declaration is sustained because the remedy is in equity, the action is defeated by a defect of form, within Pub. St. c. 136, § 12, providing that, if an action commenced against an executor or administrator before the expiration of two years from the time of his giving bond be defeated by a defect in the form of the writ or a mistake in the form of the proceeding, plaintiff may commence a new action for the same cause within one year thereafter.

4. On a bill by a beneficiary against the executor of a trustee for an accounting, the beneficiary is entitled to an execution as at common law against the estate of the trustee in the hands of the executor for the principal sum found due, and another execution for costs against the executor personally.

REPORT from Superior Court, Suffolk county, ALBERT MASON, Judge.

Bill in equity by Ellen A. Taft against Abner M. Stow. From a decision overruling a demurrer to the bill, and from a final decree in favor of complainant, defendant appealed. Submitted on report. Decree modified and affirmed. .

The bill of complaint was as follows:

" (1) On or about March 31, A. D. 1875, the plaintiff paid over to one Lucinda E. Phillips the sum of $1,000 in bank bills the same with accumulating interest thereon to be held in trust by said Lucinda for the benefit of said plaintiff during the lifetime of said Lucinda, and the said Lucinda so received the same and agreed to hold said sum with its accumulations, in trust as above set forth;

(2) that the said Lucinda, on January 27, 1894, died, leaving a will and a large estate, which will was duly proved and allowed in the Probate Court of said county; (3) That the defendant was duly appointed executor under said will; (4) that said Lucinda has never paid over to the plaintiff said trust fund, nor any part thereof; (5) that said trust was terminated by the death of said Lucinda, and said trust fund has passed, together with the assets of said estate, into the hands of said defendant; (6) that demand has been made upon the defendant by the plaintiff for the payment to her of said trust fund, with the accumulated interest thereon, but said defendant has refused, and still refuses, to pay the same over to the plaintiff. Wherefore the plaintiff prays (1) that the defendant be ordered to pay over to the plaintiff said trust fund and the accumulated interest thereon; (2) that the plaintiff may have such further and other relief as the nature of her case requires."

Defendant answered as below:

"And the defendant admits that Lucinda E. Phillips died testate on or about January 27, 1894, and that he was appointed sole executor and residuary devisee and legatee under her will, but he denies that the said testatrix ever received or intended to receive from the plaintiff any money or other property as in and by said bill alleged; and, on the contrary, he avers that if she did or so intended, then she long since, and in her lifetime, repaid the same by supporting the plaintiff for a long series of years, and furnishing her with an education which otherwise she could not have had, and at an expense exceeding the amount of the said alleged $1,000. But the defendant further answering, says that the said testatrix became estranged from the plaintiff about the time the plaintiff came of age, and so continued until the death of testatrix; that any money paid, as alleged, accrued to a right of action, and plaintiff did not demand or sue for the same within six years after it accrued, or otherwise within the time required by statute; that testatrix did not intend to pay the plaintiff the said money other than in the manner in which she did by the support and education given the plaintiff, as alleged above, all which the plaintiff well knew, and that by her laches all her right of action, either at law or in equity, has long since expired and been barred under the statutes of limitation. And the defendant further says that plaintiff well knew that his said testatrix had become angry with the plaintiff, ordered the plaintiff to leave her (the said testatrix's) house, and never return thereto, and she knew that the said testatrix then and there never intended to pay the said money or funds to the plaintiff, and distinctly refused to do any other thing to or for the plaintiff's benefit or advantage, and continued in such determination until the testatrix's death; that thereupon a right of action arose, if it ever arose, in favor of the plaintiff against the said testatrix, but the plaintiff never prosecuted the same within six years thereafter, or at any other time, and such right of action, whether at law or in equity, has long since been barred under the statutes of limitation. And the defendant, further answering, says that, if the said testatrix ever received money from the plaintiff, as she hath alleged, and deposited the same for her in a savings bank, then such deposit was made in the Provident Institution for Savings, in the town of Boston, on or about the 31st day of March, 1875; that she then proceeded to withdraw the same, May 2, 1877, $190.29; August 23, 1882, $524; August 2, 1888, $738.84, thus closing the account and reducing the whole to her own use; and that thereupon a right of action accrued to the plaintiff to recover the said gift or the said moneys or funds from the said testatrix, so reduced to her own use as aforesaid, but plaintiff failed and neglected to avail herself of her said right of action within six years thereafter, and so the said right of action was long since barred under the statutes of limitation, and the defendant avers that the said right of action was barred as aforesaid long before the decease of said testatrix. And the defendant further says that he was appointed and qualified as executor of the will of the said Lucinda E. Phillips on or about the 23d day of February, A. D. 1894; that at that time, and for a long time afterwards, he had no notice or knowledge of the said alleged payment until the filing of said will, when he learned that plaintiff then claimed that such payment had been made; that just before the expiration of the two years' limitation, provided by law in regard to claims against estates in process of settlement by executors and administrators, to wit, on the 25th day of January, A. D. 1896, the plaintiff brought an action against the defendant in the Superior Court within and for the county of Suffolk, in which there was a judgment in behalf of the defendant on the 1st day of February, A. D. 1897; that the cause of action in the said action last above mentioned is set forth in the declaration therein, a copy whereof is hereunto annexed and marked 'Exhibit A;' that the cause of action or complaint set forth in plaintiff's said bill of complaint is the same, or substantially the same, as that set forth in the said declaration, and the same has been settled and adjudicated in and by the judgment of the Supreme Court as aforesaid, and ought not again to be litigated or brought in question by the plaintiff. And, further, answering, the defendant saith that, if the said cause of action or complaint set forth in said bill of complaint ever accrued against him, it accrued within two years after his said appointment as executor, and that said bill of complaint was not filed against him within the said two years, and ought not now to be heard or considered. And, further answering the said bill of complaint, the defendant saith that in equity and good conscience the plaintiff ought to and should have filed her said bill in good time after defendant's appointment as executor, as aforesaid, and ought not to have failed and neglected so to do till nearly four years after defendant's said appointment, and more than a year after the said judgment of the Superior Court, and that thereby she has lost her right now so to do, and the said bill of complaint ought to be dismissed. And, if their be any other matter or thing in said bill of complaint not hereinbefore admitted or denied, the defendant denies the same."

Defendant also filed the following demurrer:

"And, further answering the said bill of complaint, he demurs thereto, and alleges as causes of demurrer the following, to wit: (1) That it appears in and by said bill of complaint that the trust therein alleged or set up was terminated upon the death of the said Lucinda E. Phillips, and thereupon accrued into a right of action at law, and that no right in equity has arisen thereon; (2) that it appears in and by said bill of complaint that the said Lucinda E. Phillips died more than four years ago, and that complainant is guilty of *laches* in not proceeding against the defendant long since, and the said bill of complaint ought to be dismissed; (3) that the complainant in her prayer for relief seeks no such equitable relief as a court of equity within its jurisdiction in equity and in its discretion ought to grant; (4) that complainant in her prayer for relief seeks only such relief as a court of common law can grant, to wit, a judgment and execution for the amount due and interest; (5) and that said bill of complaint was not filed within two years from the date when defendant was duly appointed executor; (6) that complainant has a complete remedy at the common law against the defendant, in his capacity of executor, for breach of the agreement of the said Lucinda E. Phillips."

At the request of defendant, the court made the following report of facts found:

" In the above-entitled cause the court finds: (1) That on or about March 31, 1875, Lucinda E. Phillips made a valid gift of $1,000 to Ellen A. Taft, the plaintiff, and gave her possession thereof. (2) That thereafter, on the same day, the said $1,000, being then the property of said Ellen A. Taft, was delivered to said Lucinda E. Phillips, to be by her invested and held in trust for said Taft until the latter should be of full age, or, at the election of said Phillips, until the death of said Phillips. (3) That said trust fund was on the same day, with the knowledge and assent of said Taft, deposited in the Provident Institution for Savings in the name of said Phillips, as trustee for said Taft, and said trust fund subsequently gained $453.13 income from said deposit. (4) That on May 2, 1877, said Lucinda E. Phillips withdrew from the deposit of said trust fund, $190.29, and on August 23, 1882, withdrew the further sum of $524, and on August 2, 1888, withdrew the further sum of $738.84, thereby closing the account with said Provident Institution for Savings; and said Phillips commingled with her own estate the several portions of said trust fund so withdrawn, and from the time of such withdrawal, did not keep the same or any part thereof invested separately in trust for said Taft, but such withdrawals and said commingling with the trustees' own estate were unknown to said Ellen A. Taft until after the death of said Lucinda E. Phillips. (5) That said Lucinda E. Phillips died January 27, 1894. That the defendant was appointed and qualified as executor of her will February 23, 1894, and was not informed of any claim by the plaintiff that a trust had been held for her benefit by said Phillips for nearly two years after his said appointment as executor. (6) That January 25, 1896, the plaintiff, Ellen A. Taft, brought an action at law against the defendant, as executor of the said Lucinda E. Phillips, to recover said trust fund and its accumulations. Said action was brought in the Superior Court in the county of Suffolk, carried upon demurrer to the Supreme Judicial Court, the decision in that court being reported in 167 Mass. 363, and thereafter was determined by judgment for the defendant in the Superior Court, February 1, 1897, (7) That, at and before the termination of said suit at law, said Ellen A. Taft was in ill health, and not reasonably able to attend to business, and that such condition continued until shortly before the bringing this bill of complaint. That, as soon as reasonably practicable after she had so far recovered as to be able to attend to business, she instituted this suit in equity, and was guilty of no *laches* in bringing or prosecuting the same. (8) That on accounting to this 23d day of February, 1898, there has accrued as simple interest at 6 per cent. upon the portions of said trust fund commingling with the estate of said Phillips from the several dates of such commingling, the sum of $1,147.66, and the total amount of said trust fund, its accumulations of income and interest which the plaintiff is now entitled to recover, is $2,600.79."

Nason & Proctor, for plaintiff.

S. H. Dudley and *Howland Dudley,* for defendant.

MORTON, J.—Upon the facts found, we think that the plaintiff's remedy is clearly in equity. The case is not one where all that remained to be done was the payment of an ascertained sum with interest, as, for instance, in *Buttrick* v. *King* (7 Metc. [Mass.] 20). It is found that the testatrix received the money in trust, to be invested and held by her for the plaintiff until the plaintiff became of full age, or, at the election of the trustee, until the latter's death. Pursuant to the trust, the money was invested by the trustee in the Provident Institution for Savings with the knowledge and assent of the plaintiff. Subsequently it was drawn out by the trustee without the knowledge of the plaintiff, and mingled by the trustee with her own estate, and not kept invested for the plaintiff, as the terms of the trust required. An account would have to be taken, therefore, in order to determine the amount for which the estate of the testatrix should be held liable, and it is well settled that in matters relating to trusts that can be done only in equity. (*Johnson* v. *Johnson,* 120 Mass. 465; *Davis* v. *Coburn,* 128 id. 377; *Norton* v. *Ray,* 139 id. 230; 29 N. E. 662; *Upham* v. *Draper,* 157 id. 292; 32 N. E. 2; 2 Perry Trusts [4th ed.], § 843.) The bill, as framed, is very meager, and with advantage might have set

out the facts more fully. But sufficient appears from it to show
that there was a trust, that the fund impressed with the trust
passed to defendant as executor, and that the trust is still open.
An action for money had and received could not be maintained by
the plaintiff, and the plaintiff would not have a plain and adequate
remedy at law. (*Norton* v. *Ray, supra; Davis* v. *Coburn, supra;
Johnson* v. *Johnson, supra; Upham* v. *Draper, supra;* 2 Perry
Trusts [4th ed.], § 843.) The demurrer was rightly overruled.
The cause set out in the declaration in the action at law is the
same, we think, as that set out in the bill in this suit, though stated
somewhat differently. In each case the plaintiff seeks to recover
the sum of $1,000, with its accumulations, alleged to have been
held in trust for her by the testatrix during the life of the latter;
and there is no claim that more than $1,000, with its accumula-
tions, was ever so held by her. We also think that the action at
law was defeated by a defect in form (*Taft* v. *Stow,* 167 Mass.
363; 45 N. E. 752), and that the provisions of Pub. St. ch. 136,
§ 12, apply. The original of that section was St. 1855, ch. 157,
§ 1, subsequently re-enacted in Gen. St. ch. 97, § 7, and again in
the Public Statutes, with some change in each case by way of
condensation of the previous statute, but without any intention,
we think, to change the scope of the law as it originally stood.
It is plain that this case would have come within the terms of that
statute, and we think that the present statute should be construed
so as to include it. Moreover, this construction would put this section in harmony with Pub. St. ch. 197, § 13, as St. 1855, ch. 157,
§ 1, was no doubt intended to be, and, as there is no reason why
§ 12, ch. 136, Pub. St., should not be. The result is that we
think that the conclusion to which the Superior Court came was
correct, but that the terms of the decree should be modified so
that the plaintiff should recover of the defendant, as he is the
executor of the will of Lucinda E. Phillips, the principal sum which
is found due, and that execution should issue as at common law
for the sum so found due against the goods and estate of said
Lucinda E. Phillips, deceased, in the hands of said Stow as executor, and that another execution for costs, to be taxed by the clerk,
issue against said Stow personally. (*Tyler* v. *Bingham,* 143 Mass.
410; 9 N. E. 750.)

So ordered.

LORING *et al. vs.* WILSON *et al.*

LORING *vs.* BLAIR *et al.*

[Supreme Judicial Court of Massachusetts, July 3, 1899; 174 Mass. 132;
54 N. E. Rep. 502.]

POWERS — WILLS — CONSTRUCTION — TRUSTS — LEGACIES —
PAYMENT — DEBTS OF TESTATOR.

1. Where one conveys property in trust, to be held for the benefit of such
"charitable corporations" as he may appoint by will, a testamentary
direction to his executor, an individual, to expend a certain sum in
providing free excursions for poor children is valid, and the executor
may give the money to a charitable corporation to be so expended.

2. Where one conveys property in trust, to be held for the benefit of such
persons sustaining a specified relation to him as he may appoint by will,
a testamentary appointment of a person not within the class is invalid.

3. Where one conveys property to be held in trust for the benefit of such
persons as he may appoint by will, and he dies seized of general assets,
and in disposing of the latter he makes a legacy, the trust estate is not
liable therefor.

4. Testator's mother created a trust in his favor, giving him a general
power of appointment by will. He conveyed other property in trust,
reserving a power of appointment by will, and died, seized of general
assets. His will first purported to dispose of the property included in
the trust created by his mother, and his own property, giving a pecuniary legacy, and bequeathing the "residue" to another legatee: It
then purported to dispose of the estate conveyed by testator in trust,
and in doing so enumerated certain chattels that had always been used
in connection therewith, but which, in fact, were included in the trust
created by the mother. *Held,* that said chattels passed by the latter
clause, and not to the residuary legatee named in the former.

5. The latter devise, including the gift of the chattels, having been charged
with certain pecuniary legacies, the legatees waived all right to have
their legacies paid out of any real estate or chattels included in the trust
created by the testator's conveyance. *Held,* that the chattels included
in the trust created by the mother, and given by the latter clause of the
will, were not thereby exempted.

6. Testator's debts were payable, first out of his own property, and then
out of that included in the trust created by his mother of which he
disposed in the former clause of the will, and then out of the chattels
which were included in the trust created by the mother, but which were
disposed of in the latter clause of the will.

CASES reserved from Supreme Judicial Court, Suffolk county; JAMES M. BARKER, Judge.

Bills in equity by Augustus P. Loring and William A. Hayes, trustees, against William P. Wilson and others, and by Augustus P. Loring, executor, against Thomas Blair and others. Both cases were reserved on the pleadings, an agreed statement of facts, and a stipulation.

Decree advised.

R. M. Morse, for petitioner A. P. Loring.

J. B. Warner, for defendant Massachusetts Horticultural Society.

W. A. Hayes, 2d, for defendants Sarah Shurtleff and others.

Philip Dexter, for defendant Thomas Blair.

Arthur Lord, for defendant W. P. Wilson.

HAMMOND, J.—The first suit is by the trustees under the deed of trust executed by Francis B. Hayes, on June 12, 1889, for instructions in regard to their duties under such deed. The second suit is by the executor of the will of Francis B. Hayes, for instructions in regard to his duties under the will. Both cases were reserved on the pleadings, agreed statement of facts, and a stipulation on file, and the same questions arise in each case.

The agreed statement of facts is as follows:

" The trustees under the trust of June 12, 1889, have paid all the pecuniary legacies appointed in Mr. Hayes' will, except those to Blair, Loring, Miss Shurtleff, two of Comley's children, Comley's wife, and that for the benefit of poor children, which are the legacies about which instructions are asked in the bill. They have also paid out of the trust fund to the executor of the will, towards his expenses incurred in establishing the will, the sum of $66,000; this payment being made with the consent of the Massachusetts Horticultural Society, to whom the residue of the trust is appointed. They have paid to the horticultural society, on account of the residue, $200,000. They have retained in their hands, awaiting the decision of the questions raised by this bill, and the decision of the full court on the question whether interest is payable on legacies,.the sum of $61,967.16, and, in addition, real estate valued at about $4,000. The executor holds in his hands, from the trust fund established by the testator's mother, over which he had general power of appointment by will, about $7,000, and also holds, as assets of the estate never in any trust, about $6,900, and a claim on real property of the estimated value of $2,500; making in all, money and property held by the executor to the amount of $16,400. In 1891 Hayes, acting with the consent of the trustees under the trust of June 12, 1889, set apart his library, which had previously formed a part of that trust, upon a new and specific trust for the payment of such debts as he might owe at his death. This library was supposed to be worth from $25,000 to $40,000. The debts due from Hayes' estate at his death in 1895 were about $17,000, all of which had been incurred since the trust deed of 1889 was executed. Since the bill in this cause was filed, the library has been sold, and has yielded only about $10,000, which will be insufficient to meet his debts and the interest thereon by about $10,000. During the lifetime of the testator, Francis B. Hayes, and in or about the years 1889 and 1890, said Hayes, being then engaged in litigation with the family of his wife and others, and being desirous of purchasing a residence at Ascutneyville, state of Vermont, Mrs. Margaret M. Hayes, his mother, purchased a certain estate in said Ascutneyville for the use of the testator, taking a conveyance to herself, and the testator then entered on said estate, expended large sums on improvement thereof, lived thereon, and had his residence and paid taxes thereon for some time afterwards. After the death of Mrs. Hayes this title descended to her heirs at law, or was devised to her residuary legatees, who are the half brothers and sisters of the testator. There being some doubt as to the question in what manner this property should be treated, it was referred by the executor to arbitration, and the arbitrator found that the amount expended by Mrs. Hayes in the purchase of said estate for the use of her son, with interest and expenses, amounting in all to about $6,600, should be charged as a debt to the estate of the testator, Francis B. Hayes. This has never been paid, and is included in the $10.000 balance of indebtedness which is stated as due in the first agreement of facts in this case. The arbitrator also found that, on the payment of said in-

debtedness to said heirs at law or residuary devisees, the executor
would then be entitled to conveyance of said real estate, and this
amount is also referred to in said agreed statement of facts as 'a
claim on real property of the estimated value of $2,500.' The title
has not yet been conveyed by the heirs or devisees of Mrs. Hayes,
but they are ready to convey it to the executor, or as he may direct,
on receiving payment of the sum found by the arbitrator, and,
when conveyed, it will be a part of the general assets of the testator
not covered by any trust.   There also remains unpaid a balance of
about $15,000 of the expenses incurred by the executor in establish-
ing the will.   Of the money spent by the trustees since the testator's death in the care of the property at Lexington known as
'Oakmount' (over $18,000), a part was spent in necessary repairs
on the buildings, taxes, and insurance, and a part in the care of
chattels, plants, and shrubs which never formed a part of the trust
of 1889, were not attached to the estate, and did not pass by the
appointment of Oakmount, and the remainder was spent in maintaining the grounds about the mansion house, or the extensive
ornamental grounds surrounding a gentleman's residence, with
trees and shrubs, lawns, drives, walks, and the surroundings of
an expensive country seat."

The stipulation is as follows:

"It is agreed by the several parties as follows: (1) The legacies or gifts bequeathed or appointed in the will of Francis B.
Hayes to Thomas Blair, Augustus P. Loring, Sarah Shurtleff,
Eliza J. Comley, and Antoinette J. Horch, respectively, are not
within the limits of the power of appointment reserved by said
Hayes to himself by his trust deed of June 12, 1889; and the said
legatees, respectively, waive and abandon all claim to have said
legacies or gifts charged upon any of the real estate which is devised by the first paragraph of the second part of said will to William P. Wilson for life, and after his death to other persons, or
to have such legacies or gifts satisfied out of said real estate, or
out of any chattels included in said trust, or to have the payment
of them made a condition to the conveyance of such real estate to
the devisees named in said paragraph.   (2) The expenses incurred
in the care and preservation of the furniture and other chattels at
Oakmount since the death of Mr. Hayes shall be repaid to the
trustees out of the proceeds of those articles now in the hands of

the executor. (3) The entire expenses of establishing the will shall be borne by the three funds interested in setting up the will, in proportion to their size; that is, by the general assets of the estate never in any trust, the proceeds of property in the trust established by Margaret M. Hayes, and the fund in the trust of 1889, —not including in this fund the real estate called 'Oakmount,' which is specifically devised. (4) An agreement having been made by the parties in interest disposing of all questions concerning the provision made in said will for the benefit of James Comley and Harriet E. Comley, his wife, and disposing, also, of the question respecting the payments made by the trustees since the death of said Hayes in the care and maintenance of his real estate, no question respecting these matters now remains for argument in this case. (5) The only questions presented by the bill for instructions in this cause, or by the bill in the cause of Loring, executor, against Blair and others, which now remain to be passed upon by the court, are: First, the question respecting the bequest for excursions for poor children; second, the question whether the legacies to Blair, Loring, Miss Shurtleff, and the daughters of Comley are to be satisfied out of the fund covered by the trust of 1889, though not within the powers of appointment reserved by the testator over that fund; third, the question raised by the amendment to the bill respecting the payment of a sum from the trust fund to the executor to satisfy the debts of the testator, or some part of them, so as to exonerate the general assets of the estate; fourth, the question how the residue of the general assets of the estate, not derived from any trust, shall be applied to the satisfaction of debts and legacies; fifth, the question how the cash and the residue of the proceeds of the furniture and chattels included in the trust established by the will of Margaret M. Hayes shall be applied to the satisfaction of debts and legacies, including the question whether the furniture and chattels were specifically bequeathed with Oakmount."

The deed of trust of June 12, 1889, contains no power of revocation on the part of Francis B. Hayes without the consent of the trustees, and therefore we think that it is valid against Hayes himself and against the devisees and legatees found in his will. In that deed of trust it is provided that "upon and after the death of the said Francis B. Hayes," the trustees are "to hold the said trust property, original and substituted, and any accumulations thereof, and any additions thereto, and also said homestead estate and books and library, to the use or for the benefit of such one or more of the following persons and corporations, and in such manner as the said Francis B. Hayes may by will appoint, namely: Any wife of his, his blood relations, their husbands and wives, the children of said husbands and wives, persons at any time employed as domestic servants or gardeners by himself or by his parents, and also charitable corporations. And in default of such appointment," etc. This limited power of appointment Francis B. Hayes executed in his will in the manner hereinafter mentioned. By the will of his mother, Margaret M. Hayes, certain property of hers was given to a trustee for the use of Francis B. Hayes during his life, and "upon and after the death of said Francis B. Hayes to hold such trust fund or property, original or substituted, or any accumulation thereof, or any addition thereto, to the use and. for the benefit of such persons or such corporations as my said son may, in whole or in part, by will or any instrument in the nature of a will, appoint; and in default of such appointment," etc. This general power of appointment Francis B. Hayes also executed by his will.

In his will, in the clause before the first article, Francis B. Hayes proposes to dispose of the property referred to and designated in the will of his mother, over which he was given a general power of appointment, and also to dispose of all the estate, real, personal, and mixed, of which he should die seized and possessed, exclusive of the property in trust under the deed of June 12, 1889, and of any property situate in England. Out of this property of himself and of his mother he gives, by the first article of the will, $10,000 to Thomas Blair. He next gives, by the second article, $2,500 to Thomas Blair in trust, which legacy he revokes by a codicil. He next, by the first clause of the third article, gives, devises, bequeaths, and appoints the residue of the said property and estate to the Massachusetts Horticultural Society. The testator was here speaking of the residue of the property referred to in the will of his mother, over which he had a general power of appointment, as well as of all the property of which he should die seized or possessed, except the trust property under the deed of trust of 1889, and any property of his situate in England. It does not appear that Francis B. Hayes died seized or possessed of any property in England. After making these dispositions of the property under his mother's will, over which he had a power of appointment, and of his own property not included in the deed of trust and not situate in England, he proceeds, in the remainder of the third article of the will, to execute the limited power of appointment reserved in said deed of trust in the following manner: "Now, therefore, pursuant to and by virtue of the said power so given, limited, or reserved to me in and by the said indenture of the twelfth day of June, one thousand eight hundred and eighty-nine, and every other power and authority in me vested, or in any wise enabling me hereunto, as to all the property referred to and designated in the said indenture of trust as aforesaid, and now remaining subject to the trusts thereof, I give, devise, bequeath and appoint the same in manner following; that is to say," etc. After making twenty-two devises and bequests of the property included in said deed of trust, by the twenty-third section he devises, bequeaths, and appoints "all the rest, residue, and remainder of the said property, comprised in or now subject to the trusts of the said indenture of the twelfth June, one thousand eight hundred and eighty-nine," to the Massachusetts Horticultural Society. The first section under this third article of the will contains a devise of the homestead called "Oakmount" to William Power Wilson for life, with remainder in tail to his issue, "together with all the household furniture and effects, plate, plated goods, linen, china, books, prints, and pictures thereunder, with the live stock and cattle and greenhouse plants thereon," etc. This section ends as follows: "And I declare that the said gift is made upon the further condition, so far as I am able to impose such a condition, that the said William Power Wilson do and shall pay or cause to be paid any legacies bequeathed by this, my will, which, from any cause whatever, cannot be paid to the respective legatees out of the property and in the manner in which such legacies are, or purport to be, bequeathed by this, my will." The third section under this article is as follows: "Third. I give to the said James Comley, my gardener, ten thousand dollars, and to each of his children living at my decease five hundred dollars. And I further direct that the said James Comley and his wife be allowed to continue to occupy, free from all rent or other charge, the dwelling house now occupied by them on my estate in

Lexington, during their joint lives and the life of the survivor of them." The fifth section under this article is as follows: "Fifth. I give to Sarah Shurtleff the sum of two thousand dollars." The nineteenth section under this article is as follows: "Nineteenth. I direct my executor, hereinafter named, to appropriate and use the sum of five thousand dollars, in such amounts and at such times, not exceeding three years from the date of his appointment, as he shall determine, in providing free excursions for poor children in the city of Boston." The twenty-second section under this article is as follows: "Twenty-second. And I give and bequeath to Augustus P. Loring, my executor hereinafter named, the sum of five thousand dollars, if (but not otherwise) he shall accept the office of executor of this, my will."

The first question is whether the bequest for free excursions for poor children is valid, as being within the power reserved to Francis B. Hayes in the deed of trust to appoint to charitable corporations. The executor is not a charitable corporation, but the purpose of the gift is charitable; and we think that the executor can pay the money to some charitable corporation for the purpose of carrying the provisions of this section into effect. It is a direction to use money in a way in which charitable corporations could use it, and the section need not fail because the executor is not himself a charitable corporation.

The legacies given to each of the children of James Comley by the third section, to Sarah Shurtleff by the fifth section, and to Augustus P. Loring by the twenty-second section, are to persons not within the power of appointment reserved to Francis B. Hayes in the deed of trust. They cannot, therefore, be paid out of the property comprised in that deed, and we are of opinion that they cannot be paid at all, except as hereinafter stated.

The legacy given by the first article of the will to Thomas Blair is given out of his own property and that of his mother over which he had a power of appointment, and must be paid, except as hereinafter stated, subject to the debts of the testator and certain specific bequests to Wilson, hereinafter named, out of these properties.

Some of the chattels given to William Powell Wilson by the first section under the third article of the will are not properly included in the deed of trust, but are property which formerly belonged to the testator's mother, and were included in the trust for his benefit in her will, and over which he had a general power of appointment; and one of the questions is whether these articles passed to Wilson under that section. We are of the opinion that they did so pass. The testator starts out at first to dispose of his own property and that over which he had a testamentary power of appointment under the will of his mother, and, after some special bequests, gives the residue to the Massachusetts Horticultural Society. Evidently supposing that there is nothing further to be done as to that property, he goes on to act under the power reserved in the trust deed. He begins specifically, and the very first thing which comes to his mind is Oakmount, and the personal property used and connected therewith; and then, in plain and explicit terms, he declares his will to be that Wilson shall have the articles particularly described by classes in this section. It is the first time these articles are particularly mentioned. There can be no question that he intended all this property to go to Wilson. It is not reasonable to suppose that he thought he had already disposed of it, or any part of it, under a general residuary clause the words of which had just passed from his lips. Oakmount was to go to Wilson, and it was natural that the articles which always had been associated in the mind of the testator with that estate, and were its natural and usual adjuncts, should go with it. He was mistaken in the nature of the title under which he held them, but his intention to pass to Wilson whatever title he could stands out plainly and distinctly, and is not overcome by the mere fact that the clause wherein the intent is manifest comes after the clause where another intent is supposed to be lurking in general language. He was thinking, rather, of what he should do with the property, than of the particular power under which he was acting. The dominant intent was that Wilson should have that specific property, and we think that intent can be carried out without violating any sound rule of construction. But this bequest of Oakmount and the chattels connected therewith was incumbered with the condition, " so far as [the testator] could impose such a condition," that Wilson should " pay or cause to be paid any legacies bequeathed by this, my will, which, from any cause whatever, cannot be paid to the respective legatees out of the property and in the manner in which such legacies are, or purport to be, bequeathed by this, my will."

The various legatees " waive and abandon all claim to have said
legacies or gifts charged upon any of the real estate which is devised by " this section of the third item, or to have them " satisfied
out of said real estate, or out of any chattels included in the trust "
created by the deed, or " to have the payment of them made a condition to the conveyance of such real estate to the devisees named
in said paragraph." But this waiver does not apply to such of the
chattels as were the property of the mother over which the testator
had the general power of appointment; and as to such chattels we
think they pass to Wilson, subject to the condition that the legacy
to Blair, the legacies to the children of James Comley by the third
section, to Sarah Shurtleff by the fifth section, and to Augustus
P. Loring by the twenty-second section, be paid. The debts of
the testator, we think, are primarily payable out of the property of
which he died seized and possessed, and out of the property which
he derived from his mother's will, over which he exercised the general power of appointment. These properties are more than sufficient to pay all the debts in full.

One contention has been that, for the sake of paying debts, the
deed of trust of June 12, 1889, is voidable by the creditors of Francis B. Hayes, and that they should first be paid out of the property
comprised in this deed of trust, in order that Blair may receive his
legacy in full. But whether, if there were no other property for
the payment of the debts of Francis B. Hayes, the property included in the deed of trust could be applied to the payment of his
debts, we find it unnecessary to decide, because the property of
which he died seized and possessed, and the property of his mother
over which he had and exercised a general power of appointment,
are sufficient to pay all the debts; and we think the debts are primarily to be paid out of these properties. There must be included
in this property of the mother certain chattels mentioned in the
devise and bequest in the third article to William Power Wilson.
The debts must first be paid out of the testator's absolute property;
then out of the property of the mother over which the testator had
a general power of appointment, which he exercised; then the bequest of the specific articles formerly belonging to his mother's estate, which in the third article is made to Wilson, is to stand; then
the legacy to Blair must be paid out of these properties, so far as
it can be paid; and, if anything is left of these properties, it falls

into the residue, and is payable to the Massachusetts Horticultural Society. (*Olney* v. *Balch*, 154 Mass. 318; 28 N. E. 258.) See *Loring* v. *Society* (171 Mass. 401; 50 N. E. 936); *White* v. *Institute* (171 Mass. 84, 96; 50 N. E. 512); *Emmons* v. *Shaw* (171 Mass. 410; 50 N. E. 1033).

The debt due to the estate of the mother of Francis B. Hayes, under the arbitration had with reference to the real property at Ascutneyville, in Vermont, stands on the same footing as any other debt; and that estate, when conveyed to the executor of the will of Francis B. Hayes, his heirs and assigns, must be regarded as real property belonging to Francis B. Hayes.

The legacies out of the property included in the deed of trust to Augustus P. Loring, executor, by the twenty-second section, to the children of James Comley by the third section, and to Sarah Shurtleff by the fifth section, are void.

Decree accordingly.

CROCKER *vs.* SHAW, State Treasurer.

[Supreme Judicial Court of Massachusetts, September 11, 1899; 174 Mass. 266; 54 N. E. Rep. 549.]

TRANSFER TAX—GIFT TO TAKE EFFECT ON DONOR'S DEATH—CONSTRUCTION OF INSTRUMENTS—EXECUTION BEFORE ENACTMENT OF STATUTE.

1. Property conveyed in trust to pay the income to the grantor during her life, and the principal on her death to be transferred to such persons as she should appoint by her will, when such will has been executed and has taken effect by her death, and the appointees are within the terms of St. 1891, ch. 425, is subject to the collateral inheritance tax imposed thereby, as property passing "by deed, grant, sale or gift made or intended to take effect in possession or enjoyment after the death of the grantor;" the will in such case being referred to the instrument creating the power of disposition, and being regarded as a disposition made by the donor of such power, whether such donor is the testatrix or another.

2. The fact that the instrument creating the trust and the power of appointment was executed prior to the passage of the statute is immaterial; the transfer having been thereby made to take effect in possession

and enjoyment only on the grantor's death, which took place after the statute became effective.

APPEAL from Probate Court, Suffolk county.

Petition by one Crocker, trustee, for instructions. From the judgment of a justice affirming the judgment of the Probate Court in favor of Shaw, state treasurer, petitioner appeals.

Affirmed.

Frank Brewster, for appellant.

Arthus W. De Goosh, Asst. Atty -Gen., for appellee.

MORTON, J.—This was a petition for instructions to the Probate Court by the appellant as trustee under two indentures, dated in 1865 and 1885, respectively, and executed by Frances W. Ladd and her husband, Alfred Ladd, by which certain property was conveyed by the said Frances to the petitioner in trust to pay over the net income to her during her life, and after her death, subject to a provision in favor of her daughter, which has become inoperative by reason of the daughter's death before that of the mother, to convey and transfer the principal to such persons as she should appoint by her last will. Frances W. Ladd died in 1895, leaving a will which has been duly proved in Suffolk county. By her will she directed that a large portion of the trust property should be paid over and transferred to such persons that it is liable to a collateral inheritance tax, if St. 1891, ch. 415, and the acts in amendment thereto, are applicable. It is agreed that the said Frances was domiciled in Boston at the time of her death, and when the trust indentures were executed, and that at each of those dates the trust estate was within the jurisdiction of this commonwealth. The Probate Court ruled that the property was subject to the payment of the tax. The trustee appealed, and the case was heard on agreed facts by a justice of this court, who affirmed the decree of the Probate Court, and the trustee thereupon appealed to the full court.

The questions are whether the property passed " by deed, grant, sale or gift, made or intended to take effect in possession or enjoyment after the death of the grantor," whether the statute is constitutional as applied to cases like this, and whether the statute applies to cases where the deed was made before it went into effect, although the property vested after that event.

It seems to us clear that the property passed by a deed intended to take effect in possession or enjoyment after the death of the grantor. Mrs. Ladd's will is to be referred, as was held in *Emmons* v. *Shaw* (171 Mass. 410; 50 N. E. 1033), to the instruments creating the power under which it was executed, and is to be regarded as a disposition made by the donor of the power. It makes no difference that the donor of the power and the person executing it are one and the same. If the provisions contained in the will of Mrs. Ladd had been incorporated into the trust indentures, there can be no doubt that the property in reference to which this controversy has arisen would have passed under a deed intended to take effect in possession and enjoyment, quoad that property, on the death of the grantor. The grantor would have taken a life estate, and the various gifts would have taken effect in possession and enjoyment at her death. (*In re Green's Estate*, 153 N. Y. 223; 47 N. E. 292; *In re Seaman's Estate*, 147 N. Y. 69, 77; 41 N. E. 401.)

We see no difference in principle between property passing by a deed intended to take effect in possession or enjoyment on the death of the grantor, and property passing by will. In either case it is the privilege of disposing of property after the death of the grantor or testator which is taxed, though the amount of the tax is determined by the value of the property. The constitutionality of the law in regard to taxing property passing by will was fully considered in *Minot* v. *Winthrop* (162 Mass. 113; 38 N. E. 512), and that case, we think, is decisive of this.

It is immaterial, it seems to us, in this case, as it would be in the case of a will, that the indentures were dated and executed before St. 1891, ch. 425, took effect. It is the vesting of the property in possession and enjoyment on the death of the grantor, and after the statute took effect, that renders it liable to the tax, and both of those things happened in this case. (*In re Green's Estate, supra; In re Seaman's Estate, supra.*)

The appellant has pointed out some difficulties that might arise in a supposable case, but it is enough to say that they do not exist in this case. No interest vested in this case, either in possession or enjoyment, in any of the legatees, till after the death of the grantor. It was held in *Cushing* v. *Aylwin* (12 Metc. [Mass.] 169), that Rev. St. ch. 62, § 3, applied to a will made before that law took effect, "when the will had not taken effect before that time by the death of the testator." We think that that case applies to this, and, if authority is needed, is sufficient to justify the conclusion to which we have come. It is true that in New York there is an express provision, by which the statute is applicable whether the transfer was made before or after the passage of the act. But it is evident, we think, that the conclusion arrived at in the cases to which we have referred would have been the same without that provision.

Decree of Probate Court affirmed.

Note.—INHERITANCE TAX.

(a) Foundation principles.
(b) Rules of construction.
(c) Residence of party or *situs* of property.
(d) Exemptions.
(e) Where there are life interests and remainders.
(f) Exercise of a power.
(g) Deeds of trust.
(h) Statute not retroactive by construction.
(i) Deductions.
(j) Some illustrative cases.

(a) **Foundation principles.**—The right to take property by will or descent is derived from and regulated by municipal law; and in assessing a tax upon such right or privilege the state may lawfully measure or fix the amount of the tax by referring to the value of the property passing; and the incidental fact that such property is composed in whole or in part of federal securities does not invalidate the state tax, or the law under which it is imposed. The theory upon which this can be done consistently with the Constitution and the laws of the United States is that such taxes are regarded as imposed not upon the property the amount of which is referred to as regulating the amount of the taxes, but upon franchises and privileges derived from the state. (Plummer v. Coler, 178 U. S. 115; 20 Sup. Rep. 829.)

The opinion of the court contains a valuable review of the cases both State and Federal.

The opinion of the court in the case of Knowlton v. Moore (178 U. S. 41; 20 Sup. Rep. 747), contains an interesting and valuable historical summary and review of the law applicable to the subject of an inheritance tax. The War Revenue Act of Congress, 1898, imposed a tax on legacies and distributive shares of personal property and the constitutionality of this provision was one of the specific questions considered and determined in holding same to be constitutional, but on the special facts of the case the representatives of the estate were held entitled to some relief.

The tax imposed is not in a proper sense a tax upon the property passing by will, or under the Statutes of Descent or Distribution. It is a tax upon the right of transfer by will, or under the intestate laws of the state. It is an exaction made by the state in the regulation of the right of devolution of property of decedents which is created by law, and which the law may restrain or regulate. Whatever the form of the property, the right to succeed to it is created by law, and if the property consists of government securities, the transferee derives his right to take them as he does his right to take any other property of the decedent under the laws of the state and the state by these statutes makes the right subject to the burden imposed." ANDREWS, Ch. J. (Matter of Sherman, 153 N. Y. 1; 46 N. E. Rep. 1032.)

The tax is computed not on the aggregate valuation of the whole estate of the decedent considered as the unit for taxation, but on the value of the separate interests into which it is divided by will or by the statute laws of the state, and is a charge against such share or interest according to its value, and against the person entitled thereto. (Matter of Westurn, 152 N. Y. 93, 99; 46 N. E. Rep. 315.)

That such a law is constitutional. (Minot v. Winthrop, 162 Mass. 113; 38 N. E. Rep. 512; Magoun v. Illinois Trust Co., 170 U. S. 283, 288; 18 Sup. Rep. 594; Tyson v. State, 28 Md. 577; Matter of McPherson, 104 N. Y. 306; 10 N. E. Rep. 685.)

That it is a tax on privilege or right of succession, not on property. (Minot v. Winthrop, 162 Mass. 113; 38 N. E. Rep. 512; Magoun v. Illinois Trust Co., 170 U. S. 288; 18 Sup. Rep. 594; [the opinion gives a valuable historical summary]; State v. Hamlin, 86 Me. 495; 30 Atl. Rep. 76; Matter of Merriam, 141 N. Y. 479; 36 N. E. Rep. 505; Matter of Davis, 149 N. Y. 539; 44 N. E. Rep. 185; Matter of Hoffman, 143 N. Y. 327, 333; 38 N. E. Rep. 311; Estate of Swift, 137 N. Y. 77; 32 N. E. Rep. 1096; State v. Switzler, 143 Mo. 287; 45 S. W. Rep. 245; State v. Furnell, 20 Mont. 299; 51 Pac. Rep. 267.)

(b) **Rules of construction.**—When doubt as to whether a particular fund is subject to the tax, it should be resolved in favor of the taxpayer. (Matter of Harbeck, 161 N. Y. 211; 55 N. E. Rep. 851.)

When the question is whether a certain subject of taxation is embraced within the act and brought within the power of taxation, the statute should be strictly construed in favor of the citizen since it assumes to impose a special burden upon particular property and persons, and is not in any proper sense a general tax. But where a particular subject is within the scope of the act, and exemption is claimed on ground that the Legislature has not provided proper machinery for accomplishing the legislative purpose in the particular instance, the construction should be liberal in making effective the legislative intent. (Matter of Stewart, 131 N. Y. 274; 30 N. E. Rep. 184.)

(c) **Residence of party or situs of property.**—In England the liability of the tax is made to depend upon the domicile of the testator or intestate; if the domicile is in Great Britain the duty is payable; if not in Great Britain no duty is payable. (Re Tootal's Trusts, L. R. 23 Ch. Div. 532.)

In Thompson v. Advocate General (12 Cl. & F. 1), it was held by the House of Lords in an issue involving the imposition of a transfer or legacy tax, that personal property had no *situs* of its own and followed the domicile of its owner. And to same effect is Wallace v. Attorney-General (L. R. 1 Ch. App. 1), where it was held that a succession duty was not payable on legacies given by will of a person domiciled in a foreign country.

It matters not whether a transfer is by grant or gift so long as intended to take effect in possession or enjoyment, at or after the death of the grantor or donor, the devolution of title is subject to the tax; it is not important whether the remaindermen reside within the state or elsewhere. (Matter of Green, 153 N. Y. 223; 47 N. E. Rep. 292.) .

Decedent's domicile being in Massachusetts, it draws to it the passing of the title to personal property in the hands of his agent in New York, consisting of stocks and bonds of foreign corporations, and bonds secured by mortgage on real property in New Hampshire, and hence such property is subject to the tax in Massachusetts. (Frothingham v. Shaw, 175 Mass. 59; 55 N. E. Rep. 623.) The opinion contains a valuable review of the authorities.

Bonds of foreign as well as of domestic corporations and certificates of stock of domestic corporations (but not of foreign corporations) owned by a non-resident decedent and deposited by him with a safe deposit company within the state are subject to the tax. (Matter of Whiting, 150 N. Y. 27; 44 N. E. Rep. 715; Matter of Morgan, 150 N. Y. 35; 44 N. E. Rep. 1126.)

Stocks and bonds of foreign corporations, the certificates and bonds being within this state, but the owner and testator being a non-resident domiciled in England, are not subject to the tax. (Matter of James, 144 N. Y. 6; 38 N. E. Rep. 961.)

Stock in domestic corporations, and of national banks located within the state are subject to the tax, although the certificates are not in the state, at time of decedent's death and he is non-resident. The rights of a foreign executor or administrator, are subject to this right. (Greves v. Shaw, 173 Mass. 205; 53 N. E. Rep. 372, and see Moody v. Shaw, 173 Mass. 375; 53 N. E. Rep. 891.)

Certificates or shares of stock of domestic corporations held by a non-resident decedent at his domicile are subject to the tax. (Matter of Bronson, 150 N. Y. 1; 44 N. E. Rep. 707.)

To render personal property liable under the Pennsylvania Act it must have a *situs* within that commonwealth; bonds of United States without regard to place of deposit, cannot have any *situs* different from that of their owner. (Orcutt's Appeal, 97 Pa. St. 179.)

Stocks of foreign corporations held by an executor as such are part of the estate and right of succession thereto is subject to the tax. (Matter of Merriam, 141 N. Y. 479; 36 N. E. Rep. 505.)

Bonds of a domestic corporation held by a non-resident decedent at his domicile are not subject to the tax. (Matter of Bronson, 150 N. Y. 1; 44 N. E. Rep. 707.)

Money of non-resident invested in the state in a bond and mortgage and deposits in a savings bank are subject to the tax. (Estate of Romaine, 127 N.Y. 80; 27 N. E. Rep. 759.)

The prevailing opinion recognized no distinction between the case of a non-resident who made a will, and one who did not. There was an able dissenting opinion by Judge HAIGHT founded on this distinction in which he forcibly argued that as the property did not pass by any will, or any law of the state, being personal, its *situs* was with its owner and it was not therefore subject to the tax.

Moneys of non-resident decedent deposited by him with a trust company as trustee, are subject to the tax. (Matter of Houdayer, 150 N. Y. 37; 44 N. E. Rep. 718.)

That property situate in the state, although belonging to one domiciled in another state is subject to a succession tax. (Alvany v. Powell, 2 Jones Eq. 51 [N. C.].)

Non-residents subject to tax on property within the state. (State v. Dalrymple, 70 Md. 594; 17 Atl. Rep. 82.)

Interest of a non-resident deceased member of a limited partnership where its property is within the state is subject to the tax. (Small's Estate, 151 Pa. St. 1; 25 Atl. Rep. 23.)

Real estate situated in another state, although owned by decedent resident is not subject to the tax, nor does the doctrine of equitable conversion make it subject. Otherwise as to personal property of a resident decedent which is subject to the tax wherever situated. (Estate of Swift, 137 N. Y. 77; 32 N. E. Rep. 1096.)

Where a resident decedent directs his executors to sell real estate in another state to pay legacies in his own state, same are converted by such direction and are subject to the tax. (Williamson's Estate, 153 Pa. St. 508; 26 Atl. Rep. 246.)

But otherwise where the proceeds are directed to be invested in mortgages in such other state. (Hale's Estate, 161 Pa. St. 181; 28 Atl. Rep. 1071.)

Estates not passing by will operative within the State of Pennsylvania, or under the intestate laws thereof, or by deed or grant intended to take effect on death are not subject to the tax in that state. (Orcutt's Appeal, 97 Pa. St. 179.)

Share of a resident deceased partner in proceeds of partnership real estate in another state or country, subject to such a tax. (Forbes v. Steven, L. R. 10 Eq. 178.)

Real estate situate in another state cannot be made subject to tax. (Bittinger's Estate, 129 Pa. St. 338; 18 Atl. Rep. 132.)

Where real estate out of the state is directed by will to be sold or converted into money to pay legacies, the legacies pass as money, subject to the tax. (Miller's Estate, 182 Pa. St. 157; 37 Atl. Rep. 1000.)

But may be otherwise where the conversion is not imperative but permissive. (Handley's Estate, 181 Pa. St. 339; 37 Atl. Rep. 587.)

Where widow is given an estate upon express condition, that she pay certain legacies to collateral relatives, the gifts to the legatees are direct and subject to the tax. (Nieman's Estate, 131 Pa. St. 346; 18 Atl. Rep. 900.)

Where non-resident by will directs that land in another state should be sold to pay legacies, the proceeds of such sale are not subject to the tax. (Coleman's Estate, 159 Pa. St. 231; 28 Atl. Rep. 137.)

(d) **Exemptions.**—An amendment to the statute exempting certain charitable and other corporations applies only to domestic corporations, and foreign corporations are not exempted. The fact that such a corporation has a limited privilege by special statute to hold real and personal property within the state, does not relieve it from the legacy duty. (Estate of Prime, 136 N. Y. 347; 32 N. E. Rep. 1091; Catlin v. Trustees, 113 N. Y. 133; 20 N. E. Rep 864.)

Bequests to colleges and churches or other charitable corporations liable to pay such a tax; property not exempt until they receive it. (Baninger v. Cowan, 2 Jones Eq. 437; and see Miller v. Commonwealth, 27 Gratt. 110.)

Exemption as to religious corporations applicable only to domestic corporations. (Matter of Balleis, 144 N. Y. 132; 38 N. E. 1007; follow Prime case.)

Exemption of charitable organizations. (Hooper v. Shaw,   Mass. ; 57 N. E. Rep. 361.)

Municipal corporations are not exempt under a general description as "corporations now exempt by law from taxation." (Matter of Hamilton, 148 N. Y. 310; 42 N. E. Rep. 717.)

But now held otherwise by effect of N. Y. Tax. law 1896. (Matter of Thrall, 157 N. Y. 46; 51 N. E. Rep. 411.)

Under N. Y. Act 1892, exempting in case of " any person to whom decedent stood in mutually acknowledged relation of parent " such relation may exist where person is not of his blood, and not legally adopted. (Matter of Beach, 154 N. Y. 242; 48 N. E. Rep. 516.)

A widow is not exempt as widow, where she marries again. (Commonwealth v. Powell, 51 Pa. St. 438.)

The exemption of five hundred dollars, is a several exception of that sum from each portion of the estate passing by will or descent to persons outside the exempted classes. It applies to each taker within the class subject to the duty. (State v. Hamlin, 86 Me. 495; 30 Atl. Rep. 76.)

When *proviso* of statute is that an estate of less than five hundred dollars shall not be subject to the tax, the legislative intent is to limit the estates upon which the tax should be imposed, and not that all taxable estates should be exempt to the extent of five hundred dollars. (Estate of Sherwell, 125 N. Y. 376; 26 N. E. Rep. 464; and see Matter of Howe, 112 N. Y. 100; 19 N. E. Rep. 513; Matter of Cager, 111 N. Y. 343; 18 N. E. Rep. 866; and compare Howell's Estate, 147 Pa St. 164, 168; 23 Atl. Rep. 403.)

Where statute in terms makes subject to tax, property "of which a person may die *seised* or *possessed*," the increase or interest thereafter obtained cannot be made subject to the tax. (Matter Will of Vassar, 127 N. Y. 1; 27 N. E. Rep. 394; Williamson's Estate, 153 Pa. St. 508; 26 Atl. Rep. 246.)

(e) **Where there are life interests and remainders.**—But where the right to possession or enjoyment on death of life tenant is contingent solely as to the persons who should eventually take and the proportions to be observed, the legatees as a class being certain, the particular individuals being alone uncertain, the right of. the state (if any) attaches when the right of succession accrues but may not be enforced in advance of that future possession and enjoyment or indefeasible ownership which identifies the persons who ought to pay. (Matter of Seaman, 147 N. Y. 69; 41 N. E. Rep. 401.)

Where property is willed to widow for life *subject* to *power of disposition* by her *during her life,* with remainder to legatees dependent upon contingency whether the power of disposition was exercised by the life tenant, *held,* that the present appraisable value of the interest of such legatees was incapable of any correct or reasonably approximate valuation. (Matter of Cager, 111 N. Y. 343; 18 N. E. Rep. 866.)

Contingent interests given by will, which might never become vested, and cases where, although there may have been a technical vesting of a future estate, the estate is liable to be defeated before it comes into actual enjoyment, may require delay in proceeding to fix the tax. (Matter of Westurn, 152 N. Y. 93, 100; 46 N. E. Rep. 315.)

The true test of value by which the tax is to be measured is the value of the estate at the time of the transfer of the title, and not its value at the time of the transfer of possession. Hence, in case of a vested remainder it must be appraised at time of death of testator when title passed and not as of time of death of life tenant when possession passed. (Matter of Davis, 149 N. Y. 539; 44 N. E. Rep. 185.)

Under the N. Y. Act of 1892, where a trust fund remains in the hands of executors to feed life estates and for payment over of the remainder, the executors must pay the tax when they know against whom it is chargeable and the rate to be assessed. The state gets its tax when the legatees get their property. The appraisal should be adjourned until rights of remaindermen become fixed and actual. (Matter of Hoffman, 143 N. Y. 327; 38 N. E. Rep. 311; and see also Matter of Roosevelt, 143 N. Y. 120; 38 N. E. Rep. 281; Matter of Curtis, 142 N. Y. 219; 36 N. E. Rep. 887.)

While appraisal may be postponed, the value which is the measure is the value at time of the transfer of title and not at time of transfer of possession. (Matter of Sloane, 154 N. Y. 109; 47 N. E. Rep. 978.)

In case of contingent remainders a delay until contingency is solved is necessary and proper. (Matter of Curtis, 142 N. Y. 219; 36 N. E. Rep. 887.)

The ascertainment of the persons entitled to the property of a decedent must precede the imposition of any tax. (Matter of Westurn, 152 N. Y. 93; 46 N. E. Rep. 315.)

Where widow or life tenant has power of disposition during life, the tax can not be ascertained until after her death. (Nieman's Estate, 131 Pa. St. 346; 18 Atl. Rep. 900.)

Appraisal where life tenancy is terminated by remarriage of the widow. (Matter of Sloane, 154 N. Y. 109; 47 N. E. Rep. 978.)

In case of remainder after life estate as to value at what time, see Line's estate (155 Pa. St. 379; 26 Atl. Rep. 728.)

As to appraisal of contingent interests under N. Y. Act of 1885. (Matter of Stewart, 131 N. Y. 274; 30 N. E. Rep. 184.)

(f) **Exercise of a power.**—Bequests in exercise of a power by will, executed after the passage of a transfer tax act, but such power created by will which took effect before the passage of any taxable transfer law, are not subject to the tax, because the source of the title is the will creating the power, into which the names of the appointees must be read and their right of succession vests, not at time of execution of the power, but at time the will creating it took effect. (Matter of Harbeck, 161 N. Y. 211; 55 N. E. Rep. 851; rev'g 43 App. Div. 188; 59 N. Y. Supp. 362.)

But by special act in N. Y. in 1897, the exercise of a power is deemed a taxable transfer. (Id. 217; compare Crocker v. Shaw, 174 Mass. 266; 54 N. E. Rep. 549.)

Where the donee of a power has the right of selection, the interest appointed vests in the appointee at the time of the appointment, but his title relates to and is acquired under the will or instrument giving or creating the power. (Matter of Stewart, 131 N. Y. 274; 30 N. E. Rep. 184.)

(g) **Deeds of trust.**—Application of transfer act to deeds of trust. (Matter of Bostwick, 160 N. Y. 489; 55 N. E. Rep. 238; Matter of Edgerton, 35 App. Div. 125; aff'd 158 N. Y. 671; Line's Estate, 155 Pa. St. 378; 26 Atl. Rep. 728; and see Attorney-General v. Dodd [1894], 2 Q. B. 150.)

(h) **Statute not retroactive by construction.**—No retroactive effect. (Commonwealth v. Shimp, 53 Pa. St. 132, 137.)

An act imposing such a tax should not be made retroactive by construction. (Matter of Seaman 147 N. Y. 69; 41 N. E. Rep. 401.)

· The retroactive clause in the N. Y. Act of 1892, construed as restricted to case of gifts or grants *causa mortis* mentioned in the preceding portion of the sub-division and does not extend to transfers by will or intestacy so as to subject to taxation rights of sucession which accrued before the statute became a law. (Matter of Seaman, 147 N. Y. 70; 41 N. E. Rep. 401.)

(i) **Deductions.**—Debts, commissions and expenses of administration should be deducted from valuation. (Matter of Westurn, 152 N. Y. 93; 46 N. E. Rep. 315; Line's Estate, 155 Pa. St. 379; 26 Atl. Rep. 728; Orcutt's

Appeal, 97 Pa. St. 179; Commonwealth's Appeal, 127 Pa. St. 435; 17 Atl. Rep. 1094; Callahan v. Woodbridge, 171 Mass. 595, 599; 51 N. E. Rep. 176; Hooper v. Shaw, 57 N. E. Rep. 361; but see Pullman's Estate, 46 App. Div. 574; 62 N. Y. Supp. 395.)

Sum expended in litigation in sustaining a will should not be deducted from valuation. (Matter of Westurn, 152 N. Y. 93; 46 N. E. Rep. 315.)

Expenses of litigation not deducted. (Line's Estate, 155 Pa. St. 379; 26 Atl. Rep. 728.)

But litigation over probate of a will necessarily delays-proceedings to fix transfer tax. (Matter of Westurn, 152 N. Y. 93; 46 N. E. Rep. 315.)

The legacy tax paid to the United States under Act of Congress 1898, should be deducted. (Hooper v. Shaw, Mass. ; 57 N. E. Rep. 361.)

Transfer by will, although made for the purpose of paying a debt, and accepted as such payment is subject to the tax. (Matter of Gould, 156 N. Y. 423; 51 N. E. Rep. 287.)

(j) **Some illustrative cases.**—Personal property bequeathed by will to the United States is subject to the tax under state law. (United States v. Perkins, 163 U. S. 625; 16 Sup. Rep. 1073; aff'g Matter of Merriam, 141 N .Y. 479; 36 N. E. Rep. 505.)

It is proper to include in the valuation United States bonds for purpose of ascertaining the tax, unless excluded by specific terms of the statute in imposing the tax, as, for instance, in the New York Statute. (N. Y. Statute § 22, L. 1892; Matter of Sherman, 153 N. Y. 1; 46 N. E. Rep. 1032; Matter of Whiting, 150 N. Y. 27; 44 N. E. Rep. 715.)

A grandmother held subject to tax, although a lineal and not a collateral relative. (McDowell v. Addams, 55 Pa. St. 430.)

A policy of life insurance, on life of decedent, payable to his executors, administrators and assigns, or to his representatives, is subject to the tax. (Matter of Knoedler, 140 N. Y. 377; 35 N. E. Rep. 601; but see Abbett's Estate, 29 Misc. 567; 61 N. Y. Supp. 1067.)

As to jurisdiction of surrogate. (Estate of Ullman, 137 N. Y. 403; 33 N. E. Rep. 480; Matter of Fitch, 160 N. Y. 87; 54 N. E. Rep. 701.)

DILLARD *vs.* DILLARD *et al.*

[Supreme Court of Appeals of Virginia, Sept. 21, 1899; 97 Va. 434; 34 S.
E. Rep. 60.]

MULTIFARIOUSNESS—RES JUDICATA—WILL—CONSTRUCTION—
DISCRETIONARY POWER.

1. A bill is not objectionable as multifarious where the construction of a
will is the primary matter in controversy, around which all the matters
in issue revolve, and on which all the relief sought depends, and all
the complainants are immediately interested in the various clauses to be
construed and in all the questions involved, and defendant is concerned
in them all, and will be affected by their decision.

2. A decree dismissing a suit by one for construction of a will and for an
interest claimed thereunder, on the ground that he took nothing under
the will, is not *res judicata*, against persons joined with the executor
as defendants in such suit, where they bring a suit for construction of
the will, not claiming in the same right as the plaintiff in the former
motion, but asserting rights separate, distinct, and antagonistic to those
asserted by him, and they not being in privity with him.

3. The term "money," in a gift to testatrix's husband for life, and thereafter over to another, of "all the money that may be in the hands of
my said husband as trustee for me at my decease," includes a debt to
him as trustee for money of the trust fund which he has loaned out.

4. The discretionary power jointly confided to three trustees by name, to
give all or any part of the fund to a certain person, though coupled with
an interest, cannot, after death of one of them, be executed by the survivors; Code, § 3419, as amended by Acts 1889-90, p. 41, and Acts
1897-98, p. 687, not referring to a trust involving such power.

5. Where discretionary power is jointly given to three trustees, by name,·
to give all or any part of the fund to D., and they are also directed,
whenever and on such terms as they think proper, to sell the property
belonging to the fund and remaining unappropriated, and divide the
proceeds equally between three certain persons, one of the trustees
having died without any of the property having been given by them
to D., their only other discretion (determination of time and terms of
sale) then ceases, and the sale and division among the three persons
must be made in a reasonable time.

APPEAL from Circuit Court, Nelson county.

Suit by one Dillard and others against one Dillard. Decree for
complainants. Defendant appeals.
Reversed.

Caskie & Coleman, for appellant.

J. Thompson Brown and *A. B. Coleman,* for appellees.

RIELY, J.—There was a demurrer to the bill for multifariousness. It was overruled by the court, and this is assigned as error.

It is a general rule of chancery pleading that a party will not be permitted to embrace in the same bill distinct and separate causes of action, but, to come within the rule, the causes must be wholly distinct, and each cause, as stated, must be sufficient to sustain a bill. The courts, however, have found it impracticable to lay down any fixed rule applicable to all cases, but, where the matters in controversy are not absolutely independent of each other, they consider what is just and convenient in the particular case; and if it will be more convenient to litigate and dispose of the matter in controversy in one suit, and this can be done without injustice to any party, the objection of multifariousness will not prevail. (Story, Eq. Pl. § 530; *Segar* v. *Parrish,* 20 Grat. 672; *Hill's Adm'r* v. *Hill,* 79 Va. 592; *School Board of Albemarle Co.* v. *Farish's Adm'r,* 92 id. 156; 23 S. E. 221; *Spooner's Adm'r* v. *Hilbish's Ex'r,* 92 Va. 333; 23 S. E. 751; and *Staude* v. *Keck,* 92 Va. 544; 24 S. E. 227.)

In the case at bar the true construction of the will of Narcissa E. Dillard, deceased, is the primary matter in controversy. It is the pivot, as it were, around which all the matters in issue revolve, and upon which all the relief sought depends. All the complainants are immediately interested in the various clauses of the will to be construed, and in each and all of the questions involved; and the appellant is likewise concerned in them all, and will be affected by their decision. It is therefore manifestly both proper and convenient to litigate in the same suit the several matters in controversy. It cannot be perceived how the appellant could be prejudiced by this mode of proceeding.

The defense of *res adjudicata* is likewise untenable. It is a just maxim of the law that no person shall be twice vexed for one and the same cause of action, but the justice of the maxim requires that the judgment of decree in a former suit which is relied on as a bar to the subsequent suit must have been rendered upon the merits of the controversy. The adjudication, when so made, it may be added, constitutes a bar, not only to the points actually decided, but to every point which properly belonged to the particular matter in litigation, and which the parties might have brought forward at the time; for a party is required to present the whole of his case, and not omit a part which by the exercise of reasonable diligence he might have brought forward at the time. All those matters which were offered and received, or which might have been offered, to sustain the particular claim or demand litigated in the prior suit, and all those matters of defense which were presented or might have been introduced under the issue to defeat the claim or demand, are concluded by the judgment or decree in the former suit. It must, however, have been rendered in a proceeding between the same parties or their privies, and the matter in controversy must have been the same in the former suit as in the latter, and been determined on the merits. (*Chrisman's Adm'x* v. *Harman,* 29 Grat. 494; *Diamond State Iron Co.* v. *Alex. K. Rarig Co.* 93 Va. 595; 25 S. E. 894; and *Miller* v. *Wills,* 95 Va. 354; 28 S. E. 337.)

The decree relied upon as a bar to the present suit was not rendered upon the merits of the matters now in controversy. The former suit was brought by John T. Dillard mainly for the construction of the will of his mother, the settlement of the accounts of her executor, and the recovery of the interest he claimed under her will. He was sole plaintiff, and made, among other persons, the complainants and the executor defendants. The court decided that the plaintiff took nothing under the will of the decedent, and upon that ground alone dismissed his bill. (*Dillard* v. *Dillard's Ex'rs,* 21 S. E. 669.) This was clearly not a decision on the merits of the matters now in issue. The complainants in the present suit do not claim in the same right as the plaintiff in the former suit. All claim under the same will, but the rights asserted by them are separate, distinct, and antagonistic to those asserted by him. In no sense were they in privity with him. A decision that he was without any right to maintain the suit did not determine their right to sue, and was not an adjudication in any manner of the matters now put in issue. And no case was made by the pleadings or proof that warranted a decree between them and the appellant as co-defendants

This brings us to the merits of this controversy. The testatrix, in the latter part of the first clause of her will, devises and bequeaths as follows: "And from and immediately after the death of my said husband I hereby give and devise the tract of land * * * and all the money and other personal property in this clause given to my said trustees for the sole use and benefit of my said husband, that may be on hand and unexpended and unappropriated, to my son William S. Dillard, and his heirs and assigns, forever."

The particular matter to be decided is what William S. Dillard took under the phrase "all the money" in the above bequest. In what sense did the testatrix use the word "money," and what is embraced by it? Did she mean "money," in its natural and ordinary sense, or did she intend to include, also, debts and securities?

It seems to be well settled that a gift in a will of "money," with nothing in the context to explain or define the sense in which it is used, includes cash, bank notes, and money in bank, but does not include choses in action or securities. The word, however, is often popularly used as synonymous with "personal estate," and has been construed to include, besides money, literally so called, not only debts and securities, but the whole personal estate, and even the proceeds of realty. (1 Jarm. Wills, 724-732; *Dabney* v. *Cottrell's Adm'x,* 9 Grat. 572; and *In re Miller,* 17 Am. Rep. 422.) What is meant by the word "money" must in each case depend upon the will and its context.

In order to ascertain what money the testatrix referred to, and what she meant by its use, it is necessary to look to the prior part of the clause making the gift to trustees for the benefit of her husband. After giving to them the tract of land on which she resided, and certain personal property, she then also gives to them " all the money that may be in the hands of my said husband as my trustee at the time of my decease," and directs that they permit him to make such use and disposition of the rents and profits of the land and " of the money and other personal property as to him may seem right and proper, without stint or accountability."

It appears from the record that her husband held certain estate and funds in trust for her and had lent a part thereof in the year 1858 to Thomas J. Massie, for which he took the bond of Massie, with personal security, payable to himself as trustee for his wife, and subsequently reduced the same to judgment.

In construing a will of personal property, the terms used are to be construed according to the ordinary acceptation of language in the transactions of mankind. There is generally a wide difference in a person's meaning, when, in speaking of his "money," he is referring to money in his own possession or under his immediate control, and when he is speaking of "money" belonging to him, which is in the possession or under the control of another person. In the one case he knows of what his property consists, and knows what part of it is in ready money and what part is invested. Therefore when he is referring to his "money" in his own possession, he usually means his ready money; that is, the money which he has actually in hand, in his dwelling, or on deposit in bank. In the other case, when he is referring to his "money" in the possession of another person, as in the case of money for his use and benefit in the hands of a trustee, whose duty it is to invest or lend out the money, he generally means the fund so held in trust. In the latter case he would naturally presume that the trustee had done his duty, and lent out or invested the money, but would not be likely to know to whom it was lent, or how it was invested. It is a common expression of a *cestui que trust* to speak of his or her money in the hands of the trustee; referring, not merely to the coin or currency that may happen to be in the hands of the trustee, but meaning the trust fund or estate, in whatever shape it may be, or however invested. It was this sense, we think, in which the testatrix used the phrase "all the money that may be in the hands of my said husband as trustee for me at my decease," and that consequently the gift over to William S. Dillard includes the "Massie" debt.

By the fifth clause of her will the testatrix gave to her sons William S. Dillard and Stephen T. Dillard and her son-in-law, John C. Mundy, in trust, all her right, title, and interest in and to the tract of land on which her son John T. Dillard resided, and also the sum of $2,000, "to be held and managed by the said trustees at their own absolute discretion. They may permit my son John T. Dillard to occupy and enjoy the said tract of land, and to take to himself the profit thereof, and may pay to him the whole or any part of the principal or interest of the said sum of money, but shall not be compelled, or be liable to be compelled, to do so, either at law or in equity. * * * The said trustees are also authorized, if they think proper to do so (but they shall not be compelled, or be liable to be compelled to do so, either at law or in equity, being hereby vested with an absolute and uncontrollable discretion), to give the whole or any part of the money or of the land aforesaid to my son John T. Dillard, in fee, for life or for a term of years, subject to such conditions, limitations, and restrictions as they may think proper to annex to such gift; and I desire and hereby direct that the said trustees, whenever they may think it proper so to do, shall sell, upon such terms as they may deem best, the whole of the real and personal property belonging to said trust fund, and remaining unappropriated and still under their control, and divide the proceeds of such sale, together with any moneys belonging to said trust fund, into three equal parts; " giving one of said parts for the benefit of Elizabeth H. Dillard, another part for the benefit of Cynthia J. Mundy, and the remaining part for the benefit of the children of Terisha W. Dillard.

Stephen T. Dillard, one of the trustees, died, without the land or money, or any part thereof, having been given by them to John T. Dillard under the discretionary power conferred upon them by the trust. Two questions, therefore, arise and are presented by the pleadings in the case: First, can the discretionary power be now exercised in favor of John T. Dillard by the surviving trustees? And, second, if not, what right, if any, have the complainants to require the land to be sold, and Cynthia J. Mundy and the executor of Elizabeth H. Dillard deceased, to recover one-third each of the proceeds of sale and of the moneyed legacy?

It is manifest that the trust created by the fifth clause of the will is, as respects John T. Dillard, discretionary, and peculiarly one of personal confidence. It imposed on the trustees a most delicate duty. The testatrix, for reasons which do not appear on the face of the will, thereby placed this son, with respect to any interest in her estate, in the uncontrollable power of the trustees. For the discharge of this trust she selected two of her sons and a son-in-law. In all the other trusts created by the will, their execution was intrusted to the two sons. The power, as respects John T. Dillard, being conferred on the three trustees by name, without words of survivorship, and being one of personal confidence, it could only be conjointly exercised by all three of them, and not by a less number. The authority, being joint, is determined by the death of one of them. (Hill, Trustees, marg. pp. 211, 227, 489); 2 Perry Trusts, §§ 496, 497, 499; *Cole* v. *Wade*, 16 Ves. 27; *Walter* v. *Maunde*, 19 id. 424; and *Brown* v. *Hobson*, 3 A. K. Marsh. 380.)

If the law were otherwise, then upon the death of one of the trustees the two survivors could execute the power, and upon the death of one of them the sole survivor could do so, and might dispose of the property contrary to what the other two trustees in their lifetime always opposed and prevented, and thereby frustrate the very object of the testator in intrusting its disposition to the joint judgment of all three of them, and defeat his testamentary intent. The question here is not the same that was decided in *Sulphur Mines Co. of Virginia* v. *Thompson* (93 Va. 293; 25 S. E. 232), but very different. There the question was whether a power coupled with an interest, unexecuted in the lifetime of the donor, was revoked by his death. The question here is whether a discretionary power jointly confided to three trustees by name, though coupled with an interest, can be executed by the survivors after the death of one of the trustees or donees of the power.

Section 3419 of the Code, as amended by Acts 1889-90, p. 41, and by Acts 1897-98, p. 687, was relied upon by counsel as authority for the execution of the power by the surviving trustees. These statutes could never have been intended to refer to a trust involving discretion or personal confidence, but only to those trusts which a court may execute. Where the trust is discretionary or one of personal confidence, a court of equity has no jurisdiction to interfere with its exercise by the trustee so long as he acts in good faith, and cannot execute it; nor can any trustee appointed by it in the place of him in whom the discretion and confidence was reposed do so. (Hill, Trustees, marg. pp. 486, 488, 495; 2 Perry Trusts, §§ 499, 510, 511; *Cowles* v. *Brown*, 4 Call, 477; *Cochran* v. *Paris*, 11 Grat. 348; and *Read* v. *Patterson*, 6 Am. St. Rep. 877; and note thereto [s. c. 14 Atl. 490].)

The power to give the property or any part of it to John T. Dillard having become extinct by the death of Stephen T. Dillard, the trust became absolute for the alternate beneficiaries. The testatrix expressly directs that the trustees, " whenever they may think it proper so to do, shall sell, upon such terms as they may deem best, the whole of the real and personal property belonging to said trust fund, and remaining unappropriated and still under their control, and divide the proceeds of such sale, together with any moneys belonging to said trust fund," among the persons therein named and specified. The discretionary power not having been exercised in favor of John T. Dillard before the death of Stephen T. Dillard, and consequently not being capable of now being exercised, there remains no discretion in the trustees as to the disposition of the trust subject. The beneficiaries who are to take it are named and the manner in which they are to take it is prescribed. The only discretion allowed the trustees, if the power with respect to John T. Dillard was not exercised in his favor, was as to the time when and the terms upon which the sale of the property should be made and the distribution take place; but this discretion being confided to the three trustees jointly, like that conferred upon them with respect to John T. Dillard, it ceased with the death of Stephen T. Dillard, and the surviving trustees were thereafter without authority to postpone the sale and the division of the trust subject. Good faith required that this duty be performed within a reasonable time. It could not be indefinitely deferred. Stephen T. Dillard died April 10, 1890, and this suit was brought to September rules, 1893. The court properly decreed that the land be sold, in order that the proceeds of sale and the rest of the trust subject might be divided among the alternate beneficiaries.

The decree appealed from, however, must be reversed for the erroneous construction of the first clause of the will, and the cause remanded to be further proceeded in in accordance with the views herein expressed.

ADAMS vs. ADAMS.

[Supreme Court of Illinois, October 16, 1899; 181 Ill. 210; 54 N. E. Rep. 558.]

DECEDENT'S ESTATE—ASSETS—OWNERSHIP—EVIDENCE.

The *prima facie* presumption of D.'s ownership of a note given by R. to him as a payee, and of a certificate of deposit to his own order, arising from his possession thereof at the death of his mother, is overcome by evidence that the money for which they were given belonged to the mother, constituted nearly her whole personal estate, and had been loaned by her agent A.; that she complained to him of the irregularity of the payment of the interest, directed him to collect the principal, and told him that, as her health was poor, she would send D. to see about the collections from time to time; that A. disposed of most of the money in the bank to her order, and shortly afterwards she gave a check therefor to D., who, in a few days, loaned the money to R., taking the note in question; and that, on A. giving a check for the balance of the collection, D. deposited it, taking therefor the said certificate of deposit.

APPEAL from Appellate Court, First district.

Proceeding by John S. Adams against Robert D. Adams. From a judgment of the Appellate Court affirming judgment for the petitioner (81 Ill. App. 637), respondent appeals.
Affirmed.

C. B. Morrison, S. H. Bethea, and Henry S. Dixon, for appellant.

A. C. Bardwell, for appellee.

WILKIN, J.—This is a petition to the June term, 1897, of the County Court of Lee county, by John S. Adams, as one of the children and heirs at law of his mother, Amanda M. B. Adams, deceased, under sections 81 and 82 of the Administration Act, to compel Robert D. Adams, his brother, to transfer to the administrator of the estate of their mother certain moneys and securities held by him, amounting to about $10,000, alleged to have belonged to her at the time of her death. Mrs. Adams, a widow, died intestate on the 28th day of May, 1897, leaving her sons, Waldo, Robert D., and John S., and an adopted daughter, Maud Adams, her only heirs at law. At the time of her death she was about seventy years old. For several years before January 1, 1895, one J. C. Ayres had conducted her business affairs, loaned money for her, and collected the interest. Some time prior to November 5, 1894, she had nearly her whole personal estate invested in two mortgages, one of $8,000 and the other of about $1,600. In October of that year she informed Ayres she was tired of the irregularity of the payment of interest on the $8,000 loan, and desired to have it collected. Ayres thereupon proceeded to make the collection, and on November 5th following the sum of $8,164.71 was collected by him. On the day the money was received by him, he deposited $6,000 to her credit in the bank, and four days later $2,000 more. On January 4, 1895, he collected the other loan, amounting, with interest, to $1,758.12, which he held for the time, subject to her order. Mrs.

Adams told Ayres at their meeting in October, 1894, that, as her
health was poor, she would send her son, the appellant, to see about
the collections from time to time. On December 24, 1894, Mrs.
Adams gave appellant a check for $8,000, and on January 7th fol-
lowing he loaned it to one Rosenthal, taking the note and mortgage
in his own name, and at the same time drawing the money from the
bank on the check from his mother. On January 15, 1895, Ayres
gave appellant his check for $1,600, and on January 29th following
his check for $62.25, of the funds held by him to the credit of Mrs.
Adams. On the 17th of that month appellant presented the check
of Mrs. Adams for $1,600 to the bank, and took a certificate of de-
posit for $1,500 to his own order. After her death, letters of ad-
ministration on her estate were taken out. The administrator filed
an inventory, showing that all the property she owned at the time
of her death was a lot in the city of Dixon, valued at $500, and
household furniture of the value of $150. The object of the peti-
tion in this cause was to compel appellant to turn over the money,
notes, and mortgages received by him from the fund collected by
Ayres to the estate of his mother. Appellant answered the petition, denying that he had such money, notes, and securities belonging to his mother at the time of her death. The cause was heard
first in the County Court, and afterwards in the Circuit Court.
Upon the hearing, appellant offered no evidence on behalf of himself. The finding of the Circuit Court was for the petitioner, ordering respondent to turn over to the administrator, among other
things, a mortgage for $8,000, and the sum of $1,662.25 in cash,
as the property of the deceased. This order was affirmed by the
judgment of the Appellate Court for the Second District, where
the cause was taken on appeal. Robert D. Adams, appellant, now
appeals to this court.

As we read the evidence and the arguments of counsel in this
case, but a single question arises; that is, whether the mere possession of the assets by appellant at the time of his mother's death,
under the evidence in this case, is sufficient to establish his ownership, and entitle him to the property in his own individual right.
His sole reliance is upon the presumption of law that possession of
personal property is *prima facie* evidence of ownership. There is
no claim or pretense that the money did not belong to the deceased
at the time it was collected by Ayres, her agent, and paid over to

the bank to her credit. From the evidence there appears to be no
ground for an inference that she made a gift of the money to appellant, nor does he make this claim. He does not claim that he
paid his mother any consideration for the money. By his answer
he negatives the presumption that it was a loan to him. On the
other hand, the evidence strongly tends to prove that he, in drawing
out the money and reloaning it, acted as the agent of his mother.
From the evidence introduced, the conclusion is irresistible that the
courts below were abundantly justified in holding that the *prima
facie* presumption of ownership was overcome, and that appellant's
possession was not as owner of the property, but as agent for the
owner. We agree fully with the Appellate Court that the case of
Martin v. *Martin* (174 Ill. 371; 51 N. E. 691), cited and relied
upon by appellant, has no bearing upon the issue here. In that
case the person holding the property in dispute did not rely upon
mere possession as her evidence of ownership, but upon proof
which clearly showed that she was put in possession of the property
as the owner, and not in any sense as an agent, or in any other
capacity than that of owner.

It is urged that the County Court was without jurisdiction to
determine this matter, because there was no evidence sufficient to
establish a trust relation between appellant and his mother. On
that question we see no ground for reasonable controversy. The
Appellate Court held that such a relation did exist, and we are
satisfied the evidence warrants the finding. The cause is one provided for by the sections of the statute before referred to, and the
County Court exercised its reasonable equitable jurisdiction in the
matter. From a careful consideration of the evidence and this
whole record, we have no hesitancy in saying the judgment of
the Appellate Court is correct, and its judgment will be affirmed.

Judgment affirmed.

GULICK *vs.* GRISWOLD.

[Court of Appeals of New York, October 17, 1899; 160 N. Y. 399; 54 N. E. Rep. 780.]

POWERS—RIGHT TO SELL REALTY—TERMINATION—STATUTES—
RETROACTIVE OPERATION.

1. Where a testator authorizes his executrix, with the consent of her mother, to sell his realty, and the mother dies before consenting to a sale, the power terminates on her death.

2. Real Property Law, § 154 (Laws 1896, ch. 547), providing that where the consent of two persons to the execution of a power is requisite, and before its execution one dies, the consent of the survivor is sufficient, unless otherwise prescribed by the power, is not applicable when one of the persons whose consent was necessary to the exercise of a power died before its passage, since it has no retroactive effect.

APPEAL from Supreme Court, Appellate Division, First Department.

Submission, without action, of a controversy between Mary E. Gulick, executrix of Isaac F. Jones, deceased, as plaintiff, and John C. Griswold, as defendant. There was a judgment for defendant (43 N. Y. Supp. 443), and plaintiff appeals. Affirmed.

Franklin Pierce, for appellant.

Herbert A. Shipman, for respondent.

PARKER, C. J.—Isaac F. Jones, by his will, authorized the executrix thereof, with the consent of her mother, to sell his real estate. Jones died in 1870. The mother of the executrix died in 1875, without having given her consent to a sale, and in 1896 the executrix attempted to exercise the power. The appellate division correctly decided that at the time of the death of the mother it was the law of this state that her death operated to terminate the power of sale. (*Barber* v. *Cary,* 11 N. Y. 397.) The contention of the appellant that section 154 of the real property law establishes that it is now the law that, notwithstanding the death of the mother, the power of sale survived, and was properly executed, is not well taken in this case, as the statute was not passed until long after her death, and there is nothing in its provisions suggesting that it was intended to have a retroactive effect. The judgment should be affirmed, with costs. All concur.

Judgment affirmed.

NOTE.—TERMINATION OF POWER OF SALE.

(a) Purpose ceases—Power ceases.
(b) As to time of its exercise.
(c) Connected with trusts.
(d) Effect of death.

(a) **Purpose ceases—Power ceases.**—When the purpose ceases the power ceases. (Harvey v. Brisbin, 50 Hun, 377; 3 N. Y. Supp. 676; aff'd 143 N. Y. 151; 38 N. E. Rep. 108; Hetzel v. Barber, 69 N. Y. 1.)

When executor has sold all that was necessary to carry out provisions of a will, the power of sale is exhausted. (Swift's Appeal, 87 Pa. St. 502.)

Power ceases when estate is settled, all claims satisfied actually or presumptively by lapse of time, and no object of the testator remains to be attained. (Ward v. Barrows, 2 Ohio St. 241.)

A power to sell for an object which cannot be accomplished cannot itself be exercised. (Bates v. Bates, 134 Mass. 110; Slocum v. Slocum, 4 Edw. Ch. 613, 616; Sharpsteen v. Tillon, 3 Cow. 651.)

When power is given for a specific purpose which fails or is accomplished without a conversion, it ceases. (Sweeney v. Warren, 127 N. Y. 426; 28 N. E. Rep. 413; and see Gourley v. Campbell, 66 N. Y. 169.)

Ceases as soon as all the legacies and bequests specified in the will are satisfied. (Chamberlain v. Taylor, 36 Hun, 24.)

When power is qualified "that it must be expedient in interest of legatee" and legatee having no interest, because funds sufficient to satisfy from other sources, the power ceases. (Hovey v. Chisolm, 56 Hun, 328; 9 N. Y. Supp. 671.)

It continues until the whole of the real estate is divided among the several devisees, either by act of the parties or by legal proceedings. (Hoffman v. Hoffman, 66 Md. 568; 8 Atl. Rep. 466.)

Where the beneficiary under a power of sale is also vested as heir or devisee with the title, subject to such power, he may if competent to convey before the power has been exercised, convey the real estate—and this extinguishes the power of sale. (Roberts v. Cary, 84 Hun, 328; 32 N. Y. Supp. 563.)

Where an executor is given imperative power to sell and to distribute the proceeds the parties entitled thereto, if of age, and rights of others not affected may elect to take the land; and the purpose of the power being thus accomplished it ceases. (Prentice v. Janssen, 79 N. Y. 478.)

But an election by one without the concurrence of the others will not extinguish the power. (Mellen v. Mellen, 139 N. Y. 210; 34 N. E. Rep. 925; McDonald v. O'Hara, 144 N. Y. 566; 39 N. E. Rep. 642.)

A tender of a debt secured by a deed of trust, takes away the power of the trustee to sell. (Welch v. Greenalge, 2 Heisk. 209.)

(b) **As to time of its exercise.**—When time discretionary may be delay. (Wimbish v. Rawlins, 76 Va. 48.) In this case very nearly two years.

When entrusted in terms to the discretion of the executor as to time of its exercise, court will not ordinarily interfere, but if he fails to exercise his judgment, the court may put him in motion or act in his place. (Haight v. Brisbin, 96 N. Y. 132.)

Where there are no special or modifying facts a period of eighteen months may serve as a just standard in fixing a reasonable time for an executor to exercise his power. (Estate of Weston, 91 N. Y. 502.)

Where will directed sale of all the estate within five years, and division of proceeds, the provision as to time is directory only, and the power can be afterwards exercised. In this case testator died February, 1878, and the power of sale was exercised February, 1887. (Waldron v. Schlang, 47 Hun, 252.)

When power was imperative a lapse of twenty-nine years was *held* no objection to its exercise. (Clifford v. Morrell, 22 App. Div. 470; 48 N. Y. Supp. 83.)

Where power of a trustee is limited as to time, and exercised within that time, it cannot be exercised subsequently on first purchaser refusing or neglecting to take title. (Simmons v. Baynard, 30 Fed. Rep. 532.)

(c) **Connected with trusts.**—When power is connected with a specific trust which becomes executed or ceases, the power ceases. (Parrott v. Dyer, 105 Ga. 93; 31 S. E. Rep. 417; Bruner v. Meigs, 64 N. Y. 506; Benedict v. Webb, 98 id. 460.)

Does not cease for mere failure to exercise it. (Spitzer v. Spitzer, 38 App. Div. 436; 56 N. Y. Supp. 470.)

When power covers not only the residue but the whole estate and is unlimited as to time, and there are several trusts, the termination of one of the trusts does not extinguish the power. (Cussack v. Tweedy, 126 N. Y. 82; 26 N. E. Rep. 1023; and see McCready v. Metropolitan Life Ins. Co., 83 Hun, 526; 32 N. Y. Supp. 489; aff'd 148 N. Y. 761 [no opinion]; Cresson v. Ferree, 70 Pa. St. 446.)

Where there is a naked power, the mere fact that it might have been convenient to have exercised it in execution of the trust, does not show such connection with it, as to make it inoperative, when the trust itself has been deemed void. (Lindo v. Murray, 91 Hun, 335; 36 N. Y. Supp. 281; aff'd 157 N. Y. 697, without opinion.)

As dependent upon continuance or existence of trust see Heard v. Read (171 Mass. 374; 50 N. E. Rep. 638.)

May terminate with discharge as executor although will appoints same person trustee. Goad v. Montgomery, 119 Cal. 552; 51 Pac. Rep. 681.)

(d) **Effect of death.**—Where the power is imperative in trust for benefit of some person it does not cease with death of the executor, but may be executed by a trustee appointed by the court. (Osborne v. Gordon, 86 Wis. 92; 56 N. W. Rep. 334.)

When sole object of a power is to provide for support of a widow, it ceases with her death. (Fidler v. Lash, 125 Pa. St. 87; 17 Atl. Rep. 240; Jackson v. Elsworth, 6 Johns. 73.)

And so where she exercises her election and takes dower. (Snider v. Snider, 3 W. Va. 200.)

If the execution of a power is made dependent upon consent of a person who dies before it is exercised, the power ceases. (Barber v. Cary, 11 N. Y. 397; Kissam v. Dierkes, 49 id. 602; Piersol v. Roop, 56 N. J. Eq. 739; 40 Atl. Rep. 124.)

But see N. Y. Real Property Law, § 154; and see Phillips v. Davies (92 N. Y. 199), where in construing the particular will, the power was held to survive the death.

Where will gives widow all the property for life with power to sell and invest in discretion for benefit of an adopted daughter who is given the remainder, and the evidence showing that the power was given for the benefit of the widow as life tenant, it is not extinguished by the death of the adopted daughter. (Cotton v. Burkelman, 142 N. Y. 160; 36 N. E. Rep. 890.)

When power is in terms given to widow and another person "jointly and not singly," it ceased with death of the widow. (Herriott v. Prime, 87 Hun, 95; 33 N. Y. Supp. 970; aff'd 155 N. Y. 5; 49 N. E. Rep. 142; but the affirmance put upon the ground that the trust terminated with death of the widow, the other point not decided.)

A power of sale annexed to devise of the fee to be exercised at discretion of the devisee, expires at death of the devisee. (Sites v. Eldridge, 45 N. J. Eq. 632; 18 Atl. Rep. 214.)

Power to sell in trust to convert into money and pay over to a sole legatee, ceases on the death of such legatee. (Hannan v. Smith, 38 Fed. Rep. 482.)

Power survives death of a co-executor. (McCown v. Terrell, 9 Tex. Civ. App. 66.)

Where power of sale survived death of life tenant, see Millspaugh v. Van Zandt (55 Hun, 463; 8 N. Y. Supp. 637).

GIBSON vs. NELSON et al.

[Supreme Court of Illinois, October 13, 1899; 181 Ill. 122; 54 N. E. Rep. 901.]

WILLS—ATTESTATION—ORDER OF SIGNING.

Under statute of wills, requiring a will to be attested in the presence of the testator by two witnesses, who are present and see the testator sign the will, or to whom he acknowledges it to be his will, it is not essential that the testator sign first, if the signature and attestation be parts of the same transaction.

APPEAL from Circuit Court, Cook county; R. S. TUTHILL, Judge.

Will contest by Eva Nelson and others against James W. Gibson. There was a decree for complainants, and defendant appeals. Reversed.

George G. Bellows, for appellant.

M. C. Harper and *O. C. Peterson,* for appellees.

CARTER, J.—Upon their bill brought to contest the last will, and the probate thereof, of Leander E. Nelson, deceased, the appellees obtained a decree based upon a verdict of the jury that the will had not been signed by the testator when the attesting witnesses signed their names as witnesses to the instrument, and that it was not the last will of the deceased, and it was accordingly set aside. The record is now before us on the appeal of James W. Gibson, the principal legatee and devisee.

While there was some controversy of fact, yet we think the effect of the testimony of the subscribing witnesses was that they subscribed their names as witnesses to the instrument, as the last will of the testator, at his request and in his presence, but that he did not sign the will until after the signatures of the witnesses had been affixed; that the witnesses and the testator were all present at the time; that it was on the same occasion, and was one transaction, completed when all were present, but that in the mere order of signing the witnesses preceded the testator. On behalf of the contestants, the court gave to the jury the following instruction:

" The jury are instructed that, in order that a will be properly attested and be a valid will, it is necessary that the attesting witnesses subscribe their names to the same as witnesses in the presence of the testator and at his request, and that the name of the testator be signed to the instrument before the signatures of the attesting witnesses are attached; and you are instructed that if you find, from the evidence, that the signature of Leander E. Nelson was not attached to said instrument, so offered here as his will, until after the names of the attesting witnesses were attached thereto, then said instrument is not the last will and testament of said Nelson, and it is your duty so to find."

The question is thus presented for decision whether, under our statute of wills, an instrument intended as a will, appearing to have been executed and witnessed with all the formalities required by the statute, must fail to take effect as a will merely because the act of the testator in signing the will followed that of the witnesses, though done in their presence, on the same occasion, and as a part of one entire transaction.   Section 2 of the act in regard to wills, so far as it affects this question, provides: " All wills * * * by which any lands, * * * goods and chattels are devised shall be reduced to writing and signed by the testator or testatrix, or by some person in his or her presence and by his or her direction, and attested in the presence of the testator or testatrix by two or more credible witnesses, two of whom declaring on oath or affirmation, before the County Court of the proper county, that they were present and saw the testator or testatrix sign said will * * * in their presence, or acknowledge the same to be his or her act and deed, and that they believed the testator or testatrix to be of sound mind and memory at the time of signing or acknowledging the same, shall be sufficient proof of the execution of said will * * * to admit the same to record; * * * and every will, * * * when thus proven to the satisfaction of the court, shall, together with the probate thereof, be recorded, * * * and shall be good and available in law," etc.

It will be noticed that the statute does not in terms require the subscribing witnesses to attest or certify that the will was signed by the testator before they subscribed their own names; and in *Hobart v. Hobart* (154 Ill. 610; 39 N. E. 581), we held that, where the testator acknowledged the will to be his act and deed, that was sufficient, without acknowledging specifically and in terms that he had signed it; that, as it would not be a will without his signature, it would, in the absence of proof, be presumed from his statement that it was his will, and that he had signed it. In that case it was pointed out that decisions based upon the English statute, and the statutes of New York and other states, requiring specifically that the signature be made or acknowledged in the presence of the witnesses, were not applicable here, where the statute requires that the testator acknowledged merely the will. It cannot, of course, be presumed in the case at bar that at the precise moment when the witnesses subscribed their names to the instrument the testator had signed it, for they testified to the contrary on the trial below; but he signed it in their presence, as required by the statute, and the several acts of signing by the testator and witnesses took place on the same occasion, and constituted one transaction, viz., the execution and attestation of the will. Must the instrument be held inoperative as a will merely because the testator and the witnesses did not observe the usual order, in point of time, in signing their names? To so hold would, in our opinion, require a greater degree of nicety in the execution of wills than is required by the statute. Suppose the draftsman of a will has read it over to the testator, and the testator, having approved it, requests him to subscribe his name as a witness, and he does so at the time and in the presence of the testator, and then hands the pen to the testator, who thereupon signs the will; is there any provision of the statute or rule of law which would require the courts to take notice of the difference in the moment of time intervening between the two acts of signing, where both were parts of one transaction? We know of none. It would not be physically impossible for the testator and the witnesses to sign at the same time, yet, under the rule contended for and as held by the court below, the will would be invalid because the testator did not sign first. Undoubtedly the proper order is for the testator to sign first, for after the witnesses had signed he might never sign, or might sign on some other occasion or out of their presence, which would not be a compliance with the statute; but we are not prepared to hold that the validity of the instrument as a will can be made to turn upon the mere order in which the signatures are attached to the instrument, where all are attached at the same time. We are referred to cases, both English and American, which have so decided, but we do not regard the reasoning employed satisfactory when applied to a case arising under our statute. In *Chase* v. *Kittredge* (11 Allen, 63), while it was said that a will was not sufficiently witnessed where the witnesses signed their names before the testator signed, still the fact was, in that case, that one of the witnesses had not only signed his name before the testator had, but had signed it out of the presence of the testator. Still, it has undoubtedly been held in many cases that a will signed by the attesting witnesses before it was executed by the testator, though on the same occasion, is not entitled to probate. We are of the opinion, however, that, as applicable to cases arising under our statute, cases holding to the opposite view are sustained by the better reasoning. In *O'Brien* v. *Gallagher* (25 Conn. 229), the court said: " Where, as in the present case, witnesses are called to attest the will, and, being informed what the instrument is, subscribe their names thereto as witnesses, and the testator on his part and in their presence duly executes the instrument as his will, and all is done at one and the same time, and for the purpose of perfecting the instrument as a will, we cannot say that it is not legally executed, merely because the names of the witnesses were subscribed before that of the testator." So, also, in *Rosser* v. *Franklin* (6 Grat. 1), it was held that " the mere fact whether, in the order of time, the testatrix made her mark before or after the subscription of the witnesses, is, under the circumstance, in no wise material, insomuch as the whole transaction must be regarded as one continuous, uninterrupted act, conducted and completed within a few minutes, while all concerned in it were present, and during the unbroken supervising attention of the subscribing witnesses." So. too, in *Miller* v. *McNeill* (35 Pa. St. 217), the court said: " Our statute contemplates, undoubtedly, a signature by the testator, and then a signing by witnesses in attestation of the signature, * * * but when a transaction consists of several parts, all of which occur at the same moment and in the same presence, are we required to undo it because it did not occur in the orderly succession which the law contemplates? No language of our statute of wills imposes any such necessity upon us, and we would not decide anything so unreasonable except under stress of very positive statutory language. The execution and attestation of the will were contemporaneous, or, rather, simultaneous acts, and we will not regard the question who held the pen first,—the testator or his witnesses."

In 1 Redf. Wills (*226), it is said: "The particular order of the several requisites to the valid execution of a testament is not at all material, provided that they be done at the same time and as a part of the same transaction." These authorities, and others following them, hold, in our opinion, the more reasonable rule. To invalidate such a will, otherwise properly executed and attested, would enable a witness, after the lapse of many years, to defeat its operation by proof of an unimportant fact which few could then remember. How many witnesses to wills, unaided by presumptions and inferences which arise from the ordinary cause of procedure in the execution of wills, could remember as a fact that the testator signed the will first? While it is true, as contended, that the instrument is not a will until it has been executed by the testator, and cannot be attested as a will by the witnesses without such execution, it is also true that it is not a complete will until it has been attested by the necessary witnesses, the statute requiring both. While this attestation required by our statute includes the subscription of their names by the subscribing witnesses, it means much more; that is, that they bear witness and certify to the facts required by the statute to make a valid will. (*Swift* v. *Wiley,* 1 B. Mon. 114.) The mere physical act of signing their names does not constitute the whole, nor the most important part, of the duty of attesting witnesses. If all of the several acts required by the statute are done upon the same occasion, in the presence of the testator and the attesting witnesses, and, as said in the case cited above, under their unbroken supervising attention and as parts of one entire transaction, we cannot hold that the instrument is rendered inoperative as a will by merely proving the fact that the signatures of the witnesses were affixed before the signature of the testator. In the case at bar this fact did not appear by the testimony of the suscribing witnesses given in the Probate Court when the will was admitted to probate, but they testified to it on the hearing of the issue in this case in the Circuit Court. The will upon its face appeared to have been properly executed and witnessed, and the mere fact, which appeared by the evidence, that the testator signed it after the witnesses had signed, was rendered harmless by the further fact, shown by the evidence, that these several acts of sign-

ing were done at the same time and as parts of the same transaction. The court erred in giving the instruction in question. The
judgment will be reversed, and the cause remanded.

Reversed and remanded.

CLARK *vs.* CAMMANN *et al.*

[Court of Appeals of New York, October 3, 1899; 160 N. Y. 315; 54
N. E. Rep. 709.]

WILLS—CONSTRUCTION—VESTING OF BEQUEST—LAPSED LEGACY
—DISTRIBUTEES.

1. Under a will giving money in trust to pay the income to a niece for life,
and on her death to pay and divide the principal to and among her
children "and to their lawful representatives, forever," the issue of
any child then dead to take his parent's share, the gift to the children
will not vest if they die before their mother, leaving no issue.

2. The distributees of a lapsed legacy arising from a devise to trustees to
convert, to pay the income to testator's wife for life, and on her death
to pay the income of $10,000 thereof to a niece for life, and on her
death to divide the principal among her children, all of whom died
without issue before her, are those who were at the testator's death
entitled under the then statute of distribution.

APPEAL from Supreme Court, Appellate Division, First Department.

Action by W. Irving Clark, as trustee of Mary Ann Gillespie
under the last will and testament of Thomas L. Clark, against
Henry J. Cammann and others. From a judgment of the Appellate
Division affirming a judgment entered on the report of the referee
(43 N. Y. Supp. 575), defendants appeal.

Affirmed.

William C. Cammann and *William L. Clark,* for appellants Cammann and Johnson.

Mortimer C. Addoms, for appellant Mary A. Avery.

Henry A. Foster, for appellant Margaret A. Kane.

John Mason Knox, for appellant Christopher Wolf.

Charles S. Martin, for respondent Catharine A. Kissin and others.

Charles M. Bleecker, for respondent Edward M. Clark.

Henry A. Prince, for respondent William N. Clark and others.

Richard H. Mitchell, for respondent Isabella Hoffmire and others.

HAIGHT, J.—This action was brought to determine to whom a fund of $10,000 belongs. The facts, so far as pertinent, are in substance as follows: Thomas L. Clark died August 8, 1853, leaving a last will and testament dated March 3, 1848, which was duly proved and admitted to probate. After making certain specific bequests he gives and devises to his executors and trustee all his real estate and personal property not before disposed of, upon trust to reduce to possession, and receive the rents, incomes, and profits, to sell the real estate, and to invest the proceeds together with the personal estate, and to apply the income thereof to his wife for life. He then directs: " From and immediately after the decease of my said wife I will and direct that, as to $10,000 of the principal moneys to be invested as aforesaid, my said executors and trustees shall stand possessed of the same in trust to apply the interest thereof to the use of my niece Mary Ann, wife of my executor, George D. H. Gillespie, for and during her natural life, so as she may not anticipate the same, and from and immediately after her decease upon trust to pay over and divide the said principal sum of $10,000 unto and among all her children, share and share alike, and to their lawful representatives forever, as tenants in common, per capita; the issue of any such child who may then be dead to take his or her deceased parent's share." The testator then directs that on the death of his wife all the rest and residue of the money directed to be invested other than the $10,000, his trustee shall pay over and divide unto and among his nephews and nieces (naming them), " their respective heirs, executors, administrators, or assigns, forever, in equal shares, as tenants in common, per capita; the issue of any such child of either of my said brothers who may be then dead to take his or her deceased parent's share." He then concludes by appointing his executors and trustee. The testator's widow died in March, 1872. Mary Ann Gillespie had two sons, George Wolf Gillespie and John Clark Gillespie, and they were both living at the time of testator's death. George died in the year 1870, in the lifetime of the testator's widow, unmarried, without issue, and intestate; leaving his father, George H. Gillespie, as his only next of kin. John, the other son, died in the year 1873, after the death of the testator's widow, intestate and without issue; leaving his widow, Anna G. Gillespie, and his father, George H. Gillespie, as his next of kin. Mary Ann Gillespie died September 12, 1894. The estate of the testator passed into the hands of his trustee by reason of the trusts created by the will, and has been executed in accordance with its provisions down to the termination of the trust estates, which occurred at the death of Mary Ann Gillespie on the 12th of September, 1894, and there now remains in the hands of the trustee the principal sum of $10,000 for distribution. The defendants, either as appellants or respondents in this court, assert conflicting claims thereto. Henry G. Cammann, as one of the legatees under the will of the father of the two sons of Mary Ann Gillespie, claims that the fund vested in the sons, George and John, at the death of the testator. Walter B. Johnson, as committee of Mary A. Carroll, one of the next of kin of the widow of the son John, claims that the fund vested in the son John upon the death of the testator's widow. Christopher Wolf and Margaret Kane were the next of kin of the sons at the time of the death of their mother, Mary Ann Gillespie, and claim that the fund vested in them at that time, as the representatives of the deceased sons. Mary A. Avery was the sole surviving next of kin of the testator at the time of the death of Mary Ann Gillespie, and claims that there was no vested remainder in the fund in the sons, George and John, and that upon their death without issue the legacy lapsed and became vested in the sole surviving next of kin at the time of the death of Mary Ann Gillespie. The other claimants are the children or representatives of deceased nephews and nieces of the testator in being at the time of his decease, and they claim that the remainder did not vest in the sons, but was contingent, and the sons having both died before the termination of the life estate created by the will, without issue, the testator died intestate as to this fund, and that it should be divided among them. The referee ordered judgment in accordance with this latter contention, and the Appellate Division has affirmed such determination.

Various rules of the interpretation of wills have been invoked, among which are the following: (1) The law favors the vesting of legacies; (2) the testator is presumed to have intended to dispose of all his property, and an interpretation which results in partial intestacy will not be favored; (3) if futurity is annexed to the substance of a gift, the vesting is suspended; (4) if the gift is absolute, and only the time of payment is postponed, the gift is not suspended, but vests at once; (5) where the gift is only found in a direction to pay at a future time, time will be deemed to be of the essence of the gift, but if the amount of the gift is to be severed instanter from the general estate for the benefit of the legatee, and the interest thereon paid him until the period of distribution, a mere direction to pay at such a period will constitute a present gift; and (6) where a clause in a will is capable of two interpretations, the one should be adopted which prefers the persons of the testator's blood to strangers. While these rules are well recognized, and often control the determination of the meaning of wills, they all have exceptions, and must give way to the intention of the testator as expressed in the will.

The paramount question presented upon this review is as to whether the testator intended to vest in the sons of Mrs. Gillespie the $10,000 which was given to the trustees for her use during life. It is contended on behalf of some of the appellants that the *Brown Case* (154 N. Y. 313; 48 N. E. 537), is controlling on this question, and that under it the amount must be deemed to have vested in the sons at the death of the testator. There is, however, one important distinction between this will and the one which we had under consideration in the *Brown Case*. In that case the testator, Abraham Wing, died leaving him surviving, a widow and two daughters, each of which had children. After making certain specific bequests, he gave and devised all the rest and residue of his estate to his executors in trust, with directions to pay a certain annuity to his widow and the rest of the income to his daughters, and, in case of the decease of either of his daughters during the lifetime of his widow, then "and in such case to pay the half share of said income to the children of such deceased daughter which would have belonged and been paid to the deceased daughter had she survived." The will contained a similar provision in case both daughters should die during the lifetime of the widow, requiring the income to be paid, respectively, to the children of each. On the decease of the widow and daughters, the estate went to the grandchildren, they taking their mother's portion. It will be observed in that case there were no words of survivorship used with reference to the grandchildren, such as " their descendants," or such as " then survived," which were important considerations in determining the meaning of that will, and induced us to hold that under the statute the estate vested in the grandchildren, they all being alive at the death of the testator, and having an immediate right of possession upon the determination of the life estate. In the will we now have under consideration the provision materially differs: "And from and immediately after her decease upon trust to pay over and divide the said principal sum of $10,000 unto and among all her children, share and share alike." Had the testator stopped here, we should have regarded this will to be in substance the same as in the *Brown Case,* and should not have hesitated to hold that the legacies vested in the sons; but the testator proceeds, " and to their lawful representatives forever, as tenants in common, per capita; the issue of any such child who may then be dead to take his or her deceased parent's share." Here we have an express provision of the will which seems to negative the claim that the estate vested in the sons. The testator apparently understood that it might happen that the sons would not survive his widow or their mother, and therefore undertook to provide for such a contingency by giving the estate to the issue of the sons in case of their death. If the estate was intended to vest in the sons, then upon the death of either of them the estate would pass to their executors or administrators, and might never reach the issue of such deceased child; but here we find, seemingly, an intention disclosed that the issue of the deceased child should take, rather than the executors or administrators. It is contended that the words " and to their lawful representatives forever " are used as words of succession or substitution, and not of limitation. We are aware that the words " lawful representatives " are often intended to mean executors and administrators, but to so construe the words in this case would not only render meaningless the provision which follows, but would, as we have shown, be in conflict with the testator's evident intention of having the estate go to the issue of the sons, should they die during the lifetime of their mother.

The learned Appellate Division invokes the rule that, when the gift is found only in a direction to the trustees to pay over to the sons on the death of their mother, time is of the essence of the gift. This rule, we held, had no application in the *Brown Case*, for reasons there stated, and to which we have here already called attention; but, as we have shown, the provisions of the will in this case are materially different, and the reasons for not applying the rule in the *Brown Case* are not found in this. It is true that the rule has many exceptions, and is seldom alone relied upon. It is, however, recognized by the courts as an aid in the determination of the meaning of wills, and in a proper case should be given reasonable weight.

The view that we entertain of this will is that the testator intended the estate to go to the issue of the sons of Mrs. Gillespie in case of the death of either during the existence of the life estate. No issue of these sons were in being at the death of the testator, and it was uncertain as to whether they would ever have issue. The remainder was therefore contingent, and not vested, for the reason that the persons to whom or the event upon which the estate was limited to take effect remained uncertain until the termination of the life estate. Futurity was annexed to the substance of the gift, and the vesting was suspended.

A discussion of the authorities we do not consider necessary. There is a long line of cases in which it has been held that the remainders were vested, and another line of cases, equally as long, holding remainders contingent, which cases have been disposed of under the peculiar phraseology of the wills under review in those cases. Our attention has been called to no case in which the precise language of this will has been considered in this court. *In re Baer* (147 N. Y. 348; 41 N. E. 702); *In re Allen* (151 N. Y. 243; 45 N. E. 554); and *McGillis* v. *McGillis* (154 N. Y. 532; 49 N. E. 145), are among the recent cases in which remainders have been held to be contingent, and in some respects form a precedent for the conclusion which we have reached in this case.

The sons of Mrs. Gillespie having died without issue during the lifetime of their mother, and before they became vested with the estate, the question arises as to what disposition, if any, has been made of the estate. Under the provisions of the will, after the death of the testator's widow the sum of $10,000 was continued in the hands of the executors and trustees, to apply the interest or the income to Mrs. Gillespie during life; and all the rest and residue of the estate, other than the $10,000, the executors and trustees were directed, at that time, to pay over and divide among the eight nephews and nieces of the testator (naming them). These nephews and nieces were given no part or interest in the $10,000 reserved for the benefit of Mrs. Gillespie, and there was no other residuary estate created or provided for into which the $10,000 item could fall. It therefore follows that in case there are no persons who can take as remaindermen, under the will, the testator died intestate as to this sum. Intestacy exists as to everything not disposed of, or which turns out not to be disposed of, by the will, whether by reason of the inability of an attempted disposition, or other accident. There being no disposal of the estate by the will, it follows that it must be distributed under the statute of distribution. (*Lefevre* v. *Lefevre*, 59 N. Y. 447.)

Among the conflicting claims made to this fund, we find one in . which it is insisted that the testator's next of kin at the time of the termination of the life estate are the persons to whom the distributions should be made, and not to those who were next of kin at the time of the testator's death, or their personal representatives. Chancellor WALWORTH, speaking upon this subject, says: " Where a reversionary interest in personal property is not disposed of by the will of the testator, it does not necessarily belong to those who may happen to be his next of kin at the termination of the particular estate or interest in such property which is bequeathed by him, but, as an interest in the property undisposed of by the will, it belongs to the widow and next of kin of the decedent who were entitled to the distributive shares in such unbequeathed interest at the death of the testator. (*Hoes* v. *Van Housen*, 1 Barb. Ch. 379; *In re Kane*, 2 id. 375; *Greenland* v. *Waddell*, 116 N. Y. 234, 245; 22 N. E. 367.)

An argument is presented to the effect that there was no intestacy as to this fund at the death of the testator, and no invalidity in the bequest for the lives of the widow and Mrs. Gillespie; but such intestacy occurred at the death of Mrs. Gillespie, who left no children her surviving, or issue of such children, and until the happening of that event it could not be determined who was entitled to the fund, and consequently those who occupied the relation of next of kin at that time were the persons entitled. Such might have been the case if the estate had passed under the will, but, inasmuch as the will fails to dispose of the fund, it must be disposed of under the statute, which must be resorted to in order to determine the interest, as well as the persons among whom distribution must be made. The persons and the only persons who are entitled to take by virtue of the statute are those who answer to the legal definition of next of kin at the time of the death of the intestate. If, for any reason, the bequest made ultimately fails to take effect according to the testator's intention, the property remains undisposed of by the will, and the testator has died intestate as to such property, and it immediately reverts to his personal representatives, appointed or to be appointed, in trust for his next of kin. The rights of persons claiming under a will are to be ascertained and determined in view of all its provisions, and by the application of settled rules of construction governing such instruments. If, on such constructions, no rights of property can be claimed under the will, the provisions of the statute of distribution must control, and alone determine the rights of the parties.

We think the case was properly disposed of below, and that the judgment should be affirmed. In view of the fact that the case is somewhat complicated, we think that the plaintiff should recover costs, payable out of the estate. All concur.

Judgment affirmed.

NOTE.—VESTING.

(a) General rules of construction.
(b) Immediate and absolute gift as test.
(c) Direction for future division or payment.
(d) Gift to a class.
(e) Gift of money.
(f) Words of survivorship.
(g) Effect of bequest, of interest or income.
(h) Gift through trustee.
(i) Effect of a power.
(j) Convenience of estate.
(k) Use of word " heirs."
(l) Use of words " from and after."
(m) Illustrative cases—Holding vested.
(n) Illustrative cases—Holding not vested.

(a) **General rules of construction.**—Under the rule by which a modern will speaks as of the date of the death of the testator, every gift to a person who is alive at that date vests at once, in the absence of an expression of an intention that the vesting shall be postponed. It will be presumed where the testator does not expressly or by implication indicate that the vesting of the title is to be postponed, that he meant it to vest at once upon his death. The rule that the executory estate shall be construed to be vested rather than contingent is the result of that other very old rule of the common law that the fee shall never be in abeyance if it can possibly be avoided. (2 Underhill on Wills, § 861 [ed. 1900]; and see Harvard College v. Balch, 171 Ill. 275; 49 N. E. Rep. 543; Bethea v. Bethea, 116 Ala. 265; 22 So. Rep. 561.)

There are two well known rules of construction: (1) Where the only words of gift are found in the direction to divide or pay at a future time, the gift is future, not immediate; contingent and not vested. (2) Where the gift is of money and the direction to convert the estate is absolute, the legacy given to a class of persons vests in those who answer the description and are capable of taking at the time of the distribution. To these general rules of construction there are exceptions, and the cases noting them can be grouped under two heads: (1) If the postponement of the payment is for the purpose of letting in an intermediate estate, then the interest shall be deemed vested at the death of the testator and the class of legatees is to be determined as of that date for futurity is not annexed to the substance. of the gift; (2) Where there are words importing a gift in addition to the direction to executors or trustees to pay over, divide or distribute, in other words where from the examination of the whole will it is apparent that it was the intention of the testator that the estate should vest in the beneficiaries immediately upon his death, the rule governing where there is merely a direction to divide at a future time is subordinated to that broader rule which requires that the intention of the testator should control where it can be ascertained " within the four corners of the will." (Matter of Crane, 164 N. Y. 71, 76; 58 N. E. Rep. 47; rev'g 36 App. Div. 468; 55 N. Y. Supp. 822.)

If the person to take a remainder is in being and ascertained and it is to take effect by words of express limitation on the determination of the preceding particular estate, it will be vested. It is the present capacity of taking effect in possession if the possession were to become vacant, and not the certainty that the possession will become vacant before the estate limited in remainder determines that distinguishes a vested from a contingent remainder. (Burton v. Gagnon, 180 Ill. 345, 356; 54 N. E. Rep. 279.)

(b) **Immediate and absolute gift as test.**—Where a devise is made or a legacy given, of which the enjoyment is postponed the leading inquiry upon which the question of vesting or not vesting is whether the gift is immediate, and the time of payment or enjoyment only postponed, or is future or contingent, depending upon beneficiary arriving at age, or surviving some other person, or the like. (Goebel v. Wolf, 113 N. Y. 405, 412; 21 N. E. Rep. 388.)

If futurity is annexed to the subject of the gift, the vesting is suspended; but if it appear to relate to the time of payment only, the legacy vests instanter; and words directing division or distribution between two or more objects at a future time are equivalent to a direction to pay. (Everitt v. Everitt, 29 N. Y. 75.)

Where the gift is absolute and time of payment only postponed; time not being of the substance of the gift but relating only to the payment, does not suspend the gift, but merely defers the payment. (Warner v. Durant, 76 N. Y. 133; Matter of Mahan, 98 id. 372; McGillis v. McGillis, 154 id. 532, 540; 40 N. E. Rep. 145.)

The mere fact that a remainder may be contingent does not prevent vesting on death of a testator. Rules of the common law as changed or modified by statute considered. (Hennessy v. Patterson, 85 N. Y. 91.)

Mere postponement of time of payment of a positive direct gift does not prevent vesting. (Bushnell v. Carpenter, 92 N. Y. 270; Williams v. Williams, 73 Cal. 99; 14 Pac. Rep. 394; Little's Appeal, 117 Pa. St. 14; 11 Atl. Rep. 520; Perrine v. Newell, 49 N. J. Eq. 57; 23 Atl. Rep. 492.)

The intent to postpone vesting must be clear and manifest and must not arise by mere inference or construction. (Moores v. Hare, 144 Ind. 573; 43 N. E. Rep. 870.)

(c) **Direction for future division or payment.**—When the gift is created simply by directing the payment, division and distribution at some future period of time after the decease of the testator, or upon the happening of the contingent event, and there is no provision in the will for vesting the legacy immediately, then the future time fixed or the happening of the contingency is of the essence of the gift and it does not vest. (Willet v. Rutter, 84 Ky. 317; 1 S. W. Rep. 640; Farnam v. Farnam, 53 Conn. 261, 283; 2 Atl. Rep. 325; 5 id. 682; Warner v. Durant, 76 N. Y. 133; Smith v. Edwards, 88 id. 92, 108; Loder v. Hatfield, 71 id. 92.)

But this rule yields to an intention otherwise. (Matter of Young, 145 N. Y. 538; 40 N. E. Rep. 226; Goebel v. Wolff, 113 N. Y. 405, 412; 21 N. E. Rep. 388; Miller v. Gilbert, 144 N. Y. 73; 38 N. E. Rep. 979; Matter of Seebeck, 140 N. Y. 241, 246; 35 N. E. Rep. 429; McGillis v. McGillis, 154 N. Y. 512, 539; 49 N. E. Rep. 145; Matter of Seaman, 147 N. Y. 74; 41 N. E. Rep. 401; Matter of Brown, 154 N. Y. 325; 48 N. E. Rep. 537; Paget v. Melcher, 156 N. Y. 399, 407; 51 N. E. Rep. 24; Steinway v. Steinway, 163 N. Y. 183; 57 N. E. Rep. 312 [this volume, p. 599]; Carr v. Smith, 25 App. Div. 214; 49 N. Y. Supp. 351; aff'd 161 N Y. 636 [no opinion]; Canfield v. Fallon, 43 App. Div. 566; 57 N. Y. Supp. 149; aff'd 161 N. Y. 623; 55 N. E. Rep. 1093; Aldridge v. Aldridge, 43 App. Div. 413; 60 N. Y. Supp. 69; Staples v. Hawes, 39 App. Div. 552; 57 N. Y. Supp. 452; aff'g 24 Misc. 475; 53 N. Y. Supp. 860.)

(d) **Gift to a class.**—General rule of construction that a future and contingent devise and bequest to a class takes effect on the happening of the contingency on which the limitation depends only in favor of those objects who at that time come within the description. (Matter of Allen, 151 N. Y. 247; 45 N. E. Rep. 554.)

Where will on death of life tenant directs sale and conversion into money, and be distributed or divided as such among a class of persons vests in those who answer the description and are capable of taking at time of distribution. (Delaney v. McCormack, 88 N. Y. 174.)

Where the direction is to pay to and divide among a class only those persons who are members of the class at the date fixed for distribution take, and their interests do not vest until that period. (Geisse v. Bunce, 23 App. Div. 291; 48 N. Y. Supp. 249; Teed v. Morton, 60 N. Y. 503.)

Where final division and distribution is to be made among a class the benefits of the will must be confined to those persons who come within the appropriate category at the date when the distribution or division is directed to be made. (Matter of Baer, 147 N. Y. 348; 41 N. E. Rep. 702.)

Where there is a limitation or remainder over after devise to a life tenant to a class, which may include persons not yet born, the time of the distribution defines the members that are to constitute the class, and there is no vesting until that time arrives. (Haskins v. Tate, 25 Pa. St. 249.)

When will on death of wife directs " the property to be equally divided between my children," the " class " doctrine has no application and property vests. (Owens v. Dunn, 85 Tenn. 131; 2 S. W. Rep. 29; Thomman's Estate, 161 Pa. St. 444; 29 Atl. Rep. 84.)

Gift to children as a class. (In re Hannam [1897], 2 Ch. 12.)

(e) **Gift of money.**—When the gift is of money and trustee is to divide the proceeds of a sale of land among the persons entitled on death of the life tenant, that is the period fixed for the division, and it is a general rule of construction that words of survivorship in bequests of personal estate are to be referred to the period of division and enjoyment, unless there is a special intent to the contrary. (Teed v. Morton, 60 N. Y. 503.)

Where the only gift or devise of property is contained in the implication resulting from a direction to pay or divide a fund then to come into existence at a future time, futurity is annexed to the substance of the gift and no title or interest vests until the arrival of the specified period. (Geisse v. Bunce, 23 App. Div. 291; 48 N. Y. Supp. 249; Aldridge v. Aldridge, 43 App. Div. 412; 60 N. Y. Supp. 69.)

Two circumstances strengthen the application of general rule as to not vesting when gift consists only in direction to divide, etc.

(1) That property was not in existence in the form or shape it was ultimately to reach the beneficiaries, and

(2) During the whole continuance of the trust a contingency existing which rendered it uncertain whether they would ever take at all. (Geisse v. Bunce, 23 App. Div. 292; 48 N. Y. Supp. 249.)

When upon death of the wife the executor is empowered and directed to sell land and divide the proceeds, it is *money* which is the subject of the bequest; the actual conversion not to take place until after the death of the widow. In such a case not only is there no bequest before the widow's death, but the subject matter did not then exist in the shape and form in which it is given; there is no vesting until death of the widow. (Vincent v. Newhouse, 83 N. Y. 505, 511.)

The distinction between a bequest of a sum of money at a particular specified time, and a similar bequest, payable or to be paid at the same time, is somewhat refined, and it is probable seldom exists in the mind of a testator; but it is established by so long a series of decisions that it must now be regarded as a constituent part of the law. In the second case the gift is immediate and only its payment is postponed. In the first, the gift itself is postponed. In the language of the books, the time in the second case is annexed to the payment, in the first to the substance of the gift. The first is a contingent, the second a vested legacy. DUER, J. (Andrew v. N. Y. Bible Society, 4 Sand. 156, 173.)

When will on death of wife directs sale and after payment of certain items that balance should " then " be divided into parts and paid over to associations which testator knew at time of making of his will had no legal existence, and evidently contemplated a future incorporation, *held*, no vesting until death of widow and creation of fund provided for. (Shipman v. Rollins, 98 N. Y. 311.)

In this case stress was laid on the fact that the fund out of which the legacies were to be paid had no legal existence until the decease of testator's widow. It was upon the happening of that event that it was to be created, and it was only then that it could be ascertained what the fund would be. It might be more or less according to the exigencies provided for by the will, and it might be nothing, and it was only in case a balance remained that the same was to be divided as directed. It was then to be disposed of or given away, and not before that time.

When gift is after life interest of widow to trustees to be converted into money and divided among several persons named and the survivors or survivor of them, those only are entitled who survive the widow. (Hoghton v. Whitgreave, 1 Jac. & W. Ch. 146.)

As this seems to be a leading English case cited and relied upon as the foundation of the doctrine in this country, it may be well to quote the will. It read: " And I further direct that the moneys arising from the sale of my real estate and all the rest of my personalty shall be paid and equally divided amongst my nephews and nieces (naming them) and the survivors or survivor of them; and I do hereby give and bequeath the same to them and to the survivors or survivor of them, after the decease of my wife, and in manner aforesaid."

(f) **Words of survivorship.**—Words of survivorship unless contrary intention appears construed as relating to death of testator. (Canfield v. Fallon, 43 App. Div. 568; 57 N. Y. Supp. 149; aff'd 161 N. Y. 623; 55 N. E. Rep. 1093.)

Words of survivorship in bequests of money or personal property are to be referred to the period of distribution and enjoyment unless there is a special intent to the contrary. (Vincent v. Newhouse, 83 N. Y. 505, 511; citing Teed v. Morton, 60 N. Y. 502.)

The presumption is that a testator intends that his dispositions are to take effect either in enjoyment or interest at the date of his death, and unless the language of the will by fair construction make his gifts contingent they will be regarded as vested. Words of survivorship and gifts over on the death of the primary beneficiary are construed, unless a contrary intention appears, as relating to the death of the testator. (Nelson v. Russell, 135 N. Y. 137; 31 N. E. Rep. 1008; and see as to words of survivorship, Mullarky v. Sullivan, 136 N. Y. 227; 32 N. E. Rep. 762.)

When will after death of widow directs estate "to be equally divided between ———— and the survivors and survivor of them," *held*, that it referred to survivors at death of the widow. (Dutton v. Pugh, 45 N. J. Eq. 426; 18 Atl. Rep. 207; aff'd on opinion of the Chancellor as Jones v. Jones, 46 N. J. Eq. 554; 21 Atl. Rep. 950. But see able dissenting opinion of Dixon, J.)

When will directed on death of the widow a division "between my *surviving* children," there is no vesting at death of the testator. (Roundtree v. Roundtree, 26 S. C. 450; 2 S. E. Rep. 474.)

And so where the devise was to sisters and at their death "to descend to their children respectively, and to be equally divided among them or the survivors of them." (Spear v. Fogg, 87 Me. 132; 32 Atl. Rep. 791; Estate of Winter, 114 Cal. 186; 45 Pac. Rep. 1063.) And so where the direction was to pay over to "my *surviving* nephews" on termination of a life interest. (Denny v. Kettell, 135 Mass. 138.) And so where the direction on termination of the life interest is "to divide between my children *then* living." (Wilhelm v. Calder, 102 Iowa, 342; 71 N. W. Rep. 214.) And see Smith v. Block (29 Ohio St. 488); Thomson v. Ludington (104 Mass. 193).

When will provided for an equal division of income among children and upon death of all the children devise to "such of her grandchildren as may then be alive," the grandchildren do not take the vested estate. The idea of survivorship prevailing in the residuary clause "to grandchildren" generally is potent in giving to it the same construction. (Hopkins v. Keazer, 89 Me. 347; 36 Atl. Rep. 615.)

In Moores v. Hare (144 Ind. 573; 43 N. E. Rep. 870), the court says: "It is settled law that words of survivorship in a will, unless there is a manifest intent to the contrary always relate to the death of the testator."

(g) **Effect of bequest of interest or income.**—The allowance of the entire income during the period from decease of the testator to final delivery or distribution of the *corpus* of the estate, is deemed sufficient evidence that the estate shall vest at the decease. (Kelly v. Dike, 8 R. I. 436, 451.)

When the gift is to be severed *instanter* from the general estate, for the benefit of the legatee, and in the meantime the interest thereof is to be paid to him; that is indicative of the intent of the testator that the legatee shall at all events have the principal, and is to wait only for the payment until the time fixed. (Warner v. Durant, 76 N. Y. 133.)

The rule that if the intermediate gift of interest is not co-extensive with the whole amount of the interest on the legacy provided for, or is made out of another fund, the legacy will not vest before the day fixed for payment of the legacy itself, does not require absolutely that the specific fund shall yield the named interest; so long as it is substantially a gift of the whole interest received from the legacy, vesting may take place. (Id. 138.)

Effect of bequest of income or interest as determining vesting of *corpus* or principal. (Andrew v. N. Y. Bible Society, 4 Sand. 174; Zartman v. Ditmars, 37 App. Div. 178; 55 N. Y. Supp. 908; Hopkins v. Keazer, 89 Me. 354; 36 Atl. Rep. 615; and see Patton v. Ludington, 103 Wis. 629; 79 N. W. Rep. 1073.)

(h) **Gift through trustee.**—Where futurity is annexed to substance of the gift and the future interest is devised not directly to a given person, but indirectly through the exercise of a power or title conferred upon trustees, the devise to a class as children or heirs is designed to be contingent, and survivorship at the time of distribution is an essential condition to the acquisition of an interest in the subject of the gift. (Matter of Baer, 147 N. Y. 348, 354; 41 N. E. Rep. 702.) And case where a trustee is directed to sell and divide money. Teed v. Morton (60 N. Y. 503).

And see Staples v. Hawes (39 App. Div. 552; 57 N. Y. Supp. 452).

Trustee having the power to appropriate the entire trust estate to the purposes of the trust, take the fee during the continuance of the trust, and only the residue remaining unspent at the termination of the trust vests in any other person. (King v. King, 168 Ill. 273, 285; 48 N. E. Rep. 582.)

Where the entire estate is vested in trustees during life of widow, and without a direct gift to the children, simply a direction to divide among them after the death of the widow, there is no vesting in the children during life of the widow. (Delafield v. Shipman, 103 N. Y. 463; 9 N. E. Rep. 184.)

A testamentary trustee takes a legal estate commensurate with the equitable estate bestowed and outside thereof there may be remainders and future estates or powers of sale adequate to terminate the trust. (Matter of Tienken, 131 N. Y. 391; 30 N. E. Rep. 109.) And see Matter of Tompkins (154 N. Y. 634; 49 N. E. Rep. 135).

A trust to invest personalty and pay over income during life or lives is no obstacle to vesting of the principal fund in testator's next of kin as of time of testator's death when he dies intestate as to the principal. (Doane v. Mercantile Trust Co., 160 N. Y. 495; 55 N. E. Rep. 296.)

In order that the interest of the beneficiary may vest at once there must be in addition to the direction to the trustee either express words of gift, or circumstances from which may be fairly inferred an intention to appropriate at once the subject of the gift to the use of the beneficiary, although the full enjoyment thereof is postponed to a later date. (Geisse v. Bunce, 23 App. Div. 292; 48 N. Y. Supp. 249.)

Intervention of a trust estate for benefit of life tenant does not prevent vesting. (Murtha v. Wilcox, 47 App. Div. 526; 62 N. Y. Supp. 481.)

Power of sale in trustees does not prevent vesting. (Matter of Tienken, 131 N. Y. 391; 30 N. E. Rep. 109.)

Where several distinct trusts, with fee vested in trustee. (Salisbury v. Slade, 160 N. Y. 278; 54 N. E. Rep. 741.)

And see fee in trustee. (Hale v. Hale, 146 Ill. 227; 33 N. E. Rep. 858.)

(i) **Effect of a power.**—A power of appointment does not prevent vesting of remainder subject to its exercise. (Thorington v. Thorington, 111 Ala. 237; 20 So. Rep. 407; Sandford v. Blake, 45 N. J. Eq. 247; 17 Atl. Rep. 812; Harvard College v. Balch, 171 Ill. 275; 49 N. E. Rep. 543.)

And so where the power is in executor or trustee. (Lehnard v. Specht, 180 Ill. 208; 54 N. E. Rep. 315; Railsback v. Lovejoy, 116 Ill. 443; 6 N. E. Rep. 504.)

Where power to sell real estate is given to executors after expiration of life estate, with direction to divide among the *testator's* "legal heirs," the heirs are vested with the fee subject to execution of the power. (Sayles v. Best, 140 N. Y. 368; 35 N. E. Rep. 636.)

(j) **Convenience of estate.**—Where it is apparent that the postponement of payment or possession is merely for the convenience of the estate, it will not prevent vesting. (Wedekind v. Hallenberg, 88 Ky. 114; 10 S. W. Rep. 368; Heilman v. Heilman, 129 Ind. 60; 28 N. E. Rep. 310; Harvard College v. Balch, 171 Ill. 276; 49 N. E. Rep. 543.)

Where postponement of division and distribution was chiefly for benefit of father of testator during his life, to enable the estate to meet the burden imposed upon it in his behalf, that does not prevent vesting. (Murtha v. Wilcox, 47 App. Div. 526; 62 N. Y. Supp. 481.)

And as to application of the doctrine of convenience of estate see Loder v. Hatfield (71 N. Y. 92); Matter of Tienken (131 N. Y. 391; 30 N. E. Rep. 109).

(k) **Use of word "heirs."**—The word "heirs" when uncontrolled by the expressed intention of the will has the effect to vest a legacy which might otherwise be contingent. (Little's Appeal, 117 Pa. St. 14, 27; 11 Atl. Rep. 520.) And see Crews v. Hatcher (91 Va. 378; 21 S. E. Rep. 811.)

When the word "heirs" of a living person not named or referred to otherwise in a will is used to point out legatees, unless context shows testator used it in a different sense the primary legal meaning of the word will be given to it; the legacy does not vest until upon the death of such person it can be determined who are his heirs. (Cushman v. Horton, 59 N. Y. 149.)

Whenever "heirs" used primary meaning given unless contrary intention. (Leake v. Watson, 60 Conn. 506; 21 Atl. Rep. 1075.) And see Bolton v. Bank (50 Ohio St. 290; 33 N. E. Rep. 1115).

(l) **Use of words "from and after."**—The words "from and after" the specified death of the life tenant in connection with a limitation over indicate an intention to postpone the vesting. (Cherbonnier v. Goodwin, 79 Md. 55; 28 Atl. Rep. 894.)

The words "from and after" in gift of remainder following gift of life estate, do not prevent vesting, when there is nothing else to indicate postponement of vesting. (Hersee v. Simpson, 154 N. Y. 496; 48 N. E. Rep. 890.)

But may be evidence of such intent in connection with other clause in will. (McGillis v. McGillis, 154 N. Y. 512, 541; 49 N. E. Rep. 145.)

The words "from and after" used in a gift of remainder following a life estate, do not afford sufficient ground in themselves for adjudging that the remainder is not vested, and unless their meaning is enlarged by the context they are regarded as defining the time of enjoyment simply and not of vesting the title. (Nelson v. Russell, 135 N. Y. 137; 31 N. E. Rep. 1008.)

"From and after," etc., relate to time of enjoyment and not to time of vesting; especially in construction of devises of real estate. (Canfield v. Fallon, 43 App. Div. 568; 57 N. Y. Supp. 149; aff'd 161 N. Y. 623; 55 N. E. Rep. 1093.)

The words "then and in that case" in a gift of remainder do not necessarily postpone the period of ascertaining the parties entitled to the remainder. (Wadsworth v. Murray, 29 App. Div. 198; 51 N. Y. Supp. 1038; aff'd 161 N. Y. 274; 55 N. E. Rep. 910.)

(m) **Illustrative cases—Holding vested.**—Gift direct and immediate and time of payment only postponed. (Matter of Gardner, 140 N. Y. 122; 35 N. E. Rep. 439.)

After bequest of all his property to his wife for life, testator added, "then they are to descend to my legal heirs." *Held* to create a vesting remainder in fee in the legal heirs of *testator living* at the *time* of *his death.*

(Bunting v. Speek, 41 Kans. 424.) · The opinion contains an interesting and valuable summary and review of the authorities.

When will on death of life tenant directed division into as many parts as he should "then have children living, the issue of any deceased child to represent their parents" and gave to each a part, *held* to vest. (Womrath v. McCormick, 51 Pa. St. 504.)

In Hogan v. Hogan (102 Mich. 641; 61 N. W. Rep. 73), where it was held that the remainder vested, there was no estate or title vested in the executors as trustees, nor was there any power of sale given to them.

In Matter of Mahan (98 N. Y. 372), where legacy was held to vest the bequest of the residue in question was "I do then give, devise, etc., to my children John, Thomas, and Mary, the survivor or survivors of them, share and share alike."

In Matter of Brown (154 N. Y. 313; 48 N. E. Rep. 537), where it was held to vest there was nothing in the will making the provision dependent upon survivorship at time of distribution. And see cases holding vested. Shangle v. Hallock (6 App. Div. 56; 39 N. Y. Supp. 619); Miller v. Von Schwarzenstein (51 App. Div. 18; 64 N. Y. Supp. 475); Zartman v. Ditmars (37 App. Div. 178; 55 N. Y. Supp. 908); Emburg v. Sheldon (68 N. Y. 227); Ritter's Estate (190 Pa. St. 102; 42 Atl. Rep. 384); Caswell v. Robinson (21 R. I. 193; 42 Atl. Rep. 877); Howard v. Trustees (88 Md. 292; 41 Atl. Rep. 156); Hill v. True (104 Wis. 294; 80 N. W. Rep. 462).

(n) **Illustrative cases—Holding not vested.**—When residue clause called for division among grand-children *per stirpes—not vested.* (Hale v. Hobson, 167 Mass. 397; 45 N. E. Rep. 913.) Construing same will as in Hale v. Hale (125 Ill. 399; 17 N. E. Rep. 470; 146 Ill. 227; 33 N. E. Rep. 858); Hobson v. Hale (95 N. Y. 588).

Where the gift is conditioned upon death of life tenant without lawful issue, there can be no vesting and the gift is future. (Delaney v. McCormack, 88 N. Y. 174.)

Where in gift of remainder language indicates intention of substituting the issue for the parent in the event of the death of latter where testator could not have contemplated the death of the parent during the testator's life—no vesting. (Lyons v. Weeks, 53 App. Div. 212; 65 N. Y. Supp. 818.)

Where will on termination of life tenancy of a daughter "after her death to be equally divided among her children, *if she shall leave children*, and if *not* then to be equally divided among my other children," the remainder to latter is contingent not vested. (Rosenau v. Childress, 111 Ala. 214; 20 So. Rep. 95.)

But where devise was to wife for life and on her death "to be divided among all my children, and the heirs of such as may *then* be deceased," there is no vesting until death of the wife. (Hunt v. Hall, 37 Me. 363.)

Where the devise on termination of life interest to widow is to four children specifically named "*if living*," no vesting until death of widow as it was impossible to tell who would take. (Robinson v. Palmer, 90 Me. 246; 38 Atl. Rep. 103.)

In Mercantile Trust Co. v. Brown (71 Md. 166; 17 Atl. Rep. 937), where it was *held* that the vesting was postponed the language was on termination of the life estates "child or children as may be living at the time this part is *intended to vest*."

In Plymouth Society v. Hepburn (57 Hun, 161; 10 N. Y. Supp. 817), where legacy was held not to vest, the bequest was "upon the decease of my said wife and son, he not leaving lawful issue then surviving I give and bequeath to, etc.," the executor being then authorized and empowered to sell.

In Cox v. Wisner (43 App. Div. 591; 60 N. Y. Supp. 349), the devise was "upon the decease of my said wife, to such of my children as shall then be living and the lawful issue of such as may then be dead equally as tenants in common." *Held* that this language clearly indicated an intention that only those children and grandchildren should take who outlived the widow.

˙AMBROSE *et al vs.* BYRNE.

[Supreme Court of Ohio, October 31, 1899; 61 Ohio St. 146; 55 N. E. Rep. 408.]

JUDGMENT LIEN—DEATH OF DEBTOR—ISSUE OF EXECUTION— PRIORITY IN PROCEEDS OF LAND — LIMITATIONS — ACTION AGAINST EXECUTORS.

1. Where a judgment is a subsisting lien on the lands of the debtor at the time of his death, it is not necessary thereafter to issue execution upon it in order to preserve the lien. It is entitled to share in the proceeds of the land, when sold by the personal representative, according to its priority at the time of the debtor's death, although execution be not issued thereon within five years from its rendition or the date of the last execution. ·

2. The allowance of the claim by the personal representative, or its presentation to him for that purpose, is not requisite to the judgment creditor's right to share in the fund.

3. Pleading the lien by the judgment creditor, in an action brought by the personal representative to sell the land for the payment of debts, is not the commencement of an action, within the purview of the statute limiting the time within which actions may be commenced against executors and administrators.

(Syllabus by the court.)

ERROR to Circuit Court, Franklin county.

˙Action by Luke G. Byrne, executor, against Samuel Ambrose and others. From a judgment sustaining a demurrer to defendants' answer, they bring error.

Reversed.

On the 21st day of July, 1888, Luke G. Byrne, as executor of the last will and testament of Elizabeth J. Kent, deceased, commenced an action in the Court of Common Pleas to bring to sale the real estate of which the testatrix died seized, for the payment of her debts, she having left no personal property of any consequence. Charles Higgins, and Edward J. Dowdall, as executor of the estate of Joseph Dowdall, deceased, who, it was alleged, claimed a judgment lien on the land, were made defendants. Their lien was set up by Higgins and Samuel Ambrose, who had become the administrator *de bonis non* of the estate of Joseph Dowdall, by filing the following pleading: " The said Ambrose, as such administrator, and the said defendant, Charles Higgins, jointly represent to the court that heretofore, to wit, on the 24th day of October, 1876, in a certain action in this court then pending, wherein the Central Bank of Columbus, Ohio, was plaintiff and the said Elizabeth J. Kent, then in full life, this defendant, Charles Higgins, and the said Joseph Dowdall, then in full life, were defendants, prosecuted upon a certain promissory note, upon which the said Elizabeth J. Kent was principal and the said Joseph Dowdall and said Charles Higgins were her sureties, said bank recovered a judgment against the defendants to said action, by the consideration of this court, upon said note, for the sum of $201.30, with interest thereon from that day, together with its costs therein expended, taxed at $10.10. On the 14th day of November of said year 1876, the said Central Bank caused an execution to be issued upon said judgment to the sheriff of said Franklin county, Ohio, who, for want of goods and chattels of the said Elizabeth J. Kent whereon to levy for the satisfaction thereof, levied the same upon certain real estate then owned by the said Elizabeth J. Kent in said county of Franklin, of which real estate the premises described in the petition form a part. Afterwards, to wit, on the 20th day of April, A. D. 1880, the said Central Bank sold and assigned to the said Charles Higgins and the said Joseph Dowdall said judgment for a full and valuable consideration, and the said Charles Higgins and the said Joseph Dowdall became the owners, both at law and equity, of said judgment. Afterwards, to wit, on the 1st day of Nevember, A. D. 1881, said Charles Higgins and said Joseph Dowdall caused an alias execution to be issued on said judgment against the said Elizabeth J. Kent, which said execution was returned unsatisfied. The said Elizabeth J. Kent died in 1883, as averred in the petition, and said judgment lien, acquired by said judgment and the levy of execution on said real estate, was in full force at the time of the death of said Elizabeth J. Kent, and has ever since so remained, the same not having been paid, either in part or whole, and there is due and payable thereon to this defendant, the said Charles Higgins, and the said Samuel Ambrose, as administrator as aforesaid, jointly, from the estate of said Elizabeth J. Kent, the sum of $211.40, with interest thereon from the 24th day of October, 1876. These defendants therefore say, by reason of the sale and assignment of the said judgment by the said Central Bank to the said Charles Higgins and the said Joseph Dowdall, that they should be here subrogated to all the rights of the said bank in and to the said judgment at the time of the said sale, and should now be here adjudged to hold both a lien at law and in equity upon said real estate to the extent of said judgment, with interest thereon as aforesaid, together with the amount of said costs. These defendants therefore here pray that the court may find and adjudge their said claim to be a valid lien on said premises, and that the said executor may be ordered to allow and pay the same out of the proceeds of said property, when sold by him, according to its priority, with other liens thereon. These defendants pray for such other and further relief to which, in the premises, they may be entitled." The Court of Common Pleas sustained a general demurrer filed by the plaintiff to this pleading, and dismissed the same, and that judgment was affirmed by the Circuit Court.

G. J. Marriott, for plaintiffs in error.

W. H. English and *Luke G. Byrne*, for defendant in error.

WILLIAMS, J. (after stating the facts).—The principal question to which the arguments of counsel have been directed is whether the lien of the judgment set up by the plaintiffs in error was lost by their failure to have execution issued upon it within five years from the date of the last preceding execution. On the one hand, it is contended by counsel for the defendant in error that the judgment below, holding the lien was so lost, is in accordance with section 5380 of the Revised Statutes, which provides that: "If execution on a judgment be not sued out within five years from the date of the judgment, or if five years intervene between the date of the last execution issued on such judgment and the time of suing out another execution thereon, such judgment shall become dormant and shall cease to operate as a lien on the estate of the judgment debtor." On the other hand, it is the claim of the counsel for the plaintiffs in error that under section 6165 the fund arising from the sale made by the executor should be distributed to the liens in the order of their priority as they existed at the time of the testatrix's death. That section reads as follows: "The money arising from the sale of real estate shall be applied in the following order: First. To discharge the costs and expenses of the sale, and the per centum and charges of the executor or administrator thereon, for his administration of the same. Second. To the payment of mortgages and judgments against the deceased, according to their respective priorities of lien, so far as the same operate as a lien on the estate of the deceased, at the time of his death; which shall be apportioned and determined by the court, or reference to a master or otherwise. Third. To the discharge of claims and debts, in the order mentioned in this title." Though these two sections are found in different divisions of the codification of the statutes, they are so in *pari materia* that they should be construed with reference to each other, and so that each may receive its appropriate effect. There is some apparent discrepancy between them, but it is not wholly irreconcilable. The former contains the general provision with respect to the dormancy of judgments, and the steps necessary to keep their liens alive; while, by the latter, special provision is made in regard to the manner, judgment and other liens shall be paid, and the order in which they shall be entitled to share in the distribution of trust funds in particular cases. And in accordance with a well-settled rule, the special provision may be regarded as an exception to the more general one, and as controlling in the particular class of cases to which it relates. (*Doll v. Barr*, 58 Ohio St. 113, 120; 50 N. E. 434.) It becomes of some importance, then, to determine the proper scope of section 6165. Some confusion arises from the use of the word " operate " in the second clause, and the courts below transposed the language to read as follows: " To the payment of mortgages and judgments against the deceased, according to their respective priorities of lien, at the time of his death, so far as the same operate as a lien on the estate of the deceased; " thus using the word " operate " in the present tense,—that is, as of the time of distribution, or the commencement of the action to sell the land; and holding that a judgment lien not kept on foot until that time by executions issued thereon every five years is not entitled to payment out of the fund arising from the sale of the land, although the lien was a subsisting one at the time of the judgment debtor's death. The confusion in the section largely disappears when the letter " d " is added to the word " operate," and that, we find, was the form of the section at the time of the codification, and had been since the Administra-

tor's Act of 1831. (3 Chase's St. 1781; Swan & C. St. 594.)
The dropping of that letter in the codification may have been acci-
dental, but, if not, we cannot presume it was intended to change
the meaning and construction of the statute. In that form of the
section the transposition of its language alluded to is of no importance. Reading it as so transposed, or without making the transposition, the section requires the payment of the liens out of the
proceeds of the sale in the order of their priority as they existed at
the time of the decedent's death; and that requirement cannot be
complied with unless they are treated as subsisting liens on the
fund in that order when the distribution is made. There is much
reason why that should be so. The death of the debtor stops ordinary process, and administration becomes the appropriate proceeding for the payment of his debts. And, though there may be cases
where judgment creditors who obtained a levy on the land of the
debtor before his death have been allowed to proceed thereafter to
sale and confirmation, yet that is an extraordinary remedy, which
may complicate administration and prejudice the rights of the
heir or devise. The personal estate is nevertheless the primary
fund for the satisfaction of liens, as well as other debts of the deceased. The title of the personal representative to the assets,
whenever appointed, relates back to the time of the death, and in
contemplation of law, the estate is in process of administration
from that time. The real estate, so far as may be necessary to pay
any lien upon it, or other debt, becomes assets in his hands, and,
the proper and usual method of subjecting it to the payment of the
liens is by a proceeding of the personal representative for that purpose. The law makes ample provision for such proceedings, and
enjoins the duty of diligence on the representative, with a view of
bringing the estate to a speedy settlement; and the prompt performance of that duty the lienholder has the right to expect, and
may accordingly rely on the security of his lien as it existed at the
time of his debtor's decease. In this respect the consequences of
the transfer of the debtor's property, by operation of law, upon his
decease, are much the same as those resulting when a voluntary assignment of property incumbered by liens is made by a debtor for
the benefit of his creditors. In each case the trust attaches at once
to the property; its administration is under the control of the
court; and similar specific regulations are prescribed by statute for

the disposition of the property, the adjustment of the liens, and the payment of the creditors. It was held in *Scott* v. *Dunn* (26 Ohio St. 63), that in the case of an assignment "the priority of judgment liens is to be determined as the liens existed at the time the assignment took effect." The question was whether a judgment which was the superior lien on land at the time of its assignment for the benefit of creditors, lost its priority over a junior judgment, also a lien on the land, by the failure to have execution issued upon the former within a year from the date of its rendition. The year had not expired when the assignment took effect, but thereafter expired before the sale of the property by the assignee. The following is the provision of the statute under which it was held the liens were preserved as they existed when the assignment took effect: " The Probate Court shall order the payment of all incumbrances and liens upon any of the property sold, or rights and credits collected, out of the proceeds thereof, according to priority, provided, that the assignee may, in all cases where real estate to be sold is incumbered with liens, or where any questions in regard to the title require a decree to settle the same, file his petition for the sale of such real estate, in the Court of Common Pleas of the proper county, making all persons in interest parties to such proceedings; and, upon hearing, such court shall order a sale of the premises, the payment of incumbrances, and determine the questions involved in regard to the title to the same; and the proceeds of the real estate so sold by order of the Court of Common Pleas, after payment of liens and incumbrances, as ordered by such court, shall be reported to the Probate Court by the assignee, and disposed of as provided in this act." (Swan. & S. Rev. St. 396, § 9.) And the statute then in force relating to the order of liens among judgments (now section 5415 of the Revised Statutes) provides that: " No judgment on which execution is not issued and levied before the expiration of one year next after its rendition, shall operate as a lien on the estate of the debtor to the prejudice of any other *bona fide* judgment creditor." It may be observed that the statute which was held to fix the legal status of the liens on the assigned property as of the time of the taking effect of the assignment does not do so with more certainty than are the liens preserved on the judgment debtor's land as they existed at the time of his death by the provisions of section 6165. And section 5415 is not less explicit in its provision that judgments shall cease to operate as liens in the given cases by failure to comply with its requirement than is section 5380, when its provisions are not met. So that, upon the question here involved, this case seems indistinguishable in principle from that of *Scott* v. *Dunn* (*supra.*)

It is also contended the demurrer was properly sustained because the claim of the plaintiffs in error was not presented to the executor for allowance; and, furthermore, that it was barred because the pleading was not filed within the time required by section 6113 of the Revised Statutes, after the executor qualified and gave notice of his appointment. Neither position appears to be tenable. The requirement of section 6115 that the executor make distribution to the lien of the plaintiff in error according to its priority at the time of the testatrix's death dispensed with any necessity for its presentation for allowance, if it were otherwise required; and pleading the lien, in the action brought by the executor, in order that it might receive its proper share of the proceeds of the land on which it was charged, is not the commencement of an action against the executor within the purview of the statute which limits the time for bringing actions against executors and administrators.

Judgment reversed, and cause remanded.

PENN *et al. vs.* FOGLER *et al.*

[Supreme Court of Illinois, October 25, 1899; 182 Ill. 76; 54 N. E. Rep. 192.]

ADMINISTRATOR WITH WILL ANNEXED—POWER TO EXECUTE TRUST —TRUSTEE DE SON TORT—PROPER INVESTMENT OF TRUST FUNDS —LIABILITY OF PARTNERSHIP FOR TRUST FUNDS IMPROPERLY INVESTED IN FIRM BY A MEMBER—LIABILITY OF INCOMING AND OUTGOING PARTNERS—EQUITY—BILL— RELIEF— EVIDENCE — BENEFICIARY OF TRUST—ACQUIESCENCE IN MANAGEMENT OF PROPERTY—LACHES.

1. The duties and powers imposed on an executor as a trustee, being in the nature of a personal trust or confidence reposed in him by the testator, do not devolve on the administrator with the will annexed.

2. A decree giving generally to an administrator with the will annexed " all the powers, rights, duties, and authority that an executor could or might have, if named and mentioned in said will," limits such administrator to duties belonging properly to the office of executor, and does not clothe him with power to execute a trust created by the will.

3. Where an administrator with the will annexed executes, without authority, a trust created by the will, he becomes a constructive trustee or a trustee *de son tort*.

4. An administrator with the will annexed, holding stock of a national bank in trust, has no power or authority to invest it in a private banking partnership.

5. Where a partner, who is a trustee, improperly employs trust funds in the partnership business, or in the payment of partnership debts, the *cestui que trust* is entitled to reimbursement by the firm, if the other partners had knowledge of the nature of the fund at the time of the misapplication.

6. Where an incoming partner, at the time of entering the firm, has knowledge that trust funds have been improperly invested in the business and are being used by the firm, he becomes liable for such misapplication thereof as occurs after he becomes a member.

7. Where an outgoing partner knew that trust funds were improperly employed in the firm business, he is liable therefor to the extent of his interest which he afterwards sold.

8. A bill need not charge all the circumstances which may conduce to prove the general charge, as these are matters of evidence.

9. Relief which is consistent with the allegations and proof is properly granted, though it may be different from that specifically prayed for.

10. Where a bill makes a case for account, evidence which discloses other facts in addition to those charged should be considered, when the facts disclosed strengthen the right claimed, and merely expand the measure of accounting.

11. A beneficiary of a trust, whose interest does not accrue under the will until after the death of the last survivor of life annuitants, being a mere remainder, cannot acquiesce in the management of the property until his interest comes into possession.

12. Where a cause of action arises from a fraud, the bar created by *laches* does not apply in equity until the fraud is discovered by the exercise of reasonable diligence.

13. The failure to use diligence in discovering fraud is excused where there is a relation of trust and confidence which renders it the duty of the party committing the fraud to disclose the truth to the other.

APPEAL from Appellate Court, Fourth District.

Bill by W. M. Fogler and others against John Penn, trustee, and others. From a judgment of the Appellate Court (77 Ill. App.

365), affirming a decree of the Circuit Court in favor of complainants, defendants appeal.

Reversed.

This is a bill in chancery, filed September 1, 1896, by W. M. Fogler and George W. Brown, the latter being administrator with the will annexed of the estate of Nathaniel M. McCurdy, deceased, and others, stockholders or partners in a certain banking firm known as the "Bank of Vandalia," against certain other stockholders or partners therein, and Imogene Marr, Harrietta Marr, McKendree College, and the Church Extension Society of the Methodist Episcopal Church, beneficiaries under the will of the said Nathaniel M. McCurdy, deceased, for the purpose of winding up the partnership affairs of said firm under the direction of the court, and for the appointment of a receiver of the firm assets, and for the distribution thereof after the payment of the firm liabilities, and for general relief.

The bill sets up the existence of the National Bank of Vandalia in Vandalia prior to April 2, 1883, and alleges that it did a general banking business under the charter issued to it under authority of the national banking act, with a paid-up capital stock of $100,000; that on April 2, 1883, the stock was controlled and owned in certain proportions by certain persons, and that among them the Nathaniel M. McCurdy estate, of which George W. Brown was the administrator with the will annexed, owned $40,000 of the stock; that the bonds deposited for the guaranty of the circulating currency were called in for redemption; that, the premiums on the bonds being at that time very high, the stockholders surrendered the charter, and continued the banking business as a co-partnership from April 2, 1883, to May 1, 1895, with the same persons and the same capital, with certain exceptions therein set forth; that the partners were to share in the losses and profits in proportion to the amount invested by each, respectively; that Lydia A. Fogler withdrew on June 8, 1887, her capital stock of $15,000; that certain stockholders died in 1890, 1894, and 1895, leaving heirs and representatives, upon whose estates administrators and executors were qualified; that certain stock was sold, and the purchasers admitted as partners; that, on the dissolution of the firm, the interests of its members were two-fifths thereof, or $40,000, in the McCurdy estate, and the other three-fifths in certain other persons, whose respective interests are named; that real estate was taken in settlement of bad debts; that the firm has notes and other evidences of indebtedness; that the assets should be reduced to money to pay creditors and to make distribution; that no settlement of the partnership affairs has ever been made; that the will provides for the payment of an annuity to Harrietta and Imogene Marr during their lives out of the earnings of the capital invested in the banking business, and that at their death such capital is to be divided between said college and said church extension society. A decree was made, appointing a receiver, and ordering him to take charge of the partnership assets.

One John Penn, trustee, who had been appointed trustee in a proceeding in chancery, commenced by McKendree College and the board of church extension against George W. Brown and the annuitants as defendants, and to whom, as such trustee, George W. Brown was ordered to account for such fund and pay the same over, was made a party defendant to the original bill, and granted leave to answer and file a cross bill. John Penn, trustee, in his answer, alleged that, when the partnership was formed, on April 2, 1883, Brown was admitted as a general partner, and held the stock of the National Bank as an administrator of the estate, or the proceeds thereof, and contributed it to, and it was received by, said partnership as assets; that the persons composing the firm at that time knew that said fund did not belong to Brown, but was held by him as administrator, and was subject to the order of the County Court of Fayette county. The answer further avers that Brown had no authority to make such investment, denies the dissolution of the firm, admits that the co-partners agreed to share the profits and losses, but denies that the legatees of McCurdy made any such agreement.

Penn filed a cross bill, praying that the said sum of $40,000, together with lawful interest thereon, be decreed to be a liability of said partnership, and a prior lien on the firm assets, and that, if the assets are insufficient to discharge the liabilities, a money decree be rendered against the defendants to the cross bill for the residue, and prayed for general relief. The cross bill makes parties defendant thereto all the parties to the original bill, except McCurdy's legatees. The cross bill avers that Nathaniel M. McCurdy died testate, September 29, 1876; that his will was admitted to probate; that, at the time of his death, he owned 400 shares of the capital stock of the National Bank of Vandalia, which he bequeathed to McKendree College and the Board of Church Extension of the Methodist Episcopal Church, subject to the payment of certain legacies and annuities out of the earnings of the stock; that at his death said shares of stock were worth no less than $100 per share; that no trustee was appointed to execute said trust; that Mary K. Marr was to be paid an annuity from the earnings of the stock during her life, and at her death the same was to be paid to her two daughters, Harrietta and Imogene, in equal parts, and, at the death of either, the survivor was to receive the whole during life; that Mary K. Marr is dead, and her daughters still survive; that George W. Brown has been appointed and is acting as adminis- trator with the will annexed; that the estate is still unsettled; that the stock came into Brown's hands as administrator, and, when re- ceived by him, was worth no less than $40,000; that the charter of the bank was surrendered on April 2, 1883, and a partnership was formed by said stockholders and Brown to transact a banking business; that the said firm had a partnership fund called " capital stock "; that Brown contributed the proceeds of said 400 shares to the partnership; that the same was received by said partners, and each of them knew that no part thereof belonged to Brown, but was the property of McCurdy's legatees; that Brown was the cashier of said National Bank and of the Bank of Vandalia, and continued as such until the firm ceased doing business, in May, 1895; that said firm has assets and liabilities; and that among its liabilities is the said sum of $40,000, with lawful interest up to the filing of the cross bill, which is due cross complainant, as trustee.

Answers were filed by all the defendants to the cross bill of John Penn, trustee, but the answer of George W. Brown thereto was separate from the others. The joint and several answer of the defendants, except Brown, to the cross bill, sets up that the National Bank of Vandalia ceased to do business, but that the same business was carried on, with the same directors and the same stockholders, at the same place, and with the same assets, and with no change except in name; that the continuation of the business by the partnership was in accordance with the will. The answer denies that Brown contributed to the firm $40,000 belonging to the

McCurdy estate, or that defendants had notice thereof, or that the partnership is indebted to the beneficiaries of McCurdy, or that the defendants agreed to pay the liabilities of the bank existing when they became interested therein, except ordinary deposits, or that the cross complainant is entitled to a prior lien on the assets or to any relief whatever. The answer further avers that whatever use was made of said fund by either of the banks or the firm was well known to McKendree College and to the board of church extension; that the latter consented thereto and acquiesced therein. The answer also sets up *laches* and the ten-year and five-year statute of limitations as a defense. George W. Brown, in his separate answer, avers that, at the time of the surrender of its charter, the National Bank had a large amount of real estate taken for bad debts, which had depreciated, and that by reason thereof the McCurdy stock was not worth $40,000; that the charter was surrendered because the bonds securing the bank's circulation were called in for redemption, and it would have been detrimental to buy other bonds, on account of the high premium they commanded; that the total amount received on the sale of the bonds when the charter was surrendered was less that $10,000; that the organization of said partnership and the continuation of the banking business were what prudent and careful business men would have done; that the college and the board of church extension consented to and acquiesced in and ratified the investment of the funds in the copartnership. An amendment was filed to the answer of W. M. Fogler to the cross bill of John Penn, which sets up that at the February term, 1877, of the Circuit Court of Fayette county, George W. Brown, administrator, etc., filed a bill for the construction of the will, and for the appointment of a trustee to sell the real estate and carry out the provisions concerning the bank stock; that the college and the church extension society were defendants thereto, and entered their appearances; and that a decree was entered therein on March 10, 1877, the substance of which is set out in the opinion.

Upon the hearing of the case, the court below made a final decree, sustaining the investment made by Brown in the partnership known as the " Bank of Vandalia," and, in general, denying the relief prayed for in the cross bill. By the terms of the final decree, it was ordered that the receiver proceed to execute the decree under which he was appointed; that out of the assets in his hands, or to come into his hands, he should first pay the costs of the receivership, and next the creditors of the firm in 'full; that, after such indebtedness is paid in full, he shall deliver to John Penn, trustee, two-fifths of the remaining assets, and to each of the remaining complainants in the bill, except Brown, their ratable proportion, according to their respective interests; and that the receiver should pay all the costs of this proceeding. The complainants in the cross bill of John Penn, trustee, excepted to the decree.

A writ of error was sued out from the Appellate Court to review the decree so entered by the Circuit Court, and the Appellate Court affirmed the decree of the Circuit Court. The present bill is prosecuted from such judgment of affirmance entered by the Appellate Court.

The will of Nathaniel M. McCurdy, above referred to, is as follows:

" I, Nathaniel Masters McCurdy, of the city of Vandalia and county of Fayette, in the state of Illinois, being in good health and of sound and disposing mind and memory, calling to mind the uncertainty of life, and in view of a contemplated excursion through the Lake Superior, beset, as it must be, with dangers of both waters and land, and being desirous of so disposing of the little property with which a kind Providence has intrusted to my hands as to avoid litigation and waste, that it may be the source of the greatest good to others, I make and publish this, my last will and testament, hereby revoking and making null and void all other wills and testaments by me heretofore made.

" And first, I desire and direct that my mortal body, wheresoever it may be that the immortal spirit departs therefrom, shall be transported to the vault prepared for the purpose near the McCurdy M. E. Church in the city Vandalia, in the state of Illinois, and placed by the side of the remains of my deceased wife, and that my epitaph be cut upon the same stone as that of my departed wife. And that there may be a legal as well as a moral obligation resting upon the trustees and society of the McCurdy M. E.· Church to respect the repository of the dust of myself and deceased wife, by keeping the tomb in decent repair and good condition, I give, devise, and bequeath to the said trustees and their successors in office $3,000 in cash, to be continually invested so as to realize therefrom the highest legal interest, to be regularly paid semiannually, and such interest invested in—First, the premium on insurance against loss by fire, and to be kept unremittingly effective on an amount not less than $12,000, embracing the parsonage as well as the church; secondly, the purchase and hanging a bell in the place where now hangs the bell I bought for that church sold to Michael Lynch, and which bell may now be sold to pay in part for the new bell under contemplation, which new bell shall weigh not less than twelve hundred pounds, and as much more as the trustees may think the church steeple is capable of sustaining; thirdly, the placing of a good and substantial iron fence in front of, and on the two sides of, the church lot, including the tomb or vault; fourthly, the roofing of the entire church and parsonage with slate as soon as the accruing interest will admit of the payment for these enumerated objects; and until then the interest is not to be expended for any other purpose whatever, but, after these objects are procured and paid for, the balance of accruing interest forever shall be applied to the repairs of the church and parsonage, and the tomb, as occasion may require. If the lot on which stands the tomb should ever be sold, it can only be done in accordance with a provision of the discipline of the M. E. Church, which requires the proceeds of such sale to be reinvested in another lot and church, and in such case I demand and require that my tomb shall be removed to the new lot, and re-erected thereon, and preserved and taken care of as I expect and require to be done on the lot where it now stands; and as an evidence that the trustees of the church, for themselves and their successors in office, fully agree to perform the above requirements, they accept the $3,000 with the conditions annexed. The $3,000 shall be paid by my executors hereinafter to be named as soon after my decease as they may be able to discharge all other bequests I make in this will, out of my dividends on my bank stock in the National Bank of Vandalia.

"Also I give and bequeath unto my sister Mary K. Marr, now of Portland, state of Maine, $3,000 annually, out of dividends to be made on the earnings of my shares of stock of the N. B. of V., or semiannually, if so preferred by the bank, beginning as soon after my decease as may be convenient, and continued as long as she may live, which cannot, in the common course of nature, be long, and after her death the same to be divided between her two daughters,

Imogene Marr and Harrietta Marr as long as they may both live. At the death of either, let the same be paid to the survivor as long as said survivor shall live, at the death of whom it shall cease.

" The means to meet and discharge all the legacies in this will hitherto devised will be found in the earnings of my bank stock, and, when they are all fully discharged, I hereby will, bequeath, and devise unto the proper government of McKendree College, for the use and behoof of said college, to endow and support and maintain and continue in use a professional chair, to be known as the ' McCurdy Professorship of the Pure and Applied Sciences,' two hundred shares, of $100 each, to be transferred on the books of the National Bank of Vandalia to the credit of said McKendree College, the earnings of which shall be appropriated exclusively to the salary of the professor and the purchase of apparatus for use of such chair, in such proportions as the government of the college may agree upon.   The said stock shall ever be considered as a perpetual endowment of said professorship, and no part thereof shall ever be diverted to any other use, but it shall be kept upon the best interest obtainable, and the interest alone annually expended. After the transfer of stock to the college or its authorized agent is made, and the college becomes the legal proprietor of that amount of capital stock, it (the college) will be entitled to a participancy in the management of the National Bank of Vandalia, and may continue so, or sell out the stock and invest elsewhere, as they may determine for the benefit of the endowment; but, as the condition of things now is, I would advise that it be kept as stock in the bank so long as the bank may hold an existence as such, and then seek other investment.

" I also give, devise, and bequeath to the Church Extension Society of the Methodist Episcopal Church, a body corporate under the laws of the state of Pennsylvania (the corporate name of the society may at this writing be somewhat changed, but let it be understood that I mean the society once known by the above title), two hundred shares of the capital stock of the National Bank of Vandalia, together with all the rights and privileges thereunto belonging or in any way appertaining; and as it is but a natural desire on the part of most men to have kept alive the name and remembrance of departed loved ones, and that it may induce others to follow my example, I make it a condition in receiving this legacy on the part of the church extension society that it shall ever be known, in both law and equity, as the ' McCurdy Fund for Church Extension.'

" I also will and ordain that my executors shall, on the best terms they can make, and within a reasonable time after my death, sell all the property, real, personal, and mixed, of which I may die seized and possessed, or to which I may be entitled at the time of my decease, and the avails of such sale, after all expenses and charges shall be fully met, and all just demands against my assets are discharged and paid, and the money received kept on interest when the amount is too small to meet a legacy, shall be divided and paid over to the proper persons authorized to receive the same, as follows: To the Fayette County Bible Society, of which I acted as secretary for twenty years, $300; to the sisters Imogene and Harrietta Marr, both of Portland, Maine, $3,000 each if both shall be living at the time when the money may be ready for distribution, but if one should be dead the survivor shall be entitled to receive the share of the other; and to Elizabeth Pingree, also of Portland, Maine, $3,000; and to Mrs. Eliza Watson, now of Cairo, Illinois, $1,000; and to the four daughters of Samuel McCurdy, all of Augusta, state of Arkansas, $1,000 each if all shall be alive, but if one or more be dead the whole to go to the survivors in equal proportions. And all the rest, residue and remainder of my estate and effects, whether personal, real, or mixed, whatsoever and wheresoever, not hereinbefore otherwise effectually disposed of, I do give, devise, and bequeath unto the Missionary Society of the Methodist Episcopal Church."

Merrills & Mooneyham and *G. A. Kœrner,* for appellants.

Patton, Hamilton & Patton, for appellees.

MAGRUDER, J. (after stating the facts).—1. The will in this case appointed no executor or trustee. George W. Brown, who was then cashier of the National Bank of Vandalia, was appointed by the County Court of Fayette county administrator with the will annexed of the estate of Nathaniel M. McCurdy, deceased, and filed his inventory, as such administrator, on January 8, 1877. The estate has not yet been settled by the County Court. At the February term, 1877, of the Circuit Court of Fayette county, George

W. Brown filed a bill, and in the suit commenced by the filing of said bill the decree of March 10, 1877, was entered. The bill itself and other papers in the case have been lost, and there is some dispute between the parties as to the contents of the bill and as to the object sought by it. The appellees claim that the object of the bill was to construe the will and determine the powers of Brown under it to conduct the business, including the bank stock. The appellants claim that the bill merely asked for authority to sell real estate. Without deciding what was the real character of the bill, we will confine ourselves to the language and finding of the decree of March 10, 1877.

Counsel on both sides discuss the question whether the administrator *cum testamento annexo* had the power to execute and carry out the provisions of the will in regard to the 400 shares of bank stock. Executors are often required by the terms of the will appointing them to act in a double capacity: First, as executors by virtue of their office; and, second, as agents or trustees under a warrant of attorney. An executor is often charged, not only with the duties and liabilities appertaining to that office, but also with certain duties in the execution of a trust which is imposed upon him by the will. The general rule is that the duties and powers of an executor, which result from the nature of his office as executor, devolve upon the administrator with the will annexed. But the duties and powers which are imposed upon an executor as a trustee are in the nature of a personal trust or confidence reposed in him by the executor, and do not devolve upon the administrator with the will annexed, inasmuch as they cannot be delegated. (*Hall* v. *Irwin*, 2 Gilman, 176; *Nicoll* v. *Scott*, 99 Ill. 529.)

It is clear, therefore, that George W. Brown, acting under his appointment as administrator with the will annexed as made by the County Court, would have had no power to take upon himself the execution of the trust in regard to the bank stock. The question then arises whether such power was conferred upon him by the decree of the Circuit Court of Fayette county, rendered on March 10, 1877, in the proceedings brought therein by the filing of the bill by Brown against the life annuitants, Mary A. Marr, Harrietta Marr, and Imogene Marr, and the remaindermen, or those entitled to take after the death of the annuitants, to wit, McKendree College and the Church Extension Society of the Methodist Episcopal Church. Brown had the right, as administrator with the will annexed, to apply to a court having equitable juris-diction to have a trustee appointed to carry out those provisions of the will which did not strictly devolve upon him as such adminis-trator. (*Wenner* v. *Thornton*, 98 Ill. 156.)

The decree of March 10, 1877, did not give a definite construc-tion of the will, so far as it related to the duties of the executor or trustee in relation to the bank stock. It will appear from the find-ings of the decree, as set forth in the reciting part thereof, that the object of the bill upon which the decree was founded was to get the permission of a Court of Chancery to sell the real and personal property of the estate. The decree finds that the legatees in the will of Nathaniel M. McCurdy, deceased, were the Marrs and the col-lege and the church extension society above named; that said Mc-Curdy left a large amount of real and personal estate, which had been inventoried and reported to the County Court by Brown, but that no executors were named in the will; and the finding portion of the decree then proceeds as follows: "And it further appearing that said testator desired all of his real and personal property sold, conveyed, or transferred, to enable the specified legacies to be dis-charged; and of said personal estate there are four hundred shares of bank stock in the National Bank of Vandalia, valued at $100 a share, and the following described real estate, to wit: (Here fol-lows description of real estate.)" The ordering part of the decree is that Brown, the administrator with the will annexed, "transfer and dispose of said bank stock as in said will specified, and that it be so transferred and disposed of for the uses and purposes in said will mentioned; and that said administrator is hereby fully author-ized and empowered to sell all the other property of Nathaniel M. McCurdy, deceased, including real estate, personal and mixed prop-erty, and to collect what is due said estate, and to disburse the same as directed by said will; that said real, personal, and mixed prop-erty may be sold; * * * and said complainant (Brown) shall have generally all the powers, rights, duties, and authority that an executor could or might have, if named and mentioned in said will and said administrator shall report all his actions and doings to the County Court of said Fayette county, as provided by law in refer-ence to administrators."

It is claimed by the appellees that, inasmuch as the decree gave

Brown generally "all the powers, rights, duties, and authority that an executor could or might have, if named and mentioned in said will," Brown was thereby clothed with power to manage the bank stock in accordance with the terms of the will.   But it was expressly held by this court in *Hall* v. *Irwin* (*supra*), that those words did not confer upon an administrator *cum testamento annexo* the right to exercise the trust powers conferred upon an executor, but only the powers appertaining strictly to his office as executor. In *Hall* v. *Irwin* (*supra*), the case of *Conklin* v. *Edgerton's Adm'r*, (21 Wend. 430),—where words in a New York statute precisely similar to the words used in this decree were construed as being limited to duties belonging properly to the office of executor, and as not extending to anything to be done by the executor as trustee,— was approved by this court.   Counsel for appellees insist that the case of *Conklin* v. *Edgerton's Adm'r* (*supra*), has been since modified, if not overruled, by a subsequent decision made by the New York Court of Appeals.   But we consider ourselves bound by the doctrine announced in *Hall* v. *Irwin* (*supra*), because the case of *Hall* v. *Irwin* was subsequently indorsed and approved by this court in *Nicoll* v. *Scott* (*supra*).

That the provision in the decree which gave Brown the powers, rights, duties, and authority that an executor could or might have if one had been named in the will, did not confer upon him any other powers than those strictly appertaining to the nature of his office as executor, is apparent from the requirement that he shall report all his actions and doings to the County Court as provided by the law in reference to administrators.   Section 112 of the Illinois Administration Act (Starr & C. Ann. St. p. 242), provides that executors and administrators shall exhibit their accounts for settlement to the County Court at the first term after the expiration of one year after the date of their appointment, and in like manner every twelve months thereafter.   If the decree was intended to make Brown a trustee for the purpose of executing the trust in regard to the bank stock, and not a mere administrator to discharge the duties of administration, it would seem that he should have been required to report to the Chancery Court which appointed him. The decree undoubtedly gave him power to sell the land with a view to paying the legacies to be paid out of the proceeds of the sale thereof, but the decree leaves it in doubt what duty was intended to be imposed upon him in relation to the bank stock. He was merely required to "transfer and dispose of said bank stock as in said will specified," and "for the uses and purposes in said will mentioned." There is nothing in the language of the decree that necessarily empowered him to hold the stock as administrator with the will annexed until Mrs. Marr and both her daughters should die, and then transfer it to the college and the church extension society. Such a construction of the decree would give him the right to hold and manage the stock for a long period of years, or until the survivor of the three annuitants should die. The decree, on the contrary, seems to contemplate immediate action; and a fair construction of it would lead to the conclusion that it was his duty to have either himself or another person appointed trustee by a Court of Chancery, and transfer the stock to such trustee.

If the decree did not confer upon Brown, administrator *cum testamento annexo*, the authority to execute the trust in regard to the bank stock, his acts in so doing constituted him a constructive trustee or a trustee *de son tort*. Where one without authority undertakes to execute a trust requiring the investment of a fund, he must himself carry all the risks, and make good all the losses, and have none of the profits, and his co-investors are equally liable. "A person may become a trustee by construction by intermeddling with, and assuming the management of, trust property without authority. Such persons are trustees *de son tort*." (Perry, Trusts, [3d ed.] § 245; *Morris* v. *Joseph*, 1 W. Va. 256; *Piper* v. *Hoard*, 107 N. Y. 73; 13 N. E. 626.) "During the possession and management by such constructive trustees, they are subject to the same rules and remedies as other trustees; and they cannot avoid their liability by showing that they were not, in fact, trustees, nor can they set up the Statute of Limitations." (Perry, Trusts, [3d ed.] § 245.)

2. But, for the purposes of this case it may be conceded that Brown had authority, under the terms of the decree, to manage the trust in regard to the bank stock. Did he do his duty as trustee, if he had the authority of a trustee in the management and investment of the trust fund in his hands?

The testator, Nathaniel M. McCurdy, owned 400 shares of stock in the National Bank of Vandalia, each share being $100, and the whole amounting to $40,000. At the time of his death, on September 29, 1876, this stock had a par value of $100 per share and was worth more than par. The shares were probably at the time at a premium. By the terms of his will, he gave to his sister Mary K. Marr $3,000 annually out of the dividends to be made out of the earnings on these shares of stock, to be continued during her life, and after her death the same to be divided between her two daughters, Imogene and Harrietta Marr, as long as they might both live; at the death of either, the same to be paid to the survivor as long as the latter should live. By the terms of the will, after the legacies charged against the bank stock should be paid, the testator bequeathed and devised to McKendree College 200 shares of the stock, to be transferred on the books of the National Bank of Vandalia to the credit of said college, and 200 shares of said stock to the Board of Extension of the Methodist Episcopal Church, a corporation organized under the laws of Pennsylvania. When Brown was appointed administrator with the will annexed, he took possession of these 400 shares of bank stock; represented it at the meeting of the directors and shareholders of the bank; collected the dividends thereon; paid the legacies to the Methodist Episcopal Church in Vandalia; and paid the annuities up to the time of the surrender of the bank's charter, as hereinafter stated.

The National Bank of Vandalia did business as such until the 1st day of April, 1883. At the latter date the National Bank surrendered its charter, pursuant to a resolution adopted by its stockholders on January 11, 1883. That bank did no further business after April 3, 1883. The reason assigned for the surrender of its charter was that the government bonds pledged to secure its circulating currency or bills had matured, and were called in for redemption, and that the premium on bonds which could then be purchased to be substituted for those retired was 28 per cent. It is said that, in view of the high premium which it was necessary to pay in order to purchase new bonds, it was not for the interest of the stockholders to continue the existence of the bank as a national bank. Accordingly, on April 2, 1883, the stockholders of the National Bank organized a co-partnership under the firm name and style of the " Bank of Vandalia," and continued doing business at the same stand formerly occupied by the National Bank of Vandalia. The new firm, by the agreement of the parties, succeeding to the business of the National Bank, took possession of its assets, and assumed its liabilities. At the time of the surrender aforesaid, Brown, administrator with the will annexed of the estate of Nathaniel M. McCurdy, still had in his hands the 400 shares of the capital stock of the National Bank of Vandalia. When the new firm was formed under the name of the " Bank of Vandalia," he went into said firm as a partner in his capacity as administrator, and permitted the fund, consisting of said 400 shares of bank stock, to go into the business of the new firm, and to be continued therein as a part of the assets of said firm.

The report of the National Bank of Vandalia made by Brown to the Comptroller of the Currency on December 30, 1882, showed the total resources of the bank to be $330,673.96, and the total liabilities to be $190,928.27, leaving the net resources $139,545.69. It is contended by the appellees that of these resources, about $69,-000 afterwards proved to be a loss. But the evidence shows that, if such a loss occurred it could have been avoided in large part by proper management. The directors and stockholders, who were debtors to the firm, were settled with in such a negligent way as to involve a loss to the firm, and one or more of the stockholders was allowed to withdraw his or her capital to the detriment of the firm.

Whether the reason assigned for surrendering the charter of the National Bank was a good one or not, it was done by a vote of the necessary number of stockholders; and the question arises whether Brown made a proper investment of the funds of the estate, theretofore consisting of the 400 shares of bank stock, when the surrender took place. The new firm, which was organized under the name of the " Bank of Vandalia," was a mere partnership. It was none the less a partnership because articles of association were entered into. The evidence is clear that Brown invested the trust fund in his hands in the new venture or partnership. The Bank of Vandalia was not subject to the restrictions which were imposed by act of Congress upon the National Bank of Vandalia. Brown made the investment of the trust fund in the new firm upon his own judgment, and without applying for permission to do so, either to the County Court or to the Circuit Court. The fund in his hands belonged to McKendree College and the Board of Church Extension of the Methodist Episcopal Church, subject to the rights of Mrs. Marr and her two daughters to receive $3,000 a year from the income of the fund so long as any one of them was alive. It was the duty of Brown, as administrator with the will annexed, to protect the principal, or *corpus*, of the fund for the college and board of extension, as only the income thereof was to go to the annuitants, Mrs. Marr and her two daughters. He, however, formed a new firm or organization, and paid out dividends which trenched upon and depleted the *corpus* of the fund. The law is that, where a monthly or yearly allowance is to be paid from the income of a fund, the *corpus* of the estate cannot be resorted to for the purpose of making up the accruing deficiencies in the allowance. (*Einbecker* v. *Einbecker*, 162 Ill. 267; 44 N. E. 426.) The new partnership not only continued the same banking business at the same stand, but substantially with the same capital and the same stockholders, as had been in and connected with the National Bank of Vandalia. The firm known as the " Bank of Vandalia " continued in business up to May 1, 1895, when it ceased to do business, and a new bank was organized, and called the " First National Bank of Vandalia." Brown was cashier of the National Bank of Vandalia from some time in 1866, soon after its organization, down to the surrender of its charter, in April, 1883. He was also cashier of the partnership known as the " Bank of Vandalia," and also became cashier of the First National Bank of Vandalia. It does not appear that any of the trust fund in question went into the latter bank, which was organized with a capital stock of $50,000. The capital stock of the National Bank of Vandalia was $100,000, and the same amount was invested in the new firm known as the "Bank of Vandalia." The interest of the McCurdy estate in the National Bank of Vandalia was $40,000, or two-fifths of its capital stock, and it had the same interest in the capital invested in the new firm.

Brown was required by the decree of March 10, 1877, to report his actions and doings to the County Court of Fayette county. He made three reports. The first one was filed March 8, 1879, and covered the period from November 30, 1876, to March 8, 1879. In this first report he charges himself with a balance of $50,471.50, and says, " Included in the above balance is $40,000 bank stock." In this report he also charges himself with dividends on the bank stock. In the report he charges himself with items of receipts, embracing personal property, which includes the bank stock, and refers to this personal property as being embraced in the inventory filed by him in the County Court. The inventory describes the bank stock as follows: "Four hundred shares in the National Bank of Vandalia, at $100 per share, par value $40,000." His second report is dated March 17, 1884, and embraces the period from March 8 1879, to February 18, 1884. It will be observed that a part of the time embraced in the latter period was after the surrender of the charter of the National Bank, which took place in April, 1883. In this report he says nothing about the surrender of the charter of the National Bank, and nothing about the formation of a new partnership known as the "Bank of Vandalia," nor anything about his investments of the trust funds in said partnership. On the contrary, he uses the following words: "Balance due, being bank stock held in trust, $40,000." He also refers to the annuities paid Imogene and Harrietta Marr. At the time this report was made, there was really no bank stock existing in the National Bank of Vandalia, because that bank had gone out of existence in April, 1883. Whatever stock then existed was stock in the Bank of Vandalia, or, rather, a two-fifths interest in the partnership doing business under that name. The report, however, treats the bank stock as though it was still existing in the National Bank of Vandalia. The report, taken in connection with the previous report and the inventory referred to therein, can have no other interpretation than that of describing the 400 shares of National Bank stock as still existing. There was nothing in the report to inform the County Court that the stock in his hands was not National Bank stock. The report was calculated to deceive the court as to the character of the investment, and the author of the report must be held to have intended to make the impression which the language of the report creates. The third report made by Brown was filed in March, 1896, and covers the period from February 18, 1884, to February 18, 1896,—12 years. In this third report he mentions, among the items of receipts, the following: "February 12, 1884 four hundred shares bank stock, par value $100 each, $40,000." References are made to dividends on the bank stock and to items paid out to Imogene and Harrietta Marr. The report asked the court to reduce the rate of interest to be paid to the annuitants from 10 per cent. per annum to 4 per cent. per annum and refers to his compensation, using the following words: "Until the conditions requiring the transfer of the bank stock to the final purpose intended by the deceased, viz., to the McKendree College and the Extension Society of the Methodist Episcopal Church." This third report makes no mention of the formation of the new firm, and refers to a contemplated transfer of bank stock at some time in the future to McKendree College and the board of church extension. It is true that, in the last sentence of the report, the following words occur: " The four hundred shares of bank stock in the Bank of Vandalia, at $100 per share, total principal $40,000, held in trust as administrator with the will annexed." No provision was made in the will for the transfer of any stock except national bank stock and such transfer was to be made upon the books of the National Bank of Vandalia. When the third report was made, the National Bank of Vandalia had long since gone out of existence, and no transfer of stock could ever be made upon its books. No transfer of stock was directed by the will to be made upon the books of the Bank of Vandalia. It follows that the report was misleading, and, although the words " Bank of Vandalia " were used in the last sentence of the report, all the language, taken together, was calculated to make the impression upon the County Court that the administrator was dealing with the same stock which was referred to in the will, and which had been mentioned in his former reports. The conclusion is inevitable that this administrator with the will annexed not only failed to ask the advice of any court as to the investment of the trust funds in his hands in the new partnership venture, but that he sedulously concealed from the court the fact that he had made such investment after it was made.

Under the law, Brown, as administrator with the will annexed, holding this bank stock in trust, had no power or authority to invest it, or the proceeds of its sale, if it had been sold, in the new partnership. The evidence is clear that he did so invest it, and that he put it into the partnership, as trust funds in his hands as administrator with the will annexed. A trustee will not be protected from loss in investing trust funds, unless he invests in government or real estate securities, or other securities approved by the court, to which he is accountable. (*Simmons* v. *Oliver*, 74 Wis. 633; 43 N. W. 561.) A trustee should not invest the money of others in his care in the stock or shares of any private corporation, nor has he any right to employ trust funds in a private business, and thereby subject them to the fluctuations of trade, even though such investment is approved of by his own judgment and is made with honest intent. It is the duty of a trustee to make investments of trust funds in real estate securities or government securities, whether of the national or state government, or, if he is acting under the direction of a court, to select such securities as the court approves of. (11 Am. & Eng. Enc. Law, pp. 819, 835; *Gray* v. *Fox*, 1 N. J. Eq. 259; *White* v. *Sherman*, 168 Ill. 589; 48 N. E. 128; *Mattocks* v. *Moulton*, 84 Me. 545; 24 Atl. 1004; *King* v. *Talbot*, 40 N. Y. 76; 2 Pom. Eq. Jur. § 1074.)   In *King* v. *Talbot* (*supra*), the court said: " It is not denied that the employment of the fund as capital in trade would be a clear departure from the duty of trustees. If it cannot be so employed under the management of a co-partnership, I see no reason for saying that the incorporation of the partners tends in any degree to justify it."

It is claimed that, by making an investment of the trust fund in the partnership formed under the name of the " Bank of Vandalia," it was continued as an investment in the banking business, and that the testator in his will showed a preference for an investment in bank stock. The will, however, shows a preference on the part of the testator for an investment in the stock of a national bank, and not in the stock of a private bank. He says in his will: " I would advise that it be kept as stock in the bank so long as the bank may hold an existence as such, and then seek other investment." This language refers to stock in a bank so long as it should exist as a national bank, subject to such examinations and other restrictions as are imposed by the national banking law. There is nothing in the will to indicate that the testator ever intended the investment to be changed from one in the National Bank to one in the stock or shares of a private banking partnership. Changes in investments or reinvestments should not be made by trustees, as a general thing, unless they are ordered by a Chancery Court, and in such case the trust fund may be withdrawn and reloaned. (11 Am. & Eng. Enc. Law, p. 824.) It is not claimed that the Bank of Vandalia was organized under any private banking charter granted by the Legislature before the present Constitution was adopted; and the present act, permitting the organization of corporations with banking powers, did not exist in April, 1883, when the firm known as the " Bank of Vandalia " was formed. That act was not adopted until 1887.

3. The question arises as to the liability of those who were partners with Brown in the firm known as the " Bank of Vandalia.''
They are called " stockholders," but it is apparent that they were
mere partners. When the firm known as the " Bank of Vandalia "
was dissolved, on May 1, 1895, George W. Brown, as administrator
with the will annexed of the McCurdy estate, owned an interest of
two-fifths or $40,000, in the firm; and other parties, whose names
appear in the record, owned the other interest of three-fifths, in
various amounts, ranging all the way from $15,000 to $500. From
the time when the firm was organized up to the time of its dissolution a few changes in the stockholders took place, through death,
and, in three instances, through transfers of stock.

Where a partner, who is a trustee or executor, improperly employs the money of his *cestui que* trust in the partnership business,
or in the payment of partnership debts, the *cestui que* trust will be
entitled to reimbursement by the firm, if the other partners have
knowledge of the nature of the fund at the time of the misapplication. The other partners, at the election of the *cestui que* trust,
are placed, with the misappropriating partner, in the attitude of
trustees of the fund, and they are regarded as having connived at
the violation of the trust. If they know that the fund belongs to an
estate, they are bound to inquire upon what terms it is held. The
liability, when incurred, is a joint and several one. (17 Am. & Eng.
Enc. Law, pp. 1071, 1072.) The rule is thus stated by Story in his
work on Partnership (5th ed. § 368) : " If one partner is separately intrusted with trust money, and he, with the knowledge and
consent of his partners, applies it to partnership purposes, it will
constitute a joint debt against the partnership, at the election of the
cestui que trust or beneficiary." See, also, T. Pars. Partn. (4th
ed.), § 104. Where all the partners know that the fund invested
is trust money, they are implicated in the breach of trust. If they
know that such money is being employed in the partnership business for the common benefit, they will all be bound for the money
so employed, and be made answerable for the breach of trust committed by their co-partner with their acquiescence. (*Englar* v.
Offutt, 70 Md. 78; 16 Atl. 497.) Bates, in his work on the Law of
Partnership (volume 1, §§ 481, 483), thus lays down the rule: " If
a partner has possession of the funds of others in trust, * * *
and he properly uses the trust funds for the benefit of the firm, the

nature of the co-partner's liability depends on whether they participated in the breach of trust. * * * But, if the other partners have knowledge of the nature of the funds at the time of such misappropriation, they are implicated in the breach of trust, and become themselves, at the election of the *cestui que* trust, his debtors, or even trustees of the fund, as having connived at the violation." (1 Lindl. Partn. [5th ed.] pp. 161, 162; *Jaques* v. *Marquand,* 6 Cow. 497; *Hutchinson* v. *Smith,* 7 Paige, 26; *Guillou* v. *Peterson,* 89 Pa. St. 163; *Emerson* v. *Durand,* 64 Wis. 111; 24 N. W. 129; *Durant* v. *Rogers,* 87 Ill. 508; *Renfrow* v. *Pearce,* 68 id. 125.) .

The evidence is clear to the effect that all the partners or stockholders in the partnership known as the " Bank of Vandalia " had notice of the fact that Brown held the funds in his hands as administrator with the will annexed of the McCurdy estate, and that he invested the trust funds in the business of the new firm. Therefore these other partners are brought within the scope of the liability announced in the foregoing authorities. The other partners in the accounting which is to take place when the case goes back shall be charged with the value of the interest belonging to the estate of the deceased testator which had been represented by 200 shares of National Bank stock before April 2, 1883, as such value existed when the new partnership was formed. When the new firm was formed in April, 1883, W. M. Fogler owned $5,000 of the stock, and Mary I. Henninger owned $2,000 of the stock. On January 14, 1892, Mary I. Henninger transferred $500 of her stock to W. M. Farmer, and $500 thereof to J. J. Brown, and on March 5, 1892, W. M. Fogler transferred $4,000 of his stock to Mary Wagner. The rule, announced in some of the text books, that, where the misuse of the trust funds has taken place before the admission of a partner into the firm, he will not be liable because not a participator in the misuse, is invoked in behalf of these transferees. This rule is based upon the case of *Twyford* v. *Trail,* (7 Sim. 92). The examination, however, of the facts of that case will show that, at a certain date, two persons were admitted as partners into a firm, and knew that certain trust money remained in the firm, but they afterwards retired, and other partners were admitted, and, upon the failure of the firm, these two persons were held not to be responsible for the breach of trust committed by their co-partners. No such state of facts exists in the case at bar. W.

M. Farmer and J. J. Brown and Mrs. Wagner acquired their interest in the firm in 1892. The firm continued to do business thereafter for three years, and these transferees remained in the firm during that time. They did not retire from the firm to be succeeded by other partners, as was the case of the partners held not to be liable in *Twyford* v. *Trail*, (*supra*). Farmer and J. J. Brown, as we understand the record, were lawyers, who has been consulted by G. W. Brown during his administration of the estate. Mrs. Wagner and J. J. Brown and Farmer knew that the funds which George W. Brown had put into the firm were trust funds. Those funds were used for the benefit of the firm during the three years following their entrance into it. It cannot be said of them that they were not participators in the misuse of the trust funds. The liability of the firm to these beneficiaries, the McKendree College and the board of church extension and the daughters of Mrs. Marr, existed when the new partners came into the firm, and continued to exist thereafter. The incoming partners should not be chargeable with liabilities for the violation of the trust which occurred before they became members of the firm, but the partners who sold to them their interests are to remain affected with such liabilities to the extent of their interests so sold.

4. It is claimed by appellees that the cross bill does not contain such allegations as are sufficient to authorize an inquiry into the mismanagement of the trust fund by the partnership. We think that the bill is sufficient to authorize the granting of the relief asked for by it. It is a bill for account and relief. It traces the trust fund into the hands of defendants, and avers that "the trust fund and interest thereon is a liability of the partnership." It charges that the defendants should "in equity and good conscience, be held to account to your orator for the said sum of $40,000 so received by the defendants as aforesaid." It is not necessary in a bill to charge all the circumstances which may conduce to prove the general charge, for these circumstances are matters of evidence. This is especially true where the circumstances are of such a nature as to be peculiarly within the knowledge of the defendants, as was the case here. When the relief granted is not repugnant to the facts alleged and proved, it is properly granted, although not specifically prayed for under the prayer for general relief. (Story Eq. Pl. § 28; *Stanley* v. *Valentine*,

79 Ill. 544; *Pope* v. *Leonard*, 115 Mass. 286; *Hopkins* v. *Snedaker*, 71 Ill. 449.) Moreover, the defendants here did not challenge the sufficiency of the cross bill by a demurrer, nor did they make any motion to make its allegations more specific. Nor did they raise the question of its sufficiency upon the admission of the evidence, and thereby furnish an opportunity for amending the bill. The proof, which is now claimed to be improper under the allegations of the bill, was allowed to go in without objection. Such proof discloses a case for relief which is not inconsistent with the object and scope of the bill, and therefore may be given proper effect in entering the decree. Although the relief granted may be different from the relief specifically prayed, yet, if it is consistent with the allegations and proof made, it is properly granted. (*McNab* v. *Heald*, 41 Ill. 326; *Morrison* v. *Smith*, 130 id. 304; 23 N. E. 241; *Hopkins* v. *Snedaker*, *supra*.) As, in the case at bar, the statement and charging part of the bill make a case for account, it is not proper to refuse to consider evidence which discloses other facts in addition to those charged, when the facts disclosed strengthen the right claimed, and merely expand the measure of accounting.

5. It is further claimed that the beneficiaries whose rights are here in controversy, to wit, the daughters of Mrs. Marr and Mc-Kendree College and the board of church extension are estopped from complaining of the conduct of these defendants, by reason of alleged acquiescence and *laches* on their part. So far as Mc-Kendree College and the board of extension are concerned, their interests were not to accrue under the will until the death of the last survivor of the life annuitants. They are therefore mere remaindermen, and under the law, a remainderman cannot acquiesce until his interest fall into possession. (Perry, Trusts [3d ed.] § 467; *White* v. *Sherman*, 168 Ill. 589; 48 N. E. 128.) So far as Imogene and Harrietta Marr are concerned, we have been pointed to no evidence, and have discovered none, which shows that they had any notice or knowledge of the improper investment made of these funds by the administrator with the will annexed. There is nothing in the record to show that any of the beneficiaries acquiesced in the wrong here complained of, and therefore the principles announced in *White* v. *Sherman*, (*supra*), upon this subject are precisely applicable here.

6. Where a cause of action arises from a fraud, the bar created

by *laches* will not apply in equity until the discovery of the fraud, or until the fraud could have been discovered by the exercise of reasonable diligence. The failure to use diligence is excused where there is a relation of trust and confidence, which renders it the duty of the party committing the fraud to disclose the truth to the other. (*Farwell* v. *Telegraph Co.* 161 Ill. 522; 44 N. E. 891.) There is nothing here to establish the fact that any of these beneficiaries were guilty of *laches* after their discovery of the improper conduct of the trustee. *Laches* cannot be here pleaded against any equitable right of the college or against the board of extension because they are not asking that they be put into possession of the fund, but that it be secured. The lapse of time is no bar or evidence of *laches* against them, because, as remaindermen, they had not come into possession at the time of the wrongful investment and continuance of the same. (*Bennett* v. *Colley*, 5 Sim. 181.) Our conclusion is that John Penn, trustee, the complainant in the cross bill below and one of the appellants here, and the beneficiaries in the trust which he represents, are entitled to the relief prayed for in the cross bill. Accordingly, the judgment of the Appellate Court and the decree of the Circuit Court are reversed, and the cause is remanded to the Circuit Court, with instructions to proceed in accordance with the views herein expressed.

Reversed and remanded.

NOTE.—POWERS OF ADMINISTRATOR WITH WILL ANNEXED.

  (a) Power to sell land.
  (b) As limited by a leading case.
  (c) Illustrative cases.

  (a) **Power to sell land.**—Power to sell land only where given to the executor by virtue of his office as such. (Harrison v. Henderson, 7 Heisk. 316, 351.)

Power to sell land construed as a personal trust or confidence reposed in an executor and therefore not to be exercised by an administrator with will annexed without aid of the court. (Nicoll v. Scott, 99 Ill. 529; Mitchell v. Spence, 62 Ala. 450; and see Tarver v. Haines, 55 Ala. 503; Simpson v. Cook, 24 Minn. 187.)

Administrator with will annexed may sell land if the executor could have sold it as such. (Kidwell v. Brummagin, 32 Cal. 436; Lantz v. Boyer, 81 Pa. St. 325; Davis v. Hoover, 112 Ind. 423; 14 N. E. Rep. 468; Venable

v. Mercantile Trust Co., 74 Md. 187; 21 Atl. Rep. 704; Schroeder v. Wilcox, 39 Neb. 137; 57 N. W. Rep. 1031; Green v. Russell, 103 Mich. 638; 61 N. W. Rep. 885; Dilworth v. Rice, 48 Mo. 124; Jackman v. Delafield, 85 Pa. St. 381, 384.)

Under Illinois statute no power to sell land, without aid of court. (Nicoll v. Scott, 99 Ill. 529.)

Nor will such power devolve on the administrator unless such intention is expressed in the will or unless statute changes the rule. (Hodgin v. Toler, 70 Iowa, 21; 30 N. W. Rep. 1.)

(b) **As limited by a leading case.**—Where a power of sale is given to executors for the purpose of paying debts and legacies, or either, and especially where there is an equitable conversion of land into money for the purpose of such payment and for distribution, and the power of sale is imperative and does not grow out of a personal discretion confided to the individual, such power belongs to the office of executor, and under the statute passes to and may be exercised by the administrator with the will annexed. (Mott v. Ackerman, 92 N. Y. 540. The opinion by FINCH, J., reviews the cases and disagreement of the courts. And see previous decisions, Conklin v. Egerton's Adm'r, 21 Wend. 430; Roome v. Phillips, 27 N. Y. 357; Dominick v. Michael, 4 Sand. 374; Van Giesen v. Bridgford, 83 N. Y. 356.)

Where power to sell is discretionary in the executor it cannot be exercised by the administrator with will annexed. (Clifford v. Morrell, 22 App. Div. 471; 48 N. Y. Supp. 83; citing Greenland v. Waddell, 116 N. Y. 234, 240; 22 N. E. Rep. 367; and see Cooke v. Platt, 98 N. Y. 39.)

And so where duties are active as applied to trusts the executor is deemed a trustee, and such power cannot be executed by the administrator. (Greenland v. Waddell, *supra*.)

Powers do not include such as vested in the executor as testamentary *trustee*. (Dunning v. Ocean National Bank, 61 N. Y. 497; Harrison v. Henderson, 7 Heisk, 316, 349.)

Involving an element of personal confidence. (Hayes v. Pratt, 147 U. S. 567; 13 Sup. Rep. 503.)

(c) **Illustrative cases.**—Power ceases when will is set aside. (Kilton v. Anderson, 18 R. I. 136; 25 Atl. Rep. 907.)

Does not become a trustee merely by virtue of his appointment. (Knight v. Loomis, 30 Me. 204.)

When power is given to executor as such, it survives death of the executors, and may be exercised by administrator with will annexed. (King v. Talbot, 36 Miss. 367.)

If confidence or trust is reposed specially in the executor named, power will not devolve on administrator. (Dilworth v. Rice, 48 Mo. 124.)

Limited to duties and powers which are not necessarily connected with a personal trust or confidence reposed in the executor. (Farwell v. Jacobs, 4 Mass. 634.)

Where the will imposes upon the executor named duties foreign to those which come within the scope of an executor's ordinary functions, such powers do not pass to the administrator unless it be clear that it was the intention of the testator to make him a donee of the power. (Ingle v. Jones, 9 Wall. 486.)

The Maryland statute involved in this case, while it authorized the appointment of an administrator was silent as to his powers. (Id. 497.)

When statute is silent as to his powers the common law limits them to the personal estate unadministered by his predecessor. (Ingle v. Jones, id. 499.)

It seems that person named as executor may decline that office and still act as trustee under the will and have power of sale as such, notwithstanding appointment of an administrator with will annexed. (Clark v. Tainter, 61 Mass. 567.)

Where trustee dies the trust devolves upon the court and it has jurisdiction to appoint new trustees to execute the trust. (Royce v. Adams, 123 N. Y. 405; 25 N. E. Rep. 386.)

So when there is a power of sale, which is a power in trust and discretionary in the executor and trustee. (Cooke v. Platt, 98 N. Y. 39; and see Greenland v. Waddell, 116 N. Y. 243; 22 N. E. Rep. 367.)

NIEMAN *et al. vs.* SCHNITKER.

HESEMAN *et al. vs.* VOGT *et al.*

[Supreme Court of Illinois, October 16, 1899; 181 Ill. 400; 55 N. E. Rep. 151.]

WILLS—CONTEST—TESTAMENTARY CAPACITY—EVIDENCE — INSTRUCTIONS.

1. Declarations of testator, made before or after the execution of will, are admissible to show his mental condition at the time the will was executed.

2. In a contest over the validity of a will on the ground of want of testamentary capacity, a previous will, made when the soundness of testator's mind was unquestioned, and which disposed of property approximately the same as the 'contested will, is admissible in evidence as tending to show soundness of mind when the contested will was executed.

3. Where previous wills, made by a testator, are in evidence as showing mental soundness at the time a contested will was made, proof of the mental soundness of testator when such previous wills were executed is admissible.

VOL. V—16

4. In a contest over the validity of a will on the ground of want of testamentary capacity, the jury were instructed that the opinions of subscribing witnesses to a will as to testator's mental soundness are not entitled to greater weight than opinions of other witnesses, equally credible, who had better opportunities of observing testator. There was no evidence that other witnesses were present when the will was executed, nor that there were others who had better opportunities for observing deceased. *Held,* that the instruction was erroneous, as suggesting that other witnesses had better opportunities of observing deceased than the subscribing witnesses.

5. In a contest over the validity of a will on the ground of want of testamentary capacity, it is error to instruct the jury that " unsoundness of mind embraces every species of mental incapacity from raging mania to delicate and extreme feebleness of mind," because a testator's mind might be in a partial sense unsound, and yet not incapacitate him from making a will.

6. In a contest over the validity of a will on the ground of want of testamentary capacity, it is error to give an instruction that, " if the will was made under the influence of partial insanity, and is the product of it, it is invalid," when there is no evidence that the testator was laboring under any delusion or mania.

7. In a contest over the validity of a will on the ground of want of testamentary capacity, it is not within the province of the jury to determine whether the will is a reasonable and proper distribution of the testator's property, and an instruction giving the jury such an understanding is ground for reversal.

APPEAL from Circuit Court, Washington county.

Bill by Caroline Vogt and others against Caroline Heseman and others to contest the validity of a will. Dismissal was entered by all complainants except Wilhelmina Schnitker. From a judgment annulling the will, defendants appeal.

Reversed.

James A. Watts, for appellants.

Charles T. Moore, F. P. Tscharner, and *F. M. Vernor,* for appellees.

PHILLIPS, J.—The will of Henry Nieman was admitted to probate in the County Court of Washington county on the 6th day of August, 1898, and on the 28th day of September, 1898, this bill was filed to contest the validity of the will, on the sole ground as alleged in the bill, of want of testamentary capacity. The evidence shows that on May 24, 1898, the testator made his will, which was duly witnessed by Prof. Fassbender and Fred Hoffman, who testified that at the time of the execution he was of sound and disposing mind. The evidence shows that the town assessor called on him the same day, and the testator made his personal property schedule,—*i. e.*, the schedule of his individual property and of property held by him as guardian,— giving a description and statement of the property from recollection. Some twelve witnesses who saw the testator before and after this will was signed, within a short time of that event, and who had known him for a number of years, testified to having conversations with him, and of observing his manner and condition; and their evidence tends to show that he was of sound and disposing mind. On the 29th day of May he took the sacrament, and the preacher who administered the sacrament testified that he would not take part in that religious ordinance with one not of sound mind; that he conversed with the testator for the purpose of learning of his condition of mind, and states that, in his opinion, he was of sound mind. Another witness testifies that ten days before the execution of the will the testator stated that he intended to will the appellants here just what he did give to them. Six or seven witnesses called by the contestant, among them the attending physician, testify that about the time of the execution of the will they had conversations with, and observed the condition of the testator, and that, in their opinion, he was not of sound mind. Others called by the contestant, who shortly prior and shortly after the execution of the will conversed with the testator, testify that at times he knew and at other times he did not know of what he was speaking. Other witnesses were called, both by proponents and contestant, who testified to certain acts and conversations with the testator both prior and subsequent to the execution of the will, but expressed no opinion as to the soundness or unsoundness of his mind. Without expressing any opinion as to the weight of evidence in this case, it is sufficient to say that the evidence is sharply conflicting. The testator, at the time of his death, on June 19, 1898, was about seventy-nine years of age. He had made three or more wills, one of date August 17, 1897, one of date April 23, 1898, and the one sought to be contested, May 24, 1898. The two former wills were offered in evidence, and were objected to by the contestant, and the objections were sustained, to which the proponents excepted. Numerous instructions were submitted to the jury on behalf of contestant and proponents, to which, respectively, exceptions were taken. The jury found that the instrument purporting to be the last will of Henry Nieman was not his last will and testament, and the court entered a decree accordingly. Error is assigned to the admission and execution of evidence, in giving and refusing instructions, in entering the decree and overruling the motion for a new trial, etc.

From what appears in this record, we are compelled to reverse this decree, and, inasmuch as the case must go before another jury, we refrain from expressing any opinion on the evidence, and as to which side has a preponderance. The declarations and statements of a testator, made, both or either, before or after the execution of his will, may be proved for the purpose of showing his mental condition at the time of the execution of the will. (*Craig v. Southard,* 148 Ill. 37; 35 N. E. 361; *Petefish* v. *Becker,* 176 Ill. 448; 52 N. E. 71; *Hill* v. *Bahrns,* 158 Ill. 314; 41 N. E. 912; *Taylor v. Pegram,* 151 Ill. 106; 37 N. E. 837.) And, where the testator has made previous wills, his declarations and statements made about the time of the execution of those former wills, upon the subject of or manner in which he had therein disposed of his property, have been held to be competent evidence. (*Taylor* v. *Pegram, supra.*)   Where a previous will has been made at a time when the soundness of mind of the testator is unquestioned, and the disposition of property as made by such previous will is approximately the same as made by a will sought to be contested on the ground of unsoundness of mind, such previous will so approximately disposing of property when such soundness of mind is unquestioned is the strongest character of evidence to show a condition of soundness of mind at the time the contested will was made.   The wills sought to be offered in evidence, objections to which were sustained by the court, approximately disposed of the property of the testator in the same way as the contested will, and the declarations of the testator made prior to the execution of the contested will show a purposed change of the will for the correction of minor errors and mistakes appearing in the will. Such former wills are a stronger character of evidence than the mere declarations and statements of a testator, made at about the time of their execution, as to their contents and as to their purpose, depending on the mere recollection of witnesses. The condition of mind of the testator at the time of making such former wills might be properly proved, and, when such evidence shows him to have been of sound mind at that time, and where there has been but slight change in the disposition of his property under the former wills and under the contested will, such former wills furnish exceedingly strong evidence of the mental soundness of the testator at the time of the execution of the contested will. Proof of the mental soundness of the testator at the time of the execution of such former wills was competent evidence, as were also the wills themselves. The court erred in excluding testimony as to the mental soundness of the testator at the time of the execution of such former wills, and in excluding the wills themselves.

.The first instruction given for the contestant was to the effect that the mere fact that a person is a subscribing witness to a will does not entitle his opinion as to the competency of the testator to execute the same to any more weight than the opinion of any other witness equally credible and intelligent, and with equal opportunities of judging; and " his testimony may not be entitled to as much weight as that of some other witness who had better opportunities of observing the deceased at or about the time the will was executed." There is nothing in the record showing that any other witness than the subscribing witnesses was present at the time of the execution of the will, nor is there evidence showing there were other witnesses who had better opportunities of observing the deceased at that time. The question of the weight of the testimony of the witnesses is a question to be determined by the jury, and their province should not be invaded by the court, as is done by this instruction, where it is stated that the testimony of the subscribing witnesses is not entitled to as much weight as that of some other witness who had better opportunities of observing the deceased. Whether there were any other witnesses who had better opportunities of observing the deceased, and the weight of their testimony, were both questions for the jury, and not for the court, and this instruction impliedly suggests to the jury that some other witness or witnesses had better opportunity of observing the deceased than the subscribing witnesses. It was error to give this instruction. (*Brown* v. *Riggin,* 94 Ill. 560.)

It was error to give the fourth instruction for contestant, which is as follows: " Unsoundness of mind embraces every species of mental incapacity from raging mania to that delicate and extreme feebleness of mind which approaches near and degenerates into unconsciousness." The mind of a testator may be affected in a degree, and may be in a partial sense unsound, but as a matter of law, that alone would not incapacitate him from making a valid will if he yet possesses the capacity to know and understand what disposition he will make of his property, and upon whom he will bestow his bounty. (*Freeman* v. *Easly*, 117 Ill. 317; 7 N. E. 656.) The instruction as given would take away from a testator who is feeble from sickness, but who possesses capacity to know and understand what disposition he desires to make of his property, the right to do so as a matter of law, if every species of mental incapacity from raging mania to delicate and extreme feebleness of mind which approaches near to and degenerates into unconsciousness constitutes want of testamentary capacity. The instruction ignores the extent of the unsoundness of mind, because, in effect, it states " every species of mental incapacity " is embraced in the term " unsoundness of mind." This states the rule of law broader than warranted by the authorities of this state. It was error to give this instruction.

The fifth instruction given for the contestant was as follows: " The law recognizes the difference between general and partial insanity, and if the jury believe, from the evidence, that the will offered was made under the influence of partial insanity, and is the product of it, it is as invalid as if made under the effects of insanity ever so general." There was no evidence in the record tending to show that there existed any delusion in the mind of the testator as to any particular matter or a mania on any particular subject. The evidence can only be considered as presenting the question as to whether the condition of mind was occasioned by senility or softening of the brain. The instruction suggests, what was not suggested by the evidence,—that the will offered was made under the influence of partial insanity,—and in this respect the instruction was misleading. As held in *Chambers* v. *People* (105 Ill. 409 [on p. 418]): " The fact that the court assumes to state the law applicable to particular states of case is of itself an assumption that those states of case exist, for it is not to be presumed a court would give the law to a jury, while trying a case, with reference to questions not believed to be before them." In the absence of evidence as to any delusion or mania, there was no basis on which the jury could find that the will was made under the influence of partial insanity, and it was error to give this instruction.

The seventh instruction given for the contestant is as follows: " That a person may have, upon some subjects, and even generally, mind and memory and sense to know and comprehend ordinary transactions, and yet upon the subject of those who would naturally be the objects of his care and bounty, and of a reasonable and proper disposition as to them of his estate, he may be of unsound mind." It is not the province of the jury to determine whether the will is a just, wise, and proper disposition of the testator's property. (*Carpenter* v. *Calvert*, 83 Ill. 62.) In *Freeman* v. *Easly*, this court said (page 321, 117 Ill., and page 658, 7 N. E.) : " In this case the testator suffered greatly from severe bodily disease, and no doubt his mind was affected to a degree it might be, at least in a partial sense, unsound; but the jury should not, for that reason alone, be told, as a matter of law, that would incapacitate him to make a valid will. That would be to state the rule of law on this subject broader than the authorities in this and other states will warrant. * * * It accords with common observation that in contests concerning wills, where the testator has made, or has seemingly made an unequal or inequitable disposition of his property among those occupying the same relation to him, by consanguinity or otherwise, there is a disposition in most minds to seek for a cause for holding the will invalid. The inclination in this direction that is found to exist in the minds of most, if not all, jurors, cannot always be controlled by instructing them there is no law requiring a testator, nor is he bound, to devise his property equitably, or in equal proportions, among his heirs. Of course, the law is, he may make such disposition of his property as he sees fit, and he may bestow his bounty where he wishes, either upon his heirs or others. While this is undoubtedly the law, the common mind is disinclined to recognize it, and jurors will too frequently seize upon any pretext for finding a verdict ·in accordance with what they regard as natural justice." This instruction is much more vicious than the one to which the foregoing lan-

guage was applied, and is, of itself, sufficient on which to base a
reversal of this case.   For the errors indicated, the judgment must
be reversed, and the cause remanded.

Reversed and remanded.

ELDRED *et al. vs.* MEEK.[1]

[Supreme Court of Illinois, October 25, 1899; 183 Ill. 26; 55 N. E.
Rep. 536.]

WILLS—CIRCUIT COURT—JURISDICTION—DISPOSITION OF PROP-
ERTY—GENERAL SCHEME—VOID CLAUSE—CONTINGENT RE-
MAINDERS—PERPETUITIES.

1. Where a will directs that a trustee shall transfer parts of testator's estate to beneficiaries on the happening of certain contingencies, and in
   the meantime keep the lands rented and the personalty invested, pay
   taxes, repair and rebuild buildings, etc., and apply the balance of the
   income to the maintenance and education of such beneficiaries, it
   creates an active trust, and not a naked power only, and the Circuit
   Court has jurisdiction to construe it.
2. Where certain provisions of a will constitute a general scheme for the
   disposition of testator's property to a class of beneficiaries, and one is
   void as a perpetuity, such provision invalidates the others connected
   with it, though, standing alone, they would be valid.
3. A will directed a trustee to transfer a portion of testator's estate to
   grandchildren on their arrival at twenty-five years of age, and declared that, if one or more of such grandchildren should die without
   issue before arriving at twenty-five, his or their interest should be paid
   to the survivors, and, if any should die under twenty-five leaving issue,
   the interest of such a one should go to his issue on arrival at twenty-
   five. *Held* that, since the grandchildren's interest was a contingent
   remainder, the clause providing for the disposition of the interest of
   one who should die before twenty-five leaving issue would postpone
   the vesting of such interest longer than a life or lives in being and
   twenty-one years, and hence such provision was void as a perpetuity.
   CARTWRIGHT, J., dissenting.

APPEAL from Circuit Court, Greene county; ROBERT B. SHIR-
LEY, Judge.

---

[1] Rehearing denied December 18, 1899.

Appeal by Ella Meek against John L. Eldred, executor, etc., and others. From a decree in favor of plaintiff, defendants appeal. Affirmed.

The controversy in this case grows out of a bill filed by Ella Meek to construe the will of her mother, Mary Brace, who died leaving the complainant as her only child, and Alva B., Charles, and Wilbur Meek, complainant's children and decedent's grandchildren, who at the time of decedent's death were respectively, twelve, seven, and four years of age. The will is as follows: " I, Mary Brace, of the city of Carrollton, county of Greene and state of Illinois, sixty-three years of age, sound in mind and of disposing memory, do hereby revoke such former wills as I may have made, and make, declare, and publish this instrument as my last will and testament: Item First. All of my estate, real and personal, of whatever nature or kind, I give, bequeath, and devise unto John L. Eldred, the executor of this my last will and testament, as herein below nominated and appointed, his successor, etc., forever; but in trust, nevertheless, for the full performance of this said instrument at my decease, concerning the foregoing estate; that is to say: (1) To pay my funeral expenses and others of my legal debts. (2) To give, transfer, and deliver to my daughter, Ella Meek, an equal one-fourth (¼) part of my personal estate. (3) To give, transfer, and deliver to each of my grandchildren, Alva B. Meek, Charles T. Meek, and Wilbur Meek, an equal one-fourth (¼) part of my personal estate upon their becoming, respectively, twenty-five (25) years of age. (4) To execute and deliver a good and sufficient deed, in fee simple, to said Alva B. Meek, as soon as he shall become twenty-five (25) years of age, conveying to him all that part of the east half of the northwest quarter of section twenty-two (22) lying north of the public road that leads west from the north side of the public square of the foregoing city of Carrollton, together with that part of the southeast quarter of the southwest quarter of section 15 as joins on the north and inclosed with said east half, except a strip of land some one hundred feet off of the west side of said part of said east half occupied as a road, all in township 10 north, range 12 west of the third principal meridian, situated in the county of Greene, aforesaid. (5) To execute and deliver a good and sufficient deed, in fee simple, to said Charles T. Meek, upon his becoming twenty-five (25) years of age, conveying to him all that part of the east half of the northwest quarter of section twenty-two (22) lying south of the foregoing public road, in township ten (10) north, range twelve (12) west of the third principal meridian, together with lot No. one (1) in Rainey's second addition in the town (now city) of Carrollton, all situated in said county of Greene.   (6) To execute and deliver a good and sufficient deed, in fee simple, to said Wilbur Meek, upon his becoming twenty-five (25) years of age, conveying to him the northwest quarter of the northwest quarter of section thirteen (13), township ten (10) north, range twelve (12) west of the third principal meridian, together with the undivided one-half (½) interest of twenty-seven (27) feet off of the east side of lot No. twenty-one (21) in the city of Carrollton, as described in the original plat of the town of Carrollton, all situated in the county of Greene and state of Illinois.   (7) In case of the death of said Ella Meek before I should die, my said executor shall give, transfer, and deliver, in equal parts, my said daughter's bequest aforesaid to my said grandchildren upon their, respectively, becoming twenty-five (25) years of age.   (8) In case of the death of any one of my said grandchildren without leaving a legitimate child or children, (then) my said executor shall give, transfer, etc., and deliver to the remaining live ones of said grandchildren, upon their becoming twenty-five (25) years of age, respectively, an equal one-half part each that said deceased grandchild would have received under the will in case he had not died, etc.   (9) In case any two of my said grandchildren shall die prior to or after my decease, and leaving no legitimate child or children, then, as soon as said live grandchild shall arrive at the age of twenty-five (25) years, (then) my said executor, etc., shall give, transfer, deed, etc., and deliver to said grandchild the whole of the estate or parts of which said deceased grandchildren would have been entitled under this will in case they had lived, etc.   (10) In case any of my said grandchildren shall die before arriving at twenty-five (25) years of age, leaving legitimate child or children, then my said executor shall, upon said child or children becoming twenty-five years of age, respectively, give, transfer, deed, etc., and deliver to each child, or equally divide among said children, their said father's share which he would have received under this will in case he had l.ved, etc. (11) In case of the death of all my said grandchildren, and leaving no child or children, then my executor is to fully see and provide so that my daughter, Ella Meek, shall have a full and complete life estate in the whole of my estate, and at her death my said executor shall give, transfer, and deliver to the Methodist Episcopal Church (or whatsoever its name is or may be) of said city of Carrollton the sum of one thousand dollars ($1,000), and the balance of my estate shall be equally divided, given, transferred, deeded, etc., and delivered, respectively, among the son and daughter of my brother, Henry Robley, and the children of my sister, Emily Twitchell, or their respective heirs, of the foregoing parties, etc., (of this eleventh division of my will). (12) That in deeding, etc., lands under this will, as aforesaid, my said executor shall adjust the difference out of my personal property in lands received by the grantee or grantees, and those lands to be received by the others, etc. (13) Of such of my estate as shall be held in trust, as aforesaid, my said executor shall keep the lands duly rented, and the personal property, as near as may be, loaned at the highest legal rate of interest, and good and sufficiently secured by mortgages upon lands located in said county of Greene, and out of the proceeds of my said estate pay all legal taxes and assessments, and well repair the buildings, fences, and other improvements of said property; also rebuild any of same, when for the best interest of said estate; and, further, keep fully insured the buildings of same. The balances of said proceeds to be equally applied in the necessary care, maintenance, and education of those entitled to the actual benefit of the respective trusts, under the terms and provisions of this will, etc. Such balances as may come to the said trustee he shall loan as aforesaid, and in time distribute under this instrument. Item Second. I do hereby nominate and appoint John L. Eldred, of the city of Carrollton, county of Greene and state of Illinois, to be the executor of this, my last will and testament. In witness whereof I have hereunto set my hand and seal, including the words, 'and to my niece Julia Fain' erased, and the words 'personal,' 'and delivered,' '100,' 'interest,' 'one,' 'life,' 'Henry,' 'and daughter,' 'located in,' 'legal,' 'equally,' added, this 15th day of December, in the year of our Lord one thousand eight hundred and ninety-six. Mary Brace. [Seal.] "

The appellant John L. Eldred, together with the three grandchildren and others, were made parties defendant. Answers were filed by said Eldred, and also by the other defendants, and by the minor defendants, who enter by Henry T. Rainey, their guardian *ad litem.*

The decree of the Circuit Court finds that by the general scheme of the will of the testatrix, Mary Brace, the said testatrix did not intend, by the third, fourth, fifth, sixth, eighth and ninth clauses, to vest the property therein devised and bequeathed in the several devisees with the enjoyment postponed, but that the right to the property so devised was contingent upon their arriving at the age of twenty-one; that there was no antecedent or other gift to such devisees; that the seventh clause of the will is inoperative, Ella Meek having survived the testatrix; that by the third, fourth, fifth, sixth, eighth, ninth, and tenth clauses of said will the property so devised might be taken out of commerce for a longer period than a life or lives in being and twenty-one years thereafter, and that the same are perpetuities, and are therefore void; that the eleventh, twelfth, and thirteenth clauses are dependent for their validity upon the third, fourth, fifth, sixth, eighth, ninth and tenth clauses of the will, as a part of the general scheme of the testatrix, and that she did not intend that they should be operative unless the last-named clause should be operative also, and finds that they are void; that as to all the property of the testatrix to be devised by said will she died intestate, except as to the property bequeathed in the first and second clauses thereof, but as to said property in the first and second clauses she died testate; that by the several provisions of the will the trust attempted to be created was an active trust, and that a court of equity will construe the will. It is therefore ordered that the third, fourth, sixth, seventh, eighth, ninth, tenth, eleventh, twelfth and thirteenth clauses of item 1 of the will of Mary Brace, deceased, and the probate thereof, be, and the same are hereby, set aside and vacated, and declared to be wholly null and void, and of no effect; and as to all the real estate owned by her, and as to all the personal property remaining after the payment of debts and costs of administration and the legacy mentioned in clause 2 of item 1, the said Mary Brace died intestate; and that Ella Meek, as the only heir at law of said Mary Brace, deceased, have and hold in fee all the real estate of which the said Mary Brace died seized; and that said complainant, as said heir, take and hold all of the personal estate of said Mary Brace, deceased, mentioned in the third clause of item 1 of said will, and take the property mentioned in said second clause of item 1 as legatee; that John L. Eldred surrender possession of all the real estate to the complainant within thirty days from this date, and that he turn over to her all such personal estate mentioned in clauses 2 and 3 of item 1 of said will, in due course of administration. From this decree the appellant John L. Eldred, and the infant defendants, by their guardian *ad litem*, prosecute an appeal to this court.

The errors assigned on the record are to the effect—First, that the Circuit Court erred in finding that the will violated the rule against perpetuities; second, that by the third, fourth, fifth, sixth, eighth, and ninth clauses the testatrix did not intend to devise property devised to the several devisees with the enjoyment postponed; third, in finding that the testatrix died intestate except as to the property decreed in the first and second clauses; fourth, in finding that the trust attempted to be created was an active trust, and not a naked trust or a passive trust; fifth, in holding that Ella Meek took and held as heir all the personal property mentioned in the third clause of item 1; sixth, in decreeing that John L. Eldred should surrender possession of the real estate held by him within thirty days from the date of the decree; and, seventh, in holding that the Circuit Court had power to construe the will

Henry T. Rainey, for appellants.

Frank A. Whiteside, for appellee.

PHILLIPS, J. (after stating the facts).—We shall consider the fourth and seventh assignments of error above first. Appellants contend that the Circuit Court had no power to grant the relief asked in the bill, even if the contentions in the bill were well founded, and insist that the controversy involves only legal titles, and hence only legal remedies can be invoked; that by the will the trustee is clothed with only naked power to execute deeds under certain contingencies, and that if he failed to execute them the law would unite the use and the trust; and that, as the bill seeks no other relief than that the will be construed, the bill should have been dismissed. The recent cases of *Harrison* v. *Owsley* (172 Ill. 629; 50 N. E. 227; and *Minkler* v. *Simons* (172 Ill. 323; 50 N. E.

176), are cited as conclusive of this contention. We do not concur in this view. Appellants seem to overlook the thirteenth clause of the will, which directs that the executor (trustee) shall keep the lands rented, and the personal property lent at the highest legal rate of interest, and well secured upon farm mortgages; that he shall pay legal taxes and assessments, repair buildings, etc., and rebuild, when for the best interest of the estate, and keep the buildings insured; and that he apply the balance of the proceeds equally in the " necessary care, maintenance, and education of those entitled to the actual benefit of the respective trusts under the terms and provisions of the will." The duties imposed upon the trustee are more than passive. They are active duties, vesting and holding the title in him pending the period mentioned, and constitute him more than a mere naked trustee, and hence would authorize a Court of Chancery to direct and control the mode and manner of execution. (*Steib* v. *Whitehead*, 111 Ill. 247; *Minkler* v. *Simons, supra; Knox* v. *Jones*, 47 N. Y. 389.)

On an examination of the will above, the first question for consideration is, what is the nature of the estate given to the grandchildren? Appellants contend that under the provisions of the will they take a vested interest, with the enjoyment only postponed. The tendency of courts is to consider limitations as vested. (Gray, Perp. 402, § 673.) " The event upon which a contingent remainder is limited may happen, and the contingent become a vested remainder, but not to be enjoyed in possession until some fixed time, or until the dropping out of an existing estate for life. There is a difference between ' vesting ' and ' the enjoyment of possession,' and it is sufficient if the contingent becomes a vested remainder within the time limited by the rule against perpetuities, although the enjoyment may be postponed beyond such time. (*Madison* v. *Larmon*, 170 Ill. 65; 48 N. E. 556.) In *Knight* v. *Pottgieser* (176 Ill. 368; 52 N. E. 934), we held that an immediate right of present enjoyment is not essential to a vested remainder; that it is sufficient if there is a present vested right to future enjoyment; that the vesting of a gift in remainder will not be postponed, but will vest at once, the right of enjoyment only being deferred; that the principle which applies to and controls the vesting of bequests of personal property is, in general, equally applicable to devises of real estate. If a remainder is vested,—that is, if it is ready to take

effect whenever and however the particular estate   ted as void.
is immaterial that the particular estate is determinable b   no error
gency which may fall beyond a life or lives in being. For ı   dered
if an estate is given to the unborn child of A. until he die
changes his name, and to B. and his heirs, B. has a vested remain
der; for he will take the estate whether the child dies or changes
his name, although the contingent determination of the estate before the child's death depends upon an event which may not take
place until beyond the limits prescribed by the rule against perpetuities.   And it makes no difference whether the provision for termination be expressed in the form of a condition or a limitation.
So, a remainder to a person ascertained and his heirs after a term
of years, however long the term or whatever be the conditions to
which the term is subject, is not too remote. (Gray, Perp. 148,
§ 209.)   " It is a general rule in regard to vesting of personal legacies that if there is no independent bequest, but only a direction to
pay at a future time or upon the happening of a certain event, the
vesting will be postponed until the event has occurred or the time
arrived. But the general rule is subject to an exception so well established and universally recognized as to practically constitute another general rule, which is: Though a gift arises wholly out of
directions to pay or distribute in *futuro*, yet if such payment or distribution is not deferred for reasons personal to the legatee, but
merely because the testator desired to appropriate the subject matter of the legacy to the use and benefit of another for and during
the life of such other, the vesting of the gift in remainder will not
be postponed, but will vest at once, the right of enjoyment only
being deferred. (*Scofield* v. *Olcott*, 120 Ill. 362; 11 N. E. 351;
Carper v. *Crowl*, 149 Ill. 465; 36 N. E. 1040.)   The principles
which apply to and control vesting of bequests of personal property ·
are in general equally applicable to devises of real estate." (*Knight*
v. *Pottgieser*, 176 Ill. 368; 52 N. E. 934.)   A gift to a person if or
when he shall attain a certain age will not vest until that age is attained. (*Scofield* v. *Olcott*, 120 Ill. 362; 11 N. E. 351; 2 Jarm.
Wills [Rand. & T. ed.], 458; Theob. Wills, 412; *In re Bennett's
Trust*, 3 Kay & J. 280; *In re Johnson's Estate*, 185 Pa. St. 179; 39
Atl. 879.)   " There is a distinction between a gift of a legacy to a
person to be paid to him at a future time and a direction to pay or
transfer the legacy to him at a future time. In the former case,

the legacy is considered as vesting in him immediately, but where the gift is merely by a direction to pay to him at a future time the legacy does not vest forthwith.   Until the time arrives he has no vested interest in the bequest."   (*Scofield v. Olcott, supra; Jones v. MacKilwain,* 1 Russ. 223; *Kingman v. Harmon,* 131 Ill. 171; 23 N. E. 430; *Loan Co. v. Bonner,* 75 Ill. 315.)   Thus, a direction to trustees to pay (transfer, deed, etc.) to certain devisees " when they should arrive at twenty-five years of age," or " upon their becoming twenty-five years of age," has been held to convey a contingent interest only.   (*Leake v. Robinson,* 2 Mer. 363.)   In *Coggin's Appeal* (124 Pa. St. 36; 16 Atl. 584,), the court says: " In a doubtful case it would be persuasive, but where the nature of the interest is clear it is entitled to but little weight.   There is abundant authority that, where the attainment of a certain age forms part of the original description of the devisee, the vesting is suspended until the attainment of that age, even though the limitation over is only to take effect in case of his death under that age without issue."

Had the testatrix closed her will at the end of the seventh clause, it might be held that a reasonable interpretation would be that the grandchildren take a vested interest; but the intention of a testator is to be arrived at, not by considering portions of the will, but by an examination of the entire will or the system of bequest, giving due consideration to each and every part thereof.   Courts must construe a will according to its own terms.   They cannot make a new will, or build up a scheme for the purpose of carrying out what might be thought was or would be in accordance with the wishes of the testator.   (*Tilden v. Green,* 130 N. Y. 29; 28 N. E. 880; *Lawrence v. Smith,* 163 Ill. 149; 45 N. E. 259.)   It is true that parts of a will which are valid will be sustained though other parts are rejected as invalid, if no violence is done to the parts sustained. (*Lawrence v. Smith, supra;* Gray, Perp. 166, 283, §§ 233, 423; *Howe v. Hodge,* 152 Ill. 252; 38 N. E. 1083; 1 Jarm. Wills [4th ed.], 297.)   But this rule should apply only when the first gift is absolute.   And bequests of a will valid in themselves will be rejected with the invalid ones where the retention of them would defeat the testator's wishes, as evidenced by the general scheme adopted, or where manifest injustice would result to the beneficiaries.)   (*Lawrence v. Smith, supra.*)

In the light of the above authorities, an examination of the subsequent provisions of this will indicates to us clearly that the testatrix did not intend that the grandchildren should take a vested interest. By the eighth and ninth clauses it is provided that, if one or both grandchildren should die without leaving legitimate child or children, his or their estate shall be paid to the survivor or survivors upon reaching the age of twenty-five years. By the tenth clause it is provided that if any grandchild shall die before arriving at twenty-five years of age, leaving legitimate child or children, then the executor shall, upon said child or children becoming twenty-five years of age, respectively, give, transfer, and deliver to said child, or equally divide among said children, their said father's share which he would have received under the will in case he had lived. If any effect is to be given to these clauses whatever, they mean that the right of either of the three grandchildren to enjoy the property devised to them, respectively, is contingent upon their reaching the age of twenty-five years, and that failing to do so, but leaving issue, their respective issue shall not enjoy the property until they shall arrive at the age of twenty-five years. These clauses, taken together, comprise one entire, clear and distinct scheme of devise, and it were to do violence to the will to reject any one of them in the construction of the others. The eleventh, twelfth, and thirteenth clauses of item 2 strengthen the views we have above expressed. In *Lawrence* v. *Smith* above cited, this court said: "We see no way by which a division of the trust created by this will can be made, and part held valid and the rest invalid, without doing violence to the intention of the testator. It is all one entire scheme, and, although the trust is an instrument to effect the beneficial purpose of the testator, it is made the most prominent feature of the will." See, also, *Post* v. *Rohrbach* (142 Ill. 600; 32 N. E. 687). In *Tilden* v. *Green* (130 N. Y. 29; 28 N. E. 880), the court, after reviewing a number of authorities, say: "The rule, as applied in all reported cases, recognizes this limitation: That when some of the trusts in a will are legal and some illegal, if they are so connected together as to constitute an entire scheme, so that the presumed wishes of the testator would be defeated if one portion was retained and other portions rejected, * * * then all the trusts must be construed together, and all must be held illegal and must fall." *In re Butterfield* (133 N. Y. 473; 31 N. E. 515), the court, while holding that a valid testamentary trust may be relieved from the peril of some unlawful incident or limitation by disregarding it, say: " This can only be done where the vicious provision is clearly separable from the valid demise or trust, and may be disregarded without maiming the general frame of the will or the testator's substantial and dominant purpose." *In re Johnson's Estate* (185 Pa. St. 179; 39 Atl. 879), a testator devised his real estate to his executors in trust for the period of seventy-five years, giving to the executors power in the management of the estate, and directing them to pay all charges against the land, and all legacies, out of the rents and profits. After all the charges and legacies were paid out of the rents, he directed his children to select a trustee, and directed that such trustee should collect the rents and profits of the land, and, after paying for repairs and taxes, should distribute the balance to his children and their legal descendants, until the expiration of the seventy-five years, at the expiration of which time the trustee was authorized to sell the land, and the proceeds were to be distributed " to and among all my children, share and share alike, that may be then living, and the legal descendants of any of my said children that may be then dead, the legal descendants of such deceased child or children to take, however, only such share and portion of the said proceeds as their deceased parent would have taken if then living." It was held (1) that the particular estate—the term of seventy-five years given to the trustee—did not violate the rule against perpetuities; (2) that the gift of the ulterior estate in remainder was a future contingent interest, repugnant to the rule against perpetuities, and therefore void for remoteness; (3) that as the testator's general scheme was to keep his estate entire for an unlawful period, and as the particular estate was created for this purpose only, the particular estate must fall with the ulterior estate;

that the testator died intestate as to his real estate, which accordingly passed at his death to his heirs at law. The above rule has been applied in *Fosdick* v. *Fosdick* (6 Allen, 48), and *In re Walkerly* (108 Cal. 627; 41 Pac. 772). The rule being that if provisions of a testamentary character are such that under them a violation of the rule against perpetuities may possibly happen the devise is void, it is clear that the tenth provision of item 1 offends this rule, as providing for a disposition of the estate upon contingencies which may not happen within the life or lives of persons in being or twenty-one years thereafter, and it follows that all of item 1 of the will after the first and second clauses must be treated as void. (Gray, Perp. 146, § 207; Jarm. Wills, 814.) We find no error in the decree of the Circuit Court of Greene county as rendered and the same is affirmed.

Decree affirmed.

CARTWRIGHT, C. J. (dissenting).—I do not concur in setting aside the entire will on account of the invalidity of the tenth clause, which is the only one violating the rule against perpetuities. The fourth, fifth, and sixth clauses devise separate specific tracts of real estate upon contingencies which are lawful. The testatrix separated the gifts, and the contingencies upon which they are limited, and the provisions of the will are independent of each other. The wishes of the testatrix should be sustained if possible, and in such a case there is no difficulty in upholding the valid provisions. (Gray, Perp. 239-245, §§ 341-355; *Howe* v. *Hodge*, 152 Ill. 252; 38 N. E. 1083; *Lawrence* v. *Smith*, 163 Ill. 149; 45 N. E. 259.)

HAMBEL *et al. vs.* HAMBEL *et al.*

[Supreme Court of Iowa, October 21, 1899; 109 Iowa, 459; 80 N. W. Rep. 528.]

WILLS—DEVISE IN FEE—PRECATORY WORDS.

A devise was of all testator's property, unconditionally, to his widow, with full power, as executrix, to sell and convey, followed by directions to divide the property remaining at her death among his children, and, in case she re-married, two-thirds of the property then remaining to be divided among his children. *Held*, that the widow took a fee under the first clause, and the subsequent directions must be treated as precatory.

On rehearing. For former opinion, see 75 N. W. 673.

Action for the interpretation of the will of James W. Hambel, deceased, and for other relief. A demurrer to the petition was overruled, and, the defendants refusing to plead further, a decree was rendered in favor of the plaintiffs. The defendants appeal.

Reversed.

ROBINSON, C. J.—The will in question was made on the 18th day of January, 1890, and the portions material to a determination of the questions presented are as follows: " First. I devise and bequeath to my wife, Lucelia A. Hambel, all my property, both real and personal, of every kind and description, that I may own at my decease. Second. I further direct that at the decease of my said wife all the property then remaining shall be equally divided between my children, except W. O. Hambel, youngest son, that may be living at the time of my decease. Third. I nominate and appoint my wife, Lucelia A. Hambel, my sole executrix, with full power to settle my estate and execute this, my will, with full power to sell and convey all real and personal property of which I may die possessed; and I hereby direct that she shall not be required to give bonds or report to court as executrix. Fourth. I further desire and direct that, in case my said wife shall marry after my decease, then upon said marriage two-thirds of my said property then remaining shall be equally divided between my said children, as directed in second part herein." In January, 1896, the testator, then a resident of Marshall county, died, and his widow became the executrix of his estate, pursuant to the terms of his will. He had been twice married, and had three children by each wife. The children by the first wife were the plaintiffs, Melvin D. and Marcus B. Hambel, and W. O. Hambel, mentioned in the will, who died after the will was made, but before the death of his father. The three children by the second marriage are daughters, all of whom, with the husbands of two who are married, are joined with the executrix and the widow as parties defendant. It is contended by the plaintiffs that the will gave to the widow but a life estate in the property of the decedent, and by the defendants that the will gave to her the unqualified and absolute title to the property. The District Court adjudged that the widow was entitled to a free and unlimited control, management, and use of the estate of the decedent during her lifetime, with full power to use, control, and dispose of it, and of the income therefrom " for her personal use, comfort, benefit, pleasure, support, and maintenance," provided she should remain unmarried; and that at her death each of the children of the deceased who survived him should take an undivided one-fifth of the property of the estate then remaining; and that in case of the marriage of the widow each of said children should receive an undivided one-fifth of an undivided two-thirds of so much of the estate of the decedent as should then remain. The decree further provided that none of the estate should be disposed of by the widow, except for her personal use, benefit, comfort, and pleasure, and for the benefit of the estate. On a former submission of this cause an opinion was filed, but, a petition for a rehearing having been presented and sustained, the cause is again submitted for our consideration. The decree is criticised by the appellants as being indefinite and uncertain, and calculated to lead to controversy and further litigation; but, in view of the conclusion we reach, the form of the decree is not important. For the purposes of this appeal we shall treat the ruling of the District Court on the demurrer and the decree as an adjudication to the effect that the will gave to the widow but a life estate in the property of the testator in case she did not remarry, or an undivided one-third of it if she did.

The appellees contend that the will in controversy falls within the rule which governed in *Iimas* v. *Neidt* (101 Iowa, 348; 70 N. W. 203); *Jordan* v. *Woodin* (93 Iowa, 453; 61 N. W. 948); *Stivers* v. *Gardner* (88 Iowa, 307; 55 N. W. 516), and similar cases, but we are of the opinion that a comparison of the provisions of the wills construed in those cases with the one in controversy will disclose clear and controlling differences. The primary rule of all the cases has been to ascertain and give effect to the intent of the testator. (*Westcott* v. *Binford,* 104 Iowa, 645; 74 N. W. 18.) The will involved in *Iimas* v. *Neidt* contained the following: " I give and bequeath to my youngest daughter, Katherine Kline," land, which was duly described. That provision, not modified, would have given to the devisee the fee title to the land to which it referred, but subsequent provisions gave to the widow the use of the land during the minority of the children, and made it liable for the payment of certain money. These and other provisions of the will showed that the testator did not intend to give to his daughter Katherine absolute power to dispose of the property, and that she did not take the fee. The will considered in *Jordan* v. *Woodin* (*supra*), was of a somewhat similar character. It contained provisions, which, taken alone, would have transferred the absolute and unqualified title to the property to which they referred, but the will as a whole showed that the testator did not intend that the provisions referred to should give an unconditional and absolute title.

The will considered in *Stivers* v. *Gardner* (88 Iowa, 307; 55 N. W. 516), gave to the husband of the testatrix certain land. The language, " I give and devise," if unmodified, was sufficient to convey title in fee with power of sale, but provisions which followed showed that the testatrix did not intend that the husband should have power to dispose of the land. On the contrary, other provisions showed that he was to have the use of the property only during his lifetime, and so long as he should remain unmarried, and that after his death it was to go to a son of the testatrix, subject to a lien to secure the payment of a bequest to a daughter of the testatrix. Other cases relied upon by the appellees are of a similar character.

The will in controversy belongs to a different class. The provision, " I devise and bequeath to my wife, Lucelia A. Hambel, all my property, both real and personal of every kind and description, that I may own at my decease," was sufficient, if unmodified, to give to the widow the absolute and unqualified title to all the estate of the decedent not required to pay debts, with unlimited power to sell and convey it. It is insisted that the estate thus conveyed is limited by the second and fourth paragraphs. It will be observed, however, that each of those paragraphs refers, not to any specific property or share, but to the property which should remain when the event referred to should take place, thus recognizing the right of the widow to dispose of property belonging to the estate. Therefore the case is governed by the rules which were stated in *Bills* v. *Bills* (80 Iowa, 269; 45 N. W. 748), as follows: " First. When an estate or interest in land is devised, or personalty is bequeathed, in clear and absolute language, without words of limitation, the devise or bequest cannot be defeated or limited by a subsequent doubtful provision inferentially raising a limitation upon the prior devise or bequest. Second. When there is an absolute or unlimited devise or bequest of property, a subsequent clause, expressing a wish, desire, or direction for its disposition after the death of the devisee or legatee, will not defeat the devise or bequest, nor limit the estate or interest in the property to the right to possess and use during the life of the devisee or legatee. The absolute devise or bequest stands, and the other clause is to be regarded as presenting precatory language. The will must be interpreted to invest in the devisee or legatee the fee simple title of the land and the absolute property in the subject of the bequest." Those rules have been applied frequently by this court, and, although some of its members have thought they were departed from in one or two cases, a careful examination of all the cases will show that the rules have been uniformly applied in cases which fell within their scope. In *Halliday* v. *Stickler* (78 Iowa, 388; 43 N. W. 228),—a case which involved a provision which gave to the husband of the testatrix all her real and personal property which was not otherwise disposed of, and provided that whatever of it should be left at his decease should be equally divided among his children and their heirs,—it was held that the husband took an absolute title to the property devised and bequeathed to him, and that the direction respecting that part which he should leave at his death was without effect. It was said that this court had repeatedly held that, " if the first devisee has power, by the terms of the will, to dispose of the property, he must be considered the absolute owner, and any limitation over is void for repugnance." The same rule was clearly announced in *Rona* v. *Meier* (47 Iowa, 607), and has been followed in numerous cases cited in those to which we have referred, and in the recent case of *Law* v. *Douglass* (Iowa; 78 N. W. 212). We would not be justified in reviewing all the cases to which our attention has been called, but have referred to the most important of those decided by this court upon which the parties rely. It is sufficient to say that those relied upon by the appellees are not governed by the rules which are applicable in this case. There can be no doubt that the will in question gave to Lucelia A. Hambel all the property of the estate, with unlimited power to dispose of all of it which was not required to pay claims against the estate, and the second and fourth paragraphs must be regarded as precatory merely. It follows, from what we have said, that the plaintiffs were not entitled to any relief, and that the demurrer to the petition should have been sustained. The decree of the District Court is therefore reversed.

GRANGER and GIVEN, JJ., dissenting.

NOTE.—PRECATORY TRUSTS.

(a) General rules of construction.
(b) As affected by discretion.
(c) Cutting down absolute gift.
(d) Use of word " wish."
(e) Illustrative cases holding no trust.
(f) Illustrative cases holding a trust.

(a) **General rules of construction**—" Each will must be construed according to its peculiar phraseology. The only general rule which it is safe to enunciate is that, where a gift is bestowed in *absolute* terms, and the use, employment or disposition of the property is left to the discretion of the legatee, so that he may consume or expend the whole for his own benefit, no trust is created by the language of the testator recommending, exhorting, desiring or entreating him to give a part to another. If the conferring of the pecuniary benefit is relegated to the discretion or good judgment of the legatee, or if he may do ' as he thinks *proper* ' or prudent, as he ' *may think just and right,*' as he ' *may think best,*' or ' *may see fit,*' or as ' *sense of justice and Christian duty shall dictate,*' and if the testator directs that the legatee is to be under no legal responsibility to any court or person for the use of the money, he takes an absolute title unfettered by any trust, although the strongest words of desire, suggestion or recommendation have been used. * * * The current of the decisions both in England and in the United States, indubitably shows that precatory trusts are not to be favored nor is their extension to be encouraged by the courts." (2 Underhill on Wills, §§ 794, 796.)

Theobald says, p. 398 (ed. 1895), " the inclination of the courts is not to construe doubtful words into a declaration of trust, and many of the earlier cases in which a trust has been held to be created would probably now be differently decided." (And see Re Diggles, 39 Ch. Div. 253.)

" I conceive the rule of construction to be that words accompanying a gift or bequest expressive of confidence or belief or desire or hope that a particular application will be made of such bequest will be deemed to import a trust upon these conditions: First, that they are so used as to exclude all option or discretion in the party who is to act as to his acting according to them or not; secondly, the subject must not be too vague or indefinite to be enforced." Lord Chancellor TRURO, in Briggs v. Penny (3 Mac. & G. 554), cited and followed by the U. S. Supreme Court in Colton v. Colton (127 U. S. 313; 8 Sup. Rep. 1164), with this comment added by latter court, " the most recent declarations of the English courts do not modify this statement of the law."

The intention of the testator is a controlling element and if a trust be sufficiently expressed, which does not require technical or set language, it is not rendered invalid as such because precatory words are used. When property is given absolutely without restriction, a trust is not to be lightly imposed upon new words of recommendation and confidence; but if the objects are definite and property clearly pointed out, and if the relations between the parties are such as to indicate a motive to provide, and if the precatory clause of wish, entreaty or recommendation warrant the infer- ence that it is peremptory, then it may be held to create a trust. (Colton v. Colton, *supra;* and see Noe v. Kern, 93 Mo. 367; 6 S. W. Rep. 239; Jones v. Jones, 124 Ill. 254; 15 N. E. Rep. 751.)

Cases turn upon one important and vital inquiry, and that is whether the alleged bequest is so definite as to amount and subject matter as to be capable of execution by the court, or whether it so depends upon the dis- cretion of the general devisee as to be incapable of execution without superseding that discretion. In the latter case there can neither be a trust or charge, while in the former there may be, and will be if such appears to have been the testamentary intention. (Phillips v. Phillips, 112 N. Y. 197, 204; 19 N. E. Rep. 411.)

Three things must be shown: (1) The words of the testator must be construed as mandatory; (2) The person intended to be the beneficiary must be certain; (3) The subject to which the obligation relates must be certain. (Webster v. Wathen, 97 Ky. 318, 323; 30 S. W. Rep. 663.)

Tendency of modern decisions is not to extend the rule or practice which from words of doubtful meaning, deduces or implies a trust. (Foose v. Whitmore, 82 N. Y. 406; Re Hutchinson, L. R. 8 Ch. Div. 540.)

" It would, however, be an entire mistake to suppose that the old doctrine of precatory trusts is abolished. Trusts, *i. e.,* equitable obligations to deal with property in a particular way, can be imposed by any language which is clear enough to show an intention to impose them." LINDLEY, L. J. (Re Williams [1897], 2 Ch. 12, 18.)

(b) **As affected by discretion.**—Where the direction is positive, point- ing out the fund for which the amount for support and benefit is to be taken out from time to time, the sum necessary being alone left to the dis- cretion of the wife, the fact that such discretion is imposed by precatory words offers no obstacle to a court of equity. There is a trust and if the discretion be not honestly and intelligently exercised a court of equity will compel it. (Collister v. Fassitt, 163 N. Y. 281; 57 N. E. Rep. 490.)

In order to effectuate the testator's intention, words of request, recom- mendation or hope may be treated as imperative; and shall be so treated when the objects of the precatory language are certain, and the subjects contemplated are also certain, unless a clear discretion or choice to act be given, or the prior disposition of the property import absolute or uncon- trollable beneficial ownership. (Harrison v. Harrison, 2 Gratt. 13.)

Precatory words will not convert a legatee of an absolute gift into a trustee, unless it affirmatively appear that they were intended to be im- perative. (Burt v. Herron, 66 Pa. St. 400.)

Nor will trust be implied when legatee has discretion to apply property to other purposes. (Lefroy v. Flood, 4 Ir. Ch. 1; Curtis v. Rippon, 5 Mad. 434.)

(c) **Cutting down absolute gift.**—Whether precatory words in a will shall be accorded such force as to deprive the donee of the absolute right of disposal and thereby qualify the beneficial interest in the gift, must be determined in connection with what may be gathered from the rest of the will as an intention reconcilable with the idea of a trust imposed upon the legal estate, when to impose such a trust would nullify previous expressions in the will and create a repugnancy between its different parts, the rules of construction forbid the attempt. (Clay v. Wood, 153 N. Y. 134; 47 N. E. Rep. 274.)

Under authority of this case the words "wish" and "request" were *held* insufficient to create a trust. (Street v. Gordon, 41 App. Div. 439; 58 N. Y. Supp. 860; and see note "Cutting Down Devise," 4 Prob. Rep. Ann. 121.)

(d) **Use of word "wish."**—"Wish" may be the equivalent of command or will. (Phillips v. Phillips, 112 N. Y. 197; 19 N. E. Rep. 411; Riker v. Leo. 115 N. Y. 98; 21 N. E. Rep. 719; Murphy v. Carlin, 113 Mo. 112; 20 S. W. Rep. 786; Decker v. High Street Church, 27 App. Div. 410; 50 N. Y. Supp. 260.)

But there must be testamentary intention. (Matter of Keleman, 126 N Y. 73, 80; 26 N. E. Rep. 968.)

(e) **Illustrative cases holding no trust.**—A "request" construed as a recommendation and to create no trust. (Durant v. Smith, 159 Mass. 230; 34 N. E. Rep. 190; and see Re Whelen's Estate, 175 Pa. St. 23; 34 Atl. Rep. 329; Mitchell v. Mitchell, 143 Ind. 113; 42 N. E. Rep. 465; Foose v. Whitmore, 82 N. Y. 405, 408.)

Where gift absolute mere expressions of desire, recommendation or confidence not sufficient. (Van Amee v. Jackson, 35 Vt. 173; Hoxsey v. Hoxsey, 37 N. J. Eq. 21; Re Whitcomb, 86 Cal. 265; 24 Pac. Rep. 1028; Rowland v. Rowland, 29 S. C. 54; 6 S. E. Rep. 902; Sale v. Thornberry, 86 Ky. 266; 5 S. W. Rep. 468; Fullenwider v. Watson, 113 Ind. 18; 14 N. E. Rep. 571; Bills v. Bills, 80 Iowa, 269; 45 N. W. Rep. 748; Clark v. Hill, 98 Tenn. 300; 39 S. W Rep. 339; Aldrich v. Aldrich, 172 Mass. 101; 51 N. E. Rep. 449; Hill v. Page, 36 S. W. Rep. 735 [Tenn.], affirmed orally by Supreme Court; Nunn v. O'Brien, 83 Md. 198; 34 Atl. Rep. 244; Hopkins v. Glunt, 111 Pa. St. 287; 2 Atl. Rep. 183; Gilbert v. Chapin, 19 Conn. 342; Boyle v. Boyle, 152 Pa. St. 108, 113; 25 Atl. Rep. 494; Orth v. Orth, 145 Ind. 184, 195; 42 N. E. Rep. 277; Matter of Gardner, 140 N.Y. 122, 128; 35 N. E. Rep. 439; Cheston v. Cheston. 89 Md. 465; 43 Atl. Rep. 768.)

Expression of the object or motive of an absolute gift do not create trust. (Randall v. Randall, 135 Ill. 398; 25 N. E. Rep. 780; Rose v. Porter, 141 Mass. 309; 5 N. E. Rep. 641; Cressler's Estate, 161 Pa. St. 427. 433; 29 Atl. Rep. 90, 95. Compare Riker v. Leo, 115 N. Y. 98; 21 N. E. Rep. 719.)

It depends upon intention as expressed in the will. (Riker v. Leo [second appeal], 133 N. Y. 519; 30 N. E. Rep. 598.)

No such trust will be implied when it is uncertain who or what testator meant by such general words as "family," "relations," or "heirs." (Harland v. Trigg, 1 B. C. C. 142; Wright v. Atkyns, 17 Ves. 255; Greene v. Greene, I. R. 3 Eq. 90, 629.)

Expression that legatee will dispose of property according to the testator's wishes, none being stated, there is no trust. (Reid v. Atkinson, I. R. 5 Eq. 162, 373; Creagh v. Murphy, I. R. 7 Eq. 182.)

Nor will trust arise if it is not clear what the property is; for instance, if requested to give "whatever she can transfer" (Flint v. Hughes, 6 Barb. 342), or the bulk (Palmer v. Simmonds, 2 Dr. 221), or when "no longer required by her" (Mussoorie Bank v. Raynor, 7 App. Cas. 321), or if the words apply to all the property of the legatee as well as to that given by the will. (Parnall v. Parnall, 9 Ch. Div. 96; and see Parnall v. Parnall, 11 Cl. & F. 513.)

Mere expression of a desire that the legatee will be kind to (Buggins v. Yates, 9 Mod. 122); remember (Bardsnell v. Bardsnell, 9 Sim. 319); consider (Sale v. Moore, 1 Sim. 534); deal justly by (Pope v. Pope, 10 Sim. 1); educate and provide for (Macnab v. Whitbread, 17 Beav. 209: Morrin v. Morrin, 19 L. R. Ir. 37); take care of (Re Moore, 55 L. J. Ch. 418); a certain class of persons will raise no trust.

In Lawrence v. Cooke (104 N. Y. 632; 11 N. E. Rep. 144), where it was *held* no trust created the words were "I enjoin her to make *such provision* for * * * in *such manner* at *such times* and in *such amounts* as she may deem *expedient.*"

And so where the husband was "desired to make certain gifts as he had been verbally named and requested," being at most discretionary. (Rose v. Hatch, 125 N. Y. 433; 26 N. E. Rep. 467.)

Expression of hope and trust "that legatee will not diminish the property," create no trust. (Howard v. Carusi, 109 U. S. 325, 725; 3 Sup. Rep. 575.)

Words of recommendation desire as to use of income for benefit of children. "as she may deem proper and just," *held* to create no trust. (Van Gorder v. Smith, 99 Ind. 404.)

"Also wish and desire" held dispositive to give a vested interest. (Brasher v. Marsh, 15 Ohio St. 103.)

"Any present that she may need and that my estate can afford" too uncertain to create a trust. (Webster v. Wathen, 97 Ky. 318; 30 S. W. Rep. 663.)

In Maught v. Getzendamer (65 Md. 527; 5 Atl. Rep. 471), the bequest was " * * * and desired him to use and appropriate same for such religious and charitable purposes and objects and in such sums and in such manner as will in his judgment best promote the cause of Christ," *held* void as too vague and indefinite.

In re Williams ([1897] 2 Ch. 12), the bequest was absolute to the wife "in the fullest trust and confidence that she will carry out my wishes in the following particulars," etc.; and it was *held* that the wife took free from any trust.

So *held*, however, on construction of the particular will as to the particulars which included the *wife's own property* as well as *testator's;* and the court upon the whole will determined that it was the intention to trust to *discretion* only. (Id. 22.)

(f) **Illustrative cases holding a trust.**—In Noe v. Kern (93 Mo. 367; 6 S. W. Rep. 239), the words were "in full faith that my husband will provide for" (two children) "whom we have undertaken to raise and educate."

The gift was of income for life to her husband "in the full confidence that he will as he has heretofore done, continue to give and afford my children such protection, comfort and support as they may stand in need of." *Held,* that the income was subject to a trust. (Warner v. Bates, 98 Mass. 274.)

Where devise was to the wife "as a home for herself and the children" and that all the income of estate to be paid to her as she should require for support and education of the children, *held,* to create a trust. (Cole v. Littlefield, 35 Me. 439; and see Harrison v. Harrison, 2 Gratt. 1.)

Bequest was to wife of use of real estate for life and personal estate absolutely, "having full confidence that she will leave the surplus to be divided at her decease justly among my children," *held,* to create a trust. (McConkey's Appeal, 13 Pa. St. 253. But this case appears to be overruled by Boyle v. Boyle, 152 id. 108, 113; 25 Atl. Rep. 494.)

In Colton v. Colton (127 U. S. 300; 8 Sup. Rep. 1164), the bequest was to the wife absolutely and clause added "I recommend to her the care and protection of my mother and sister, and request her to make such gift and provision for them as in her judgment will be best." *Held,* to create a trust.

In re Osburn's Estate.

Fowle *et al. vs.* Osburn.

[Supreme Court of Nevada, November 8, 1899; Nev.; 58 Pac. Rep. Rep. 521.]

ADMINISTRATORS — FINAL ACCOUNT — RECORD ON APPEAL — TRANSCRIPT—CLOSING OUT ESTATE—ATTORNEY'S FEES—COMPENSATION OF ADMINISTRATOR—BURIAL EXPENSES.

1. The filing of an account by an administrator makes the inventory on which it is predicated a part of the record, and it is properly included in the transcript on appeal, though not offered in evidence.

2. The petition for letters, order appointing administrator, his bond, and the order of distribution, not being necessary parts of the administra-

tor's report, are not a part of the record unless offered in evidence, and, if included in the transcript on appeal, will not be considered.

3. Where an administrator files a final account, showing he has administered the estate, he is estopped to deny his representative character, or liability to account.

4. Where an estate was disposed of by auction and private sale, and the administrator shows that it was impossible to keep an account of each article sold, or of the purchasers' names, as required by Hill's Ann. Laws, § 1173, the court, if convinced that the administrator made an honest effort to sell for the best interests of all concerned, will treat the account as the final settlement of the estate.

5. Under Hill's Ann. Laws, § 1144, authorizing the court to order an administrator to sell at private sale, it may order him to sell a stock of goods, and close it out in the regular course of business, and for this purpose to incur the necessary expense of lighting, clerk hire, etc.

6. But the court has no authority to authorize the administrator to replenish the stock by the purchase of other goods.

7. Where an estate is appraised at $2,400, an order approving an expense of $31 for carriages, hearse, and caring for the body of deceased will not be disturbed.

8. Under Hill's Ann. Laws, § 1178, authorizing the administrator to incur reasonable attorney's fees, an allowance of $100 is not an abuse of the court's discretion.

9. Under Hill's Ann. Laws, § 1180, authorizing the court to allow an extra amount for extraordinary services, an allowance of $200 for eight months' work in closing out a stock of goods under the court's order will not be disturbed.

10. Where decedent, at his death, had goods in his stock, the title to which was to remain in the vendor till paid for, and which the administrator, without knowledge of the terms, sold, the court had no authority to direct payment therefore in full; and, they not being secured, nor in the preferred class, and the estate being insolvent, the vendor must prorate with other creditors.

11. *Ex parte* orders of the court, directing the administrator to pay bills, found to be unauthorized, can afford no protection to the administrator in his final account, under Hill's Ann. Laws, § 1173, requiring notice of the final account and the day for the hearing of objections thereto.

12. Though the final report of an administrator did not state that he had disposed of and accounted for all the goods that came into his possession, yet where, as a witness, he testified that such was the fact, and was corroborated by the final report, which showed that he received within a small amount of the appraised value of the goods, he was not charged with the appraised value, but with the amount received only.

BEAN, J., dissenting.

APPEAL from Circuit Court, Douglas county; J. C. FULLERTON, Judge.

In the matter of the estate of A. G. Osburn, deceased. From a judgment of the Circuit Court affirming an order approving the final report of Grace Osburn, administratrix, Fowle & Daley, creditors of the estate, appeal.

Modified and affirmed

This is a controversy arising out of the settlement of an estate. A. G. Osburn having died intestate, the County Court of Douglas county appointed his widow, Grace Osburn, administratrix of his estate, which consisted of a stock of boots, shoes, and furnishing goods, valued by the appraisers at $2,558.04; but the inventory improperly included the " shoe bill of Isaac Farris, $180.80," as an asset of the estate, so that the value of all the goods rightfully appraised was $2,377.24. Said court having ordered that the merchandise be sold at private sale, and " as in regular course of business," the administratrix commenced selling the goods as ordered, keeping an account of the daily receipts, but not of the articles sold, nor the names of the purchasers, and, after conducting the business in this manner about eight months, sold the remaining goods at public auction, realizing for the entire stock the sum of $2,333.15. She thereupon filed her final account, showing that claims had been allowed against the estate amounting to $2,631.73, upon which she had paid by order of the court, the sum of $759.90; that the funeral charges and expenses of administration were $1,301.49, and that there remained on hand for disbursement the sum of $271.76. Messrs. Fowle & Daley, creditors of the estate, whose claim had been allowed, filed objections to many items of the account, and issue being joined thereon resulted in the approval of the account, except an item of $40, paid to May Aubery for clerk hire, which was disallowed. From this decision an appeal was taken to the Circuit Court, and, the order complained of being affirmed, said creditors appeal to this court.

William R. Willis and *A. M. Crawford*, for appellants.

J. W. Hamilton, for respondent.

MOORE, J. (after stating the facts).—As a preliminary matter, respondent's counsel move to strike from the transcript the petition for letters of administration, the order appointing the administratrix, her undertaking, the inventory, and the order of the County Court directing a *pro rata* distribution of the funds of the estate; contending that neither of these papers was offered in evidence. The inventory constituted the first item of charge against the administratrix, and was the foundation of her account (Hill's Ann. Laws Or. § 1176; 11 Am. & Eng. Enc. Law [2d ed.], 1200; 2 Woerner, Adm'n, § 510), the filing of which made the inventory upon which it was predicated a part of the record, and it was properly included in the transcript without having been offered in evidence. As to the order of distribution, the respondent is evidently mistaken, as the transcript shows it was in evidence. The other papers, however, not having been offered in evidence, and not being a necessary part of the final report, will not be considered; but this conclusion cannot change the result, for, the final account having been filed by Mrs. Osburn, showing that she had administered upon the estate, she is estopped from denying her representative character, or her liability to account accordingly. (*Damouth* v. *Klock,* 29 Mich. 289.)

When an estate is fully administered, the executor or administrator is required to file his final account, which must contain a detailed statement of the amount of money received and expended by him, from whom received, and to whom paid, and refer to the vouchers for such payments, and the amount of money and property, if any, remaining unexpended or unappropriated. (Hill's Ann. Laws Or. § 1173.) Inasmuch as it does not appear from the final account from whom the money was received, or what property if any, remains undisposed of, or that the estate is fully administered, counsel for appellants contend that the account should be set aside, and the administratrix charged with the appraised value of the estate. No memorandum having been kept of the goods sold, or the separate amounts received for the different articles disposed of, it is impossible to check up the sales with the inventory, so as to be able to say with any degree of certainty that any goods remain on hand, or whether they were sold for more or less than their appraised value. The administratrix, as a witness, testifies that it was impossible to keep an account of what each article sold for at the auction, and impracticable, and almost impossible, to keep an account of the names of the persons to whom the property was sold, whether at the private sale or the public auction. If it were possible to obtain a corrected report, it would be the duty of the court to set aside the account, and require the administratrix to file one conforming to the ·requirements of the statute; but, since a corrected report cannot be made, we have concluded that the ends of justice can better be subserved by treating the account as the final settlement of the estate, believing that the administratrix made an honest effort to dispose of the property for the best interests of all concerned.

It is insisted that the County Court had no authority to order the merchandise sold at private sale in the regular course of business, and that the amounts paid clerks, for rent of store, electric light, and other expenses, in attempting to sell the goods in the manner indicated, should be disallowed. When it appears to the court that it would be for the interest of the estate, it may order that the executor or administrator sell all the personal property of the estate, or any article thereof, at private sale. (Hill's Ann. Laws Or. § 1144.) By this grant of power the County Court is vested with discretion in the matter of ordering sales of personal property of an estate, and, while the sale was greatly prolonged by the administratrix, we do not think there has been such an abuse of her trust as to warrant us in charging her with the expenses connected therewith, and hence the compensation of the clerks, the rent of the store, and other expenses connected therewith are allowed.

Objection is made to certain items of funeral expenses, among which is the sum of $2 paid to the Eugene *Register* for funeral notices, $14 for carriages, and $15 for hearse and caring for the body of the deceased. The burial of the dead is a necessity which the preservation of the health of the living enjoins, and the reasonable expenses connected therewith constitute a preferred charge upon the decedent's estate. What is a reasonable charge in such cases must be determined by the apparent condition of the estate which is burdened therewith. (2 Woerner, Adm'n, § 359.) We think the estate left by the deceased warranted the administratrix in incurring the charges on account of the burial, and hence these items are approved.

Appellants also object to the allowance of $100 as an attorney fee. The statute provides that " an executor or administrator shall be allowed, in the settlement of his account, all necessary expenses incurred in the care, management, and settlement of the estate, including reasonable attorney fees in any necessary litigation or matter requiring legal advice or counsel." (Hill's Ann. Laws Or. § 1178.) The County Court, being thus authorized to make allowances on account of attorney fees, is vested with discretion in the matter, and, being cognizant of the services performed is generally able to make a proper allowance; and, the sum awarded being considered no abuse of such discretion, it will not be disturbed.

Objection is also made to the extra compensation of the administratrix for eight months' service in the store conducting sales, amounting to the sum of $200: The statute prescribes the compensation allowed by law to an executor or administrator on account of the ordinary services demanded of him in the performance of his trust, but in all cases such further compensation as is just and reasonable may be allowed by the court or judge thereof for any extraordinary or unusual service not ordinarily required of an executor or administrator. (Hill's Ann. Laws Or. § 1180.) In the case at bar the administratrix made an honest effort to sell the merchandise in her possession in the ordinary course of business, and was engaged eight months in carrying out the court's order, in view of which we think the sum allowed her is not unreasonable.

Objection is made to the items of $15.25 and $53.67, paid to Valentine & Goldsmith and Williams, Marvin & Co., respectively, for merchandise purchased by the administratrix to enable her to dispose of the stock belonging to the estate. Osburn having died intestate, the business in which he was engaged was thereby terminated, and the court was powerless to authorize the purchase of goods to replenish the stock, and its order, being void in this respect can afford no protection to the administratrix, who will be charged with having paid these sums on her own account.

Objection is also made to the claim of the Douglas County Bank, amounting to $136.05, on account of goods purchased by the decedent, which were in his store at the time of his death, the title to which was to remain in the bank until the goods were paid for. The administratrix, not knowing the terms of the delivery, sold these goods, whereupon the court ordered her to pay the bill in full. This debt was not secured, nor included in the preferred class, and the court was without authority to direct the payment of more than the *pro rata* share thereof. (2 Woerner, Adm'n, § 520.) The administratrix was authorized, by the order of the County Court, to pay only 25 per cent. of the claims allowed by her, and, having paid said bank in full, she overpaid it $102.04, which sum will be · charged to her.

The *ex parte* orders of the County Court directing the administratrix to pay these bills afford her no protection when brought in question, and found to be unauthorized, for it is the duty of the court or judge, upon the filing of the final account, to make an order directing that notice thereof be given, and to appoint a day for the hearing of objections to such final account and the settlement thereof. (Hill's Ann. Laws Or. § 1173.) These statutory requirements show that all persons interested in the settlement of an estate are to have a day in court before their rights can be adjudicated.

The final report does not state that the administratrix had disposed of and accounted for all the merchandise that came into her possession, but as a witness she testifies that such was the fact, and her testimony is corroborated by her final report, which shows that she received on account of sales within $44.09 of the appraised value of the goods, and this being so, she will not be charged with the value as given by the appraisers, but with the amount received only. The final account shows that the administratrix had in her hands for distribution, the sum of $271.76, which is increased by the County Court disallowing the claim of $40, and will be further augmented by the disallowed payments to Valentine & Goldsmith of $15.25, Williams, Marvin & Co. $53.67, and the Douglas County Bank, $102.04, making a total of $482.72, which latter sum will be distributed *pro rata* among the creditors of the estate whose claims have been allowed, paying each 18.3 per cent., including Mrs. Osburn's as the equitable assignee of the claim of the Douglas County Bank. The decree of the Circuit Court must therefore be modified as hereinbefore indicated, but in all other respects affirmed.

BEAN, J. (dissenting).—As at present advised, I am unable to concur in the view that the County Court has authority to permit an administrator to sell and dispose of a stock of merchandise belonging to the estate in the usual course of business, and therefore withhold my judgment upon that point.

APPEAL OF TURNER.

[Supreme Court of Errors of Connecticut, October 5, 1899; 72 Conn. 305; 44 Atl. Rep. 310.]

WITNESSES—CROSS-EXAMINATION—TRIAL—STRIKING OUT EVIDENCE—WILLS—TESTAMENTARY CAPACITY—OPINIONS—CONFIDENTIAL RELATION—ATTORNEY AND CLIENT—APPEAL AND ERROR.

1. A witness testifying to certain facts on direct examination cannot be asked on cross-examination if at a former trial he was not present when another testified to different facts, and he did not correct such testimony.

2. When witnesses' answers, material to the case, are stricken out because they are not responsive to questions, there is no error when such witnesses, under proper questions, are afterwards allowed to testify to the same matters so stricken out.

3. Where the record does not clearly state the grounds upon which questions and answers were excluded, nor upon which they were objected to, and the Appellate Court cannot say with certainty that the rulings were erroneous, the trial court will be affirmed.

4. In a will contest the opinion of a nonexpert witness as to the mental condition of the testator is not receivable until the witness is shown to have had sufficient knowledge and opportunities of personal observation to form a correct conclusion as to the testator's mental condition, or until he has testified to sufficient particular facts upon which to base such opinion.

5. In a will contest a qualified witness may be asked whether, in his opinion, the testator possessed sufficient understanding to transact ordinary business matters incident to the management of his household affairs and property.

6. One may make a valid will, if he understands the nature and elements of such a transaction, although he is mentally incapable of transacting business generally.

7. Where testamentary capacity was involved, a lawyer testified that he knew the testatrix for many years, and had frequent opportunities of observing her, and frequent conversations with her. When asked to detail the conversations, objection was made on the ground that they were confidential communications, but no evidence was offered to show that they were of a professional nature. The objection being overruled, witness detailed conversations concerning the settlement of an estate, and stated that she inquired about her interests therein, seeking information as to facts, and that subsequently she strenuously objected to a charge for fees against said estate, and that he appeared

for her and contested the same, but it did not appear that he was being consulted professionally in the prior conversation. *Held,* that admitting said testimony was not error.

8. The rule forbidding an attorney disclosing as a witness matters communicated in professional confidence should be strictly construed, as tending to prevent a full disclosure of the truth in court.

9. It is not error to refuse an instruction that the verdict must be for the contestant of a will if the evidence shows that the testator lacked testamentary capacity, when in the court's charge it properly defines such capacity, states that the burden of proving it is on the proponent, and that, if there is any uncertainty as to the side upon which the evidence preponderates, the verdict must be against the party having the burden of proof.

10. Where the ground of a will contest is undue influence, it is not error to refuse an instruction which assumes a confidential relation between the executor and the testator, when such relation is not admitted, and the court leaves the question of its existence to the jury, with the charge that, if the relation is proven, it is incumbent upon the executor to prove that he acted fairly, and took no advantage of it to procure the making of the will in his favor.

11. To establish undue influence, the testator's free agency and independence must be overcome, and some domination or control exercised over his mind must have constrained him to do, contrary to his will, what he was unable to refuse, or too weak to resist.

12. Neither mere kindness of treatment by a legatee towards a testator, nor moderate and reasonable solicitation, amount to undue influence, when yielded to intelligently, from a sense of duty, and without restraint.

13. Stating reasons of appeal to be that the court erred in his charge to the jury as to burden of proof, and as to amount of preponderance of evidence necessary to establish a will, is not in compliance with Prac. Book, 258, rule 14, § 1, requiring the precise matters of error to be set forth.

14. In a will contest there is no error in a charge when it refers to evidence of the testator's weakened mind in connection with other evidence indicating his mental condition, and all evidence bearing on testamentary capacity is unqualifiedly submitted to the jury, although the submission is made in such manner as to intimate the judge's opinion on the weight of the evidence, if such intimation is not a practical withdrawal of the evidence from the jury.

APPEAL from Superior Court, New Haven county; MILTON A. SHUMWAY, Judge.

Proceeding by Jane Turner and others contesting the probate of the last will and testament of Caroline Warner, deceased. The will was admitted to probate in the Probate Court, from which an appeal was taken to the Superior Court of New Haven county, where a like judgment was rendered, and said Jane Turner appeals.

Affirmed.

There was evidence to show: That the testatrix, Caroline Warner, died in 1898, at the age of seventy-nine years, leaving an estate of about $14,500. She had never married, and her nearest surviving relatives were cousins. Jane Turner, a cousin of the testatrix, eighty-five years old, and who received by the will a legacy of $500, appealed from the probate of the will upon the ground of the want of testamentary capacity and of undue influence. That the testatrix had executed three wills before the one in question, which were drawn by Judge Bishop, who was a witness at the trial. That the executor of the present will was a second cousin of the testatrix, and occasionally attended to some of the business of the testatrix at her request, and according to her directions, and that, when she decided to make some changes in her then last will, he accompanied the testatrix, at her request, to the office of Judge Bishop, and, not finding him, went with her to the office of Mr. Webb, and introduced the testatrix to him, and that Mr. Webb prepared for her a will, of which he (Webb) was made the executor. That within a few weeks the testatrix, having decided to make some changes, consulted with one Mix and his sister, Mrs. Potter, concerning them, and that at the request of the testatrix said Mix called upon Mr. Webb, and furnished him with a memorandum of the changes she desired, and arranged with him to meet the testatrix at the residence of Mr. Mix's daughter, to complete the preparation and execution of a new will, and that in accordance with such arrangement Mr. Webb soon after met the testatrix at said place, having before prepared only such parts of the new will as were to be like the former one, and, after having consulted the testatrix about the changes she desired, completed the present will, which was executed in August, 1891. That, at the request of the testatrix, Mr. Mix, with his team, drove the testatrix and the said Mrs. Potter to the said house, but that he was not present during the consultations between the testatrix and Mr. Webb, nor when the will was prepared. That at the suggestion of Mr. Webb, Mr. Mix was made executor of this will. Said

Mix, at the trial in the Superior Court, having testified that he
accompanied the testatrix to the office of Mr. Webb, and arranged
for the preparation of the present will, including the taking to Mr.
Webb of the memorandum aforesaid, and upon cross-examination
having testified that he was present at the hearing upon the probate
of the will, at which hearing Mr. Webb testified as a witness, was
asked if it was not true that he heard Mr. Webb testify that he
went to the residence of Mr. Mix's daughter, and did all his writing there from directions given him by the testatrix, and that he
(Mr. Mix) made no corrections.   Upon objection the question was
excluded, and the appellant excepted.   Charles H. Webster, a witness for the appellant, having testified that for six months prior
to April, 1887, he had lived in the same house with the testatrix,
and saw her frequently every day, was asked if she had sufficient
mind to intelligently dispose of her property.   Upon objection of
the appellee this question was excluded, and the appellant excepted
to the ruling of the court.   The further examination of this witness by the appellant was as follows: " Q. Do you think she was
of sound and disposing mind at that time?   A. Well, her mind
was weak."   Upon motion of the appellee this answer was stricken
out as not responsive.   The appellant excepted.   " Q. You may
state what her condition was during the time you lived there.   A.
Well, this time, as I say, her mind was weak.   *   *   *"   This
witness further said upon direct and cross-examination: " I cannot say about her mind.   *   *   *   Her mind was weak at the
time we went there."   When asked if he thought her mind was
unsound, the witness said, in substance, that he could not say as
to the soundness of her mind, further than that her mind was
weak.   In the deposition of Dorcas Webster, wife of the last witness, the following question was asked by the appellant: " Do
you think, the time you lived in the house there with her, she was
capable of transacting business?"   The witness answered: " I
don't think she was capable of making a will.   *   *   *"   The
question having been repeated, she answered: " I don't know what
you mean by 'transacting business.'"   These two questions and
answers were excluded upon objection, and the appellant excepted.
The following answers of this deponent were read: " She was
capable of paying her grocery bill, but, as for doing legal business
I don't think she was.   I don't think she could go on and do busi-

ness, make a will, or anything like that." "I don't know as I think she was of unsound mind, anyway." Margaret Newton, a witness for the appellant, who had testified that she was acquainted with the testatrix, and had visited her and conversed with her frequently, was asked upon direct examination whether she thought that the testatrix, during the last ten years of her life, was able to transact business. Upon objection this question was excluded upon the ground that the opinion of the witness as to the ability of the testatrix to transact business generally was immaterial, but the court ruled that, after the witness had stated her knowledge of the testatrix and her opportunities of observing her, she might state whether or not, in her opinion, she was of sound and disposing mind. The same witness upon direct examination subsequently testified: "Her mind was not as it was once, and she was not able to do as she was once,—transact business, or much of anything else;" and upon cross-examination: "I shouldn't call her mind strong enough to transact business alone, from what I knew of her." Judge Bishop, a witness for the appellee, having testified to his acquaintance for many years with the testatrix, his means of observation, and frequent conversations with her, was asked: "Do you recollect any of the conversations had with her at that time,—any of the subjects you talked about?" The witness answered: "She would talk about what her share was under the law. * * * In substance, it was, she wanted to know how much there was in the estate, how much she was likely to get out of it, and the details of the settlements of the estates, and we would talk those matters over." "My recollection of it is that I went to the Probate Court, saw Mr. Burgess, afterwards. * * * Told her the amount there was in the estate as appeared by inventory, and told her what Mr. Burgess had said about it; also, what the judge of probate had said, * * * and what her distributive share would be after the final settlement of the estate. That was the substance of our talk." "Later on the account of Sherman Warner was filed, and I submitted that report to her; and on that, I remember, she objected very strenuously to Mr. Burgess's fees, and gave me instructions to ask that those fees be reduced, and in pursuance of that instruction I did go before the Probate Court upon that question." The appellant objected to this testimony upon the ground that the witness was the attorney of the testatrix, and was testifying to confidential communications made to him by his client. The court admitted the evidence, and the appellant excepted.

The appellant requested the court to charge the jury as follows: " (1) That if the jury shall find that it is more probable than not that decedent at the time of the execution of the will did not sufficiently appreciate and comprehend her relations to the appellant and the beneficiaries under said will, the character and consequences of the provisions of said will, and the nature, extent, and effect of the business which she was transacting, their verdict should be for the appellant. (2) That it is admitted that Norris W. Mix was in the habit of transacting the decedent's business, and stood in confidential relations with her, and that said Mix and his sister, Mrs. Potter, brought and accompanied the decedent to the house of the daughter of Mr. Mix, where the will was executed; that Mr. Mix procured the services of the attorney who drafted the will, and the witnesses to the will; that under these circumstances the burden of proof is upon the appellees, who are benefited by the provisions in favor of Mr. Mix and Mrs. Potter, to show that decedent was not unduly influenced by them in the making of these provisions." " Under these circumstances, the burden of proof is upon Mr. Mix to show that decedent was not unduly influenced by him, in so far as the will operates in his favor." The court did not charge as requested in the second request.

 The court charged the jury, in part, upon the subject of the burden of proof, that, before the will should be approved as a valid will, it should appear to the jury that the statutory formalities of its execution had been complied with, and that the testatrix was at the time of sound and disposing mind and memory; that the burden of proving the testamentary capacity of the testatrix rested upon the proponents of the will; that the law did not require that this fact should be proven with absolute certainty; that at the end there might perhaps exist in the minds of the jurors nothing further than a strong probability that the fact was so; that the rule for determining whether the fact of testamentary capacity had been proven was that the proponents of the will must prove the fact by a fair preponderance of evidence (that is, that " more or more satisfactory evidence must be produced in favor of the existence of that fact than is produced against it ") ; that if there should be an uncertainty in the minds of the jury, so that they could not say upon which side of that issue the evidence preponderated, then " the issue should be found against the party upon whom rested the burden of proving it," but that, " if the evidence preponderated one way or the other, the issue should be found as the evidence preponderated ; " that, although the burden of proof rested upon the proponents of the will on the issue of the capacity of the testatrix to make a will, yet the jury should not find that issue in favor of the contestants " unless the evidence of the contestants overcame that given by the proponents in rebuttal, and was evenly balanced in the minds of the jury with all the evidence of the proponent, including the evidence of the subscribing witness, by which the proponents had made out a *prima facie* case in the first instance ; " that the burden of proving that undue influence had been exercised upon the mind of the testatrix was upon the contestants ; that the existence of undue influence was not often susceptible of direct proof, but was generally proved by " the facts and circumstances surrounding the testator, preceding, pending, and following the making of the will," and that as bearing upon that question the jury might consider " the testatrix's family relations, her condition of health, her relations to the persons claimed to have influenced her, her dependence upon and subjection to the control of such persons, and the opportunity of the latter to wield such influence," and the provisions of the will ; that while from such facts, and others of a like nature, undue influence might be inferred without direct proof, " yet such inference was not to be drawn unfairly or unreasonably ; " that " the facts and circumstances ought to be of such a nature as to lead justly and reasonably to the inference that such undue influence existed, and was exercised upon the testatrix, so that her mind and will were affected by it ; and that she was led thereby to make a different will from what she would have made if it had not existed." The court said: " But this burden upon the question of undue influence may be shifted or discharged whenever the business relation existing between the testatrix and the persons specially benefited by the will, or having drawn the will, or having been shown to have any part in procuring it to be drawn, is such as denotes special confidence, and gives to the party so benefited a controlling influence with the testatrix." " If the evidence discloses to you that his (Norris B.

Mix's) relations to the testatrix were of especial confidence and trust, and that he has been benefited by his act, then * * * it is incumbent upon the proponents of the will to show that he acted fairly, and that he took no advantage of his position to induce or to procure the making of the will, or any part of it, in his favor." In defining " undue influence " the court said in its charge: " Her free agency and independence must be overcome, and she must, by some domination or control exercised over her mind, have been constrained to do what was against her will, and what she was unable to refuse and too weak to resist. Mere kindness of treatment of a testatrix by a legatee would not; nor would moderate—any reasonable—solicitation, entreaty, or persuasion, though yielded to, if done intelligently, without restraint and from a sense of duty, vitiate a will in other respects valid." Upon the question of testamentary capacity the court charged the jury, in part, that it was sufficient if the testatrix had such a mind and memory as would enable her to recollect and understand " the nature and condition of her property; the persons who were or should be the natural objects of her bounty, and her relations to them; the manner in which she wished to distribute it among or withhold it from them; and the scope and bearing of the provisions of the will she was making." The court further used the following language: " Mere physical weakness or disease or eccentricities, blunted perceptions, weakening judgment, failing memory or mind, are not necessarily inconsistent with testamentary capacity. One's memory may be failing, and yet his mind not be unsound. One's mental powers may be weakening, and still sufficient remain to make a will." " Now, the evidence which has been offered before you as to the mental condition of the testatrix at the time the will was made, and both before and after, has been given to aid you in placing before your minds a mental picture of the testatrix at the time the will was made; and if the evidence shows that the testatrix was physically and mentally weak, that her mind or memory was impaired, that it was less than it may have been at some former period of her life, that she was odd, and that she was peculiar or eccentric, or that she may have said that she feared that she might go to the poorhouse, or that she may have had an incorrect belief as to the wrongs that may have been inflicted upon her, it does not necessarily follow that she had not testamentary capacity. You should not, and you doubtless will not, confound oddities and eccentricities and peculiarities with incapacity. Oddities, peculiarities, and eccentricities are one thing. Incapacity is the question which you are to pass upon, and say whether the testatrix was incapable, in the meaning of the law, of making a will. Nor should you mistake a mind that is only weakened for one that is lost."

The rulings of the court in excluding the questions aforesaid asked the witnesses Mix, Mr. and Mrs. Webster, and Margaret Newton, and in excluding and striking out their answers as aforesaid, in admitting the testimony of Judge Bishop, and in refusing to charge as above requested, were assigned as reasons of appeal. The thirteenth and fourteenth reasons of appeal were in the following form: " (13) The court erred in his charge to the jury as to the burden of proof. (14) The court erred in his charge to the jury as to the amount of preponderance of evidence necessary to establish a will." Other reasons of appeal alleged error as to parts of the charge above set forth, regarding the preponderance of the evidence, the definition of " undue influence," and the failure of the court to instruct the jury that disease, eccentricities, and other failings or peculiarities named by the court as not inconsistent with testamentary capacity in the testatrix, were facts which should be considered by the jury as evidence bearing upon the question whether the testatrix possessed testamentary capacity.

Henry G. Newton and *E. P. Arvine,* for appellant

William H. Williams and *Isaac Wolfe,* for appellee.

HALL, J. (after stating the facts).—The question asked the witness Mix on cross-examination, if he had not heard Mr. Webb testify to certain facts in the Court of Probate without correcting him, was properly excluded. It does not appear that Mr. Mix was present when the last will was prepared, nor that he had testified to what occurred at that time. The facts implied in the question did not, therefore, contradict his testimony. Nor would Mr. Mix have been called upon to correct a witness in the Court of Probate who he may have thought was testifying incorrectly. Such inquiries should not be permitted when their evident purpose is to intimate that some other witness has testified differently from the one under examination.

The rulings of the court excluding certain questions asked the witnesses Mr. and Mrs. Webster and Mrs. Newton, and excluding or striking out their answers, do not furnish sufficient grounds for granting a new trial—first, because, if such rulings were erroneous, the errors seem to have been corrected by afterwards permitting these witnesses to fully answer the questions which had been excluded; and, second, because the record does not so clearly state either the grounds upon which the questions and answers were excluded, nor upon which they were objected to, that we can say with certainty that the rulings were erroneous. The inquiries excluded called for answers from non-expert witnesses, in the nature of opinion evidence, concerning the mental condition of the testatrix. The mere opinions of such witnesses are never received. They are admissible only after either a sufficient statement of the particular facts upon which they are based, or after the witness has been shown to have sufficient means and opportunities of personal observation to enable him to form a reasonably correct conclusion. They are received rather as statements of impressions or conclusions in the nature of facts of which the witness has knowledge, than as opinions. Their reception is rendered necessary because of the difficulty of so detailing and so reproducing the numerous particular facts upon which they are founded as to produce upon the triors the impression received by the witness, or to enable them to draw a fair inference from such facts. The value of such a statement, when given by a candid and impartial witness, depends largely upon his intelligence and upon his opportunities and habits of observation. (1 Greenl. Ev. § 440, and note; *Town of Cavendish* v. *Town of Troy*, 41 Vt. 99; *Insurance Co.* v. *Lathrop*, 111 U. S. 612-619; 4 Sup. Ct. 533; *Sydleman* v. *Beckwith*, 43 Conn. 9; *Ryan* v. *Town of Bristol*, 63 id. 26; 27 Atl. 309; *Kimberly's Appeal*, 68 Conn. 428; 36 Atl. 847.)

The record before us does not assume to give the examination of these witnesses in full. If the trial court excluded these questions because the witnesses had not been shown to have had sufficient opportunities of observation to qualify them to express an opinion or conclusion upon the subject of the inquiries, we cannot

from the testimony as set forth in the finding, hold that such decision was erroneous. When, in trials involving the question of testamentary capacity, it is desired that a witness who has testified to
sufficient facts should also give his opinion as to the mental condition of the testator, a common and proper form of inquiry is, "Was
or not the testator, in your opinion, a person of sound mind?"
For the purpose of showing the extent of mental impairment, it is
not unusual or improper to ask a duly qualified witness whether,
in his opinion, the testator possessed sufficient understanding to be
able to transact the ordinary business matters incident to the management of his household affairs and property. (*Keithley* v. *Staf-
ford*, 126 Ill. 507-520; 18 N. E. 740.) The mental power required
to attend to such ordinary affairs may be regarded as so much a
matter of common knowledge and experience as to be a fair standard of comparison, readily understood by both witness and jury,
by which to illustrate the degree of intelligence of one whose
mental condition is the subject of investigation. It has been held
to be proper to permit a witness to compare the mental power of
the testator to that of "an average child of seven or eight years."
(*Richmond's Appeal*, 59 Conn. 226-242; 22 Atl. 82.) A witness
may, of course, always testify to the fact, when such fact is within
his personal knowledge, that the testator's mental state was such
that he was or was not able to transact business, or to do any other
particular act which would indicate the condition of his mind. It
is not error to refuse to allow a non-expert witness to state his
opinion whether a testator was capable of making a will. (*Crowell*
v. *Kirk*, 14 N. C. 355-358; *Farrell's Adm'r* v. *Brennan's Adm'x*,
32 Mo. 328; *White* v. *Bailey*, 10 Mich. 155-159; *Fairchild* v. *Bas-
comb*, 35 Vt. 398-414; *Schneider* v. *Manning*, 121 Ill. 376-386; 12
N. E. 267.) What constitutes testamentary capacity is a question
of law, which witnesses and jurors are not ordinarily competent to
answer correctly. Their views upon that question would probably
differ from each other, as well as from the rule laid down by our
law upon that subject. Various tests of the capacity essential to
enable one to make a valid will have been adopted even by the
courts. It was formerly held that imbecility of mind not amounting to idiocy or lunacy would not incapacitate one from making a
will. (*Blanchard* v. *Nestle*, 3 Denio, 37; *Stewart* v. *Lispenard*,
26 Wend. 255.) Some courts have held the mental ability to exe-

cute a valid deed or contract to be the proper measure of testamentary capacity. (*Stewart* v. *Elliott*, 2 Mackey, 307; *Coleman* v. *Robertson's Ex'rs*, 17 Ala. 84.) Others, that the possession of sufficient mind and memory for the transaction of ordinary business is the true test of capacity to make a valid will. (*Barnes* v. *Barnes*, 66 Me. 286.) In this state, one may make a valid will, though mentally incapable of transacting business generally. The test which we apply is the ability of the testator at the time of the execution of the will to understand the nature and elements of the particular transaction of making a will, in which he is engaged; and it is a part of the duty of the court, in charging the jury, to instruct them as to the elements of the act of intelligently disposing of one's property by will, which the testator should have been capable of comprehending. (*St. Leger's Appeal from Probate*, 34 Conn. 434-448.) It was not error to exclude the answer of the witness, Mrs. Webster, that she did not think the testatrix capable of making a will.

The fact that the testatrix's mind was weak, testified to by Charles H. Webster in answer to the question of appellant's counsel, was material and relevant to the issue; and, having been claimed by counsel examining the witness, the answer should not have been stricken out, upon motion of the opposing counsel. merely because it was irresponsive. Such an order of the court, however, furnishes no ground for complaint, when, as in this case, counsel is permitted to put another question, to which the excluded answer is responsive.

There was no error in the ruling of the court admitting the testimony of Judge Bishop concerning his conversations with the testatrix. The burden rested upon the appellant to show that the conversations occurred while the testatrix was consulting the witness professionally as an employed attorney. (*Carroll* v. *Sprague*, 59 Cal. 655.) At the time of the objection no preliminary examination seems to have been made for the purpose of proving that fact, nor has that fact been found by the court. The only facts found in connection with the ruling are that the witness had testified to his acquaintance with the testatrix for many years; to having had frequent opportunities of observing her, and frequent conversations with her. That the facts which appear elsewhere in the record with reference to his having acted as her attorney were known to the court when the objection was made cannot be assumed. Even those facts fail to show that these conversations occurred while the testatrix was consulting Judge Bishop as her attorney. But the rule which forbids an attorney from disclosing as a witness matters communicated to him in professional confidence should be strictly construed, as tending to prevent a full disclosure of the truth in court; and we think that the testimony admitted does not amount to a disclosure by the witness of a confidential and privileged communication made to him, as an attorney, by his client, even if we assume the existence of the relation of attorney and client between them at the time of the conversation in question. (*Foster* v. *Hall*, 12 Pick. 89-98; *Gower* v. *Emery*, 18 Me. 79.) The testimony was, in substance, merely that she talked to him about the settlement of an estate; that she wished him to ascertain for her how much she was likely to receive from it, which he did; and that she directed him to appear before the Court of Probate to procure the reduction of certain fees to which she objected. Such a request by a client to his attorney, made for the purpose of obtaining information for the former's benefit upon a matter of fact, and not for the purpose of asking the attorney's advice, ought not to be regarded as a privileged communication. (Weeks, Attys. at Law [2d ed.], 328.) An attorney may properly be required to testify by whom he is employed, and in what capacity. (*Satterlee* v. *Bliss*, 36 Cal. 489; *Gower* v. *Emery*, 18 Me. 79.)

The appellant has no reason to complain of the failure of the court to charge in the language of the first request. The court correctly defined testamentary capacity, and charged that the burden of proving that the testatrix possessed such capacity at the time of the execution of the will rested upon the proponents of the will.

The court further charged that in case there should be " an uncertainty in the minds of the jury, so that they could not say upon which side of that issue the evidence preponderated, their verdict should be against the party upon whom rested the burden of proving it." This was more favorable to the appellant than the instruction asked for, which was, in effect, that the appellant was entitled to a verdict if the evidence showed a want of testamentary capacity.

The court properly refused to charge in the language of the second request. The record discloses no admission by the appellee of the facts stated in the request. It was incumbent upon the appellant to prove the asserted confidential relations. (*Richmond's Appeal,* 59 Conn. 226; 22 Atl. 82.) The court rightly left it to the jury to decide whether the claimed relations of confidence and trust existed between the testatrix and Mr. Mix, and correctly instructed them that, if the evidence disclosed the existence of such relations, it became " incumbent upon the proponents of the will to show that he (Mix) acted fairly, and that he took no advantage of his position to induce or to procure the making of the will, or any part of it, in his favor."

The language of the charge defining " undue influence " was approved by this court in the case of *Dale's Appeal* (57 Conn. 127-145; 17 Atl. 757).

The thirteenth and fourteenth reasons of appeal present no questions for our consideration. Clearly, it was not intended by these assignments of error to say that parts of the charge manifestly favorable to the appellants were erroneous, as, for example, that the burden of proving testamentary capacity rested upon the appellee, and that it should be proved by a fair preponderance of evidence. The purport of these reasons of appeal is that there was error in something which the court said in its charge upon these subjects. They fail to comply with the rule. (Prac. Book, 258, rule 14, § 1; *Simmonds* v. *Holmes,* 61 Conn. 1-9; 23 Atl. 702.) In *Richmond's Appeal* (*supra*), the trial judge in his charge to the jury made use of this language: " Mere physical weakness or disease, old age, eccentricities, blunted perceptions, weakening judgment, failing memory or mind, are not necessarily inconsistent with testamentary capacity. One's memory may be failing, and yet his mind not be unsound. One's mental powers may be weakening, and still sufficient testamentary capacity remain to make a will." In granting a new trial upon an appeal, this court said concerning that part of the charge: " This is undoubtedly true, but such facts are admissible in evidence upon the question of capacity, and it was mainly by proof of their existence that the appellants sought to establish the want of such capacity. The court, therefore, in charging as it did, and in entirely failing to make reference in any portion of the charge to the significance of such facts as evidence, would seem, rather, in effect, to have withdrawn them from under the eyes of the jury, and from their consideration of them as such evidence, and thereby may, and, we fear, must, have misled the jury to the injury of the appellants." The appellant claims that the court made the same mistake in the case at bar. A distinction may be drawn between this case and *Richmond's Appeal*. In this case the court did not entirely fail to refer to the evidence of a weakened mind, etc. On the contrary, it directly refers to the evidence of these facts in connection with the other evidence indicating the mental condition of the testatrix as proper to be considered by the jury in passing on the question of testamentary capacity, which was accurately defined by the court. All the evidence bearing on the question of capacity was unqualifiedly submitted to the jury for their consideration. The court may properly submit the evidence in such manner as to intimate an opinion in respect to its weight, as undoubtedly was done in this case, so long as it does not exceed the limits of its powers by a practical withdrawal of competent evidence from consideration by the jury. (*Kimberly's Appeal*, 68 Conn. 428, 441; 36 Atl. 847; *Baptist Church* v. *Rouse*, 21 Conn. 160, 167; *State* v. *Rome*, 64 id. 329, 337-339; 30 Atl. 57; *State* v. *Smith*, 65 Conn. 283; 31 Atl. 206.) In *Richmond's Appeal* there was a total absence of any reference to the evidence on which the appellant relied. There was error in the admission of testimony, and error in other parts of the charge, which were mainly relied on for obtaining a new trial. Indeed, the error in not commenting on testimony of a weakened mind, etc., is hardly specified in the reasons of appeal, and but slightly referred to in briefs of counsel. It would be difficult, however, to distinguish the two cases, if the portion of the opinion above quoted is treated as establishing a rule of law. We think it should not be so treated. The failure to caution the jury in respect to the weight of evidence is error *per se*, in the case of the admission of the testimony of an accomplice, but ordinarily the propriety of comment on testimony depends on the circumstances of each case. It is not true that a failure to comment on the weight of evidence of a weakened mind, etc., in connection with a statement that such facts, if proved, do not necessarily establish testamentary incapacity, must always be treated as error. The circumstances of a case may be such that a total failure to comment may seem to be equivalent to a withdrawal of the evidence, and so mislead the jury to the injury of a party, as we thought in *Richmond's Appeal;* but the circumstances

may be such that a slight reference to such testimony is not equivalent to its withdrawal, but is simply a proper exercise of the discretion of the judge in intimating his opinion as to the weight of evidence, as is the case at bar.   The question is always largely one of
fact,—does the charge of the court, in view of all the circumstances, pass beyond the limit of proper comment, so as to submit
the testimony unfairly, or practically invade the province of the
jury in passing on the weight of evidence?   If so, a new trial may
be granted.   The charge of the court below does not call for a new
trial for such reason.   There is no error.

The other judges concurred.

DOBIE et al. vs. ARMSTRONG et al.

[Court of Appeals of New York, November 21, 1899; 160 N. Y. 584; 55
N. E. Rep. 302.]

WILLS—MENTAL CAPACITY—INSANE DELUSION—EVIDENCE.

Testator's son, who had been educated at his father's expense, became intemperate and improvident, and took his mother's part in divorce proceedings, consulted with an attorney who was his father's bitter foe,
and wrote a letter to an uncle in which he abused his father, and spoke
of him as being fit for the penitentiary.   After the divorce he lived with
his mother, and never again saw or communicated with his father, who
died fourteen years later.   The father had, without reason, while in
anger, called the son a bastard, but doubtless as a countercharge to his
wife, who had accused him of adultery.   Five years before his death
testator conveyed property to a college, and later made a holographic
will, leaving the bulk of his estate to the college.   To this a codicil was
added, slightly changing the conditions, and before his death he made
another will to the same effect.   He was a man of extraordinary intellectual vigor, managed his estate until his death with ability, and his
letters to the college trustees showed a purpose, formed several years
before his death, so to dispose of his property.   *Held*, not to show a
mental delusion, with respect to the son's character and habits, sufficient to justify submission of the testator's capacity to make a will to
the jury.

APPEAL from Supreme Court, Appellate Division, Fourth Department.

Action by David S. Dobie, individually and as executor of the will of Thomas Armstrong, deceased, and others, against Emmett Armstrong and another. From a judgment for plaintiffs affirmed by the Appellate Division (50 N. Y. Supp. 801), defendant Emmett Armstrong appeals.

Affirmed.

T. F. Conway, for appellant.

Richard L. Hand, for respondents.

GRAY, J.—The plaintiffs, who are executors of, and also legatees and devisees under, the will of Thomas Armstrong, deceased, brought this action to establish the validity of the testamentary probate. The testator died in December, 1895, and his will was probated in the Surrogate's Court of Clinton county in May, 1896. In the present action Emmett Armstrong, the only child and son of the deceased, and Harriet Armstrong, a divorced wife, were made defendants. The latter disclaimed all interest in the testator's personal estate, and, upon the trial, the judgment divorcing her from the deceased was conceded to be valid. The son, to whom the will gave nothing, contested its validity, upon the ground that his father was of unsound mind and incompetent to make a will. At the conclusion of the trial, the court directed the jury to find a verdict in favor of the plaintiffs, and a judgment was entered thereupon establishing the validity of the will. The Appellate Division has affirmed the judgment, and an appeal has been taken to this court.

It is insisted upon by the appellant that the evidence was sufficient to raise a question of fact as to the testamentary capacity of the testator, which should have been submitted to the jury. His contention is that the evidence proved, or strongly tended to prove, that the testator was influenced in making his will by a mental delusion with respect to his son's character, conduct, and habits. I think it unnecessary to indulge in any extended discussion of the facts of this case, inasmuch as they were quite fully reviewed, first, by the learned trial judge upon his direction of the verdict, and, again, at the Appellate Division.

Thomas Armstrong was seventy-six years of age at the time of his death. He came to this country a poor and friendless boy, and commenced to work at his trade of a tailor. In 1842 he married his first wife, the defendant Harriet, and soon commenced the study of the law. In 1847, he took up his residence in Clinton county, in this state, became a member of the bar, and attained a position of eminence thereat, and, generally, in the community. At one time he was district attorney for his county, and during the war of the Rebellion he had served as the colonel of a volunteer regiment. In the course of his life he accumulated an estate of some $250,000, and, alone, managed his business affairs until his death. Emmett Armstrong, the testator's son, was born in 1848, and was educated in part at Union College, in this state, and in part in Europe. He was permitted to travel considerably in Europe by his father, who seems to have had much affection for him, and to have exhibited some pride in his attainments. Early in life he appears to have contracted habits of intemperance, and was inclined to be improvident and lax in money matters. In 1882 the testator and his wife ceased to live together, and considerable litigation ensued between them. She was seeking to obtain an absolute divorce here, and he obtained such a judgment in the Dakota courts, in 1883, by default. As the final outcome of negotiations, an agreement was entered into between them to the effect that the default obtained by him should be opened; and she should appear in the action; and that, in case a judgment of divorce should be finally rendered in his favor, it should provide for the payment to her of the sum of $15,000 as alimony and in lieu of dower. Such a judgment was entered, and thereafter Mrs. Armstrong removed to Pennsylvania, where she invested the moneys received by her, and supported herself and their son, Emmett, who had accompanied her.

In 1889, the testator married another woman, with whom, it may be inferred from the evidence, he had previously become infatuated. In 1890 he conveyed by deed certain real estate to Union College; the income of which, amounting to about $6,650, was to be applied towards maintaining professorships and the support of students who should be farmers' sons from Clinton county. In 1891 a second deed of the same property to the college was executed, jointly, by the testator and his wife, which recited the obligation of the college to pay the sum of $1,000 a year to her during her life. In 1893 the testator made a holographic will, which, after some small bequests, gave the residue of his estate to Union College for the purpose of establishing certain annual prizes and certain scholarships for the sons of farmers of Clinton county. Judge Landon, a justice of the Supreme Court of the state and a trustee of the college, and Dr. Webster, then president of the college, were made residuary legatees as to all property not legally disposed of. Afterwards, the testator executed a codicil, whereby he gave to his wife an annual income of $1,000, which, with the provision in the college deed, would assure her an annual income of $2,000. In May, 1895, he executed a second holographic will, which gave the remainder of his estate to the college for the same objects as previously expressed, and provided, as in the former will, that, as to any part of his estate not legally devised, it should go to Judge Landon and to Dr. Raymond, then the president of the college, in succession to Dr. Webster. These were the three testamentary papers which were admitted to probate.

With respect to the disposition of his estate in favor of Union College, it may be observed that the interviews and correspondence had between Armstrong and Judge Landon show the formation and development of such a purpose for several years prior to the former's death. In the evidence furnished by the testimony of persons who had known the deceased and had had intercourse, in business and other ways, with him, and by the latter's letters and documents, we have indisputable proof that, in the conduct of his life, the testator had been a man of extraordinary intellectual vigor and ability. His characteristics were those of a self-willed, proud, and passionate man; who certainly made little, if any, effort to govern his impulses, or to exert any control over a very bad temper; who frequently engaged in bitterness of speech, or in making defamatory statements; and who was cruel, and, at times, even brutal, in his conduct. He was most eccentric in his habits, and in entertaining singular, and often extravagant, theories. He was highly sensitive and susceptible to offense, and his pride, or vanity, was such as, probably, to prevent him from making advances. For several years prior to his death his health was affected by a disease of the kidneys; but though, at times, greatly prostrated by its attacks, he seemed to have had remarkable powers of recuperation. His emotions were easily excited, and he would be effusive in his demonstrations of affection or of grief. The appellant has brought together a multitude of instances exhibiting these various and peculiar characteristic traits of the deceased, and he claims to have shown that his mind was unbalanced, and incapable of that soundness of judgment which the testamentary disposition of his property required.

Ordinarily, the burden of proof is upon the party propounding a will; but section 2653a of the Code of Civil Procedure, which is the authority for the maintenance of this action, places the burden upon the defendants, who contest the validity of the will, of establishing the testamentary incapacity of the testator. The probate of the will by the surrogate is made *prima facie* evidence of its due execution and validity. The affirmative was with this appellant upon the question of the case, whether a delusion, or an insane belief, existed in the testator's mind with respect to his domestic relations, and, especially, with respect to his son, which incapacitated him from validly willing away his estate. The burden was upon him to adduce evidence which would be sufficient to uphold a verdict that the testator was the victim of such a delusion, with respect to his son, as to prevent his affections from operating in their natural channel. He assumed the burden of showing that there was no cause for his father's changed feelings, in facts or in actual circumstances, and therefore that they could only have had their origin in some figment of the brain.

Up to 1881, the testator and his wife lived together, as husband and wife, although their relations had become strained. The son was then thirty-three years of age. He had disappointed his father by his refusal to engage in business. From his wife's letters, from reports, and from observation, the testator believed that his son was intemperate and gambled. These ideas were not enough, however, to turn him against his son, and would not, necessarily, have done so, had not the events from 1881 to 1886 supervened. During those years, when litigation existed between him and his wife, his feelings of dislike for the latter were accentuated by mortification at the charges made by her against him, and his affection for his son was destroyed from various causes. His son had espoused his mother's side, and among the many things, in addition to that, which might be alluded to as contributing towards the destruction of his affection, were, possibly more prominently, these: That he consulted upon his mother's matters with Mr. Smith M.

Weed, a lawyer, who was conspicuous in public life, a political antagonist of his father, and for whom the deceased entertained hostile feelings; that he wrote a letter to an uncle, in which, after much abuse of his father, he spoke of him as being fit to be sent to the penitentiary; and that from 1881 to the time of his father's death, in 1895, a period of fourteen years, there were absolute silence and an estrangement on his part.

Stress is laid upon the fact that the testator was known to have called his son a bastard, without any reason; but that, evidently, was not his belief. He, undoubtedly, said so in anger and excitement, and when he wrote to his wife, in 1882. That letter, however, was after his wife had charged him with adultery, and, quite possibly, was a counter attack on his part, to deter her from prosecuting the charges. If it was true that he believed his son to be a bastard, he could not have written to him with such affection and consideration as he certainly had often done.

It is plain that the will, in its provisions, was not the result of any sudden impulse, but, rather, of a definite purpose, formed in prior years and while the estrangement existed between him and his son. The experts who testified in the case for the contestant seemed practically forced to concede that, without the assumption of the existence in the testator's mind of a delusion as to his son, he could not be regarded as mentally unsound at the time of making his will. The hypothetical question, which was answered by the experts for the contestant in favor of his contention that the testator was mentally unsound, resumed a quantity of isolated facts and expressions during a great number of years. When brought together in this question, they are made to present that appearance of continuity, with respect to the testator's state of mind, which makes the question unfair, as describing the self-made and successful man with whom we are made acquainted through the evidence. The assumption in the hypothetical question of the existence of an insane impulse with regard to his son, from his having characterized him as a drunkard and as an otherwise worthless character, was not warranted by the evidence. There was not an absence of facts, or of circumstances, for the formation of such impressions by the deceased.

Apparently, at times, entertaining irrational opinions and views of men and of affairs, eccentric and arbitrary in conduct, the evidence, as a whole, shows that the testator was quite capable of personally managing his various interests, and that he could not be regarded as insane, however different he might be from other men.

It seems to me that this was not a case which should have been submitted to the decision of the jury. The contestant had not met the burden cast upon him by the statute of impeaching the validity of the testamentary act. The evidence does not prove, or even tend to prove, that the testator was insane when he executed the testamentary instruments in question. It fails to prove that he was influenced by any insane delusion in his domestic relations. The proof is abundant that they were sufficiently unfortunate and unhappy, whether attributable to his behavior or not, to embitter him, and, with his peculiar temperament, to harden his affections against the son, who had disappointed his ambitions, and who, turning against him in his latter years, had passed out of the sphere of his life.

When we consider what was the intellectual strength of his mind, and his self-sufficiency, as shown through his long life, and the reasons, good or bad, which undoubtedly existed for his making the disposition of his property complained of, it is impossible to say that there was any substantial foundation in the proofs for a judgment that the testator's mind was so diseased as to incapacitate him from making this will. A man's testamentary disposition of his property is not invalidated because its provisions are unequal or unjust, or the result of passion, or of other unworthy or unjustifiable sentiments. It is natural, and therefore usual, to make provision for a child; but, under our governmental institutions, no obligation to do so is imposed upon the parent, and the presumption of validity is not affected by the failure to do so, alone. Nor is the presumption in favor of a will overcome by showing that the testator was of advanced age, or of enfeebled condition of mind or body. (*Horn* v. *Pullman*, 72 N. Y. 269.) That the testator may have received some unjustifiable impression, which had actuated him in making his will, does not warrant us in calling it a delusion. A man may even have an insane delusion, and yet be able to make a valid will; for the will, to be invalid, must be the result itself of the delusion, and it is not a delusion which incapacitates, if the proof of its existence depends upon external and observable facts, giving rise to impressions which, upon investigation might be proved to be unjust. *In re White* (121 N. Y. 406; 24 N. E. 935), where it was the proposition of the contestants that, when the will was made, the testator was laboring under the insane delusion that his son was engaged in a conspiracy to injure and to defraud him, and that the will was the offspring of such a delusion and therefore invalid, it was observed that "delusion is insanity, where one persistently believes supposed facts, which have no real existence except in his perverted imagination, and against all evidence and probability, and conducts himself, however logically, upon the assumption of their existence. * * * But if there are facts, however insufficient they may in reality be, from which a prejudiced or a narrow or a bigoted mind might derive a particular idea or belief, it cannot be said that the mind is diseased in that respect. The belief may be illogical or preposterous, but it is not, therefore, evidence of insanity in the person."

I cannot bring my mind to the conclusion that the evidence was sufficient, in this case, to warrant its submission to the jury. Whether it was sufficient was a question of law for the court, and the trial judge, in holding as he did, in my opinion, committed no error. The trial court was not required to submit the question of the testator's mental capacity to the jury, merely because some evidence had been introduced by the party bearing the burden of proof. (*Dwight* v. *Insurance Co.* 103 N. Y. 341; 8 N. E. 654; *Linkauf* v. *Lombard*, 137 N. Y. 417-425; 33 N. E. 472.) The Legislature never could have intended, and the statute does not compel the construction, that courts should hold that every case which is brought under section 2653a of the Code must be submitted to the arbitrament of a jury. Experience has shown that verdicts are frequently unduly influenced by considerations based upon sentiment and sympathy, and no wise policy demands that, in cases of such importance and of such far-reaching consequences, the jury should determine the controversy upon any showing of the contestants. Their verdict should proceed upon such evidence as would warrant the court, in its review of the facts, in holding that it actually tended to prove such mental unsoundness in the testator, when proceeding to make a testamentary disposition of his property, as, by reason of the existence of some delusion, to render him incapable of forming a judgment as to the condition of his property, or of apprehending his true relations to the person whom his will deprives of the share in the estate which was reasonably, or naturally, to have been anticipated. Such cases are fraught with the gravest consequences, and I do not believe that a solemn testamentary disposition of property should be left to the decision of a jury upon mere surmise, or upon inferences from facts which are as consistent with the one view as with the other. I think that the evidence produced by the contestant was not of a nature that the jury could have properly proceeded to find a verdict upon it in his behalf, and, further, that, if such a verdict had been rendered, it could not have stood the test of a motion addressed to the court to set it aside. I advise the affirmance of this judgment.

All concur, except PARKER, C. J., not sitting.

Judgment affirmed.

IN RE POTTER'S WILL.

[Court of Appeals of New York, November 28, 1899; 161 N. Y. 84; 55 N. E. Rep. 387.]

WILLS — CONTEST — EVIDENCE — CONVERSATIONS WITH DE-CEASED—UNDUE INFLUENCE—MENTAL INCAPACITY—TRIAL— OBJECTION TO EVIDENCE — NECESSITY OF OFFER.

1. Code Civ. Proc. § 829, declaring that no person interested in a suit shall be examined in his own behalf or interest, against the survivor of a deceased person, concerning a personal transaction or communication between the witness and the deceased, does not render the testimony of legatees inadmissible on the part of contestants in a proceeding to set aside the will.

2. In a will contest, the contestants may prove entire conversations between deceased and the legatees, which tend to show undue influence and mental incapacity of the testator, and it is error to restrict such evidence to what the legatees said, and exclude what deceased said.

3. Where, in a will contest, objections are sustained to competent questions as to undue influence and mental incapacity, the case will be reversed, although no offer of proof or showing is made revealing what the rejected evidence is, or how it is material, although Code Civ. Proc. § 2545, provides that a decree upon an issue of fact shall not be reversed for error in admitting or rejecting evidence unless it appears that appellant was necessarily prejudiced thereby.

APPEAL from Supreme Court, Appellate Division, Third Department.

Proceedings for the probate of the will of Orra Potter, deceased. From an order of the appellate division affirming a surrogate's decree admitting the will to probate (45 N. Y. Supp. 563), William P. Potter and others appeal.

Reversed.

J. B. McCormick, for appellants.

C. H. Sturges and *Jurden E. Seeley,* for respondents.

BARTLETT, J.—The decree admitting the will of Mrs. Orra Potter to probate is attacked upon the ground that the learned surrogate rejected competent and material evidence on the trial before him. The facts surrounding the controversy have an important bearing upon this question. The testatrix was nearly eighty-nine years of age at the time she executed this will. She left, her surviving, seven children,—four daughters and three sons. The residuary legatees are her son Seaman G. and her daughter Caroline M. A trifling legacy of personal property is given to her son John D., and to his wife a cash legacy of $50. She gives to the wife of Seaman G. a legacy of $100 in cash, and to her residuary legatee Caroline M. Potter the residue of her household furniture, wearing apparel, etc. It thus appears that three daughters and one son take nothing under the will. They are the contestants in this proceeding. It was proved that the testatrix lived in the same house with her son John D. Potter, and her unmarried daughter Caroline M. Potter. Her son Seaman G. Potter resided within a few rods of John's house. The contestants attack this will upon the grounds of undue influence on the part of the children with whom the testatrix resided or was brought into immediate and constant contact. Mental incapacity is also charged. In support of the issues, the contestants' counsel called to the stand Seaman G. and Caroline M. Potter, presumably hostile witnesses, and sought to prove by them conversations with the deceased prior to the execution of the will, and which tended to show improper influence on their part over the free will of the testatrix. Many questions were addressed to these witnesses by the counsel for the contestants, seeking to draw out the substance of these conversations, but objections to them were uniformly sustained on the ground that the evidence was incompetent, under section 829 of the Code of Civil Procedure. As these witnesses were not called in their own behalf or interest, but were testifying against their interests, it is clear that this evidence was improperly rejected. (*Bank* v. *McCarty*, 149 N. Y. 71, 84; 43 N. E. 427; *Carpenter* v. *Soule*, 88 N. Y. 251, 257.) The learned Appellate Division affirmed this decree of the surrogate by a divided court, the prevailing opinion holding, substantially, that, while the evidence was improperly rejected, the contestants were not necessarily prejudiced thereby, and therefore the decree should not be reversed; citing Code Civ. Proc. § 2545. By that section it is provided that a decree upon the trial of an issue of fact " shall not be reversed, for an error in admitting or rejecting evidence, unless it appears to the Appellate Court that the exceptant was necessarily prejudiced thereby." The opinion goes on to state that it was incumbent upon the exceptant to have the case show, in substance by way of offer or otherwise, what the rejected evidence was as only in that way could it be made to appear whether or not there was prejudice to his case.

It was also suggested that the contestants did not avail themselves of the qualified ruling of the surrogate on the admissibility of this evidence, wherein he stated that he would permit them to show what the witness said to the testatrix, but would exclude the statements of the latter to the witness. In respect to the last suggestion, it is sufficient to say that these entire conversations between the witnesses and testatrix, tending to show undue influence or mental incapacity, were clearly competent, and the contestants were not compelled to place before the court a garbled and one-sided account of a colloquy.

As to the other suggestion, that the contestants were bound to show, by way of offer or otherwise, that the rejected evidence was material, there are complete answers: (1) The contestants did make an offer to show, when Caroline was upon the stand, that prior to the making of the will she had talks and conversations with the deceased, and directed her how she wanted this will made, and that it was made in accordance with the instructions and views of the witness, and that such talks were had prior to the making and execution of the will and on the same day; (2) it was not necessary to make an offer, as the practice is not favored by the court. A trial court is not bound to rule upon an offer of testimony, but it is a matter within its discretion, and it has the right, at least, when the opposite party requires it, to decide that the witness shall be produced, and questions asked tending to establish the matter embraced in the offer. (*Manufacturing Co.* v. *Colby*, 120 N. Y. 640; 24 N. E. 282.) It is difficult to conceive of evidence more competent or material under the issue of undue influence or mental incapacity. Furthermore, it may be said, generally, that the contestants rested under no positive obligation to disclose, by offer or otherwise, the character of the evidence to be adduced. As the examination of the witnesses progressed, unless the evidence bore upon the issue of undue influence or mental incapacity, it would be rejected or stricken out under objection, and it cannot be presumed that counsel examining a hostile witness will be able to state in advance, with accuracy, what he can prove. The defenders of the will are abundantly protected by the right to object to each question calling for an answer immaterial to the issues. We have here witnesses with whom the testatrix resided, a will that was wholly in their favor, and that disinherited the four other children. Under these circumstances, the greatest latitude should be accorded the contestants. It would have been competent for the surrogate, if satisfied that these witnesses were hostile, to have accorded to the contestants the privilege of a cross-examination. There is a marked difference in the situation presented to an appellate court between evidence improperly received or rejected. In the former case, the evidence is upon the record, and the court may readily determine whether its reception was prejudicial or not; but in the latter case, as already pointed out, it is quite impossible to acquaint the court with the full scope and character of the evidence that might have been adduced from hostile witnesses.

There are other grounds of alleged legal error discussed in the appellants' brief, but, as we are of opinion that a new trial must be granted, it is unnecessary to examine them. We do not wish to be understood as expressing any opinion as to the merits of this controversy, as the only question before us is whether there was legal error in the rulings of the surrogate. The judgment appealed from and the decree of the Surrogate's Court should be reversed, and a new trial ordered, with costs in all the courts to abide the event.

All concur, except O'BRIEN, J., not voting.
Judgment reversed, etc.

NOTE.—EVIDENCE OF TRANSACTIONS WITH DECEASED.

(a) Late criticism and tendency in construction.
(b) Test of interest.
(c) When evidence admitted.
(d) Relating to probate and executor's accounts.
(e) Attorney's claim for services.
(f) Action by administrator for death by wrongful act.
(g) Some illustrative cases.

(Reference is made to the full and elaborate note on this subject in 3 Prob. Rep. Ann. 347.)

The following references and selections only serve to illustrate the tendency of modern decisions and limitations or exceptions in application of general rules. It would take a book as large as this volume to treat the subject at length and even attempt to reconcile the decisions in all the states under different statutes.

(a) **Late criticism and tendency in construction.**—It is a significant fact that in the last Edition of Greenleaf on Evidence (1899) it is said in speaking of the statutes excluding evidence of the survivor of a transaction with the deceased " as a matter of policy this survival of the now discarded interest-disqualification is deplorable in every respect; for it is based on a fallacious and exploded principle, it leads to as much or more injustice than it prevents, and it encumbers the profession with a mass of barren quibbles over the interpretation of mere words," and reference is made to the opinion of CORLISS, J., in St. John v. Loffland (5 N. D. 140), which is well worth reading as showing a tendency to limit the operation of such laws, and not to broaden them by interpretation.

(b) **Test of interest.**—The test of interest that will exclude a witness not a party from testifying is that he will either gain or lose by the direct legal operation of the judgment, or that the record will be legal evidence for or against him in some other action. It must be a present, certain and vested interest, and not one that is uncertain, remote or contingent. (Connelly v. O'Connor, 117 N. Y. 91; 22 N. E. Rep. 753.)

An agent is not a " person interested in the event." (Nearpass v. Gilman, 104 N. Y. 506; 10 N. E. Rep. 894; and see Cheney v. Pierce, 38 Vt. 515.)

Nor is the mother of a plaintiff in an action of ejectment claiming as son and heir, disqualified from giving evidence of her marriage. (Eisenlord v. Clum, 126 N. Y. 552; 27 N. E. Rep. 1024.)

An interest in the question is not enough to disqualify; it must be in the event. (Albany County Savings Bank v. McCarty, 149 N. Y. 84; 43 N. E. Rep. 427.)

Witness liable on note in suit as surety is interested in the event. (Munz v. Colvin, 35 App. Div. 188; 54 N. Y. Supp. 781.)

Interested in the event. (Carpenter v. Romer & Tremper Co., 48 App. Div. 363; 63 N. Y. Supp. 274.)

(c) **When evidence admitted.**—While party may be prohibited from testifying to particular communications or transactions with deceased, he is not precluded from testifying to extraneous facts which tend to show that a witness who has testified to such a transaction has testified falsely, or that it is impossible that his statement can be true. (Pinney v. Orth, 88 N. Y. 447; and see Lewis v. Merritt, 98 id. 206; Clift v. Moses, 112 id. 438; 20 N. E. Rep. 392; Burns v. Mullin, 42 App. Div. 116, 122; 58 N. Y. Supp. 933; Cowan v. Davenport, 30 App. Div. 130, 134; 51 N. Y. Supp. 478.)

If a party calls the adverse party and examines him as to a personal communication or transaction with the deceased in reference to which he would be precluded from testifying in his own behalf, the witness is entitled to state the whole transaction or conversation and thereby explain or qualify the testimony called out by the other party. (Nay v. Curley, 113 N. Y. 575, 579; 21 N. E. Rep. 698.)

Plaintiff administratrix in suit in action for goods sold, may call defendant to prove the purchase but if she does so he may be cross-examined as to whether he had not made payment. (Mahoney v. Jones, 35 App. Div. 84; 54 N. Y. Supp. 488.)

Where an executor, who is a plaintiff, testifies in his own behalf to a personal transaction between the deceased and the defendant, then the defendant becomes a competent witness in his own behalf with respect to the *same* transaction, but not to other or different transactions. (Rogers v. Rogers. 153 N. Y. 343. 350; 47 N. E. Rep. 452; Russell v. Russell, 47 App. Div. 144; 62 N. Y. Supp. 108.)

Proof of declarations of deceased by competent third parties is not within the meaning of the statute as the *testimony* of a deceased person, and it does not open the door for the admission of what would otherwise be plainly incompetent evidence. (Lyon v. Ricker, 141 N. Y. 225; 36 N. E. Rep. 189; Matter of Calister, 153 N. Y. 306; 47 N. E. Rep. 268.)

Admission against interest of a living person is competent although the *admission* itself may include reference to a transaction with a deceased party. (Hirsh v. Auer. 146 N. Y. 13; 40 N. E. Rep. 397; and see Comins v. Hetfield, 80 N. Y. 261; Leaptrot v. Robertson, 37 Ga. 586; Hanna v. Wray. 77 Pa. St. 27.)

(d) **Relating to probate and executor's accounts.**—Upon settlement of an executor's account involving a claim by him of a credit on account of a payment made by him to a third party as against a contesting residuary legatee, he is precluded from testifying to conversations with the testator concerning such claim. (Matter of Smith, 153 N. Y. 124; 47 N. E. Rep. 33.)

Where probate of will is contested a legatee may become a competent witness by execution of a valid release. (Loder v. Whelpley, 111 N. Y. 239; 18 N. E. Rep. 874.)

A release of interest will not necessarily make witness competent where plaintiff derives part of title and interest by virtue of such release. (Bennett v. Bennett, 50 App. Div. 127; 63 N. Y. Supp. 387.)

When probate of will is contested on ground of no publication, a beneficiary under it is incompetent to testify to any conversation or transaction in his presence at the time of its execution and publication, even though the witness took no part in the conversation and it was wholly between the testator and the attesting witnesses. (Matter of Bernsee, 141 N. Y. 389; 36 N. E. Rep. 314.)

(e) **Attorney's claim for services.**—Where the contract of employment is established by other competent evidence an attorney in action against the estate for services rendered may testify as to what he did in detail so long as it does not necessarily involve a personal transaction with the deceased. If the employment or request for services in any manner or to any extent rested upon an inference drawn from the acts done, the evidence is incompetent. In such a case it is proper to ask the plaintiff " What was done by you, excepting personal transactions or communications with the deceased from the time you first commenced your labor down to his death?" If any objectionable testimony is given in reply, the remedy is by motion to strike out. (Lerche v. Brasher, 104 N. Y. 157; 10 N. E. Rep. 58; and see Nay v. Curley, 113 N. Y. 581, 582; 21 N. E. Rep. 698; Clift v. Moses, 112 N. Y. 436; 20 N. E. Rep. 392; Matter of Powers, 124 N. Y. 365; 26 N. E. Rep. 940; Matter of Rowell, 45 App. Div. 325; 61 N. Y. Supp. 382; Moses v. Hatch, 38 App. Div. 143; 56 N. Y. Supp. 561; Denise v. Denise, 110 N. Y. 562; 18 N. E Rep 368.)

(f) **Action by administrator for death by wrongful act.**—In action brought by administrator to recover damages for death of intestate, the defendant is precluded from testifying to personal transactions or communications between himself and the deceased. (Abelein v. Porter, 45 App. Div. 307; 61 N. Y. Supp. 144; citing Forbes v. Snyder, 94 Ill. 374; Consolidated Machine Ice Co. v. Keifer, 134 id. 841; 25 N. E. Rep. 799; Sherlock v. Alling, 44 Ind. 184; Hudson v. Houser, 125 id. 309; 24 N. E. Rep. 243; Quin v. Moore, 15 N. Y. 432)

(g) **Some illustrative cases.**—If no objection on the trial to such evidence, force and effect may be given to it. (Stern v. Ladew, 47 App. Div. 336; 62 N. Y. Supp. 267.)

Neither a mortgagee. nor his assignee is a person deriving his title or interest from, through or under a deceased mortgagor. (Holcomb v. Campbell, 118 N. Y. 46; 22 N. E. Rep. 1107; and see Squire v. Green, 38 App. Div. 431; 56 N. Y. Supp. 551.)

What witness can not testify to directly can not be testified to indirectly, for instance upon an issue of title to a bank deposit that she had seen the bank book exhibited to her in a tin box. (O'Connor v. Ogdensburg Bank, 51 App. Div. 70; 64 N. Y. Supp. 501.)

Testimony as to possession of a deed, and that signature was in hand-writing of deceased does not necessarily involve a personal transaction. (Simmons v. Havens, 101 N. Y. 433; 5 N. E. Rep. 73; and see Wadsworth v. Heermans, 85 N. Y. 639.)

In St. John v. Lofland (5 N. D. 140; 64 N. W. Rep. 930), the action was by an administrator who succeeded a deceased administrator to whom as such note and mortgage in suit had been given by the defendant. The defense was payment and it was *held* that defendant might testify that he paid the note and mortgage to the first administrator.

Fox *et al. vs.* Martin.

In re Stickney's Will.

[Supreme Court of Wisconsin, November 24, 1899; 104 Wis. 581; 80 N. W. Rep. 521.]

Wills—Undue influence—Confidential relations—Secrecy—Instructions.

1. Instructions should be limited to a statement of the law applicable to the particular question which the jury are called on to decide on the evidence; and there should be no suggestions as to evidentiary facts, pointing to their probable existence, when there is no evidence to support that view.

2. Suggestion of confidential relations between testator and M. and his wife,—the latter a sister of testator,—should not be made in instructions to the jury on the question of undue influence, the evidence being that testator had no confidential relations with any one; that he was exceptionally self-willed down to and including the time he made his will; that he did his own thinking, and on the occasion of making the will expressed fully the reasons for his conduct; that he had lived alone for many years, except a short period of unsatisfactory association with two of his children; that he was at the house of M. when the will was made, without solicitation or influence on their part; that he was taken sick while on an ordinary visit to his sister, where it was more natural to go than elsewhere, as she lived on their father's old homestead, where she had been his associate more recently than any other member of their family; and that shortly after being taken sick he sent M. to get B. to draw some papers for him, and instructed him (B.) as to drawing the will.

3. It is no evidence that the testator's sister prejudiced his mind against his daughter, that she advised him to send the daughter away if he could not get along with her, and that she did not encourage the daughter's presence when he was sick; he having endeavored to live with his daughter and her children, and being so annoyed by them that he had to send them away; and the daughter having never afterwards visited him, though living in the neighborhood, till he was on his death-bed; and the sister not having told the daughter that testator was not in condition to see her till she had communicated with him, and he not having afterwards inquired for her; and he having, after providing for one of his children, said that it made little difference what he gave the others, as they would not be satisfied till it was all wasted.

4. Secrecy in the making of a will does not raise an inference of undue influence, testator's mind not being weak or susceptible to undue influence.

APPEAL from Circuit Court, Waukesha county; JAMES J. DICK, Judge. ·

The will of W. H. Stickney, proposed for probate by Everett Martin, was contested by Ellen A. Fox and others. From a judgment of the Circuit Court reversing a judgment of the County Court, and declaring the will void, proponent appeals.

Reversed.

Appeal from a judgment of the Circuit Court of Waukesha county reversing a judgment of the County Court of such county respecting the validity of the will of Warren H. Stickney, and decreeing such will void on the ground of undue influence. Mr. Stickney was possessed of a small amount of personal property, a farm consisting of 190 acres in Waukesha county, and a tract of land in Dunn county, the latter supposed, from the consideration named in the deed, to have been worth about $900. He had three children, all adults,—two sons, Joseph Hollis Stickney and Percy Warren Stickney, and a widowed daughter, Ellen A. Fox, who had two children and was in very poor circumstances. The testator had eight brothers and sisters. Before making his will he made a deed and left it in possession of the person who drew it, conveying the Dunn county land to his son Hollis. He also made a bill of sale, conveying to Everett Martin, a brother-in-law at whose home he lay sick, his personal property. He willed his homestead to his three children, his brother-in-law

Martin, and five of his brothers and sisters, including Mrs. Martin, in equal shares. Elva J. Nicolai, a sister living a short distance from the home of the Martins, Volney J. Stickney, a brother, and Alice M. Fraser, a sister, all living near, were not remembered by the testator in his will. On the trial the foregoing facts appeared, and the following, upon which the contestants rely to establish their claim that Everett Martin and wife unduly influenced the testator to make the will as he did. None of the testator's children or his brothers and sisters, outside of the Martin home, were notified of the making of the will so they could be present. Martin and his wife were present and were remembered to a much greater extent than the other relatives. The testator made statements during the later years of his life that he intended that his children should have his property. There was evidence tending to show that Mrs. Martin did not like the daughter Ellen, and had advised the testator, while Ellen and her children were living with him, to get rid of her if he could not get along otherwise. There was also evidence tending to show that when the daughter called to see her father after the will was drawn, Mrs. Martin told her that he was not in a condition to be seen. Mr. Martin, by direction of Stickney, procured the presence of Thomas F. Bayley for the purpose of preparing some papers for Stickney. Stickney was fifty-seven years of age at the time of his death. He was divorced from his wife about 1885, the custody of his three children being awarded to the wife, with whom they resided most of the time thereafter. After the divorce the testator lived for about two years with his father and sister Ida (who afterwards became the wife of Everett Martin), on the father's homestead in Waukesha county, Wis. He then, under a deed from his father, took possession of the land devised by his will, and resided thereon alone till 1887. In the meantime his father died. In 1887 he induced his daughter Ellen and son Hollis to live with him, because of the fact that he was becoming too feeble to work his farm and get along alone, though he was at that time able to do considerable work. In March, 1898, he required his children to go away because he could not bear the presence and noise of the daughter's children. He lived alone on his farm thereafter til July 31, 1898. On that day he went to the home of the Martins for a visit. He was accustomed to make such visits and to take his washing to his sister to be done. At this time the testator, though

able to do considerable work and all his business, was enfeebled
physically by rheumatism caused by an old injury to his knee, and
some other complaints.   He walked by the use of a cane, and
sometimes two canes.   Soon after he arrived at the Martins on the
date stated, he was taken quite ill.   The next day he was worse,
and, quite early, he sent Martin to procure Bayley to draw some
papers for him.   Bayley lived some three miles away.   On the
journey to procure Bayley, Martin stopped at Mr. Nicolai's, a
brother-in-law of Mr. Stickney, with whom his son Hollis resided.
Martin left word at Nicolai's that Stickney was dangerously ill
and wanted Nicolai to come and settle for some potatoes for which
he was indebted.   There was some dispute in the evidence as to
whether Martin inquired for Hollis or left word specially for him.
Mr. Bayley arrived at Martin's place about nine o'clock of the day
mentioned and before seeing Stickney requested Martin to find out
about the papers that were to be drawn.   Martin then interviewed
Stickney and thereafter gave instructions for a deed to be drawn
conveying the Dunn county land to Hollis, but said nothing about
a will.   Bayley, after drawing the deed, conversed with Mr. Stickney about the will, no one being present but the two.   After receiving Stickney's instructions he drew the will and read it over to him,
no one else being present, and the testator expressed his satisfaction with its provisions.   Martin and Charles Haese were then
called in and the will was executed, the former knowing nothing
about its contents.   Mr. Stickney sat up in bed, getting to that position without help.   Martin sat behind him so that he could steady
his body by leaning back, and then, with a piece of board on his lap
and the draft of the will on the board, he wrote his name to the
paper.   He then lay down and the piece of board was placed on the
side of the bed, and using that as a rest for the will, Charles Haese
and Mr. Bayley, at the testator's request, signed as witnesses, each
in turn kneeling down at the bedside when writing his signature.
In the position they occupied when writing their names the testator
could not see them write, which caused him to remark: " I suppose
you are signing, but I could not swear what you are doing," whereupon Mr. Bayley told him that it was not necessary that he should
be able to swear to that fact; that it was sufficient that the witnesses
were able to swear that they signed the will as witnesses in his presence.   Mr. Martin, after consultation with Mr. Stickney, paid for

drawing the papers, and told Bayley to keep the will. Mr. Nicolai, in response to the request to come over and settle for the potatoes, happened in during the time the papers were being drawn, and made such settlement, doing the business with Mr. Martin. Nothing was said to him about the will. The son Hollis visited his father in the afternoon but was not told about the execution of the papers referred to. No directions were given by Stickney as to what to do with the bill of sale or the deed. Martin took the former and Bayley kept the letter to perfect it for record by affixing thereto a revenue stamp and to then deliver it to Hollis, which he did after some delay on account of difficulty in procuring the stamp, but not till after Stickney's death, which occurred the eighth day after the papers were made. Stickney was a very eccentric man, who had his own peculiar notions and carried them out, customarily, in his own way. He was of sound disposing mind and memory when he made the will. The court, added to some advisory findings by the jury, found as facts that Mr. Stickney executed the will with full knowledge of its provisions, and was of sound mind and testamentary capacity; but that he was very ill, suffering from pain, and that the will was not his free and voluntary act, but an act performed by him under undue influence exerted upon his mind by Everett Martin and his wife to obtain special benefits to themselves to the detriment of the testator's children.

Judgment was rendered accordingly.

Tullar & Lockney, for appellant.

Ryan & Merton, for respondents.

MARSHALL, J. (after stating the facts).—Is the finding of fact that the will was procured by undue influence, and for the benefit of Everett and Ida F. Martin, supported by the evidence? Answer to that is conclusive of this appeal.

The challenged finding, as indicated in the statement of facts, was primarily made by a jury. It became the decision upon which the judgment rests by adoption by the trial court. A careful reading of the evidence fails to disclose the foundation for it, keeping in mind that reasonable probabilities, arising from such evidence, excluding mere speculation and conjecture, must govern. Looking elsewhere than to the evidence for a solution of the inquiry as to where the jury went for the inference embodied in their verdict, the instructions given by the trial court seem to furnish a key to the situation. They cover some twenty-four printed pages, about half as much as the entire evidence in the case. On the particular question under consideration they are quite exhaustive, referring to almost every circumstance said in the books to be evidentiary of undue influence. In that regard the instructions indicate much learning and industry, but as a clear, concise statement of the law applicable to the particular question which the jury were called upon to decide on the evidence, they are very misleading. It is the better practice, in submitting questions to a jury, to observe the rule that instructions should be confined to such a statement of the law as to each question as is called for by the evidence, and necessary to enable the jury to answer it intelligently. A long, argumentative discussion of principles, full of suggestions as to evidentiary facts, pointing to their probable existence, though there be no evidence to support that view, is quite likely to result in a miscarriage of justice, especially where the situation of the parties is such as to stimulate sympathy for the one and prejudice against the other. In such circumstances juries will easily reach a conclusion that suggested probabilities in favor of the weaker party exist and are of sufficient probative power to warrant a finding of the existence of the ultimate fact in issue, when, if pains were taken to fence their deliberations securely within the limits of the evidence produced, and to submit to them only questions in regard to which there are reasonably conflicting inferences from such evidence, and to give to the jury the law applicable thereto and none other the result would rarely be other in fact than in theory,—the safest and most just test of where the truth lies. The mischief of a contrary course is rarely better illustrated than in this case. It not only led, as it seems, to a finding of fact upon suggested probabilities not arising from evidence produced, but the trial judge adopted the result as his deliberate conclusion, and rendered judgment thereon.

The suggestions referred to, not warranted by the evidence, in the main are: (1) The existence of confidential relations between the testator and the Martins; (2) creation of prejudice by the Martins in the mind of Mr. Stickney against his children; (3) the Mar-

tins were guilty of solicitation and procuration in regard to securing a will favorable to them and were particularly active in that
regard; (4) the testator made an unnatural disposition of his
property; (5) the will was made in secret, the Martins being in-
strumental in excluding the testator's children and other relatives
from his presence, instead of notifying them that a will was to be
made so they might be present and protect their interests.

On the subject of confidential relations, the evidence is without
dispute that Mr. Stickney was a man who did not have confidential
relations with any one; that he was exceptionally a self-willed man
down to and inclusive of the time when the will was made; that he
did his own thinking, came to conclusions by his own peculiar pro-
cesses of reasoning, and, on the occasion in question, he expressed
fully the reasons for his conduct, as will be more fully stated hereafter. He was a very peculiar and eccentric man. He had lived
alone for many years prior to the time he was taken sick, except a
short period of very unsatisfactory association with two of his
children, particularly with his daughter Ellen. He was at the Martin home when the will was made without solicitation or influence
on their part. He was unexpectedly taken sick while making an
ordinary visit to his sister, where it was more natural to go than
elsewhere, as the Martins lived on the old Stickney homestead
where he had spent much of his life and where his
sister Ida had been his associate more recently than any other
living member of the Stickney family. Soon after he was taken
sick, realizing that the sickness was liable to be serious, he sent
Mr. Martin to obtain the presence of Mr. Bayley to draw some
papers for him, and of his brother-in-law, Nicolai, to settle a business transaction respecting some potatoes. When Bayley arrived
Mr. Martin received the sick man's directions as to the deed to be
made to Hollis and reported the same to the former. It does not
appear that he gave any directions whatever regarding the bill of
sale. For aught that appears that was the result of a conversation between Mr. Stickney and Mr. Bayley. When Nicolai arrived
to settle for the potatoes Mr. Martin received the money to avoid
disturbing Mr. Stickney, as he was in some pain and evidently en-
grossed with the business in hand of having his papers drawn by
Bayley. It will be seen that the Martins were not in any position of
confidence with Mr. Stickney, which they could have abused for

their own advantage. The situation cannot properly be called one of confidential relations, precluding an occurrence for the benefit of one to the detriment of others without the former being responsible for showing that his conduct was free from fraud.

On the subject of prejudicing Mr. Stickney against his children evidence is entirely wanting. True, Mrs. Martin told her brother that if he could not get along with his daughter Ellen she would advise sending her away; further, she did not encourage the presence of the daughter when Mr. Stickney was sick, but the state of minds of the father and daughter explains that and shows that Mrs. Martin was in no way responsible for it. Stickney endeavored to live with his daughter and her children, but they annoyed him so intensely that he felt obliged to secure peace of mind by sending them away. Mr. Nicolai, an unfriendly witness, testified that he knew in advance that Mr. Stickney would not be able to live with his daughter and her children and advised strongly against attempting it. After the daughter was sent away she did not visit her father or pay any attention to him till he was on his death-bed. All the indications are that he did not then care to see her. Mrs. Martin, after communicating with him, told the daughter that he was not in a condition to be seen. He did not inquire for her after that, and she did not visit him even to inquire, till the night he died, though he needed attention night and day for a period of some eight days, and he had ample opportunity to express his wishes as to her to his son Hollis. The son went to his father's bedside on the day the will was drawn and was there much of the time afterwards till death occurred. He had ample opportunity to communicate with his father about the will and to know his father's wishes as to Ellen without any interference whatever from the Martins. The other son was in Missouri. Mr. Stickney had seen but little of any of the children since they were quite young, and evidently had no warmth of affection for any except Hollis. After the will was drawn he said that Hollis was a nice boy and he had provided for him so as to give him a good start; that it made little difference what he gave the other children, because they would not be satisfied till it was all wasted. That shows, clearly the state of Mr. Stickney's mind, as it was privately made known to the man who drew the will, uninfluenced by anybody. Such condition of mind seems quite natural in view of the eccentric character of the man and his history as shown by the uncontroverted evidence. Much significance is given to the fact that the daughter was obliged to take in washing and do other hard service to support herself and her children; but it appears that Mr. Stickney wanted her to go to some other part of the country, and that her remaining in the neighborhood, working as she did, under the circumstances, tended to annoy him. He considered that she thereby willfully brought discredit upon him among his neighbors, as it seems.

On the subject of unnatural disposition of the property, sufficient has already been said to show that, the will in that regard was made exactly in accordance with the bent of the testator's mind. He was a man of strong prejudices and was eccentric to a high degree. He remembered his children as he viewed their deserts and then gave some of his property to such of his brothers and sisters as he desired to remember in that way, providing more particularly for his sister Ida and her husband than for any of the others, which is readily explained by the fact that such sister stood nearest to him in family regard. As before indicated, she lived on the old homestead and to her he felt more free to turn than to the others, as is evidenced by the fact that he had customarily taken his washing to her home to be done and had been accustomed to visit her frequently. On the whole, considering the mental characteristics of the testator and the relations he sustained to his relatives, the disposition of his property was perfectly natural and intelligent.

On the subject of solicitation and procurement to secure the making of a will favorable to the Martins, we fail to find any circumstances to create a suspicion. It does not even appear, definitely, that Mr. Martin, when he went on the errand to secure the presence of Mr. Bayley, was aware a will was to be drawn. It affirmatively appears that all the directions, as to how the property was to be disposed of in the will, were given by Mr. Stickney privately to his scrivener, that the will was approved by him when drawn, such approval being accompanied by statements explanatory of his conduct, that he was very decided as to all he wanted done, and was so thoughtful throughout, that when the witnesses came to sign he called Mr. Bayley's attention to the fact that he was not in position to see their signatures as they were writing, and had to be assured that it was sufficient if the witnesses actually signed in his presence. From first to last Mr. Martin was not consulted as to how the will should be drawn, did not know its contents till it was read in probate court, and did not make any inquiries of Mr. Bayley as to its contents. His conduct throughout appears to have been free from criticism.

On the subject of the will being made in secret, and the other relatives being excluded instead of being called in so as to protect their interests, there is the same lack of evidence as in respect to the other circumstances mentioned. Reasonable efforts were made to notify the son Hollis and Mr. Nicolai of the illness of Mr. Stickney. The other relatives heard of the illness in due time and visited and conversed with the sick man freely, when, as they testified, he was in the full possession of his faculties and conversed as usual. Inasmuch as the will was made without solicitation or influence on the part of the Martins, and they were ignorant of its contents, and there was no question but that Stickney was perfect master of himself in doing as he liked, there was no occasion for any one to be called in to protect him against the Martins, or for their protection against suspicion of wrongdoing in the event of the will being favorable to them. There is liable to be far too much significance given to the circumstance of a person making his will in private. It would be a strange doctrine to adopt, that a person, in making his will, for safety against its being impeached for fraud must call in his relatives or neighbors. Of all the things that a person about to make a final disposition of his property would think of, if in the full possession of his faculties, that is not one of them. Men usually make their wills in private and try to keep their provisions profoundly secret so long as they live. The circumstance that a will is thus made is not of itself suspicious in the absence of proof that the mind of the testator was weak and susceptible to undue influence. The presence of others than the favored beneficiary is not for the purpose of consultation with the testator, but to exclude the idea that may otherwise exist, that one was favored because of his solicitation or procuration, or other improper influence. The idea that as a rule, relatives must be called in when a person is about to make his will, is out of harmony with the testamentary right. and contrary to reason and common sense. The adjudications referring to the making of a will in secret as a

badge of fraud have no application to situations where the circumstances are not such as to suggest need of protection for the testator in order that he may express his will instead of the will of
some other person. To refer to the perfectly natural circumstance
of a person making a will in private as a badge of fraud, where
there is no reason for publicity to insure protection to the testator
from those standing near to him, and security to them against the
charge of procuring the will for selfish purposes, is not justified by
the law and tends to destroy the testamentary right.

No further discussion of the evidence seems to be necessary.
The learned court misled the jury by the nature of the charge, and
then adopted their finding and passed judgment as before indicated.
The instructions led the jury away from the evidence into the
realms of conjecture and speculation, and even worse, as it suggested the probability of the existence of evidentiary circumstances
of fraud where the evidence shows conclusively that the will was
the free intelligent act of the testator. It seems to have been forgotten that, where the circumstances, to which the court referred as
evidentiary of undue influence, exist, calling for explanation their
effect is entirely destroyed by affirmative proof that the will was the
free and intelligent act of the testator.

A brief reference to the cases decided by this court will emphasize what has been said, particularly on the question of the significance of want of publicity in the making of a will and the circumstances under which that tends to raise an inference of undue influence. In *Watkins* v. *Brant* (46 Wis. 419, 1 N. W. 82), the validity of a deed was questioned. The grantor, a weak-minded,
partially deaf married woman, entirely unacquainted with business
matters, possessed of eighty acres of land, all the property of the
family, was secretly induced to convey part of it to a strong-minded,
energetic sister without consideration or knowledge of her husband.
The grantee worked upon the grantor's mind by interviews and
solicitations, continued for a considerable period of time, pledging
the latter, during such time, not to talk with her husband about
the matter. Finally the grantee, by aid of her mother, induced the
grantor to go to an attorney's office and sign a deed for 60 acres of
land, believing it was a deed for 20 acres.

In *Davis* v. *Dean* (66 Wis. 100; 26 N. W. 737), the validity of
a deed was in question. The grantor was a woman 80 years of

age and was incompetent to do business. She had been uncon-
scious, or partially so, for some days before the paper was made,
and was in that condition most of the time afterwards till she died.
She conveyed all her property to a man not her son, but whom
she and her husband had reared and educated, disinheriting her
daughter and several families of grandchildren. The time of the
transaction was between 9 o'clock in the evening and midnight.
The grantee worked upon the grantor's mind by interviews and
therefore, to secure absolute secrecy from the other relatives, by
selecting nightime for the transaction, procuring the presence of a
justice of the peace and the doctor, and inducing two gransons,
who expected to sit up with their grandmother that night, to go
home.

In *Cole* v. *Getzinger* (96 Wis. 559; 71 N. W. 75), the victim
of undue influence was an old man, eighty-eight years of age, too
infirm in mind and body to intelligently attend to business matters
of importance without assistance. The only persons concerned in
obtaining the deed, or who had knowledge of it, were beneficiaries,
two of whom, however, a daughter and son-in-law pretending to be
acting in the interest of the grantor.

In *Baker* v. *Baker* ([Wis.] 78 N. W. 453), the testator was
seventy-three years of age, so weak mentally as to be easily influenced by his wife, who practically dictated his will, leaving to
her nearly all of his property.

In *re Derse's Will* ([Wis.] 79 N. W. 46), the testatrix was an
old lady, seventy-three years of age, who had suffered two strokes
of paralysis and was helpless and irresponsible. There was no
question but that her mind was greatly impaired when she made
the will. She had twelve children. The one son with whom she
resided, by numerous acts prior to the making of the will, exhibited a disposition to obtain possession of his mother's property.
He finally secured the execution of a will very favorable to himself, in place of one previously made leaving the testatrix's property to her children share and share alike.

It will be observed that in each instance there was a subject unquestionably susceptible to undue influence, and there was clear
evidence of a disposition on the part of the favored person to exercise such influence. In such a situation the secrecy of the transaction was said to be a significant circumstance, evidentiary of fraud.

Lay aside the two elements mentioned, and the mere circumstance of secrecy ceases to be evidentiary of undue influence, and becomes consistent with the usual way in which such business transactions occur. In *Disch* v. *Timm* (101 Wis. 179; 77 N. W. 196), quoting from *In re Wheeler's Will* (5 Misc. Rep. 279; 25 N. Y. Supp. 314), it was said, " Where interest, opportunity, and a disposition to influence a testator improperly are shown, a presumption of undue influence arises." It follows that, where opportunity does not exist, for want of a subject susceptible to undue influence, mere secrecy does not create suspicion or give sufficient significance to the other circumstances stated, standing alone, to create a presumption of fraud. Further, quoting, it is said, in regard to the situation when the presumption of undue influence exists, " the burden is then on the party charged therewith to show that the will was testator's voluntary act." Here, as has been seen, the alleged fraud was not established so as to cast upon the defendant the burden of rebutting it. Nevertheless, the fact was established, affirmatively, that the will of Mr. Stickney was his free, voluntary and intelligent act.

The judgment of the Circuit Court is reversed and the cause remanded with directions to affirm the judgment of the Probate Court admitting the will to probate.

NEW YORK LIFE INSURANCE & TRUST CO. *vs.* VIELE *et al.*

[Court of Appeals of New York, November 21, 1899; 161 N. Y. 11; 55 N. E. Rep. 311.]

REVIEW — REFERENCE — FINDING OF DOMICILE — WILLS—CONSTRUCTION—WHAT LAW GOVERNS.

1. A finding of a referee on a question as to the domicile of a testatrix, unanimously affirmed below, is conclusive on appeal.
2. Where a testatrix resided in New York, but was temporarily settled in Saxony when she executed her will, it will be interpreted according to the laws of New York, her domicile.
3. Testatrix, whose domicile was in New York, in 1855 went to live with a married daughter in Saxony, where she executed her will in 1878,

bequeathing a portion of her estate on her daughter's death to her daughter's "then living lawful issue," if any; otherwise, to testatrix's grandchildren. No reference was otherwise made to an adopted child of her daughter, who was then forty years of age, and had no living issue. This child had been legally adopted in 1873 by the daughter and her husband under the laws of Saxony, and after her mother's death claimed under the will as "lawful issue." *Held,* that such term referred alone to her daughter's offspring, and hence did not include children by adoption.

APPEAL from Supreme Court, Appellate Division, First Department.

Action by the New York Life Insurance & Trust Company, trustee under the will of Mary Griffin, deceased, against Terese Viele and others. From a judgment on a decision of the court construing the will, affirmed by the Appellate Division (47 N. Y. Supp. 841). Anna Maria Louisa Natalia Reichelt and others appeal.

Affirmed.

Charles E. Hughes, for appellants.

Severyn B. Sharpe, for respondents.

O'BRIEN, J.—This appeal involves the construction of the third clause of the will of Mary Griffin, who died on the 9th day of March, 1888, at Dresden, in the kingdom of Saxony, one of the states of the German empire. She was the widow of Francis Griffin, of the city of New York, who died there in the year 1852, and the bulk of the property which the testatrix disposed of by the will in question came to her from her deceased husband. This will bears date July 6, 1878, and a codicil thereto July 28, 1882. Both instruments were executed at Dresden, where the testatrix had resided for over thirty years prior to her death, and, relate to both real and personal property. The real estate is situated within this state, and the personal, consisting of bonds, stocks, and other securities, was all substantially under the control and management of the plaintiff, the testatrix receiving the rents and income thereof. The will was executed according to the laws of this state, and has been proved here, and the executors appointed resided here. The execution of the trusts and the management of the estate have devolved on the plaintiff, under certain provisions of the will framed for that purpose. The testatrix, after making certain specific bequests, disposed of the residuary estate in trust for the benefit of her children and grandchildren. The true meaning and construction of the trust provision for her daughter Emily has given rise to the present controversy, and that is the only question involved in the appeal. This provision is found in the third item of the will, and is in the following language: " Item Third. I direct my said executors to safely invest and keep invested one equal one-third part of my residuary estate, and to receive and collect the rents, issues, and profits thereof, and to apply the net income derived therefrom to the use of my daughter, Emily S. Lengnick, during her natural life. Upon her decease I direct that the principal of such share be paid over or transferred by my executors to her then living lawful issue, if any, and, if she leaves her surviving no such issue, I direct that the same be then added in equal parts or proportions to the principal of the several shares of my residuary estate hereinafter directed to be held in trust for my ten grandchildren hereinafter named. But if, at the decease of my daughter Emily, leaving her surviving no lawful issue, either of these ten grandchildren shall be deceased and there shall be living lawful issue of him or her, I direct that the part or proportion which would so be added to the share held in trust for such grandchild, if living, be then paid over or transferred by my executors to such issue (*per stirpes*). And, if either of my said ten grandchildren shall die before my daughter Emily, leaving no lawful issue who so survive her, I in that case direct that the part or proportion which would so be added to the share held in trust for such grandchild, if living, be paid over or transferred by my executors upon the decease of my said daughter to such of my said grandchildren as are then living, and to the then living lawful issue (taking *per stirpes*) of such of them as are then deceased." The record shows that Emily was married in the year 1857 to Carl Emil Lengnick, an officer in the Saxon army, with whom she lived until her death, on August 3, 1893. There were but two children of this marriage, both of whom predeceased the testatrix, dying in the year 1872. It will be seen by the clause of the will above quoted that a remainder was limited upon the life estate of Emily in favor of her " lawful issue," if any survived her, but, if not, then over to the other grandchildren of the testatrix for whose benefit trusts were created by other clauses of the will.

The courts below have determined that, since Emily died without descendants, the remainders limited upon her life estate devolve upon the other grandchildren in the proportions specified in the provision quoted. The correctness of this determination could hardly be questioned but for a peculiar state of facts existing when the will was made, and at the time of the death of the testatrix. It appears that in the year 1876 the defendant Olga Felicitas Heinicke, a niece of Emily's husband, was legally adopted by them in accordance with the law of the kingdom of Saxony, and taken into their family with all the rights conferred by such relation under the law of that country. The legal status conferred upon this adopted child by the law of the place will sufficiently appear from the following provisions of the Saxony Code, which, it is admitted, are based largely upon the doctrines of the civil law:

" Sec. 1787. The taking into the relation of children, adoption, can only take place by contract made or acknowledged in court and approved by the sovereign of the adopting party."

" Sec. 1797. The reciprocal legal relationship between an adopted child and the adopting party is the same as that between a child of the marriage and its parents, in so far as it is not otherwise provided in the contract of adoption."

" Sec. 1808. Children begotten during wedlock and born during the lifetime of their father are from their birth under the paternal power. The same is true of illegitimate children on the subsequent marriage of their parents, accompanied by a decree of legitimacy by the sovereign, and adopted children on the approval by the sovereign of their adoption, unless they stand in the relations which according to sections 1832 and 1833, would abolish the paternal power."

" Sec. 2044. Adopted children inherit from the adopting party the same as children of marriage, unless otherwise provided in the contract of adoption, subject to the restriction contained in section 2568."

" Sec. 2046. If before the death of the adopting party an adopted son dies leaving descendants born in wedlock, or an adopted daughter dies leaving descendants born in or out of wedlock, such descendants inherit the same share which their father or mother would have taken."

" Sec. 2567. Adopted children and their descendants have the same right to an obligatory share against the party adopting them as descendants of marriage, unless otherwise provided in the contract of adoption."

The articles of adoption and the royal decree approving the same appear in the record, and they contain nothing limiting or restricting in any way the rights conferred by the code upon the children by adoption. Subsequently, Emily and her husband took into their family two other nieces of the husband, who were cared for and treated as children, but were never legally adopted. They have been brought in as defendants in this action, but we do not understand that any serious claim to share in the estate in question has been or can be made in their behalf. But the learned counsel who has appeared for Olga has presented to the court her claim to the remainder, limited on the life estate of her parent by adoption, in a very learned and elaborate argument. It is not too much to say that his industry has explored practically every source of knowledge on the subject. The reasoning in support of his contention, and the collection of authorities to sustain it, has given to the question involved an interest beyond what it would seem to merit from first impressions. The proposition sought to be established is that Olga is the lawful issue of Emily, though not related to her by blood, and so entitled to take the remainder, under the terms of the will, in the trust share of her parent by adoption. The main postulate in support of this contention is that the legal status of an adopted child, acquired by the law of adoption, is by the law of comity recognized in every other jurisdiction where such status becomes material in determining the right to take property by will or inheritance. The authorities cited seem to give much support to this proposition, and, so far as it is involved in or material to this case, we need not question it. (*Miller* v. *Miller*, 91 N. Y. 315; *Ross* v. *Ross*, 129 Mass. 243; *Burrage* v. *Briggs*, 120 id. 103; *Buckley* v. *Frasier*, 153 id. 525; 27 N. E. 768; *Sewall* v. *Roberts*, 115 Mass. 262; *Tirrell* v. *Bacon* [C. C.] 3 Fed. 62; *Hartwell* v. *Tefft*, 19 R. I. 644; 35 Atl. 882; *Warren* v. *Prescott*, 84 Me. 483; 24 Atl. 948; 17 L. R. A. 435; *Patterson* v. *Browning*, 146 Ind. 160; 44 N. E. 993; *Markover* v. *Krauss*, 132 Ind. 294; 31 N. E. 1047; 17 L. R. A. 806; *Atchinson* v. *Atchinson's Ex'rs*, 89 Ky. 488; 12 S. W. 942; *In re Rowan's Estate*, 132 Pa. St. 299; 19 Atl. 82; *Humphries* v. *Davis*, 100 Ind. 274; *Power* v. *Hafley*, 85 Ky. 671; 4 S. W. 683; *Gray* v. *Holmes*, 57 Kan. 217; 45 Pac. 596;

Van Matre v. *Sankey,* 148 Ill. 536; 36 N. E. 628; 23 L. R. A. 665.)

It is said that the status of Olga must be determined by the statutes of Saxony, construed with reference to the doctrines of the civil law upon which they are based, and, thus construed, she has all the rights of a child born in wedlock. In the language of the civilians, being an agnate of the adopting parents, she has become a cognate of the members of the family, and so the conclusion is reached that she is, in law, not only the child of Emily, but the grandchild of the testatrix. If the will in question was to be construed according to the foreign law, or the civil law, the argument would doubtless be much stronger than it is, although even then the construction placed upon the Saxon Code by the aid of the civil law, which confers upon an adopted child the status of a child of the marriage, not only with respect to the adopting parents, but all the other members of the family as well, would be difficult to maintain, since there is no finding of fact that gives such construction to the words of the code, and foreign laws must be construed in the same light as facts.

But we do not consider it important to determine the precise status of this adopted child, since, in the view we are disposed to take of the case, it is not material whether she would be considered, under the law of the country of her adoption or under the civil law, to be the lawful issue of Emily or not. Whatever status was conferred upon her by the act of adoption was purely conventional. The meaning and intention of the testatrix in the use of the words " lawful issue " in her will must be ascertained by the application of the rules and principles sanctioned by the courts of this state in the construction and interpretation of wills. The will in question is not a foreign, but a domestic, will. The fact that the deceased resided in Saxony for over thirty years does not affect the legal character of the instrument by which she disposed of her property. The referee who tried the case found as a fact that the testatrix never changed, or intended to change, her domicile of origin, but that when she made the will, and up to the time of her death, her legal domicile was in the city of New York. This finding, unanimously affirmed in the court below, concludes us with respect to the domicile of the testatrix, and it is so well settled that the law of the domicile must prevail in the interpretation of wills that any discussion of that principle is unnecessary. (*Dupuy* v. *Wuriz,* 53 N. Y. 556; *Moohouse* v. *Lord,* 10 H. L. Cas. 283.) An inquiry in regard to the legal domicile of a party, involving, as it generally does, the intention to abandon one or acquire another, presents a question of fact to be determined upon all the circumstances of the particular case, and certainly this case is no exception to that rule. We must accept the finding of the referee upon that question, since the constitution and the statute so command, even if the facts and circumstances upon which the finding is based were not so satisfactory and persuasive as they appear to be. The words "lawful issue," when used in a domestic will, primarily and generally mean "descendants." *Palmer* v. *Horn,* 84 N. Y. 519; *Chwatal* v. *Schreiner,* 148 id. 683; 43 N. E. 166; *Palmer* v. *Dunham,* 125 N. Y. 68; 25 N. E. 1081; *Soper* v. *Brown,* 136 N. Y. 244; 32 N. E. 768; *Drake* v. *Drake,* 134 N. Y. 220; 32 N. E. 114; 17 L. R. A. 664; *Johnson* v. *Brasington,* 156 N. Y. 181; 50 N. E. 859.) Where there is nothing to the contrary to be found in the context of the instrument, or in extraneous facts proper to be considered, that is the sense in which they are presumed to be used in a will. The real question in this case is whether the testatrix used them in that sense or in some other sense. In giving construction to the words used by the testatrix in a domestic will, we cannot assume, without the clearest evidence, that she used the words "lawful issue" in the sense that they might possibly bear in the Code of Saxony, or that they might be understood by the Roman civilians. Therefore the question is not what was the precise status of Olga as an adopted child under the Saxon law or under the civil law, but what the testatrix meant when she devised the remainder to the "lawful issue" of Emily. We think that the context of the instrument shows quite clearly that she used these words in their primary and general sense, as including descendants, and not children by adoption.

The ten grandchildren of her own blood, for whose benefit she constituted the other two trusts in her will, represented two families, descendants of her husband, from whom the property came. They were the children of another daughter, still living, and of a son who died before the testatrix. It seems that the relations between this daughter and her mother were not friendly, and the only provision made for the former was in the form of an annuity, to which the share of her children was subject by the terms of the will. The grandchildren constituting these two families, ten in all, are carefully enumerated in the will by name as life beneficiaries of two-thirds of the residuary estate, with remainder to their lawful issue. The testatrix, when she made the will and codicil, knew of Olga's adoption, and of her relations to the family of Emily, the other daughter, and her husband. It is quite difficult, in view of these facts, to believe that, if the testatrix intended to make a gift to a child by adoption of a remainder in one-third of the estate, she would omit to mention her name in any part of the will, whereas she did name all her grandchildren by blood. If Olga was intended to be included in the words " lawful issue," she would take after the death of Emily, one-third of the residuary estate in fee, whereas each of the ten grandchildren by blood would take a life estate only in about one-fifteenth. In the distribution of her property by the testatrix, such a marked discrimination in favor of an adopted child of her daughter and son-in-law, who was in no way related to her by blood, and against her own descendants, would seem to call for some explanation, and none appears either upon the face of the will or in the surrounding circumstances. A construction of the will should not be favored that would impute to the testatrix an intention apparently so unjust and improbable. If there was any intention to make a gift to Olga of any part of the estate, it is reasonable to suppose that the testatrix would have mentioned her by name, as she did her grandchildren in blood. It would be an extreme and almost fanciful construction that would impute to her an intention to make a gift of such a large portion of her estate to one who occupied no other relation to her than that arising from the fact that she had been legally adopted by her son-in-law and his wife. The words " lawful issue," when applied to Olga, became so ambiguous, at least, that they could not have been used by the testatrix for the purpose of making a gift to her daughter's adopted child, without at the same time contemplating that they must create and be followed by litigation and discord in the settlement of the estate.

But there is another provision of the will which shows quite clearly that the testatrix could not have intended that the adopted child of Emily should take the remainder in her share. That provision is as follows: " Item Sixth. If my daughter Emily dies before me, I direct that the one-third part of my residuary estate directed to be held in trust for her by the preceding third item of my will be added to the other two shares of my residuary estate, so as that one-half of the one-third part or share shall be controlled and disposed of by the fourth and the other one-half thereof by the fifth item of this my will." In the fourth and fifth items of the will, above referred to, trusts are created in the remaining two shares of the estate for the benefit of the ten grandchildren already mentioned, and the sixth item above quoted provides that, in case Emily died before her mother, then her share should go, not to Emily's adopted child, but should be added to the shares of the ten grandchildren. It would be difficult to conceive of a clearer indication of the purpose of the testatrix to transmit the whole estate to her own descendants. The meaning and intention of the testatrix with respect to the remainder which was limited upon the life estate of Emily is not, we think, very difficult to perceive. She evidently had in mind what was quite possible, if not probable— that her daughter Emily might have another child, or other children, born to her before the will would take effect, in which event the remainder would vest in them, but, in default of such issue, then the other grandchildren, her own descendants, were to take. This is altogether the more reasonable construction to place upon the words " lawful issue " in her will, and this view is re-enforced by the settled rule of law which favors such an interpretation as will permit the estate to pass to those persons who are in the line of ancestral blood. (*Knowlton* v. *Atkins*, 134 N. Y. 313; 31 N. E. 914; *Wood* v. *Mitcham*, 92 N. Y. 375; *Quinn* v. *Hardenbrook*, 54 id. 83; *Scott* v. *Guernsey*, 48 id. 106; *Kelso* v. *Lorillard*, 85 id. 177; *Van Kleeck* v. *Dutch Church*, 20 Wend. 457.) Moreover, if Olga had been adopted under the statutes of this state, she would be precluded from taking anything under this will by the express words of the law regulating domestic relations (§ 64), and the same result would follow under the decisions of the courts in cases quite analogous. Under the language of the will, and the law governing its interpretation, the expression "lawful issue" denotes the offspring of Emily only. (*Barnes* v. *Greenzebach*, 1 Edw. Ch. 41; *Schafer* v. *Eneu*, 54 Pa. St. 304; *Wyeth* v. *Stone*, 144 Mass. 441; 11 N. E. 729.) We think that the judgment of the court below is right, and should be affirmed, with costs to all parties appearing who were awarded costs on the appeal below; to be paid out of that part of the residuary estate disposed of by the third item of the will. All concur, except MARTIN, J., not sitting.

Judgment affirmed.

NOTE.—WHAT LAW GOVERNS.

(a) As to real estate.
(b) As to personal property.
(c) Construction.
(d) Powers.
(e) Bequests to foreign corporations.

(a) **As to real estate.**—As to real estate the law of State where situated governs as to the capacity or incapacity of the testator the extent of his power of disposition, and the forms and solemnities necessary to give the will its due authority and effect. (Carpenter v. Bell, 96 Tenn. 294; 34 S. W. Rep. 209; Robertson v. Pickrell, 109 U. S. 608; 3 Sup. Rep. 407; Applegate v. Smith, 31 Mo. 166; Walton v. Hall, 66 Vt. 455, 461; 29 Atl. Rep. 803; Ford v. Ford, 70 Wis. 19; 33 N. W. Rep. 188; Otis v. Doty. 61 Iowa, 25; 15 N. W. Rep. 578; Richards v. Miller, 62 Ill. 418; Harrison v. Weatherby, 180 Ill. 418; 54 N. E. Rep. 237; Levy v. Levy, 33 N. Y. 97; White v. Howard, 46 id. 144; Knox v. Jones, 47 id. 389; Hobson v. Hale, 95 id. 589; Vogel v. Lehritter, 139 id. 223; 34 N. E. Rep. 914; United States v. Fox, 94 U. S. 320; Proctor v. Clark, 154 Mass. 45; 27 N. E. Rep. 673; Williams v. Kimball, 35 Fla. 49; 16 So. Rep. 783; De Puy v. Standard Mineral Co., 88 Me. 202; Penfield v. Tower, 1 N. D. 216; 46 N. W. 413.)

Land whether held as a chattel interest or for a freehold interest remains real estate. (Freke v. Lord Carbury. L. R. 16 Eq. Cas. 461.)

(b) **As to personal property.**—The validity of a bequest or disposition of personal property by will must be governed by the law of the testator's domicile at the time of his death and this includes not only the form and mode of the execution of the will, but also the lawful power and authority of the testator to make such disposition. and especially is this true where the testator's domicile at time of making his will continues to be same until time of his death. (Ford v. Ford, 70 Wis. 45; 33 N. W. Rep. 188; Fellows v. Miner, 119 Mass. 544; Harrison v. Nixon, 9 Pet. 483; Whitney v Dodge, 105 Cal. 192; 38 Pac. Rep. 636; Bloomer v. Bloomer, 2 Bradf. 339; Bascom v. Albertson, 34 N. Y. 584; Chamberlain v. Chamberlain, 43 id. 433; Wi'l of Booth, 127 id. 109; 27 N. E. Rep. 826; Cross v. United States Trust Co., 131 N. Y. 330; 30 N. E. Rep. 125; Damert v. Osborn, 140 N. Y. 30; 35 N. E. Rep. 407; and see on motion for reargument, 141 N. Y. 564; 35 N. E. Rep. 1088; Enohin v. Wylie, 10 H. L. Cas. 19; Bolling v. Bolling,

88 Va. 524; 14 S. E. Rep. 67; Penfield v. Tower, 1 N. D. 216; 46 N. W. Rep. 413; Crawford v. Thomas, 54 S. W. Rep. 197 [Ky.].)

The law of the testator's domicile controls as to the formal requisites essential to the validity of the will as a means of transmitting property, the capacity of the testator and the construction of the instrument. Personal property has no locality and therefore the law of the domicile of the owner governs its transmission either by last will and testament or by succession in case of intestacy. ALLEN, J. (Chamberlain v. Chamberlain, 43 N. Y. 424; cited and followed, Simonson v. Waller, 9 App. Div. 514; 41 N. Y. Supp. 662.)

The validity of the execution of a will of personal property depends upon the law of the place where the testator was domiciled at time of his death, not at time of execution of the will. (Dupuy v. Wurtz, 53 N. Y. 556.)

Whether a person dies intestate or not is determined by the law of the place where he has his domicile *at time of his death.* (Moultrie v. Hunt, 23 N. Y. 394; Enohin v. Wylie, 10 H. L. Cas. 1.)

In cases of intestacy under foreign wills, questions relating to the distribution of personal property must be determined according to the foreign law of the domicile of the intestate. (Simonson v. Waller, 9 App. Div. 503; 41 N. Y. Supp. 662.)

(c). **Construction.**—It is a general rule that the law of the testator's domicile governs the interpretation or construction of wills, which are supposed to speak the sense of the testator according to the received laws and usages, of the country where he is domiciled, by a sort of tacit reference, unless there is something in the language which repels or controls such a conclusion; and this rule applies to real estate so far as limited to ascertaining the intention of the testator from the language employed in the will. (Ford v. Ford, 70 Wis. 45; 33 N. W. Rep. 188; and see Harrison v. Nixon, 9 Pet. 483; Keith v. Eaton, 58 Kans. 732; 51 Pac. Rep. 271. Opinion in this case is valuable as tracing origin and reason of the rule. Richards v. Miller, 62 Ill. 418; Caulfield v. Sullivan, 85 N. Y. 154; Enohin v. Wylie, 10 H. L. Cas. 1.)

Construed according to intent of testator. (Lincoln v. Perry, 149 Mass. 368, 374; 21 N. E. Rep. 671; Codman v. Krell, 152 Mass. 218; 25 N. E. Rep. 90.)

(d) **Powers.**—Executor under power in a will may convey land situate in another state; and may be compelled by a court of equity having jurisdiction, of his person. (Newton v. Bronson, 13 N. Y. 587.)

As to a power executed by will in another State, it is sufficient if it complies with laws of state where situated. (Sewall v. Wilmer, 132 Mass. 131.)

As to personalty the question whether the power has been exercised and the appointment made must be decided according to the law of the domicile of the *donor* of the power. (Cotting v. De Sartiges, 17 R. I. 668; 24 Atl. Rep. 530.)

And as to execution and construction of power see (Olivet v. Whitworth, 82 Md. 258; 33 Atl. Rep. 723.)

Where land has been sold by an executor in a foreign country under a power of sale in the will, valid under the laws of such country, such laws have no application to the proceeds of sale. (Re Piercy [1895], 1 Ch. 83.)

A person where domicile is in a foreign country may by will execute a power invalid in such country, yet operative in another where the trust fund or personalty is. (Goods of Huber [1896], Prob. 209.)

But where a domiciled Englishman executes by will a general power of appointment created by a *Scotch* will, the case is governed by the law of Scotland, and consequently the appointor does not thereby make the appointed property part of his general estate so as to be assests for creditors. (Re Bald [1897], 66 L. J. Ch. 524.)

(e) **Bequests to foreign corporations.**—Where laws of a state do not prohibit a testamentary bequest to a foreign municipality, the ability to take depends upon the law of the legatee's domicile. (Matter of Huss, 126 N. Y. 537; 27 N. E. Rep. 784.)

And so where bequest is of a charitable nature. (Hope v. Brewer, 136 N. Y. 126; 32 N. E. Rep. 558.)

DOBLER et al. vs. STROBEL.

[Supreme Court of North Dakota, November 21, 1899; 81 N. W. Rep. 37.]

ADMINISTRATOR—ACCOUNTING.

A party who has been appointed as administrator of an estate, and received letters of administration therein, and has seized and misappropriated and dissipated the property of the estate, cannot evade an accounting upon the ground of the nullity of his appointment.
(Syllabus by the Court.)

APPEAL from District Court, McIntosh county; W. S. LAUDER, Judge.

Action by Gottlieb Dobler and David Dobler, by A. W. Clyde, special guardian, against Gottlieb Strobel. Judgment for plaintiffs. Defendant appeals.
Affirmed.

L. T. Boucher, for appellant.

A. W. Clyde, for respondents.

BARTHOLOMEW, C. J.—The facts upon which the questions of law here involved rest are as follows: On November 24, 1897, Matthias Dobler died intestate in McIntosh county, in this state. That he left surviving him, and as his only heirs at law, two sons, —Gottlieb Dobler, aged fourteen years, and David Dobler, aged ten years,—the respondents herein. That on December 18, 1897, the petition of Jakob Dobler was presented to the county judge of said county, which petition set forth the death of said Matthias Dobler, and named the respondents as his children, and stated that petitioner was a brother of deceased, and that deceased left certain specified personal property and certain real estate, and asking the appointment of Gottlieb Strobel as administrator of said estate. Upon the same day the bond of Gottlieb Strobel as such administrator was filed and approved, and letters of administration were issued to him by the said county judge, and his oath of office filed, and appraisers were appointed and filed their oaths of office. Three days later, to wit, on December 21, 1897, an inventory and appraisement of the personal property was filed, and on the following day the administrator filed an application for leave to sell the personal property. The record is then silent until November 9, 1898, when A. W. Clyde filed in said County Court an application to be appointed special guardian for Gottlieb and David Dobler, alleging that he was a friend of said minors, and that they had no general or special guardian, and that he desired to commence a special proceeding before said court against said administrator, as such special guardian, upon a petition, a copy of which was annexed to, and formed a part of, the application. The sufficiency of such petition is not questioned. After setting forth the appointment of said administrator in manner and time as before stated, and without any citations to or appearance upon the part of said minors, the petition continues: "That nevertheless said Gottlieb Strobel assumed the duties of administrator of said estate, and took possession of the property, and assumed to act as such administrator in the management and settlement of the estate, and in so doing has wrongfully misappropriated the personal property belonging to the deceased at the time of his death, the same being property exempt by law from the payment of his debts, which misappropriation he has made by omitting and neglecting to have the exempt personal property aforesaid appraised and set apart as

such to the use and benefit of your petitioners, and by wrongfully
selling and disposing of the same without authority of law or the
order of the County Court, and by wrongfully misapplying the
same, or the proceeds thereof, to divers persons claiming or pretending to be creditors of said deceased." And the prayer of the
petition is as follows: " Petitioners pray that said Gottlieb Strobel
may be required to render a full account of all his doings as such
administrator, and that his account may be fully settled by the
court, and that thereupon his letters of administration may be revoked; that a successor may be appointed to complete the administration of the estate;, and that he be ordered and directed to pay
over to his successor all money and property for which he is justly
accountable, as determined by the court, to the end that the rights
of your petitioners may be duly observed; and for such other and
further relief as may be just and proper." The application was
granted when presented, and the special guardian was authorized
to verify and file the petition; and upon the same day a citation
was issued to the administrator, returnable December 5, 1898,
requiring him to appear and answer the petition. On the return
day both parties appeared, and the administrator asked for further time, to enable him to employ an attorney and make answer.
The time was allowed, and the hearing adjourned to December
10, 1898. Upon that day the administrator failed to appear,
whereupon the petitioners, by their special guardian, asked that he
be adjudged in default for want of an appearance and answer, and
that the court proceed with the hearing upon the petition. The
court denied this request, and upon its own motion entered an
order setting aside and canceling, and declaring null and void, all
proceedings theretofore had in the matter of said estate, including
the appointment of the administrator and the appointment of the
special guardian. The court based its action upon the ground
that its record and the petition of the minor heirs showed that the
court never acquired jurisdiction to act in the matter. The petitioners appealed from such order to the District Court, and in that
court the order of the County Court was reversed and set aside
in toto. From the order of the District Court the administrator
appeals to this court.

The questions for decision upon these facts are simple: Was
the action of the County Court in appointing the administrator

regular or irregular, or absolutely void? And, in taking possession of the estate, did the appellant act as an administrator *de jure,* or as an administrator *de facto,* or as a bald trespasser? The learned District Court appears to have entertained but little sympathy for the position of the administrator in this case. We adopt the following language found in the opinion of that court: " The respondent was appointed administrator of this estate. He was duly commissioned by the court to take into his possession, all and singular, the property thereunto belonging. This he did, and did it under the mandate of the County Court. On the face of the record, it appears that most of the property was exempt to the two minor heirs. The petition of the special guardian, asking for an accounting, alleges under oath that the property of the estate has been willfully and unlawfully diverted from the purpose to which the law assigns it; that it has been disposed of without authority of law, and, unless protected by the court, the minor heirs will be defrauded of their just rights. If the position taken by the County Court is correct, there has been no administrator, no bond, and no case in the County Court; and even though all the property belonging ultimately to the minor heirs has been seized and disposed of, and this under the orders of the County Court, these same heirs are without remedy, except eventually in a personal action against the respondent, who, for aught that appears, is insolvent. To assume that such is the law is, in my opinion, a reproach upon the administration of justice. Helpless children cannot be juggled out of their rights by any such legal legerdemain. The County Court seems to have confounded jurisdiction of the case; that is, of the property of the estate, the *res,* and jurisdiction of the persons interested. Section 6183, Rev. Codes, provides that the County Court obtains jurisdiction of the case by the existence of certain facts, and the filing the petition setting forth such facts, and then provides how jurisdiction of the interested persons may be obtained. The distinction between jurisdict'on of the subject-matter and jurisdiction of the person is as clearly drawn in Probate Court as in any other. The original petition, while confessedly not artistically drawn, was clearly sufficient to give the county judge jurisdiction of the case. This being so. the proceedings in reference to appointment of an administrator, the property of the estate, etc., were not null and void. Doubtless, upon application of the heirs, the respondent would have been restrained from acting further, and removed, because of the irregularity of his appointment; but, until such proceedings were had, respondent would continue to be in fact and in law administrator, and obliged to account when called upon." It will be conceded that the appointment of appellant was extremely irregular, and must have been set aside upon application of any party entitled to attack it. Here it is the administrator himself who is seeking to sustain the order declaring the appointment void on the ground of want of jurisdiction in the court making the appointment. In the case of *Culver* v. *Hardenbergh* (37 Minn. 225; 33 N. W. 792), where the acts of an administrator were being attacked by interested parties on the ground that his appointment was void, the court said that the authorities were not agreed as to whether there might or might not be an administrator *de facto*. But the court also said that it could see no reason why there might not be an administrator *de facto* as well as a probate judge *de facto*. The point was not decided, but the court clearly inclined to the affirmative of the proposition. In *Succession of Dougart* (30 La. Ann. 268), the court said: "As to the illegality of the appointment of the executrix, it is only necessary to say that the question cannot be raised in this indirect and collateral way. Whether legally or illegally done, she was appointed and qualified, and must be treated as the lawful executrix until her appointment is revoked in a direct action." In *Cloutier* v. *Lemee* (33 La. Ann. 305), the court said: "Inquiries touching the legality of defendant's appointment are irrelevant. While actually exercising the office, he must perform its duties, and the illegality of his appointment will not vitiate his acts." In *Succession of Robertson* (49 La. Ann. 80; 21 South. 197), the court cited the foregoing and many other authorities, and said: "Adhering to this line of authority, we are of opinion that the acts of the qualified and acting executrix must be recognized as valid, and that the subsequent nullity of her appointment would not vitiate them." All these were cases where parties interested in the estate were attacking appointments made by the Probate Court. In *Appeal of Ela* ([N. H.] 38 Atl. 501), which was a case where an administrator sought to avoid an accounting upon the ground that his appointment was a nullity, the court said: "Another consideration fatally adverse to the plaintiff is that a party cannot set up the invalidity of a decree under which he has obtained and holds property as a defense to an accounting for that property. It is useless to argue such a self-evident proposition. What is clearly apparent need not be proved." That meets the precise question here involved. To permit this appellant, who, on the record before us, and pursuant to the order and authority of the County Court, has taken the property of this estate, belonging to these minor heirs, and misappropriated and dissipated the same, to entirely escape an accounting on the ground that his appointment was a nullity, would be such a manifest outrage upon justice that it requires neither authority nor discussion to show that it cannot be done. The order of the District Court is in all things affirmed.

All concur.

PECK *vs.* AGNEW *et al.*

[Supreme Court of California, November 9, 1899; 126 Cal. 607; 59 Pac. Rep. 125.]

DISMISSAL—ABATEMENT—NOTICE OF APPEAL.

1. Where, in an action, no summons is served, and part of the defendants appear by demurrer, the court has no jurisdiction, under section 581, Code Civ. Proc., providing that, if appearance has been made by defendants within three years, such action may be prosecuted as if summons had been issued and served, to dismiss such action, on motion of defendants, as to those defendants who demurred.

2. While the issue whether certain lands belonged to the estate of plaintiff's intestate is pending and undetermined, the action does not abate by reason of the revocation of the special letters of administration granted to the plaintiff.

3. Where plaintiff, as special administratrix, was served with a motion to dismiss the action, she has the right to appeal from the judgment against her on such motion, although her special letters had been revoked prior to taking the appeal.

4. Service of a copy of the notice of appeal instead of the original notice, is sufficient.

5. It is not necessary to serve a notice of appeal upon defendants, who were not served with summons and who did not appear.

DEPARTMENT I. Appeal from Superior Court, Santa Cruz county.

Action by M. Elizabeth Peck, as special administratrix, against H Agnew and others. From an order allowing defendants' motion to dismiss the action, plaintiff appeals. Motion to dismiss appeal denied.

Modified.

J. F. Utter, J. J. Scrivner, and *A. H. Cohen,* for appellant,

Jeter & McKinney and *Chas. B. Younger,* for respondents.

HARRISON, J.—This action was commenced in the Superior Court, December 12, 1895, against a number of defendants, by the plaintiff, as special administratrix of the estate of Martina Castro Depeaux, deceased, for the purpose of having it declared that they have no interest in or title to the land described in the complaint, and that it belonged to the estate of her intestate, and that she recover possession thereof. It does not appear from the record, except inferentially, whether a summons was ever issued upon the complaint, or that it was ever served upon either of the defendants, but within ten days after the commencement of the action a demurrer was filed on behalf of several of the defendants. It does not appear that any action has been taken by the court upon this demurrer. December 19, 1898, a motion was made on behalf of seven of the defendants named in the complaint who had not demurred thereto to set aside the summons and the service thereof, and to dismiss the action, upon the ground, among others, that the summons had not been returned within three years from the commencement of the action. At the hearing the court granted their motion and dismissed the action, and the plaintiff has appealed therefrom.

The appellant does not controvert the right of the persons who made the motion to have the action dismissed as to them, nor does she object to the action of the court, so far as it may be limited to them. At the time the motion was granted she excepted thereto " upon the ground that said court had no jurisdiction to dismiss said action, except as to the defendants who had not or who did not appear in said action by the demurrers," and she now contends that to the extent that the dismissal purports to embrace those who had appeared in the action it was erroneous, and that in this respect the judgment should be modified.

With this contention of the appellant we agree. The failure of the plaintiff to return the summons did not affect her right to continue the action against those defendants who had demurred to the complaint. It is declared in the concluding sentence of section 581, Code Civ. Proc., that "all such actions may be prosecuted if appearance has been made by the defendant or defendants within said three years, in the same manner as if summons had been issued and served." This provision does not prevent a dismissal, when some of the defendants have appeared, as to those who have not appeared, nor does it require an appearance by all of the defendants in order to deprive the court of all power of dismissal, but it is to be construed as authorizing a dismissal as to those defendants who have not appeared, and a prosecution of the action against those who have made such appearance whenever the court would be authorized to render a judgment against them in the absence of the other defendants. The defendants who demurred were entitled to have the issue presented by their demurrer passed upon by the court, and had chosen attorneys for that purpose, as well as to represent them in all proceedings that might be had in the action. It was not competent for the court to dismiss them out of the action upon the motion of other defendants, with whom they were in no wise connected. Nor did the fact that the motion was made by the same attorneys that represented them in the demurrer affect their rights. The motion was made on behalf only of defendants who had not demurred,—seven in number,—and without any notice to the demurrants.

Whether the property described in the complaint belonged to the estate of the decedent, was an issue to be tried in the case, and could not be determined upon a motion to dismiss the action. While this issue was pending and undetermined, the action did not abate by reason of the revocation of the special letters that had been granted to the appellant.

A motion to dismiss the appeal was made herein upon the ground that at the time of taking the appeal the appellant had ceased to be the special administratrix of the estate, and her powers as such had been revoked, and she was therefore not authorized to take an appeal. It is a sufficient answer to this motion to say that the respondents recognized her right to represent the estate by serving their motion for a dismissal of the action upon her. The orders which they now invoke as a reason why she had no right of appeal were made long prior to such service, and no change has taken place in her relation to the estate since the action of the court upon their motion.   If the Superior Court was authorized to entertain their motion and render judgment against her, she is authorized to seek a reversal of that judgment in this court.

The further ground urge$_d$ for a dismissal of the appeal, viz. that the notice of appeal has not been served upon the respondents, is contradicted by the transcript, in which there is printed a copy of an affidavit of this service.   The correctness of the affidavit, as printed in the transcript, is not disputed, and, from the nature of the act, proof of such service would not be a part of the judgment roll.   The objection to the statement therein that a " copy " of the notice of appeal, rather than the original, was served upon the respondents, is without merit.

It was not necessary to serve the notice of appeal upon the defendants who had not appeared.   They were not parties to the proceedings in the Superior Court, and their interest in the action will not be injuriously affected by a modification of the judgment as asked by the appellant.   (*Clarke* v. *Mohr* [Cal.], 58 Pac. 176.) The motion to dismiss the appeal is denied.   The Superior Court is directed to modify its judgment in accordance with the views herein.

We concur: GAROUTTE, VAN DYKE, JJ.

MEDILL *et al. vs.* SNYDER *et al.*

[Supreme Court of Kansas, November 11, 1899; 61 Kans. 15; 58 Pac. Rep. 962,]

WILLS—CONTEST—ESTOPPEL—ACCEPTANCE OF BENEFITS—EVIDENCE—FINDINGS—INSANITY—HARMLESS ERROR—QUESTIONS OF FACT.

1. The general rule is that one who receives and retains property and benefits under a will thereby recognizes its validity, and is estopped to deny or contest it; but this rule does not apply where such person acted

in ignorance of the facts showing invalidity, and of her rights in the premises.

2. In such case if, when a legatee learns the facts of invalidity as to her rights, she returns or offers to return what has been received under the will, she may institute a proceeding to set the will aside, and assert her rights in the estate under the law.

3. In an action to set aside a will the court may call a jury to aid it in determining disputed questions of fact, but it is optional with the court whether it will adopt the findings of the jury, or ignore them, and make findings of its own. When the court gives independent consideration to the evidence, and makes its own findings of fact, upon which judgment is rendered, errors committed by the jury become immaterial.

4. A hypothetical question may be based upon any assumption of facts which the testimony tends to prove, and it is *held* that there was evidence to sustain the assumed facts in the questions asked.

5. There may be an insane delusion although the belief entertained is not, in the nature of things, a physical impossibility; but, if such belief is entertained against all evidence and probability, and after argument to the contrary, it affords grounds for inferring that the person entertaining it labors under an insane delusion.

6. The credibility of witnesses and the probative force of the facts as to testamentary incapacity were for the determination of the trial court, and, it appearing that there is legal evidence to support the findings, these matters are not open for further consideration.

(Syllabus by the court.)

ERROR from District Court, Leavenworth county; LOUIS A. MYERS, Judge.

Action by E. W. Snyder, administrator, and others, against Sherman Medill and others, to set aside a will. Judgment for plaintiffs, and defendants bring error.

Affirmed.

Waggener, Horton & Orr, A. H. Horton, O. C. Phillips, and *Wm. Dill*, for plaintiffs in error.

Wm. C. Hook, John H. Atwood, and *James A. Reed*, for defendants in error.

JOHNSTON, J.—On the 3d day of July, 1894, James Medill died in Leavenworth, having, on the 12th of the previous month, made a will devising to his family an estate the estimated value of which was $80,000. He gave to his daughter, Nana Medill, the home

in Leavenworth, and the furniture therein, and directed that $15,-
000 of mortgages and securities should be set aside for her use,
the income of which should be paid to her semiannually during her
life, the fund to be managed by the son, Sherman Medill, who was
made executor.   The day before his death a codicil to the will
was executed by him, adding $2,000 to the fund set aside for Nana,
and swelling it to the sum of $17,000.   The will provided that at
her death the trust fund should go to the heirs of her body, if any,
and, if there were none, it should be paid to the heirs of Sherman
Medill.   The will also set apart $5,000, the income of which
should be paid to Fairy M. Hollingsworth, the child of a deceased
daughter of the testator, and the management of the same was
also placed in Sherman Medill, and it was provided that, if her
marriage should be unsatisfactory to him, or she should die, the
fund or property should go absolutely to, and become the property
of, Sherman Medill.   The sum of $3,000 was devised to a son of
Sherman Medill, and all the residue of the estate was devised absolutely to Sherman Medill.   The will was probated on July 6,
1894, and in the succeeding month $17,000 in value of securities
were set apart for the use of Nana, and were approved and accepted by her.   On September 5, 1895, Nana brought this action,
alleging that her father was not of a sound and disposing mind
when the will and codicil were executed, and that in the execution he was subjected to undue and improper influences by Sherman Medill, to whom most of the estate was devised; and for these
reasons she asked that the will be set aside.   Fairy M. Hollingsworth appeared by her guardian, and in her answer attacked the
will, alleging that when it was made the testator did not have sufficient mental capacity to execute a will, and, further, that undue
influence was exerted upon him.   Sherman Medill denied these .
averments, and pleaded that Nana, having selected certain securities in pursuance of the will, and having in writing accepted them,
as well as other benefits under the will, is estopped to maintain an
action to contest and set it aside.   A jury was called to aid the
court, and on the testimony produced the jury found against
Sherman Medill, and returned the following special findings of
fact: " (1) Was the testator, James Medill, of sound mind and
memory at the time he executed the will in question? Answer.
No. (2) Was the testator, James Medill, of sound mind and

memory at the time he executed the codicil to the will in question? Ans. No. (3) Was the execution of the will in controversy due to and the result of undue influence exerted upon the testator? Ans. Yes. (4) When the plaintiff Nana Medill received property and money from her father's estate under the provisions of the will in question, did she do so in ignorance of her rights, and without having knowledge of, or being advised of, the facts urged by her as grounds for setting aside the said will? Ans. Yes." The court thereupon approved, ratified, and confirmed the verdict and findings of the jury, and on its own motion, and from the evidence adduced in the cause, made its findings of fact as follows: " First. That at the time of the signing of the will in question the testator, James Medill, was not of sound mind and memory. Second. That at the time of the signing of the codicil to the will in question the testator, James Medill, was not of sound mind and memory. Third. When the plaintiff Nana Medill received property and money from her father's estate under the provisions of the will and codicil in question in this cause, she did so in ignorance of her rights, and without having knowledge of, or being advised of, the facts urged by her as grounds for setting aside the said will and codicil, and that she did not have such knowledge and was not so advised until shortly before the commencement of this action". The court thereupon entered a judgment vacating and annulling the will, and directing that the estate should be administered as though James Medill had died intestate.

The first point contended for is that Nana Medill, having received and retained property under the will, has recognized its validity, and is estopped to deny it. That is conceded to be the general doctrine, but it can have no application if she acted in ignorance of the facts and her rights in the premises. It is true, she did not institute a contest until more than a year after her father's death, and that during that time she proceeded as though the will was valid, accepting and using the property and funds set apart for her as the will provided. Her testimony tended to show, however, that she did not learn the important facts relied upon to show testamentary incapacity, nor what her rights were, until about the time the action was begun. She was acquainted with some of the circumstances cited to show unsoundness of mind, but there is testimony that many of the controlling facts indicating incapacity were unknown to her, and that she did not understand or learn that she could attack the will upon such grounds until about the time that action was taken. As soon as she learned the facts, and understood her rights, she challenged the validity of the will, and tendered back what she had already received under the will. It would seem from the testimony that her conduct did not induce a change of position by Sherman Medill, nor operate as a fraud upon him, and it cannot if all that she received under the will is restored to the estate. This is an essential element of equitable estoppel. *In Re Peaslee's Will* (73 Hun, 113; 25 N. Y. Supp. 940), it was held that " where a legatee named in a will is paid a portion of her legacy by the executors therein, she is not in a situation to attack the will until she puts the parties in a position where, whatever the result may be, no one can be the loser because of the payment originally made to her." Here the legatee who accepted the benefits has offered to restore what was received, and, as we have seen, no one can be prejudiced or be the loser by her conduct. *Hamblett* v. *Hamblett*, (6 N. H. 333), decides that a party who has received a legacy under a will cannot be permitted to contest the validity of such will without repaying the amount of the legacy or bringing the money into court. *Holt* v. *Rice* (54 N. H. 402), holds that the receipt of a legacy is, to a certain extent, an affirmance of the will, but that it is not an absolute bar to an action to annul the same. A party desiring to attack the will should make restitution of the money or benefits received, when the contest may proceed. The Supreme Court of Pennsylvania holds that an election in pais to take under a will should be intelligently made, and should be unambiguous and positive in its character to amount to an estoppel. " The rule seems to be that a legatee who has received his legacy, and afterward concludes to contest the will, may return the legacy of the executors, and so relieve himself from the operation of the general rule that forbids him to take under the will that which the testator gave him, and at the same time deny its validity as to others." (*In re Miller's Estate,* 159 Pa. St. 562; 28 Atl. 441.) The offer of restoration made by Nana Medill in her pleading was sufficient in a case of this character. (*Thayer* v. *Knote,* 59 Kan. 181; 52 Pac. 433.) We think that she ought not to be concluded if she did not comprehend her rights, nor understand the facts bearing upon the invalidity of the will; and the trial court correctly instructed the jury that her acceptance of benefits would not conclude her if they found " from the evidence that such act was done in ignorance of her rights, and without having knowledge of, or being advised of, the facts urged by her as grounds for setting aside the will."

A vigorous attack is made upon the finding that James Medill was not of a sound and disposing mind when the will was executed. We find much in the testimony strongly tending to show that he was sane and capable until shortly before his death, and, if we were the triors of the fact, we might hesitate, on the testimony in the record, to find testamentary incapacity. However, many circumstances were shown, and much expert and other evidence produced, going to show unsoundness of mind, and tending to sustain the findings. The credibility of witnesses and the probative force of the facts were for the trial court, and, it appearing that there was legal evidence to support the finding, the question is not open to further consideration.

There is very little testimony which tends to show that the execution of the will was the result of undue influence exerted upon the testator, but, as the judgment of the court rests on testamentary incapacity alone, the point of insufficiency of evidence to establish undue influence is no longer material. While the jury found undue influence, the court, acting independently upon the testimony, and probably not being satisfied with the testimony offered to support that ground, did not find that there was undue influence. The action of the court in calling the jury was discretionary. For its own convenience, or to satisfy its conscience, it can refer questions of fact to the jury; but the court is not bound by the findings made, and may ultimately determine for itself all the questions in the case. It may accept and adopt the findings of the jury in whole or in part, or it may ignore them, and, upon independent consideration of the evidence, make findings of its own; and, when the latter course is pursued, the mistakes of the jury may be of little consequence. If the court had tried the case as though a jury trial was a matter of right, and had accepted and adopted as its own the findings of the jury without giving independent consideration to the facts, the errors of the jury might be worthy of consideration as grounds of reversal. (*Vickers* v. *Range Co.*, 60 Kan. 598; 57 Pac. 517.) It is contended that the court in this instance adopted the findings of the jury, and that, therefore, the errors committed by the jury are available in this court. The record shows that, after the general and special findings of the jury were returned, the court approved and ratified them, but it is clear from what followed that the court was unwilling to adopt or make them its own. The court afterwards, on its own motion, took up the entire case, and upon the evidence made independent findings, upon which its judgment is based. The finding as to testamentary incapacity at the time the will was executed is the same as that of the jury, while that as to undue influence was entirely omitted, and the finding that Nana Medill accepted benefits in ignorance of her rights differs from the one made by the jury on that subject, and enlarges it by the finding that she did not have such knowledge, and was not so advised, until shortly before the commencement of the action. The action of the court in determining the facts from the evidence for itself renders the objections to the findings made by the jury unimportant, as well as several other objections urged against rulings made in presenting the case to the jury. (*Rich* v. *Bowker*, 25 Kan. 7; *Delaney* v. *City of Salina*, 34 id. 532; 9 Pac. 271; *Stickel* v. *Bender*, 37 Kan. 457; 15 Pac. 580; *Franks* v. *Jones*, 39 Kan. 236; 17 Pac. 663; *Hudson* v. *Hughan*, 56 Kan. 152; 42 Pac. 701; *Caldwell* v. *Brown*, 56 Kan. 566; 44 Pac. 10.) It disposes of the point that the finding of testamentary incapacity negatives the finding of undue influence. We are not prepared to assent to the proposition that the two issues were irreconcilably inconsistent, but, however that may be, there is no such inconsistency where the judgment annulling the will rests on the ground of testamentary incapacity alone.

We find nothing substantial in the objection to the rulings on evidence. A number of extended hypothetical questions were submitted to expert witnesses, and it is contended that they did not correctly state the facts brought out in the evidence. Our examination of the record leads us to the opinion that they were within the range of the testimony offered by the parties attacking the will. While the proof in support of some of the facts was slight, " a hypothetical question may be based upon any assumption of facts which the testimony tends to prove according to the theory of the examining counsel." (8 Am. & Eng. Enc. Pl. & Prac. 757.) There appears to have been some evidence sustaining the assumed facts, and we cannot say that the questions were objectionab!e in form.

Complaint is made of an instruction to the effect that the testator might be capable of transacting the ordinary business affairs of life, and sane on other matters, but that, if the will was influenced, and the direct offspring of an unfounded and insane delusion, it could not be sustained. Plaintiff in error says that a " delusion is a belief in something impossible in the nature of things or the circumstances of the case," and it is argued that supposed relations and a prospective marriage between Nana and her brother-in-law, who was greatly disliked by the testator, were not impossible. While the definition given may be found in the books, it is too narrow a conception of the term to say that it is a belief in something that is impossible. (1 Bouv. Law Dict. 537; Whart. Cr. Law, 37.) The things believed may not exist, and there may be no grounds whatever for the belief, and yet their existence may not be a physical impossibility. An instance cited is the persistent and wholly unfounded notion that a wife is guilty of adultery. Another example is where a parent, without the slightest pretense or color of reason, unjustly persists in attributing to a daughter a gross vice, and uses her with uniform unkindness. Another is where a person without cause or reason insists that those who had administered medicine to him in sickness had given him poison. These things are not physical impossibilities, but, if such a belief is entertained against all evidence and probability, and after argument to the contrary, it would afford grounds for inferring that the person entertaining it labored under an insane delusion. We think the instructions cannot be regarded as erroneous, and, since the court made its own findings of fact from the evidence, the instruction is not of great consequence. We find nothing in the admission of evidence or in the instructions of the jury that furnishes ground for reversal, nor is there anything substantial in the objections that there was misconduct of the prevailing parties and by the jury. The important questions in the case arise upon the facts, and, these having been determined in favor of the defendants in error upon sufficient evidence, we are constrained to affirm the judgment.

All the justices concurring.

Note.—DELUSIONS.

(a) Will must be result of delusion.
(b) Eccentricities and peculiarities.
(c) Concerning relations, husband, wife, children—Cases holding delusion or evidence of it.
(d) Same—No delusion.
(e) Spiritualism or witchcraft, cases holding delusion or evidence of it.
(f) Same—No delusion.
(g) Miscellaneous illustrative cases holding no delusion.

(a) **Will must be result of the delusion.**—Existence of delusions do not destroy testamentary capacity unless they are such as dictate or substantially affect the provisions of the will itself. (Shreiner v. Shreiner, 178 Pa. St. 60; 35 Atl. Rep. 974; Will of Cole, 49 Wis. 179; 5 N. W. Rep. 346; Redfield's Estate, 116 Cal. 637; 48 Pac. Rep. 794; Peninsular Trust Co. v. Barker, 116 Mich. 333; 74 N. W. Rep. 509; Potter v. Jones, 20 Ore. 239; 25 Pac. Rep. 769; Taylor v. Trich, 165 Pa. St. 586; 30 Atl. Rep. 1053; Hemingway's Estate, 195 Pa. St. 291; 45 Atl. Rep. 726; Bonard's Will, 16 Abb. Pr. N. S. 128; Dobie v. Armstrong, 160 N. Y. 584; 55 N. E. Rep. 302; Will of White, 121 N. Y. 406; 24 N. E. Rep. 935; Riggs v. American Tract Society, 95 N. Y. 503; Matter of Iredale, 53 App. Div. 51; 65 N. Y. Supp. 533; Smee v. Smee, L. R. 5 P. D. 84; Banks v. Goodfellow, L. R. 5 Q. B. 549; cited and followed by Lord Coleridge, C. J., in Murfett v. Smith, L. R. 12 P. D. 116.)

There is a distinction between general insanity and the existence of an insane delusion. (Taylor v. Trich, *supra*.)

Only when false beliefs are such as a reasonable man would not under the circumstances entertain, that they become (evidence of) insane delusions. (Appeal of Kimberley, 68 Conn. 428; 36 Atl. Rep. 847.)

(b) **Eccentricities and peculiarities.**—Eccentricities or peculiarities or radical or extreme notions or opinions upon religion, colleges, education or masonry and secret societies may be evidence of delusion but do not establish same necessarily. (American Bible Society v. Price, 115 Ill. 623; 5 N. E. Rep. 126.)

That eccentric or peculiar acts or conduct do not constitute insane delusion, see Pilkington v. Gray ([1899] A. C. 401); Schneider v. Manning (121 Ill. 376; 12 N. E. Rep. 267); Fulbright v. Perry Co. (145 Mo. 432; 46 S. W. Rep. 955); Kelly v. Miller (39 Miss. 17).

(c) **Concerning relations, husband, wife, children—Cases holding delusion or evidence of it.**—Conduct and motives of daughter. (Ballantine v. Proudfoot, 62 Wis. 216; 22 N. W. Rep. 392.)

Belief that wife and children had conspired to injure him without foundation in fact. '(Riggs v. American Tract Society, 95 N. Y. 503.)

Evidence of strong dislike and bitter feeling on testator's part towards the father of contestants. (Cotton v. Ulmer, 45 Ala. 378.)

Belief that his children were his enemies conspiring to rob him of his property. (Matter of Dorman, 5 Dem. 112.)

Prejudice and hostility against an adopted son when the will was the direct offspring of such a delusion. (Merrill v. Rolston, 5 Redf. 220.)

And so in case of a niece. (Miller v. White, id. 320.)

Insane delusion in respect to a child. (See Segur's Will. 44 Atl. Rep. 342 [Vt.].)

Hostility and aversion to those who are bound to one by tie of kindred and blood, may be evidence of delusion. (Brown v. Ward, 53 Md. 376; American Bible Society v. Price, 115 Ill. 623; 5 N. E. Rep. 126; Thomas v. Carter, 170 Pa. St. 272; 33 Atl. Rep. 31.)

Testator's belief that principal legatee was his son when testator and wife both being white the son showed peculiar marks of a negro—color that of a mulatto and his hair woolly. (Florey v. Florey, 24 Ala. 241.)

Belief that wife and children had entered into a conspiracy, had attempted to poison him, and send him to an asylum. (Matter of Kahn, 1 Connoly, 510; 5 N. Y. Supp. 556.) But in this case the fact of insanity was established by murder of his wife and attempted suicide. (Id.)

Where a testator disinherits a daughter upon the belief that she is a bad woman, or that she is not his own offspring, or a son upon the belief that he is a drunkard, or his grandchildren upon the belief that their father (the testator's son-in-law) has threatened to kill him, and it appears that there is no foundation in fact for such beliefs, and that they are mere delusions, the will is void, notwithstanding testator was sane upon all other subjects and fully competent to manage his business affairs. (Rivard v. Rivard, 109 Mich. 98; 66 N. W. Rep. 681; and see Cotton v. Ulmer, 45 Ala. 378.)

Unfounded and absurd belief that his wife in her old age had violated her marriage vows; and an insane belief that the natural objects of testator's bounty had long been conspiring against his happiness and life. (Seamen's Friend Society v. Hopper, 33 N. Y. 619.)

In Dew v. Clark (3 Add. 79), is a lengthy analysis of the evidence and subject of insane delusions with special application to a child—daughter—and will was decreed void on that account. In this report are cited several curious cases of mental delusions.— One, where the sufferer fancied himself the Duke of Hexham and became the agent of his own committee for the management of his own estate, and managed it not incorrectly. Another instance related by Lord Erskine where a witness had stood his cross-examination for quite a period, with remarkable manifestations of mental vigor and shrewdness when at the end on an affected expression of apology for the examination the witness exposed his mental weakness and delusion by saying with great gravity and emphasis, " I forgive you, I am the Christ."

(d) **Relations, husband, wife, children,—Cases holding not delusion.**—Mistaken belief in treatment of relatives. (Estate of Carpenter, 94 Cal. 407; 29 Pac. Rep. 1101.)

Prejudice against children and unjust remarks without facts or cause. (Schneider v. Manning, 121 Ill. 377; 12 N. E. Rep. 267.)

Unfounded belief that her sons had defrauded her. (Hemingway's Estate, 195 Pa. St. 291; 45 Atl. Rep. 726.)

Hostility and prejudice towards son. (Dobie v. Armstrong, 160 N. Y. 585; 55 N. E. Rep. 302.)

Mistaken belief as to a grandchild. (Martin v. Thayer, 37 W. Va. 38; 16 S. E. Rep. 489.)

A belief that the contestant had wronged the testatrix in the settlement of her father's estate. (Bull v. Wheeler, 6 Dem. 123.)

Belief that his son being a member of the masonic order against which testator was bitterly prejudiced, had leagued with other Masons to cheat him out of his land. (Will of White, 121 N. Y. 406; 24 N. E. Rep. 935.)

Not sufficient to justify rejection of a will that a 'estator, otherwise competent, entertained the mistaken idea that one of his daughters was illegitimate, if it was not the effect of insane delusion, but of slight and inadequate evidence acting upon a jealous and suspicious mind. (Clapp v. Fullerton, 34 N. Y. 190.)

Capricious, frivolous, mean or even bad motives which may disinherit children do not necessarily constitute insane delusion. Harsh, unreasonable judgment of children may go beyond the limit, and a parent's repulsion may proceed from some mental defect. (Boughton v. Knight, L. R. 3 P. D. 64.)

An erroneous belief does not of itself amount to an insane delusion. (Matter of O'Dea, 84 Hun, 591; 33 N. Y. Supp. 463.)

So *held* where testator believed that son of his wife was not his son, founded on rumors which he had heard. (Re Smith's Will, 24 N. Y. Supp. 928.)

Foolish caprices or ungrounded suspicions of husband by wife. (Matter of Blakely, 48 Wis. 294; 4 N. W. Rep. 337.)

Talking foolish or delusions as to " greenbacks " or that testator's wife had maltreated him. (Rice v. Rice, 50 Mich. 448; 15 N. W. Rep. 545.)

Wife's delusions as to the conduct and affection of her husband; and as to want of affection toward her of some of her children, that they wanted to confine her in an asylum. (Coit v. Patchen, 77 N. Y. 533.)

A husband may conceive false and unjust notions of his wife's character and conduct and may be prompted by mean and unworthy motives in making his will and yet fall short of establishing an insane delusion, making it invalid. (Phillips v. Chater. 1 Dem. 533.)

(e) **Spiritualism or witchcraft—May be delusion or evidence of it.** —Where through belief in spiritualism one is led into the delusion that another is a divinity or gifted with supernatural powers, the believer is insane on that subject and a will prompted by that delusion cannot be sustained. (Orchardson v. Cofield. 171 Ill. 14; 49 N. E. Rep. 197; distinguishing Whipple v. Eddy. 161 Ill. 114; 43 N. E. Rep. 789; and see to same effect where will was induced by spiritualism, Lyon v. Home, L. R. 6 Eq. 655.)

May be found in surrender of the will to imaginary directions regarded by the victim as the directions of God; or of spirits, speaking to him from another world, or to the control of an impulse due to an imaginary state of facts.· (Taylor v. Trich, 165 Pa. St. 586; 30 Atl. Rep. 1053.)

Expression of belief that will was dictated by a deceased husband, and the idea that the husband of her only child was possessed of a familiar demon that enabled him to control his wife's affections and alienate them from her mother—evidence proper to be submitted to jury. (Robinson v. Adams, 62 Me. 369.)

(f) **Spiritualism, witchcraft, etc.—Cases holding no delusion.—** Belief in witchcraft. (Van Guysling v. Van Kuren, 35 N. Y. 71; Fulbright v. Perry County, 145 Mo. 432; 46 S. W. Rep. 955; Kelly v. Miller, 39 Miss. 17.)

Belief that souls of men after death passed into animals. (Bonard's Will, 16 Abb. Pr. N. S. 128.)

Belief that he was personally molested by a man who had long been dead, and that he was pursued by evil spirits. (Banks v. Goodfellow, L. R. 5 Q. B. 549. The opinion by COCKBURN, C. J., contains a valuable review of the cases.)

Delusion that testator was guided by spirits of the dead through mediums, when nothing to show that subject of spiritualism entered his mind in connection with the will. (Whipple v. Eddy, 161 Ill. 114; 43 N. E. Rep. 789; McClary v. Stull, 44 Neb. 175; 62 N. W. Rep. 501.)

Eccentricity and belief in power of spirits of deceased persons to communicate with the living. (Will of Smith, 52 Wis. 543; 8 N. W. Rep. 616; 9 id. 665.)

Belief in spiritualism. (Brown v. Ward, 53 Md. 377; Middleditch v. Williams, 45 N. J. Eq. 726; 17 Atl. Rep. 726; Otto v. Doty, 61 Iowa, 23; 15 N. W. Rep. 578.)

Unless respecting matters of fact connected with the making of the will or the objects of his bounty. (McClary v. Stull, *supra;* Whipple v. Eddy, 161 Ill. 114; 43 N. E. Rep. 789; Re Spencer, 96 Cal. 448; 31 Pac. Rep. 453; La Bau v. Vanderbilt, 3 Redf. 385; Matter of Halbert, 15 Misc. 308, 316; 37 N. Y. Supp. 757; Re Rohe's Will, 50 N. Y. Supp. 392; 22 Misc. 415.)

Testatrix died at advanced age of seventy-seven years. It was shown that her physical powers had been gradually failing; that she was miser'y in disposition and at times uncleanly; that she had been a believer in witchcraft, frequently talked of buried treasures, had seen the headless horseman, gave absurd recipes and advice to others; pretended to have had personal interviews with the deity and evil one; to have entered heaven and conversed with its inhabitants; and expressed a desire to be robed like the angels when she died. On the other hand it appeared that she was prudent and sensible in the management of her household affairs, shrewd at a bargain, a consistent church member, interested in religious work and an affectionate wife; the dispositions of her will were in accord with natural claims on her bounty. Will admitted. (Matter of Vedder, 6 Dem. 93.)

(g) **Miscellaneous illustrative cases, holding no delusion.**—A simulated opinion which is but a fleeting vagary. (Redfield's Estate, 116 Cal. 637; 48 Pac. Rep. 794.)

Erroneous, foolish and even absurd opinions on certain subjects. (Thompson v. Thompson, 21 Barb. 107.)

Erratic conduct and talk; change of mind, manifestations of temper or anger. (Prentis v. Bates, 88 Mich. 568; 50 N. W. Rep. 637.)

Error of judgment or want of reasoning power, does not establish want of intellect on the subject. (Potter v. Jones, 20 Ore. 239; 25 Pac. Rep. 769.)

Mistaken belief of hostility. (Re Ruffino's Estate, 116 Cal. 304; 48 Pac. Rep. 127.)

Unfounded and unreasonable prejudice. (Barnes v. Barnes, 66 Me. 286; Carter v. Dixon, 69 Ga. 82.)

Groundless and absurd suspicions not influencing the will. (Will of Cole, 49 Wis. 179; 5 N. W. Rep. 346.)

Capricious and arbitrary likes and dislikes. (Re Spencer, 96 Cal. 448; 31 Pac. Rep. 453.)

Delusions as to poverty. (Benoist v. Murin, 58 Mo. 318.)

Mental delusion as to physical condition does not constitute testamentary incapacity. (Hollinger v. Syms, 37 N. J. Eq. 221.)

Delusions of an old person as to strange people being in the house not in any way connected with his will. (Shreiner v. Shreiner, 178 Pa. St. 57; 35 Atl. Rep. 574.)

Temporarily imagining that people were tearing down and carryi away his fences. (Boyer's Estate, 166 Pa. St. 630; 31 Atl. Rep. 359.)

VOORHEES vs. BAILEY et al.

[Court of Chancery of New Jersey, November 3, 1899; 44 Atl. Rep. 657.]

ADMINISTRATOR'S SALE—PURCHASE BY ADMINISTRATOR—BONA FIDE INTENT—ESTOPPEL.

An auctioneer at an administrator's sale, being interested in having the property bring its full value, by fictitious bidding ran the bids up to about the full value, and then knocked it off to one who had made no bid, whereupon the administrator, who had had no intention of buying, but who had advertised the sale thoroughly, and thereupon acted in good faith, publicly assumed the bid, took possession at once, and made valuable improvements. The heirs were all of age, and lived near, and complainant made no objection to the court's approval of the sale a month later; exceptions being first taken to the administrator's account charging himself with the amount bid. The account was approved, and no bill to set aside the sale was filed for over a year, during which time complainant saw the administrator making improvements of a substantial character. *Held*, that complainant was estopped to claim that the sale was invalid, or have it vacated.

Suɪᴛ by David V. Voorhees against George Bailey and others.

Decree for plaintiff.

The complainant is one of nine children who are the heirs at law of Hendrick Voorhees, late of the county of Monmouth, who died on the 29th of October, 1896, intestate. The defendant George Bailey is one of the administrators of said deceased, and the other eight defendants are the brothers and sisters of the complainant, and co-heirs at law of said deceased; and one of them (Nelson T. Voorhees) is co-administrator with Bailey. The object of the bill is to set aside a sale of real estate by the defendants Bailey and Nelson T. Voorhees, as administrators of Hendrick Voorhees, made on the 24th of March, 1897, by virtue of a previous order of the Orphans' Court of Monmouth county for that purpose, to one Asher Curtis, and by him subsequently conveyed to the defendant George Bailey, on the ground (1) that the sale was fraudulently conducted by the administrators in such a manner as to prevent the property bringing its full value; and (2) that it was bought in at the sale by Curtis as the agent and figurehead of Bailey, and subsequently conveyed to him. The bill calls for an answer from the administrators under oath. The administrators severed in their answers, and each denies the fraud, or that there was any agreement or understanding bewteen Curtis and Bailey, before or at the sale, that Curtis should buy the property for Bailey. The allegation of the bill is as follows: " And your orator further shows that the said Asher Curtis is a friend and a brother sea captain of the said George Bailey, one of the administrators aforesaid, and that it was arranged and agreed by and between them, the said George Bailey and Asher Curtis, prior to said sale, and at the time of the same, that he, the said George Bailey, one of the administrators as aforesaid, should himself become the purchaser of the said land, and that the same should be struck off and conveyed to the said Asher Curtis, and that he should then convey the same to the said George Bailey." The answer of Bailey, the principal defendant, on this subject, is as follows: "This defendant admits that said Asher Curtis is a friend of this defendant, but this defendant denies that there was any arrangement or agreement entered into or made or had between them at the time of or prior to said sale that this defendant should be or become the purchaser of said tract of land, or that said premises should be struck off and conveyed to said Asher Curtis, and that he should then convey them to this defendant." And there is an interrogatory annexed to the bill, addressed to both defendants as follows: "Had you, or either of you, any conversation or understanding with Asher Curtis, either before, or at, or during the time of the putting up and crying said lands for sale, in reference to, or in any way concerning, the purchase of said lands? If so, what was that conversation, or the substance of it, and the whole of that substance? Did you. or either of you, direct, ask, or request said Asher Curtis to bid for said lands at any time? Did you, or either of you, bid for said lands? Did you, or either of you, intimate to, authorize, or direct said Asher Curtis, or anyone else, either by word, language, wink, nod, motion or expression of any kind at any time to bid for or buy said homestead and lands of said Hendrick Voorhees, deceased?" Bailey's answer to that interrogatory is as follows: "I had no conversation or understanding with Asher Curtis before or at the sale, or the time of the putting up and crying of the lands known as the 'Homestead,' in reference to, or in any way concerning, the purchase of said lands. At the sale the complainant attempted to buy the property for a small sum, and I said to Asher Curtis, 'I will make him pay for it;' but I did not direct, ask, or request said Curtis to bid on said lands at any time, and I did not do this by an intimation or authorization, or by a direction by word, language, wink, nod, motion, or expression of any kind, or any other indication which might suggest itself to the complainant to buy or bid on the lands of said Hendrick Voorhees." The answer also denies all allegations of mismanagement at the sale, or contrivance to prevent the property from bringing its full value. The sale took place March 24, 1897, in complainant's presence, who was at once aware that Curtis's bid was assumed by Bailey. It was duly reported to the Orphans' Court, and by it confirmed on April 29th without objection. Bailey took immediate possession, and after the confirmation made considerable improvements. The administrators filed their account, charging themselves with the amount bid at the sale. Complainant filed exceptions thereto, and, after the allowance of the account by the Orphans' Court, this bill was filed, April 19, 1898.

William I. Chamberlain and *H. Chamberlain,* for complainant.

Charles J. Parker, for defendants George Bailey and Nelson T. Voorhees.

PITNEY, V. C. (after stating the facts).—The decedent died possessed of two tracts of land situate in Monmouth county. The tract here in question was called the " Homestead," and consisted of about one acre of land, with a house and barn and some outbuildings; and the other tract was about thirty acres, mainly wood land, situate detached from the house lot. This property was all heavily mortgaged at the time of his decease, and he was indebted, besides that, to various individuals,—mainly to his own children; and, as I infer from the evidence, most of that indebtedness was for services which they had rendered him, with one notable exception, however, namely, that the complainant had been security for him on a note of $250, and had been obliged to pay it in cash. I infer from the evidence that each of these separate tracts was separately mortgaged, and then that there was a blanket mortgage covering both tracts. ·The administrators applied for and obtained an order to sell the land for the payment of debts, and, although it did not appear affirmatively at the hearing that they were directed to sell the lands free of the mortgages, in point of fact they did so sell them. (See *In re Voorhees* [N. J. Prerog.] 42 Atl. 567.) All of the charges of mismanagement of the sale entirely failed. There was a suggestion made that the lot on which the house stood should have been divided and sold in parcels, but no serious request was made to the administrators so to do; and there was no proof made at the hearing that the " Homestead," as it was called, would have brought a better price if divided, but the contrary appeared. It may be here said that the children were all of age, and lived in the neighborhood. For the purposes of the sale, the administrators caused the wood land to be divided into lots by a surveyor. The property was thoroughly advertised, not only in the formal legal method, but by large posters set up in the neighborhood, and every reasonable effort was made by the administrators to cause it to bring a full price. It was well attended. There is not the least particle of proof in the case that Capt. Curtis, who was a personal friend of Capt. Bailey, the defendant, made any bid whatever upon the homestead. Both he and the auctioneer deny it. It was struck off to him by the auctioneer without the least authority on Curtis' part. The fact is that the auctioneer, who was a real-estate and insurance agent, and a reasonably shrewd man of business, was guarantor on the blanket mortgage upon the premises, and anxious on that account to have the property bring its full value. When the homestead was put up, the complainant bid $500 for it. The defendant Capt. Bailey said to the auctioneer: "Don't start the property at $500. Make it $1,000." The auctioneer then cried it as on a $1,000 bid, and then the bids were advanced. So far as the evidence shows, only two *bona fide* bids were made after that by separate bidders, the auctioneer crying fictitious bids that were never made, until he got a *bona fide* bid of $1,500 from a Mr. Longstreet, who owned the adjoining property; then another of $1,525 from a Mr. Austin Voorhees (not a relative of the heirs), who lived in the neighborhood, and desired to buy. Then he cried it on a bid of $1,550, which was made by no person, and, when he could not get a further bid was obliged to strike it off on that bid, and without any authority from Curtis whatever declared him to be the purchaser. Curtis assented thereto, but shortly afterwards Bailey being appraised of the situation, assumed the bid, and said he would take it at that price. The sale, however, was reported to the Orphans' Court as having been made to Capt. Curtis, and was so confirmed, and a deed was actually made and executed by the administrators to Capt. Curtis. There was not the least concealment of the fact that Capt. Bailey, the defendant, had taken the bid from Capt. Curtis, and become the real purchaser. He himself at once avowed it, and, so far as appears, it was known to all the heirs. The complainant knew of it at once, and Capt. Bailey took immediate and open possession. No objection was made to the confirmation of the sale on account of its having been improperly conducted, that it did not produce a sufficient price, or that it had been made in reality to Capt. Bailey. All persons interested seemed to be satisfied with it, and it was duly confirmed by the court on April 29th. Shortly after the sale the administrators filed their account, charging themselves with the purchase price. A dispute then arose among the heirs as to their several claims, and Capt. Bailey got them together, and induced them to agree among themselves as to how much their various claims should be. After this was done a large batch of exceptions was filed by complainant to the administrators' account in the Orphans' Court, which, of course, produced litigation; and when the whole thing was finally settled the net amount of the estate remaining was only sufficient to pay a fraction short of eighty cents on the dollar on the several claims. After this litigation in the Orphans' Court, and on the 19th of April, 1898, more than a year after the sale, the complainant filed his bill for relief against the sale itself. The value of the property was gone into, and, while one or two witnesses swore that it was worth $2,000 or upward, the great weight of the evidence was that $1,550 was a full price for it. I am satisfied from the evidence that Capt. Bailey is truthful in his sworn statement that he had no expectation or desire to purchase the homestead property, that he gave no authority to Capt. Curtis or to the auctioneer to bid for it, that there was no arrangement between them that he should bid in the property for him, and that Capt Curtis did not bid on it at all, but that it was really the bid of the auctioneer. The latter swore that, if Capt. Curtis had not assumed the bid, he (the auctioneer) would have assumed it.

There is another set of facts introduced into the case by the defendant Bailey's answer which seems worthy of notice. While he had no idea of purchasing the homestead, he did desire to purchase, and did purchase through Capt. Curtis, one of the pieces of wood land. Capt Curtis at his request bid upon that property, which was put up and struck off before the homestead. He was outbid by one Cook, as the auctioneer declares, who denied that he made the bid, and it was struck off to Curtis, and Curtis subsequently conveyed it to Capt. Bailey. Now, strange as it may seem, I am satisfied that Capt. Bailey was not aware that he was, in this action, doing anything wrong, dishonest, or contrary to the principles of a court of equity. The fact, which I think came to the knowledge of the auctioneer, that Capt. Curtis had just bid off the piece of wood land for Capt. Bailey, emboldened the auctioneer to declare Curtis to be the purchaser of the homestead without any authority from either. In this case, as in the other, there was no concealment, and as soon as the sale was confirmed he proceeded to expend a considerable sum in clearing and fertilizing it. Capt. Bailey, in his answer, sets out this purchase by him of the wood lot, and offers to give up the title to both properties, if made whole for the amount of improvements he had put upon each. Complainant, however, declared at the hearing that he was satisfied with the sale of the wood lot, and did not wish to disturb it. Not only did Capt. Bailey, as I have stated, avow himself the purchaser immediately after the sale, but he took immediate possession, and as soon as the sale was confirmed by the Orphans' Court he commenced to make improvements, and spent upon the property a little over $200 in cash, or its equivalent, and has paid the accruing taxes. Besides these improvements, he purchased an adjoining piece of land, situate in the rear of the homestead, and which, united with it, greatly increased the value of both, In fact, the homestead lot was ill shaped. It was an isosceles triangle, or nearly so, with a narrow base, and one of the long sides bounded on the highway, so that it had but little depth. After making this addition he moved one of the outbuildings of the Voorhees lot up to and adjoining the barn, and placed it so that a portion of it now stands upon the adjoining lot since purchased by him. The changes he has made are such as to render the outbuildings suitable for use in connection with a small farm, rather than for a mere dwelling house and garden spot. Of course, in order to separate the homestead from the additional purchase, it will be necessary to again move the outbuildings above mentioned; and it is to be inferred that the purchase of the land in the rear of the homestead would not have been made, but for use in connection with it.

The fundamental principle governing all dealings with property held in trust is that the *cestui que trust* is entitled to the best efforts of the trustee to further in all legitimate ways the interests of the *cestui que trust*. It is the duty of the trustee to use and exercise such care and diligence in dealing with the trust estate as a prudent, sagacious man would bestow upon his own. The trustee is not permitted to have any interest in the subject of the trust antagonistic to, or in any degree inconsistent with, that of the *cestui que trust*. It follows from this that, where there is a trust for sale, the trustee cannot become, either directly or indirectly, a purchaser at his own sale, even though the sale be at auction, and so conducted as to insure the best price, and in point of fact the price actually paid appear to be a fair and full one. The principal reasons for extending the restriction so far are (1) that the trustee shall not be subjected to the least temptation to abate any reasonable efforts to procure the best price for the trust property; (2) the danger that the trustee may have become possessed, in the course of his dealing as trustee, of some secret information of facts and circumstances affecting the value of the trust property, which he may take advantage of for his own benefit; and (3) the difficulty of ascertaining whether in fact all proper efforts have been made by the trustee to procure the best price. It is at once apparent that it is of the essence of this rule that the obnoxious, inconsistent position of the trustee should exist before or at the time of the sale, which period, in a sale at auction, is the moment of striking off the property to the highest bidder, and declaring him the purchaser. The trustee must entertain the intention or desire to purchase before or at the moment of the sale, in order to place himself in a position antagonistic to his *cestui que trust*. If the trustee advertises and prepares for the sale with proper care and diligence, and in good faith, without entertaining the least intention or expectation of becoming a purchaser, and, in case of a sale at auction, does not in fact, directly, or indirectly, bid for the property and it is struck off in good faith to another person then there is a complete absence of any of the elements of danger to the interests of the *cestui que trust* which underlie the restrictive rule in question.

The leading authorities in this state which support the foregoing propositions are the following: *Scott* v. *Gamble* (9 N. J. Eq. 218, at pages 235, 236); *Mulford* v. *Bowen* (9 id. 797, at page 798); *Staats* v. *Bergen* (17 id. 554, at pages 558, 559, 560); *Bassett* v. *Shoemaker* (46 id. 538; 20 Atl. 52, and cases there cited); *Wortman* v. *Skinner* (12 N. J. Eq. 358, at pages 371, 372). I will quote the language of the late Justice VREDENBURGH in speaking for the Court of Errors and Appeals in the last case cited, at pages 371, 372, since it is relied upon by the defendant herein: " Let us first see, before considering the evidence, what this doctrine, as applied to the case before us, really is. My understanding of it is this: That if an administrator, at public or private sale, sells land to another, upon an agreement made before or at the sale that such person shall buy or bid off, not for himself or for others, but for the administrator, that the purchase money is to come from him, and the deeds made from him to the bidder and by the bidder back again to the administrator, in pursuance of said agreement, then equity will set aside the proceedings as fraudulent in law. But if the purchaser bids, not for the administrator, but for himself, or for the heirs of the deceased, or for anybody else, then the principle does not apply. The rule was made from considerations of public policy, to prevent the land from being sold under value by the secret machinations of the administrator; and therefore such agreement and arrangement must be made and exist before and at the very instant of the sale. Any agreement made, however soon after it is struck off by the administrator to the purchaser, is not within the letter, the spirit, or the meaning of the rule. The rule has then had its operation upon the sale, and the land is again instantly free for all the world to purchase. The very reason for establishing the original rule requires this construction of it; otherwise, it would produce the very evil it was intended to guard against, by restricting to that extent the power of the purchaser to alienate. Applying these principles to the case before us, if Cooper and Emmons on the 2d July, 1825, bid off this property for the complainant, which was carried out by the subsequent execution of the deeds to the complainant, then the complainant was at that time, and has been ever since, but a trustee for the defendants, and his title is voidable in equity. But if such was not the fact,—if the purchase was made on the 2d July, 1825, not for the complainant or for his benefit, but for the benefit of Cooper and Emmons or of the heirs of N. Skinner, and the deed from Cooper and Emmons to the complainant was by virtue of an arrangement made after the 2d July, 1825,—then there was no legal fraud in the transaction. Immediately after the property was struck off on the 2d July, 1825, the complainant had as good a right to buy from those to whom the property had been struck off as anybody else, and it would then be in him fraud neither actual nor legal." In that case the property was struck off by

Wortman, the administrator, to two purchasers, who were mere nominal bidders, even if they bid at all, at the best price to be had at the time, but which was not satisfactory to the heirs; the object being to have the affair in such shape as to be able to make title at any moment when a purchaser at a satisfactory price could be obtained, without incurring the expense of a readvertisement. Several years afterwards the administrator bargained with a portion of the heirs for the premises at an advance over the amount bid, procured the original sale to be confirmed, made a conveyance to the original nominal bidders, who at once conveyed to him, and accounted to the Orphans' Court for the amount of the advanced price for which he bargained with some of the heirs, and used the consideration money to pay the debts of the deceased, most of which he had already advanced out of his own pocket. Though the facts of that case are somewhat different from those in hand, yet it is quite difficult to distinguish it in principle. In both cases there was absent the important obnoxious element of previous intention on the part of the trustee to become a purchaser; in both there was no actual sale to the nominal bidder; in both the trustee became the purchaser after' the bidding was closed and a purchaser declared. But in the older case years elapsed before the trustee intervened to purchase, and in the present but a few moments of time. There were other circumstances in the older case which may have influenced, and probably did influence, the minds of the judges. Under these circumstances, I feel disinclined to hold that the present case is governed by that of *Wortman* v. *Skinner*. I am afraid that the precedents so set might lead to abuses, and open a way by which trustees might actually manage to become purchasers at their own sales, in pursuance of a previous intention, without being detected in so doing. I therefore decline to decide the case on that ground.

But there is another ground upon which I think the defendant must prevail, and that is acquiesence and practical confirmation of the sale. While it is of the greatest importance for the security of infants and other helpless persons that the strict rules governing the conduct of trustees shall not be relaxed, it is equally important, in administering those rules, to bear in mind that trustees have the same right to equitable treatment at the hands of *cestuis que trustent* that the latter have against the former. In the case in hand the complainant and the other *cestuis que trustent* had the option either to hold Capt. Bailey to his purchase, and require him to hold the title and charge himself, as administrator, with the purchase price, and thereby affirm and confirm the sale, or to disaffirm the sale, object to its confirmation by the Orphans' Court, and refuse to accept, directly or indirectly, the purchase price. This option in my judgment, it was necessary for such of them as had knowledge of the facts (all were adults) to promptly exercise. Apparently all, unless we except the complainant, did exercise their option to have the sale stand, and require the administrators to charge themselves with the purchase price. And, in my judgment, the same must be said of the complainant. If he intended to disaffirm the sale and have it set aside on the grounds now sought, it was, in my judgment, his duty to do so promptly. He could not speculate,—wait in silence to see which course was most to his advantage,—while Capt. Bailey was acting in good faith on the assumption that complainant was satisfied with the sale. It must be remembered that complainant was not laboring under any disability or lack of knowledge of the true state of the case; and when the sale was confirmed by the Orphans' Court, without the least objection on his part or that of any one else, it seems to me that Capt. Bailey was entitled to conclude that the sale was approved and accepted by the complainant as well as by all the other adult heirs, and was justified in proceeding to make the improvements and changes on and in the premises which he did. If there had been any actual conscious misconduct on Capt. Bailey's part, upon which he might be properly charged with actual fraud, the conclusion just stated might not—I do not say would not —result. But the facts show the contrary. We have seen that there was no previous intention on the part of Capt. Bailey to become the purchaser of this lot. We have seen that he used every reasonable endeavor to procure a full price for the premises. In all that, his conduct is entirely above criticism. We have seen, also, that there was no concealment on his part. The complainant himself swears that he heard Capt. Bailey almost immediately declare that he had become the purchaser. We have seen that he immediately took possession and acted as owner. We have seen that the sale was duly confirmed by. and that he accounted for the purchase money to, the Orphans' Court, and that the heirs at law, who are the principal creditors, have had the benefit of that money. The complainant was cognizant of the fact that Capt. Bailey took possession, and does not deny that he saw him making improvements. Those improvements were of a character which will render it difficult to adjust the value of them, as between Capt. Bailey and the complainant, if the sale shall be set aside. They are, as we have seen, not such as to improve the house and lot as such, but to render it more convenient for use in connection with the cultivation of a small farm, to which Capt. Bailey has devoted it. He appears to have purchased land in the rear of the lot in question to use in connection with it, and to have so arranged one of the buildings in connection with this additional purchase that it will be difficult to disconnect it without loss.

The counsel of complainant was asked during the progress of the case why objection was not made to the confirmation, or the bill filed sooner, and the only excuse he could make was that the deed from the administrators to Capt. Curtis was not promptly put on record, and he had no certain knowledge that Capt. Bailey was the purchaser. But this want of knowledge is contradicted by the facts in the case, which, as we have seen, show that the complainant knew that Capt. Bailey was the purchaser, and took immediate possession and spent money upon the premises. Besides, in my judgment, it was his duty to make his objection to the judicial confirmation of the sale. The facts with regard to the deed from the administrators to Curtis not being put immediately upon record are these: The deed for the home lot was prepared by the auctioneer. The deeds for the wood lots were prepared by the surveyor, who made the partition for the purposes of the sale, and they were executed at different times, and became separated. The surveyor who had charge of the wood lots saw that those deeds were immediately recorded. The deeds from Capt. Curtis to Capt. Bailey were not executed at the same time that the deeds from the administrators to Curtis were executed, but a few days intervened; and, while the deed for the homestead from Capt. Curtis to Capt. Bailey was almost immediately recorded, that from the administrators to Curtis for this lot was left in the hands of the auctioneer for record, and was mislaid by him. That there could have been no object in keeping the deed from the records is manifest from the fact that the one to Capt. Curtis for the wood lot was immediately recorded.

I think the excuse that the deed was not put on record is entirely insufficient to account for the complainant's delay, and that it is, in this case, inexcusable.

That the facts above stated are sufficient to charge the complainant with acquiescence and confirmation, we have the authority of *Scott* v. *Gamble* (*supra*). There a sale was made in 1843 by an executor, under power in the will, and, of course, was not judicially confirmed. The fund produced belonged to the complainants, who were then infants. After they had arrived at age, and three or four years after the sale, and with full knowledge of all the facts, they accepted the bonds which were given by the trustee for part of the purchase money, in payment of their shares of the estate. The circumstances are set forth on pages 241 and 242 of 9 N. J. Eq.; and at page 242 Chancellor WILLIAMSON uses this language, which I think applies here: " The question arises, under these circumstances, and after having received, with full knowledge of the facts, the proceeds of the sale, is the complainant entitled to have the sale set aside, and a resale of the property? The fact of her having received the purchase money is not an absolute estoppel to the complainant's right of avoiding the sale; for, no matter what the ratification by her might have been,—whether by the mere receipt of the purchase money, or by a more solemn act of release under seal,—if such ratification had been without a knowledge of the facts, and in ignorance of her rights, it would be no obstacle to her obtaining relief. But, on the contrary, when such act of ratification is done with deliberation, and with a knowledge of the fact which would avoid the sale, it is a bar to any relief which this court might otherwise have afforded." It is true that in this case no money was paid directly to the complainant as the price of the land, but, in effect, it was so paid; for the complainant was an heir at law and one of the creditors of the estate, and the money was accounted for and paid, and he received his share,—whether in the shape of his claim against the estate, or in the shape of the payment of the debts of the decedent, it seems to me, matters not. Chancellor WILLIAMSON cites in support of his opinion the case of *Belton* v. *Briggs* (4 Desaus. 463). decided by the Court of Appeals of South Carolina. which held that the mere receipt by an adult of the price of land agreed to be sold by his mother during his infancy was a confirmation of the contract, and bound him to convey in pursuance of his mother's agreement. The argument from *Scott* v. *Gambel* to the present case is *a fortiori,* for in that case the complainant was a helpless infant female at the time of the sale, and was not chargeable,either in fact or in law, with knowledge of the facts of the case, which showed an actual contrivance by the husband of the executrix to have the premises sold and conveyed to a third person as a figurehead, and by him to the husband. It was in fact somewhat similar, in some of its aspects, to *Bassett* v. *Shoemaker (supra).* The case was put by the learned chancellor solely on the ground of the acceptance of the purchase price by the complainants after they became of age, with knowledge of the facts. As to the effect of complainant standing by in silence while Capt. Bailey made his improvements, I refer to *Sumner* v. *Seaton* (47 N. J. Eq. 103, 111; 19 Atl. 884 *et seq*), and authorities there cited. I am of the opinion that the complainant's case fails, and will advise that the bill be dismissed, with costs.

HOFFMAN *et al. vs.* ARMSTRONG *et al.*

[Court of Appeals of Maryland, November 24, 1899; 90 Md. 123; 44 Atl. Rep. 1012.)

EXECUTORS AND ADMINISTRATORS—FAILURE TO COLLECT DEBTS— INSOLVENT DISTRIBUTEE — ACCOUNT — RESTATEMENT — ORPHANS' COURT—JURISDICTION—TRUSTEES IN INSOLVENCY.

1. Where executors have distributed to an insolvent legatee indebted to their testator his share under the will, without deducting therefrom his indebtedness to the estate, and the share thus distributed has been sold by the legatee's trustees in insolvency to third parties for value, and without notice, the executors should not be allowed to restate their account, in order to enable them to make a claim against the purchasers.

2. That trustees of an insolvent legatee could have appealed from an order of the Orphans' Court allowing an executors' account does not prevent the court from setting such order aside within the time allowed for appeal, on the trustees' application.

3. That trustees of an insolvent legatee did not object to an order allowing executors to restate their account does not affect their right to object to the account as restated.

4. Under Code, art. 93, § 224, providing that "the bare naming an executor in a will shall not operate to extinguish any just claim which the deceased had against him," it was error for the Orphans' Court, in an order allowing executors to restate an account, to provide that they should not retain any of the distribution to which one of the executors might be entitled on account of any alleged indebtedness from him to the estate, where such executor was indebted to the estate as a surviving partner of the deceased.

5. Where the failure of executors to collect an amount due their testator from a distributee was due to their negligence, they should be charged with the amount.

6. Though all the trustees of an insolvent should ordinarily unite in judicial proceedings, yet where one of the trustees was an executor and distributee of an estate in which his insolvent was also a distributee, and such trustee was acting against the interests of his insolvent, it was proper for the court, in a matter involving the insolvent's rights as distributee, to act at the instance of the remaining trustees.

APPEAL from Orphans' Court, Washington county; LUTHER R. SPANGLER, SOLOMON NEWCOMER, and SAMUEL D. MARTIN, Judges.

Action by Mary Hoffman and others, executors, of Joseph T. Hoffman, against Alexander Armstrong and another, permanent trustees, etc. From an order setting aside the executors' account, they appeal.

Modified.

Argued before McSHERRY, C. J., and FOWLER, BRISCOE, PAGE, BOYD, BOND, PEARCE, and SCHMUCKER, JJ.

J. C. Lane and *W. H. A. Hamilton,* for appellants.

J. A. Mason and *Armstrong & Scott,* for appellees.

BOYD, J.—It will perhaps simplify the questions raised by this appeal to make a somewhat full statement of the facts: Joseph T. Hoffman appointed his wife, Mary Hoffman, and his three eldest sons, Charles W., Edward, and Ernest, executors of his last will and testament which was proven in the Orphans' Court of Washington county in June, 1891. On November 17, 1896, the executors stated their third account, in which they distributed certain shares of stock of corporations and some cash to each of the seven

children of the deceased. In October, 1897, the three remaining
,executors (Edward having been removed) filed a petition in the
Orphans' Court, in which they stated that the above-mentioned
account was erroneous, in that they should have claimed credit for
an item of $2,518.36 as a debt due to the estate by Edward Hoff-
man as surviving partner of Joseph T. Hoffman & Son,—he
having converted it to his own use,—and that they should have
charged themselves with the appraisement of certain furniture, etc.,
which they inadvertently omitted, and that they should not have
made any distribution to Edward, as he was indebted to the estate.
They asked that the account should be restated. The Orphans'
Court refused to grant their petition, and on an appeal to this court
the order was reversed. (*Hoffman* v. *Hoffman*, 88 Md. 60; 40
Atl. 712.)

After the cause was remanded the court passed an order requiring the children of the testator to answer the petition, which they
did, admitting the allegations therein, excepting Worthington W.
Hoffman, an infant, whose guardian filed the usual formal answer.
Alexander Armstrong and J. A. Mason, two of the permanent trustees of Edward Hoffman, who had been adjudicated an insolvent
(Ernest Hoffman being the third trustee), filed a petition asking
leave to answer the petition of the executors; and the Orphans'
Court passed an order making the trustees of Edward Hoffman
parties, and granting them, or such of them as desired, leave to
answer. The order was doubtless passed in that form because the
petition alleged that Ernest Hoffman was one of the trustees, and
also one of the executors. Those two trustees then filed their
answer, alleging among other things that the executors had turned
over to the trustees of Edward Hoffman the stocks distributed to
him in the third account; that they had sold them, and distributed
the proceeds in the insolvent court. Testimony was taken, and on
the 7th day of October, 1898, the Orphans' Court passed an order
setting aside the third account of the executors, and directed them
to restate it, correcting the errors set forth in their petition. The
executors then filed a petition asking that distribution be made under the direction of the court. An order was passed naming the
20th day of October, 1898, as the day for the distribution, and directing a summons to issue for the distributees and the trustees of
Edward Hoffman. The record does not show whether the summons

was issued or served, but on the 15th day of November, 1898, the third account, as restated, was approved by the court; and in it the executors charged themselves with some additional personalty, and Edward Hoffman's share was distributed to the executors, to be applied in part payment of his indebtedness to the estate; there being $640.31 distributed to each distributee, and there being claimed to be an indebtedness of Edward Hoffman amounting to $1,154.28. The distribution to each distributee included five shares of the Danzer Lumber Company's stock, appraised at $450; five shares of Interstate Hedge-Fence Company stock, appraised at 0; seventeen shares of the hosiery company's stock, appraised at 0; six shares of the Beaver Creek & South Mountain Turnpike Company's stock, appraised at $30; and $160.31 in money. That was the same distribution made in the original third account, excepting the first only included $40.95 of money to each distributee. On the 22d day of November, 1898, the two trustees filed another petition, in which they stated they were advised that the executors had produced to the court certain certificates of stock of the Danzer Lumber Company and the Beaver Creek & South Mountain Turnpike Company, in the name of Joseph T. Hoffman; that said certificates did not truly represent the manner in which the stock stood, but long prior to the time the account was restated the executors had made distribution of said stock, and transferred it on the books of the companies to the heirs and legatees of Joseph T. Hoffman; that they had no knowledge until after the ratification of the account that the executors had produced to the court said certificates of stock; and they prayed that the account be reopened, in order that the court might be advised of the real circumstances in regard to said stock, etc. The executors answered the petition, neither admitting nor denying the allegations therein, but alleging that the account was restated after testimony had been taken, and due consideration by the court. Testimony was again taken " at hearing of April 6, 1899." The secretary of the Beaver Creek, etc., Company testified that Joseph T. Hoffman was at the time of his death the holder of forty-two shares of stock in that company, and that on the stock book there was an assignment by the three remaining executors of six shares to each of the seven children (naming them and including Edward Hoffman). That transfer was made May 21, 1897. A certificate was issued to Edward for the six shares, and afterwards, as attorney in fact for the trustees, the secretary transferred them, together with four and one-fifth other shares in the name of Edward Hoffman, to Norman G. Scott. William C. Danzer, president of the Danzer Lumber Company, testified that on or about January 2, 1897, the executors produced a certified copy of the order of the Orphans' Court, dated November 17, 1896, directing the stock held by Joseph T. Hoffman in that company to be transferred; and on that day a certificate for five shares was issued to Edward Hoffman, at the request of the executors, which was afterwards transferred by the trustees to the Peoples' National Bank. On the 18th day of April, 1899, the court passed an order setting aside and annulling the said third account, approved on November 15, 1898, and again ratifying the third account as originally stated on the 17th of November, 1896, excepting as to the item of household articles and distribution of the Hagerstown Steam-Engine & Machine Company, as to which the executors were directed to state a further account. An opinion was filed by the court, in which they gave their reason for their action. In it they state that inasmuch as there had been a mistake in the original third account, as to the household furniture, they determined to reopen it, " and informed the executors, their counsel being present, but out of the presence of the said trustees or their counsel, that they must produce the true certificates, showing in whose name said shares of capital stock were issued, as mentioned in said third account. This the counsel for the executors agreed to do, and upon this understanding we passed the order of October 7, 1898. Upon November 8, 1898, the executors restated said third account, but this court would not approve the same, for the reason that the executors had not produced said certificates. However, between the 8th and 15th of November, 1898, they did produce in this court certificates of shares of said stock which stood in the name of the decedent, Dr. Joseph T. Hoffman, and this court ratified said third account as restated. After its restatement we informed the counsel for the said two insolvent trustees, as we saw, to do justice and right, we should have notified them before ratifying said third account as restated."

The executors originally charged themselves with $2,518.36, as the appraised value of property of the firm of Joseph T. Hoffman & Son; and certainly as early as when the second account was passed, on the 10th day of March, 1893, Edward Hoffman had sold that property, yet he was paid his distribution of $1,577.32; and when the third account was stated, in November, 1896, they obtained credit for the whole of the $2,518.36, as " not disposed of," —two of the three executors swearing that " the foregoing account, as stated, is just and true." So long as Edward Hoffman was receiving the distributions, no question seems to have been raised as to his right to do so; and the court was not only not informed that he was indebted to the estate, but the action of the executors was calculated to lead it to believe he was not indebted as surviving partner, as they stated that the property was not disposed of. In the meantime the rights of innocent parties have intervened, and, so far as they are concerned, it would seem to be clear that the executors are not entitled to relief merely for their own protection. Although it has been decided in many cases, including that of *Hoffman* v. *Hoffman* (*supra*), that the Orphans' Court has the power to reopen accounts of executors and administrators, and correct errors therein, that power should be very cautiously exercised, if there be danger of thereby prejudicing the rights of parties who have innocently acted under the account as originally stated. In the case before us the stock distributed to Edward Hoffman was delivered to his trustees, and sold by them. Neither of these two trustees nor the purchasers are shown to have had notice of any claim that was held by the executors against the stock. The purchasers paid for it, and the companies in which it was held issued new certificates of stock to them, and the proceeds were distributed by the trustees. Under such circumstances, it would be manifestly unjust to restate the account at the instance of the executors, to enable them to make a claim against innocent persons who have been led into the transaction by the act of the executors themselves. The Orphans' Court ought not, under such facts, to have approved the account which was restated in November, 1898; and, as is shown by their opinion, when they found they had done so under a misapprehension of the facts, which was occasioned by the production of the certificates in the name of Joseph T. Hoffman, without the knowledge of the trustees, they very properly granted the petition of the trustees to set aside and annul their former order ratifying that account, especially when they ascertained that they had not been correctly informed as to the true

status of the stock.   It is true that the trustees might have appealed
from the order ratifying that account, but, as they filed their petition within the time they could have appealed, there was no question about the right of the Orphans' Court to act on it.   The fact
that no appeal was taken from the order of October 7, 1898, cannot
affect their right to object to the account after it was restated.   So
much of the order passed April 18, 1899, as set aside and annulled
that account, which was approved November 15, 1898, was therefore properly passed.

The order, however, also provided " that the executors are not
allowed to retain in any manner in their hands any of the distribution to which Edward Hoffman or his legal representatives might
be entitled on account of any alleged indebtedness from the said
Edward Hoffman to the estate."   In that there was error.   It was
undoubtedly the duty of the executors to deduct from the distributive share of Edward Hoffman in his father's estate any indebtedness due by him to it.   By section 224 of article 93, it is provided
that " the bare naming an executor in a will shall not operate to extinguish any just claim which the deceased had against him; but it
shall be the duty of every such executor accepting the trust to give
in such claim in the list of debts "; and, after providing for the
method of establishing a claim against him if he fails to give in
such claim, it further provides " that if the executor shall give in
such claim or any part thereof be established, as aforesaid, he shall
account for the sum due in the same manner as if it were so much
money in his hands and on failure his bond may be put in suit."
Without stopping to discuss the effect of such a provision when
there is more than one executor, the statute is explicit in declaring
that the fact that such party has been named executor does not operate to extinguish a debt due the deceased; and it is well settled
that it is the duty of executors or administrators to retain from the
share of a distributee the amount due by him to the deceased.
(Smith v. Donnell, 9 Gill, 84; Manning v. Thruston, 59 Md. 218.)
Such right also exists when the debt has been incurred to the estate itself by the distributee, as administrator, after the decedent's
death.   (Gosnell v. Flack, 76 Md. 423; 25 Atl. 411; 18 L. R. A.
158.)   And it would seem to be equally clear that such is the case
where the indebtedness is from a surviving partner of the deceased,.
who is a distributee. In Smith v. Donnell (supra), it was expressly
decided that the trustee of an insolvent legatee was only entitled

to the balance after deducting the amount due the deceased by the legatee.   The insolvent law then in force was as broad as the one under which Edward Hoffman was adjudicated an insolvent, so far as this question is concerned.   It was therefore the plain duty of the executors to deduct the amount due by Edward Hoffman from his distributive share in his father's estate, and although, as we have said above, that cannot now be done to the extent of disturbing the distribution which the trustees in the insolvent proceeding got possession of and disposed of, the executors can deduct from distributions not yet paid over to the trustees any sums due by him. The evidence sufficiently shows that he is indebted to his father's estate, and therefore the order of the Orphans' Court, in so far as it affects distributions not yet made, must be reversed.

As the failure to collect the amount due by Edward as surviving partner of Joseph T. Hoffman & Son was manifestly owing to the negligence of the executors, they should be charged with the amount he owes his father's estate, as well as the appraised value of the household articles, etc., spoken of, and other sums not accounted for by them.   They should not make any further distribution to Edward Hoffman until the distributions to the other distributees are equal to the amount he owes the estate.

It may be well to add that ordinarily all the trustees of an insolvent should unite in petitions or other proceedings in courts, but as in this case Ernest Hoffman was one of the executors of his father's estate, as well as one of the distributees, and was acting against the interest of the insolvent estate of his brother Edward, the court very properly acted at the instance of the other two trustees.   The proper course for Ernest Hoffman to have pursued was to ask the insolvent court to discharge him from further acting as such trustee, as his interests, both as distributee and executor, were in clear conflict with his duties as trustee.   Section 12 of article 47 of the code gives the court ample authority to discharge trustees appointed in insolvent proceedings, as well as to remove them for misconduct.   Order passed the 18th day of April, 1899, affirmed in part, and reversed in part, and cause remanded; the costs in this court and the court below to be paid out of the estate.

PRICE *vs.* WARD.

[Supreme Court of Nevada, November 8, 1899; 58 Pac. Rep. 849.]

ACTION RESPECTING INTESTATE'S LAND—ADMINISTRATOR'S RIGHT
TO MAINTAIN.

An administrator appointed in this state cannot sue to redeem from a
mortgage on land of his intestate in another state by setting off against
the mortgage debt waste committed thereon by the mortgagee in possession after the death of the intestate, nor to recover for damages to
or trespass committed on the land, since he is not entitled to the possession thereof, and it is not assets in his hands for the payment of
debts.

BONNIFIELD, C. J., dissenting.

APPEAL from District Court, Washoe county; B. F. CURLER,
Judge.

Action by Albert F. Price, as administrator of the estate of William E. Price, deceased, against M. E. Ward. From an order sustaining a demurrer to the complaint, and the judgment rendered
thereon, plaintiff appeals.

Affirmed.

Torreyson & Summerfield and *F. H. Norcross,* for appellant.

A. E. Cheney, for respondent.

MASSEY, J.—The complaint in this action consists of two counts.
By the first count the appellant, as administrator of the estate of
William Price, deceased (appointed as such by a Probate Court of
this state), seeks by a decree in equity to have a deed absolute on
its face to lands in the state of California declared a mortgage, to
redeem said lands from the same by setting off against the debt
secured thereby damages in waste committed by the respondent in
possession thereof as mortgagee after the death of the intestate,
the mortgagor, and for a judgment over for the balance of the
damages after the satisfaction and discharge of the mortgage debt.
By the second count the said appellant seeks a judgment against
the respondent for damages for waste or trespass committed by the

respondent, after the death of the intestate, to the same lands in his possession under the deed absolute on its face, but alleged to have been given as a mortgage. The specific acts complained of are cutting and selling the timber growing upon said lands. A demurrer to the complaint was interposed and sustained. The appeal is from the order sustaining the demurrer, and the judgment rendered thereon.

Waste, as understood in law, is permanent or lasting injury done or permitted to be done by the holder of a particular estate to the inheritance, to the prejudice of any one who has an interest in the inheritance. (*Duvall* v. *Waters*, 18 Am. Dec. 350; *Dooly* v. *Stringham*, 4 Utah, 107; 7 Pac. 405; *Davenport* v. *Magoon*, 13 Or. 3; 4 Pac. 299; Cooley, Torts. 302; 28 Am. & Eng. Enc. Law [1st ed.], 862.) Waste and trespass are easily distinguished. Briefly stated, waste is the permanent or lasting injury to the estate by one who has not an absolute or unqualified title thereto. Trespass is an injury to the estate, or the use thereof, by one who is a stranger to the title. (*Duvall* v. *Waters, supra; Lander* v. *Hall*, 69 Wis. 326; 34 N. W. 80; High, Inj. [3d ed.] § 650.) Our statutes have in no manner changed the definition of waste as above given. We have also been unable to find any provision of the statutes that in any manner changes the distinction made by the authorities above cited. The only change made by the statute in action for waste, if it can be called a change, is found in that provision giving a right of action, to " any person aggrieved," for waste committed by a guardian, tenant for life or years, joint tenant, or tenant in common of real property. (Gen. St. § 3274.) It will be observed that this section in no manner changes the rights of a mortgagor or mortgagee in such action as they existed at common law. At common law no person could maintain an action for waste but he who had the immediate estate of inheritance, without any interposing vested freehold. (28 Am. & Eng. Enc. Law [1st ed.] 904.) Also, at common law a mortgagee in possession as such might commit waste, unless he had expressly covenanted against it; but he would be required to apply the timber cut to the interest and principal of the mortgage debt, in an action to foreclose or redeem. (2 Greenl. Cruise, 111; Hill. Mortg. [4th ed.] § 1123; 28 Am. & Eng. Enc. Law [1st ed.] 897; *Hanson* v. *Derby*, 2 Vern. 392; *McCormick* v. *Digby*, 8 Blackf. 99; *Onderdonk* v. *Gray*, 19

N. J. Eq. 65.) " Although a mortgagee in fee in possession has a right at law to commit any kind of waste, because he is considered as the absolute owner of the inheritance, yet he will be restrained in equity; and the Court of Chancery will also decree an account to be taken of the trees cut down, and direct the produce to be applied first in the payment of interest due on the mortgage, and then in reducing the principal." (2 Greenl. Cruise, *supra*.) In *Onderdonk* v. *Gray* (*supra*), it is said: " A mortgagee in possession is bound to account for all rents, issues, and profits received by him, and for all waste and destruction of the premises, and must deduct the allowance for these matters from the amount due on his mortgage; and Gray has adopted the proper course to entitle him to such allowance,—filing a cross bill, and praying for such account, and to be allowed to redeem on paying the balance. But such allowances can only be claimed either on a bill to foreclose or a bill to redeem against a mortgagee in possession, and in possession as a mortgage. He cannot be called to account in such suits for trespass committed by him; nor if he is in possession as a tenant of a mortgagor under a lease from him, which a mortgagee may take as well as a stranger, can the mortgagee claim an allowance for rent due on the lease or waste committed as a tenant." (See, also, *Guthrie* v. *Kahle*, 46 Pa. St. 331.)

Keeping these general principles in mind, we come to the main question presented by the averments in the first count of the complaint,—the right of the administrator to maintain an action to redeem. Generally such action can be maintained by those who have an interest in the mortgaged premises, and would be losers by foreclosure. " Any person who holds a legal estate in the mortgaged premises, or any part thereof, derived through, under, or in privity with the mortgagor, and any person holding either a legal or equitable lien on the premises, or any part thereof, under or in privity with the mortgagor's estate, may also in like manner redeem from a prior mortgage." (Pom. Eq. Jur. 280.) " No person can come into a court of equity for a redemption of a mortgage but he who is entitled to the legal estate of the mortgagor, or claims a subsisting interest under him. * * * If the respondents have shown no interest in themselves, or a right to redeem the mortgage on their own account, or on account of others with whom some connection is shown, and whose interest they have a right to represent, their claims cannot be supported, notwithstanding some other person might have a right to enforce the same claim." (*Grant* v. *Duane*, 9 Johns. 611.)   At common law the real property of a decedent could not be subjected to the payment of simple contract debts, and was not subject to administration; but in this, as in nearly all of the states, this rule has been changed by statute, and the real property, while descending to the heirs, is made subject to the payment of debts in the course of administration, and becomes assets in the hands of the administrator for that purpose.   Hence it has been held that the administrator may have such an interest in the lands of the decedent as would entitle him to redeem, and therefore entitle him to maintain such an action.   In one case it is said: "It is also claimed that the suit is improperly brought by the administrator, and that the heirs should have been made parties.   Whether in such cases the heirs are ever necessary parties, under our system, where the bill is filed for redemption, or to remove an alleged cloud in the shape of an undischarged mortgage, it is not now important to examine.   * * *   The administrator, being entitled under the statute to the possession of the lands of his intestate, has such an interest as entitles him to redeem or to compel a release of a satisfied mortgage; and, if the heirs would have been proper parties, the decree is nevertheless valid, inasmuch as it does complete justice as it stands, provided it is sustained by the proofs." *Enos* v. *Sutherland*, 11 Mich. 541.)   Discussing the same question in another case, the court says: "It is said that this bill cannot be maintained by the administrator of Leach.   In England, where the real estate upon the death of the intestate passes directly to the heir, and is not assets in the hands of the administrator for the payment of debts, the bill should be brought by the heirs.   But with us the law is different.   The action of ejectment is given to the administrator, and the heirs cannot have the action until there has been a division of the estate under a decree of the Probate Court in cases where a division is necessary.   It is the duty of the administrator to pay off the debts out of the personal estate, if sufficient for that purpose, and prepare the estate for distribution among the heirs.   To discharge this duty he must, of necessity, be permitted to maintain a bill of this description, as the only means of ascertaining what may be due, if anything, on the mortgage." (*Merriam* v. *Barton*, 14 Vt. 513.)

It will be noted that the right of the administrator to maintain an action to redeem the intestate's lands from a mortgage is based upon the express provisions of the law making the lands assets in his hands to be administered upon, and giving to him the right of possession thereof for the purposes of administration. Notwithstanding our statute gives the administrator appointed thereunder the right of possession of the lands of the intestate not exempted, and the right to the rents, issues, and profits thereof for the purpose of administration, and the same become assets in his hands for the payment of debts, it cannot be claimed or maintained that he is entitled to the possession of lands in another state, and under another jurisdiction, or that such lands become assets in his hands for the purposes of administration. Discussing the power of administrators, the Supreme Court of Iowa uses the following language: " The administrator appointed in this state derives his powers from the statutes of this state. He succeeds to none of the powers or rights of the Pennsylvania administrator. His appointment empowers him to collect such assets of the estate as may be found in this state, and he may make such disposition of them as is directed by the laws of this state; and he is not answerable for his conduct either to the foreign administrator or to the power from which his authority is derived, but is independent of both. There is privity neither in law nor estate between them, and there is no general principle of law under which it can be held that a judgment against the one is binding upon the others." (*Creswell* v. *Slack,* 68 Iowa, 113; 26 N. W. 42.) The Supreme Court of the United States, in *Johnson* v. *Powers* (139 U. S. 160; 11 Sup. Ct. 526), discussing the same question, quotes with approval from the opinion of Mr. Justice GRIER in *Stacy* v. *Thrasher* (6 How. 58), in which he uses the following language: " The administrator receives his authority from the ordinary or other officer of the government where the goods of the intestate are situate, but coming into such possession by succession to the intestate, and incumbered with the duty to pay his debts, he is considered in law as in privity with him, and therefore bound or estopped by a judgment against him. Yet his representation of his intestate is a qualified one, and extends not beyond the assets of which the ordinary had jurisdiction." (*Johnson* v. *Powers,* 139 U. S. 160; 11 Sup. Ct. 526.) The following authorities hold to the same effect: 1 Woerner, Adm'n

(§ 158; 8 Am. & Eng. Enc. Law [1st ed.], 427); *Taylor* v. *Barron* (35 N. H. 496); *Deery* v. *Cray* (5 Wall. 803); *Braithwaite* v. *Harvey* ([Mont.] 36 Pac. 39); *State* v. *Fulton* ([Tenn. Ch. App.] 49 S. W. 297).

If, then, an action to redeem lands from a mortgage by setting off and applying damages in waste committed by the mortgagee in possession as such can only be maintained in an action to foreclose or redeem, and if the administrator can only maintain an action to redeem as to such lands as are assets in his hands for the purpose of administration, or to which he is entitled to the possession, then it cannot be claimed that he has any power or right to maintain such action as to lands which are not assets in his hands, and the possession of which he is not entitled to. Considering now the right of an administrator appointed under the law of this state to maintain an action for damages in the nature of waste committed after the death of the intestate by a mortgagee upon the mortgaged premises situated in another state, it is clearly apparent that, if the rule laid down in the authorities above cited prevails here, no such authority, power, or right exists. If such claim for allowance for damages by waste can be made only in actions to foreclose or redeem under the reason given, then the administrator cannot maintain an action for waste committed by a mortgagee upon the mortgaged premises in an independent action. It may with show of reason be claimed that the rights of the mortgagee and a mortgagor with reference to the possession of the mortgaged premises have been changed by our statute which declares that a mortgage of real property shall not be deemed a conveyance, whatever its terms, so as to enable the owner of a mortgage to recover the possession of the real property without foreclosure and sale. (Gen. St. § 3284.) The mortgagee, under the above provision, not having the right to recover the possession of the mortgaged premises before foreclosure and sale, has no right to the possession. Therefore his entry upon the mortgaged premises and cutting the timber thereon were without authority of law,—a trespass for which he should be held liable in damages to the proper parties in a court of competent jurisdiction. If this be the correct view of the law, then he must be held liable for such damages under that section of our statute which gives a right of action to the " owner of such land " against any person who shall cut down or carry away any of the trees or timber thereon without lawful authority. (Gen. St. § 3275.) Can it be claimed under these provisions of the law that the administrator appointed by the District Court of this state is in any sense such an owner of the lands situated in California, upon which the respondent, after the death of the intestate, committed the alleged trespass, as would entitle him, as such administrator, to maintain an action therefor? The title of the intestate to these lands upon his death vested, under our statute, in his heirs. It certainly cannot be pretended that the title to real estate in California upon the death of the intestate vested in the administrator in this state for any purpose whatever. Neither would the law of this state, under the authorities cited, vest in the administrator the right of possession, or the right to recover the possession, of said lands. If the administrator can have no title to the lands in California by virtue of his appointment as administrator in this state,—if he is not entitled to the possession of the same under his appointment,— he can have no right, title, or interest whatever in them, and therefore cannot be called the " owner " thereof, in any sense or meaning of that word. This court, in giving an interpretation to the word "owner" as used in our statutes, has been very liberal; holding that one who had the right of possession to be the owner thereof. For a full and exhaustive discussion of the question, see *State* v. *Wheeler* (23 Nev. 143; 44 Pac. 430). If, then, the administrator cannot, under these statutes, maintain the action, we must look to other provisions of the law to ascertain whether such authority is given. By sections 165, 166, pp. 144, 145, St. 1897, the Legislature has conferred authority upon administrators to maintain certain actions. In the last-named section is found authority to maintain actions for trespass committed upon the real estate of the deceased while living. The facts shown here do not make a case within this provision, and the right of the administrator to maintain an action for trespass committed upon the lands of the deceased situated in this state can only arise by implication from his right to the possession, and the rents, issues, and profits, as conferred by preceding sections of the same act (sections 94 and 164), or by giving to the words " owner of such lands," of section 3275, above cited, an interpretation that would allow the party entitled to the possession of such lands a right of action. We must therefore conclude that an administrator appointed under the laws of this state holds no such right, title, or interest in and to the lands of his intestate situated in another state as would authorize him to maintain an action to redeem from a mortgage thereon by setting off against the mortgage debt waste committed thereon by the mortgagee in possession thereof as mortgagee after the death of the intestate; nor has such administrator such right, title, or interest in said lands as would authorize him to recover for such damage committed as aforesaid; nor has he such power or authority conferred by our statutes to maintain an action for damages in trespass committed by the respondent upon said lands after the death of the intestate. The admitted wrong is not without its proper remedy, and the right of action can be maintained by the proper parties.

The judgment and order will be affirmed.

BELNNAP, J., concurs.

BONNIFIELD, C. J. (dissenting).—A demurrer to the plaintiff's complaint was sustained by the District Court on the grounds that said complaint " does not state facts sufficient to constitute a cause of action in favor of the plaintiff and against the defendant." Judgment was given to the effect that the plaintiff recover nothing from the defendant, and that the defendant recover his costs of the plaintiff, taxed at the sum of three dollars. This appeal is taken from the judgment and from the order sustaining the demurrer.

It appears from the complaint that said William Price died intestate in October, 1897, at Washoe county, state of Nevada, the place of his residence; that said Albert F. Price was duly appointed administrator of the estate of said deceased by the District Court of said county, and that he duly qualified and entered upon his duties as such administrator; that in the year 1894 said William Price borrowed $1,000 of the defendant, a resident of said county, and then and there executed to defendant his promissory note therefor, and thereupon, to secure the payment of said note, executed to the defendant a mortgage on a certain section of timber land belonging to said Price, containing 640 acres, and situated in Nevada county, state of California; that in January, 1897, default having been made in the payment of said note, Price, at the request of the defendant, executed and delivered to him at said Washoe county, a deed of conveyance for said land and premises; that said deed was absolute in form, but executed by Price and received by the defendant only as security to secure the payment of said promissory note, and other sums advanced by defendant on account of said land; that said deed was duly recorded in the office of the county recorder of said Nevada county, state of California, on the 9th day of January, 1897; that at the time of the execution of said deed and at the date of the death of William Price said land was heavily timbered with trees suitable for the manufacture of lumber, sawed timbers, and firewood; that said land, with the timber standing thereon, was worth at said dates $12,000; that the defendant, since the death of said Price, and without the permission of any one representing said estate, and without authority from any source, willfully entered upon said land, erected thereon a sawmill, cut down a large number of the trees standing on said land, manufactured the same into lumber and sawed timbers, removed and carried said lumber and sawed timbers away from said land, and converted the same to his own use; that said lumber and timbers manufactured, removed, carried, and converted as aforesaid by the defendant were and are of the net value of $6,000; that there is due the defendant on said promissory note, and for certain payments made by the defendant on account of said land, the sum only of $1,700 in the aggregate. The plaintiff prays for judgment for treble the said sum of $6,000, less the said sum of $1,700, and for costs of suit, for a decree requiring the defendant to surrender to plaintiff said promissory note, and to execute, acknowledge, and deliver to him, as such administrator, a conveyance of said land, and for general relief.

It is said in the decision on demurrer: " This is an action on the part of Albert F. Price, as administrator of the estate of William E. Price, deceased, appointed in the District Court of the Second judicial district of the state of Nevada, in and for Washoe county, against M. E. Ward, a resident of this jurisdiction, to obtain a decree of this court declaring a deed executed in this jurisdiction by William E. Price, in his lifetime, of property situated in Sierra (Nevada) county, state of California, a mortgage; to compel a conveyance of said property to said Albert F. Price, as administrator; and for triple damages for waste committed on said property by said defendant." It is further said: " Taking all of the allegations of the complaint as true, it simply amounts to a declaration that this property is the property of the estate of William

Price, deceased, in the state of California, subject to administration in that state, and gives a right of action, not to the administrator appointed in the state of Nevada, but to the administrator appointed, or that should be appointed, in the state of California. The claim for damages for waste rests upon the same basis."

That this deed, in effect, is simply a mortgage, under the allegations of the complaint, is not controverted, and needs no citation of authorities. That some one is entitled to a decree declaring it to be a mortgage seems clear. It seems clear that the defendant is liable to account to some one, in some court, for the net value of said lumber and sawed timber that he removed from the mortgaged premises and converted to his own use, alleged to be the sum of $6,000. It likewise appears that some one is entitled to a personal judgment against the defendant for the difference between said net value of $6,000 and said $1,700 due from said estate to defendant, and to a conveyance of said land from the defendant, so as to put the title in the true owner, the estate of William Price, and to have said promissory note given up. To recover the net value of said property so converted, or a judgment for the difference between said value and the $1,700 due the defendant, the action would have to be prosecuted in a court having jurisdiction of the person of the defendant. No court in the state of California can acquire jurisdiction of the person of the defendant in the state of Nevada, the place of his residence, by the service in this state of any process or notice that it may issue. We cannot presume that the defendant would voluntarily appear in such action and submit his person to the jurisdiction of such court. An administrator appointed in California could not maintain such an action in a court in the state of Nevada. If such action cannot be maintained in a Nevada court, then the defendant may retain said lumber and timber, or the proceeds of the sale thereof, to his own use, although, as shown by the complaint and admitted by the defendant, as the case now stands the same is not his property. In *Edwards* v. *Ballard* (14 La. Ann. 362), it is held that, although no real action would lie in Louisiana for lands sold in Mississippi, yet a suit brought to recover the proceeds of those lands from a defendant domiciled in Louisiana would fall within the jurisdiction of the Louisiana courts. In most of the states, under the common law and the statutes, the real estate of the deceased person descends directly to the heir or devisee, without passing through the custody of the executor or administrator. Upon this rule counsel seems to base his contention that the plaintiff could not maintain an action against the defendant on any cause accruing with respect to real estate after the death of the intestate, even though the property was situated in this state; that the right of action would belong solely to the heir or devisee. But in several of the states, including Nevada, California, Alabama, and Minnesota, the personal representative is entitled to the possession and control, for the purpose and during the term of the administration, of the real as well as the personal property of the decedent. (Woerner, Adm'n, § 337; St. 1897, 119) For particular purposes the letters of administration relate back to the time of the death of the intestate, and vest the property in the administrator from that time. On this principle an administrator may maintain trespass for injuries to the goods of the intestate committed after such death, and before his appointment. (Woerner, Adm'n, § 173,) And where the administrator, under the statute, is put into possession of the real estate as well as the personal estate, any action necessary to protect the same against wrongdoers, or to recover damages for injuries thereto, including ejectment for possession, must lie in favor of the administrator. (Id. § 293, and cases cited in note 2.) When he has properly asserted his right to the possession, he may maintain possessory action in his own name, even against the heirs or devisees, or recover the rents, incomes, or profits, or for injury to the land or anything severed from it, or for injuries committed before he took possession, and after the death of the decedent. (Id. § 337.) " An executor or administrator may maintain an action to recover timber logs cut and removed by a trespasser from the lands of the estate, although the heir or devisee may also maintain an action on failure of the personal representative to assert his statutory rights." (Leatherwood v. Sullivan, 81 Ala. 458; 1 South. 718.) " A personal representative who has taken possession of the real estate of the decedent can maintain an action for injuries to such realty committed post mortem decedentis. This is so even if the injuries were committed before he took possession, and before his letters of administration were granted." (Noon v. Finnegan, 32 Minn. 81; 19 N. W. 391.) " If the premises are vacant and unoccupied, the bringing of such action would be equivalent to taking possession."

(Id. 29 Minn. 418; 13 N. W. 197.) " The whole estate, real and personal, under our system, is assets, and may be, if required, applied to the payment of the debts of the estate." (*Washington* v. *Black*, 83 Cal. 295; 23 Pac. 300.) I think said contention of counsel, and the inference sought to be drawn therefrom against the rights of the administrator in this case, are without merit.

It is argued by the trial court and by counsel that a decree declaring said deed to be a mortgage, and requiring the defendant to execute a deed to the plaintiff by the District Court of Washoe county, would be meddling or interfering with the devolution of the property of the estate in the state where it is located, and that the courts of that state would disregard such decree and deed, and that the defendant would be still liable to an action for waste by an administrator appointed in California. The answer to this contention is: First. That such deed would in no manner meddle with the devolution of the property of the estate situated in California, or interfere with the administration of the estate there. A deed from the defendant to the plaintiff as administrator would simply take the title out of the defendant and place it in the plaintiff as administrator, showing that the property belonged to the estate of the deceased, whereas it now appears of record in the recorder's office of Nevada county, Cal., to belong to the defendant. It would form the basis for, and facilitate, the administration of the estate of William Price in that state. Second. There would be no occasion for the administrator, when appointed in California, to bring a suit to have said deed to the defendant decreed to be a mortgage, and thus determine the true ownership of said land. Third. Such administrator could not recover judgment against the defendant for waste, or for the value of said lumber and timbers converted as aforesaid, unless the defendant voluntarily placed himself within the jurisdiction of a California court. The contention that the courts of California would pay no attention whatever to any such deed from the defendant is simply an assumption of counsel. It seems well established by the authorities cited by appellant's counsel that, when the court has acquired jurisdiction of the parties in a matter of proper equitable cognizance, it may, by acting *in personam*, compel the conveyance of interests in real property, and administer other relief in the furtherance of justice, notwithstanding the property or interest involved may be situated without the state. From the allegations of the complaint, it appears that the defendant has unlawfully appropriated a portion of said property of said estate. The deed prayed for would be a means to prevent further unlawful appropriation, and preserve the remainder of said property to said estate, which equity and good conscience demand. That the complaint shows that some one is entitled at least to recover a personal judgment against the defendant for said value of said lumber and timbers, less the said sum due the defendant, and a decree declaring that said deed to defendant is a mortgage, and requiring him to execute a deed to said land, and to give up said promissory note, I think cannot be reasonably disputed. The vital question in the case is, is the plaintiff entitled to such a judgment and decree? If so, he can prosecute this action therefor. The moneys collected on such judgment by the plaintiff would properly be assets of said estate, and subject to the payment of resident and non-resident creditors of the intestate who have presented, or who may present, their claims in pursuance of the provisions of the statute. The policy of the law in every state is to subject all the property of the decedent, real and personal, to the payment of the creditors of the decedent, except certain reasonable exemptions for the benefit of his family. If the plaintiff cannot maintain this action to recover such judgment, then the heirs alone may sue the defendant, and recover the value of said lumber and timber for their own use, and deprive all of said creditors thereof, in contravention of said policy; for, if the administrator could compel the heirs to account for the moneys collected of the defendant for the value of said property, I see no reason why he may not maintain the action against the defendant for said value. Such judgment in favor of the plaintiff would inure to the benefit of all creditors of the deceased, and to all his heirs, in the manner contemplated by the law, and would be no injury to any one. And the deed prayed for would benefit all parties who have any interest in the estate situated in California, by placing the title beyond dispute in the estate there, and thus aid in the prompt administration thereof, while, as I think I have shown above, the defendant can be in no manner injured in any of his rights, or subjected to a second recovery for the value of said property so converted by him.

NOTE.—POWER OF ADMINISTRATOR OVER LAND.

(a) Summary by late writer.
(b) Must be derived from statute.
(c) Not assets.
(d) As to rents.
(e) When power ceases.
(f). Illustrative cases.

(a) **Summary by late writer.**—At common law and under the statutes of most of the states, real estate descends directly to the heir without passing through custody of the administrator. But in a number of the states by statute a personal representative is entitled to possession or control for the purposes, and during the term of the administration, but in most of them the representative's powers are more restricted. In these states the common law rights of the heir remain unaffected until the personal representative exerts the power derived from the statute. Unless the statute confers the power the administrator is not entitled or bound to take charge of or in any wise to interfere with or protect the real estate of the intestate, until he is ordered to do so by the Probate Court for the purpose of selling or leasing it, to enable him to pay debts. If personal property be insufficient for such purpose, real estate becomes assets, practically by statute in all the states, in the hands of the personal representatives. Hence, his interest is that of a naked power to sell according to the statute upon the happening of the contingency. (2 Woerner Administration, §§ 337, 338 [ed. 1899].)

(b) **Must be derived from statute.**—It is obvious from a review of the cases that whatever power may exist in the administrator in connection with real estate it must be found in a statute, and strictly followed as therein prescribed. (McKay v. Broad. 70 Ala. 378; Walbridge v. Day, 31 Ill. 379; Burr v. Bloemer, 174 id. 638; 51 N. E. Rep. 821; Merkel's Estate, 131 Pa. St. 584; 18 Atl. Rep. 931; Gibson v. Farley, 16 Mass. 280; Jones v. Billstein, 28 Wis. 221; Humphreys v. Taylor, 5 Ore. 260; McClead v. Davis, 83 Ind. 265; Reeves v. McMillen, 101 N. C. 479; 7 S. E. Rep. 906; Clark v. Bettelheim, 144 Mo. 259; 46 S. W. Rep. 135; Hall v. Farmers' Bank, 145 Mo. 418; 46 S. W. Rep. 1000; Duryea v. Mackey, 151 N. Y. 204, 207; 45 N. E. Rep. 458; Cooley v. Jansen, 54 Neb. 33; 74 N. W. Rep. 391.)

(c) **Not assets.**—Although lands may be subject to payment of intestate's debts they are not assets until made so by proceedings prescribed by statute for sale. (Haines v. Price, 20 N. J. L. 480.)

(d) **As to rents.**—The administrator has discretionary power to take possession and collect the rents and profits; the power to sell is an independent power. (Jones v. Billstein. 28 Wis. 221.)

The right to take possession and collect rents and profits is limited to a case of necessity for its exercise. (Rough v. Womer, 76 Mich. 375; 43 N. W. Rep. 573.)

Administrator taking rents and paying debts with same, is not relieved
from responsibility to the heirs, unless he has followed the statute. (Mc-
Clead v. Davis, 83 Ind. 263; and see Heed v. Sutton, 31 Kans. 620; 3
Pac. Rep. 280; Lucy v. Lucy, 55 N. H. 9; State v. Barrett, 121 Ind. 92;
22 N. E. Rep. 969; McPike v. McPike, 111 Mo. 216; 20 S. W. Rep. 12;
Kimball v. Sumner, 62 Me. 305.)

An administrator who has collected rents cannot set off his own claim
against the intestate as a debt, in action brought by the heirs. (Baker v.
Reese, 150 Pa. St. 44; 24 Atl. Rep. 634.)

No right to rents from real estate accruing after decease of the intestate. (Gibson v. Farley. 16 Mass. 279, 286; Merkel's Estate, 131 Pa. St.
584; 18 Atl. Rep. 931; Ball v. First National Bank, 80 Ky. 501; Brown v.
Fessenden, 81 Me. 522; 17 Atl. Rep. 709.)

(e) **When power ceases.**—Power of administrator continues not only
against heirs and devisees, but purchasers from them, until decree closing
the administration. (State v. Ramsey County Probate Court, 25 Minn. 22.)

But the rights of heirs should not be prejudiced by neglect of the administrator. (Stewart v. Smiley, 46 Ark. 373.)

When power over lands is conferred by statute, duty of administrator to
take proper steps within reasonable time and to act in that regard as a
prudent man would under like or similar circumstances. (Clark v. Knox,
70 Ala. 609.)

(f) **Illustrative cases.**—May maintain ejectment when necessary.
(Dundas v. Carson, 27 Neb. 634; 43 N. W. Rep. 399.)

May maintain ejectment or bill for specific performance, or to stay
waste, or to prevent trespass. (McKay v. Broad, 70 Ala. 379; Sullivan v.
Rabb, 86 Ala. 433; 5 So. Rep. 746.)

May lease from year to year. (Grady v. Warrell, 105 Mich. 310; 63
N. W. Rep. 204.)

Only during the period of administration. (Smith v. Park, 31 Minn.
70; 16 N. W. Rep. 490.)

When land is exempt from intestate's debts (for instance homestead)
his administrator can have no power over it. (Cooley v. Jansen, 54 Neb.
33; 74 N. W. Rep. 391.)

Cannot maintain action for its recovery unless shown that it is needed
for payment of debts. (Volk v. Stowall, 98 Wis. 385; 74 N. W. Rep. 118;
and see Roberts v. Morgan, 30 Vt. 319.)

Cannot maintain action to remove cloud from title. (Ryan v. Duncan,
88 Ill. 144.)

Cannot maintain specific performance, unless necessary to pay debts.
(Carpenter v. Fopper, 94 Wis. 146; 68 N. W. Rep. 874.)

Cannot maintain action for trespass unless he has first taken possession
under the statute. (Noon v. Finnegan, 29 Minn. 418; 13 N. W. Rep.
197; compare Leatherwood v. Sullivan, 81 Ala. 459; 1 So. Rep. 718.)

If right to recover not limited to the amount necessary to pay debts;
may recover the whole damage. (Noon v. Finnegan [second appeal], 32
Minn. 181; 19 N. W. Rep. 391.)

for answer to the first count of plaintiff's petition, admits that he is the administrator of the estate of said Harvey M. Vaile, deceased, as stated in said petition. He admits that said Harvey M. Vaile furnished the plaintiff with her board and clothing from the 14th day of February, 1883, to the 4th day of June, 1894. This defendant denies that said Harvey M. Vaile became indebted to the plaintiff in the sum of $5,608.30, or in any sum whatever, on account of service rendered by her as general housekeeper, or in attending to his business in or about his home place in Independence, Mo., or on account of any services of any kind whatever rendered by her for him. This defendant avers the fact to be that said Olivia Sprague is cousin of said Harvey M. Vaile; that she lived with the family of the said Harvey M. Vaile during the time mentioned in said first count of said petition as a member of his family, and that whatever services she performed, if any there were, were rendered gratuitously as such member of his family, and without any expectation on the part of the plaintiff at the time of making a charge therefor, or on the part of said H. M. Vaile of paying anything therefor; that the said H. M. Vaile considered plaintiff as a member of his family, and furnished her with said clothing and board as such, and as such, by his last will and testament, bequeathed to her, the said plaintiff, an annuity for and during her natural life of $500 per annum, and provided by his said will that said sum of $500 should be paid to her each year out of his said estate. Defendant denies each and every allegation in said first count of plaintiff's petition not hereinbefore expressly admitted. Wherefore defendant asks that plaintiff take nothing by her said first count, and that defendant have and recover his costs herein expended." The second defense is the same to the second count. Reply was a general denial. The cause was tried to a jury in the Circuit Court of Jackson county, and resulted in a verdict for plaintiff for $5,802.86. Defendant appeals.

John A. Sea and *R. T. Railey*, for appellant.

Warner, Dean & McLeod, for respondent.

GANTT, P. J. (after stating the facts).—It appears that Harvey M. Vaile, for many years previous to his death, lived near Independence, in Jackson county. His residence was one of the handsomest and largest in said county. The grounds were extensive, and ornamented with the choicest shrubbery and flowers. He was also an extensive breeder of pedigreed cattle. He traveled much, and during his absence Miss Sprague, the plaintiff, superintended his business. as well as his household affairs. The house contained about twenty rooms. Besides herself, only two servants were employed to run it. About fifteen workmen were usually employed on the premises, and took their meals there. It is a conceded fact that during all the time for which she sues plaintiff was the housekeeper. Mr. Vaile in his last will, recites that " Miss Olivia Sprague has looked after my household affairs for many years." Plaintiff's evidence tended to prove that her services were well worth $500 a year. The theory of the defense, as it is gathered from the answer and instructions asked by the defendant, is that Miss Sprague being a relative of the decedent, did not expect compensation for her services, and did not intend to charge therefor when she rendered them; that the decedent promptly paid all his bills, and it was a fair presumption that one so punctual in meeting his obligations would not have let this matter of plaintiff's wages run for ten years; that the testator intended to and did provide for plaintiff by a provision in his will, and that the board and clothing furnished and this provision in his will were a full satisfaction for the services rendered. Various errors are assigned in two briefs by the defendant.

1. The demurrer to the evidence was properly overruled. It is elementary law that if I employ a person to do business for me, or perform any work, the law implies that I undertook or contracted to pay him as much as his labor is reasonably worth; and in an action like this, on the common count of *quantum meruit* for work and labor done and performed at the instance and request of the defendant's intestate, proof that the services were performed, and that he accepted the work, makes a *prima facie case*. It was abundantly established that plaintiff, with the knowledge and approval of Mr. Vaile, looked after his household and other business affairs during all the time for which she sues, and that her labors were reasonably worth $500 a year. Granting that there was no evidence of an express contract, the law implies an agreement on the part of deceased to pay the reasonable value of her services. Cer-

tainly, the mere fact that she was a second cousin in and of itself raised no presumption that she was rendering her services gratuitously, but it was a question of fact properly submitted to the jury whether or not she was to be compensated therefor.

2. The objection now urged that plaintiff was not a competent witness for any purpose in the case was not raised in the Circuit Court, and hence it cannot avail defendant in this court. (*Kash* v. *Coleman*, 145 Mo. 645; 47 S. W. 503.) Defendant did object to certain specific questions which tended to bring out facts between the deceased and plaintiff, and these the court sustained in almost every instance. Two questions only, that we recall, were answered over objections, and these were merely as to the number of servants employed on the farm and the length of time Mr. Vaile was absent from the place. These facts were fully established *aliunde,* and we can safely say that no possible harm resulted from permitting them; and in such case the statute forbids this court to reverse the case. (*Young* v. *Hudson,* 99 Mo. 106; 12 S. W. 632; *Lane* v. *Lane,* 113 Mo. 507; 21 S. W. 99.)

3. It is also insisted that Mrs. Minnie Taylor's evidence should have been excluded because it was an opinion as to an ordinary every-day matter. Mrs. Taylor had testified: That she was the daughter of Gen. Caldwell, of Leavenworth. She had often visited Mr. Vaile. That Miss Sprague had entire charge of the house and about the place outside. She did all the housekeeping, and made all the purchases for the house; directed all the servants. That it required a great deal of labor; and did what in other houses of like size they employ a house girl to do, and, in addition, superintended putting up fruit, and making butter. Witness had kept house herself for her father some fourteen years. She was then asked, taking the character of the duties performed, the size of the house, and all the circumstances, what, in her opinion, would be a reasonable value for such services. Defendant objected, because she was not qualified, and no foundation laid for the question. The objection was overruled, and the witness answered the services were worth $500 a year. It would cost that if you hired it done. This exception cannot work a reversal, for two reasons: The objection itself is too indefinite to advise this court upon what ground it was deemed incompetent. If, however, it be sufficient to raise the point that a non-expert witness is incompetent to give his or her opinion

after stating all the facts upon which such opinion is based, it must be remembered that the rule that a non-expert witness cannot give his opinion has well-established exceptions. In *Straus* v. *Railroad Co.* (86 Mo. loc. cit. 433), this court said: " Where the value of property is in question, a witness who states that he is acquainted with the value of that kind of property may give his opinion of the value of the property in dispute. So, where the question of the sanity of a person is involved, a witness may give his opinion, provided he states the facts upon which it is founded." In *Kelly* v. *Rowane* (33 Mo. App. loc. cit. 446), the St. Louis Court of Appeals, in a case in which objection was made to the testimony of carpenters as to the value of the services of some boys employed to aid carpenters work, on the ground that they were not experts, said: " The value of ordinary labor is a matter of such common knowledge that almost any intelligent citizen may be presumed to know it, and one who employed such labor constantly may well be regarded competent to testify concerning it." Certainly, there is no special science, art, or trade about housekeeping, or the value of ordinary services in so doing. " Employers of labor are competent to testify as to the value of one in like employment." (Rog. Exp. Test. [2d ed.] 379.) " So it has been held that neighbors, who had employed servants to do like work, are competent to testify as to the value of services of a girl employed to do housework, and that the value of the services of a farm laborer may be shown by the testimony of those who had employed him." (Id. § 380.) Mrs. Taylor had had large experience in housekeeping and hiring domestic servants, and, after detailing her knowledge of the work done by Miss Sprague, its character, etc., we think she was competent to give her opinion of its value.

4. For the plaintiff the court gave the following instructions: " The court instructs the jury that, where services are rendered, a contract or obligation to pay will be presumed, but a presumption may arise from the relationship of the parties that the services rendered are acts of gratuitous kindness, and in this case it is a question for the jury, taking into consideration all of the circumstances, including the nature of the degree of the relationship of the plaintiff to the deceased, Harvey M. Vaile, and their circumstances in life, to determine whether there was an implied contract for compensation or not; and if you find from the evidence

that the plaintiff rendered services to the deceased, Harvey M. Vaile, in attending to his business in and about his place near the city of Independence, in the county of Jackson, and state of Missouri, and that it was understood between them that the plaintiff should receive pay for such services to said Harvey M. Vaile, then you will find the issues on the first count of the petition herein for the plaintiff, and allow her in your verdict such sum as you may believe from the evidence in this case she is entitled to, not exceeding the sum of five hundred dollars a year, with interest thereon at the rate of six per cent. per annum from the 25th day of August, 1895, the date of the filing of her petition herein." "If you find the issues on the first count in the plaintiff's petition, under the last foregoing instruction, for the plaintiff, in ascertaining what compensation you will allow her you must confine yourselves to compensation for such services as you may believe the plaintiff to have rendered for the deceased, H. M. Vaile, between the 14th day of February, 1883, and the 4th day of June, 1894, and allow her for such services as you may believe to have been rendered a sum not exceeding five hundred dollars a year." Also two others, numbered 3 and 4, substantially like the foregoing, and one numbered 5, as follows: "The court instructs the jury that under the pleadings in this case it is admitted that the only compensation received by the plaintiff from the deceased, Harvey M. Vaile, for such services, if any you may find from the evidence were rendered by the plaintiff for such deceased, Harvey M. Vaile, was her board and clothing, and the defendant is bound by such admission." It is objected to these instructions that they were not confined within the limits of the pleadings. The objection is obviously not tenable as to said instructions numbered 1 and 2. It is difficult to see how they could have been more pertinent to the case in hand. They are substantial rescripts of the instruction approved in *Reando* v. *Misplay* (90 Mo. 252; 2 S. W. . 405.) The argument of defendant, orally and in the briefs, assaults the fifth instruction as notably vicious in misstating the admission in defendant's answer, in that the essential fact, to wit, the board and clothing were given as a compensation or payment, embraced a hypothesis not within the pleadings, and that this error was aggravated by telling the jury that defendant was bound by the admission in his answer. This assignment can best be tested by reproducing the part of the answer referred to and the instruction in juxtaposition:

The answer is in these words:

" This defendant denies that said Harvey M. Vaile became indebted to the plaintiff in the sum of $5,-608.30, or in any sum whatever, on account of services rendered by her as general housekeeper, or in attending to his business in or about his home place in Independence, Mo., or on account of any services of any kind whatever rendered by her for him. This defendant avers the fact to be that said Olivia Sprague is cousin of said Harvey M. Vaile; that she lived with the family of the said Harvey M. Vaile during the time mentioned in said first count of said petition as a member of his family, and that whatever services she performed, if any there were, were rendered gratuitously as such member of his family, and without any expectation on the part of the plaintiff at the time of making a charge therefor, or on the part of said H. M. Vaile of paying anything therefor; that the said H. M. Vaile considered plaintiff as a member of his family, and furnished her with said clothing and board as such, and as such, by his last will and testament, bequeathed to her, the said plaintiff, an annuity for and during her natural life of five hundred dollars per annum, and provided by his said will that sum of five hundred dollars should be paid to her each year out of his said estate."

The fifth instruction is as follows:

" The court instructs the jury that under the pleadings in this case it is admitted that the only compensation received by the plaintiff from the deceased, Harvey M. Vaile for such services, if any you may find from the evidence, were rendered by the plaintiff for such deceased, Harvey M. Vaile, was her board and clothing, and the defendant is bound by such admission."

Counsel for defendant insists that this fifth instruction told the jury that plaintiff never received anything for her services except her board and clothing. We think this is so, and the question is, was it not justified by the answer? The court had clearly told the jury that they were to determine whether her services were rendered gratuitously, and without expectation of reward, or under an understanding and implied contract that she should receive what her services merited. Looking to the answer, we think the court correctly construed it. There is no claim in it that plaintiff ever received anything but her board and clothing, and any claim that she had would have been utterly inconsistent with the allegations of the answer. We think the criticism of the instruction is not sustained by the record. This we say independently of the contemporaneous construction placed on the answer by defendant himself at the trial when he asked and obtained from the court the instruction No. 2 for defendant: " (2) The court instructs the jury that, if you believe from the evidence that the plaintiff rendered services for H. M. Vaile, yet if you further believe that she was to be fully compensated therefor by her board and clothing and a provision for her in his will, and that he did so provide for her, then she cannot recover, and your verdict must be for the defendant." A party is held in this court to the theory in which he tries his case in the Circuit Court. Now, independently of the answer of the defendant, there was no such issue tendered in the pleadings as he tenders in this instruction. If it was not his theory that plaintiff had been fully compensated by her board and clothing for her services, then he ought not to have asked this instruction, and received the full benefit for that contention. Unless defendant intended by his answer to tender the issue that plaintiff's board and clothing had been received as compensation, then nothing can be clearer than that this instruction was absolutely without the limits of the pleadings, and for that reason erroneous.

Counsel also urges that the instructions are palpably inconsistent. Granting that this is true, defendant obtained the erroneous instruction, and it is the settled law of this state that a party is estopped from complaining of an error of his own creation, and committed at his request. (*Reardon* v. *Railway Co.*, 114 Mo. 384; 21 S. W. 731; *Wilkins* v. *Railway Co.*, 101 Mo. 105; 13 S. W. 893; *Baker* v. *Railroad Co.*, 122 Mo., loc. cit. 599; 26 S. W. 39; *Francis* v. *Railroad Co.*, 127 Mo., loc. cit. 675; 28 S. W. 846, and 30 S. W. 129; *Hahn* v. *Dawson*, 134 Mo., loc. cit. 591, 592; 36 S. W. 235.) For the same reasons instruction No. 3 for defendant was erroneous. There was no plea of payment, and by obtaining it defendant obtained an instruction on an issue outside of his answer.

On the whole case the verdict is obviously for the right party, and the judgment is affirmed.

BURGESS, J., concurs. SHERWOOD, J., absent.

McMILLAN *et al. vs.* COX.

[Supreme Court of Georgia, November 2, 1899; 109 Ga. 42; 34 S. E. Rep. 341.]

WILLS—CONSTRUCTION—POWERS OF EXECUTRIX—MORTGAGE AND SALE OF ESTATE.

1. When, by the terms of a will, real and personal property is given to the wife for life, with remainder to the children of the testator, a power conferred on the executrix, who was the wife of the testator, to sell any or all of the property devised, and reinvest the proceeds, expressed in language which plainly and unequivocally limits the purpose for which any sale can be made to that of reinvestment only, does not, notwithstanding the will may have contained broad and liberal provisions as to the manner in which this power may be exercised, empower the executrix to mortgage the property devised, nor to convey the title of such property as security for a debt created by her.

2. When, after expressly conferring such a power, the will also declares that "no part of the *corpus* of said estate is to be spent unless, in the judgment of my said wife, the same shall be necessary for the proper maintenance and education of my minor children," nothing more than an implied authority to use a portion of the *corpus* if necessary for the maintenance and education of the testator's minor children is given. The language quoted cannot be construed so as to confer upon the executrix authority to borrow money for any purpose.

3. The court erred in holding that the will authorized the executrix to borrow money and secure the same by a mortgage on property of the estate, and in appointing a receiver, and granting the injunction.

(Syllabus by the court.)

ERROR from Superior Court, Fulton county; J. H. LUMPKIN, Judge.

Suit by Kate Cox against Janie McMillan and others. Judgment for plaintiff. Defendants bring error.

Reversed.

Dorsey, Brewster & Howell and *Arnold & Arnold*, for plaintiffs in error.

Abbott, Cox & Abbott, for defendant in error.

LITTLE, J.—Mrs. Cox filed an equitable petition, in which she made the following case : McMillan died testate in Fulton county, and the first item of his will, which was duly probated, is as follows : " I give and bequeath all of the property, of every kind whatsoever, both real and personal, that I may own or to which I may be entitled at the time of my death, including all land, movable property, money, notes, or other choses in action, rights or credits of whatever character or description, and no matter where or in what shape the same may be, to my beloved wife, Janie H. McMillan, during her life and at her death to be divided equally among my children, to wit, Lula, Harry, William, John, Archie, Jennie, Nannie, Robert, and an infant daughter, now three months old, with full power in my said wife without any order of court to sell and convey, in her discretion, any or all of said property, upon such terms as to her may seem proper, and reinvest the proceeds, subject to the same limitations; the purchaser from her receiving the fee simple title unincumbered by any remainder interest; and her said power to sell and reinvest continuing and running through all subsequent investments made by her; the remainder interest of my said children attaching to all property purchased by her, and lost upon all sold by her.   This wide discretion is vested in my wife with the belief that she will use it for the best interest of herself and my children, so that my said estate shall be taken care of and kept together while my wife lives, and then be divided among my children. No part of the *corpus* of said estate is to be spent unless, in the judgment of my said wife, the same shall be necessary for the proper maintenance and education of my minor children." Janie H. Millan was appointed executrix of the will and guardian of the minor children. Testator died in October, 1882. At the time of his death, McMillan was possessed of a large and varied estate, consisting of merchandise, book accounts, and the undivided one-half interest in the notes and accounts of the firm of McMillan & Snow, and also an undivided one-half interest in lot No. 25 on Marietta street in the city of Atlanta, Ga., together with other lands; also money and solvent debts. In 1892 the executrix induced petitioner to loan her the sum of $6,000, for which she gave a promissory note, signed " Janie H. McMillan, Executrix of J. C. McMillan," becoming due March 1, 1897, and also executed and delivered certain interest notes for $240 each. For the purpose of securing said loan, Janie McMillan individually and as executrix of the will of her testator made and delivered to petitioner her deed conveying an undivided one-half interest in lot No. 25 on Marietta street in the city of Atlanta, on which was situated a storehouse. The petition alleges that the loan obtained from petitioner was for the purpose of improving the estate left by the testator by erecting buildings and making other improvements rendering the estate productive; that the principal borrowed—$6,000—is now due, together with interest on the same according to the contract; that the defendant now sets up that she had no power, as executrix, to bind the estate of her testator for the payment of the sum borrowed, nor to convey title to the land as security, and she therefore refuses to pay the same; that by proper conveyances from certain of the remaindermen Janie H. McMillan individually has now a one-third interest in the land conveyed in fee simple; that she is insolvent, is in possession of the property, and receiving the rents; that her individual interest therein is not sufficient to pay petitioner the amount which is due; that she has not paid the taxes on the property, but has wasted and squandered the income. She prays for a receiver to take charge of the property conveyed, to collect the rents, and that the defendant be enjoined from interfering with such property; that the interest in the property belonging to Janie McMillan individually be sold, and the proceeds applied to the payment of the indebtedness; that two-thirds of an undivided one-half in the land conveyed be decreed to be bound for the payment of such balance as may be due petitioner after the sale of the individual interest of said Janie McMillan. There was also a prayer for general relief. The defendant answered, and denied that she had any power to bind the estate by contracts for improving the same; admits that the loan was made to her individually, but denies that the estate is bound; admits the execution of the deed; and avers that the money was borrowed for her own purposes, and was used in operating a store, and was of no benefit to the estate.   She denies that she has any life estate which can be disposed of, her only interest being as trustee for her children during her life; that the income during her life belongs to the children.   The deed from McMillan to Mrs. Cox was executed on March 1, 1892.   It purports to convey the undivided one-half interest in the lot on Marietta street, and recites that it is made under section 1969 of the Code of Georgia, for the purpose of securing a loan of $6,000, which is obtained for the purpose of improving the estate left by J. C. McMillan under his will by building and other improvements, rendering said property productive, and obviating the necessity of sale and reinvestment for such purpose.   On the hearing this deed was put in evidence; also the promissory notes, and the will of McMillan.   It was also shown that Mrs. McMillan had neglected to pay the premiums for insurance on the property; that the state and county taxes for a number of years were not paid by the executrix, but were transferred to different parties, and are still outstanding.   It was agreed that Mrs. McMillan was insolvent, and that three of the children, remaindermen under the will, are yet minors.   The presiding judge appointed a receiver for one-half undivided interest in the land, and the receiver was directed to collect the rents, and hold the property for the further order of the court.   An injunction was also granted, and to these rulings of the trial judge the plaintiff in error excepted.

1. The question made and passed upon by the judge in the court below was whether the power conferred on Mrs. McMillan by the will of her husband authorized her to borrow money for the purpose of improving the estate left by the testator in his will by building and making other improvements rendering said property productive, and obviating the necessity of sale and reinvestment for such purpose.   The judge of the Superior Court held that the powers conferred did so authorize the executrix, and under that construction he appointed a receiver for the entire interest in the property purporting to be conveyed by the deed.   One of the prayers of the original petition was that the interest belonging to Janie H. McMillan individually should be sold, and the proceeds applied to the payment of the indebtedness due the petitioner.   Inasmuch as the separate question as to what interest Janie McMillan individually owned in the property, and whether it, under the terms of the

will, passed by her deed, was not considered and passed
upon by the trial judge, we confine ourselves to the consideration of the construction of the will to ascertain whether the
executrix had the power to convey the interest for the purposes
expressed in the deed. If she did, then the ruling made below,
and the appointment of the receiver, were proper. If she did not
have such power, then, the court committed error in appointing the
receiver and granting the injunction. It is said that the power
given to the executrix is very broad, and that the language shows
that the testator intended to trust very much to her discretion. This
is undoubtedly true, but as we read the first item of the will, while
the discretion given the executrix is very broad, its exercise is
limited to a narrow field. Undoubtedly, by the terms of the will,
the wife took a life estate in all of the property of the testator, and
the children took as remainder-men. To arrive at the intention of
the testator, it is necessary that the whole will shall be construed
together. We find that the testator, after the devise to his wife and
children, and after conferring the powers named on the executrix,
declares: " No part of the *corpus* of said estate is to be spent unless, in the judgment of my said wife, the same shall be necessary
for the proper maintenance and education of my minor children."
Here is a declaration that but one contingency shall authorize the
diminution of the *corpus* of the estate; that is, when it becomes
necessary to properly maintain and educate the minor children.
True, the judgment of the executrix must determine when such
maintenance and education require the use of a part of the *corpus*,
but that judgment cannot be exercised in conveying away any part
of the estate except for maintenance and education of the children.
When properly construed, we think, there is no other clause of the
will which gives the wife any power to diminish the *corpus* of the
estate. She is invested with full power, and in her discretion without any order of court, to sell and convey any or all of the property
on such terms as she may see proper, and reinvest the proceeds.
If the power is exercised according to the evident intention of the
will, then the discretion vested in the executrix only enables her
to exchange property of the estate for other property to belong to
the estate, because immediately following the provision granting
power to sell and convey and reinvest the proceeds the will in terms
requires the property in which the proceeds are invested shall be

subject to the same limitations which qualified the devises to the wife and children. It is said, however, that in the exercise of this power of sale and reinvestment the grantee in a conveyance from her would not be bound to see to the actual investment. This is undoubtedly true, because the power to invest was intrusted to her discretion, with which the grantee has nothing to do. Besides, the will provides that the purchaser who receives from her a fee simple title takes it unincumbered. But it is nevertheless true that the power of sale is by this portion of the will confined to the purposes of reinvestment. We do not undertake to say that, if she had conveyed any portion of this property for the declared purpose of reinvestment, that title would not have passed, notwithstanding the reinvestment never was made. But how can the petitioner take any benefit from the power given to sell for the purpose of reinvestment? It is not claimed at all that the defendant in error purchased the property attempted to be conveyed. The purpose specified in the deed which she received was not a sale for the purpose of reinvestment, but a loan of money to be used for building upon the land and otherwise improving the property. Therefore without regard to the question as to whether the money borrowed was devoted to building and making other improvements of the property, it does not seem to have been authorized under a power which limited the right to sell and convey to a purpose of investing the proceeds after such sale in property which should belong to the estate. But it is claimed that a power to sell and convey carries with it the right to create a mortgage. In his learned and able opinion the judge who presided on the hearing in this case says that he " does not find it necessary to hold that, as a rule, a simple power to sell, in a deed or will, without more, necessarily includes a power to mortgage." Much might be said to the contrary. In the case of *Adams* v. *City of Rome* (59 Ga. 768), Judge BLECKLEY uses this language: " If the power to sell and convey stood alone, it would probably comprehend the power to mortgage; " citing *Wayne* v. *Myddleton* (2 Kelly, 404; 3 P. Wms. 9). Counsel for plaintiff in error has cited us to the cases of *Wayne* v. *Myddleton* (2 Kelly, 383); *Miller* v. *Redwine* (75 Ga. 130), and *Henderson* v. *Williams* (97 id. 709; 25 S. E. 395), to support the contention that the power to sell and convey in this case carries with it a right to create a mortgage on the property. It appeared in the *Case of Wayne* (*supra*), that certain slaves were given to a trustee, for the use of the grantor's wife during her life, and after her death to her children. The *cestui que trust,* with the approbation of her trustee, purchased a tract of land, growing crop, stock, cattle, etc., and a payment was secured by a mortgage on the four slaves conveyed by the deed of trust, and also by a mortgage on the land. The crop, cattle, etc., and the services of hired slaves were received by the *cestui que trust.* The mortgage was foreclosed, and the slaves sold. It was held that the *cestui que trust* was competent to make the contract. The deed authorized the *cestui que trust,* with the consent of her trustee, to sell and dispose of the trust estate whenever she shall deem it proper to do so, and to reinvest the proceeds upon like trusts. It will be noted that the power given in this case was to sell and dispose of the trust estate at any time the *cestui que trust* thought proper to do so, and to reinvest. The facts of the case show that, as consideration for the debt which she secured by mortgage she received other property; not, it is true, as it turned out, of the full value of her note, but a very considerable amount. In the case of *Miller* v. *Redwine* (*supra*), the lease of a hotel, the furniture contained in it, and the live stock about it were conveyed by a will to a daughter-in-law and her children through the medium of a trustee, with the right in the trustee " to sell said property, and reinvest the same, for the benefit of his *cestui que trust,* at any time, without an order of court for that purpose." It was held that the mortgage to Redwine was legal, it having been made to raise money to carry on the hotel business, and this decision was placed on the ground that the trustee is invested with sufficient power to execute the trust, and, in order to determine the power, the court will look to the character of the trust estate. In the case of *Henderson* v. *Williams* the trustee had power and authority to allow the *corpus* of the estate to be used on the written consent of the *cestui que trust,* when it became desirable to use any part of the *corpus* of the trust estate for the improvement thereof, or for the more comfortable support of said *cestui que trust.* Under this power the trustee procured supplies to enable him to make a crop, and with the written consent of the *cestui que trust* made a deed to secure the payment of the note so given. This was held to be a proper exercise of the power. Whether these cases rule the principle clearly and explicitly that a power to sell includes the power to mortgage is a question we do not now have to decide. The decision in each of them seems to be made upon the facts as shown, rather than to settle the principle broadly, but they do not, in our opinion, afford authority which will support the deed made by Mrs. McMillan under the powers and restrictions of the will. Of this we are clear. If A. should give to B. a power of attorney to sell a piece of property, it could hardly be claimed that B., under such power, could execute a mortgage on the property to secure a loan. We think that the true principle is that a power to sell and convey may include the power to mortgage, but it does not necessarily do so; and whether such power is or is not included depends upon the character of the estate, the words granting the power, and the purposes for which the debt was created. We are satisfied, however, that when, by the terms of a will, the power of sale is given only for the purpose of reinvestment, with a provision restricting the expenditure of the *corpus* of the estate to a single purpose, and the further provision that the same uses and restrictions which attached to the property devised should also attach to the property purchased with the proceeds of property which should be sold under the power given, that no right or power is given to the executrix to create a mortgage on the property of the estate to secure a loan of money. The intention to grant that power is not consistent with the restricted power of sale given by the will, and the expressed purpose of the testator to limit the expenditure of the *corpus* of his estate to one other single purpose.

2. It may be further said that, as a general rule, an executor cannot contract debts which will bind the estate he represents. (*Palmer v. Moore*, 82 Ga. 177; 8 S. E. 180.) In order to make such debts valid charges on the estate he represents, there must be express authority so to do, and, if the executrix in this case had the right to borrow money, and charge the estate she represented with its payment, she must have had express power to do so. The power given by the will is that which we first quoted,—that no part of the *corpus* is to be spent unless, in the judgment of the executrix, it became necessary to do so for the maintenance and education of the children. Certainly it cannot be claimed that power to borrow money was conferred by this clause of the will. It was but an effort on the part of the testator to prevent making his estate liable

for any debt, and preventing any part of his property from being expended unless it became necessary for the maintenance and education of his children. There is no condition of the will which authorizes the executrix to spend any portion of the *corpus* of the estate, except when necessary for the maintenance and education of the children. The intention gathered from the entire will is that his wife and children shall be supported from the rents and profits of the estate of which he was possessed; that, inasmuch as it was probable that the estate would remain under the control of his executrix for a considerable length of time, and as some of his children were young, and had to be reared and educated, if such rents and profits were not sufficient to maintain and educate the children, then he gave the power to his executrix to sell such a part of his estate as was necessary for this purpose. In the meantime, if it became desirable to sell any particular pieces of property, or all of it, and with the proceeds to procure other property—power was given to the executrix so to do for the benefit of his devisees; but the testator nowhere in his will used language which fairly construed, showed that he intended to give his executrix power to borrow money and contract debts with the incident risk of dissipating an estate which he set aside for the support and maintenance of those whom he left dependent upon it.

Judgment reversed. All the justices concurring.

BURNEY *et al. vs.* ALLEN *et al.*

[Supreme Court of North Carolina. November 28, 1899; 125 N. C. 314; 34 S. E. Rep. 500.]

WILLS—EXECUTION—WITNESSES—INSTRUCTIONS.

1. A testator must actually have seen, or been in a position to see, not only the witnesses, but the paper writing itself, at the time the witnesses signed it.
2. In the execution of a will, it is not necessary, in the absence of statutory requirement, for the testator to request the witnesses to sign. Such request may be made by any person, so long as the testator acquiesces or approves it, or by his conduct such acquiescence or approval can be implied.

APPEAL from Superior Court, Bladen county; ROBINSON, Judge.

Action by Sarah A. Burney and others against Edna Allen and others. Judgment for plaintiffs, and defendants appeal. Reversed.

C. C. Lyon and *Jones & Stewart*, for appellants.

R. O. Burton, for appellees.

MONTGOMERY, J.—Nathan Jones, one of the subscribing witnesses to the script which purports to be the last will and testament of the decedent, Henry Allen, testified that he subscribed it in the presence of the decedent and at his request, and in the presence of W. F. Devane, the other subscribing witness, and that Devane also subscribed it in the presence of the decedent and at his request. Devane testified as follows: " I was witness to Henry Allen's will. I signed it in the presence of the testator, Nathan Jones, and A. M. McNeill. Emma Jones came for me, and I went to Allen's house. Emma Jones is sister to Widow Allen. When I went, don't recollect that Henry Allen spoke to me. I don't think he spoke to me at all. I saw him when he signed the will. He was lying flat on his back when he signed it. Allen made his mark. I don't know what I signed. I asked McNeill to let me read it, but he said it was not necessary. I do not know whether Allen could see me when he signed it or not. He could see me, but don't think he could see the paper. He was on the bed, in the east corner of the room, and I was at the west corner of the same room, at a table. I was standing with my side or back to him; I don't know which. I am satisfied that he could not see the paper writing at the time I signed it, but he could see me." A. M. McNeill testified: " Allen was very sick, and suffered greatly. He was on his bed. I wrote his name, and he made his mark to the paper writing. I don't know whether his eyes were open or not. I don't know the condition of his mind. He could have seen the parties when they signed the paper as witnesses, but could not see the paper. Allen did not ask any one to sign it. I wrote his will at his dictation." The following issue was submitted to the jury: " Is the paper writing, or any part thereof, the last will and testament of Henry Allen? "

An exception was made by the defendants, the propounders, to

that part of the charge of the court which is in the following words:
" That the deceased, Allen, must actually have seen, or have been
in a position to see, not only the witnesses, but the paper writing
itself, at the time the witnesses signed the same, and that, if the
jury should believe that he did not see the paper writing at the
time the witnesses signed it they should answer the issue, ' No.' "
The instruction was in harmony with the decision of this court
made in the case of *Graham* v. *Graham* (32 N. C. 219). In that
case it appeared that the decedent was very sick and lying in bed
at the time the paper writing propounded as the will of the decedent
was alleged to have been subscribed by the witness. The witnesses
withdrew into another room, and there, at a large chest, signed
their names. The testator, as he was lying in bed, could, by turning
his head and looking around the side of the door between the
rooms, have seen the backs of the witnesses as they sat at the chest,
writing; but he could not have seen their faces, arms, or hands,
or the paper on which they wrote, a view of those being obstructed
by the partition wall. After the witnesses had signed, they went
back, with the will, into the room where the decedent was, and
informed him that they had witnessed it, and he asked one
of the persons present to take charge of it. Upon that evidence
the court directed the jury that, " though the testator could have
seen enough of the persons of the witnesses while they were subscribing the will to enable him to recognize them, yet, if he
could not have seen what was going on whilst they were in the act
of attestation, the paper was not properly executed and attested."
And this court (RUFFIN, C. J., delivering the opinion), in reviewing that instruction, declared that while it was a rigid construction
of the terms " in his presence," which were used in the act, yet it
was in conformity with the cases theretofore decided on that subject, and that it was consonant with the policy and meaning of the
statute. In that opinion the true principle of the statute was settled to be " that a subscribing by the witnesses must be in such
a situation, whether within or without the testator's room, as will
enable the testator, if he will look, to see that the paper signed
by him is the same which is subscribed by the witnesses. * * *
The statute meant that he should have evidence of his own senses
to the subscribing by the witnesses, just as he should to a signing
for him by another by his direction and in his presence, so as to

exclude almost the possibility of imposition by substituting one paper for another without detection by the testator himself upon his own ocular observations, and without exposing him to any risks from undue confidence." And the opinion concludes in this language: " We believe, indeed, that there is no instance in which a paper has been sustained where the attestation was under such circumstances that the testator could not see what was done, so as to protect himself, upon his own knowledge, against any dishonest substitution by the people whom he is obliged by the law to select and depend upon as subscribing witnesses to his will." In the next volume of our Reports (33 N. C. 632), in the case of *Bynum* v. *Bynum,* the court, with its personnel unchanged, and the same judge delivering the opinion, reversed the judgment below because his honor instructed the jury that, " as to the formal execution of the script, it was not necessary it should be proved that the party deceased saw the paper at the time it was subscribed by the witnesses, but it was necessary she should be in such a situation that she could see it if she wished, and that, if the jury believed she could not see it at the time, it was not subscribed in her presence, within the meaning of the law." In that case the decedent was raised up in bed, and in that position she signed the script, and then laid down. The witnesses then subscribed their names in the same room, and within two or three feet of the decedent; but the witnesses said that they were not certain whether, from the position in which she was lying, she could see the paper at the time it was being subscribed, and that they thought another paper might have been substituted for the one she signed, without her knowing it. In the discussion of that case the court, without in so many words overruling the case of *Graham* v. *Graham* (*supra*), adopted an entirely different course of reasoning, and arrived at an entirely different conclusion from the principle announced in the last-mentioned case. In *Bynum* v. *Bynum* (*supra*), it is held, substantially, that, provided the subscribing by the witnesses is done in the same room, " openly and without any clandestine appearance about it," the attestation would be good, whether the decedent could actually see the paper or not. So, too, the declaration in *Graham* v. *Graham* (*supra*), that the testator should have evidence of his own senses (that is, the power to look and see from his present position, if he wished to do so), so as to exclude " almost the possibility of imposition by substituting one paper for another without detection by the testator upon his own ocular observation, and without exposing him to any risks from undue confidence," is substituted in the case of *Bynum* v. *Bynum* by the declaration: "It is not, therefore, the feasibility of obtaining another paper which will avoid the attestation, when all passes in the same room, so that the party has opportunity of watching for him or herself, for under those circumstances the attestation is *prima facie* good." In *Jones* v. *Tuck* (48 N. C. 202), the principle enunciated in *Graham* v. *Graham* (*supra*), was followed fully, and that case was cited as authority for the decision in *Jones* v. *Tuck*. In *Cornelius* v. *Cornelius* (52 N. C. 593), the court instructed the jury that: "If they believed that the attestation was made by the subscribing witnesses in the room in which the deceased was lying, and in such a situation as, by turning his head in the manner described by them, he could see the paper writing at the time of the attestation, and that he had the ability to do so, there was an attestation in his presence. It was an attestation in his presence as required by the act of assembly." This court said in reviewing that case that: "After reviewing the authorities upon this point, we think that the strictest interpretation of the law has gone no further than to require that the testator should be in a position and have power, without a removal of his person, to see what was done. It is not necessary for him, in point of fact, to see." The court also referred to the opinion in *Bynum* v. *Bynum* (*supra*), where it was held "that the attestation, being done openly and without any clandestine appearance about it, in the same room with the testatrix, and within two or three feet of her, when she had her senses, and nothing intervened between her and the witnesses, is good, under the statute. It was done, both literally and substantially, in her presence." But the court, it seems to us, clearly showed a mistrust of that position, as is shown by the following language: "There are authorities going to the extent of holding that, the transaction being openly done, there can be no question of presence, where the parties are all in the same room." (Best, Pres. 83.) But, however this may be, it is clear, upon authority, if it be affirmatively established that the testator might have seen, that the attestation is good. (Pow. Dev. 96; *Tod* v. *Earl of Winchelsea*, 12 E. C. L. 227.) And, too, in *Cornelius* v. *Cornelius* (*supra*), the doctrine laid down in *Jones*

v. *Tuck* (*supra*), was not questioned, for the court said there: " We are not disturbing at all the case of *Jones* v. *Tuck* (48 N. C. 202), to which our attention has been called. In that case it appeared that the testator could not have turned himself so as to have seen the attesting witnesses subscribe, without danger, and acting contrary to the advice of the physician. In the case before us the turning of the head would have sufficed to enable the testator to see, and that, according to the testimony, he could do without pain or difficulty."

Upon a review of these cases, we are of the opinion that there was no error in the instruction of his honor which we have been considering, and that the principle announced in *Graham* v. *Graham* (*supra*), is the correct one. The decedent must be in such a situation—such a position—as will enable him, if he will look, to see the paper writing which he has signed, as it is being subscribed by the witnesses. He must have the opportunity, through the evidence of ocular observation, to see the attestation of the paper from the position or situation in which he is, if he will look, and this so as to exclude the almost impossibility of a substitution of the paper which he has signed with another by some other person. In the case before us, it does not appear whether the decedent was able to turn his head to one side or not. Two of the witnesses said that, if he had turned his head to one side, he could have seen the paper. If he could have done so without risk or danger, or not contrary to his physician's advice, and was of testamentary capacity (and there is no proof before us to the contrary), then there was a compliance with the statute in reference to the attestation. (*Cornelius* v. *Cornelius, supra.*) But even if he was of testamentary capacity, and there was no fraud or undue influence, yet, if he was unable to partly turn his head, so that he might look and see the paper writing as it was being subscribed, the attestation was not according to the requirements of the statute.

The court further instructed the jury " that the deceased must have actually requested the witnesses to sign the paper writing as witnesses, and if the jury should believe from the evidence that he did not so request them, or either of them, then the paper writing was not properly executed as a will, and they should answer said issue, ' No.' " We think the instruction was given in language too broad, and that it was therefore erroneous. There is nothing in the statute (Code, § 2136) which requires that the decedent shall ask or request the witnesses to subscribe; and we can see no reason why the draftsman of the will, or any other person, in the presence of the testator, and with his acquiescence and approval, and with a clear knowledge of what is going on, should not make the request of the witnesses to sign the script. Nor can we see any good reason why the request should not be implied from the testator's conduct or well-understood signs. Such implied requests have been frequently held by the courts to be sufficient. (29 Am. & Eng. Enc. Law, 205, and cases there cited.) In New York the statute requires that the witnesses must sign at the request of the testator; but it was held in *Gilbert* v. *Knox* (52 N. Y. 125), that the words of request or acknowledgment may proceed from another, and will be regarded as those of the testator, where the circumstances show that he adopted them, and that the party using them in his presence was acting for him with his assent. In *Peck* v. *Cary* (27 N. Y. 9), the draftsman of the will in the presence of the testator requested the witnesses to witness the will, and they thereupon signed it, and it was held to have been done at the request of the testator. There was error in the instruction of his honor which we have last discussed.

Error.

FURCHES, J. (concurring in the judgment of the court, but not in the conclusion arrived at in discussing the first proposition).—As the case goes back for a new trial, he will not enter into a discussion of that question now, further than to say that the opinions in *Bynum* v. *Bynum* and *Cornelius* v. *Cornelius* carry the doctrine of " being signed in the presence of the testator " as far as he is willing to go. Something must be left to personal confidence. Were this not so, neither a blind man nor an illiterate man could make a will. Though an illiterate man may see the witnesses sign the paper he has signed with a cross mark, yet he only knows it is his will because he has confidence in the party who wrote it and read it to him.

FAIRCLOTH, C. J.—I concur in Justice FURCHES' view.

VANDEVEER *vs.* HIGGINS *et al.*

[Supreme Court of Nebraska, December 6, 1899; 80 N. W. Rep. 1043.]

WILL—REVOCATION BY MARRIAGE.

1. Whether the devise of her separate real estate by a married woman will exclude the husband's estate by curtesy not decided, because not directly involved.
2. A will executed by a single woman is revoked by her subsequent marriage, at least to the extent it would operate to exclude her husband from his right as tenant by curtesy in any lands of which she died seized in her own right of an estate of inheritance.

(Syllabus by the court.)

ERROR to District Court, Nemaha county; LETTON, Judge.

Petition by Absalom Vandeveer against Daniel Higgins and others. Judgment for defendants, and plaintiff brings error. Reversed.

G. W. Cornell, for plaintiff in error.

W. H. Kelligar, for defendants in error.

HARRISON, C. J.—The facts in which the matters in litigation in this case originated are undisputed. It appears that Eliza M. Kimberly, a widow, the owner of some real estate, to which she had title in fee, made her will, by which she devised to certain defendants in error the lands. She subsequently intermarried with the plaintiff in error, and some time afterwards died. After her death the will was presented to the County Court of Nemaha county, and, in the due course of regular procedure in such matters, was admitted to probate. The plaintiff in error, by what is designated a "Petition," filed in the County Court, in which certain of the facts were stated, asserted his claim to the real estate as tenant by curtesy. Answers were filed by the adverse parties, to which there were replies for the plaintiff. A trial in the County Court resulted in the defeat of the plaintiff, who appealed to the District Court, where judgment was rendered against him on the pleadings. · The will involved in controversy was of date November 6, 1893.· The marriage of plaintiff and Eliza M. Kimberly occurred November 13, 1894, and her death was on February 6, 1895.

The two questions raised and argued are,—the main one, did the marriage of Eliza M. Kimberly to plaintiff revoke her prior will? another, on the answer to which it is contended the settlement of the first necessarily depends or hinges, can a married woman, by devise of her separate real estate, defeat the husband's right to take at her death as tenant by curtesy? It is argued that if the will of a married woman, by which there is a devise, to a person other than her husband, of real estate of which the wife is seized in her own right, will exclude the husband as tenant by curtesy, the reason for the rule by which the marriage would have revoked a will of the woman, made before that event, by which real estate was devised, ceases; for if she could, after marriage, make a will with the same effect as before, no reason exists for a revocation, by law, of the prior will. The questions must be solved probably mainly by an application to our statutory provisions on the subject involved, and it may be best to review, to some extent, the course and history of legislation which has culminated in the present statutory provisions.

In 1855 it was of the enactments that any person of full age and sound mind might, by will, dispose of all of his property, except sufficient to pay his debts, and the allowance, as a homestead or otherwise, given by law to his wife and family; the revocation to be by cancellation, actual destruction with intention to revoke, or by subsequent will. (Sess. Laws 1855, p. 63.) In the act approved January 26, 1856, it was stated all persons of full age, except idiots and persons of unsound mind, may by will dispose of all their property. The marriage of a testator after the will made, and issue born either before or after his death, if his wife be living at his death, revoked the will, unless the issue was provided for by some settlement or in the will. A will of an unmarried woman was revoked by her subsequent marriage. (Sess. Laws 1856, p. 93.) In 1860-61 it was enacted that a married woman might by will dispose of any property to which she was entitled in her own right, and alter or revoke the same in like manner that a person under no disability might; provided, to be valid, the will or any alteration or revocation of it, must have the consent of the husband in writing annexed to it, executed with the same formalities as the will. There was also a general provision in regard to revocation of wills, which was as follows: "No will, or any part thereof, shall be revoked unless by burning, tearing, canceling or obliterating the same with the intention of revoking it, by the testator, or by some person in his presence and by his direction; or by some other will or codicil in writing, executed as prescribed in this chapter; or by some other writing signed, attested and subscribed in the manner provided in this chapter, for the execution of a will; excepting only that nothing contained in this section shall prevent the revocation implied by law from subsequent changes in the condition or circumstances of the testator." This general provision has been continually in force to, and inclusive of, the present time. (Sess. Laws 1861, p. 77, ch. 5, § 10.) The portion of the statute in regard to the will of a married woman to which we have just referred was so amended in 1881 that no consent of the husband was necessary to either the will or its voluntary revocation. (Sess. Laws 1881, p. 233.) As then amended, the section has been continued, and is now in force. In an enactment on the subject of real estate and its alienation, approved January 26, 1856, there appeared a section which was as follows: "Any real estate belonging to a married woman, may be managed, controlled, leased, devised or conveyed by her by deed or by will in the same manner and with like effect as if she were sole." (Sess. Laws 1856, p. 88, ch. 31, § 50; Sess. Laws 1864, p. 67, ch. 12, § 48.) This, with no change except the use of the word "single" instead of "sole," has been and is now in force. (Rev. St. 1866, p. 290, ch. 43, § 47; Gen. St. 1873, p. 880, ch. 61.) In 1855 it was enacted, in regard to the disposition of real estate of decedents, that the one-third of all real estate in which a husband, at any time during the existence of the marriage, had a legal or equitable interest, not sold on execution or judicial sale, and to which the wife had not relinquished her rights, should be set apart to her after the death of her husband, if she survived him, to be so set off as to include a home and homestead; and in another section this appears: "All the provisions hereinbefore made in relation to the widow of a deceased husband, shall be applicable to the husband of a deceased wife. Each is entitled to the same rights of dower in the estate of the other and like interest shall in the same manner descend to their respective heirs. The estate by curtesy is hereby abolished." (Sess. Laws 1855, p. 75, § 185.) The following was approved January 26, 1856: " When any man and his wife, shall be seized in her right of any estate of inheritance in lands, the husband shall, on the death of his wife, hold the lands for his life, as tenant thereof, by the curtesy provided." (Sess. Laws 1856, p. 133, ch. 44, § 31.) In 1887 this was so amended as to read: " When any married woman seized in her own right of any estate of inheritance in lands shall die leaving no issue, the land shall descend to her surviving husband during his natural lifetime as tenant by curtesy." (Sess. Laws 1887, p. 383; ch. 34, § 29.) It has been since and is now the same. In 1871 (Sess. Laws 1871, p. 68), was passed the act relating to the rights of married women, by which they were given the right to bargain, sell, convey, control, and manage all the property they had at time of the marriage, and which they acquired thereafter by descent, devise, or bequest, or the gift of any person except the husband, and it was to remain their sole and separate property. This, with some amendments which do not materially affect the main purpose, is now and has been the law. The estate of a husband by curtesy was in an early day abolished. (Sess. Laws 1856, *supra.*) Then, by act approved January 26, 1856, an estate by curtesy was created. (Sess. Laws 1856, *supra.*)

The estate is, then, a statutory one. The other matters of the execution of a will by a married woman, and its revocation, and the revocation of the will of a woman made before marriage by the latter event, are also subjects of statutory provisions. As we view the matter before us, it may be conceded that a married woman may make a will, and it will be with like effect as if she was at the time single, pass at her death the whole estate, and cut off a husband's rights by curtesy which would otherwise accrue. We do not decide this, however, as it is not directly involved. In the decision of the case of *In re Tuller* (79 Ill. 99), it was stated: " It is the old and well-settled rule of the common law that the will of a *feme sole* is revoked by her subsequent marriage, and it is contended that under this rule the will was revoked. The reason of the rule was that a will is in its nature ambulatory during the testator's life, and can be revoked at his pleasure. But the marriage destroys the ambulatory nature of the will, and leaves it no longer subject to the wife's control, and it is against the nature of a will to be absolute during the testator's life. It is therefore revoked, in judgment of law, by such marriage. (4 Kent, Comm. 527; 2 Greenl. Ev. 684.) That reason does not exist under our present statute of 1872, which gives to every female of the age of eighteen years the power to devise her property by will or testament." In *Baacke* v. *Baacke* (50 Neb. 18; 69 N. W. 303), some of the cases were cited which countenanced the doctrine just quoted, and it was held: " The common-law doctrine that the revocation of a will may be implied from subsequent changes in the condition or circumstances of the testator obtains in this state, in so far as it has not been modified by statute."

It but remains for us now to determine whether or not the will here in question was, by the subsequent marriage of the testator, revoked at least to the extent, by its terms and effect, it would exclude the husband's estate by curtesy; and it seems that the query mainly is, what was the intention of the legislature in its enactments on the subject of revocation of wills ? It will be borne in mind, as we have hereinbefore shown, there was a specific provision that marriage, subsequent to the making of a will by a woman, worked a revocation; and there was also a statement of the changes of condition and circumstances which revoked a prior will of the man, of which marriage, in connection with the occurrence of another event, were mentioned; and, further, that a subsequent legislature enacted the general rule in lieu of the specific one, and this general provision has been continued throughout the legislation, by which all the restrictions which existed upon the power of a married woman to convey and dispose of her separate property have been removed. The only difference in the specific rules in regard to the revocation of wills to which we have directed attention and the general one is that the former more clearly expressed the intention than the latter. The first were expressed, the second implied. From a review, which we have given a somewhat wide range, of the legislation, directly or indirectly affecting the subject-matter of the litigation, we are convinced that the intention of the lawmakers was to continue in force the rule as generally understood, *i. e.* that changes of conditions and circumstances include that of marriage. It follows that the marriage of the testatrix revoked her prior will to the extent it would have excluded her husband from an estate by curtesy in the real estate of which she died seized, and the judgment of the District Court is reversed, and the cause remanded for further proceedings in accordance with the views herein expressed.

Reversed and remanded.

NOTE.—EFFECT OF MARRIAGE ON WILL.

(a) English statute and common law.
(b) As affected by marital rights of husband.
(c) Effect of statutes conferring property rights on married women.
(d) Rule in New York.
(e) Will of married woman or widow.
(f) Effect of ante-nuptial agreement.
(g) Effect of a power.
(h) Some illustrative cases.

(a) **English statute and common law.**—In England the Act 1 Vict. 1837 marks the certain change effected by statute. This law reads " that every will made by a man or woman shall be revoked by his or her marriage, except a will made in exercise of a power of appointment, when the real or personal estate thereby appointed would not, in default of such appointment, pass to his or her heir, executor or administrator, or persons entitled as next of kin." See this act commented upon and the rules at common law. (McAnnulty v. McAnnulty, 120 Ill. 26; 11 N. E. Rep. 397; and see Sloniger v. Sloniger, 161 Ill. 270; 43 N. E. Rep. 1111; Hudnall v. Ham, 183 Ill. 486; 56 N. E. Rep. 172; Ingersoll v. Hopkins, 170 Mass. 401, 404; 49 N. E. Rep. 623; Hulett v. Carey, 66 Minn. 341; 69 N. W. Rep. 31.)

The English act is quoted because it is the foundation of legislation in a number of the states; the writer of these notes has never considered that the local *statutes* of the several states should be inserted because it is assumed that the lawyer making use of the note knows the statute bearing on the particular matter. The cases following are selected mainly as being helpful as tracing the origin of the common law and modifications made by the general tendency of legislation.

The statutes of the several states vary so much in language that it would extend a note beyond all reasonable bounds to point out their differences.

In Brush v. Wilkin (4 Johns. Ch. 506), Chancellor KENT reviews the common law rule as to revocation by marriage and birth of child.

Walker v. Hall (34 Pa. St. 183), reviews and summarizes the changes made by statute both in England and in Pennsylvania.

(b) **As affected by marital rights of husband.**—The rule that marriage of a woman revoked a will made by her before marriage does not apply where a considerable portion of the property disposed of by the will remained in her, unaffected upon her death by any marital rights of her husband, who survived her. (Morton v. Onion, 45 Vt. 145.) So held upon an issue of probate. But see Re Polly Carey's Estate (49 Vt. 236, 245), involving same will, where it was held that it was revoked by the marriage so far as personal property was concerned, on account of husband's rights therein. And see Colcord v. Conroy (40 Fla. 97; 23 So. Rep. 561), where the subject is considered at length and conflict in the cases pointed out.

(c) **Effect of statutes conferring property rights on married women.**—Since statute conferring property rights on a woman notwithstanding her marriage, the will of a *feme sole* is not revoked by marriage. (Re Tuller, 79 Ill. 99. But this rule was changed by statute in Illinois, id. 106.)

Where statute confirms title and separate estate in married woman, then marriage no longer revokes a will previously made. (Roane v. Hollingshead, 76 Md. 369; 25 Atl. Rep. 307; McCall v. Wells, 55 Mich. 173; 20 N. W. Rep. 890.)

Will of a woman not revoked by her marriage where statute confers power on her as a married woman to make, alter, or revoke a will. (Re Emery, 81 Me. 275; 17 Atl. Rep. 68; Well v. Jones, 36 N. J. Eq. 163). There is a valuable note by the reporter to this case upon the subject. (Id. pp. 164-166; Re Lyon's Will, 96 Wis. 339; 71 N. W. Rep. 362; Fellows v. Allen, 60 N. H. 439; Roane v. Hollingshead, *supra*.)

(d) **Rule in New York.**—The provision of the New York statute that the will of an unmarried woman is revoked by her subsequent marriage is not abrogated by subsequent statutes conferring upon her testamentary capacity, thus taking away reason of the rule at common law. The courts cannot dispense with a statutory rule because it appears that the policy upon which it was established has ceased. (Brown v. Clark, 77 N. Y. 369.)

(e) **Will of married woman or widow.**—Where a married woman or widow executes a will, and subsequently marries again it operates as a revocation. (Colcord v. Conroy, 40 Fla. 97; 23 So. Rep. 561.) The opinion in this case gives an interesting and valuable review of the common law and of the decisions in England and in the various states. (Craft's Estate, 164 Pa. St. 520; 30 Atl. Rep. 493.)

Where statute provides that a " will executed by a married woman is revoked by her subsequent marriage, and is not revived by the death of her husband " it only applies to a will which is executed by a woman who is unmarried at time of its execution, and does not apply to a will executed by a married woman, and such will is not revoked by her second marriage, subsequent to the execution of the will. When married woman has power by statute to make a will, it can be revoked only in one of the modes prescribed by statute. (Re Comassi, 107 Cal. 1; 40 Pac. Rep. 15.)

During her second marriage a woman made a will giving her property to children of the first marriage. Afterwards she married a third time and died leaving her third husband surviving. There was no issue of the second or third marriages. *Held,* that as she had absolute right under the statute to dispose of her property, will was not revoked by third marriage. How it would have been if will had been in favor of a stranger, suggested but not decided. (Will of Ward, 70 Wis. 251; 35 N. W. Rep. 731.)

A will executed by a *married* woman is not revoked by her subsequent remarriage after an intervening widowhood. Matter of McLarney, 153 N. Y. 416; 47 N. E. Rep. 817; aff'g 90 Hun. 361; 35 N. Y. Supp. 893; and see Matter of Burton's Will, 4 Misc. 512; 25 N. Y. Supp. 824.)

A widow is an "unmarried woman" within meaning of statute providing that will of an unmarried woman shall be revoked by her subsequent marriage. (Matter of Kaufman, 131 N. Y. 620; 30 N. E. Rep. 242; aff'g 61 Hun, 331; 16 N. Y. Supp. 113.)

(f) **Effect of ante-nuptial agreement.**—The execution of a power by an appointment by will before the marriage pursuant to an ante-nuptial agreement is not revoked by the marriage. (Osgood v. Bliss, 141 Mass. 474; 6 N. E. Rep. 527.) This subject now governed by statute 1892, see Ingersoll v. Hopkins (170 Mass. 401; 49 N. E. Rep. 623); and see as to effect of an ante-nuptial agreement, Stewart v. Mulholland (88 Ky. 38; 10 S. W. Rep. 125); Stewart v. Powell (90 Ky. 512; 14 S. W. Rep. 496); Corker v. Corker (87 Cal. 643; 25 Pac. Rep. 922); McAnnulty v. McAnnulty (120 Ill. 26; 11 N. E. Rep. 397); Hudnall v. Ham (172 Ill 76, 82; 49 N. E. Rep. 985; second app. 183 Ill. 486; 56 N. E. Rep. 172); Lant's Appeal (95 Pa. St. 279); Bradish v. Gibbs (3 Johns. Ch. 523); Lathrop v. Dunlap (4 Hun, 213; aff'd 63 N. Y. 610).

(g) **Effect of a power.**—Power not affected by marriage. (Mutual Ins. Co. v. Shipman, 108 N. Y. 19; 15 N. E. Rep. 58; and see Bradish v. Gibbs, 3 Johns. Ch. 523; Goods of Russell, L. R. 15 P. D. 111.)

(b) **Some illustrative cases.**—Governed by law of the state where domiciled at the time of death. (Matter of Coburn, 9 Misc. 437; 30 N. Y. Supp. 383.)

Will of testator revoked by subsequent marriage and issue without provision for same. (Baldwin v. Spriggs, 65 Md. 373; 5 Atl. Rep. 295 [reviews the cases and common law].)

Revocation of will of woman by her marriage is presumptive only. (Miller v. Phillips, 9 R. I. 141.)

Marriage of a woman revokes her will though it occurs on same day and within few hours after will was executed. (Ellis v. Darden, 86 Ga. 368; 12 S. E. Rep. 652. The opinion contains a valuable collection of authorities on the general subject.)

Where statute provides that revocation may be implied by law "from subsequent changes or circumstances of the testator" the will of a woman is revoked by her subsequent marriage. (Swan v. Hammond, 138 Mass. 45; Nutt v. Norton, 142 Mass. 242; 7 N. E. Rep. 720; and see Colcord v. Conroy, 40 Fla. 97; 23 So. Rep. 561.)

Will in bequest to wife read "having the utmost confidence in her integrity, and believing that should a child be born to us, she will do the utmost to rear it to the honor and glory of its parents," *Held*, no provision for his child subsequently born sufficient to prevent revocation as to the child. (Walker v. Hall, 34 Pa. St. 483.)

Marriage of testator after making of a will is by operation of law a revocation of. it, even though no issue born. (Duryea v. Duryea, 85 Ill. 42; following Tyler v. Tyler, 19 Ill. 151; American Board of Missions v. Nelson, 72 Ill. 564.)

Marriage of testator, whether or not it be followed by birth of an heir is operative to revoke any will which he has antecedently made. (Brown v. Scherrer, 5 Col. App. 255; 38 Pac. Rep. 427.)

Rule by the common law that will of an unmarried man is revoked by his subsequent marriage and birth of a child, unless provision is made for them is not abrogated by statutory provision in Kansas. (Shorten v. Judd, 60 Kans. 73; 55 Pac. Rep. 286.)

The rule that subsequent marriage operates to revoke the will of testator when such will makes no provision for such marriage does not in this state (Illinois) when the husband and wife are heirs to each other, owe its existence to the statute, but was a recognized rule of the common law prior to the statute. (Hudnall v. Ham, 172 Ill. 76; 49 N. E. Rep. 985; second appeal, 183 Ill. 486; 56 N. E. Rep. 172.)

Where under a statute a widow and child not provided for in the will are entitled to share of estate as if testator had died intestate, a previous will of the testator is not revoked by his marriage. (Hoitt v. Hoitt, 63 N. H. 475, 496; 3 Atl. Rep. 604; and see Fidelity Trust Co.'s Appeal, 121 Pa. St. 1; 15 Atl. Rep. 484), where, under a similar statute it is *held* that the widow has the option to take under the will or under the statute.

Although under statute a wife may inherit from her husband, it has not changed the common law rule that the will of a man is not revoked by his subsequent marriage alone, without birth of issue. (Hutell v. Carey, 66 Minn. 328; 69 N. W. Rep. 31.)

The opinion by Judge Mitchell in this case contains an interesting and valuable summary of the rules of the common law, and see Bowers v. Bowers (53 Ind. 430); Belton v. Summer (31 Fla. 139; 12 So. Rep. 371).

IN RE DAHLMIER *et al.*

UNKE *vs.* DAHLMIER *et al.*

[Supreme Court of Minnesota, December 12, 1899; 78 Minn. 320; 80 N. W. Rep. 1130.]

GUARDIAN—ACCOUNTING.

A widow married a second husband, and he with a child by his former marriage, and she and her minor children by her former marriage all resided on her homestead as one family. He was appointed guardian of her children, and for ten years thereafter cultivated the farm, consisting of said homestead and other land belonging to her and her children, and still other land conveyed to him, but purchased with the money of her children. He apparently treated the crops of all of this land as his own, never kept any separate account of the crops or profits of any part of it, but the crops were mingled together, and the family were supported out of the common mass. There was no evidence as to what arrangement he had with his wife as to the cultivation of her part of the land, and he never made any arrangement with her as to who should support her children, or what funds should be applied for that purpose. In a proceeding to settle the guardian's account, *held*, he was the head of the family, and a finding that the wife's children boarded with her and that she supported them during the ten years is not sustained by the evidence.

(Syllabus by the court.)

APPEAL from District Court, Morrison county; L. L. BAXTER, Judge.

In the matter of the guardianship of Henry Dahlmier on an accounting by Charles Unke, as guardian of Henry Dahlmier and others. From an order denying a new trial after judgment ordered against the guardian, he appeals.

Reversed.

Geo. W. Stewart and *E. S. Smith,* for appellant.

Lindberg, Blanchard & Lindberg, and *E. P. Adams,* for respondents.

CANTY, J.—An appeal was taken from an order of the Probate Court settling the account of Unke, as guardian of the five Dahl-

mier children.   On the trial in the District Court, judgment was
ordered against Unke in the sum of $3,268.50, and he appeals from
an order denying a new trial.   In 1886, Henry Dahlmier died intestate, leaving his widow and four children surviving him.   His
fifth child was born shortly after his death.   He left one hundred
and sixty acres of land, eighty acres of which was his homestead,
so that his wife had a life estate in this eighty and an undivided one-
third of the other eighty.   In June, 1887, the widow married the
appellant, Unke, and thereafter he resided with her on her said
homestead.   Her five children resided with them, as also did a
child of his own by a former marriage.   On January 1, 1888, he
was appointed guardian of her five children, and, as such guardian,
received at that time promissory notes payable to the deceased
amounting to $1,250, the same having come to the children as a
part of their share of their father's estate.   Some time afterwards,
but just when does not appear, Unke collected the notes, and used
the money to buy another eighty acres of land, the title to which
he took in his own name.   He cultivated this eighty, and the Dahlmier one hundred and sixty, thereafter, until January 1, 1898, when
he resigned or was removed as such guardian.   When he was appointed guardian, the oldest of the Dahlmier children was ten
years of age.   They resided in the family during all of the time of
said guardianship, except that in December, 1893, when the oldest
boy was sixteen years of age, he left the family home, and thereafter resided elsewhere.   The District Court ordered a judgment
against Unke for the $1,250, and interest thereon at the rate of
seven per cent. since he was appointed guardian.   The court found
that during all of the ten years of said guardianship he received a
profit of $80 per year from the cultivation of said undivided two-
thirds of said eighty acres which the five wards inherited from
their father, and ordered judgment against Unke for those amounts
also.   He was allowed $25 for attorney's fees and some taxes that
he had paid for the wards, but he was allowed nothing for the support, maintenance, or clothing of the wards, although he presented
a claim therefor, and the main question which it is necessary to
consider is whether the court erred in refusing to allow him anything therefor.   The court found that during all of the ten years
of the guardianship the five wards " continued to live with her
(their mother), as a part of her family, and to be supported by

her," and for this reason the court refused to allow appellant anything for the support, maintenance, or clothing of the five wards.

In our opinion, the evidence does not sustain the finding above quoted. The evidence is that appellant, his child, his five stepchildren, and his wife all lived together as one family; that hè cultivated the Dahlmier one hundred and sixty acres and said other eighty acres; apparently treated all of the crops raised on all of this land as his own; never kept any account of the amount produced or the amount of the profit realized from any particular part of the land; and supported and maintained the family out of the produce of all of the land, regardless of whether it came from one part of the land or another. While the evidence on these points is very meager, it is uncontradicted, and, in our opinion, will not support the finding made. As his son and his stepsons grew old enough to do so, they assisted him in the cultivation of all the different parts of the farm. The evidence is wholly silent as to what arrangement or agreement he had with his wife under which he cultivated her share of the land, and there was no express agreement between them as to whose means should be used to support her five children. On this evidence, it must be held that appellant was the head of the family. A widow, on her marriage to a second husband, is not liable for the support of her minor child, but is entitled to have its income applied thereto (*In re Besondy*, 32 Minn. 385; 20 N. W. 366), and, whether the evidence would sustain a finding that the five wards were supported by funds and produce furnished partly by the mother and partly by the stepfather, we will not consider; no such finding is made. In *Haslett* v. *Babcock* (64 Minn. 254; 66 N. W. 971), the husband raised crops on his wife's land, and we held that, on the evidence in that case, it was a question for the jury whether the crops belonged to the husband or the wife. Conceding, without deciding, that the evidence in this case warranted a finding that all of the crops raised on the wife's land belonged to her, still it cannot be held on the evidence that the five wards were supported and maintained wholly from these crops, as all of the crops on all of the land were mingled together, and the family was supported from the common mass.   ·

Again, conceding that the evidence would warrant a finding that appellant was in *loco parentis* to these five wards, that he received them into his family under circumstances such as to raise a presumption that he intended to support them gratuitously (see *In re Besondy, supra*), still there is no finding to that effect, and the evidence is certainly not conclusive that he intended to support them gratuitously. As the evidence will not support the finding above quoted, a new trial must be granted. In our opinion, it sufficiently appears by the settled case that it contains all the evidence.

Order reversed, and a new trial granted.

LAMB'S ESTATE *vs.* HALL.

[Supreme Court of Michigan, December 12, 1899; 80 N. W. Rep. 1081.]

WILLS—CONSTRUCTION—CONDITIONAL ESTATES.

A testatrix gave all her estate to her brothers and sisters, providing that, should any die "previous to the probating or execution" of her will, the share of the decedent should go to his or her surviving children. *Held*, that unless a brother or sister lived until testatrix's estate was settled and distributed, he or she took nothing under the will.

ERROR to Circuit Court, Van Buren county; HARSEN D. SMITH, Judge.

In the matter of the estate of Catherine Lamb, deceased. Her will was construed by the Probate Court on petition of James H. Hall, the executor, and Annetta Tillou, claiming as a child of Carlton Ray, one of the devisees and legatees, appealed to the Circuit Court, where there was a decree construing it in her favor, and the executor brings error.

Affirmed.

Catherine Lamb died testate. Her will provided as follows: " I give and bequeath to Benjamin Ray, Carlton Ray, Samuel Ray, Nancy Sumner, Marilla Smith, Julia Hopkins, Mary Carnes, Jane Hoffman, and Levinia Taylor (all of whom are my brothers and sisters) all the real and personal estate of which I may be possessed at the time of my decease, to be equally divided between them, share and share alike. But in case of the death of any of the above-named legatees previous to the probating or execution of this, my last will and testament, then I desire, will, and bequeath that the share of such deceased brother or sister shall revert to, and become the property of, the children of said deceased legatee; but, if said deceased legatee has no children living at the time of my decease, then the said deceased legatee's share of property bequeathed to him or her by the terms of this will shall revert to, and become a part of, the general fund to be divided among the surviving legatees named in this, my last will and testament." She died March, 1898. Her will was admitted to probate, and letters testamentary were granted to defendant, June 13, 1898. Carlton Ray died December 18, 1898, before the distribution of the estate. Prior to the probating of the will, Mr. Ray assigned to his wife all his interest as devisee and legatee under the will. He left two children. January 21, 1899, the executor filed a petition in the Probate Court praying a construction of the will. From the decision of the Probate Court an appeal was taken to the Circuit Court, and judgment entered holding that Mr. Ray's share did not pass by his assignment to his wife, and that it passed to his children, since he died before the estate was finally administered and settled.

A. J. Mills, for appellant.

B. F. Heckert, for appellee.

GRANT, C. J. (after stating the facts).—The decision depends upon the construction to be placed upon this clause of the will: " But, in case of the death of any of the above-named legatees previous to the probating or execution of this, my last will and testament, then I desire, will, and bequeath that the share of such deceased brother or sister shall revert to, and become the property of, the children of said deceased legatee." Manifestly, the term " execution " does not apply to the act of signing and publishing her will. It refers to something to be done after her decease. Certain cardinal rules must be kept in mind. The intention of the testator must be determined from the four corners of the instrument. (*Bailey* v. *Bailey,* 25 Mich. 185, 188; *Fraser* v. *Chene,* 2 Mich. 82,

88.) Wills must be construed so that the distribution will conform as nearly to the general rule of inheritance as the language will permit. (*Rivenett v. Bourquin*, 53 Mich. 10; 18 N. W. 537, and authorities cited.) Words must be given their ordinary significance, and testators must be held to have meant something by the words used, unless the contrary clearly appears. To probate a will is not to execute it. To probate involves only a determination that the will was duly signed and published, and that the testator was competent to make it. It simply establishes the validity of the will. Its execution comes after its probate. The executor has no control over the estate until the probate of the will. The executor is the person appointed to "carry the will into effect after his decease, and to dispose of his property according to the tenor of the will." (1 Burrill, Law Dict. 584.) Counsel concede that Mr. Ray took a conditional estate,—the condition being that he live until the proof or probate of the will. This construction would eliminate from the will the words " or execution," as it would leave them no office to perform. We cannot hold that the testatrix used the word " execution " as synonymous with " probating." Persons of common intelligence know what it is to probate a will. We think it manifest that the intention was to devise her property to her brothers and sisters, and to their children in case of their death before her will was executed. The term " execution " was, in our judgment, used with reference to the act of the executor in executing the will by settlement of the estate under the provisions of law for the settlement of estates of deceased persons, and distributing the property to her legatees. At her death Mr. Ray received an estate upon the sole condition that he live until the will was executed, and the property ready for distribution. This was the construction placed upon similar language in *Scott v. Guernsey* (60 Barb. 163, 175), and *Lambert v. Harvey* (100 Ill. 338), and is not in conflict with *Calkins v. Smith's Estate* (41 Mich. 409; 1 N. W. 1048). The word " or " is often construed to mean " and," and its use is a common mistake in wills as well as elsewhere. (2 Jarm. Wills, *471 ; 2 Burri'l, Law Dict. 263.) We think the court reached the correct conclusion. Decree affirmed, with costs.

The other justices concurred.

ZUNKEL *vs.* COLSON *et al.*

[Supreme Court of Iowa, December 14, 1899; 109 Iowa, 695; 81 N. W. Rep. 175.]

VENDOR AND PURCHASER—EXECUTORY CONTRACT—FORFEITURE—WAIVER—RESULTING TRUST—ADMINISTRATION—WIDOW'S ALLOWANCE — WAIVER — ABATEMENT — ADVERSE POSSESSION—LIMITATIONS—PARTITION—LACHES.

1. A vendor's right to a forfeiture for the purchaser's default in the payment of an installment on an executory contract for a sale of land was waived by his subsequent acceptance of payment, and the execution of a deed.

2. Where a widow collected money from her deceased husband's estate, and paid the balance due on land which he had bought and partially paid for, and took the deed in her own name, she holds the land in trust for his heirs.

3. Where the widow fails, until discharged as administratrix, to apply under the statute for a necessary allowance out of the estate for support during twelve months after her husband's death, she waives all claim thereto.

4. A widow's claim to an allowance for support pending administration abates with her death.

5. The statute of limitations does not begin to run in favor of one holding land in trust, as against the beneficiary, until the former has clearly notified the latter that he claims the land adversely.

6. The execution of a mortgage by one holding the legal title to land in trust will not be regarded as a repudiation of the trust, and an act of adverse possession, where it was intended to benefit the estate, and was soon after satisfied by the trustee.

7. The act of a trustee in giving a third person an option, unavailed of, to buy minerals underlying land constituting the trust estate, was not an act of adverse possession, as against the beneficiary.

8. Where an heir permitted his stepmother to continue in possession of land which she held in trust for him and other heirs, and to appropriate its rents and profits for the necessary support of herself and such other heirs, without demanding or suing for his interest therein until eight or nine years after he became of age, he is not guilty of such *laches* as will defeat his suit for partition.

APPEAL from District Court, Boone county; S. M. WEAVER, Judge.

Action for partition. The answer put in issue the plaintiff's title, and from a decree in his favor the defendants appeal. Affirmed.

Dyer & Stevens, for appellants.

A. J. Holmes and *Crooks & Snell,* for appellee.

LADD, J.—The parties to this action are the children of Ferdinand Zunkel, who died March 18, 1876, leaving as his heirs the plaintiff, a son by his first wife, and the defendants, the issue of his second union. The mother of the defendants survived him until January 18, 1896. Ferdinand settled on the eighty acres of land in controversy prior to 1875, broke about fifty acres, built a house and fenced it, and June 23d of that year entered into a contract of purchase with Edwin C. Litchfield, agreeing to punctually pay therefor $400 November 1, 1875, and $380 in six equal annual payments, beginning November 1, 1876. Time was of the essence of this agreement, and, upon failure to comply with any of its conditions, it was to be void, without declaration of forfeiture. No payments were made during the lifetime of Ferdinand Zunkel, and Litchfield had the undoubted right to treat it as a nullity. But the ·provisions relating to forfeiture were for the benefit of the vendor (*Barrett* v. *Dean,* 21 Iowa, 426; *Sigler* v. *Wick,* 45 id. 690; see *Mahoney* v. *McCrea,* 104 id. 735; 74 N. W. 699), and might be waived. (*Lessell* v. *Goodman,* 97 Iowa, 682; 66 N. W. 917; see *Davidson* v. *Insurance Co.* 71 Iowa, 532; 32 N. W. 514.) That they were in fact waived appears from the record before us. All the payments were subsequently made by Mrs. Zunkel on the original contract, and a deed executed to her in pursuance of the sale made to her deceased husband. As she derived the money used for this purpose from the sale of property left by him, the collection of notes due him, and the rents and profits of the land, she took title as trustee for his heirs. (*Fox* v. *Doherty,* 30 Iowa, 334; *Robinson* v. *Robinson,* 22 id. 427; *Murphy* v. *Murphy,* 80 id. 740; 45 N. W. 914.) That she so did is put beyond controversy by the inventory and final report filed by her as administrator of his estate. From the former it appears that he left personal property valued at $638.90, while the latter shows its value to have been $783.52. Out of this she paid $57.79 taxes on this land, and $569.53 on the contract. She listed it as real estate of the deceased. In her final report she represented herself and children as living on the land, and prayed the court to approve of these payments. The agent of Litchfield is deceased, but his accounts were identified, and confirm the final report, in showing that payments were made on the original contract, and a deed executed to Mrs. Zunkel in pursuance of the sale made to Ferdinand.

2. The widow doubtless might have acquired some property left by the deceased for the support of herself and children during the twelve months after his death. But our statute required her to make application therefor, and directed a necessary allowance, rather than a specified sum. Until there is a judicial determination, the claim is contingent and uncertain. The right to it cannot vest until the amount has been fixed. As a general rule, such an application can only be entertained during the time support is intended. (*Kingman* v. *Kingman*, 31 N. H. 182.) And, by failing to apply therefor prior to her discharge as administratrix, she waived all claim thereto. (See *Davis' Appeal*, 34 Pa. St. 256.) Besides, it has been repeatedly held that, as the allowance is intended solely to furnish the widow means of support until her share in her husband's estate has been set apart (*Newans* v. *Newans*, 79 Iowa, 32; 44 N. W. 213), her claim thereto abates with her death (*Simpson* v. *Cureton*, 97 N. C. 114; 2 S. E. 668; *Tarbox* v. *Fisher*, 50 Me. 238; *Adams* v. *Adams*, 10 Metc. [Mass.] 170; 1 Woerner, Adm'n, 86-92). It cannot then be said that she had other interest in the estate of her husband than her distributive share.

3. This action was begun March 12, 1897—more than twenty years after the death of Ferdinand Zunkel. The plaintiff had lived on the land with his stepmother until eighteen years of age, and thereafter frequently visited her, up to the time of her death. Her possession under the deed of June 16, 1881, was that of her *cestui que trust;* also, of her cotenant in common. Until she " in some unmistakable manner had given plaintiff notice, or sufficient reason to know," that she claimed the property adversely to him, the statute of limitations did not begin to run. (*Murphy* v. *Murphy, supra; Gebhard* v. *Sattler*, 40 Iowa, 157; *Potter* v. *Douglass*, 83 id. 190; 48 N. W. 1004; *Peters* v. *Jones*, 35 Iowa, 512; *Otto* v. *Schlapkahl*, 57 id. 229; 10 N. W. 651.) She stood in *loco parentis,*

and he had the right to assume, at least during his minority, in the absence of knowledge to the contrary, that she would not undertake to devest him of his inheritance. In April, 1882, she executed a mortgage to Schlister, but soon thereafter satisfied it. The money derived by giving this security was devoted to the improvement of this land, and was repaid from its income. The transaction, then, was for the benefit, not only of the widow, but also of the plaintiff and other heirs of the deceased. Under such circumstances, the execution of the mortgage ought not to be regarded as a repudiation of the trust. In September of the same year she gave one Brown the option of buying the minerals underlying the land within four months, and in December following extended this time sixty days. Brown never went into possession, nor did he avail himself of the privilege of buying. This transaction cannot possibly be construed into anything more adverse to the plaintiff than a mere threat to disavow in part her obligation as trustee,—an unexecuted threat. The possession of the widow with her children, the defendants, was uninterrupted up to her death; and the record discloses no act of hers prior to July 23, 1893, which was necessarily inconsistent with the recognition of plaintiff's interest in the land. If she had any intention of repudiating the trust in 1882, she failed to carry it out, and it was abandoned long before the plaintiff arrived at the age of majority. The statute of limitations, then, was not put in motion before the sale of the coal underlying forty acres in 1893; and whether that amounted to a disavowal of the trust as to all the land is not involved in this action.

4. We need only add that this is not a proper case in which to apply the doctrine of *laches*. To do so would be to repudiate the virtues of parental respect and gratitude, that all approve. Doubtless the defense of *laches* may be availing in cases of implied trusts, but lapse of time is only one of many circumstances by which it may be established. (*Reynolds* v. *Sumner* [Ill. Sup.], 18 N. E. 334; 1 L. R. A. 327; *Boone* v. *Chiles*, 10 Pet. 177; *Michoud* v. *Girod*, 4 How. 510; Perry, Trusts, 229.) In permitting his stepmother, who had reared him, to continue in possession of the land, and to appropriate its rents and profits for the necessary support of herself and minor children during the eight or nine years after he became of age, without demanding or bringing an action for his interest therein, he was not guilty of such delay as ought to defeat his suit

for partition. (*Paschall* v. *Hinderer*, 28 Ohio St. 568. See *Tyler* v. *Daniel*, 65 Ill. 316.)

Affirmed.

GRANGER, J., not sitting.

NOTE.—LACHES.

(a) General principles.
(b) Effect of change in conditions.
(c) A question of pleading.
(d) Effect of statute of limitations.
(e) As affecting relief against purchase by administrator or executor.
(f) As affecting right to have land sold for debts.
(g) Several illustrative cases.

(a) **General principles.**—"A court of equity which is never active in relief against conscience or public convenience has always refused its aid to stale demands, where the party has slept on his rights, and acquiesced for a great length of time. Nothing can call forth this court into activity but conscience, good faith, and reasonable diligence." Lord CAMDEN in Smith v. Clay (3 Brown Ch. 638; and see 1 Pomeroy Eq. §§ 416, 417).

While a court of equity may deny relief because of *laches* in suing, although plaintiff commenced his action within the period limited by statute for actions at law, still the granting or refusing relief, upon that ground, must depend upon the special circumstances of each case. (Bryan v. Kales, 134 U. S. 126, 135; 10 Sup. Rep. 435.)

No inflexible rule can be laid down, each case must be judged upon its own merit. (Kipping v. Demint, 184 Ill. 166; 56 N. E. Rep. 330; and see Haddaway v. Hynson, 89 Md. 305; 43 Atl. Rep. 306.)

(b) **Effect of change in conditions.**—A delay which may be of no consequence in an ordinary case may be amply sufficient to bar the title of relief where the property is of a speculative character, or is subject to contingencies, or where the rights or liabilities of others have, in the meantime, been varied. If the property is of a speculative or precarious nature, it is the duty of a party complaining of the fraud to put forward his complaint at the earliest possible time. He cannot be allowed to remain passive, prepared to affirm the transaction if the concern should prosper, or to repudiate it, if that should prove to his advantage. (Benson v. Demster, 183 Ill. 297, 306; 55 N. E. Rep. 651.)

In this case a delay of thirty-eight years was held fatal to relief and the court says (p. 307) that delay for much shorter period will bar relief.

Heirs cannot stand silently by for years while occupant is making valuable and lasting improvements, without being chargeable with *laches*. (Evans v. Snyder, 64 Mo. 516.)

Changes which lapse of time make in value of property and in situation of the parties, are potent elements in determining when *laches* are involved, that it would be inequitable to grant relief. (Willard v. Wood, 164 U. S. 503; 17 Sup. Rep. 176; and see Mooers v. White, 6 Johns. 369; Pairo v. Vickery, 37 Md. 469; Penn. Mutual Ins. Co. v. Austin, 168 U. S. 699; 18 Sup. Rep. 223.)

Where party seeks relief by bill in equity to correct errors of law or fact in settlements of decedent's estate, he is chargeable with fault or neglect if he had knowledge of facts which should have put a person of ordinary prudence on inquiry. (Cawthorn v. Jones, 73 Ala. 82.)

(c) **A question of pleading.**—Courts of equity withhold relief from those who have delayed the assertion of their claims for an unreasonable time; and this doctrine may be applied in the discretion of the court, even though the *laches* are not pleaded or the bill demurred to. (Willard v. Wood, *supra.*)

As regards pleading such is the rule in the United States courts but *query* whether such a defense should not be pleaded to be available in those states at least, which have a Code of Procedure.

(d) **Effect of statute of limitations.**—In a suit in equity to enforce a purely equitable demand the defense of the statute of limitations can have no application of itself, or by analogy to any limitation in courts of law. Such cases must be determined by courts of equity upon rules and principles of their own. While in such cases *laches* and lapse of time are elements which cannot be safely disregarded, they are not always the most important considerations. Where the lapse of time is less than twenty years the most important considerations in support of this defense generally are: (1) the death of the parties to the original transactions to be investigated, or the intervention of the rights of third persons: (2) the loss of evidence where the transactions are complicated, so as to render it difficult if not impossible to do justice; and (3) the character of the evidence; for instance, if important facts rest upon mere parol testimony; this will be a consideration of much weight, but if upon written or documentary evidence it will be entitled to very little weight. Courts may deny relief after the lapse of much less than twenty years, and relief may be granted after a period greater than twenty years. (Cranmer v. McSwords, 24 W. Va. 595.)

The opinion gives the English origin of the rule as to *laches* and reviews the cases.

In determining whether there has been *laches* on the part of a complainant a court of equity is not necessarily controlled by the period of limitations as fixed in actions at law. A delay for a less period than that prescribed by the statute of limitations will according to the circumstances of the case, be held to be *laches* and to bar relief. When a court of equity is asked to lend its aid in the enforcement of a demand that has become stale, there must be some cogent and weighty reasons presented why it has been permitted to become so. Good faith, conscience and reasonable diligence of the party seeking its relief are the elements that call a court of equity into activity. In the absence of these elements, the court remains passive and declines to extend its relief or aid. It has always been the policy to discountenance *laches* and neglect. (McMillan v. McMillan, 184 Ill. 230, 235; 56 N. E. Rep. 302.)

Courts of equity will refuse relief even in cases of breach of trust on account of *laches* or unreasonable delay of those concerned to apply for relief. This doctrine is somewhat in analogy to the statute of limitations at law. But the time which constitutes the *laches* depends on the circumstances. In this case suit was commenced seventeen years after the oldest son of the intestate, and five years after the youngest son came of age, and it was under the circumstances *held* not to be such *laches* as should bar relief. (Smith ∖ Drake, 23 N. J. Eq. 302.)

Analogy to statute of limitations. (Killough v. Hinton, 54 Ark. 68; 14 S. W. Rep. 1092; Ricard v. Williams, 7 Wheat. 59; Gregory v. Rhoden, 24 S. C. 90, 99.)

Within what time a claim for relief in equity will be barred depends upon the peculiar circumstances of each case, and these are always examinable. Relief may be denied on ground of lapse of time within the period fixed by the statute of limitations. (Obert v. Obert, 12 N. J. Eq. 423.)

Whether the equitable doctrine of *laches*, as distinguished from the statute of limitations, now exists in New York, is open to serious doubt. (Cox v. Stokes, 156 N. Y. 511; 51 N. E. Rep. 316.)

The statute of limitations in New York prescribes limit for *equitable* as well as legal causes of action. (See Gilmore v. Ham, 142 N. Y. 1; 36 N. E. Rep. 826. But compare 1 Pomeroy Eq. § 417.)

A statute of limitation unless restricted may be equally binding upon courts of law and equity. (Bland v. Fleeman, 58 Ark. 84, 96; 23 S. W. Rep. 4.)

(e) **As affecting relief against purchase by administrator or executor.**—Sale by administrator to himself is voidable at election of *cestui que trust*, but if the *cestui que trust* receive the proceeds of sale or any part thereof, with knowledge of all the facts, he thereby confirms and ratifies the sale, and cannot afterwards avoid it. (Axton v. Carter, 141 Ind. 673; 39 N. E. Rep. 546.)

And so where the administrator paid full value, and the creditors received the proceeds, the widow and heirs have no equitable ground to have sale set aside and the administrator decreed a trustee for them. (Highsmith v. Whitehurst, 120 N. C. 123; 26 S. E. Rep. 917.)

Where action is brought by heir against an administrator to recover land of decedent purchased by him at his own sale, lapse of time is no defense, unless based upon some statute of limitation. Upon general principles mere lapse of time is not material to the case. (Morgan v. Wattles, 69 Ind. 260.)

But possession after such sale by the administrator open and notorious for thirty years after final settlement, of itself constitutes a complete defense. (Harney v. Donohoe, 97 Mo. 141; 10 S. W. Rep. 191.)

A party cannot be charged with *laches* in asserting his right to have an

has been unreasonable, though less than ten years have elapsed. (State v. Probate Court, 40 Minn. 296; 41 N. W. Rep. 1033.)

Settled doctrine of this court that a delay, when not satisfactorily explained for seven years after the granting of letters of administration, in proceeding to sell land by the administrator to pay debts, is such *laches* as will bar relief. (McKean v. Vick, 108 Ill. 373; Brogan v. Brogan, 63 Ark. 405; 39 S. W. Rep. 58.)

But a probate allowance is a judgment within the meaning of a statute fixing a period of limitation at ten years, which runs from time of discharge of the administrator. (Brown v. Hanawer, 48 Ark. 277; 3 S. W. Rep. 27.)

In Abbott v. Downs (168 Mass. 481; 47 N. E. Rep. 94), proceedings by administrator to sell land were sustained when brought nearly *seventeen* years after petitioner was appointed administrator the court finding that one of the parties who claimed title by deed took same with full knowledge of all the equities, and that petitioner had not been guilty of *laches*.

g) **Several illustrative cases.**—*Laches* may arise from failure in diligent prosecution of a suit. (Willard v. Wood, 164 U. S. 502; 17 Sup. Rep. 176.)

Law presumes legacies to have been paid, satisfied or abandoned after twenty years from time when suit might have been instituted for their recovery. (Cox v. Brower, 114 N. C. 422; 19 S. E. Rep. 365.)

While an infant is not chargeable with his own *laches*, yet where time has commenced to run against an ancestor it continues to run against his infant heir. (Gibson v. Herriott, 55 Ark. 86; 17 S. W. Rep. 589.)

COUSENS *vs.* ADVENT CHURCH OF CITY OF BIDDEFORD.

[Supreme Judicial Court of Maine, December 5, 1899; 93 Me. 292; 45 Atl. Rep. 43.]

WILL—PROBATE—EQUITY—JURISDICTION.

1. This court, sitting in equity, cannot establish an unprobated will.
2. If, after probate of a will, a later will, which revokes the first, is found, it should be presented for probate to the Probate Court. From the decree of that court an appeal lies to the Supreme Court of Probate.
3. The prior probate of the earlier will does not preclude the probate of the later will. If the later will revokes the former, upon its probate the court authorized to admit wills to probate has authority to revise or revoke the former decree so far as to give effect to the last will.

(Official.)

EXCEPTIONS from Supreme Judicial Court, York county.

Bill by James H. Cousens against the Advent Church of the City of Biddeford, praying that the defendant corporation be required to pay to the plaintiff a legacy of $3,000, and other sums and bequests, which he claimed were due him under the will of Charles E. Rumery, deceased, made in 1884, and alleged to have been fraudu· lently suppressed or destroyed by Eliza A. Rumery, his wife, and never probated.

The defendant answered and demurred to the bill, and, the presiding justice having sustained the demurrer, the plaintiff took exceptions to this ruling and order of the court.

Exceptions overruled.

Argued before PETERS, C. J., and HASKELL, WISWELL, STROUT, and FOGLER, JJ.

J. M. Stone and *C. S. Hamilton*, for plaintiff.

J. O. Bradbury and *Geo. F. & Leroy Haley*, for defendants.

STROUT, J.—Demurrer to the bill was sustained by the justice hearing the case, and exception taken.   The only question is whether the case made by the bill, if proved, affords ground for the equitable relief sought.

The bill alleges: That Charles E. Rumery made his will on the 16th day of January, 1870, and died on May 14, 1885.   This will was admitted to probate by decree of the Probate Court, and, on appeal by complainant, by the Supreme Court of Probate.   That under this will Eliza A. Rumery, his wife, took all of the estate of Charles, and that by her will she gave it to defendant, who since her death has received and still holds the same.

It alleges: That in the summer or fall of 1884 Charles E. Rumery made another and later will, in which he gave complainant $3,000, and, he believes, other valuable gifts; that Charles exhibited this will to his wife, and told her that he had given complainant $3,000.   That thereupon she became very indignant, and said complainant should never receive a cent of it.   That this last will was fraudulently concealed or destroyed by Eliza, and has never been found.   That at the time of the probate of the will of

1870 complainant was unable to prove the execution and contents of the later will of 1885, but that he has since discovered, and is now able to make, such proof. That defendant has already received, as legatee of Eliza, a little over $6,000, and will receive $1,000 more on the death of this complainant, which is now held by a trustee. It charges that by law the defendant holds this sum of $6,000 in trust to pay the complainant the $3,000 legacy to him, and other sums given him by the will of 1884. The prayer is that defendant be decreed to pay complainant " three thousand dollars, and such other sums and bequests as were therein given to him in the last will and testament of said Charles E. Rumery," and for other relief.

Wills do not become operative until proved and established in some court having jurisdiction for that purpose,—in this state, by allowance by the Court of Probate, or the Appellate Supreme Court of Probate. No other tribunal can give effect to a will. Until established in that forum, it has no life. This court, sitting in equity, cannot establish and execute an unprobated will. The first step for complainant to take is to prove his later will in the Probate Court.

But the complainant says he cannot do this, because an earlier will has been admitted to probate, and the judgment in that case is final, conclusive, and cannot be revoked. It may be that what has been done by the executor under that will, and its probate, will protect the executor; but it does not follow that, upon the probate of a later will which revokes the earlier, the estate may not be followed in the hands of the legatees who received it under the earlier will. Our statutes make no provision for a new trial or review in case of an appeal allowing a will. But if a will admitted to probate is afterwards found to be a forgery, or the testator proves to be alive, or a later will is discovered, it would be a reproach to the law to hold that such erroneous decree must stand. If it is to be corrected, it would seem it should be done in the court having jurisdiction of the subject-matter,—in the Probate Court in the first instance, and by appeal in the Supreme Court of Probate. This course is more convenient and much more logical than an appeal to a court of equity to annul or revise the decree of another court of special and exclusive jurisdiction in such matters. It is said in *Gale* v. *Nickerson* (144 Mass. 415; 11 N. E. 714): " There is an inherent power in probate courts, in cases where justice clearly requires it, to revise such a decree. Thus, if, after a will is proved, a later will or codicil is discovered, or if there is newly-discovered evidence proving that a will is forged, the court may reopen the case and revise the decree." It is also there said that "it is more in harmony with our system, and more convenient in practice, that a motion for a new trial or rehearing of a decree of the Probate Court affirmed by the Supreme Court of Probate should be heard in the first instance in the Probate Court."

The same question is fully discussed in *Waters* v. *Stickney* (12 Allen, 1, 12, 13), and the same result reached. In that case it is said: "A Court of Probate has no more power by a decree establishing one testamentary instrument to preclude the subsequent probate of a later one, never before brought to its notice, than by a decree approving one account to discharge an administrator from responsibility for assets not accounted for. * * * There is no reason why the probate of a will which does not express the last intentions of the testator should be held irrevocable, more than letters of administration issued upon the supposition that the deceased died intestate."

In *Bowers* v. *Johnson* (5 R. I. 119), the Supreme Court of Rhode Island held that the power to revoke a probate once granted, though nowhere expressly recognized in the statutes of that state, was a just and necessary power to be implied from the statute granting general authority to "take the probate of wills and grant administration on the estate of deceased persons," and might be exercised incidentally to an application for the probate of a later will. See, also *Muir* v. *Trustees* (3 Barb. Ch. 481). So it is held that after probate of a will a later will may be admitted to probate by the court which granted the first probate. (*Clogett* v. *Hawkins*, 11 Md. 281; *Schultz* v. *Schultz*, 10 Grat. 358.)

The power of the Probate Court to revoke a decree granting administration is recognized in Rev. St. ch. 64, § 19, which requires an administrator to give a bond with the condition, among others, "to deliver the letters of administration into the Probate Court, in case any will of the deceased is thereafter proved and allowed." In the same chapter (section 7) provision is made for admitting to probate lost or suppressed wills, on the testimony of the subscribing witnesses, or "by any other evidence competent to prove the

execution and contents of a will." For a construction of this statute, see opinion of PETERS, C. J., in *Rich* v. *Gilkey* (73 Me. 603).

To grant the prayer of the bill would require ths court, sitting in
equity, to assume the jurisdiction of the Probate Court, and establish and execute a will never presented to a Court of Probate. This
is beyond the province of equity. (*Wolcott* v. *Wolcott*, 140 Mass.
194; 3 N. E. 214.)

The complainant must seek relief by proving the later will in the
Probate Court in the first instance.

Exceptions overruled. Demurrer sustained.

Bill dismissed, with costs.

COLE *vs.* PROCTOR *et al.*

[Court of Chancery Appeal of Tennessee, December 2, 1899; 54 S. W. Rep.
674.]

LEGACY—CHARGE ON REAL ESTATE.

A will giving to testator's daughter certain land, " also $1,000, if, after the
payment of the debts of my estate, there should be that much left,"
making certain specific legacies, and then providing, " The bulk of my
estate, after carrying out the above directions, I give to " the daughter,
charges the $1,000 legacy on the real estate; the personal property
at testator's death, and presumptively when the will was made, being
worth less than $1,000, and the debts exceeding it.

APPEAL from Chancery Court, Montgomery county; A. R.
GHOLSON, Special Chancellor.

Suit by Henry Cole against Winnie Proctor and others. Decree for complainant on bill and cross bill. Defendants appeal.
Reversed.

Leech & Savage and *H. P. Gholson,* for complainant.

Thos. F. Martin, for defendants in original suit.

Gholson & Lyle, for complainants in cross bill.

Leech & Savage, H. P. Gholson, and *T. F. Martin,* for defendants.

NEIL, J.—Stephen Cole died November 3, 1898, leaving a last will, which was probated on the 16th day of November, 1898. This will reads as follows: " I give to my daughter, Winnie Proctor, the place on which she lives, containing seven acres, more or less; also one thousand dollars, if, after the payment of the debts of my estate, there should be that much left. (2) I give to my son, Henry Cole, two dark mules, about fifteen hands high, the same he is now working on the farm, and fifty dollars. (3) I give to my nephew's son, Norman Johnson, the dark year-old filly, so long as he conducts himself. properly, and request my friend Dr. T. D. Johnson to say if it shall remain in his possession, and fifty dollars. (4) The bulk of my estate, after carrying out the above directions, I give to my daughter, Winnie Proctor, and Henry Cole, my son; but, fearing the capacity of business of my son, Henry, I request the county judge to select some one to act as agent for him." This will is dated June 6, 1896. It turns out that the personal estate is insufficient to pay the legacy of $1,000, to say nothing of debts; hence there is no source from which Mrs. Proctor can receive her entire legacy of $1,000, except from the realty. It does not appear that there is any material difference between the amount of the personal property now and at the time the will was made. The proof does not show the amount of the debts now nor at the time the will was made. There is a statement in a cross bill filed by the administrator that the debts are $1,304.77, but it is also there stated that these debts are disputed by the devisees, and there is no proof upon the point. On the face of the cross bill it appears that $127.77 of this indebtedness accrued after the making of the will. The total personal assets stated upon the face of the cross bill amount only to the sum of $816.71. The only question before us is whether, under a true construction of the will, the $1,000 was charged upon the realty, and therefore whether Mrs. Proctor can resort to the realty in view of the insufficiency of the personalty. It appears that the testator owned, besides the seven acres, other realty as follows: Fifty-five acres near Clarksville; some real estate in the city of Clarksville; also a tract of land on the south side of Cumberland river, in Montgomery county. It does not appear what the

value of this land is, but it is conceded in the answer of Winnie
Proctor that the lands were much more valuable than the
personalty, but what their value was is not shown.   In aid of the
construction of the will the following proof was introduced in behalf of Mrs. Proctor: That Stephen Cole was ill about two years
with paralysis, and Mrs. Proctor lived with him, and paid him the
most devoted attention, and that he needed a great deal of attention;
that the testator's son, complainant Henry Cole, neglected his
father, and his father complained of this neglect; that Stephen Cole
was much attached to his daughter, Mrs. Proctor, and often so expressed himself, and said he was going to make a difference between his children; that he spoke of giving her the seven acres mentioned in the will, and particularly of the $1,000, and that the latter
was to build a house for her on the seven acres; that he spoke of
this both before he made the will and afterwards; that he spoke of
his personal property, and mentioned one note for a balance of
$630, another of $300 of doubtful character, and another of $40,
but never at any time stated how much he thought his personal
property would be worth after the payment of his debts.   It is also
proven that he knew of the existence of several small debts.   Dr.
T. D. Johnson, who wrote the will, was introduced, and testified that
at the time he wrote the will testator stated to him that he had been
for a long time intending to will his daughter and her husband a
home upon the place where they then lived, and to give them $1,000
for the purpose.   He was then asked this question, and answered
as follows: " Q. Please state what he said in connection with the
fourth and last article of his will, which begins thus: ' The bulk
of my estate,' etc. A. After preparing the three previous articles
of his will, he said that was all he wanted to give away at present.
I told him he had not disposed of the bulk of his estate. He seemed
to be under the impression that it was an immediate disposition of
his property. When I explained to him that none was disposed of
until his death, he directed me to write the fourth clause as it is
worded. Q. Did he (Stephen) undertake, while talking to you,
to draw any distinction between his real property and personal
estate, and did you, in drafting the will, undertake for him to draw
any such distinction? A. He did not, and neither did I. In fact I
did not think we separated the two at the time. Q. In what meaning did you use the word 'estate,' and how did Stephen, from what

he said, intend it to be used? A. He meant all of his property of which he died possessed; his entire estate. I supposed—and I thought he did—that he intended that all of his estate of all kinds should be turned over to the executor or administrator, and division made according to the will. I don't remember his exact language, but do not think he intended to draw any distinction between personal property and real estate. I know I knew of no such distinction at the time until this suit came up." The above testimony was all objected to in the court below by the complainant, but the attention of the chancellor was not called thereto, nor was it acted upon by him, so far as the record shows. The chancellor, however, decreed: " That it was the intention of the testator, Stephen Cole, as expressed in his will, that the legacy of one thousand dollars to his daughter, Winnie Proctor, was not a charge upon the real estate left by him, but said legacy was to be paid out of the personalty of the estate after payment of debts; that the place on which the said Winnie Proctor lived contained seven acres, more or less, passed to said Winnie Proctor by the terms of said will; that the two mules and the fifty dollars bequeathed to Henry Cole by the second item of the will were the property of said Henry Cole; that there is no question raised as to the third item of the will, and the court does not pass on that; that it was the intention of the testator by the fourth item of said will to give all the remainder of his estate absolutely to his daughter, Winnie Proctor, and his son, Henry Cole, equally, to share alike." The court therefore, decreed that the estate should be settled in accordance with the construction above given to the will. Mrs. Proctor and her husband prayed and were granted an appeal " from so much of this decree as holds the said legacy of one thousand dollars is not a charge on and payable out of the real estate owned by testator, but the payment of said legacy must be made from the personalty left after the payment of said debts." The question raised by this appeal is the only question before us.

Looking at the face of the will alone, and leaving out the paragraphs and all unnecessary words, the following reading will clearly bring out the meaning: " I give to my daughter, Winnie Proctor, the place on which she lives, containing seven acres, more or less; also one thousand dollars, if, after the payment of the debts of my estate, there should be that much left. I give to my son,

Henry Cole, two dark mules, about fifteen hands high, the same he is now working on the farm, and fifty dollars. I give to my nephew's son, Norman Johnson, the year-old dark filly * * * and fifty dollars. The bulk of my estate, after carrying out the above directions (that is, after my debts are paid, and after my daughter receives one thousand dollars, and my son, Henry Cole. receives the two dark mules and fifty dollars, and Norman Johnson receives the dark filly and fifty dollars), I give to my daughter, Winnie Proctor, and Henry Cole, my son." It is clear the case falls within the authority of *Hutchinson* v. *Gilbert* (86 Tenn. 464; 7 S. W. 126). The syllabus of that case expresses its contents, and is in the following words: "Where a testatrix, after directing payment of her debts and funeral expenses, gives a general pecuniary legacy, and then disposes of the residue of her property, real and personal, in one mass, she indicates her intention to charge her real as well as her personal estate with such legacy." In the present case there is no specific direction for the payment of debts, but the expression, "if, after the payment of the debts of my estate," etc., is equivalent to a direction to pay debts, or at least is the expression of a purpose that the debts should be paid out of the estate. The language of the fourth item, " The bulk of my estate, after carrying out the above directions, I give," etc., is, in substance, a disposition of the residue of the property after the payment of debts and the pecuniary legacies and the special legacies mentioned prior to the fourth item of the will. Likewise, by the words, "the bulk of my estate," it is clear the testator referred to his estate, both real and personal. The presumption is against intestacy, and the word " estate," when not qualified or restricted, is always construed to embrace every description of property, real, personal, and mixed. (*Gourley* v. *Thompson*, 2 Sneed, 388, 393.) Again, when we look to the facts surrounding the testator at the time, the meaning becomes even more plain. It is evident from the face of the will that the testator intended that his daughter should have the seven acres of land and $1,000 more than his son. It is fair to presume, under the facts stated, that the personal property of the testator was about the same at the time the will was made as it was when he died. In each instance it was less than $1,000. It would not be fair to presume that the testator intended to do an idle thing when he bequeathed $1,000 to his daughter. It could not be supposed that he intended that she should get this out of a fund that did not exist in a sufficient amount to pay the legacy. We are of the opinion that many of the facts stated are immaterial, and we have based nothing on them, although we have set them out because the position assumed by counsel, and the relief attempted to be based thereon, make it proper to set them out, so that full benefit of them may be had upon appeal to the Supreme Court. We have had the benefit of the chancellor's opinion in this case, which was sent up with the record, and have given the reasons therein stated full consideration. Those reasons are thus stated in that opinion: " The personal estate is by law primarily liable for the payment of decedent's debts and legacies. True, a testator may, if he sees fit, make the payment of a money legacy a charge upon his real estate; but when he has not seen fit to do so he must be held to have contemplated its payment out of his personal estate. I think, in view of the language used, testator meant that, if, after his debts were discharged, there was enough personalty left, his daughter should be paid one thousand dollars; if not, she could not go on the real estate to make up the deficit. Evidently there was in his mind some doubt as to whether, after the payment of his debts, there would be as much money left as would pay her one thousand dollars. The proportion which his indebtedness bore to the value of his personal estate might raise such a doubt in his mind; but, if you add his real estate to his personalty, the amount would so far exceed his indebtedness as to render such a condition on which the one thousand dollars were to be paid to his daughter wholly inappropriate and unnecessary. I therefore hold that, after the payment of his debts out of the personal property, what is ' left ' (to use the language of the will) should be paid on the thousand dollar legacy to his daughter; but she cannot go on the real estate for the same. He intended to apply in payment of this legacy what might remain of his personal estate after his debts were paid. I think the fourth item of the will was intended by testator, after the payment of the legacies mentioned in the previous items of the will, to divide the remainder of his property, real and personal, between his daughter, Winnie Proctor, and his son, Henry Cole." As we understand this, the eminent special chancellor who tried this case placed the stress of the argument on the fact that there might be a doubt as to whether there would be a sufficiency of the personalty left, after the payment of debts, to pay the legacy of $1,000, but that, putting the personalty and the realty together, there could have been no doubt in the testator's mind upon this subject. There is no sufficient basis of fact in the record upon which this argument, if otherwise sound, can rest, because, if we take the debts and assets as stated in the cross bill to be the true amounts, there could never have been any doubt that there would be nothing left whatever out of the personalty, after the payment of debts, to go upon the legacy; indeed, it would appear from these facts that the debts were more than the personal property, even after deducting the $127.77, which certainly accrued afer the making of the will. Thus, so far from there being any doubt in the testator's mind upon this subject, there would be a certainty that there would be nothing left of the personalty to pay the legacy which he bequeathed to his daughter; and that would involve the testator in the predicament of making a bequest which he knew could never be paid out of his estate. It is true that, under the concession in Winnie Proctor's answer (to the effect that the real estate was worth more than the personalty, there being nothing else to show the value of the realty), if we put the personal property at $816.16, the realty at that much at least, and the debts at the figure stated in the cross bill, there could have been no doubt in the testator's mind but that on such putting together of the realty and personalty there would be a surplus left after the payment of debts. Hence, an impression might arise in the mind of one considering the case that the testator could not have intended that the legacy of $1,000 should come out of the joint estate, inasmuch as it was apparently contemplated by him that the property out of which the legacy should come might prove insufficient after the payment of debts. It is argued this could not happen if realty and personalty were considered together; it might happen if personalty were considered alone; *ergo,* testator referred to personalty alone. But the impression referred to is not well based, and the argument to support it is not sound. It is a necessary assumption in the argument that the testator knew, at the making of his will, the amount of debts he would owe at his death. As a matter of fact he did not and could not know this, and it does not yet appear in this record what these debts were. With the amount of the debts left out, the whole argument breaks down. Again, if we assume that the debts were as stated in the cross bill, still this would not interfere with the operation of the rule laid down and applied in

Hutchinson v. *Gilbert* (*supra*), and we have already shown that the language of the will in this case brings it within the authority referred to.   Furthermore, even upon the facts stated upon which rests the argument we are considering, the testator, as already pointed out, would be placed in the position of making a mere hollow pretense of giving a legacy to his daughter, placing it upon a portion of his estate which he knew would be wholly consumed in the payment of debts, and then devising the entire residue of the estate.   A construction which leads to such a result must necessarily be wrong.   It is true, as stated in the special chancellor's opinion, that personal property is primarily chargeable with general pecuniary legacies (*Evens* v. *Beaumont*, 16 Lea, 713), but even in this case it is conceded that, if there is a direction that the residue of the estate shall go in a certain direction after the payment of legacies, this would be sufficient to constitute a charge upon the real estate (id. 717, 718).   For the reasons given, we are of the opinion that the decree of the chancellor should be reversed.   A decree will be entered here construing the will as indicated above, and the cause will be remanded to the Chancery Court of Montgomery county for further proceedings.   The costs of this court will be paid by Henry Cole.   The costs of the court below will be paid as may hereafter be decreed by the chancellor.   All the judges concur.

Affirmed orally by Supreme Court, December 23, 1899.

BARNES *vs.* ROCKEY *et al.*

[Supreme Court of Oregon, December 16, 1899; 36 Ore. 279; 59 Pac. Rep. 464.]

ADMINISTRATORS—REMOVAL—PETITION—WAIVER OF OBJECTION.

1. Objection that petition for removal of an administrator does not allege that his neglect had or would result in loss to petitioners, or set out the facts showing that petitioners are creditors of the estate, or that the person whom the court is asked to appoint administrator was a resident of the county, is waived by the administrator appearing and submitting an excuse, without objection to sufficiency of the petition.

2. Failure of an administrator to comply with Hill's Ann. Laws, § 1131, making it his duty, immediately after appointment, to publish notice to present claims within six months, and section 1112, requiring him to file an inventory within one month after appointment, is sufficient ground, in the discretion of the court, for his removal, under sections 1094, 1100, providing that he may be removed for unfaithfulness or neglect of his trust, to the probable loss of persons interested in the estate.

APPEAL from Circuit Court, Multnomah county; JOHN B. CLE-LAND, Judge.

In the matter of the estate of Laura Marie Barnes, deceased. A. E. Rockey and another petitioned for removal of W. St. M. Barnes as administrator. From a decree of the Circuit Court affirming the County Court's order of removal, the administrator appeals. Affirmed.

This is an appeal from a decree of the Circuit Court of Multnomah county affirming an order of the County Court of that county removing the appellant as administrator of the estate of Laura Marie Barnes. The facts are that Mrs. Barnes died intestate on the 16th of April, 1897, and on the 28th of the same month her husband (the appellant herein) was appointed as administrator of her estate. On November 2, 1897, A. E. Rockey and J. T. Walls filed in the County Court a petition averring that they were creditors of the estate; that, although more than six months had elapsed since the appointment of the appellant as administrator, he had failed and neglected to publish a notice of his appointment, as required by law, or make and file an inventory of the property belonging to the estate, and in fact had done nothing towards the settlement thereof; that their verified claims had been presented to the administrator some time before the filing of the petition, but he had not passed upon the same, although he had sufficient time, and had been requested so to do; and asking that his letters be revoked, and one J. B. Bridges, the father of the deceased, be appointed in his stead. Upon the filing of this petition an order was made citing the appellant to appear and show cause why it should not be granted, and on the 16th of November he appeared, and, without making any objection to the petition, or denying any of its allegations, averred: " That the principal cause of delay in proceeding

with the administration has been absence from the city, and press
of business; that, since having his attention called to the fact that
interested parties were desirous of having the administration progress, he has caused notice of his appointment, etc., to be published,
has prepared an inventory of the estate, and filed a petition in the
County Court asking for the appointment of appraisers, and is
ready to proceed with the administration of the estate as expedi-
tiously as possible." A reply was filed denying each averment
in the answer, and the matter was submitted upon the pleadings.
On the following day the court entered a decree finding that the petitioners were creditors of the estate; that, although the appellant
was appointed as administrator on the 28th of April, 1897, he had,
up to the time of filing the petition for his removal, failed to publish
notice of his appointment, or to make or file an inventory, and had
neglected and failed to take any steps towards the settlement of the
estate; that no order or application to the court had been made
for an extension of time in which to file the inventory or for the
appointment of appraisers; that, by reason of the neglect of the administrator, the creditors were uninformed of the condition or value
of the estate, which was alleged in the petition for his appointment
to be $1,000, and had suffered probable loss in not being able to col-
lect their claims; that the administrator had failed to show cause
why his negligence should be excused; and thereupon entered a
decree removing him, and appointing J. B. Bridges, whom it found
to be a resident of Multnomah county, and a suitable person, as administrator of the estate. An appeal was taken to the Circuit Court,
where the order of the County Court was affirmed, and the administrator appeals to this court.

J. R. Stoddard, for appellant.

F. S. Grant and *E. Mendenhall,* for respondents.

BEAN, J. (after stating the facts).—The contention of the appellant is that the petition filed in the County Court for his removal
was not sufficient to authorize the court to make any order whatever in the matter, because: (1) It does not allege that the neglect
of the administrator to publish notice of his appointment or file an
inventory within the time required by law had resulted or would
result in probable loss to the petitioners; (2) the bare allegation

that the petitioners are creditors of the estate was insufficient, but the facts constituting their claim ought to have been averred; and (3) it does not aver that Bridges, whom it asks to have appointed administrator, was a resident of Multnomah county. But these objections, if they ever possessed any merit, were waived by the administrator when he appeared and submitted an excuse for his negligence, without objection to the sufficiency of the petition. The statute provides that an executor or administrator may be removed upon the application of an heir, legatee, devisee, creditor, or other person interested in the estate, for unfaithfulness or neglect of his trust, to the probable loss of the applicant (Hill's, Ann. Laws, § 1094), and the court may, for like cause, upon its own motion, remove such officer (id. § 1100; *in re Partridge's Estate*, 31 Or. 297; 51 Pac. 82). When therefore, the appellant, in obedience to a citation regularly issued, appeared, admitted his delinquency, and submitted to the court the sufficiency of his excuse for the failure to discharge the duties of his trust, it became its duty to determine whether he should be removed or not, and its decision in that regard will not be reviewed on appeal unless abuse appears. (*In re Holladay's Estate*, 18 Or. 168; 22 Pac. 750; *McFadden* v. *Ross*, 93 Ind. 134; *in re Graber's Estate*, 111 Cal. 432; 44 Pac. 165; 1 Woerner, Adm'n, 572.) The law makes it the duty of the administrator immediately after his appointment to publish a notice requiring all persons having claims against the estate to present them with the proper vouchers within six months from the date of such notice (Hill's Ann. Laws, § 1131), and also to file an inventory of the property belonging to the estate which shall come into his possession or knowledge within one month after the date of his appointment, or such further time as the court or judge may allow (id. § 1112). It is admitted that the administrator in this case failed and neglected to comply with either of the sections referred to, and such failure was a sufficient ground, in the discretion of the court, for his removal. (*In re Holladay's Estate, supra; in re Mills' Estate*, 22 Or. 210; 29 Pac. 443.)

It follows that the decree of the court below must be affirmed, and it is so ordered.

NOTE.—EFFECT OF OMISSION TO FILE INVENTORY.

(a) As breach of a bond.
(b) Effect of omission.
(c) Remedy by accounting.
(d) Some illustrative cases.

(a) **As breach of a bond.**—Failure to file constitutes breach of a bond, and it is not necessary for a legatee plaintiff to prove actual damages, in order to sustain his action on the bond. (Forbes v. McHugh, 152 Mass. 412; 25 N. E. Rep. 622.)

General rule is that to entitle an administrator to defend on ground of insufficiency of assets there must be an inventory filed and a settlement of his account. (McKim v. Haley, 173 Mass. 112; 53 N. E. Rep. 152; and see Hodge v. Hodge, 90 Me. 508; 38 Atl. Rep. 535; Ellis v. Johnson, 83 Wis. 394; 53 N. W. Rep. 691; Sherwood v. Hill, 25 Mo. 391), where not only failure to file an inventory was considered a breach, but the actual receipt of the money by the executor was involved as an element.

In State v. Smith (52 Conn. 557), the breach of a bond in failing to file inventory was held technical in suit by a plaintiff who had no interest beyond costs.

Nor can the administrator defend the breach of his bond by the excuse that his omission was caused by belief and advice of counsel. (Bourne v. Stevenson, 58 Me. 499.)

Where failure to file inventory is relied upon as breach of the bond it must be averred that *some* property came into the hands of the administrator; plaintiff should show that damage has been sustained through the administrator's neglect. (Walker v. Hall, 1 Pick. 19.)

(b) **Effect of omission.**—Omission of assets from inventory may be a fraud or its equivalent. (McNeal's Estate, 68 Pa. St. 412.)

But not where money or property is omitted under an honest although mistaken legal belief that it belonged to the administrator personally and not to the estate. (Speakman's Appeal, 71 Pa. St. 25.)

Under such circumstances a Probate Court should not compel the insertion of the property in question in the inventory, but leave parties to their remedy on an accounting. (Greenhough v. Greenhough, 5 Redf. 191; and see Stewart's Estate, 137 Pa. St. 175, 181; 20 Atl. Rep. 554.)

The omission to file is a strong circumstance in support of a charge of improper conduct. (Hart v. Ten Eyck, 2 Johns. Ch. 62, modified on appeal but not on above ground; id. 121; and see *note* 1 Cow. 743, 744.)

As affecting right to commissions see Eppinger v. Canepa (20 Fla. 264).

(c) **Remedy by accounting.**—Where no personal estate has come to possession of the administrator, and he has no knowledge of the existence of any, filing an inventory is a useless formality; and parties who allege the contrary should be left to their appropriate remedy on an accounting.

(Estate of Langton, 16 Phil. 369; Walker v. Hall, 1 Pick. 19; and see Matter of Ryalls, 74 Hun, 205, 208; 26 N. Y. Supp. 815.)

And as to remedy on accounting. (Montgomery v. Dunning, 2 Bradf. 220; Greenhough v. Greenhough, 5 Redf. 191; Sheerin v. Public Administrator, 2 Redf. 421; Matter of Mullon, 145 N. Y. 98; 39 N. E. Rep. 821; Grant v. Reese, 94 N. C. 720.)

Where an administrator has disposed of all the assets in payment of funeral expenses and debts, a motion to compel an inventory may be denied, and proper and sufficient relief be obtained on an accounting. (Matter of Robins, 4 Redf. 144.)

But this case so far as it was founded on reasoning based upon an appraisal being impracticable as part of the inventory appears to be overruled by Silverbrandt v. Widmayer (2 Dem. 263).

(d) **Some illustrative cases.**—May be waived by parties in interest. (1 N. Y. Civ. Proc. 59.)

Failure to file does not affect a purchaser at the executor's sale. (Cooper v. Horner, 62 Tex. 356, 364.)

Clause in a will relieving executors and trustees from filing an inventory is invalid as against public policy. (Potter v. McAlpine, 3 Dem. 109.)

Omission to include property in an inventory is not evidence of title as against the estate. (Lewis v. Lusk, 35 Miss. 696.)

Omission to include interest of deceased in a partnership, does not charge an executor with its nominal value; its real value may be shown. (Moses v. Moses, 50 Ga. 9.)

In Heirs of Adams v. Adams (22 Vt. 50), on a bill in chancery by heirs it was held that a charge against an administrator of not making an inventory and appraisal of *choses in action* was of no importance.

Where statute prescribes time within which an inventory must be filed, and gives court power to revoke letters, such power is discretionary only, and revocation does not follow as matter of course. (Re Graber, 111 Cal. 432; 44 Pac. Rep. 165.)

If administrator omits to file he has no power over personal estate and no right to release a debt due the estate. (Jeroms v. Jeroms, 18 Barb. 24.)

But right to maintain action to enforce debts due the estate does not depend upon filing of an inventory. (Leland v. Manning, 4 Hun, 12.)

Omission to file does not affect jurisdiction of surrogate to order a sale of real estate. It is proper to refuse such order until such omission has been supplied; but if such sale is ordered without, the act of the surrogate cannot be questioned in a collateral proceeding. (Schneider v. McFarland, 4 Barb. 139.)

HAYS *vs.* FRESHWATER *et al.*

[Supreme Court of Appeals of West Virginia, December 2, 1899; 34 S. E. Rep. 831.]

EXECUTORS—SURCHARGING ACCOUNTS—LACHES—WILL—CONSTRUCTION.

1. J. M. C., by his last will and testament, appointed two executors, who qualified, and entered upon their duties, and made the first settlement of their accounts on the 13th of December, 1883, and the second settlement on the 16th of June, 1888. After the death of one of the executors, H., one of the distributees under said will, at October rules, 1894, filed her bill to surcharge and falsify said accounts. The *laches* of plaintiff are so great in the circumstances that the relief prayed for will be denied.

2. The cardinal rule for the construction of a will is to ascertain the intent of the testator from the entire instrument.

3. Where a testator, in his will, makes advancements to his children, and directs that they shall be charged interest thereon, it is proper to charge such interest in making distribution of his estate.

(Syllabus by the Court.)

APPEAL from Circuit Court, Hancock county; JOSEPH R. PAULL, Judge.

Suit by Virginia B. Hays against E. A. Freshwater and others. Decree for plaintiff, and defendant Freshwater appeals.
Affirmed.

John R. Donehoo and *Melvin & Ewing,* for appellant.

Palmer & Palmer, for appellee.

ENGLISH, J.—On the 27th day of April, 1878, James M. Campbell, of Butler, Hancock county, W. Va., made his last will and testament, and appointed his brother, George W. Campbell, and his son-in-law, E. A. Freshwater, executors thereof, and on December 1, 1880, he added a codicil thereto. After the death of said James M. Campbell, said executors qualified, and gave bond, and took upon themselves the duties attending the administration of said estate, and continued to act as such executors jointly until some

time in the year 1890, when said George W. Campbell died, and
R. H. Campbell and Howard N. Campbell were appointed and
qualified as his executors. After the death of said George W.
Campbell, nearly all of the business connected with the settlement
of the estate of said James Campbell was transacted by said E. A.
Freshwater, surviving executor of said last will and testament.
On the 13th of December, 1883, said George W. Campbell and E.
A. Freshwater made a settlement of their accounts as such executors before a commissioner of the County Court of Hancock
county, finding a balance due said estate as of September 17, 1883,
of $1,340.18, which report was unexcepted to, and was, on the 4th
day of February, 1884, confirmed by the County Court of said
county. Said executors again made a settlement of their accounts
before the same commissioner on the 16th day of June, 1888, who
found a balance due said executors of $5.74. On the first Monday
in October, 1894, Virginia B. Hays, a daughter and legatee of
said James M. Campbell, filed her bill in the Circuit Court of Hancock county, having for its object a settlement of the accounts of E.
A. Freshwater as surviving executor of said James M. Campbell,
and of R. H. and Howard N. Campbell, executors of the last will
and testament of George W. Campbell, deceased, to surcharge and
falsify the accounts of E. A. Freshwater and George W. Campbell
which had been settled before a commissioner, and to recover such
balance as might be found in the hands of the said surviving
executor, or R. H. and Howard N. Campbell, executors of said
George W. Campbell, deceased, and seeking a construction of said
will. To this bill the appellant E. A. Freshwater, as executor of
James M. Campbell, filed his demurrer, claiming therein that so
much of said bill as sought to surcharge and falsify said first settlement of accounts made by said executors was barred by the
laches of the plaintiff, more than ten years having elapsed between
the date of said settlement and the commencement of this suit; and
also demurred to so much of said bill as relates to said second settlement, because more than six years had elapsed between the date of
said second settlement and the commencement of this suit; and for
other reasons assigned,—which demurrer was overruled, and the
defendants were ruled to answer. On the 5th of December, 1874,
said Freshwater, executor, as aforesaid, filed his separate answer to
complainant's bill, claiming therein that the plaintiff was barred by

her *laches* from surcharging and falsifying either of said accounts settled as aforesaid, and assigned other reasons why the plaintiff's bill could not be maintained, and put in issue the material allegations of the plaintiff's bill. R. H. and Howard N. Campbell, executors of George W. Campbell, also filed their answer, relying on the *laches* of the plaintiff, stating various reasons why the plaintiff's bill could not be maintained, and putting in issue the material allegations of the plaintiff's bill. On the 24th of July, 1895, the cause was heard upon the bill and answers together with the papers theretofore filed. The court, proceeding to construe said will, held that the plaintiff was entitled to have the accounts of E. A. Freshwater and George W. Campbell, executors, and the accounts of E. A. Freshwater, surviving executor, restated and settled to conform to the construction placed upon said will by said decree, and directed that the cause be referred to a commissioner of the court to restate and settle said accounts, with leave to either party to surcharge and falsify the settlements of the accounts as already made by said executors. In pursuance of this decree an account was taken, and reported to the court, which was excepted to by said executors for various reasons, and on the 11th of April, 1896, a decree was entered in said cause sustaining some of the exceptions to said report and overruling others, ascertained the sums which it considered properly chargeable to the devisees of James M. Campbell as advancements, and also the amount which the plaintiff, Virginia B. Hays, was entitled to as a devisee of James M. Campbell; also found the balance in the hands of E. A. Freshwater, executor, on November, 1893, was $2,140.75, and directed that, so far as the said R. H. and Howard N. Campbell, executors, as aforesaid, should pay the amounts therein recovered by Virginia B. Hays and Hannah G. Miller, or either of them, they, the said executors of George W. Campbell, should be reimbursed, and recover against said E. A. Freshwater, not exceeding the sum of $2,140.78, and interest thereon from the 15th of November, 1893; and from this decree the defendant Freshwater, executor, etc., obtained this appeal.

The first error assigned and relied upon by the appellant is claimed to have been in the action of the court in its decree of November 15, 1894, overruling appellant's demurrer to the plaintiff's bill: First, because the settlement made in 1883 by appellant and his co-executor was regular, and regularly confirmed, and, having remained unchallenged for more than ten years before the institution of this suit, plaintiff was barred by her *laches* from surcharge or falsification of any part of it; secondly, for the reason that, their second settlement having been made in June, 1888, more than six years before the commencement of this suit, a similar bar is raised. Our Code (chapter 87, § 22), speaking of the report of settlements of accounts of fiduciaries, says: " The report to the extent to which it may be so confirmed shall be taken to be correct, except so far as the same may in a suit in proper time be surcharged or falsified." Now, it appears, as we have seen, that the executors of the estate of James M. Campbell, deceased, settled their accounts as such before a commissioner on the 13th of December, 1883, which settlement was confirmed by the County Court December 23, 1883, and this suit was not instituted until October, 1894. This first settlement was unexcepted to, and dealt with all the items that are now sought to be surcharged and falsified. A second settlement was made, as before stated, on June 16, 1888, which was retained by the commissioner for ten days for exceptions, but which remained unexcepted to. The balance found due from said executors on the first settlement was $1,340.18. In the 'second settlement the executors are charged with this amount, and the interest collected at different times on $3,000, invested for the benefit of the widow of said James M. Campbell, and the interest on $999.39 used by E. A. Freshwater, one of the executors, for three years and four months; and they were credited with certain amounts disbursed by them, ascertaining a balance in favor of said executors of $5.74. Now, the only criticism made upon this second settlement of accounts appears to be that the same was not made in the time required by law, and for that reason said executors should not be allowed commissions; and because it does not charge the proper balance carried over from the former settlement, which balance should be corrected in the manner indicated in the objections raised to the first settlement; so that it appears that the entire effort to surcharge and falsify said accounts was directed against the items charged in the first settlement, with the exception of the objection to the commissions charged in the second settlement on the ground that the settlements were not made in time. Was this suit instituted in time to raise these questions? It has become a maxim that equity favors the vigilant, and looks with discountenance upon stale demands, and it has been frequently held that long delay, and sometimes a delay less than the period of the statute of limitations, will be treated as *laches* sufficient to deny the aid of equity. As was said by Lord CAM-DEN *in Smith* v. *Clay* (3 Brown, Ch. 640, note): " A court of equity, which is never active in. relief against conscience or public convenience, has always refused its aid to stale demands where the party has slept upon his rights, and acquiesced for a great length of lime. Nothing can call forth this court into activity but conscience, good faith, and reasonable diligence. Where these are wanting, the court is passive, and does nothing. *Laches* and neglect are always discountenanced." So, in the case of *Pusey* v. *Gardner* (21 W. Va. 470), this court held (Syl., point 6) that: " Even where there is no absolute bar from lapse of time or by the statute of limitations, it is a principle of courts of equity not to take cognizance of an equitable claim after a great lapse of time ; and where, from the death of parties and witnesses, there is danger of doing injustice, and there can no longer be a safe determination of the controversy." And in point 7: " Lapse of time, when it does not operate as a positive statutory bar, operates, in equity, as an evidence of assent, acquiescence, or waiver." See, also, *Bland* v. *Stewart* (35 W. Va. 518; 14 S. E. 215) ; and *Bill* v. *Schilling* (39 W. Va. 108; 19 S. E. 514). In the case of *Cranmer* v. *McSwords* (24 W. Va. 595), this court held that: " In a suit in equity to enforce a purely equitable de-mand, the defense of the statute of limitations can have no applica-tion, of itself or by analogy, to any limitation in courts of law. Such cases must be determined by courts of equity upon rules and principles of their own. While in such cases *laches* and lapse of time are elements which cannot be safely disregarded, they are not always the most important considerations. Where the lapse of time is less than twenty years, the most important considerations in support of this defense generally are: First, the death of the parties to the original transaction to be investigated, or the inter-vention of the rights of third persons ; second, the loss of evidence when the transactions are complicated so as to render it difficult, if not impossible, to do justice," etc. In the case under considera-tion more than ten years had elapsed between the date of the confirmation of the first settlement and the institution of this suit and more than six had elapsed since the last settlement was made before the suit was brought. One of the executors had died, and the suit had to be defended by his executors, who were necessarily unacquainted with many of the transactions. Under the provisions of the will, as understood by the executors, it appears they proceeded to administer the estate without reference to the $3,000 directed to be loaned out and the interest applied to the support of the widow, the appellee herself receiving a considerable portion thereof, so far as appears, without objection, and, after acquiescing in the distribution thus made by the executors for so many years, she files her bill, praying another and different distribution, at variance with the settlements made by said executors, when they were both in life.

ON REHEARING.

After hearing the arguments, I am led to the conclusion that the plaintiff is entitled to a construction of the will, and especially the fifth clause thereof, in pursuance of her prayer asking therefor. The cardinal rule in construing a will is to seek from the entire instrument the intention of the testator. The law is stated thus in *Hinton* v. *Milburn's Ex'rs* (23 W. Va. 166) : " In the construction of a will the intention of the testator is to be ascertained by taking the whole will together. * * * The manifest intention must have effect, unless some rule of law is violated thereby." And in *Couch* v. *Eastham* (29 W. Va. 784; 3 S. E. 23), this court held that: " When the language of the testator is plain, and his meaning clear, the courts can do nothing but carry out the will of the testator, if it be not inconsistent with some rule of law." Now, when this will is examined, it is found that the testator, after providing for the payment of his just debts and funeral expenses, and making certain provisions for his widow, in the third clause says, " To my children [naming them] I bequeath equal portions of my estate, share and share alike," after speaking of certain advancements he had made and intended to make. In the fourth clause he says, " I hereby authorize and direct my executors to make such disposal of the balance of my personal property not herein bequeathed as shall cause my heirs to share and share alike in the same," and in the fifth clause he directs that the sum of $3,000, which was to be placed at interest for the benefit of his wife, should, at her death, be equally distributed among his heirs therein named. So, the testator in several places clearly manifests his intention of dividing his property equally among his children therein named, and the intention should be carried out, if possible. The said sum of $3,000 seems to have been loaned out by the testator to create an annuity for the benefit of his wife, and, the party to whom it was loaned becoming involved, some labor and expense was necessary in collecting the same; and, in fact, the sum was reduced to some extent by the cost of its recovery. The question which now presents inself for solution is: What must be regarded as the share of the plaintiff in the estate of James M. Campbell; and, if she has not already received it from the hands of the executors, can she require its payment out of said $3,000, loaned for the benefit of said widow? Looking at the entire will for the intention of the testator, we must hold that at the death of the widow this $3,000 became a general fund in the hands of the executors, to be distributed as the other personal estate; and if, in the distribution made by the executors, which may be ascertained by reference to their accounts, settled as aforesaid, or by extraneous evidence, it is found that the appellee has not received what she was entitled to under the provisions of said will, she can recover from the executors whatever balance may be found due her out of the assets in their hands. The court, in its decree directing an account in this cause, held that the plaintiff was entitled to have the accounts of Freshwater and Campbell, executors of James M. Campbell, deceased, and the accounts of Freshwater, surviving executor, restated and settled to conform to the construction of the will therein made, and referred the cause to a commissioner to settle said accounts, with leave to either party to surcharge and falsify the settlements as already made by said executors; and that said settlements should be regarded as *prima facie* correct, except so far as they might not conform to the construction of the will announced in said decree. This, as before stated, we regard as error, under the rulings of this court in *Bland* v. *Stewart* (35 W. Va. 518; 14 S. E. 215); *Pusey* v. *Gardner* (21 W. Va. 469); and *Trader* v. *Jarvis* (23 id. 100). Under these authorities the *laches* of the plaintiff would prevent her from surcharging the first two settlements made by the executors. Under this decree the commissioner proceeded to settle said account, but did not surcharge in any material manner the former settlements made by said executors, and the appellants are not prejudiced by the action of the commissioner in that regard, or by the decree allowing said accounts to be surcharged and falsified. In ascertaining the amount the respective parties were chargeable with by way of advancement, the commissioner charged interest on the amount received from the date of its reception, and while the general rule is that interest is not charged upon advancements during the lifetime of an intestate, as held in this court, in *Kyle* v. *Conard* (25 W. Va. 760); and *Knight* v. *Yarborough* (4 Rand. 569), yet where a testator, in his will, directs interest to be charged on advancements, it is proper to do so. (See 1 Am. & Eng. Enc. Law, 785; also, *Treadwell* v. *Cordis*, 5 Gray, 341; *Nichols* v. *Coffin*, 4 Allen, 27.)

It is also claimed that the court erred in decreeing that the executors of G. W. Campbell recover against appellant such sum, not exceeding $2,140.78, as they might pay of the amount recovered against them and appellant, there being no allegation in the bill, and no proof warranting such recovery, on the ground that there can be no decree between co-defendants unless the equities between the defendants arise out of the pleadings and proofs between the plaintiff and defendant. The proof in this case, however, shows that this money was paid over to Freshwater by his co-executor, and was in his hands as part of the assets, and for that reason I regard the decree correct.

The only remaining error is in regard to the commissions which the commissioner refused to allow the executors, which action was confirmed by the court. The statute being so imperative that commissions shall not be allowed where personal representatives fail to make their settlements in proper time, we cannot disturb the decree in that respect, and for these reasons the same is affirmed.

KERN vs. KERN et al.

[Supreme Court of Indiana, January 9, 1900; 154 Ind. 29; 55 N. E. Rep. 1004.]

WILLS — WITNESSES — ATTORNEY AND CLIENT — COMMUNICA-
TIONS—LOST WILL—REVOCATION.

1. An attorney who drew decedent's will, and was a subscribing witness thereto, is qualified to testify as to its contents in an action between decedent's heirs and his devisees, though Burns' Rev. St. 1894, § 505, prohibits attorneys from testifying to communications by clients, made in the course of business; since such rule does not apply after the client's death.

2. Under Burns' Rev. St. 1894, § 2729 (Rev. St. 1881, § 2559), providing that the revocation of a second will does not revive a prior will unless the intention to revive appears from the terms of the revocation, the testator's first will was not revived where a second will, which had revoked the first, could not be found.

APPEAL from Circuit Court, St. Joseph county; LUCIUS HUB-
BARD, Judge

Proceeding by Catharine Kern against Ella Kern and others to set aside the probate of the will of Amon S. Kern, deceased. From a judgment for defendants, plaintiff appeals.
Reversed.

Agnew & Kelly, for appellant.

A. L. Brick, and *Stuart McKibben,* for appellees.

DOWLING, J.—This was an action to contest a will. It was tried by the court without the intervention of a jury, and a finding was made in favor of the appellees, who were the defendants below. Over a motion for a new trial the court rendered judgment upon the finding. The contestor appealed, and the decision of the court overruling appellant's motion for a new trial is the error assigned.

The contestor was the mother of the testator. The widow, and other beneficiaries under the will, were the defendants. The facts set out in the complaint are, in substance, as follows: On the 20th

day of September, 1897, Amon S. Kern died in the city of South
Bend, St. Joseph county, Ind., leaving an estate of the value of
$75,000 in real and personal property, situated in said city of
South Bend. He left surviving him no children, and no father; his
only heirs at law being his mother, who is the appellant, and his
widow, Ella Kern. On the 24th day of September, 1897, an instrument purporting to be the last will and testament of the said
Amon S. Kern, and bearing date of April 6, 1890, was admitted to
probate in the St. Joseph Circuit Court in said St. Joseph county,
Ind., then in session. By the terms of said will the whole estate
was devised and bequeathed to the widow of the said testator, subject to a residuary bequest to three other relatives, one of whom
died without descendants before the said Amon S. Kern. The appellant, as the mother of the said Amon S. Kern, is by law entitled
to inherit the undivided one-fourth of his estate, and the said Ella
Kern, as the widow of the said Amon S., is entitled to take the undivided three-fourths of his estate, if the said Amon S. Kern died
intestate. The supposed will of April 6, 1890, was invalid, and was
wrongfully admitted to probate, for the reason that it was revoked
by a subsequent will, duly executed in 1894, by the said Amon S.
Kern, either expressly or by an inconsistent disposition of his
estate. Prayer that the probate be set aside, etc. The complaint
was duly verified, and an undertaking for costs was given, as required by the statute. The defendants appeared, and filed a joint
answer in denial. By consent the cause was submitted to the court,
and, as has been stated, the trial resulted in a finding and judgment sustaining the will of 1890. The grounds of appellant's motion for a new trial were that the finding was contrary to law, and
was not sustained by sufficient evidence, and that certain errors of
law occurred on the trial in the rulings of the court in striking out
evidence given for the appellant.

On the trial, Andrew Anderson, a witness for appellant, testified
that he was a practicing lawyer of South Bend, Ind.; that he was
acquainted with Amon S. Kern; that Kern was dead; that some
three or four years before the date of the trial Kern came to the
office of witness, and said that he wanted to make a will disposing
of his estate; that witness thereupon called Mr. Bast, who was his
stenographer, and dictated the will to him; that the stenographer
brought the will into the front room of the office; that Mr. Kern

signed it, and that he (Anderson) and Bast signed it as witnesses. Kern paid witness for his services, and carried the will away with him. Witness never saw it afterwards. Kern lived in South Bend. He owned a store. He was married, and he left as his widow the lady who was his wife when the will was executed. After proof by another witness that the will drawn by Anderson and executed by Kern could not be found after Kern's death, the witness Anderson was asked to state the contents of that will. The question was objected to for the reason that the contents of the will were made known to Anderson as a privileged communication, notwithstanding the fact that the attorney became a subscribing witness to the will at the request of the testator. The court, not being prepared to pass upon the question raised by the objection, permitted the witness to state the contents of the will, but held the evidence under advisement. Anderson stated that in the first part of the will Kern disposed of all his estate in the following manner: Provision was made for his wife equivalent to one-third of his estate, and, in addition thereto, he gave her the use of the dwelling house in which he lived. The remainder of the estate was devised to two brothers. The entire estate was given away. He made his brothers his residuary legatees. Robert W. Bast, the stenographer in the office of Anderson, who took down the will in shorthand, and afterwards reduced it to print, and who also was a subscribing witness to the will, was asked to state the contents of the will. The question was objected to upon the ground that the communication was a privileged one as to Anderson, the attorney, and that the privilege extended to the knowledge acquired by the witness as the law clerk of Anderson. The objection was overruled, and the witness testified substantially as Anderson had done. Appellant gave in evidence the will of Amon S. Kern, dated April 6, 1890, with the probate of the same, whereby the testator devised the whole of his estate to his wife, Ella Kern, subject to residuary interest in one-half of what might remain at her death devised to three nephews. Ella Kern was nominated as sole executrix. Other evidence was introduced by appellant, but it is not necessary that we should set it out. The plaintiff be'ow having rested, the defendants introduced evidence as to the finding of the will of 1890, and the ineffectual search for the will prepared by Anderson. At this point the court announced its decision upon the objections to the testimony of

Anderson and Bast, and struck out all of the evidence relating to the contents of the will drawn by Anderson.

The question is presented whether communications between a testator and his solicitor or attorney in reference to the testator's will are privileged, after the death of the testator, in a contest between his heirs at law and the beneficiaries under the will. The statute of this state in regard to confidential communications made to an attorney in the course of his professional business, and as to advice given in such cases, has not changed the rule of the common law. (Burns' Rev. St. 1894, § 505.) This rule does not apply to testamentary dispositions where the controversy is between the heirs and devisees of the testator. In such cases it is said that the very foundation upon which the rule proceeds seems to be wanting. The leading case upon this subject is *Russell* v. *Jackson* (9 Hare, 387), in which Lord Justice TURNER says that: " The disclosure in such cases can affect no right or interest of the client. The apprehension of it can present no impediment to the full statement of his case to his solicitor, and the disclosures, when made, can expose the court to no greater difficulty than presents itself in cases where the views and intentions of persons or of objects for which the disposition is made are unknown." In Hageman Privil. Com. (§ 86), the rule laid down in *Russell* v. *Jackson* (*supra*), is concisely stated thus: " That communications between a testator and his solicitor in reference to the testator's will are not privileged after the death of the testator. *Contra,* as to communications between the same solicitor and executors." *Russell* v. *Jackson* is cited with approval in Wharton on Evidence, and in treating upon the subject of professional privilege it is said: " The privilege, it should also be remembered, is meant to protect the living in their business relations, and cannot be invoked when the question arises as to the intentions of a deceased person in respect to the disposition of his estate. (Whart. Ev. [3d ed.] § 591.) In *Graham* v. *O'Fallon* (4 Mo. 338), it is said that an attorney who draws up a will is entirely competent to testify to its contents in order to set it up as a lost will, and his testimony is not subject to the objection that it discloses the confidential communications of a client. This view of the rule as to such communications, and the competency of the solicitor to testify to them, is sustained by the decisions in the following, among other cases:

Blackburn v. *Crawfords* (3 Wall. 186; 18 L. Ed. 186); *Scott* v. *Harris* (113 Ill. 447); *Sheridan* v. *Houghton* (6 Abb. N. C. 234; 16 Hun, 628); *Pence* v. *Waugh* (135 Ind. 152; 34 N. E. 860); *Denning* v. *Butcher* (91 Iowa, 425; 59 N. W. 69); *Doherty* v. *O'Callaghan* ([Mass.], 31 N. E. 726).

It is urged, however, on behalf of the appellees, that this court has held that evidence of this character is inadmissible, and we are referred to the cases of *Gurley* v. *Park* (135 Ind. 440; 35 N. E. 279); *Pence* v. *Waugh* (135 Ind. 152; 34 N. E. 860); *Brown* v. *McAllister* (34 Ind. 375); and *Turner* v. *Cook* (36 Ind. 129),— as authorities sustaining such ruling. *Gurley* v. *Park* (135 Ind. 440; 35 N. E. 279), was an action to set aside a will on account of the unsoundness of the mind of the testatrix, and because its execution was procured by undue influence. The court say (on page 442, 135 Ind., and page 279, 35 N. E.): "In *Heuston* v. *Simpson* (115 Ind. 62; 17 N. E. 261), it was said: 'The law forbids the physician from disclosing what he learns in the sick room, no matter by what method he acquires his knowledge.' See other authorities cited in the same case. Also, *Pennsylvania Co.* v. *Marion* (123 Ind. 415; 23 N. E. 973)." "For a similar reason, the evidence offered by the attorney who drew the will was properly excluded." "In *Jenkinson* v. *State* (5 Blackf. 465), it was held that, when an attorney is consulted on business within the scope of his profession, the relation of attorney and client exists, and the communications on the subject between him and his client should be treated as strictly confidential. And this ruling has always been adhered to by this court. (*Bigler* v. *Reyher*, 43 Ind. 112.)" "The client may waive the privilege, but otherwise it is inviolable. (*Pence* v. *Waugh*, 135 Ind. 143; 34 N. E. 860; *Bank* v. *Mersereau*, 3 Barb. Ch. 528.)" While the rule announced by the court in *Gurley* v. *Park* is doubtless the correct one in disputes between the client's representatives on the one hand and strangers on the other, we do not think it applies where both the litigating parties claim under the client. The attention of the court does not appear to have been called to this distinction, and none of the cases bearing upon it is referred to in the opinion. We regard this qualification of the general rule as a very material one, and, to the extent that the opinion in *Gurley* v. *Park* conflicts with the view we have expressed, that case is overruled. In *Pence*

v. *Waugh,* it was held that by selecting the attorney who drew
the will as one of the subscribing witnesses, the client waived the
objection to the competency of the witness arising from the professional relation such witness sustained to the client.   In the
opinion the court cites, in support of its conclusions, the decision
in *Re Coleman's Will* (111 N. Y. 220; 19 N. E. 71), and *Alberti*
v. *Railroad Co.* (118 N. Y. 77; 23 N. E. 35).   The court says, in
the course of the opinion: " The privilege of the statute requires
no express waiver in this state, and it may be waived not only by
express waiver, but by implication."   This case lends no support
to the position of counsel for appellees.   The cases of *Brown* v.
McAllister (34 Ind. 375), and *Turner* v. *Cook* (36 id. 129),
decide only that it is not necessary to the due execution of a will
that the testator should in any manner indicate to the witnesses
who attest it that the instrument is the will of the person executing it.

The next question we are called upon to determine is the legal
effect of the revocation by the testator of the will of 1894. Was the
will of 1890 thereby waived?   There is no doubt that at common
law the revocation of a subsequent inconsistent will, revoking a
former will, operated to revive the former, when such former will
was not destroyed by the testator.   In *Harwood* v. *Goodright* (1
Cowp. 92), Lord Mansfield said: " If a testator makes one
will, and does not destroy it, though he makes another at any time
virtually or expressly revoking the former, if he afterwards destroy the revocation, the first will is still in force and good."   In
29 Am. & Eng. Enc. Law, 288, it is said: " Where the latter of
two inconsistent wills was revoked by the testator in his lifetime,
it was held by the courts of common law that the earlier will was
thereby revived, and, unless afterwards revoked by some subsequent act, came into operation on his decease, whether the latter
will contained an express clause of revocation or not.   In the
ecclesiastical courts it was held that the revocation of the latter
will raised no presumption in favor of the revival of the earlier
will, but that the question depended upon the intention of the
testator as shown by the peculiar facts and circumstances of the
case, and was open to decision either way.   The statute of Vic-
toria abolished the doctrine by expressly providing that no will or
codicil, or any part thereof, which shall be in any manner revoked.

shall be revived otherwise than by the re-execution thereof, or by a duly executed codicil showing an intention to revive the will. In several of the states similar statutes exist under which the revocation of the second will does not revive the first unless such intent appear in the terms of the revocation, or the first will be duly republished afterwards. In the absence of such legislation, the rule varies greatly in different states." Commenting on this subject, it was well said by BURKS, J., in *Rudisill* v. *Rodes* (29 Grat. 149) : " The effect of the rule in the law courts was to exclude arbitrarily all extrinsic evidence of intention upon the question of revival, and thus oftentimes to set up a will contrary to the intention of the testator; while the rule in the ecclesiastical courts threw the door wide open to the admission of such evidence, and suffered the intention of the testator to be determined by ' the uncertain testimony of slippery memory.' It was the object of the English statute, by the twenty-second section, to abrogate both of these rules, which were attended with the mischiefs just indicated, and to establish in their stead a safer rule, by which the intention of the testator would be manifested with more certainty, and be less liable to be defeated by acts and circumstances of an equivocal character." The statutes of this state establish the rule governing this case. (Burns' Rev. St. 1894, § 2729; 2 Rev. St. 1852, p. 308, § 19; Rev. St. 1843, p. 491, § 30.) The provision of the statutes, to which alone we must look, declares that: " No will, in writing, nor any part thereof, except as in this act provided, shall be revoked unless the testator, or some other person in his presence, and by his direction, with intent to revoke, shall destroy or mutilate the same; or such testator shall execute other writing for that purpose signed, subscribed, and attested as required in the preceding section. And if, after the making of any will, the testator shall execute a second, a revocation of the second shall not revive the first will, unless it shall appear by the terms of such revocation to have been his intent to revive it, or, unless, after such revocation he shall duly republish the previous will." (Burns' Rev. St. 1894, § 2729 [Rev. St. 1881, § 2559; Horner's Rev. St. § 2559].) The execution by Kern of the will of 1894, which made a disposition of his estate inconsistent with that of the will of 1890, operated to revoke the first will. (*State* v. *Crossley*, 69 Ind. 203; *Burns* v. *Travis*, 117 id. 44; 18 N. E.

45.) The will of 1894, having been in the possession of the deceased, and not having been found after the death of Kern, the presumption is that it was destroyed by him *animo revocandi*. (*McDonald* v. *McDonald*, 142 Ind. 55; 41 N. E. 336; *In re Mitcheson*, 32 Law J. [Prob. & Mat.] 202.) The first will having been effectually revoked, it could be revived only (1) by a writing executed by him for that purpose, signed, subscribed, and attested as in the case of a last will; or (2) by due republication of such previous will. There is no claim on the part of appellees that any such writing was executed, and it cannot be said that there was proof of the republication of the will of 1890. The preservation of the will of 1890, and the fact that it was found in a conspicuous place among the valuable papers of the deceased, did not constitute a republication. No oral declaration by the decedent, or other unequivocal act indicating an intention to republish the will of 1890, was shown. (Schouler, Wills, §§ 441, 442, 444, 445; *Abney* v. *Miller*, 2 Atk. 599; *Barker* v. *Bell*, 46 Ala. 216; *In re Lones' Estate*, 108 Cal. 688; 41 Pac. 771; *Wolf* v. *Bollinger*, 62 Ill. 368; *Beaumont* v. *Keim*, 50 Mo. 28.) We conclude, therefore, that the will of 1890 was not republished, or otherwise revived, by any act of the decedent, within the meaning of section 2729 of the statute.

We have carefully examined the cases of *Randall* v. *Beatty* (31 N. J. Eq. 643); *Flintham* v. *Bradford* (10 Pa. St. 82); *Neff's Appeal* (48 id. 501); *Peck's Appeal* (50 Conn. 562), and *Cheever* v. *North* (106 Mich. 390; 64 N. W. 455); and all other authorities referred to in the several briefs of counsel for appellees. There is a conflict among the decisions upon the questions arising in this case, but the great weight of authority seems to sustain the views we have expressed. For the error of the court in striking out the evidence of Anderson and Bast, and for the reason that the finding of the court was contrary to law, the judgment is reversed.

NOBLE et al. vs. JACKSON.

[Supreme Court of Alabama, December 20, 1899; 26 So. Rep. 955.]

WITNESS — COMPETENCY — EXECUTORS — COMMISSIONERS — ATTORNEY'S FEES — INTEREST.

1. A claim of an executor for services rendered testator in his lifetime having been paid by the executors, one of the executors is incompetent, by reason of interest in maintaining the payment, to give testimony, on a proceeding for settlement of the administration, to establish the claim.

2. Under Code, § 219, providing that executors may be allowed such commissions on receipts and disbursements by them as may appear to the Probate Court a fair compensation for their trouble, risk, and responsibility, not to exceed two and one-half per cent. on the receipts and the same percentage on disbursements, the discretion of the court has but two limitations,—the allowance must be a fair compensation, and must not exceed said percentage.

3. Executors who institute a suit in good faith and on reasonable grounds are entitled to reimbursement of costs and expenses of litigation, though unsuccessful. So, too, they are entitled to reimbursement for a reasonable amount paid by them to an attorney to represent them in a proceeding to require them to give a bond, or for their removal, they having in good faith and on reasonable grounds defended against it.

4. Where an agreement is made by executors with the residuary legatee, the only other person interested, that they pay themselves $2,400 as commissions, subject to their right to have the amount increased and the legatee's right to have it reduced, the executors, on the amount being reduced to $1,800, should not be charged interest thereon.

5. Executors who do not distribute the assets at the end of eighteen months after grant of letters will be charged interest on all the amount in their hands, except such as they might reasonably have retained to meet the claims against the estate which were disputed, and on which suits were threatened.

APPEAL from Probate Court, Montgomery county; J. B. GASTON, Judge.

Proceeding for settlement of the administration of George D. Noble and others, executors of Jesse Hooker, deceased. From an adverse decree, all of the executors except Mrs. James H. Jackson, appeal.

Reversed.

Gordon Macdonald, for appellants.

Gunter & Gunter, for appellee.

TYSON, J.—The matter of controversy in this case grows out of the refusal of the court to allow the payment of certain claims to G. D. Noble and Ruth Hooker, two of the appellants; second, the amount of commission allowed by the court to the executors and executrices; third, the disallowance, as a credit, of amounts paid to Gordon Macdonald, Esq., as attorney's fees; and, fourth, the matter of interest charged against the executors. It appears that Jesse Hooker died in June or July, 1896, leaving an estate, consisting entirely of personal property, of the value of about $90,000, leaving a will naming the appellee as residuary legatee and the appellants and Mrs. Jackson executors and executrices of his will, which was probated in Montgomery county. The debts of the estate are shown to have been only $1,098.04. Of this amount $905.15 were for expenses incurred in and about the purchase and improvement of a lot in the cemetery, the purchase of casket, clothing, etc. The remaining indebtedness of $193.89 comprised small bills due and owing by the testator, contracted by him. The property comprising the assets of the estate consisted of bonds, stocks, mortgages, notes, and money.

1. The claim of appellant Noble for $600 for services rendered the testator during his lifetime was attempted to be established by the testimony of Mrs. Hooker, the wife of the testator, and one of the executrices. It appears that this claim had been paid Noble by the executors and executrices, and the purpose of the testimony to establish it was to have the court allow them a credit for the amount paid him. The court properly excluded the testimony, for the obvious reason that Mrs. Hooker, being interested in maintaining the payment which she and the others had made, so as to get a credit for it as against the estate, was an incompetent witness. (*Hullett* v. *Hood,* 109 Ala. 345; 19 South. 419.) There was no proof to support the claim of Mrs. Hooker, and for this reason it was properly disallowed. The refusal of the court to allow Noble his claim for special or extraordinary services is not assigned as error, and we cannot consider the action of the court in that regard. But, had it been, in the absence

of the will of the testator from the record we would have been compelled to treat the question as pertaining to the administration of the estate in the ordinary mode of administering estates under the law.

2. The next question presented for consideration is the one involved in the assignment of error based upon the allowance of commissions. Compensation or commissions allowed administrators and executors for ordinary services are governed by section 219 of the Code, which reads as follows: "Executors and administrators may be allowed such commissions on all receipts and disbursements by them, as such, as may appear to the Probate Court a fair compensation for their trouble, risk and responsibility, not to exceed two and one-half per cent. on the receipts, and the same percentage on the disbursements; and the court may also allow actual expenses, and, for special or extraordinary services, such compensation as is just." Section 220 provides that: "Upon the appraised value of all personal property, and the amount of money and solvent notes distributed by executors or administrators, they shall be allowed the same commissions as upon disbursements." By the terms of these statutes it is manifest that a discretion as to the amount of commissions is lodged in courts charged with their allowance, and that but two limitations upon the exercise of this discretion are imposed: The allowance must be a fair compensation for the trouble, risk, and responsibility of the executor or administrator, and it must in no case exceed two and one-half per cent. on receipts, disbursements, personal property appraised, and notes and money distributed. The statute is equivalent to a legislative declaration that a fair compensation for the ordinary duties and responsibilities of an executorship cannot exceed the two and one-half per cent. which the court is authorized to allow; or, in other words, that no case can arise in which that maximum would not furnish sufficient compensation. Being thus sufficient in the most extreme cases, its allowance in many instances would afford more than that fair compensation contemplated and provided for by the lawmakers. This, in our opinion, is not such a case. The estate here being administered was, at the death of the testator, it is true, quite a large one, amounting to something like $90,000. It consisted, as we have heretofore stated, of money, mortgages, and other readily convertible securities. The executors were charged

with the duty of collecting up the assets, paying the debts of the testator, and distributing the residue to the legatee under the will. It is clear to our minds that the full statutory commission on receipts and disbursements—that is, two and one-half per cent. on $180,000—would be excessive. Their services in performing those duties in respect to this estate would not be worth nearly so much as $4,500. Since the case must be reversed upon another point, we will not forestall the probate judge's discretion in fixing the amount upon another hearing.

3. One of the contentions here as against the allowance of a credit of $1,542.50 paid Gordon Macdonald, Esq., for services rendered as attorney, is that no itemized claim was presented showing the items comprising the account, and the value of each item; in other words, the amount or value of the whole was proved in gross, and unless all of the services were proper charges, none can stand. We entertain no doubt as to the correctness of this proposition, provided the objection to the allowance proceeded on the ground that no sufficient statement of the services rendered and paid was made in the court below. There appears, however, in the record before us from the opinion, this statement: " In the original account filed in this court, I find the following under the head of ' Amounts Paid Out': ' The executors also file with their vouchers, marked " No. 61," account presented to them by Gordon Macdonald, Esq., which shows a balance due him of $432.50. The executors ask that we be allowed to pay such balance. The account and voucher marked " No. 61 " is an itemized account for services to Geo. D. Noble et al., executors of Jesse Hooker, deceased, amounting to $1,975, with credits amounting to $1,542.50, leaving a balance of $432.50.' " We have quoted this extract from the opinion solely for the purpose of showing that the court had an itemized statement of the claim before it, and considered it; and doubtless was influenced by this statement in his opinion as being sufficient in striking from the bill of exceptions the accounts and vouchers filed by the executors, which would, of course, disclose it otherwise in the record, if they had been permitted to remain in the bill of exceptions. So, then, it may be said that an itemized statement of the services rendered by the attorney and the value of each item of services was before the court. It is true that Mr. Macdonald testified to the various items of services rendered by

him, but testified to the value of only one of them; while the witnesses Crum and Winter, examined on behalf of the executors, testified to the value of such services in gross, and not to the value of each item. There was no objection by the appellee to the testimony of either of these witnesses, nor does the record disclose that the objection to the allowance of the credit proceeded upon the ground here contended for. On the contrary, the cross-examination of the witness Macdonald by appellee's counsel in the court below shows that the credit asked was resisted upon the grounds that the service rendered by him was not for the benefit of the estate, or to protect the executors against the unjust or wrongful claims or demands of the appellee or others. This same contention is made here in this language: "Trustees have no right to employ a lawyer to show them how to squander the estate, or how to retain them in possession of the assets for the purpose of coercing the payment of unjust demands." Indeed, the judge trying the cause enters into quite an extended discussion to show that the tax suit could not have been maintained. This record does not contain the record in that case, but it does appear from the testimony that it was the honest opinion of their attorney that the suit was a meritorious one, and that the result accomplished was an adjustment of the amount of the taxes claimed by the paying of a very much smaller sum by the appellee. We do not understand the rule to be that executors are allowed an allowance for counsel fees paid by them only when they are successful in the prosecution of suits brought by them, or in the defense of suits brought against them. Such a rule would make them, in a measure, at least to the extent of the expense incurred by them in the prosecution or defense of all suits to which they are parties, insurers. The rule, as we understand it, is that an executor who institutes a suit in good faith and on reasonable grounds is entitled to reimbursement of the costs and expenses of the litigation, notwithstanding his failure of success, provided there does not appear to have been a want of proper diligence. (*Holman* v. *Sims,* 39 Ala. 710.) In *Taylor* v. *Kilgore* (33 Ala. 214), it is said: "In the institution of the suit in South Carolina the guardian had no conceivable motive or interest to induce him to act *mala fide*. In the institution of the suit he acted under the advice of counsel learned in the law, and of unquestioned integrity, who appears to have been fully informed of all facts pertaining to the case which were known to the complainant. There is, therefore, no just reason for the imputation of bad faith." The testimony shows services rendered by Macdonald for the executors in a proceeding instituted by this appellee to require them to give a bond as such, which resulted in a judgment for them. Enough is shown in the record to justify the finding that the executors were relieved of giving bond by the terms of the will, and doubtless the proceeding set on foot by this appellee, the sole residuary legatee under the will, to require them to give bond, was instituted under subdivision 1 of section 67 of the Code. Manifestly, the testator regarded it of importance to the administration of the affairs of the estate that the persons named by him as executors and executrices should administer them. And so, too, it would seem that the legislature considered it highly important that these executors should be trusted with its administration without bond, as no bond can be required of them except when the interest of a legatee is or will be endangered for want of security, or they are likely to commit a waste, to the prejudice of some person interested. Nor could their removal be had except for incapacity, failure to return inventory or account of sales, to make settlements, or to do any act as such when lawfully required by the judge of probate; wasting, embezzling, or other maladministering of the estate, or using funds of the estate for their own benefit. These safeguards for their protection as the representatives of the testator were not enacted for the personal benefit of the executors, but for the benefit of the estate. This being true, where a proceeding is instituted to require them to give a bond, or for their removal, and they in good faith and on reasonable grounds defend against the proceeding, and employ an attorney to represent them, and pay him, they are entitled to be reimbursed out of the estate the amount so paid him, if reasonable. Or, to state the principle abstractly and broadly, it may be said: " Whether involved in litigation or not, any trustee is entitled to the assistance and advice of counsel in the performance of his duties, and there is neither justice nor good conscience in charging him with the compensation of such counsel. The care and diligence the trustee is required to exercise is not for his own interest, but for the interest of the *cestuis que trustent.* The counsel assists and advises for them, and for their protection. Of course, in seeking such advice and assistance, and in the amount of compensation, good faith must be observed. The protection of the trustee and the preservation of the trust estate are alone considered in determining the propriety of an allowance of the compensation to the counsel he may employ to aid and advise him. An administrator or executor, under the system prevailing in this state, should have the assistance and advice of counsel in many of the duties devolving on him. The advice and supervision of intelligent, conscientious counsel is to his protection, and the prevention of future litigation. So many of the proceedings he must take are statutory, and their value dependent on their conformity to the statutes authorizing them, so many of them are practically *ex parte,* and there is and has been such a ' lamentable looseness ' in keeping the records of the court before which he must proceed, that a prudent man, even at his own expense, would prefer the aid and assistance of counsel to the hazards he would incur in acting without it. When, therefore, an administrator or executor procures the aid and advice of counsel in his administration, in good faith, for his own protection and that of the estate, paying only such compensation as is fair and reasonable when considered in connection with the value of the estate and the services rendered, he should be allowed a credit for such compensation. * * * Nor is it material that the services rendered were for the benefit of the administrator, unless it appeared he was seeking a personal benefit, in opposition to his duty as trustee. If that appeared, he would not only be refused an allowance of such compensation, but would be subjected to a loss of compensation for his own services. Any advice and assistance rendered a trustee is, in a narrow sense, for his benefit. It may protect him in action or in passiveness. A good reason for making a fair and just allowance to him for the aid of counsel is that he is acting wholly in a fiduciary capacity, for the benefit of others, and so long as he is honest and diligent, should not be subjected to the dangers of personal liability. That he guards himself from such liability, and keeps within the line of his duty, and thereby secures a personal benefit, is a reason for, and not against, the allowance of such compensation." (*Smyley* v. *Reese,* 53 Ala. 99.) Without further consideration in detail of the items of service rendered these executors and executrices, it would seem that what we have said is a sufficient guide for the determination of every question likely to arise out of this particular claim upon another trial.

4. The remaining question to be considered grows out of the various charges of interest decreed by the court against the appellants upon certain items; and it is for an error clearly committed by the court in this respect that the case must be reversed. One of the charges against the appellants was of interest on $2,400 paid to them as commissions under the agreement of October, 3, 1896. It appears from the recitals in this agreement that all the special legacies had been paid, and the remainder of the estate, amounting to about $20,000, was to be paid to this appellee upon a final settlement of the estate. One of the terms of the agreement was to authorize the executors to pay themselves this sum of $2,400 as commissions, subject, however, to their right to have the amount increased by the court or reduced by the appellee. The court reduced the amount of the commissions to $1,800, $600 less than the sum authorized to be paid under the agreement. It is doubtless true that, in the absence of this agreement, the commissions were not payable until ascertained by the court, but we know of no rule of law or policy which prohibits parties *sui juris* from making this contract. The payment being made under it, and authorized by it, the executors were not chargeable with interest thereon. The use of the money, being by the express consent of the sole party interested in the estate, was not in violation of their duties as trustees, and constituted no breach of trust by them. As to whether they should pay interest on the $600 and $194.71 paid to Noble, the $171 paid Mrs. Hooker, and the amount paid as counsel fees, depends, of course, upon their allowance as credits against the estate. The court below—and it is complained of here—charged the executors with interest upon all money in their hands, whether used by them or not, from the 1st day of March to the date of the settlement. The theory upon which this charge was made against them was that they should have made a final settlement of the estate at the expiration of eighteen months after grant of letters, or should have distributed the assets in their hands to the appellee to the extent of at least a retention by them of only a sufficient amount to meet in any emergency the claims asserted by Graham & Steiner and the tax collector. It appears that Graham & Steiner's claim was $500, for legal services rendered the executors, which they dis-

puted the correctness of as to amount; and the tax matter of about $50. It was on account of these claims, and the just anticipation of suits upon them, that the executors undertake to justify their delay in making a final settlement. As each of these claims, if just, and paid by them, would have been a proper charge against the estate, they could not have been required to distribute the entire assets of the estate; yet they were not justified in retaining so large a sum as $20,000, or, for that matter $4,500, thereby making it unproductive. This principle is clearly announced in (*Clark* v. *Knox* (70 Ala. 620), where it is said: "What will constitute unseasonable delay in making a settlement, rendering the executor or administrator liable for interest, must depend upon the particular facts and circumstances of each case. The inquiry is whether, in view of these facts and circumstances, a prudent man, dealing with his own funds, for his own interest, would have retained the money unproductive, or would have appropriated it as it was *prima facie* to be appropriated. The pendency or the just anticipation of suits, which, if the event of them was unfavorable, would seriously diminish the assets, complicating the accounts if there was a distribution, may be a good reason for delaying the settlement, and during the period of reasonable delay may justify keeping the moneys without a liability for interest; or, if the amounts involved in such suits are not large compared with the assets, the keeping without a charge for interest of a sum sufficient to answer the judgments which may be rendered in them. * * * These and other causes developed by the particular facts of the case may excuse a delay in making settlement, and relieve from liability for interest. * * * Diligence in making settlements, and accounting to those entitled to receive it for the money received, is as high a duty, as imperatively demanded by law, as diligence in the collection or in reducing to money by appropriate proceedings, when a legal necessity exists for the reduction of the property, real or personal, subject to administration." We are of the opinion, therefore, that the executors were properly chargeable with interest upon all money unproductive in their hands, less the amount which they would have been allowed to retain had they made a partial settlement of the estate on the first day of March, and the cost and expenses attendant upon the making of the final settlement. It appears that the court in charging interest did not cal-

independent of statutory provisions relating to costs. (Wetmore v. Parker, 52 N. Y. 450, 466; and see Re Simon's Will, 55 Conn. 239; 11 Atl. Rep. 36.)

And entitled to credit for payment of such counsel fees upon an accounting. But what constitutes reasonable counsel fees is not committed to discretion of the executor; if the actual expenditure exceeds what was reasonable and necessary, the excess must be borne by the executor personally. (Matter of Hutchinson, 84 Hun, 563; 32 N. Y. Supp. 869.)

Direction in will to employ certain attorney does not bind the executor. (Re Ogier, 101 Cal. 381; 35 Pac. Rep. 900; Young v. Alexander, 16 Lea. 108.)

When necessary expense. (Matter of Collyer, 1 Connoly, 546; 9 N. Y. Supp. 297.)

(e) **Where burden rests.**—Burden rests upon executor of showing justice of attorney's bill paid; necessity of the services, and value; when item objected to. (Matter of Hosford, 27 App. Div. 433; 50 N. Y. Supp. 550.) An executor does not become entitled to reimbursement for sums expended for legal services, by merely showing the fact of payment, nor, even in addition that he has acted honestly and in good faith. Upon objection made he must prove the necessity and value of such services. (St. John v. McKee, 2 Dem. 236; and see Journalt v. Ferris, id. 323; Willson v. Willson, id. 462; and to same effect, Munden v. Bailey, 70 Ala. 63; Johnson v. Henagan, 11 S. C. 93.)

But if charge be reasonable on its face and said to be necessarily contracted for the good and benefit of the estate sustained by proper voucher, the presumption is that it is correct, and the burden is on the objectors. (Matter of White, 6 Dem. 388.)

(f) **Must be paid first.**—Payment must precede credit or allowance on accounting for attorney's fees. (Bates v. Vary, 40 Ala. 422, 441; Shields v. Sullivan, 3 Dem. 297 [N. Y.]; Matter of O'Brien, 5 Misc. 136; 25 N. Y. Supp. 704; Matter of Bailey, 47 Hun, 477; Matter of Spooner, 86 id. 9, 12; 33 N. Y. Supp. 136.)

But it seems otherwise where the administrator dies before payment. (Perrine v. Roach, 94 Cal. 515; 29 Pac. Rep. 956; 30 id. 106.)

Or effect of statute. (Jackson v. Leech, 113 Mich. 391; 71 N. W. Rep. 846.)

(g) **Cannot act in double capacity.**—An executor or administrator who is also an attorney, cannot be allowed credit for value of his services in latter capacity. (Collier v. Munn, 41 N. Y. 143; Hough v. Harvey, 71 Ill. 72; Gray v. Robertson, 174 id. 250; 51 N. E. Rep. 248; Pollard v. Barkley, 117 Ind. 40; 17 N. E. Rep. 294; Doss v. Stevens, 13 Col. App. 635; 59 Pac. Rep. 67.) But see Morgan v. Nelson (43 Ala. 587), where the contrary seems to be *held.*

Nor can he be allowed such credit when paid to a law firm of which he is a member. (Taylor v. Wright, 93 Ind. 121.)

But the administrator or executor as an individual may employ his co-partner to do work for him outside of and independent of the co-partnership. (Parker v. Day, 155 N. Y. 383; 49 N. E. Rep. 1046, and see opinion below, 9 Misc. 298; 30 N. Y. Supp. 267.)

Where he does not share in the compensation for such services. (Matter of Simpson, 36 App. Div. 564; 55 N. Y. Supp. 697.)

(h) **Contingent fees.**—Contract by executor to pay a contingent fee of one-third of the amount recovered on account of a certain claim. (Mac-Kie v. Howland, 3 D. C. App. 461, 482.)

And as to credit for contingent fees paid attorney where claim on a disputed insurance policy. (Filbeck v. Davies, 8 Col. App. 320, 325; 46 Pac. Rep. 214.)

Where claim was against the United States. (Pike v. Thomas, 65 Ark. 437; 47 S. W. Rep. 110.)

Where claim was by administrator to recover damages under statute for death by wrongful act. (Lee v. Van Voorhis, 78 Hun, 575; 29 N. Y. Supp. 571; aff'd on opinion below, 145 N. Y. 603.)

And see similar case where the administrator was *held* to his personal responsibility, the court, however, saying that "whether the administrator was entitled to a credit for fee paid the attorney was a different question not before it." (Tucker v. Grace, 61 Ark. 410; 33 S. W. Rep. 530.)

Such a contingent agreement with an attorney cannot give him any interest in the property of the estate. (Estate of Page, 57 Cal. 238.)

But the attorney's lien may be enforced. (Lee v. Van Voorhis, *supra.*)

Compare Platt v. Platt (105 N. Y. 489, 501; 12 N. E. Rep. 22), where the power of an executor to make such a contingent agreement or to create any *lien* upon the estate is denied upon the ground that while the executor could bind himself personally, he could not bind the estate. And also Randall v. Dusenbury (39 N. Y. Supr. 174).

See where an agreement for a contingent fee was sustained where the administrator qualified as *survivor* in community property. (James v. Turner, 78 Tex. 241; 14 S. W. Rep. 574.)

Contingent fee sustained and allowed. (Noel v. Harvey, 29 Miss. 72.)

And as to contingent fees see Taylor v. Berniss (110 U. S. 42; 3 Sup. Rep. 441); Matter of Hynes (105 N. Y. 560; 12 N. E. Rep. 634); Re McCullough's Estate (31 Ore. 86; 49 Pac. Rep. 886).

(i) **Relief in equity.**—Where the administrator is insolvent and claim of attorney cannot be enforced against him individually on his contract, relief may be had in equity as against estate which received the benefit of the services. (Pike v. Thomas, 65 Ark. 437; 47 S. W. Rep. 110; and see Clopton v. Gholson, 53 Miss. 467.)

(j) **Statute directory.**—A statute requiring an executor or administrator to act under an order or direction of the Probate Court in employment of attorneys *held* directory only, and that in cases of emergency such employment might be made without waiting for an order or direction of the court. (Wassell v. Armstrong, 35 Ark. 268.)

Allowance discretionary in Probate Court, where no order in the first instance authorizing the expense. (Reynolds v. Canal Co., 30 Ark. 520.)

(k) **Illustrative cases—Where allowed.**—Services and traveling expenses of attorney. (Re Moore, 72 Cal. 336; 13 Pac. Rep. 880.)

Disbursement by trustee for legal expenses in proving will in another state. (Young v. Brush, 28 N. Y. 667, 672.)

For legal services in making application to the Probate Court for leave to expend money in erection of a monument. (Dudley v. Sanborn, 159 Mass. 186; 34 N. E. Rep. 181.)

Reasonable counsel fee paid attorney in action brought against an executor personally to recover price of a tombstone ordered by him. (Matter of Grout, 15 Hun, 361.)

A nominated executor entitled to be reimbursed out of estate, for expenses of attorney's fee incurred in attempting to have will probated, even although will rejected; otherwise as to a devisee. (Taylor v. Minor, 90 Ky. 544; 14 S. W. Rep. 544.)

(l) **Illustrative cases—Not allowed.**—Attorney's fee cannot be based on services caused by neglect of executor or administrator to perform his duty in keeping proper accounts. (O'Reilly v. Meyer, 4 Dem. 161 [N. Y.].)

Or otherwise in failing to perform his duty. (Aldridge v. McClelland, 36 N. J. Eq. 288.)

Or caused by positive misconduct. (Robbins v. Wolcott, 27 Conn. 234; Morrow v. Allison, 39 Ala. 73; Allen v. Royster, 107 N. C. 278; 12 S. E. Rep. 134; Matter of Bailey, 47 Hun, 477.)

Or caused by vexatious litigation carried on for his own exclusive benefit. (Wither's Appeal, 13 Pa. St. 582; and see Caldwell v. Hampton, 53 S. W. Rep. 14 [Ky.].)

But where the improper conduct was in good faith caused by erroneous advice of counsel, it is proper to allow as a credit an amount paid to subsequent counsel whose services became necessary on account of such irregularity. (Merkel's Estate, 131 Pa. St. 585; 18 Atl. Rep. 931.)

Not allowed where the services of attorney were not reasonably necessary because incumbent upon the executor personally in view of his statutory commissions. (Raymond v. Dayton, 4 Dem. 333 [N. Y.].)

Nor where work does not require professional skill, and which they might do themselves. (Hurlbut v. Hutton, 44 N. J. Eq. 303; 15 Atl. Rep. 417.) For instance in making an inventory. (Matter of Collyer, 1 Connoly, 546; 9 N. Y. Supp. 297.)

Not allowable for what the executor should attend to personally. (Matter of Arkenburg, 13 Misc. 744; 35 N. Y. Supp. 251.)

For services in proceeding itself of an accounting by an executor or trustee. (Hawley v. Singer, 3 Dem. 589, 596 [N. Y].)

Not allowed where paid in contesting a proper claim against him. (Anderson v. Anderson, 37 Ala. 683.)

Where services rendered for the administrator before his appointment. (Allen's Administrator, 89 Ill. 474; Matter of Collyer, *supra*.)

Not allowed where incurred by an unnecessary appeal. (Beatty v. Trustees, 39 N. J. Eq. 452.)

For unreasonably resisting an application to the court. (Matter of O'Brien, 145 N. Y. 379; 40 N. E. Rep. 18.)

Or incurred in defending a suit brought against him to recover the trust fund, wherein it appears complainant was justified in bringing suit. (Lilly v. Griffen, 71 Ga. 535; and see Sill v. Sill, 39 Kans. 189; 17 Pac. Rep. 665.)

Or for resisting claim of heir where the contest was between the legatees and an heir, and the executor had no right to litigate. (Re Jessup, 80 Cal. 625; 22 Pac. Rep. 260.)

Not entitled to allowance or credit for such services rendered in improper, unsuccessful contests with creditors or distributees. (Prior v. Davis, 109 Ala. 117; 19 So. Rep. 140.)

No part of duty of an administrator to employ counsel to prosecute the murderer of the intestate. (Lusk v. Anderson, 1 Met. 429 [Ky.]; and see Alexander v. Alexander, 120 N. C. 474; 27 S. E. Rep. 121.)

Not allowed where the executor has no voice in the distribution of fund in his hands. (Bracken's Estate, 138 Pa. St. 104, 107; 22 Atl. Rep. 20.)

For amount paid attorney in preparing an inventory in an ordinary case, it appearing that it was not a necessary expense. (Pullman v. Willets, 4 Dem. 536; and see McCullough's Estate, 31 Ore. 86; 49 Pac. Rep. 886.)

Attorney's claim may be apportioned by imposing part as a credit against the estate and balance against the executor individually. (Fox's Appeal, 125 Pa. St. 518; 17 Atl. Rep. 451.)

·

DICKINSON *vs.* HENDERSON *et al.*

[Supreme Court of Michigan, January 23, 1900;   Mich.   ; 81 N. W. Rep. 583.]

EXECUTORS—WIDOW'S ALLOWANCE—AMOUNT—WAIVER—TRUS-TEES — PAYMENT — FINAL ACCOUNT — APPROVAL — EFFECT —JUDGE'S MEMORANDUM.

1. The fact that testator's widow, entitled to the income of his estate for life, failed to claim the income during administration, until after approval of the executor's accounts, including such income as turned over to the trustees under the will, did not constitute a waiver of her right thereto, since the order approving the account merely found that a certain sum had been paid over to the trustees.

2. Where a widow was entitled to the income from her husband's estate for life, and the income arising during administration was paid over to the

trustee by the executors, the trustee was authorized to pay such income to the widow.

3. Though no formal order was made on the hearing of a widow's petition for an allowance for support, yet where the executor's final account, approved by the probate judge, showed that a certain sum had been paid therefor, such sum constituted a payment from testator's estate, and not from the widow's estate under the will.

4. Where, on hearing a widow's petition for support pending settlement of her husband's estate, the trial judge entered a memorandum in his docket, " Widow allowed net income for support," such memorandum did not constitute an order, and cannot be considered on appeal from a decree approving payments made to the widow by the executor and trustee.

5. Under a will giving testator's wife the income of his estate for life, subject to certain trusts, and appointing trustees to collect the income of the estate and to pay to the widow all net income collected, keeping the principal, etc., invested during the widow's life, she was only entitled to the income after payment of necessary expenses incurred in caring for the estate.

APPEAL from Circuit Court, Wayne county, in chancery; WILLARD M. LILLIBRIDGE, Judge.

Bill by Julian G. Dickinson, as surviving trustee under the will of Davis Henderson, against Charles D. Henderson and others. From a decree construing the will, and approving payments made by complainant as executor and trustee, defendants appeal.
Modified.

Morse Rohnert, for appellants.

John D. Conely, for appellee.

MONTGOMERY, J.—This is a bill filed to obtain a construction of the will of Davis Henderson, deceased, and to obtain an order approving certain payments made to the widow by complainant as executor and trustee. The two clauses of the will which bear on the question involved are the second and fifth. The second reads as follows: " I give, devise, and bequeath to my wife, Elizabeth Sinclair Henderson, for and during her natural life, in lieu of dower, and subject to the trusts hereinafter specified, all and singular, the rents and profits of all my real estate, and the income from all the rest and residue of my personal property and effects, of every name and nature." The fifth is in part as follows: " I hereby nominate as executors of this, my last will, my wife, Elizabeth Sinclair Henderson, and Julian G. Dickinson, and do appoint them trustees for the following purposes: To take possession of and manage all my said real estate, personal property, and effects during the life of my said wife, and during the minority of my said grandchildren. * * * To collect all moneys due and belonging to my estate, and keep the same invested in good, interest-bearing, first mortgages on real estate in the city of Detroit. To pay over to my said wife all the net income from rents and from interest col'ected on any of said investments, keeping the principal of all my personal estate invested as aforesaid during the life of my said wife." Complainant and Mrs. Henderson duly qualified as executors, and took possession of the estate, which consisted of real property valued at upward of $40,000, and personal property, securities, accounts, and money in bank amounting to $38,508.79. Pending the settlement of the estate a petition for a widow's allowance was filed, and a hearing had thereon. No formal order of allowance was made and entered, but in the judge's docket, under the head of " Remarks," is entered, " Widow allowed net income for support." On the 2d of December, 1891, the executors presented their separate final accounts, as executors, which were later allowed, as presented, by the probate judge. In this account appear items aggregating $3,700 " paid Elizabeth S. Henderson, widow, for her support." In this account complainant took credit for $25,976.41 turned over to the trustees under the will, and Mrs. Henderson took credit for $335 so transferred. During the period of administration the rents collected aggregated $2,232.16, and the interest earned $886.05, which with $230.93 earned on the Griffith mortgage prior to probate of wil!, but collected by executors, amounted to $3,349.14. Complainant, on request of Mrs. Henderson, turned over to her this entire sum of $3,349.14, considering that she was entitled to the same under the terms of the will. The present controversy concerns this payment.

It is contended by the defendants that the account of the executors having been allowed without any such payment having been made, the complainant, as trustee, had no authority to make payment thereafter, and that in no view was the widow entitled to more than the net income. On the other hand, complainant contends that Mrs. Henderson was by the terms of the will entitled to the income of the estate, as her own property; that the unsigned memoranda of the probate judge never became an order from which an appeal could be taken, or strictly an order of court; that the order approving the final accounting of the executors approved of the payments made to Mrs. Henderson for her support, and that it must be assumed that the payment was made from personal estate of deceased, and not from the income; that the order approving the account, and the payment of the trust fund into the hands of the trustees, did not change the character of the fund, or deprive Mrs. Henderson of her property right in and to the income of the estate. We are cited to the case of *Lawrence* v. *Security Co.* (56 Conn. 423; 15 Atl. 406), as sustaining defendant's contention that, failing to make any claim on the executors for the income during the administration of the estate, the widow waived her claim to such income. The case cited falls short of sustaining the contention. In that case there had been a distribution of the fund, with the sanction of the court, given by an order entered after the widow had her day in court. This order was held final. In the present case the effect of the order allowing the account was to find that there had been turned over into the hands of the trustees a certain sum of money. No order was made as to the distribution of the fund, and we think the property rights of Mrs. Henderson were not cut off by the order. The order approving the account involved an approval of the payments made to Mrs. Henderson for her support. We think this allowance must be treated as having been made from the estate left by the testator, and not from the income. The memorandum made on the petition of the widow never assumed the form of an order, and cannot be considered. (*People* v. *Probate Judge of Eaton Co.*, 40 Mich. 244.) We think so much of this fund as the will provides shall be paid to Mrs. Henderson, she had the right to have paid to her after it was placed in the hands of Mr. Dickinson as trustee.

The decree below approves the payment of the gross income, without any deduction whatever for expenses of collection, repairs, or taxes. We do not think this was intended by the will. On the contrary, the intention to preserve the estate is manifest. The decree will be modified by providing that complainant is entitled to credit for the payment made to Mrs. Henderson to the extent of the net income only. The appellants will be entitled to costs of this court. As we are convinced of the good faith of complainant, no costs will be allowed for the proceedings in the circuit to either party.

The other justices concurred.

JACOWAY *vs.* HALL.

[Supreme Court of Arkansas, January 13, 1900; 67 Ark. 340; 55 S. W. Rep. 12.]

ADMINISTRATOR'S ACÇOUNTS — DIVIDEND — ACCEPTANCE — ESTOPPEL.

1. Where, on a statement· by an administrator of his account, the court orders the payment of a dividend, out of funds shown by such report to be on hand, to creditors of a certain class, the acceptance by a creditor of the designated class of a part of her proportion, and the issuance of an execution for the collection of the balance, do not estop her to object to the settlement of the administrator's accounts, and to require the latter to pay her a further sum, on the ground that he has fraudulently withheld funds belonging to the estate, for which he should have accounted.

2. Where, after the Probate Court has rendered a judgment ordering the payment by administrator of a dividend to creditors out of funds shown by the administrator's account to be on hand, the settlement of the estate is delayed by litigation concerning the settlement of the administrator's account, limitations· do not run against the right of a creditor to procure another order directing the administrator to pay the creditor's claim.

3. Where, on a statement of an administrator's account, the court orders the payment of a dividend out of funds in his hands, a tender of a creditor's proportion on condition that he sign a receipt in full settlement of his claim against the estate is not a valid tender, as the administrator has no right to require such a receipt.

4. On settlement of an administrator's account, he is not entitled to an allowance for attorney's fees expended by him in resisting proper charges against him.

5. Where an administrator wrongfully withholds from his accounts certain funds belonging to the estate, and the court orders a distribution of the funds thereby shown to be on hand to the creditors of a certain

class, pursuant to which the administrator pays a dividend on the basis shown by the account, and takes a receipt in full settlement of the creditors' claims, he is not, on subsequently being compelled to account for the funds, entitled to the difference between the amount paid and what he should have paid had the account pursuant to which the dividend was declared been correct, as such profit accrues to the estate.

6. Where the administration of an estate is unreasonably prolonged by the fault of the administrator, he should be charged with interest on funds in his hands.

APPEAL from Circuit Court, Yell county, Danville district; JEREMIAH G. WALLACE, Judge.

Exceptions by L. C. Hall, as administrator, against W. D. Jacoway, as administrator. From a judgment of the Circuit Court, both parties appeal.

Reversed.

J. C. Hart and *Rose, Hemingway & Rose,* for appellant.

G. S. Cunningham, for appellee.

RIDDICK, J.—This case commenced in the Probate Court, and the questions involved arise on exceptions filed by certain creditors to a settlement of W. D. Jacoway as administrator of the estate of Samuel Dickens, deceased. The administration of Dickens's estate commenced in 1867, and, it seems, should have been ended long ago; but, by reason of litigation arising out of certain settlements filed by the administrator, the administration is yet unclosed. Some of the questions involved in the litigation referred to have been twice before this court, and a fuller history of the administration of this estate, and of the litigation in which the administrator became involved, can be found by reference to former decisions of this court. (See *Dyer* v. *Jacoway,* 42 Ark. 186; id., 50 id. 217; 6 S. W. 902.) It is only necessary for us to refer briefly to the history of this past litigation: During the progress of the administration the Probate Court, in 1875, after the administrator had filed his fifth account current, made an order that he should pay upon the debts of the fourth class which had been probated and allowed against the estate the sum of thirty-nine cents and eight mills on the dollar of such debts. Under this order the administrator paid to most of the creditors that proportion of their claims, and took from them receipts in full of all claims against the estate. Two of the creditors, Mrs. J. A. Johnston and A. J. Dyer, who are appellees here, refused to accept the amount offered in full settlement of their claims, and for that reason they were not paid. These parties subsequently filed a complaint in equity in the Yell Circuit Court, alleging that the said fifth settlement of the administrator was fraudulent in many respects, and asking that the court set aside and restate said settlement. At the end of this litigation many of the allegations of fraud made against the administrator were overruled, but others were sustained, and the lawsuit resulted in charging the administrator with additional items amounting in the aggregate to over $500. After the case had been remanded to the Probate Court, the administrator filed in that court what is called his seventh and final settlement, and the questions here arise on exceptions to that settlement. The case was appealed from the Probate to the Circuit Court, and from the judgment of the Circuit Court both parties appealed to this court. Counsel for the administrator have devoted several pages of their brief to a criticism of the decree made by the Yell Circuit Court in Chancery in 1893, which decree finally disposed of the questions arising in the action to set aside and restate the fifth settlement of the administrator. But as that court, we think, had jurisdiction of the case, and as no one appealed from the decree, we consider it unnecessary to notice that portion of the argument; for, in our opinion, it can have no effect upon the decision of this case.

Estoppel. After the Probate Court had ordered the administrator to pay a pro-rate of thirty-nine cents and eight mills on the dollar, Mrs. Johnston accepted $35 from the administrator upon her claim, and afterwards ordered an execution to be issued for the collection of the balance of this apportionment. Counsel for the administrator now say that by these acts on her part " she and her representatives are estopped." But in what respect they are estopped, counsel do not say. Her representative makes no claim to the $35 paid by the administrator and there is no contention as to that. As to the balance, certainly an unsuccessful effort to collect a judgment does not estop the party owning it from making other efforts in the same direction. Nor is there any inconsistency in the effort of a creditor to collect from an administrator the sum apportioned to his claim by the Probate Court in part satisfaction thereof, and a demand by him that the administrator be ordered to pay other and further sums upon said claims. It is the duty of the Probate Court from time to time to apportion among the creditors money shown by the settlement of the administrator to be in his hands after payment of expenses. A collection or an effort to collect one of these apportionments does not estop the creditor from showing that there are still other sums due from the administrator. We are therefore unable to see that the Circuit Court erred in overruling this contention.

Limitations. We concur in the ruling of the circuit judge in refusing to sustain the plea of the statute of limitations set up by the administrator. An administrator is a trustee, and pending the administration the funds in his hands are held as such for the creditors and others interested in the estate. It is a general rule that the statute of limitations does not affect the rights of the *cestui que trust* so long as the trust relation continues. In this case no final settlement had been made, and the administration was in active operation. Although the Probate Court made in 1875 an apportionment of money shown by the settlement of the administrator to be in his hands, still appellees soon afterwards attacked such settlement for fraud, alleging that they were entitled to still larger sums than those apportioned, and litigation has continued over that matter until the present time. If we should hold that the order of the Probate Court directing the administrator to make a *pro rata* payment upon the claims probated against the estate was a judgment, and barred after ten years, yet, no final settlement having been made, or the trust renounced, and the funds in the hands of the administrator being held by him as a trustee, he would acquire no right to it by such lapse of time, and the creditor could obtain another order for its payment. For these reasons, we think the Circuit Court correctly held that the statute of limitations was of no avail in this case.

Tender. The appellant also claims that in 1875 he tendered to appellees the full amounts due upon their claims. But the Circuit Court found to the contrary. It is also admitted by the administrator that he demanded, as a condition of the tender, that they should execute receipts in full of their demands against the estate. The sums tendered did not pay the claims of appellees in full, and, even if it was their full *pro rata* of the assets of the estate, still the

condition that they should execute receipts in full was one he had
no right to impose, and rendered the tender of no avail. (*Fields* v.
Danenhower, 65 Ark. 392; 46 S. W. 938; 43 L. R. A. 519.) The
administrator was entitled to a receipt for the sum paid, but he
had not the slightest right to demand of the creditors that they
should render their right to participate in any further assets of the
estate, as a condition of receiving money that already belonged to
them, and which the court had ordered him to pay.

Attorney's fees. The administrator, in his settlement, asked an
allowance for attorney's fees amounting to $1,457.75, but the Cir-
cuit Court allowed only $650 for this purpose. When a settlement
of an administrator is wrongfully assailed in the courts, it is just,
and in accordance with the decisions, to allow attorney's fees necessarily incurred in defense thereof; but no credit should be allowed for fees of attorneys paid by the administrator in resisting
proper charges against him, or in defending a suit brought against
him to compel him to perform a legal duty when he is in fault.
(11 Am. & Eng. Enc. Law [2d ed.], 1246; 2 Woerner, Adm'n
[2d ed.], 1149.) The attorney's fees for which the administrator
asks an allowance in this case were paid in defending charges of
fraud and misconduct on his part, which were in part sustained,
and in part overruled. In fixing the allowance for such fees, the
circuit judge properly took into consideration the rule that the
administrator is not entitled to counsel fees paid for defending
litigation caused by his own fault. Being familiar with the services
rendered, the judge, in fixing the allowance, could act upon his
own knowledge of their value; and we would not overturn his
finding thereon unless clearly erroneous. The amount allowed
was, we think, sufficient to cover legitimate charges for attorney's
fees, and it is approved. (*Harrison* v. *Perea*, 168 U. S. 311-326;
18 Sup. Ct. 129; 42 L. Ed. 478; *Fowler* v. *Trust Co.* 141 U. S. 411-
415; 12 Sup. Ct. 8; 35 L. Ed. 794.)

It appears that, with the exception of Dyer and Johnston, the administrator has settled with all the creditors of the estate having
fourth-class claims. The circuit judge finds that the administrator
settled with these creditors at thirty-nine cents and eight mills on
the dollar of their claims, and has their receipts in full of all demands against the estate, though he finds that the administrator
had in his hands funds sufficient to pay each of them forty-five

cents and three mills on the dollar, and that they were each entitled to that *pro rata* payment. The administrator contends that, in the absence of any demand on the part of the creditors with whom he has settled, he should be allowed to retain the difference between the amounts he paid and that to which they were entitled. This sum amounted to $557.85, and the circuit judge sustained the contention of the administrator, on the ground that "the administrator settled with the creditors at a time when there was a contention as to the *pro rata* they were entit'ed to receive." But we do not concur in this conclusion; for, if there was a dispute as to the amount to which these creditors were entitled, it was a matter between the estate and the creditor, in which the administrator had no personal interest. He represented the estate, and, if anything was gained by the compromise, it belongs to the estate, and not to him. An administrator is not allowed to make a profit for himself by buying in the claims against the estate, or by paying them at a discount. This rule was applied in this court in a case where the purchase was made by the administrator out of his own funds, and by borrowing money at high rates of interest, and when the estate was thereby saved from insolvency; the court saying that it was not an inflexible rule of equity that all profits made by a trustee in dealing with the trust estate belong to the *cestui que trust*. (*Trimble* v. *James*, 40 Ark. 393; *Wolf* v. *Banks*, 41 id. 104; 2 Woerner, Adm'n [2d ed.], 1157; 11 Am. & Eng. Enc. Law [2d ed.], 982.) It is the duty of the administrator to pay creditors of the estate as far as the assets in his hands permit, but the rule contended for here would encourage an administrator to delay and thwart the creditor in the collection of his just claim; for by so doing the administrator might force him to a compromise, and so make a profit for himself. The law wisely permits no such temptation to misconduct on the part of such trustees. We therefore hold that the Circuit Court erred in allowing the administrator credit for larger sums than were actually paid by him to the creditors. If the compromise was binding on the creditors, the profit goes to the estate, and inures to the benefit of those creditors still having valid claims against it; for the administrator can be allowed credits only for sums actually paid. (*Trimble* v. *James* and *Wolf* v. *Banks, supra.*)

The administrator having held the funds of the estate in his hands for over twenty-five years, he should, of course, be charged with interest thereon. The ruling of the Circuit Court on that point does not seem to be disputed, and is affirmed.

There are other questions raised, concerning small items, but as most of them involve questions of bookkeeping, rather than of law, we will not discuss them here, but will, if necessary, hand to the clerk directions in regard to the same. For the errors indicated, the judgment of the Circuit Court will be reversed, and the clerk of this court will be directed to restate the account in accordance with the views above stated, and report to this court the balance found due from the administrator to the estate.

STEVENS *et al. vs.* LEONARD *et al.*

[Supreme Court of Indiana, January 24, 1900; 154 Ind. 67; 56 N. E. Rep. 27.]

NEW TRIAL — WILLS — TRIAL — APPEAL AND ERROR — TESTAMENTARY CAPACITY — INSTRUCTIONS — WITNESS TO WILLS — UNDUE INFLUENCE — INSANE DELUSIONS — EVIDENCE — EXPERT WITNESS — MISCONDUCT OF JURY — ERRORS NOT DISCUSSED BY COUNSEL.

1. Since the statutory cause for which a new trial may be demanded is that the verdict is not sustained by sufficient evidence, it is not necessary, in addition thereto, to separately assign that the verdict was contrary to the evidence.

2 The trial court's refusal to grant a new trial on account of the alleged insufficiency of the evidence will not be disturbed.

3. The fact that the testator was, at the time of the making of his will, suffering great pain, would not of itself take away his testamentary capacity.

4. Where there was no evidence as to undue influence, coercion, or fraud, but the will reflected the desires and prejudices of testator, it was proper to withdraw such questions from the jury.

5. The fact that some of the relatives of the testator were needy is of itself entitled to little weight in determining whether undue influence was exercised over the testator, where he had ignored them in his will.

VOL. V—47

6. An instruction that a person who signs as a witness to a will impliedly certifies to the testator's testamentary capacity, and that, while the law will subsequently permit him to testify to the contrary, yet the jury may consider the fact of such implied contradiction in weighing his testimony, is a correct statement of the law, and does not usurp the province of the jury.

7. Where it was contended that the testator's antipathy for his brother was without substantial foundation, it was proper to admit evidence in contradiction thereof showing that such brother had stated to a crowd that deceased had improved every opportunity to take advantage of his other brothers, and had robbed them, although it was not shown that the deceased had knowledge of such statement before the making of his will.

8. The negative answer of an expert witness to a question as to whether, on the day of his execution of his will, such testator was or was not "laboring under an insane delusion, or anything of that kind," is not objectionable as being a statement of fact, and not the expression of an opinion.

9. Where the affidavit filed in support of a motion to set aside a verdict for misconduct of a juror was directly contradicted, not only by the juror, but also by the person from whom the pretended information was alleged to have been derived, the finding of the lower court will not be disturbed.

10. Errors assigned, which are not discussed by counsel, will be treated as waived.

APPEAL from Circuit Court, Lake county; JOHN H. GILLETT, Judge.

Action by Louis W. Stevens and others against James Leonard, as executor of the last will of Joseph Leonard, deceased, and others. Judgment for defendants, and plaintiffs appeal.

Affirmed.

E. D. Crumpacker, Agnew & Kelly, and *John B. Peterson,* for appellants.

A. C. Harris, A. D. Bartholomew, and *J. W. Youche,* for appellees.

DOWLING, J.—Joseph Leonard died June 5, 1895, leaving no wife or child. His heirs at law were his three brothers, James,

Alvah, and John, and the children of a deceased sister, to wit, Lewis W. Stevens, William Stevens, Clara De Motte, Eva Finney, and Elizabeth Finney. On the 10th day of June, 1895, a paper purporting to be the last will of the said Joseph Leonard, bearing date of December 13, 1888, was presented to, and admitted to probate in, the Circuit Court of Porter county, Ind., which was then in session. Afterwards, on the 25th day of March, 1896, the appellants filed their complaint to contest the said will; alleging unsoundness of mind of the said Joseph Leonard, and the undue execution of the will. There was a further allegation that a subsequent will had been executed by the said Joseph Leonard, revoking the former will; but this ground was abandoned by the contestors, and requires no further notice. The statutory requirements as to the verification of the complaint and the execution of an undertaking for costs were complied with. The appellees appeared and answered. After the commencement of the action, John Leonard, one of the brothers, died, and John Brodie, as the administrator of his estate, together with the widow and children of the said John Leonard, were by a supplemental complaint made defendants in the place of the said John. On the application of the appellants the venue of the cause was changed to Lake county. The case was tried by a jury, and a general verdict was returned, sustaining the will. A motion for a new trial was overruled, and the court rendered judgment on the verdict. The only error assigned is the overruling of the motion for a new trial.

The first cause for which a new trial was claimed was that the verdict was contrary to the evidence; and the second, that the verdict was not sustained by sufficient evidence. The latter is the proper and statutory cause for which a new trial may be demanded, and, when stated, it is not necessary to allege that the verdict is contrary to the evidence. A verdict which is contrary to the evidence is correctly described in the motion for a new trial in the language of the statute,—as not sustained by sufficient evidence. The first proposition in the argument for the appellants is that Joseph Leonard made his will under a delusion concerning the character and conduct of his brother Alvah. The complaint and answer made the question of the soundness or unsoundness of the mind of Joseph Leonard at the time of the execution of the will an issue in the cause. Hundreds of pages of evidence in the record exhibit the conflicting facts and opinions of the witnesses called to support and to combat the averment of mental infirmity. The question tried and determined by the jury was not whether Alvah Leonard was a rogue, a hypocrite, and a cheat, nor whether the aversion manifested by Joseph Leonard towards his sister's children was justifiable or well or ill founded, but whether Joseph was of sound mind when he executed his will. To maintain the issue on the part of appellants, the manifestation of bitter and unfilial sentiments by Joseph Leonard against his brother Alvah was shown; and there was evidence of expression of unkind feeling towards his sister's children. But this proof was met by testimony which proved that these sentiments and feelings were not the result of insane delusions, but that they had their origin in real grievances and apparent slights. 'The existence of bitter and implacable resentments is not incompatible with entire soundness of mind, and trivial instances of disrespect may create aversion and dislike in a mind which is either sensitive or exacting and imperious. All these facts were before the jury, and after long deliberation they arrived at the conclusion that Joseph Leonard was not of sound mind when he made his will. In our opinion, the evidence entirely fails to show that the feelings of Joseph Leonard towards his brother Alvah and the children of his deceased sister were the result of insane delusions or hallucinations. The deceased was evidently a man of coarse but vigorous mind, of strong will, illiterate, and unrefined. His prejudices were bitter, perhaps unjust, and excessive; but we find no support in the evidence for the allegation of the complaint that his mind was unsound, and that he was incapable of disposing of his estate by will. It is not within the province of this court to weigh the evidence, and, even where the preponderance against the finding or verdict is apparent and great, we cannot, under the oft-repeated rule of decision by which we are governed, disturb the conclusions of the court or jury. The circumstance that the supposed testator was at the time of the execution of the will suffering from acute pain, did not take away his testamentary capacity. (*Torrey* v. *Blair*, 75 Me. 548.) The evidence, in our opinion, fully sustains the verdict, and the court did not err in refusing to grant a new trial on account of the alleged insufficiency of the proof.

2. The appellants next complain that the court erred in giving

instruction No. 1, which was in these words: "There is no evidence to show that the testamentary instrument in question was not, in the matter of forms, gone through with, in all respects duly executed. I do not withdraw from your consideration, if you deem it important, any proof as to the extraneous influences, if any, which operated on the mind of the testator, if they did so operate; but, upon the condition of the evidence in this case, I instruct you that such influences, if any, can only be considered upon the question as to whether the testator was of unsound mind. There is therefore but one ultimate question for your consideration under the facts in this case, and that is, was the testator, at the time he signed the testamentary disposition of his property now in contest, so far of unsound mind as to invalidate the document which has been probated as his will?" Counsel say in their brief: "Of course, it is at once to be perceived that this instruction takes out of the record, as it is intended to do, the question of undue influence. This was a question upon which the appellants relied, and they now insist' that the court erred in withdrawing the question from the jury. The same question is presented in instruction No. 10, asked for by the appellants (page 61 of the record), which is as follows: ' If you believe from the evidence that at the time of making the will in question, and for several years prior thereto, Joseph Leonard was in poor health, and in a condition of nervousness and excitability; and if you further believe that during that time James Leonard, one of the defendants, took advantage of his enfeebled condition, and by words and insinuations poisoned the mind of the said Joseph Leonard against his brother Alvah, to such an extent that said Joseph possessed an intense hatred of his said brother, and was induced by said hatred to give all his property to James and his family by will,—said will is invalid and should be set aside.' " If there was evidence that the execution of the will was procured by the exercise of undue influence, then the instruction given was erroneous, because it withdrew from the consideration of the jury that element of the case. If there was no evidence of undue influence, the direction of the court was right. The burden of the proof was upon the appellants, and, if the evidence in the case entirely failed to sustain any one of the grounds upon which the validity of the will was assailed, the court had the right to withdraw the consideration of such ground, and to instruct the jury to disregard it. (*Faris* v. *Hoberg*, 134 Ind. 269; 33 N. E. 1028; *Railway Co.* v. *Dunn*, 138 Ind. 18; 36 N. E. 702, and 37 N. E. 546; *Palmer* v. *Railroad Co.* 112 Ind. 250; 14 N. E. 70.) It is necessary, therefore, to ascertain what constitutes undue influence, within the meaning of the law, and then to determine whether there was any evidence of such undue influence before the court and jury. " ' Undue influence ' has been defined as that which compels the testator to do that which is against his will, through fear, or the desire of peace, or some feeling which he is unable to resist, ' and but for which the will would not have been made as it was.' " (Redf. Wills, 530; 27 Am. & Eng. Enc. Law, 495, and notes.) Again, it is said that: " The influence must be undue, to vitiate the instrument, because influences of one kind or another surround every rational being, and operate necessarily in determining his course of conduct under every relation of life. Within due and reasonable limits such influence affords no ground of legal objection to his acts. Hence, mere passion and prejudice, the influence of peculiar religious or secular training, of personal associations, of opinions, right or wrong, imbibed in the natural course of one's experience and contact with society, cannot be set up as undue, to defeat a will, if, indeed, it were possible to gauge the depth of such influence at all. ' It is extremely difficult,' as Lord CRANWORTH *has observed*, ' to state in the abstract what acts will constitute undue influence, in questions of this nature. It is sufficient to say that, allowing a fair latitude of construction, they range themselves under one or other of these heads,—coercion or fraud.' " " Not even can the circumstance that the influence gained by one individual over another was very great be treated as undue, in our present connection, especially if the person influenced had free opportunity and strength of mind sufficient to select what influence should guide him, and was, in the full sense, legally and morally a responsible being." (Schouler, Wills, § 227; *Boyse* v. *Rossborough*, 6 H. L. Cas. 6; *Wingrove* v. *Wingrove*, 11 Prob. Div. 83.) The American editor of Jarman on Wills (6th Am. ed.), in an exhaustive note on the subject of undue influence, states the law thus: " The test to be applied is agreed to be this: Was such influence brought to bear as to take away (that is, did it take away) the supposed testator's free agency in this instance?

* * * Unfree agency in a case of undue influence is simply this: The apparent testator is but the instrument by which the mastering desire of another is expressed. The supposed will, or the particular part in question, is not the will of the supposed testator, except in the sense that he has consented to put his name to the instrument in the form in which it appears. Of course, yielding to influence is consistent with free agency. Agency is free, in the eye of the law, however much the agent is influenced by other men, until the influence amounts to domination of the will. Thus, persuasion and argument are not improper, so long as they do not overcome free agency." (1 Jarm. Wills, 66, note; *Dale's Appeal*, 57 Conn. 133; 17 Atl. 757.)   We have been unable to find in the great mass of testimony in this case any evidence of the existence of undue influence, or its exercise upon the mind or feelings of the deceased in connection with the disposition of his estate by his will.   In the course of his dealings with his brother Alvah, extending through many years, he had formed an unfavorable opinion of his character, and he cherished a feeling of resentment against him.   These sentiments were shared by James Leonard, the brother to whom the estate was devised; and, when the conduct of Alvah was the subject of conversation between the brothers, James freely expressed his antipathy to Alvah.   It does not appear that the disposition of the property of the deceased was ever mentioned by James, or that James attempted to influence his brother Joseph in any way concerning such disposition.   It was not shown that he advised Joseph to make a will, and it was proved that he was ignorant of the fact that a will had been made until January 5, 1895,—some six years after its execution.   The deceased during his life manifested but little affection for the children of his sister, and their habits and behavior were severely commented on by him.   But these impressions were the result of his own observation and experience, and there was no evidence that they had been artfully or wrongfully created by another who wished thereby to influence the mind of the deceased, and to divert from any of these relatives such portion of his estate as the deceased would otherwise have bestowed upon them.   It cannot be said that the disposition made of his estate by the deceased was an unnatural one.   He had neither wife nor child, so that his property, if not disposed of by will, would have been scattered among collateral relatives.   He had the right to favor those whom he loved and trusted, and from whom he had received nothing but respect and kindness, and to disappoint the expectations of other relatives, who had, justly or unjustly, incurred his ill will or aversion. The fact that some of the relatives of the deceased were needy is of itself entitled to little weight. In *Goodbar* v. *Lidikey* (136 Ind. 6; 35 N. E. 692), this court said: "Indeed, we think that the presumption in favor of the validity of a will should be increased, rather than diminished, from the circumstance that a bequest was made to one with whom the testator had maintained intimate and confidential relations during life. A will, in fact, is usually made in order to give property to those whom the testator desires to favor. If it were the desire that the property should go in due proportions to those equally related to the testator, then no will would be necessary. The law itself would make such distribution in the most equitable manner possible. This is particularly the case where, as in this case, the testator had neither wife nor children, and his property, if not devised, would go to collateral relations." There was no evidence whatever that the deceased was by any means constrained to do what was against his will, and what he would not do if left to himself. There was here neither coercion nor fraud. The will of the deceased faithfully reflected his desires, his passions, his prejudices, and not the desires, passions, or prejudices of another. He kept it by him for more than six years, and his purposes as expressed in the will remained steadfast during all that time. When his life and strength were ebbing away he spoke of his will, but intimated no inclination to alter or revoke it. Under this state of the evidence, the duty of the court was clear, and it did right in withdrawing from the jury the question of undue influence.

3. The third point made by counsel for appellants is that the court erred in giving to the jury instruction No. 15, in these words: "(15) A person who attaches his name as a witness to a testamentary instrument impliedly certifies that the testator is of sound mind and competent to make a will; and while the law will subsequently permit him to testify to the contrary, because the truth, if such it be, should be learned, yet the jury trying the case may consider the fact of such implied contradiction in weighing his testimony." It is said by counsel that: "This instruction is erroneous—First, because it does not state the law correctly; and,

second, even if it is correct in the abstract, it usurps the province of the jury in determining a question of fact, and in passing upon the credibility of a witness, of which the jury is the exclusive judge." While it is not necessary to the validity of a will that the subscribing witnesses should know that the instrument they attest is a will, yet, in the absence of proof to the contrary, they will be presumed to have had such knowledge when they attested it. The view of the law contained in the above instruction is sanctioned by very high authority. In *Scribner* v. *Crane* (2 Paige, 147) Chancellor WALWORTH said: "No person is justified in putting his name as a subscribing witness to a will unless he knows from the testator himself that he knows what he is doing. The witness should also be satisfied from his own knowledge of the state of the testator's mental capacity, that he is of sound and disposing mind and memory. By placing his name to the instrument, the witness, in effect, certifies to his knowledge of the mental capacity of the testator, and that the will was executed by him freely and understandingly, with a full knowledge of its contents. Such is the legal effect of the signature of the witness when he is dead or is out of the jurisdiction of the court." "It seems to be considered," says Judge REDFIELD, "that they (the subscribing witnesses to a will) are only witnesses to the act of signing. But when it is considered that the witnesses to a will must certify to the capacity of the testator as well as to the act of execution, the transaction begins to assume a somewhat different aspect. One who put his name as a witness to the execution of a will while he was conscious that the testator was not in the possession of his mental faculties placed himself very much in the same attitude as if he had subscribed as witness to a will which he knew to be a forgery, which every honorable man could only regard as becoming accessory to the crime by which the will was fabricated; so that it is not improbable that the want of proper appreciation of the discredit resulting from the act of becoming a witness to the execution of a will by one confessedly incompetent to the proper understanding of the instrument may, and probably does, result chiefly, with us, from the general misapprehension of the law upon the subject, rather than from any settled disposition to disregard its dictates, if correctly understood." (1 Redf. Wills, 96.) Lord CAMDEN early pointed out how peculiar a stress the statute of frauds had laid upon the quality

and office of witnesses to a will, as distinguished from other transactions. He says: "And the only question that can be asked in
this case is, was the testator in his senses when he made it? And
consequently the time of execution is the critical minute that
requires guard and protection. Here you see the reason why
witnesses are called in so emphatically. * * * Who, then,
shall secure the testator in this important moment from imposition? Who shall protect the heir at law, and give the world a satisfactory evidence that he was sane? The statute says, 'Three
credible witnesses.'" (*Hendson* v. *Kersey,* 4 Burn. Ecc. Law,
85, 88.) In *Tatham* v. *Wright* (2 Russ. & M. 1), where two subscribing witnesses had declared that they would testify against
the testator's capacity, TINDAL, C. J., made this severe comment:
"The real question is whether these witnesses are to be believed
upon this evidence, in contradiction to their own solemn act in the
attestation. * * * That is the problem to be solved." A
writer of great authority says: "The signature of an attesting
witness, when proved, is evidence of everything on the face of the
instrument, for it is to be presumed that the witness would not
have subscribed his name in attestation of that which did not take
place; and where there are several attesting witnesses, all of whom
are accounted for, proof of the handwriting of any one is sufficient,
without proving that of the rest." (Starkie, Ev. 519.) The same
author says elsewhere: "The law requires the testimony of the
subscribing witness because the parties themselves, by selecting
him as a witness, have mutually agreed to rest upon his testimony
in proof of the execution of the instrument, and of the circumstances which then took place, and because he knows those facts
which are probably unknown to others." (Id. 504; Chaplin, Wills,
92.) In Schouler on Wills this sensible observation is found:
"One should only subscribe as witness when he can conscientiously
testify without reserve in favor of the will and its proper execution,
and it is for the true interest of every rational testator to procure
witnesses who will stand resolutely by the transaction, against all
insidious or open opposition to the probate." (Section 181; *Pence*
v. *Waugh,* 135 Ind. 155; 34 N. E. 860.) It cannot be thought
possible that an honest man, of ordinary intelligence, would subscribe his name as a witness to an instrument executed by a person
whom he believed to be of unsound mind or under coercion or

constraint. The fact that such a man voluntarily identifies himself with the transaction as a witness is an indication that in his opinion the person executing the instrument is competent to do so. The witness must be understood to attest not merely the act of signing, but also the mental capacity of the testator to sign. A subscribing witness may, it is true, be heard to impeach the will; but, if he assumes that attitude towards it, he does so at the peril of his reputation for candor and veracity. Such an attitude is not merely inconsistent with the position he has voluntarily taken, but is suggestive of fraud and double dealing. It involves a betrayal of confidence, and, if the witness is believed, in some instances it may be attended with the most distressing consequences. The credibility of the witness becomes at once a matter of serious inquiry, and his desertion of his position as a sustaining witness is an important fact for the consideration of the jury. In such a case it is entirely proper for the court to inform the jury that they may consider the fact of such implied contradiction, if they find it exists, in weighing his testimony. A direction of this character is not an invasion of the province of the jury, nor is it objectionable on the ground that it singles out a witness for attack or criticism. It is the duty of the court in all cases to instruct the jury upon the law of the case, whether the testimony of one witness or the testimony of a score of witnesses is comprehended within the rules necessary to be stated for their guidance. In the instruction under examination, the court did nothing more than declare, as it was competent for it to do, a familiar rule of law; leaving the application of it entirely to the jury, and without giving them to understand what his own opinion on the subject was. (*Com.* v. *Selfridge*, 1 Horr. & T. Cas. 1.) " The court should not express any opinion on the weight of evidence, nor on the credibility of particular witnesses. * * * But general rules for weighing and reconciling the evidence, and as to what the jury may consider in determining the credibility of witnesses, so long as the court does not trench upon the province of the jury, may properly be given in almost any case." (Elliott, Gen. Prac. § 901, and cases cited in note 1.) Undue prominence was not given in this instruction to any particular portion of the evidence; nor was the attention of the jury directed to an isolated and prominent feature of the testimony, in such a manner as to mislead them, or indicate the opinion or bias of the court, to the injury of the appellants. The wholesome rules stated in the cases referred to by counsel for appellants were not violated, nor did the court in any respect usurp the functions of the jury. There was no dispute as to the fact that one of the subscribing witnesses was called by appellants, and that his testimony tended to impeach the will. The court might with propriety have said much more than it did. It could not, in justice to the parties, have said less, or stated an indisputable rule more fairly. (*Paris* v. *Strong*, 51 Ind. 339; *Stanley* v. *Montgomery*, 102 id. 102; 26 N. E. 213; *Insurance Co.* v. *Buchanan*, 100 Ind. 81; *Finch* v. *Bergens*, 89 id. 362; *Cheatham* v. *Hatcher*, 30 Grat. 56; 25 Am. & Eng. Enc. Law, 1017, note 2; 29 Am. & Eng. Enc. Law, 203, note 1.) In connection with instruction No. 15, the court, by instruction No. 17, clearly admonished the jury that they were the exclusive judges of the weight of the evidence, and that the court had no right to invade their province of determining what the evidence proved. They were further told that they had the right to decide upon the credibility of each witness. In the light of the authorities which we have cited, it is evident that the jury were properly instructed, and that there was no error in this part of the proceedings of the court.

4. It was also assigned as a ground for a new trial that the court permitted the following evidence to be given to the jury over the objection of the appellants: " Q. State what, if anything, he (Alvah) was saying to the crowd about the conduct of his brother Joseph in that partnership transaction. A. Mr. Leonard said that his brother Joseph had had an opportunity to take advantage of the other brothers, and that he improved every opportunity, right and left, and that he had robbed the other brothers of what was justly due them, and a variety of expressions of that sort; and he seemed very much excited about the matter, and talked in rather a loud tone of voice for him." It is objected that this evidence was inadmissible for any purpose, but we cannot so regard it. The theory of the appellants was that the unfriendly feelings entertained by the deceased towards his brother Alvah were the result of mere delusions of fancy, and were without substantial foundation in point of fact. Much testimony was introduced by appellants to show the existence of these unnatural sentiments, and, on the other hand, the appellees undertook to account for them by proving that Alvah's conduct in various business transactions had

created the enmity between him and Joseph. The actual state of the relations between Alvah and Joseph therefore became a material fact in the case; and proof that Alvah reciprocated the feelings of distrust and dislike cherished by his brother Joseph, and that he publicly denounced Joseph as a dishonest and unscrupulous man, was entitled to some weight upon the question whether Joseph's aversion for Alvah was but the figment of a disordered brain,—the hallucination of an enfeebled or distracted mind. It was not necessary, in our judgment, for the appellee to show that the accusations made by Alvah came to the knowledge of Joseph before the latter made his will. The state of Joseph's feelings towards Alvah was established. The attitude of Alvah towards Joseph was an important factor in the investigation of the question whether Joseph's dislike of Alvah was natural or unnatural,— whether it sprang from a collision of views and interests in real transactions, or was the offspring of a mental malady. We think the evidence was properly admitted, and that, as an indirect and collateral fact, it had a tendency to establish the reasonableness of the conduct and sentiments of Joseph Leonard towards his brother Alvah.

5. In the next place the appellants complain of the answer of Dr. Beer, an expert, to a question touching the mental condition of the deceased. The question and answer were as follows: "Question. Now, doctor, let me ask you this question: Whether, from your conversation with him, and from an examination of him, —his appearance, and everything, at that time,—whether Joseph Leonard on the 12th day of December (the date of the will) was or was not laboring under an insane delusion, or anything of that kind." To which question the witness answered: "No; he was not." Appellants excepted to this question and answer. The objection is made that the answer of the witness is the statement of a fact, and not the expression of an opinion. This construction of the answer seems to us entirely without warrant. The witness, having been shown to possess the requisite qualifications of an expert, and having seen, conversed with, and examined the supposed testator, was authorized, by the rule of evidence applicable in such cases, to express his opinion as to the soundness of the mind of the deceased. His answer was in the usual form, and could not have been understood by the court or jury as anything

more than an opinion, as all such evidence in inquisitions of this character must necessarily be. There was no error in the action of the court upon the exception to this evidence.

6. The last alleged error discussed by counsel for appellants is the refusal of the court to set aside the verdict because of the supposed misconduct of one of the jurors. This question, however, was tried in the court below upon affidavits and counter affidavits; and we must presume, in the absence of a very clear showing to the contrary, that the decision of the trial court was correct. It is proper to add that the record shows that the affidavit filed in support of appellants' motion was made upon information only, and that it was directly contradicted, not only by the affidavit of the juror, but also by the affidavit of the person from whom the pretended information was alleged to have been derived.

Other errors are assigned, but, as they are not discussed by counsel for appellants, they must be treated as waived.

Finding no available error in the record, the judgment is affirmed.

NOTE.—MENTAL CAPACITY TO MAKE A WILL.

(a) General rules.
(b) Test of memory.
(c) Will itself no test.
(d) As tested by other standards.
(e) Effect of age or weakened condition of mind or body.
(f) Executed in dying condition.

(a) **General rules.**—" The true rule is that if, from all the facts and circumstances considered together, it satisfactorily appears that the testator, *when making his will*, understood fully and intelligently the nature of the business in which he was engaged, comprehended generally the nature and extent of the property which constitutes his estate, and which he intends to dispose of, and recollects the objects of his bounty, he has sufficient capacity to make a will." (1 Underhill on Wills, § 87 [ed. 1900]; Kerr v. Lunsford, 31 W. Va. 662; 8 S. E. Rep. 493; Benoist v. Murrin, 58 Mo. 307; Riley v. Sherwood, 144 id. 354; 45 S. W. Rep. 1077; St. Leger's Appeal, 34 Conn. 434; Sturtevant's Appeal, 71 id. 392; 42 Atl. Rep. 70; Sharer v. McCarthy, 110 Pa. St. 339; 5 Atl. Rep. 614; Delaney v. City of Salina, 34 Kans. 532; 9 Pac. Rep. 271; Westcott v. Shepard, 51 N. J. Eq. 315; 25 Atl. Rep. 254; 30 id. 428; Gable v. Rauch, 50 S. C. 106; 27 S. E. Rep. 555; Hall v. Perry, 87 Me. 569; 33 Atl. Rep. 160; Bulger v. Ross, 98 Ala. 267; 12 So. Rep. 803; Spratt v. Spratt, 76 Mich. 384; 43

N. W. Rep. 627; Peninsular Trust Co. v. Barker, 116 Mich. 333; 74 N. W. Rep. 508; Chrisman v. Chrisman, 16 Ore. 127; 18 Pac. Rep. 6; Webber v. Sullivan, 58 Iowa, 260; 12 N. W. Rep. 319.)

It is essential that the testator has sufficient capacity to comprehend perfectly the condition of his property, his relations to the persons who were or should or might have been the object of his bounty, and the scope and bearing of the provisions of his will. He must have sufficient active memory to collect in his mind, without prompting, the particulars or elements of the business to be transacted, and to hold them in his mind a sufficient length of time to perceive at least their obvious relations to each other, and be able to form some rational judgment in relation to them. (Delafield v. Parish, 25 N. Y. 10, 29; Von Guysling v. Van Kurens, 35 id. 70; Re Lewis' Will, 51 Wis. 104; 7 N. W. Rep. 829; Reichenbach v. Ruddach, 127 Pa. St. 565; 18 Atl. Rep. 432; McCoon v. Allen, 45 N. J. Eq. 708; 17 Atl. Rep. 820; Chappell v. Trent, 90 Va. 849; 19 S. E. Rep. 314; Hoope's Estate, 174 Pa. St. 379; 34 Atl. Rep. 603; Cornwell v. Riker, 2 Dem. 368; Matter of Henry, 18 Misc. 149; 41 N. Y. Supp. 1096; and see Harwood v. Baker, 3 Moore P. C. 282.)

Will may be sustained even if the mental capacity under above rule is somewhat obscure or clouded. (Townsend v. Bogart, 5 Redf. 94, 104 [N. Y.].)

It is requisite to the testator's competency to make a will that he should possess sufficient mental capacity to comprehend what property he had to dispose of, the natural objects of his affection and bounty, to understand the nature of his acts and the effect his will would have upon the natural objects of his bounty and affection. One possessed of the understanding and mental power thus required is of sound mind and memory. (Daly v. Daly, 183 Ill. 269, 273; 55 N. E. Rep. 671.)

Must have mind and memory sufficient to understand the ordinary affairs of life, the value and extent of his property, the number and names of the persons who were the natural objects of his bounty, their deserts with reference to their conduct and treatment of him, their capacity and necessity; and have sufficient active memory to retain all these facts in his mind long enough to have his will prepared.   Bower v. Bower, 146 Ind. 398; 45 N. E. Rep. 595.)

His power to recollect his nearer kindred, and appreciate their c'aims upon him, to comprehend the amount and character of his estate, and to intelligently direct its distribution, does not appear to have been seriously impaired. Such capacity is sufficient for the making of a will. (Stoutenburgh v. Hopkins, 43 N. J. Eq. 577, 581; 12 Atl. Rep. 689.)

Sufficient if testator at time of making his will knows what he is doing and to whom he is giving his property. (Brinkman v. Rueggesick, 71 Mo. 553.)

Not essential that testator should understand meaning of technical or legal terms, if he understood meaning and effect of instrument as a whole. (O'Brien v. Spalding, 102 Ga. 490; 31 S. E. Rep. 100.)

(b) **Test of memory.**—Must have memory, but the failure of memory is not sufficient to create the incapacity unless it be total or extend to his immediate family or property. (Wilson v. Mitchell, 101 Pa. St. 495.)

The question is whether though the memory had failed " to a greater degree, the solid power of understanding remained." (Daly v. Daly, 183 Ill. 269; 55 N. E. Rep. 671; citing Chancellor KENT in Van Ast v. Hunter, 5 Johns. Ch. 148.)

(c) **Will itself no test.**—The fact that will omits natural objects of testator's bounty is not evidence of mental incapacity. (Spratt v. Spratt, 76 Mich. 384; 43 N. W. Rep. 627; and see Re Langford, 108 Cal. 609; 41 Pac. Rep. 701.)

A question of mental capacity is not determined by the reasonableness of the bequest or devise. (Watson v. Donnelly, 28 Barb. 653; and see Hollenbeck v. Cook, 180 Ill. 65; 54 N. E. Rep. 154.)

(d) **As tested by other standards.**—Need not be able to make contracts or to manage his estate. (Brinkman v. Rueggesick, 71 Mo. 553.)

Capability of transacting ordinary business implies capacity to make a will. Test is that party be capable of acting rationally in the ordinary affairs of life. (Meeker v. Meeker, 75 Ill. 260; Francis v. Wilkinson, 147 id. 370; 35 N. E. Rep. 150.)

May be capable of making a will, and yet be incapable of making a contract or managing his estate. (Jackson v. Hardin, 83 Mo. 175.)

A person may be incapacitated by age and failing memory from engaging in business affairs, and yet be able to give simple directions for his will. (Hall v. Perry, 87 Me. 569; 33 Atl. Rep. 160.)

Mind or memory may be so impaired that person is incompetent to manage his own affairs and yet he may have sufficient mental capacity to make a will. (Whitney v. Twombly, 136 Mass. 145.)

If testator has capacity to transact ordinary business the presumption is that he is capable of making a will; but such ability is not an absolute invariable test, as testator may have less mental capacity in making a will than would be required in business affairs. (Taylor v. Cox, 153 Ill. 220; 38 N. E. Rep. 656.) And as to test of ability to transact ordinary business affairs see Entwistle v. Meikle (180 Ill. 9; 54 N. E. Rep. 217); Greene v. Greene (145 Ill. 264; 33 N. E. Rep. 941); Knight's Estate (167 Pa. St. 453; 31 Atl. Rep. 682).

Tests of mental disease or capacity considered. (Smith v. Tebbitt, L. R. 1 P. & D. 398.)

(e) **Effect of age and weakened condition of mind or body.**—Weakness or feebleness of mind does not constitute incapacity. (Gable v. Rauch, 50 S. C. 95; 27 S. E. Rep. 555.)

Mind may be impaired and yet have testamentary capacity. (Bulger v. Ross, 98 Ala. 267; 12 So. Rep. 803.)

Old age, failure of memory, weakness, or habitual drunkenness does not *per se* constitute incapacity. (Thompson v. Kyner, 65 Pa. St. 368; Kerr v. Lunsford, 31 W. Va. 661; 8 S. E. Rep. 493; Riley v. Sherwood, 144

Mo. 354; 45 S. W. Rep. 1077; Francis v. Wilkinson, 147 Ill. 370; 35 N. E. Rep. 150.)

A person may be in one or several respects mentally unsound, yet if they do not enter into the will, his capacity to make it may remain unaffected. (Durham v. Smith, 120 Ind. 463; 22 N. E. Rep. 333; and see Freeman v. Easly, 117 Ill. 317; 7 N. E. Rep. 656; Delaney v. City of Salina, 34 Kans. 532; 9 Pac. Rep. 271.)

Feeble condition of body, and impairment of intellectual vigor, are not of themselves sufficient to destroy testamentary capacity. (Westcott v. Sheppard, 51 N. J. Eq. 318; 25 Atl. Rep. 254; 30 id. 428.)

A physical wreck with total want of moral nature and natural affection, and association with vilest classes, does not constitute incapacity. (Re Gorkow's Estate, 20 Wash. 563; 56 Pac. Rep. 385.)

Mind may be in some degree debilitated, memory enfeebled, understanding weak, character eccentric, and may even lack capacity to transact many ordinary affairs of life, and yet may have sufficient mental capacity to make will. (Kerr v. Lunsford, *supra.*)

Where imbecility is claimed to have existed by reason of disease, drugs, and old age, there is no presumption of continuity from such a temporary cause; otherwise if shown to be a chronic state preceding the execution of the will, in which case the burden of proving an interval of competency is cast on the proponents of the will. (Von de Veld v. Judy, 143 Mo. 348; 44 S. W. Rep. 1117.)

Mind, memory, and body may be impaired by old age or disease, and yet testator may have sufficient capacity to make a will. (Kramer v. Weinert, 81 Ala. 416; 1 So. Rep. 26; Taylor v. Pegram, 151 Ill. 106; 37 N. E. Rep. 837; Douglass's Estate, 162 Pa. St. 567; 29 Atl. Rep. 715; Ayres v. Ayres, 43 N. J. Eq. 565; 12 Atl. Rep. 621; McMaster v. Scriven, 85 Wis. 162; 55 N. W. Rep. 149; Chrisman v. Chrisman, 16 Ore. 127; 18 Pac. Rep. 6.)

Yet may be so impaired as to destroy capacity. (Gatt v. Provan, 108 Iowa, 561; 79 N. W. Rep. 357; Cornwell v. Riker, 2 Dem. 366; Horn v. Pullman, 72 N. Y. 276; Matter of Pike, 83 Hun, 327; 31 N. Y. Supp. 689; Matter of Henry, 18 Misc. 149; 41 N. Y. Supp. 1096; Matter of Iredale, 53 App. Div. 47; 65 N. Y. Supp. 533.)

(f) **Executed in dying condition.**—Sickness even extending to a dying condition does not prove want of capacity to make a will, if when aroused testator's mind acted clearly in respect to the thing to be done. (Bevelot v. Lestrade, 153 Ill. 625; 38 N. E. Rep. 1056; Hathorn v. King, 8 Mass. 371; Ayres v. Ayres, *supra.*)

In feeble health and confined to his room and bed for seventeen years. (Wood v. Lane, 102 Ga. 200; 29 S. E. Rep. 180.)

And other cases where will executed by a person in a dying condition, see Jackson v. Jackson (39 N. Y. 153); McQuire v. Kerr (2 Bradf. 248); Harwood v. Baker (3 Moore P. C. 282).

CASH *vs.* KIRKHAM.

[Supreme Court of Arkansas, January 13, 1900; 67 Ark. 318; 55 S. W.
Rep. 18.]

WITNESSES—COMPETENCY—TRANSACTIONS WITH DECEDENT.

In an action to recover for medical services to defendant's intestate, evidence of the plaintiff that he attended decedent, and operated on his
wife, and that such services are worth the amount claimed, are incompetent, since they involve a transaction with a decedent, within Const.
Schedule, § 2, prohibiting a party from testifying to "transactions"
with a decedent in an action by or against his administrator.

APPEAL from Circuit Court, Pike county; WILL P. FEAZELL,
Judge.

Action by Z. L. Kirkham against the administrator of John H.
Cash, deceased. From a judgment for plaintiff, defendant appeals.
Reversed.

John H. Crawford, for appellant.

E. B. Kinsworthy, for appellee.

BATTLE, J.—Z. L. Kirkham presented two accounts against the
estate of John H. Cash, deceased,—one for $178, and the other for
$13,—for allowance. The accounts were principally for services
rendered the deceased and his family by Kirkham. They were
disallowed by the administrator, and were then filed in the Probate
Court, when they were allowed in full. The administrator appealed
to the Circuit Court, and Kirkham recovered a judgment on them
for $120; and the administrator appealed.

Only two witnesses testified in the case: " J. P. Dunn, a witness for the plaintiff, stated: During the last illness of J. H. Cash,
deceased, plaintiff attended him as his family physician, but the
witness did not know how many times he attended him, or the
value of his services therefor.

" The plaintiff, over defendant's objection, then introduced himself. He testified: That he was the attending physician during

the last illness of J. H. Cash, deceased. That he made forty visits, at $2 per visit; and cost of operating on the wife of deceased, $25. That the total amount due upon said account was $120. The defendant objected to this testimony of the plaintiff, for incompetency,—the same being as to transactions with the defendant's intestate,—which objection was by the court overruled, and defendant at the time excepted." This was all the evidence adduced.

The only question presented for our decision involves the consideration of the correctness of the Circuit Court's ruling upon the admissibility of plaintiff's testimony. Was it competent?

The constitution of this state (Schedule, § 2) declares that " in actions by or against executors, administrators or guardians, in which judgment may be rendered for or against them, neither party sha'l be allowed to testify against the other as to any transactions with or statements of the testator, intestate or ward, unless called to testify thereto by the opposite party." The proceeding before us was an action by appellee against the appellant in his capacity of administrator of the estate of John H. Cash, deceased. The testimony of plaintiff tended to prove an implied contract with appellant's intestate. The legal effect of it as a whole, if true, was an implied promise of the deceased to pay the plaintiff the sum of $105 for services rendered. This was a transaction with the deceased,—as much so as it would have been had the deceased expressly promised to pay the $105. The only difference between the two transactions is that in one case the promise was implied, and in the other it was expressed. The testimony should have been excluded on the ground that the plaintiff was incompetent to testify as to such transaction. (*Peck* v. *McKean*, 45 Iowa, 18; *Smith* v. *Johnson*, id. 308; *Boyd* v. *Cauthen*, 28 S. C. 72; 5 S. E. 170; 3 Jones, Ev. § 793, and cases cited.)

Reversed and remanded for a new trial.

KAUFMAN *vs.* ELDER *et al.*

[Supreme Court of Indiana, February 14, 1900; 154 Ind. 157; 56 N. E. Rep. 215.]

EXECUTORS AND ADMINISTRATORS—CONVEYANCES—VACATION—
LAND NECESSARY TO PAY DEBTS—CONTRIBUTION—DEFENSES
—PLEADING.

1. In an action by an executor to set aside a conveyance of eighty acres of land by his testator, and for a decree that the land be sold to pay testator's debts, defendant's cross complaint alleged that the eighty acres was part of 241 acres owned by the testator, which testator conveyed in different parcels, at the same time and without consideration, to several beneficiaries, of which defendant was one. *Held,* sufficient to entitle defendant to a decree that the testator's indebtedness was chargeable ratably, according to value, against all the parcels conveyed.

2. In an action to set aside a conveyance by a testator, and for a sale of the property for payment of debts, evidence that other property conveyed by testator was equally bound with defendant's was not admissible under the general denial, where the grantees, other than defendant, were not made parties to the action.

3. In an action to set aside a conveyance by a testator, and for a sale of the property necessary to pay debts, an answer alleging that other property conveyed by testator was equally liable with that conveyed to defendant was insufficient.

APPEAL from Circuit Court, Vermillion county; A. F. WHITE, Judge.

Action by Samuel Elder, executor, etc., against Nancy J. Kaufman and another. From a judgment for plaintiff, defendant Kaufman appeals.
Reversed.

M. G. Rhoads and *B. S. Aikman,* for appellant.

Conley & Whitlock, for appellee Elder.

HADLEY, C. J.—The appellee Elder, as executor of Benjamin F. McRoberts, filed in the court below his petition to sell real estate to pay debts. The petition stated that the testator left neither

widow nor child; that he left a personal estate of the value of
$153, and real estate of the value of $100, and a probable indebtedness of $3,700, including a debt of $2,300 secured by the testator
on lands owned by him in his lifetime. It is then averred that the
testator, ten days before his death, by deed, conveyed a certain
eighty acres of land owned by him, of the probable value of $4,000,
to the defendant Nancy J. Kaufman during her natural life, with
remainder in fee at her death to the defendant Dana Lodge, No.
247, Knights of Pythias; that said conveyance was a gift, and
without any consideration; that the testator, at the time of said
conveyance, was indebted to various persons in the aggregate sum
of $3,700; that he had remaining, and afterwards acquired, no
other property subject to execution with which to pay his then
existing debts; that the testator, before said conveyance, had executed a mortgage on said eighty acres to secure a debt for $2,300,
which remains unpaid. Prayer that the conveyance be adjudged
fraudulent as against creditors, and that the land be ordered sold
for the payment of said mortgage and other indebtedness of the
estate. Appellant's motion to make the petition more specific was
overruled, as was also her demurrer thereto. She then filed an
answer in two paragraphs, to the second of which the executor's
demurrer was sustained. Defendant the Pythian Lodge filed an
answer in general denial. Appellant then filed a cross complaint,
which the executor unsuccessfully moved to strike from the files.
The executor's demurrer to the cross complaint was then filed and
sustained. Trial on the general issue, finding for the executor,
and, after denial of appellant's motion for a new trial, judgment
was rendered for the executor to the effect that the conveyance to
the defendants Kaufman and Pythian Lodge " is hereby declared
void as to creditors of said estate, and said real estate is hereby
made subject to sale by said executor to make assets to pay the
debts of said estate, * * * said real estate to be sold to discharge said mortgage lien and other debts, and the proceeds of
such sale shall be applied, first, to the payment of said mortgage
indebtedness, and then to the payment of other expenses and
claims, in the order of their priority, and, if anything remains after
paying all said indebtedness and expenses, the same shall be paid
into court " for further orders. The appraisement of the eighty
acres filed was $3,600.

The appellant has assigned error upon all the adverse rulings, but the real question involved arises upon the action of the court in sustaining the executor's demurrer to the appellant's cross complaint. It is averred in the cross complaint that the testator in his lifetime was the owner in fee of 241 acres of land in Vermillion county, and that before his death he prepared, signed, and acknowledged five different deeds of conveyance, one of which conveyed to the cross complainant the eighty acres in controversy, another of which conveyed to said executor, Samuel Elder, forty acres, another conveyed to Sallie A. McCown and Mary A. Ayres forty acres, another conveyed to Ed McRoberts sixty-six acres, and the other conveyed fifteen acres to the said Samuel Elder in trust to pay for the monument and other expenses of the grantor and his estate; that, after the execution of the deeds, the testator delivered all of them at the same time to one James, with instructions that he (James) should keep all of them in his possession until his (the grantor's) death, and thereafter should deliver each deed to the respective grantees therein named; that, pursuant to said instructions, James kept the deeds until the death of the testator and grantor, which occurred on the 26th day of December, 1898, and did thereafter, on the 29th day of December, 1898, deliver each of said deeds to the respective grantees named therein, and that each of said grantees then and there accepted his deed, and still holds the same; that all of said deeds were executed by the grantor without consideration, and were intended by the grantor, and accepted by the several grantees, as gifts, except that the said fifteen-acre tract was intended and accepted as a trust for the use of the grantor; that long before the execution of said deeds the grantor and testator executed a mortgage upon all of said 241 acres to secure to Malone a debt of $2,300, which is the same mortgage set forth in the petition; that prior to said conveyance the testator leased all of said 241 acres to one Robinson for one year from March 1, 1899, for a rental of $665, which the executor has not inventoried as assets; that said testator left real estate in the town of Dana, undisposed of, of the value of $200, and that the fifteen acres conveyed to Elder in trust for the testator's estate is of the value of $750. All the grantees named in said several deeds and the lessee, Robinson, are made parties defendant to the cross complaint, including the executor in his individual capacity.

Prayer, that each of the defendants may be required to answer, and, upon proof of the facts alleged, that the court order that said rental of $665 be inventoried as assets, and that the deficit in the fund created by the personalty, and by the sale of the Dana real estate, and the fifteen acres conveyed to the executor in trust, be assessed and levied ratably upon the lands of the cross complainant, and the lands of the said other grantees, conveyed to them by said several deeds, and that her title be quieted, except as against a ratable proportion of the deficit in the payment of debts and expenses of administration.

Two questions are propounded by the demurrer to the cross complaint: (1) Do the facts exhibited thereby entitle the cross complainant to a decree that the debt deficit is chargeable ratably, according to value, against all the several parcels conveyed by the testator as benefactions, at the same time and upon the same terms, or has the executor the right to have the entire burden of the deficit imposed upon a single parcel, as he may elect? And (2) may the issue be made and determined in a proceeding of this character?

Under the averments of the cross complaint, the conveyances were by the same act, at the same time, and upon the same terms, and the lien of the mortgage and general debts of the estate had equal force and effect against all the 241 acres. The equality of burden was created by the common grantor. It existed at the time the conveyances were made. Each parcel was accepted subject to the mortgage then upon it and the existing rights of creditors. The fraud that will strike down these deeds for the benefit of creditors is but constructive. There was no *mala fides* in any of the grantees, and probably none in the grantor. Exclusive of the mortgage indebtedness, by the application of the $665 of rents contracted for, and the real estate in Dana undisposed of, and the fifteen acres directed to the use of his estate, would probably make the estate clearly solvent. But, aside from all questions of fraud, the fact is clear that all the lands conveyed by said several deeds are held by the grantees impressed in the same way, and to the same extent, by the deficit in the payment of debts. In respect to such situations, " the doctrine is well established that, when !and is charged with a burden, the charge ought to be equal, and one part ought not to bear more than its due proportion, and equity will preserve this equality by compelling the owner of each part to a just contribution." (*Stevens* v. *Cooper,* 1 Johns. Ch. 425. See, also, *Falley* v. *Gribling,* 128 Ind. 110; 26 N. E. 794; *Cook* v. *Cook,* 92 Ind. 398; *Aiken* v. *Gale,* 37 N. H. 501; *Stroud* v. *Casey,* 27 Pa. St. 471; *Beck* v. *Tarrant,* 61 Tex. 40p; *Hall* v. *Morgan,* 79 Mo. 47; *Beall* v. *Barclay,* 10 B. Mon. 261, 265; *Briscoe* v. *Power,* 47 Ill. 447; *Allen* v. *Clark,* 17 Pick. 47; *McLaughlin* v. *Estate of Curts,* 27 Mich. 644.) The approved rule in such cases is that each part, under the common burden, shall stand as principal to the creditor for its proportion of the whole debt, according to the aggregate value of the lands affected, and the other parts stand as its surety; thus securing full protection to the creditor, and natural justice to the several owners. The same equitable principle is embodied in section 2738, Burns' Rev. St. 1894, relating to contribution by devisees and legatees.

If the cross complainant, to save the sale of her land, had paid off the common mortgage debt and the other general debts and expenses of administration, and thus relieved the lands of the other grantees from such charge, there would be no doubt of her right to enforce ratable contribution from all. (*Falley* v. *Gribling, supra;* and other cases cited above.) And this brings us to the second proposition: Is she entitled to her remedy in this proceeding? We think she is. It is the policy of our civil procedure to avoid a multiplicity of suits. By her cross complaint she presents no defense to the executor's petition. She confesses the charge asserted against her land, and asks only that others equally bound may be brought in, and the executor's claim lodged primarily against all those who, in equity and good conscience, ought to pay it. The issue tendered is to co-defendants, and, however determined, will neither delay nor injure the petitioner. He is therefore in no situation to say that in his suit the defendants may not litigate rights and equities among themselves in respect to his demand. The principle involved is analogous though not controlled by section 1226, Burns' Rev. St. 1894, which furnishes sureties " an easy and convenient remedy " to settle in the suit of the payee the question of suretyship among themselves and against the principal. The court has full power, irrespective of statute, sitting as a probate tribunal, to take cognizance of all equitab'e questions arising in such cases, and will so mold its orders and

decrees as will accomplish equity between the parties before it.
(*Galvin* v. *Britton*, 151 Ind. 1, 11; 49 N. E. 1064.) We cannot
agree with appellees' attorneys that all the facts pleaded in the
cross complaint might have been given in evidence under the general denial. The grantees of said several conveyances, other than
appellant, were not made parties to the petition to sell, and, without them being before the court, no question as to them could have
been litigated. Substantially the same facts pleaded in the cross
complaint were set up in the second paragraph of the answer.
These facts constituted no defense to the petition, and the demurrer thereto was properly sustained. For error of the court in sustaining the demurrer to the cross complaint, the cause must be
reversed.

Judgment reversed, with instructions to overrule the demurrer to
the cross complaint.

EUFAULA NATIONAL BANK *vs.* MANASSES.*

[Supreme Court of Alabama, January 18, 1900; 27 So. Rep. 258.]

WILLS—CONSTRUCTION—POWER OF EXECUTORS—EXECUTION—
PROPERTY SUBJECT.

1. A will creating a trust for the maintenance of testator's children, and
   empowering the executor to sell and reinvest the property when deemed
   by him expedient, confers no authority to continue a mercantile business
   of the testator, or to purchase goods for that purpose.
2. Where an executor, without authority to carry on a business of his testator, purchases goods for that purpose, the title to such goods vests in
   him individually, and they are subject to an execution against him.

APPEAL from Circuit Court, Barbour county; J. W. FOSTER,
Judge.

Action by the Eufaula National Bank against L. Manasses,
claimant, as executor of J. Manasses, deceased, of certain property

* Rehearing denied.

levied on as his individual property. From a judgment for claimant, plaintiff appeals.

Reversed.

This was a statutory trial of the right of property, which originated as follows: The appellant, the Eufaula National Bank, recovered a judgment against L. Manasses, and upon this judgment an execution was issued. Said execution was levied upon certain goods and merchandise in the possession of L. Manasses, who, as executor and trustee, interposed a claim to the property levied upon by giving a statutory affidavit and bond; said affidavit reciting that the property levied upon was the property of the estate of J. Manasses, deceased, and that affiant, as executor and trustee of the estate of J. Manasses, deceased, has a just claim to the property levied upon. Upon the trial of this case, after the introduction of the judgment, and the execution thereon, and the return of the sheriff on the execution, showing the levy upon the property involved in the suit, and the testimony of the sheriff as to such levy, the claimant, as a witness for himself, testified that the property in suit did not belong to him individually, but belonged to the estate of J. Manasses; that the said property was used by the claimant as executor and trustee under the will-of J. Manasses, deceased. The said will of J. Manasses, deceased, was introduced in evidence, and was shown to have been duly probated. The first item of the will provided for the payment of the testatrix's just debts. By the second item, the testatrix devised to her two sons, Jacob L. Manasses and August Manasses, all her property, real, personal, and mixed; but it was further provided that they should take the property as provided for in the third item of the will, which item is copied in the opinion. This will was dated December 2, 1891. The evidence for the claimant further tended to show that J. Manasses died in 1891, and that at the time of her death she was engaged in mercantile business; that the claimant continued to carry on said business as executor and trustee under the will, and was so engaged in said business at the time of the levy of the execution in this case, which was on February 11, 1897. The claimant, as a witness in his own behalf, testified that goods were purchased in said business after the death of said testatrix,—some on credit, and some for cash; that checks were drawn on

different banks to pay for said goods, and that money was also borrowed by said claimant to carry on said business; and that, to
secure the loans made at different times, L. Manasses signed said
notes in the name of J. Manasses, and put up as col'ateral notes
and mortgages received in said business. It is not deemed necessary, under the opinion on the present appeal, to set out in detail the
several rulings of the court upon the evidence to which exceptions
were reserved. Upon the introduction of all the evidence, the
plaintiff requested the court to give to the jury the general affirmative charge in its behalf, and duly excepted to the court's refusal to
give said charge as asked. At the request of the claimant, the
court gave the general affirmative charge in his behalf, and to the
giving of this charge the plaintiff duly excepted. There were verdict and judgment for the claimant. The plaintiff appeals, and
assigns as error the several rulings of the trial court to which
exceptions were reserved.

  S. H. Dent, Jr., for appellant.

  G. L. Comer and *G. W. Peach*, for appellee.

  SHARPE, J.—The authority to carry on a business in which a
decedent was engaged at the time of his death does not pass to
his executor or administrator by law. (*Foxworth* v. *White*, 72
Ala. 224; *Steele* v. *Knox*, 10 id. 608.) The power to do so may
be given by will, but it should be unmistakably expressed. (11
Am. & Eng. Enc. Law, 973; *Kirkman* v. *Booth*, 11 Beav. 273;
Burwell v. *Cawood*, 2 How. 560; 11 L. Ed. 378.) If the appellee
had authority in his trust capacity to carry on the mercantile business in which his testatrix was engaged, it must be found in the
third item of the will, which is as follows: " I hereby nominate
and appoint my husband, Leopold Manasses, executor and trustee,
to perform the trust of this will; and I bequeath to him all of my
estate, of every nature and description, of which I shall die seized
and possessed, or to which I shall be entitled to at the time of my
death, in trust, however, for my two sons, that he shall dispose of
the same to the following uses and purposes. And I hereby
authorize and empower him, if, in the performance of his trust,

it becomes, in his judgment, necessary or expedient, to sell at public or private sale, in such manner as he shall deem best for the interest of my said two sons, any part or all of the estate which shall come to his hands, and to invest and to reinvest the proceeds at his discretion. And he is to furnish and expend annually proper amounts for the maintenance and education of my two sons, and, when they arrive at the age of twenty-one, to divide the remainder of my said estate in his hands, after paying my debts, and paying for education and maintenance of my said two sons, between my said two sons, Jacob L. Manasses and August Manasses, equally." Here is created a trust, the main object of which is the maintenance and education of the testatrix's two sons, and the division between them of the property upon their attainment of the age of twenty-one years. The power to sell property and to reinvest is to be exercised only in the event that it should, in the trustee's judgment, become necessary or expedient in the performance of the main trust. Its purpose is to commit to the trustee's discretion the propriety of changing the form of the property, and to empower him to make the change without resorting to a court for authority. The continuance of the mercantile business is nowhere mentioned in the will. Such a business, it is true, involves the sale of goods and the reinvestment in other goods; but it also involves obligations, expenditures, and a degree of attention beyond mere selling and reinvesting. Debts incurred in an authorized business of a trustee may become chargeable against the trust estate, and so endanger its existence. No intention to subject the estate to the uncertain results of a mercantile business is either expressed or implied in this will. The goods in controversy were in no part those left by the decedent, she having died about five years before their acquisition.

Being without authority to carry on the business under the will, the appellant was without capacity, as trustee or executor, to purchase the goods for that purpose. The contract for their purchase bound him only personally, and the title thereby acquired vested in him individually. (*Malone* v. *Kelly*, 54 Ala. 532; *Liddell* v. *Miller*, 86 Ala. 343; 5 South. 571.)

There was error in giving the charge requested by the appellee, and in refusing that asked by the appellant. What we have said of appellee's powers under the will doubtless will determine the result of another trial, and it is unnecessary to notice the assignments of error relating to evidence.

Reversed and remanded.

NOTE.—CONTINUANCE OF BUSINESS OF DECEASED BY EXECUTOR OR ADMINISTRATOR.

(a) General rules.
(b) Intention must be clear.
(c) Continuance in winding up.
(d) Continuance by executor.
(e) By administrator.
(f) Limitation as to responsibility of assets.
(g) Creditors chargeable with notice.
(h) Executor or administrator personally liable.
(i) Relief in equity.
(j) Some illustrative cases.

(a) **General rules.**—Well settled that executors are not authorized to continue the business of their testator unless it clearly appears from the will that such is his intention, and if they do so without authority they do it at their own risk. (Smith v. Preston, 170 Ill. 179, 188; 48 N. E. Rep. 688; Hooper v. Hooper, 29 W. Va. 276; 1 S. E. Rep. 280; Lucht v. Behrens, 28 Ohio St. 231.)

An executor or administrator, not authorized by will or order of the court, no authority to continue business or trade of deceased. (Steele v. Knox, 10 Ala. 608, 613; Thompkins v. Weeks, 26 Cal. 51.)

Well settled rule that the death of a trader generally speaking puts an end to the business in which he was engaged at the time of his death; and ordinarily all that remains for his personal representatives to do is to convert the assets employed in the business into money as speedily as practicable. Rule does not apply when positive direction in will to continue the business. (Saperstein v. Ullman, 49 App. Div. 448; 63 N. Y. Supp. 626.)

(b) **Intention must be clear.**—The intention to confer on executor power to continue trade or business cannot be inferred; it must be expressed in direct, explicit and unequivocal language. (Willis v. Sharp, 113 N. Y. 586; 21 N. E. Rep. 795; and see Kinmouth v. Brigham, 87 Mass. 271; Kirkman v. Booth, 11 Beav. 273; Saperstein v. Ullman, *supra*.)

(c) **Continuance in winding up.**—An executor or administrator is not absolutely bound to make immediate conversion into money of the assets of the estate which were involved in trade. He is at liberty within reasonable limits, to make purchases and incur liabilities, if under the circumstances then existing, that course is demanded by the best interests of the estate. Whether such reasonable limits are exceeded can only be ascertained after investigation. (Matter of Sharp, 5 Dem. 516; and see to same effect Bowker's Estate, 12 Phil. 88; Cornwell v. Deck, 2 Redf. 88 [N. Y.].)

May continue for purpose of winding up. (Collinson v. Lister, 20 Beav. 356.)

Where an executrix did not commence the planting business but it was commenced by her testator, and was in progress at time of his death, and upon her qualification she continued it for the balance of the year, as any prudent, discreet person would have done, for the protection of the interest of the estate, *held*, that she was not chargeable with loss sustained. (Lawton v. Fish, 51 Ga. 647; and see Succession of Worley, 40 La. Ann. 622.) And a claim for money or goods advanced for the purpose to the executor or administrator is a claim against the estate. (Reinstein v. Smith, 65 Tex. 247; compare Succession of Sparrow, 39 La. Ann. 696; 2 So. Rep. 501.)

An executor who continued a school for eleven weeks, until end of school year, is not chargeable with losses resulting from such continuance. (Gilman v. Wilber, 1 Dem. 548.)

(d) **Continuance by executor.**—Discretion in executor conferred by deceased in continuing his business, will not be interfered with by the court unless there is good cause. (Re Rumsey's Will, 18 N. Y. Supp. 403; 63 Hun, 635 [memo. only, opinion not printed]; and see Tierney v. Tierney, 38 Atl. Rep. 971 [N. J.].) ·

When authority is conferred by will, estate is bound to indemnify the executor on account of debts properly incurred in carrying on the business. (Foxworth v. White, 72 Ala. 224.)

Where under authority in the will business is continued in name of the " Froelich Trading Company " by the executor, it was held that a judgment on a claim arising after death of testator should not be against the estate, but against the executor personally, and against the trading company represented by him. (Froelich v. Froelich Trading Co., 120 N. C. 39; 26 S. E. Rep. 647.)

Where will expressly authorizes continuance of the business of testator, in the discretion of the executors, upon settlement of their accounts, losses by bad debts, and costs and expenses incidental to carrying on such business, were properly charged against and deducted from the income payable to life tenant. (Matter of Jones, 103 N. Y. 621; 9 N. E. Rep. 493.)

Under such circumstances losses sustained as result of business risk are not chargeable to the executor. (Cline's Appeal, 106 Pa. St. 618; and see Boulle v. Tompkins, 5 Redf. 472 [N. Y.]; Allen v. Shanks, 90 Tenn. 361; 16 S. W. Rep. 715; Merritt v. Merritt, 62 Mo. 151.)

(e) **By administrator.**—Where an administrator carries on business of deceased, he does so at his own risk, and though he must account for all profits received, he must bear all losses; and liabilities growing out of his management are not claims against the estate, though he may pay them out of the increase of the business, if not resulting in loss to the estate. If charged in his account with gross receipts, he should be credited with expenses. (Re Rose, 80 Cal. 166; 22 Pac. Rep. 86; and see Matter Prescott, 1 Tuck. 430 [N. Y.].)

But the fact that two sons were the administrators of their father's estate, does not prevent them from continuing their father's business as individuals. (Matter of Mullon, 145 N. Y. 98; 39 N. E. Rep. 821.)

Where statute authorizes continuance of business for a limited period, administrator acts at his own peril beyond that and is chargeable accordingly. (King v. Johnson, 96 Ga. 497; 23 S. E. Rep. 500.)

And see a case where statute authorized executor or administrator to procure labor to be performed in connection with continuance of farming on plantation. (Powell v. Powell, 23 Mo. App. 365.)

An administrator may be allowed for what he has spent in good faith by request of *all* parties in interest, in carrying on business of intestate after his death. (Poole v. Munday, 103 Mass. 174.)

But such consent must be obtained in entire good faith upon full, fair and correct representations and information; there must be no deceit. (Ward v. Tinkham, 65 Mich. 696; 32 N. W. Rep. 901.)

An administrator has no authority in partnership affairs, except to call upon the surviving partner to close up the same and account to him. (Tompkins v. Weeks, 26 Cal. 51.)

Where business is continued by administrator it is at his individual risk and is his individual business, although he is obliged to credit the estate with all profits. (Estate of Munzor, 4 Misc. 374; 25 N. Y. Supp. 818; and see Shinn's Estate, 166 Pa. St. 121; 30 Atl. Rep. 1026, 1030.)

Carrying on of a farm is no part of an administrator's duties. (Hallock v. Smith, 50 Conn. 127.)

Nor to continue manufacture of machines under an executory contract, further than completing what was unfinished at time of intestate's death. (Pitts v. Jameson, 15 Barb. 316; and see Collinson v. Lister, 20 Beav. 365.)

(f) **Limitation as to responsibility of assets.**—Direction in a will that the business shall be continued, does not render liable to subsequent creditors that part of the estate not invested in the business, unless it should certainly appear in the will that testator so intended. (Brasfield v. French, 59 Miss. 632; and to same effect Del., L. & W. R. Co. v. Gilbert, 44 Hun. 201; aff'd 112 N. Y. 673; 20 N. E. Rep. 416; Willis v. Sharp, 113 N. Y. 586; 21 N. E. Rep. 705 [the opinion in this case contains a valuable review of the cases]; Stewart v. Robinson, 115 N. Y. 336; 22 N. E. Rep. 160, 163; Hardee v. Cheatham, 52 Miss. 48; Ferry v. Laible, 27 N. J. Eq. 146: Davis v. Christian, 15 Gratt. 11; compare Blodgett v. American National Bank, 49 Conn. 24; Laughlin v. Lorenz, 48 Pa. St. 275, 283; and see Jones v. Walker, 103 U. S. 444; Frey v. Eisenhardt, 116 Mich. 160; 74 N. W. Rep. 501; Re Gorton, L. R. 40 Ch. Div. 536; Re Johnson, 15 id. 548.)

It is not within the ordinary authority of a Probate Court to empower an administrator to continue the mercantile business of the deceased. An executor may continue such business when empowered to do so by the will, but he becomes personally liable for all the debts he contracts, and so does an administrator. But either may be entitled to credit for proper expenditures. Where advances are made by an administrator for the purpose under authority of an order of the Probate Court and credit extended by those who give him credit, upon the faith of the assets embarked in the trade or business, their remedies are confined to such assets. (Altheimer v. Hunter, 56 Ark. 159; 19 S. W. Rep. 496.)

(g) **Creditors chargeable with notice.**—Persons dealing with an ex·ecutor in connection with continuance of business of a deceased member of a firm, are chargeable with notice of any misapplication of the funds of the estate, where the will confers no authority. (Appeal of First National Bank, 7 Atl. Rep. 207 [Pa.].) And that persons dealing with executor are bound to look to the will to ascertain his authority. (See Matter of Sharp, 5 Dem. 520; Hardee v. Cheatham, 52 Miss. 48; Smith v. Ayer, 101 U. S. 320.)

(h) **Executor or administrator personally liable.**—Notwithstanding express authority in the will for continuation of the business, the executor becomes personally responsible for all debts contracted by him on account of it and suit cannot be maintained against him in his representative capacity. (Del., L. & W. R. Co. v. Gilbert, 44 Hun, 201; aff'd 112 N. Y. 673; 20 N. E. Rep. 416; Willis v. Sharp, 113 N. Y. 591; 21 N. E. Rep. 705; Sterrett v. Barker, 119 Cal. 492; 51 Pac. Rep. 695; and see Hallock v. Smith, 50 Conn. 127; Matter of Sharp, 5 Dem. 518 [N. Y.]; Re Morgan. L. R. 18 Ch. Div. 93; Austin v. Munro, 47 N. Y. 366; Re Johnson, L. R. 15 Ch. Div. 548; Laible v. Ferry, 23 N. J. Eq. 791.)

(i) **Relief in equity.**—But notwithstanding the personal liability of the executor where he continues business of testator under authority in the will, where the executor is or becomes *insolvent,* a creditor may have relief in equity as against the estate. (Willis v. Sharp, *supra.*)

As to remedy in equity. (See Wade v. Pope, 44 Ala. 690; Ferry v. Laible, 27 N. J. Eq. 146.)

Remedy of creditor in equity—subrogation. (Foxworth v. White, 72 Ala. 224; Re Gorton, L. R. 40 Ch. Div. 536; Re Johnson, L. R. 15 Ch. Div. 548; Re Evans, 34 id. 597.)

And see as to remedy in *equity.* (Fairland v. Percy, L. R. 3 P. & D. 217; Laible v. Ferry, 32 N. J. Eq. 791.)

In Owen v. Delamere (L. R. 15 Eq. Cas. 134), it was *held* that a creditor could not proceed against the estate in equity; his remedy was an action at law against the executor.

(j) **Some illustrative cases.**—Distinction between powers of an executor as such and as a trustee under the will. (O'Brien v. Jackson, 42 App. Div. 173; 58 N. Y. Supp. 1044.)

Court will refuse any authority to administrator to carry on or continue business where there are infants interested in the estate. (Land v. Land, 43 L. J. Eq. N. S. 311.)

Where executors are obliged to sue to recover·on a claim accrued in the business conducted by them under authority in the will, the moneys recoverable, being assets of the estate, they may sue as executors. (Abbott v. Parfitt, L. R. 6 Q. B. Cas. 346.)

Where an executor who is authorized by a will to continue the business, does so, incurring debts, and then dies himself, it *seems* the remedy of a creditor must be first obtained through administration of the estate of the deceased executor unless insolvent. (Fairland v. Percy, L. R. 3 P. & D. 217.)

Where executor carries on testator's business with assent either express or implied of the testator's creditors, he is entitled in priority to the testator's creditors to be indemnified; this is true where a receiver has been appointed to succeed the executor, and whether the will does or does not contain a direction to carry on the business. (Re Brooke [1894], 2 Ch. 600.)

In re ANDREWS' WILL.

[Court of Appeals of New York, February 27, 1900; 162 N. Y. 1; 56 N. E. Rep. 529.]

WILLS—EXECUTION.

1. A will offered for probate was drawn on a printed blank, folded in the middle so as to constitute four pages; the connection between them being at the left side, and not at the top or bottom. Clauses in writing, following a printed introduction, occupied all of the first page. On the next page, or the reverse side of the first, were printed forms for appointment of executors, testimonium and attestation clauses, and blanks for signatures, all of which were properly filled in, in writing. At the top of what would ordinarily be termed the third page were the words "2nd page," followed by additional clauses in writing to the end of the page. All the matter on such page could have been written after the execution of the instrument, as no sentence thereon was continued from the first page, or carried therefrom to page No. 3. At the top of the page on which the signatures of the testator and witnesses were subscribed were the words "3rd page." *Held*, that the will was not subscribed at its end, as required by the statute, and was therefore not entitled to probate.

2. Nor could pages Nos. 1 and 3 be treated as a complete will, and the matter on page No. 2 incorporated therein by reference.

APPEAL from Supreme Court, Appellate Division, Second Department.

Application for the probate of the will of Isabella Andrews, deceased. From an order of the Appellate Division affirming a decree of the surrogate (60 N. Y. Supp. 141) rejecting the will, proponents appeal.

Affirmed.

Geo. G. Reynolds and *Armour C. Anderson,* for appellants.

Frederic W. Adee, for respondents.

BARTLETT, J.—This case comes before us under circumstances so unusual that a few words of comment may not be out of place. The surrogate of Kings county refused probate to the will we are about to consider, on the ground that it was not subscribed at the end thereof, as required by the statute of wills (2 Rev. St. 63, §40; 2 Rev. St. [Banks & Bros. 9th ed.] 1877). In so doing, he followed the settled law of this court for years, and many well-reasoned English cases, when construing a statute similar to our own. (1 Vict. ch. 26.) The learned Appellate Division affirmed the surrogate's decree with a divided court, giving utterance at the same time to a protest both emphatic and unanimous. The opinion states that the conclusion reached was solely under the stress of authority, and that, unaided by the light of judicial decisions, a contrary result would have followed. One of the dissenting justices stated that, while he recognized the principle of *stare decisis,* cases sometimes arise when a judge is justified in refusing to follow a decision of the court of last resort. The other dissenting justice wrote an opinion in which he succeeded in reaching the conclusion that neither the statute of wills, nor the cases which had compelled the majority of his brethren to reluctantly affirm the surrogate's decree, called for any such result. As the opinion of the Appellate Division concedes that the question presented is not an open one in this court, we might well content ourselves with an affirmance of the judgment, did we not feel constrained by judicial courtesy to re-examine the legal situation that has been so pointedly called to our attention.

It has long been the settled policy of this state to require certain formalities to be observed in the execution of wills. These provisions are exceedingly simple, and calculated to prevent frauds and uncertainty in the testamentary dispositions of property. (*In re O'Neil's Will*, 91 N. Y. 520; *Willis v. Lowe*, 5 Notes Cas. 428.) 2 Rev. St. 63, § 40 (2 Rev. St. [Banks & Bro.'s 9th ed.] 1877), reads as follows: " Every last will and testament of real or personal property, or both, shall be executed and attested in the following manner: (1) It shall be subscribed by the testator at the end of the will. (2) Such subscription shall be made by the testator, in the presence of each of the attesting witnesses, or shall be acknowledged by him, to have been so made, to each of the attesting witnesses. (3) The testator, at the time of making such subscription, or at the time of acknowledging the same, shall declare the instrument so subscribed, to be his last will and testament. (4) There shall be at least two attesting witnesses, each of whom shall sign his name as a witness, at the end of the will, at the request of the testator." These are the only restrictions imposed upon a testator when executing his will, and they appear to be wise, reasonable, and easily understood. It has been repeatedly laid down as the rule in this state, in cases we shall presently discuss, that the intention of the testator is not to be considered when construing this statute, but that of the legislature. The question is not what did the testator intend to do? but what has he done in the light of the statute? It is undoubtedly true that from time to time an honest attempt to execute a last will and testament is defeated by failure to observe some one or more of the statutory requirements. It is better this should happen under a proper construction of the statute, than that the individual case should be permitted to weaken those provisions calculated to protect testators generally from fraudulent alterations of their wills.

It may be well, before examining the will which is the subject of this appeal, to refer to a few of the cases which construe the provision of the statute requiring the testator and the witnesses to subscribe at the end of the will. In *Sisters of Charity v. Kelly* (67 N. Y. 409), it was held that the provision of the statute requiring the testator to subscribe " at the end of the will " means the end of the instrument as a completed whole, and where the name is written in the body of the instrument, with any material portion following the signature, it is not properly subscribed, nor can it be claimed that the portion preceding the signature is valid as a will. *In re O'Neil's Will* (91 N. Y. 516), a printed blank was used, and the formal commencement was printed on the first page, and the formal termination printed at the foot of the third page. The entire blank space was filled with writing, and, apparently for want of room, a portion of a paragraph containing material provisions was carried over to, and the paragraph finished at, the top of the fourth page. The two portions were not, however, sought to be connected by means of a reference, or anything indicating their relation to each other. The name of the testator was written at the end of the printed form, and the names of the witnesses written below the formal attestation clause on the third page. This court held that there was no legal subscription of the will, and affirmed the judgment denying probate. Chief Judge RUGER, who wrote the opinion of the court, said: " While the primary rule governing the interpretation of wills, when admitted to probate, recognizes and endeavors to carry out the intention of the testator, that rule cannot be invoked in the construction of the statute regulating their execution. In the latter case courts do not consider the intention of the testator, but that of the legislature. * * * The statute fixes an inflexible rule by which to determine the proper execution of all testamentary instruments. * * * It will be seen in all of the cases cited there was no reason to doubt the testator's intention to make a valid disposition of his property, and yet in each case the will was denied probate because in the execution thereof the testator did not conform to the provisions of the statute, in failing to place his signature at the physical end of the will." *In re Conway* (124 N. Y. 455; 26 N. E. 1028; 11 L. R. A. 796), a blank form was used, the whole of which was upon one side of the paper. A space was left for the dispositions to be made, preceded by the words, " I give, devise, and bequeath my property as follows." The blank space was filled up by three complete devises. At the end of the last were underlined, in parentheses, the words, " Carried to back of will." Upon the back of the sheet was written the word " Continued." Following it were various bequests, and then the words, " Signature on face of the will." The signature of the testator appeared at the end of the testimonium clause on the face of the paper, and those of the witnesses under the attestation clause. It was held by the Second Division of this court that there was not such a subscription and signing by the testator as required by the statute, and that the will had been improperly admitted to probate. Judge PARKER, in delivering the opinion of the court, said: " The aim of the statute is to prevent fraud; to surround testamentary dispositions with such safeguards as will protect them from alteration." The learned judge also declared, in substance, that the admitted intention of the testator that the provisions appearing on the page following his signature should form a part of his will would in no way affect the question before the court. *In re Whitney's Will* (153 N. Y. 259; 47 N. E. 272), it was held that a will drawn upon a printed blank, covering only one page, and signed by the testator and subscribing witnesses at the foot of the page, is not subscribed by the testator at the end of the will, as required by the statute, when the blank space in the printed form is filled up by subdivisions marked, respectively, " First " and " Second," followed by the words " See annexed sheet," and additional subdivisions marked, respectively, " Third " and " Fourth," are written on a separate piece of paper attached to the face of the blank, immediately over the first and second subdivisions, by removable metal staples. It was held that the question presented was not an open one in this court, and that the will was not legally subscribed. The court again approved the doctrine that the existence of good faith did not affect the question pending, as the intention of the legislature, and not that of the testator, governed. *In re Blair's Will* (84 Hun, 581; 32 N. Y. Supp. 845), this court affirmed the judgment of the General Term, First Department, on the opinion below, which reversed a decree of the Surrogate's Court admitting the will to probate. This instrument consisted of eight pages. The testator signed at the bottom of the seventh page, and the witnesses signed at the end of a proper witnessing clause at the top of the eighth page. After the place for the signatures of the witnesses, but before they were actually signed or the will executed, a clause was added directing the executor to sell at private sale a certain piece of real estate, and to devote the proceeds of sale to liquidating any deficiency in interest or cash bequests under the will. The will was then executed, as before stated, and the testator signed the added clause, but the witnesses did not. (152 N. Y. 645; 46 N. E. 1145.) In each of the cases cited it was very clear that the will was not legally subscribed, and that to have admitted it to probate, by yielding to the suggestion that it was an honest attempt to make a will, would have been a practical repeal of the statute as to subscription at the end of the instrument. Our present statute of wills, requiring that a will should be subscribed at the end thereof, is similar to 1 Vict. ch. 26, which was in force in England from 1837 until 1853, when it was amended by 15 & 16 Vict. ch. 24, known as " Lord St. Leonard's Act." Prior to this amendment the English courts construed the act as strictly as our own have the present statute of wills. (*Willis* v. *Lowe,* 5 Notes Cas. 428; *In re Parslow,* id. 112; *in re Tookey,* id. 386; *Ayres* v. *Ayres,* id. 375; *Sweetland* v. *Sweetland,* 4 Swab. & T. 6; *Smee* v. *Bryer,* 6 Moore, P. C. 404.) In the latter case, Lord LANGDALE, delivering the opinion of the court, said at page 411: " It may happen, even frequently, that genuine wills, namely, wills truly expressing the intentions of the testators, are made without observation of the required forms; and whenever that happens the genuine intention is frustrated by the act of the legislature, of which the general object is to give effect to the intention. The courts must consider that the legislature, having regard to all probable circumstances, has thought it best, and has therefore determined, to run the risk of frustrating the intentions sometimes, in preference to the risk of giving effect to or facilitating the formation of spurious wills, by the absence of forms. It is supposed, and that authoritatively, that the evil of defeating the intention in some cases, by requiring forms, is less than the evil probably to arise by giving validity to wills made without any form in all cases." The reasoning of our own and the English courts find support in two states where the statute of wills is substantially the same as in New York. (*Hays* v. *Harden,* 6 Pa. St. 409; *Glancy* v. *Glancy,* 17 Ohio St. 134.)

We come, then, in view of the law as it now stands, to the will before us. The testatrix was an unmarried woman, aged about sixty years. She left her surviving, no nearer relatives than first and second cousins. No part of her estate is given to any relative. A stranger to her blood is sole executor. The will is in his handwriting, and the proceeds of sale of testatrix's house and lot in Brooklyn are given one-half to him, and one-half divided equally between two religious societies. In addition to this the testatrix gave eight money bequests,—four to religious societies and a cemetery, and the others to persons not of her blood. These bequests aggregate about $4,200. The residuary clause is as follows: "The rest, residue, and remainder of my estate I give unto my executor, to make disposition of and divide in such manner as he, in his judgment, may deem best and proper." No undue influence is charged. The estate is estimated at about $15,000. The will was drawn on a printed blank, being one piece of paper, consisting of a sheet of four pages, the two leaves of which were joined from top to bottom on the left side. The formal opening part of the will is printed on the top of the first page, leaving the rest of that page blank. The closing part, containing the clause for the appointment of the executor, and that which follows, including the attestation clause, was printed on the top of the second page of the first leaf, leaving the rest of that page and both pages of the second leaf blank. The draftsman filled the blank on the first page, and then turned to the first page of the second leaf, being the third page of the blank, and filled that, marking it at the top "2nd page." He then turned to the second page of the first leaf, containing the closing part of the will as before stated, in print, marked it at the top "3rd page," and completed the instrument, save as to its execution, by filling the blanks at the top of that page, except the blank for the date, which was left to be filled in at the time of execution. It is to be observed that a complete will was made out on the two sides of the first leaf, being the first and second pages of the blank. All of the first side of the third leaf, marked "2nd page," could have been written after execution, as no sentence thereof is continued from the first page of the will, nor carried over to the alleged third page thereof. The fourth page of the blank could have been written over in the same way. The first page of the will contains the money legacies, the direction to sell the real estate and divide the proceeds, and two legacies of personal property. The alleged second page of the will contains bequests of personal property and the residuary clause. We have here on one entire piece of paper, folded so as to make four pages, a complete will, so far as form goes, on the first and second pages; and then follows on the third page of the blank, and after the signatures of testatrix and witnesses on the second page of the blank, a page marked "2nd page," not connected with the will proper in any way, but complete by itself. The question is not whether, from the proofs in this case, the page following the signatures of the will is in fact a part of testatrix's will, by reason of her established intention, but, is the instrument so drawn subscribed at the end thereof, as the statute commands? We are of opinion that it is not legally subscribed, and that to hold otherwise would open the door to gross fraud, and be contrary to the statute and the settled law. It was suggested on the argument of this case that the effect of the statute of wills, as strictly construed by this court, is to defeat the intention of many testators, while the fraudulent addition to wills was a crime of rare occurrence. The fallacy of this argument consists in overlooking the fact that the number of frauds prevented by our wise and simple statute can never be known. We might as well ask how many commercial crimes have been prevented by the statute of frauds. The case at bar is one of the strongest illustrations of the wisdom of the statute of wills that has ever come to the attention of this court. With a complete will on the first and second pages of a blank containing four pages, there is nothing to prevent filling up the vacant third and fourth pages with any number of additional provisions, including as in this case, a residuary clause allowing an executor to dispose of the residue in such manner as he deemed proper. The defeat of testamentary intention in a few cases is not due to the statute, or the construction of it by the courts, but to the fact that scriveners and other laymen, ignorant of the simple and clear provisions of the statute are permitted to draw wills.

It is urged with much ability by the learned senior counsel for the appellants that the alleged second page of this will can be read into it by invoking the doctrine of incorporation as established in England, and to some extent in this state. We are of opinion that under the facts here disclosed that doctrine has no application. If it were otherwise, the evasion of the statute would be so easily accomplished as to render its repeal unnecessary.

We have to say in conclusion that it is quite possible we have given to this appeal undue importance, involving, as it does, a question of law settled in this court; but we desire to express in the most emphatic manner our approval of the statute of wills as now construed. The order appealed from should be affirmed, with costs to respondent and special guardian, to be paid out of the estate.

PARKER, C. J., and GRAY, O'BRIEN, HAIGHT, MARTIN, and VANN, JJ., concur.
Order affirmed.

In re LUDWIG'S ESTATE.

HAACK *et al. vs.* TOBIN.

[Supreme Court of Minnesota, February 7, 1900; 81 N. W. Rep. 758.]

WILL—EXECUTION—ATTESTATION—EVIDENCE.

1. A last will and testament, not executed in conformity with the requirements of section 4426, Gen. St. 1894, is invalid.
2. A last will and testament must be signed by the testator in the presence of the subscribing witnesses, or, if not so signed, the testator must acknowledge to such witnesses that the signature thereto attached is his, or in some other way clearly and unequivocally indicate to them that the will about to be signed by them as witnesses is his last will, and has been signed by him.
3. To "attest" the execution of a will, within the meaning of section 4426, Gen. St. 1894, is to witness and observe the execution and signing thereof by the testator, or to be expressly and clearly informed by the testator, before signing as witness, that he has signed and executed it.
4. Evidence recited in the opinion *held* sufficient to justify a finding by the trial court that the will in question was not executed as required by statute.

(Syllabus by the court.)

APPEAL from District Court, Ramsey county; OLIN B. LEWIS, Judge.

In the matter of the estate of Kate Ludwig, deceased. Eliza Haack and Fannie Gessard filed objections to probate of will. From a judgment of the District Court affirming an order denying a motion for a new trial, J. J. Tobin appeals.
Affirmed.

J. F. George, for appellant.

C. N. Bell and *Geo. E. Budd,* for respondents.

BROWN, J.—This is an appeal by J. J. Tobin from a judgment of the District Court of Ramsey county affirming an order of the Probate Court of the same county refusing the probate of the will of Kate Ludwig, and also from an order denying his motion for a new trial. It appears from the record that Kate Ludwig, at the time of her death, in July, 1898, was a widow without children, leaving surviving her, as next of kin, three sisters and the children of a deceased brother. She owned certain real and personal property at the time of her death, and attempted, at least, to dispose of it by her last will and testament. Some time after her death the appellant, J. J. Tobin, who is in no way related to the deceased, filed with the Probate Court what purports to be her last will and testament, and petitioned that it be allowed and probated. Due notice of his petition was given, and at the time set for hearing the next of kin of deceased above named appeared, and opposed the will; claiming that it had not been executed in conformity to law, and for other reasons not necessary to be stated. The Probate Court rejected the will, on the ground that it was not shown to have been executed in accordance with the requirements of the statute on the subject. The District Court, on appeal, came to the same conclusion, and this appeal is the result. To prove the execution of the will, appellant called one Shire, who testified that some time in February, 1897, the deceased requested him to draw a will for her to execute; that he did so, drawing and preparing it in accordance with her directions, and delivered it to her for execution. The subscribing witnesses were then called, and testified as follows, omitting portions of the evidence not material, to wit: Mrs. Clara Eggert: "Did you know Kate Ludwig? A. Yes, sir. Q. Did she ever speak to you about making a will? A. One time she spoke to me about making a will. Q: About when was that? A. A short time before she asked us to sign the will,—asked us into her house to sign the will. A short time before that she spoke to us about making a will, and asked us if we would be willing—my husband and I—to sign it, and I said, 'I guess so.' Q. To sign it as witnesses, do you mean? A. Yes, sir. Q. When did she next speak to you about it? A. The next time she spoke to us about it was the day that she came in, and said she was ready for us to sign. Q. Her will? A. I don't remember. I can't say positively whether she mentioned the word 'will' or not, but she spoke to us before about her will; yes. Q. She came in, and asked you— What did she say the second time? A. She gave me to understand that she was ready for us to sign, but whether she used the word 'my will' I don't remember that, but I understood that it was her will, because before she had asked us to sign her will. Q. You went into her house with your husband then, did you? A. Went into her house with my husband. Q. Do you remember how you went in there? A. We went from the little hall through the parlor, into the dining-room, and she had on her dining-room table a pen and ink stand, and paper covered over, as she said, her will, and she sat down to the table, took the pen and ink, and sat down to the table; but I couldn't see what she was doing, whether she was writing, or what she did; I can't say. Q. Did you see her do anything? A. I saw her hand move, but I didn't know what she was doing. Q. Why didn't you know? A. Well, it didn't impress me that she was writing. Q. Where were you sitting from her? A. I was sitting— Well, just as though I sat a little further back from this gentleman, right here. Q. You sat behind her? You could see the pen in her hand? A. I could see the pen in her hand. Q. And did you see her make any motion? A. I saw her go through motions, yes, as though she were writing, but it didn't impress me that she was writing at the time. Q. What did she then do, if anything? A. She then got up, and handed the pen to my husband, and he sat down, and wrote his name, and then I sat down, and wrote mine beneath it. Q. Is the paper presented to you now, the will proposed in this case, the paper which was on the table that you refer to? A. I can't say whether it is the paper, as I didn't see the paper. It was all covered up, excepting the two lines, where we wrote our names. Q. Is that your signature on that paper? A. Yes, sir; that is my signature. Q. Did you observe any other writing on the paper at that time? A. No, sir; I did not; it was all covered up with a sheet of paper. * * * The only thing I saw was my husband's name. Q. There was nothing visible to you on that paper except your husband's name? A. That was all I could see." Cross-examined: " Q. With the exception of your husband's name and your own name, did you see any writing then on the paper that you and your husband signed in Mrs. Ludwig's house? A. No, sir; none that I can think of,—none whatever. Q. Is there any writing on the paper except what you and your husband wrote, so far as you know? A. I don't know, because it was covered up. Q. If there was any, you didn't see it? If there was any writing on the paper, except your husband's name and your name, you didn't see it? A. No, sir. Q. Now, Mrs. Eggert, you have no interest in this one way or the other? A. None whatever. Q. Did Mrs. Ludwig say anything to you after you got into the house? A. All she said after we had signed the will was, 'Well, you both know that I am not crazy.' That is all she said. Q. Well, after she had finished at the table, * * * did she say anything to you? A. She just handed the pen to my husband. I don't know that she said anything. I didn't pay any particular attention to it. Q. She made no remark whether she was signing her will? A. No, sir. Q. After she got up, didn't she say that, 'I have signed this instrument; this is my will; I want you to witness it'? A. No, sir." Fred C. Eggert, the other subscribing witness, testified: "Q. What did you observe when you went into the house? A. Went into the house in the hall, and the front room, through the archway, and on the dining-room table, I guess it was, I seen this instrument there,—paper, and the pen and ink. She stepped forward, picked up the pen, went across the paper, and motioned on the paper, as I understood, to show me where to sign. Then I stepped forward to sign my name, and I then handed the pen to my wife, and she signed. Q. Did she ask you then to sign? A. Not in her house; she asked that in my house. Q. She took up the pen, and motioned over the paper, and she got up, and handed you the pen, did she? A. Yes. Q. Did you see whether she was signing or writing or not? A. No. I see, as soon as I went towards the table, I see that it was blank, and covered up,—saw it was covered up, to keep it secret,—and I stepped back, and she motioned, and I stepped forward, and I signed it. Q. You thought she didn't want you to see? A. I saw it was a secret; therefore I didn't read anything; wouldn't question to sign anything, but I trusted to Mrs. Ludwig's honesty. I trusted to her honesty that that was what she wanted us to sign. Q. What was? A. The will. Q. What makes you think it was the will she wanted you to sign? A. Because she asked us previous. Q. Did she say anything else to you about that, why she wanted you to sign a will or anything? A. Not to me. My wife,—she mentioned something to my wife, and she told me. Q. When you came to sign, did you have to open the will to sign it? A. No, sir. Q. Was there anything else visible there? A. No. Q. Didn't you see any writing at all? A. No, sir. Q. Upon the paper? A. No, sir. Q. Was the bracket and the word 'Witnesses' there afterwards? A. Not to the best of my memory. I didn't see any writing. Q. Of any kind whatever? A. No, sir. Q. Except your own signature and your wife's signature. You say that, after you and your wife got into the house there, you found the paper on the table. Did she prepare it there before you came in, apparently? A. It was all prepared. It was that way—found it that way—when we came in. Q. And all she said to you, as I understand, while you were there in the house, was, after you had signed and your wife had signed, she then says ' Now, you both see that I am not crazy?' A. That is all that was said by her. Q. Could you see the paper all the time from the time that you went in there? A. Oh, yes; yes, sir. Q. Did you see where she put the pen on the paper? A. Not exactly. I seen about where she placed it. She motioned on that paper when we signed it. Q. When you came into the dining-room, did she sit down at the table? A. Yes, sir. Q. Did you see her take the pen in her hand? A. Yes, sir. Q. Did you see her dip it in the ink? A. No, sir. Q. You saw her take the pen in her hand? A. Yes, sir. Q. Where did you stand with reference to where she was? A. I was away probably three or four feet. Q. She was sitting at the table? A. Yes. Q. You were looking at her in a casual way, were you? A. Yes, in a way, not in an interested way. She sat down, and made a motion just a moment, and got up. Q. Do I understand you to say that in making that motion your idea was that she intended to show you where to sign? A. Yes. Q. While she was sitting there at the table? A. Yes. Q. You didn't see her signature? A. No. Q. Or write? A. No, sir. Q. Did you see her cover the paper or uncover the paper? A. No, sir." Other witnesses, familiar with the handwriting of Mrs. Ludwig, testified that the signature to the will was, in their opinion, written by her. The will leaves the entire estate of the testatrix, with the exception of a few minor bequests, to Tobin, who was in no way related to her, but had occupied a room in her house for a few years prior to her death.

The question presented to this court is whether the finding of the trial court that the will was not executed as required by law is justified by the evidence, or whether such finding is so clearly against the evidence as to justify a reversal.   The particular point made by respondents against the sufficiency of the evidence is that the subscribing witnesses to the will did not attest its execution; that they did not see the testatrix sign the same, neither did they see her signature, nor know that she had signed it, when they attached their names; neither did she say or declare that she had signed it, or that the particular paper was her will.   At the time the witnesses attached their names, the paper or will was entirely concealed from their view.   It was entirely covered with another paper.   Does this evidence sufficiently show an attestation by the witnesses of the execution of the will?   Does it show a compliance with the statute?   Our statutes on the subject of the execution of wills must be strictly pursued and complied with.   (*Waite* v. *Frisbie*, 45 Minn. 361; 47 N. W. 1069.)   The section pertinent to the question under consideration is as follows: " No will * * * shall be effectual to pass any estate, real or personal, * * * unless it is in writing, and signed at the end thereof, by the testator, or by some person in his presence and by his express direction, and attested and subscribed in his presence by two or more competent witnesses. * * *" A great variety of decisions are to be found in the books, both in England and in this country, construing and expounding statutes similar to this, and in one respect they are nearly uniform, and that is that the requirements of the statutes must be followed and complied with, with reasonable strictness.   Any substantial departure, in the manner of the execution of the will, from the requisites laid down by the statutes, renders the will void.   The proponent of a will for probate has the burden of proof to show its due execution.   In this case Tobin presented the will for probate, and the heirs and next of kin of the testatrix opposed it.   The burden was on the proponent to prove that the will was executed in accordance with the statutes.   (*In re Layman's Will*, 40 Minn. 371; 42 N. W. 286.)   There is a very marked distinction between " attesting " and " subscribing " a will.   It is very clearly pointed out by ROBERTSON, C. J., in *Swift* v. *Wiley* (1 B. Mon. 114): " As the statute requires two witnesses to the publication of a will disposing of real estate, the paper subscribed by the witnesses must, of course, be completed as a legal will at the time of the attestation. To attest the publication of a paper as the last will, and to subscribe to that paper the names of the witnesses, are very different things, and are required for obviously distinct and different ends. Attestation is the act of the senses; subscription is the act of the hand. The one is mental, the other mechanical; and to attest the will is to know that it is published as such, and to certify the facts required to constitute an actual and legal publication, but to subscribe a paper published as a will is only to write on the same paper the names of the witnesses, for the sole purpose of identification. There may be a perfect attestation, in fact, without subscription." And we may add to this that there may be a subscription in fact without attestation. The Kentucky statute is identical with that of this state. It requires the will to be "attested and subscribed by three or more witnesses." We find the rule to be uniform, so far as our examination of the adjudged cases has extended, in all the states of this country having a statute similar to ours, and in England under the statute of frauds substantially the same, that to constitute a legal and valid attestation the testator must either sign the will in the presence of the witnesses, or acknowledge his signature to them, or in some other way clearly and unequivocally indicate to them that he has signed and executed the same. Otherwise, the witnesses attest nothing. In this case the will was not signed in the presence of the witnesses, they did not know that it had been signed by the testatrix, nor did she indicate to them in any way that she had signed it. She kept the entire paper from their view, and they saw nothing except their own signature. On this subject, see Schouler, Wills ([2d ed.], 330); *Swift* v. *Wiley* (1 B. Mon. 114); *Reed* v. *Watson* (27 Ind. 443); Cassoday, Wills (§ 114 *et seq.*); id. (§ 133 *et seq.*); 1 Jarm. Wills ([6th ed.], 113); *Chase* v. *Kittredge* (11 Allen 9); *In re Will of Mackay* (110 N. Y. 611; 18 N. E. 433; 1 L. R. A. 491); *Simmons* v. *Leonard* (91 Tenn. 183; 18 S. W. 280); *Chisholm's Heirs* v. *Ben* (7 B. Mon. 409); *Lewis* v. *Lewis* (11 N. Y. 220); *Combs* v. *Jolly* (3 N. J. Eq. 625; 29 Am. & Eng. Enc. Law, 209, and notes). A will is the solemn disposition of one's property, to take effect after death. We do not lose sight of the sacredness or sanctity of such an act, or of the right of the person to so dispose of his property. Such right to be upheld, and wills properly executed will be sustained, regardless of the particular disposition of the property of the testator. But we must not lose sight of or overlook the fact that the right to dispose of one's property in that manner is purely statutory. And, to be effectual, the statutory requirements must be complied with.

In the light of the authorities above cited, and the law as we believe it to be, we hold that the findings of the trial court are supported by the evidence, and the judgment and order appealed from are affirmed.

Note.—SIGNING OF WILL.

(a) Rule at common law.
(b) Signature.
(c) At end of the will.
(d) Hand guided by another.
(e) Signed by another.

(a) **Rule at common law.**—At common law if a person wrote his name in the body of the will with intent to execute it in that manner, the signature so written was as valid as though subscribed at the end of the instrument. (Matter of Booth, 127 N. Y. 109, 114; 27 N. E. Rep. 826; and see Armstrong v. Armstrong, 29 Ala. 538; Adams v. Field, 21 Vt. 256; Warwick v. Warwick, 86 Va. 596; 10 S. E. Rep. 843.)

(b) **Signature.**—What shall constitute a sufficient signature must depend largely on the custom of the time and place, the habit of the individual, and the circumstances of each particular case.· A signature by initials only, or otherwise informal and short of the full name, may be a valid execution of a will if the intent to execute is apparent. To this requirement our statute adds that the signature must be at the end, as evidence that the intent is present, actual and completed. (Knox's Estate, 131 Pa. St. 220; 18 Atl. Rep. 1021; the opinion contains an interesting review of the cases and law in regard to signatures.)

An imperfect or illegible signature may be valid. (Sheehan v. Kearney, 21 So. Rep. 41 [Miss.].)

Where testator started to sign his name and made a stroke apparently intended to be first part of the first letter of his name, when he stopped, saying " I can't sign it now," *held* not a sufficient signing as the stroke was not a signature, and the circumstances showed that it was not intended as a mark. (Plate's Estate, 148 Pa. St. 55; 23 Atl. Rep. 1038; and to same effect Goods of Maddock, L. R. 3 P. & D. 169.)

Use of a stamp impressing *fac simile* signature operates as signing. (Jenkins v. Gaisford, 3 Sw. & Tr. 93.)

Assumed name may be regarded as a *mark* of testator. (Goods of Redding, 2 Rob. Eccl. 339.)

As to signing by *mark* see *note*, 4 Prob. Rep. Ann. 258.

(c) **At end of the will.**—In Sisters of Charity v. Kelly (67 N. Y. 409), the Court of Appeals (FOLGER, J.) says: "Can we say that the end of a will has been found until the last word of all the provisions of it has been reached? To say that where the name is there is the end of the will is not to observe the statute. That requires that where the end of the will is, there shall be the name. It is to make a new law to say that where we find the name there is the end of the will. The instrument offered is to be scanned to learn where is the end of it as a completed whole; and at the end thus found must the name of the testator be subscribed."

Wherever the will ends there the signatures must be found, and one place cannot be the end for the purpose of subscribing by the testator, and another place be the end for the purpose of the signing by the witnesses. (Matter of Hewitt, 91 N. Y. 261, 264. And see as to signing at end of will, Glaney v. Glaney, 17 Ohio St. 134; Goods of Fuller [1892], Prob. 377; Matter of O'Neil, 91 N. Y. 516; Matter of Conway, 124 id. 455; 26 N. E. Rep. 1028; Matter of Whitney, 153 N. Y. 259; 47 N. E. Rep. 272; Matter of Fults, 42 App. Div. 593; 59 N. Y. Supp. 756; Re Andrews' Will, 162 N. Y. 1; 56 N. E. Rep. 529; this volume page 401; aff'g 43 App. Div. 394; 60 N. Y. Supp. 141. The opinion of the court below should be read in connection with that of the Court of Appeals and the whole combined probably present about as complete a review of the special subject, signing at *end* of the will, as it is possible to find anywhere.)

Testator's signature after the attestation clause is at end of the will. (Younger v. Duffie, 94 N. Y. 535; Matter of Laudy, 161 id. 432; 55 N. E. Rep. 914; Hallowell v. Hallowell, 88 Ind. 251; Matter of Cohen, 1 Tuck. 286.)

And so where testator signed in blank space in body of the attestation clause. (Matter of Acker, 5 Dem. 19.)

Where will is written with a final clause appointing executors, and testator's signature is before such clause, it is not signed at the end. (Wineland's Appeal, 118 Pa. St. 37; 12 Atl. Rep. 301.)

Where testator in his will appoints his sister-in-law executrix and before he signs the instrument, writes after the attestation clause, the words "My sister-in-law is not required to give bond," and thereafter signs the instrument above these words, *held* a signing at the end. (Baker v. Baker. 51 Ohio St. 217; 37 N. E. Rep. 125; and see McGuire v. Kerr, 2 Bradf. 254.)

Where testator's signature was written partly across the last line but one of the will and entirely above the last line, with the exception of one letter which touched the last line,—*held*, signed at end. (Goods of Woodley, 3 Sw. & Tr. 429.)

And so where the two last lines were somewhat below the signature—the sentence being written before a signing. (Goods of Ainsworth, L. R. 2 P. & D. 151; and see where the words similarly placed were written *after* the signing, Goods of Arthur, id. 273.)

A printed blank of one page signed by the testator and witnesses at bottom of the page, with reference in the body of the printed form to annexed pages in writing—is not signed at the end. (Matter of Whitney, 153 N. Y. 259; 47 N. E. Rep. 272.)

But in England probate may be granted of the first page of the will. (Goods of Anster [1893], Prob. 283.)

But this may be under the English statute. (Schouler on Wills, § 311 [ed. 1900]; Goods of Fuller [1892], Prob. 377; Royle v. Harris [1895], id. 163, 167; Sweetland v. Sweetland, 4 Sw. & T. 6.)

(d) **Hand guided by another.**—Person unable from palsy or other cause to write his name, may do so by another person steadying his hand in writing same or making his mark. (Vandruff v. Rinehart, 29 Pa. St. 232.)

Pen in testator's hand guided by another. (Vines v. Clingfoot, 21 Ark. 309; Cozzen's Will, 61 Pa. St. 196; Sheehan v. Kearney, 21 So. Rep. 41 [Miss.]; Van Hanswyck v. Wiese, 44 Barb. 494; Robins v. Coryell, 27 id. 556; Wilson v. Beddard, 12 Sim. 28.)

There is a distinction between the testator's own act with the assistance of another and the act of another under his authority. (Cozzen's Will, *supra*; and see Fritz v. Turner, 46 N. J. Eq. 515; 22 Atl. Rep. 125; Matter of McElwaine, 18 N. J. Eq. 500.)

(e) **Signed by another.**—Will signed by another person by testator's express direction. (Haynes v. Haynes, 33 Ohio St. 598; Herbert v. Berier, 81 Ind. 1; Ex parte Leonard, 39 S. C. 518; 18 S. E. Rep. 216; Butler v. Benson, 1 Barb. 526; and see Pool v. Buffom, 3 Ore. 438; Walton v. Kendrick, 122 Mo. 504; 27 S. W. Rep. 872.)

Where testator requested another to sign a paper as a will and he complied by signing "E. W. for R. D. at his request"—*held* sufficient signing. (Vernon v. Kirk, 30 Pa. St. 218.) Or so where will was signed "A. B. by C. D. in his presence and at his request." (Abrahams v. Wilkins, 17 Ark. 292; and see Riley v. Riley, 36 Ala. 496.)

Mere knowledge of the testator that his name is being signed by another, or that the signing is assented to by the testator, is not signing in his presence or by his express direction or show compliance with other statutory requirements. (Murry v. Hennessey, 48 Neb. 608; 67 N. W. Rep. 470; Waite v. Frisbie, 45 Minn. 361; 47 N. W. Rep. 1069.)

HUNT *et al. vs.* HUNT *et al.*

[Supreme Court of Michigan, June 26, 1900; 83 N. W. Rep. 371.]

WILLS—ESTATE IN TRUST—DEVISE—INSTRUCTIONS—LIFE ES-
TATE—TITLE IN TRUSTEE—RIGHTS OF BENEFICIARY—RULE IN
SHELLEY'S CASE—TERMINATION OF TRUST—EFFECT.

1. A devise by a testatrix of a farm to her executors, to invest the proceeds in bonds and mortgages, or in such other ways as they should
deem advisable, the income to be paid equally to her two sons as long
as they should live, and on the death of either to pay one-half of such
proceeds to his heirs, devisees, or legatees, created an active trust; and
the fact that the trustees had allowed the *cestuis que trustent* to occupy
and enjoy the property did not deprive other beneficiaries of their contingent interest in the property.

2. Under Comp. Laws 1897, § 8867, providing that, when a general and
beneficial power to devise the inheritance shall be given to the tenant
for life, such tenant shall be deemed to possess an absolute power of
disposition, a devise of a farm to executors, to invest the proceeds and
pay the interest to the *cestuis que trustent,* and on the death of either
of them to pay one-half of the same to his heirs, devisees, or legatees,
did not vest the title in fee to the trust property in the *cestuis que
trustent,* since they were not life tenants, because the will vested the
absolute title in the trustees.

3. Under Comp. Laws 1897, § 8810, providing that when a remainder shall
be limited to the heirs of the body, to whom a life estate in the same
premises shall be given, the persons who, on the termination of the life
estate, shall be heirs or heirs of the body of such tenant for life shall
be entitled to take as purchasers, where a devise was made to executors
to pay the income of the devised property to the sons of the testatrix
during their lifetime, and on the death of either to pay one-half to his
heirs, devisees, or legatees, the words " heirs, devisees, or legatees," as
used in such devise, are words of purchase, and an order terminating
the trust on the petition of one of the sons, after the death of the other,
was erroneous, since the surviving son had no interest in the property
other than the enforcement of the trust.

4. Where testatrix devised property to her executors in trust, the income
to be paid to her two sons equally, and, on the death of either, one-
half of the property to be paid to his heirs, devisees, or legatees, on
the death of one son the heirs of the surviving son are entitled to institute proceedings to protect the trust fund.

5. Where the absolute title to real estate was vested in trustees, with power
to the *cestuis que trustent* to dispose of the same by will, the fact that

after the death of one of the *cestuis que trustent* the other executed a will did not confer on him the power to terminate the trust, since he possessed no interest in the property other than the faithful enforcement of the trust.

APPEAL from Circuit Court, Wayne county, in chancery; WILLIAM L. CARPENTER, Judge.

Bill by Maria T. Hunt and others against Charles J. Hunt and others for the appointment of a trustee under the will of Maria E. Hunt, deceased. From an order terminating the trust, and declaring the defendant Charles J. Hunt owner of the trust property in fee, plaintiffs appeal.

Reversed.

Maria E. Hunt died testate. The first clause of her will reads thus: "I do hereby will, devise, and bequeath to my executors, hereinafter named, and to the survivors of them, my farm in the county of Shiawassee, and state fo Michigan, lying between Corunna and Owosso, in which Mrs. Henry Hunt, widow, has a life estate, in trust, however, for the following purpose, viz.: To sell and dispose of the same as soon as convenient after the death of Mrs. Henry Hunt and the termination of said life estate, and invest the proceeds thereof permanently in bond and mortgage, or in such other ways as may seem to my said executors safe and advisable, and pay over, as fast as received, the income and interest thereof, equally, to my two sons, Charles James Hunt and Joseph Nathan Hunt, share and share alike, as long as they shall live; and upon the death of either of them to pay over one-half of the same to his heirs, devisees, or legatees. including principal and interest." Hervey C. Parke and Mary A. Hunt were appointed executors. Miss Hunt did not qualify. Mr. Parke acted as sole executor, closed up the estate, and, as trustee under the clause above named, exchanged the land therein mentioned for real estate in the city of Detroit. Defendant Charles and his brother Joseph were permitted by the trustee to enjoy the use and control of this land. Mr. Parke having died, the complainants, who, upon the death of defendant Charles intestate, would, as heirs, become entitled to his property, filed a bill for the appointment of a trustee in place of Mr. Parke. The Union Trust

Company filed an answer, admitting the allegations of the bill, and that complainants were entitled to the appointment of a trustee. Defendant Charles answered, admitting the allegations of the bill as to the death of Mrs. Maria E. Hunt, the will, and its execution; the death of Mr. Parke; that at his death "the trusts created by the will were in full force and virtue, and that no trustees had been appointed in their place;" and further alleged that his brother Joseph died testate, having disposed of his interest in the land by will and that he (Charles) is the sole *cestui que trust* having interest in said land, and that he has the full power and authority to dispose of it. The court entered a decree appointing one Robert M. Chamberlain as trustee. By that decree the trustee, so appointed, was authorized to apply to the court for advice and direction in respect to the execution of said trust. Thereafter defendant Charles filed a petition in the original suit, asking that the trustee (Chamberlain) be summoned to show cause why the prayer of his cross bill should not be granted, and the trustee directed to convey to him the real estate so held in trust under the will of Mrs. Hunt. Upon that hearing Mr. Chamberlain, the trustee, appeared, and stated to the court that, in his opinion, the trust should be terminated. Charles had made a will devising the property to his wife, who appeared in court, and asked that the decree be made. The court entered a decree terminating the trust, and declaring that defendant Charles was the owner in fee of the land.

Le Vert Clark, Edwin F. Conely, and *Orla B. Taylor,* for appellants.

Charles J. Hunt, for appellees.

GRANT, J. (after stating the facts).—The intention of the testatrix is entirely clear. She devised the real estate to her executors as trustees, with authority to sell, and to " invest the proceeds in bond and mortgage, or such other ways as the said trustees should deem safe and advisable," the receipts therefrom to be paid over to her two sons during their lives. She empowered each of them to devise the property, whether it should be realty or personalty, but, should either fail to make a will, then it was to go to the heirs of each one. This intention of the testatrix must be carried out, unless to do so would be in direct violation of law. The trust was an active one, and the trustees and their *cestuis que trustent*—the two sons of Mrs. Hunt—could not, by any agreement or action of theirs, change the character of the estate or the fund received therefrom. (*Cuthbert* v. *Chauvet,* 136 N. Y. 326; 32 N. E. 1088; 18 L. R. A. 745; *Rift* v. *Geyer,* 59 Pa. St. 393.) It follows that even if the trustees permitted Charles and Joseph to occupy, enjoy, and manage the real estate, and receive all the rents and profits thereof, this would not change the active trust into a passive one, and deprive the other beneficiaries of the interest in the property to which, under certain contingencies, they would become entitled. It was entirely proper for the trustees to permit them the use and benefit of it.

The defendant Charles contends that the title in fee has become vested in him under section 8867, Comp. Laws 1897, which reads as follows: " When a general and beneficial power to devise the inheritance, shall be given to a tenant for life or for years, such tenant shall be deemed to possess an absolute power of disposition, within the meaning, and subject to the provisions of the three last preceding sections." The three preceding sections have no application to this case, for the reason that no estate for life or years is vested in the defendant Charles. The rule in *Shelley's Case* is abolished in this state by section 8810, Comp. Laws, which reads: " When a remainder shall be limited to the heirs, or heirs of the body of a person to whom a life estate in the same premises shall be given, the persons who, on the termination of the life estate, shall be heirs, or heirs of the body of such tenant for life, shall be entitled to take as purchasers, by virtue of the remainder so limited to them." (*Fraser* v. *Chene,* 2 Mich. 80.) Under that section the words " heirs," " devisees," and " legatees " in this will are not words of limitation, under the rule in *Shelley's Case* but are words of purchase. The mistake of Charles lies in his assumption that he is a life tenant with the devise over to his heirs. There is no life estate created by the will. The absolute title is vested in the trustees, and they alone have the right of possession. Upon them alone is the legal duty to pay the taxes, and to protect and care for the property. The interests of Charles and Joseph as *cestuis que trustent* have none of the attributes of a life tenancy. The trustees alone are charged with the control of the property, or of the fund which they are authorized to realize from its sale. They cannot surrender the trust to their *cestuis que trustent*. They can only surrender it to their successors duly by the Chancery Court. The only right Charles and Joseph can enforce against the trustees is the payment to them of the income and the faithful performance of the trust. This was all the testatrix intended they should have. There is no legal objection to such a trust. Upon Charles and Joseph she conferred the right to direct a testamentary disposition of the property upon the termination of the trust by their deaths. If they chose not to make such disposition, then the trustees under the will were directed to pay the fund or to deed the land over to the heirs of each. If there were no trust, and the devise were to Charles and Joseph for life, with the remainder over to their heirs, then undoubtedly they would take an *allodial* estate under *Fraser* v. *Chene* (*supra*). A case nearly parallel to this in its facts is *Sise* v. *Willard* (164 Mass. 48; 41 N. E. 116). In that case complainant had a life interest in the fund, coupled with the power of testamentary disposition, and the court held that she was not entitled to an absolute transfer of the fund to her.. (See, also, *Bowers* v. *Porter*, 4 Pick. 198; *Tayloe* v. *Gould*, 10 Barb. 388; *Germond* v. *Jones*, 2 Hill, 569.) We have examined the authorities cited by defendant Charles, and find that they are all cases where the courts held that all the beneficial interests were before the court, and that they had the right, by consent of the trustees, to terminate the trust, and that, under such circumstances, the court would direct a transfer of the fund to the parties entitled to it. The rule is well stated in *Sears* v. *Choate* (146 Mass. 395; 15 N. E. 786) : " There is no doubt of the power and duty of the court to decree the termination of a trust, where all its objects and purposes have been accomplished, where the interests under it have all vested, and where all parties beneficially interested desire its termination. Where property is given to certain persons for their benefit, and in such a manner that no other person has or can have any interest in it, they are, in effect, the absolute owners of it, and it is reasonable and just that they should have the control and disposal of it unless some good cause appears to the contrary." (See, also, Beach, Trusts, § 764.) It is, of course, impossible to now determine who will be the heirs of Charles at his death. In the event of his dying without children,[1] his brothers and sisters, and the children of any deceased brother or sister, will be the beneficiaries under the will. They are therefore entitled to take proceedings to protect the trust fund, to compel the appointment of trustees, and to have them properly execute the trust. The fact that Charles has made a will is of no significance. If his will were irrevocable, he would have no interest in this suit other than the enforcement of the trust. The only interest he would then have would be the income from the estate. But he may revoke his will at any time, and die intestate. His will might also be held void. In these events, the other beneficiaries would be entitled to the property. Decree reversed, and petition dismissed, but without costs.

The other justices concurred.

CAMERON *vs.* PARISH *et al.*

[Supreme Court of Indiana; June 8, 1900; 57 N. E. Rep. 547.]

WILLS—CONSTRUCTION—ESTATES CREATED.

1. Testator, before his death, purchased real property, and conveyed it to his wife in fee simple. By the second clause in his will he devised and bequeathed to his wife all his property, to use as she might desire, with power to sell and convey. By the third clause he directed that at death of his wife "all the property which she might then own" should be equally divided between his granddaughter, the defendant, and his foster son, the plaintiff, excepting one acre of land, which, by the fourth clause he directed should be vested in defendant, her mother, and plaintiff, in case his wife had not disposed of it prior to her death. *Held* that, as the second clause of the will gave to testator's wife an absolute title in fee, the limitation over was inoperative and void.

2. That the testator, in the third clause of the will, used the words "all the property which she might then own," did not show an intention to include property not within his power of disposition, so that an election by the widow to take under the will would constitute a waiver of her rights or those of her heirs to her property not acquired under the will, since the third and fourth clauses, when considered together, must be

construed to mean that the testator, under an erroneous supposition as to his power to do so, intended to direct the disposition at the death of his wife of the property then held by her under the will.

APPEAL from Circuit Court, Warren county; J. M. RABB, Judge.

Action by George Parish and another against Lena Frances Cameron to quit title. From a judgment in favor of plaintiffs, defendant appeals.
Reversed.

C. V. McAdams, for appellant.

E. F. McCabe, for appellee.

JORDAN, J.—Appellee instituted this action in the lower court against appellant to quiet his title to the undivided one-half of a certain tract of real estate situated in the town of Williamsport, Warren county, Ind. There was an answer in denial and a cross complaint upon the part of the defendant. The latter, by her cross complaint, alleged that she was the owner in fee of the entire premises in dispute, and she sought thereby to quiet her title as against the plaintiff, appellee in this appeal. Upon the issues joined under the pleadings there was a trial by the court, and a special finding of facts and conclusions of law thereon, to the effect that the appellee was the owner in fee of the undivided one-half of the premises described in the complaint, and was entitled to have his title quieted; and, over the exceptions of appellant to the court's conclusions of law upon the facts found, judgment was rendered accordingly.

The question presented is, did the court err in its conclusions of law in favor of appellee upon the facts embraced in the special finding? The pertinent and material facts disclosed by the finding are substantially as follows: William Cameron, prior to the year 1889, had been a farmer, and resided upon a farm, which he owned, in Warren county. On October 1, 1889, he purchased the real estate in controversy, paying therefor the sum of $2,100, and caused it to be conveyed in fee simple to his wife, Matilda Cameron. A short time after the purchase of said real estate, he and his wife moved onto the same, and continued to make their home thereon until the death of each. After taking up their residence upon said land, William Cameron purchased other real property in the town of Williamsport of the value of $800, the title to which he took in his own name, and continued to own and hold the same until his death. He and his wife had one child, James Cameron, who died in the year 1887, leaving surviving him as his only child, the appellant, Lena Frances Cameron; and at the time of the execution by William Cameron of the will hereinafter mentioned she and her grandmother, Matilda Cameron, were the only heirs of the said William. The appellee, George Parish, was taken by the said Cameron and his wife, Matilda, into their family when he was a mere child, and was made a member thereof, but was never in any manner legally adopted as their child; and at the death of William Cameron he was of the age of thirty-one years, and was still residing with the said William and his wife as a member of their family, and was not possessed of any property or estate of any kind whatever. On October 10, 1891, Matilda Cameron still owned the real estate in dispute, which had been conveyed to her in 1889, as heretofore stated, and continued to own the same until her death; but was not the owner, on said October 10, 1891, of any personal property save and except her wearing apparel and some household goods. On said date William Cameron was the owner of personal property of probable vaule of $4,500, and he also owned ten acres of real estate situated without the town of Williamsport, Warren county, Ind., of the probable value of $1,000, and was still the owner of the real estate heretofore mentioned as being purchased by him for the price of $800. On the said October 10, 1891, William Cameron executed his last will and testament. By said document he directed, first, that all of his just debts and funeral expenses be paid by his executor as soon after his death as possible. The second and third clauses of the will are as follows: " (2) I give, devise, and bequeath to my beloved wife, Matilda Cameron, all my property, real and personal, of every character and description, wherever the same may be situated, to use and dispose of as she may desire, with power to sell and convey the same, or do with the same as she may desire. (3) At the death of my wife I will and direct that all of the property which she may then own shall be equally divided between my granddaughter, Lena Frances Cameron, and my foster son, George Parish, share and share alike, except as herein otherwise provided to one acre of real estate." By the fourth clause he directed that, in the event his said wife, Matilda, had not, during her life, disposed of the one acre of land owned by him and situated near the Indiana Mineral Springs,—being the one acre mentioned in the third clause of the will,—then, and in that event, the title thereto was to vest in his said grandchild, Lena Cameron, her mother, Sue Cameron, and the said George Parish during their lives, and at their deaths the title thereto was to vest in fee simple in their surviving heirs. The fifth clause of the will provided that, in case the said Parish or the said Lena Frances Cameron died without issue of their bodies, or either of them, alive, then the property which they received from his wife at her death was to go and vest in George Cameron, his nephew, and Thomas Moore, a nephew of his wife; it being provided therein that the said property in all cases should be responsible for the funeral expenses of his said wife before vesting in his said granddaughter and the said Parish, and also responsible for her debts. On December 16th following the execution of the will, William Cameron died, leaving, surviving him, his wife as his widow, and his will was duly admitted to probate in the Warren Circuit Court; and C. V. McAdams, the executor therein named, duly qualified as such, and continued to administer his trust until he was regularly discharged as such executor on the 13th day of March, 1893. The court finds that the said widow, Matilda, at no time after the death of her husband, filed any written election with any one to take her interest in her husband's property pursuant to the laws of Indiana in preference to the provisions of her husband's will, but that she elected to and did take all her husband's property under his said will. The executor, pursuant to the will, turned over to her money, household goods, and a decree of foreclosure to the amount of $2,334.21. From this sum the executor paid out, under directions from her, the sum of $55.19 on taxes due upon her real estate, and the further sum of $182.71, upon a school fund mortgage existing against her real estate at the time the same was purchased and conveyed to her. It is further found by the court in its special finding that after the death of William Cameron his widow, Matilda, took possession of all the real estate of which he died the owner, and that she converted all the personal property turned over by said executor into cash, and loaned and used the same as she felt disposed; that she sold one piece of real estate owned by the testator at the time of his death, situated in the town of Williamsport, for the sum of $800, and caused a portion of the other lands owned and held by her husband at his death to be platted, and during her lifetime she disposed of sixteen other tracts or lots by warranty deed made by her as widow of the testator, and received for such conveyances the sum of $730; and at the time of her death the real estate which she had acquired under the will of her husband remaining undisposed of by her was but the one acre of land heretofore mentioned, which was of the value of $150. On the 13th day of July, 1898, Matilda Cameron died intestate, and the value of all the personal property then owned by her, all of which came to her under her husband's will, was $1,682.28, and consisted of household goods, horse and carriage, notes and money. After her death, to wit, on July 20, 1898, appellant and appellee, out of the moneys on hand at her death, fully paid and settled all her debts and funeral expenses, which amounted to $293, leaving a residue of her personal estate amounting to $1,389.22, which was then and there equally divided between appellant and appellee. At the time appellant and appellee made the division of the property acquired by Matilda Cameron under her husband's will, and which remained undisposed of at her death, as heretofore stated, they each supposed that the title to the real estate in controversy in this action was in William Cameron at the time of his death, and thereupon, acting under this supposition in regard to the title of said real estate, they leased the same to one Johnson for a term of one year at an agreed rent of $10 per month; one-half of which, by the terms of such lease, to be paid to each of them. And the said tenant took possession of the property, and has ever since held and is now in possession thereof pursuant to said lease. A short time before the commencement of this suit, appellee, George Parish, discovered the fact that the title to said real estate had always been in Matilda Cameron from the time it was conveyed to her, as heretofore stated, up to the time of her death, and was never at any time owned by William Cameron; and thereupon he communicated the information to the appellant, Lena Frances Camcron, and demanded of her that she execute to him a deed of conveyance for one-half of said real estate, which she refused to do, but, on the contrary, asserted, and still asserts, her entire ownership to the said realty as the only surviving heir at law of her grandmother, Matilda Cameron; and has demanded of said tenant that all the rents of said real estate be paid to her. At the time William Cameron executed his will he was 69 years old, and his wife, Matilda, was 68. Upon the foregoing facts the court stated its conclusions of law as follows: First, that the plaintiff, George Parish, is the owner in fee simple of the undivided one-half of the property in controversy, and is entitled to have his title quieted; second, that the defendant, Lena Frances Cameron, is the owner in fee simple of the other half of said real estate, and is entitled to have her title thereto quieted.

Appellant asserts title to the entire premises involved in this action by virtue of inheritance as the sole heir of her grandmother, Matilda Cameron, while, upon the other hand, appellee claims title to the undivided one-half thereof under the provisions of the will of William Cameron. Counsel for appellant insist that under the second clause of the will in question, when tested by the doctrine asserted in the case of *John v. Bradbury* (97 Ind. 263), the wife of the testator acquired but a life estate in the property devised thereby to her, with the power of disposing of the same during her natural life; that by the third clause it must be held that the testator intended that all the property which he devised to his wife under the previous clause remaining undisposed of at her death should go in equal parts to appellant and appellee; that by the provisions of said third clause the testator merely intended to direct in respect to the disposition of the property which his wife had acquired under his will, and which in whole or in part she might still own at the date of her death; and that said clause cannot be interpreted so as to include other property owned by the wife at the date of her death. Counsel for appellee, upon the contrary, contend that by the clause, " all the property which she may then own shall be equally divided," etc., as expressed in item 3, the testator intended to embrace all of the property owned by his wife, without regard as to whether the same came to her through or under his will or was otherwise acquired and owned by her. Consequently, it is asserted that under the equitable rule the will presented a case for election upon the part of the testator's surviving wife; that she, as a beneficiary under the will, was by its provisions clearly required to decide whether or not she would accept the benfits or bounty conferred upon her by the will, or renounce the same in toto; that, having elected to accept or take the property which the testator donated to her, she must thereby be deemed to have adopted the will as an entirety, and consented that any and all property that she owned at the date of her death should be subjected to its provisions, and disposed of as therein directed. That the second clause of William Cameron's will, standing alone, must be held, under the well-settled principles of law so universally asserted and affirmed by our own decisions and other authorities in general, to have invested his wife with an absolute title to the property thereby devised to her, cannot be successfully controverted. (*Ross* v. *Ross*, 135 Ind. 367; 35 N. E. 9; *Rogers* v. *Winklespleck*, 143 Ind. 373; 42 N. E. 746; *Mulvane* v. *Rude*, 146 Ind. 476; 45 N. E. 659, and authorities there cited; *Rusk* v. *Zuck*, 147 Ind. 388; 45 N. E. 691; and 46 N. E. 674; *Van Gorder* v. *Smith*, 99 Ind. 404.) In order to construe the will in controversy as creating a life estate only in the testator's surviving wife, with power of disposition over the property bequeathed to her, we would be required to extend the rule further than it was carried by the decision in the case of *John* v. *Bradbury* (97 Ind. 263). In *Goudie* v. *Johnston* (109 Ind. 427; 10 N. E. 296), it was said that the former case possibly carried the doctrine too far. Certainly, however, it may be asserted that the rule, as recognized and applied in *John* v. *Bradbury* (*supra*), is incompatible with the doctrine announced in the later cases of this court, especially in that of *Mulvane* v. *Rude* (146 Ind. 476; 45 N. E. 659); and the *John Case* must at least be considered as impliedly overruled by these later decisions. As the second clause of the will in effect gave to the testator's wife an absolute title in fee, consequently nothing remained of the estate from which a remainder over could be limited, as it is a well-settled proposition that a remainder over cannot be ingrafted upon or carved out of a precedent absolute estate in fee. Therefore, so far as the testator may have attempted by the third clause of his will to limit the disposition of the property donated to his wife, and not disposed of by her during her life, such attempt under that clause must be held to be inoperative, and of no effect for that purpose. For the rule is well settled that where an estate, as under the will in this case, is generally and indefinitely given to a person with full power of disposition, in the absence in the will of an express mention to show that the estate given is limited to the life of the donee, it must be held that such devise of propery carries with it a fee simple to the same, and any limitation over is inoperative or void by reason of its being repugnant to the principal devise. (*Mulvane* v. *Rude,* 146 Ind. 476; 45 N. E. 659, and authorities there cited.)

The principal point, however, involved in this appeal does not depend upon the question as to whether Mrs. Cameron took a life estate or one in fee simple in the property bequeathed to her by her husband's will, but the real question presented is: Did that instrument, under its terms and provisions, present such a case as required her, under the equitable doctrine of election, to decide whether she would accept the benefits bestowed upon her therein, and thereby adopt the will as an entirety, and by such acceptance impliedly consent that the property in controversy, owned and held by her at the date of her death under a deed of conveyance, should be subjected to the provisions of her husband's will, and, at her death, as therein provided, should go in equal parts to appellant and appellee? The doctrine of election, so far as it relates to wills and other instruments of donation, arises out of the equitable principle that a person shall not be permitted to accept under such instruments without giving all the provisions thereof full force and effect so far as such person is concerned. The doctrine of election, as between inconsistent right and its application to wills, has long been established and is firmly settled by the authorities. Story, in his Equity Jurisprudence (section 1077), in treating upon the subject, says: "In short, courts of equity in such cases adopt the rational exposition of the will that there is an implied condition that he who accepts a benefit under the instrument shall adopt the whole, conforming to all its provisions, and renouncing every right inconsistent with it." The equitable doctrine is to the effect that a person cannot be permitted to hold under a will and also to hold against its provisions; or, in other words, having once accepted beneficial interests under a will, he will be held to have confirmed and ratified every part thereof, and will not thereafter be permitted to interpose any right or claim of his own, however well founded it may be, which would defeat or in any manner prevent the full operation of such will. Where a person, under the terms of a will, has been thereby properly put to his election, and can be said to have elected to accept the benefits bestowed upon him by its provisions, he thereby binds or precludes, not only himself, but also those who claim through him, his representatives and heirs. (*Wilson* v. *Wilson,* 145 Ind. 659; 44 N. E. 665.) Of course, under the will in question, Matilda Cameron, as the widow of the testator, was, under section 2666, Burns' Rev. St. 1894, required to elect, within the time therein fixed, as to whether she would renounce the provisions made for her by her husband's will, and elect to be governed by the statute of descent in respect to her rights in her husband's estate. As it does not appear that she, within the time stipulated by the statute, expressly rejected in the manner therein provided, the provisions made for her by the will, her failure to do so must be considered the equivalent of an express election upon her part to abide by and accept the provisions of the will, and be controlled thereby in respect to her rights in her husband's estate.

It is settled that whenever it is reasonably clear that the provisions of a will are intended to be in lieu of the widow's interest in her husband's estate, under the law, if she accepts the former, she thereby waives the latter. (*Burden* v. *Burden,* 141 Ind. 471; 40 N. E. 1067; *Hurley* v. *McIver,* 119 Ind. 53; 21 N. E. 325; *Archibald* v. *Long,* 144 Ind. 451; 43 N. E. 439.) But, under the will in this case, can it be held that Mrs. Cameron, by her election to adopt and abide by the provisions made for her therein, did anything more than to waive her rights and claims in and to her husband's estate, which she had and held under the law as his widow? Can it, in reason, be further said that by this election she bound herself to permit the real estate in dispute to pass under the operation of her husband's will, and go to the parties in this action, as therein provided? We are of the opinion that this latter question must be answered in the negative. We are bound to assume, until the contrary clearly appears, that the testator, by his will, only intended to dispose of property subject under the law to his disposition, and, in order to create a proper case for election, under the equitable rule in question, his intention to dispose of property not his own must be made to clearly appear beyond a reasonable doubt from the will itself. It must be disclosed by such instrument that he therein assumed the power to dispose of the property of another person, who thereunder was also made a beneficiary. This feature of the doctrine of election, as settled by the authorities, is well stated by an eminent author as follows: " In order to create the necessity for an election, there must appear upon the face of the will itself, or of the other instrument of donation, a clear, unmistakable intention on the part of the testator or other donor to dispose of property which is in fact not his own. This intention to dispose of property which in fact belongs to another, and is not within the donor's power of disposition, must appear from language of the instrument which is unequivocal, which leaves no doubt as to the donor's design. The necessity of an election can never exist from an uncertain or dubious interpretation of the clause of donation. It is the settled rule that no case for an election arises unless the gift to one beneficiary is irreconcilable with an estate, interest, or right which another donee is called upon to relinquish. If both gifts can, upon any interpretation of which the language is reasonably susceptible, stand together, then an election is unnecessary. The instrument may declare in express terms that the gift to A. must be accepted by him in lieu of his own interest, which is thereby transferred to B. and then no possible doubt could exist. But this direct mode of exibiting the donor's purpose is not indispensable. It is sufficient if the dispositions of the instrument, fairly and reasonably interpreted, exhibit a clear intention of the donor to bestow upon B. some estate, interest, or right of property which is not the donor's, but which belongs to A., and at the same time to give to A. some benefits derived from the donor's own property. It is immaterial, however, whether the donor knew the property not to be his own, or erroneously conceived it to be his own; for, in either case, if the intention to dispose of it clearly appears, the necessity for an election exists." (1 Pom. Eq. Jur. § 472.) In *Havens* v. *Sackett* (15 N. Y. 365), on page 373 of the opinion, is said: " It must be clear beyond all reasonable doubt that he (the testator) has intentionally assumed to dispose of the property of the beneficiary, who is required on that account to give up his own gift." When tested by this rule, which is so fully affirmed and sustained by the authorities, it is evident, we think, that the will in the case at bar does not come up to the requirements, and clearly exposes by its own provisions that the testator assumed the right to dispose of property owned by his wife, and which she had in no manner acquired under or through his will. As previously said, the testator, under the second clause of his will, gave his wife an absolute and unconditional title in fee to all of his property, with the power to sell and do with the same as she might desire. It appears by the provisions of the third clause of his will that he supposed he had the power to control the disposition of the property which his wife held under and through the will undisposed of at the time of her death. That the testator, by the third item of his will, had in mind the disposition of the property only which he had devised to his wife under the previous clause, is made more manifest by the exception in the latter of the one acre owned by him, and which in the fourth clause he states is situated near the Indiana Mineral Springs, and as to which, under this latter clause, he directs, in the event his wife shall not during her life have disposed of this particular tract, that the title at her death shall vest in the parties to this action, together with the mother of appellant, during their natural lives. This one-acre tract, as the testator seems to have understood, had been devised by him under clause No. 2 of his will, along with his other property, to his wife; but as to it he appears to have desired that, if it was not disposed of by her during her life, it should go, not alone to the appellant and appellee, but that the mother of the former should have an interest therein. When this exception in clause 3 of the will is considered in connection with clause 4, we think it becomes manifest that the testator, under an erroneous supposition as to his power to do so, intended only to direct the disposition, at the death of his wife, of the property then held by her under his will, and that the provisions of the clause cannot be interpreted to have any reference to or embrace the particular property here involved. Under these circumstances, the will did not present a case of election under the equitable rule to which we have referred, and the property involved in this appeal is not affected by the fact that Mrs. Cameron accepted the provisions made for her by her husband's will.

It therefore follows, and we so conclude, that the premises in controversy in this action, under the facts found by the court, descended as an entirety to appellant, Lena Frances Cameron, as the sole heir at law of her grandmother, Matilda Cameron. The court therefore erred in its conclusions of law in holding that appellee was entitled to the undivided one-half of said premises. The judgment is ordered to be reversed, and the cause remanded to the lower court, with instructions to restate its conclusions of law upon the facts found in favor of appellant to the effect that she is the owner of the premises described in the complaint and in the cross-complaint, and under the latter she is entitled to a judgment quieting her title against appellee to the real estate in question.

SHRUM *vs.* SIMPSON.

[Supreme Court of Indiana, June 22, 1900; 57 N. E. Rep. 708.]

PARTNERSHIP—AGREEMENT BETWEEN LANDLORD AND TENANT— EXECUTORS AND ADMINISTRATORS—ACCOUNTING.

1. An agreement whereby an owner of land contracts with another to occupy and cultivate it, each to furnish a certain proportion of the seeds, implements, and stock, and to share at the end of the term equally in the products, does not create a partnership between the parties.
2. A complaint disclosing defendant's possession of money and property of the estate of a decedent, to which complainant is entitled as administratrix, and his refusal to settle, entitles complainant to an accounting.

APPEAL from Circuit Court, Washington county; W. H. PAYNTER, Special Judge.

Action by Lucy Shrum, administratrix of the estate of a decedent, against Joseph A. Simpson, to recover possession of certain property and for an accounting. From a judgment for defendant, plaintiff appeals.

Reversed.

John L. Schrum and *John C. Lawler,* for appellant.

Morris & Hottel, for appellee.

DOWLING, J.—Appellant's decedent owned and was in the possession of a farm of 160 acres, in Washington county, Ind. He entered into a farming contract with the appellee for the term of one year from March 1, 1898. The agreement was by parol. By its provisions, the appellee was to have the possession of the tract for one year from and after March 1, 1898. He was to cultivate the same, the decedent designating what crops should be planted, and in what fields they should be raised. Appellee was to have the house, the barn, and the garden plot, and was to pay $2.50 per month, as rent for them. He was to furnish all work, labor, and farming implements, excepting one-half of a mowing machine; also one-half of all seeds for all crops, excepting timothy seed for meadow, all of which was to be furnished by decedent in case he required the same to be sowed in wheat ground. Decedent was to furnish the other half of all seeds. Each crop grown on said lands was to be divided into two equal parts after it was harvested or gathered, and one of these parts was to belong to the decedent and the other to the appellee. Each party was to pay for threshing one-half of the wheat, oats, and timothy seed, and, excepting such parts of said grain and seed as the parties mutually agreed to store for later disposition in the markets or otherwise, the said grains and seed were to be equally divided at the machine. Neither party was to haul away from said lands any of the hay, corn, straw, fodder, or unthreshed oats, but the same were to be fed to the stock on the said farm. One-half of all live stock was to be furnished by each party, and appellee was to care for and feed the same. Neither party was to create any indebtedness for which the other could be made liable. The decedent was to direct when any of the stock should be sold, and upon a sale of stock appellee was to pay decedent one-half of the amount received therefor. All stock and fowls, hay, grain, and oats were to be divided, share and share alike, before March 1, 1899, and, if a division could not be agreed upon in any case, the stock not divided was to be sold, and the proceeds divided before March 1, 1899. It is alleged in the complaint that the appellee took possession of the land under this agreement, that each party furnished the seed, grain, live stock, and other articles required by its terms, and that appellant's decedent died March 11, 1898. It is further alleged that the appellant and appellee acted upon the agreement after the death of said decedent. It is charged that appellee raised upon said lands, during said term, crops of wheat, oats, hay, corn, and stock of the value of $600, a bill of the particulars of which is filed with the complaint; that the appellee sold and disposed of all the stock, grain, and fowls, corn, hay, oats, and timothy seed; that appellant has demanded from the appellee one-half of the amounts so received by him, due to said estate, but that, with the exception of one-half of the wheat grown on said lands, the appellee wrongfully retains the same in his possession. The second paragraph of the complaint does not differ materially from the first, except that it alleges a demand for an accounting, and a refusal on the part of the appellee to account, and also that the money and property belonging to the estate of said decedent in the hands of the appellee are required to pay to the widow her statutory allowance of $500. A demurrer to each paragraph of the complaint was sustained by the court, and judgment was rendered for appellee. These rulings are assigned for error.

The objections taken to each paragraph of the complaint are that it appears from the agreement sued upon that the appellee and the decedent were partners, or at least tenants in common of the property on the farm, and that in either case one of the parties having died, the appellee, as survivor, is entitled to the possession of the property so held until he has fully settled the business, and that until such settlement is made the appellant has no right to sue. (17 Am. & Eng. Enc. Law, 835; *Powell* v. *Bennett*, 131 Ind. 465; 30 N. E. 518; *McIntosh* v. *Zaring*, 150 Ind. 301; 49 N. E. 164; *Valentine* v. *Wysor*, 123 Ind. 47; 23 N. E. 1076; 7 L. R. A. 788; *Thompson* v. *Lowe*, 111 Ind. 272; 12 N. E. 476; *Needham* v. *Wright*, 140 Ind. 190; 39 N. E. 510; *Holmes* v. *McCray*, 51 Ind. 358; and *Kenyon* v. *Williams*, 19 Ind. 44,—are referred to as sustaining these objections.) Most of these cases decide nothing more than that, where a partnership is shown to exist, one partner cannot maintain an action against another for his share of the partnership assets until the business of the firm has been wound

up, the debts paid, and nothing remains to be done but to divide
the residue of the partnership property. *Kenyon·* v. *Williams*
(*supra*), holds that a partnership may exist in the business of
buying and selling real estate. The main question here is, not as
to the right of partners in partnership property, but whether the
agreement between the decedent and the appellee created a partnership. While many definitions of the term " partnership " are
given by jurists and courts, and various tests have been proposed
by which its existence may be determined, no general rule on the
subject has been or can be laid down which will apply to all cases.
An author of great and exact learning states the law thus: " In
. short, the true rule, *ex æquo et bono,* would seem to be that the
agreement and intention of the parties themselves should govern in all cases. If they intended a partnership in the capital stock,
or in the profits, or in both, then that the same rule should apply
in favor of third persons, even if the agreement were unknown
to them; and, on the other hand, if no such partnership were intended between the parties, then that there should be none as to
third persons, unless where the parties had held themselves out
as partners to the public, or their conduct operated as a fraud and
deceit upon third persons." (Story, Partn. § 49.) Such intention must, of course, be legally ascertained; and mere declarations
of the persons interested and uniting in the prosecution of a common enterprise that no partnership existed, would not be permitted to control the legal effect of acts or proceedings from
which the existence of a partnership is by the law presumed. It
is also to be observed that, where the rights of third parties are
not involved, the contract will be liberally construed with reference to the actual understanding of the parties and the objects
they had in view. (*Hitchings* v. *Ellis*, 12 Gray. 449.) There are
obvious reasons for holding that farm contracts or agricultural
agreements, by which the owner of lands contracts with another
that such lands shall be occupied and cultivated by the latter, each
party furnishing a certain proportion of the seed, implements,
and stock, and that the products shall be divided at the end of a
given term, or sold, and the proceeds divided, shall not be construed as creating a partnership between the parties. Such agreements are common in this country, are usually very informal in
their character, often resting in parol as in the present case. In

the absence of stipulations or evidence clearly manifesting a contrary purpose. it will not be presumed that the parties to such an agreement intend to assume the important and intricate responsibilities of partners, or to incur the inconveniences and dangers frequently incident to that relation.   The parties to such agreements seldom contemplate anything more than a tenancy of the land, with provision for compensation to the landlord from the fidelity, labor, and skill of the tenant.   There is no community of interest in the land, which is the principal thing in the agreement, and a division and several ownership of the crops and other products are usually provided for.   While the custom of renting farm lands upon shares is general, the courts have seldom held that such agreements create partnerships between the owner of the land and the tenant.   A large majority of the cases construe them as creating tenancies only.   (*Chase* v. *Barrett,* 4 Paige, 148; *Quackenbush* v. *Sawyer,* 54 Cal. 439; *Chapman* v. *Eames,* 67 Me. 452; *Warner* v. *Abbey,* 112 Mass. 355; *Dixon* v. *Niccolls,* 39 Ill. 372; *Alwood* v. *Ruckman,* 21 id. 200; *Putnam* v. *Wise,* 1 Hill, 234; 37 Am. Dec. 309.)   The agreement in question relates exclusively to the dealings of the parties with each other, and not with third persons.   It distinctly separates their rights in the use and occupation of the land and in the ownership of its products. Such products and live stock were to be divided in specie, except that, where a division of the live stock could not be agreed upon, it was to be sold, and the amount received therefor divided.   No debts were to be contracted by either party for which the other would be liable.   Under this agreement the authority of the appellee to make sales of the live stock was that of an agent, and not that of a partner.   Upon a fair construction of the agreement, it is evident that the appellee was the tenant and agent of the decedent, and in no sense a partner.   The complaint disclosed that the appellee had in his possession moneys and property belonging to the estate of the decedent, to which the appellant, as administratrix, was entitled.   The possession of the appellee of such money and property of his landlord being that of an agent, his failure and refusal to render an account of his dealings, and to make a settlement with the administratrix of the decedent, was a fraud upon the rights of the appellant.   The situation of the parties and the circumstances set forth in the complaint render a discovery indispensable to establish the appellant's right, the appellee being liable for the amount realized from the sale of the property if such amount exceeded its market value, or for its market value if it was disposed of by the appellee for a less sum. Upon the face of the complaint no pretext appears for the failure of the appellee to render an account, turn over the property of the decedent to the appellant, and pay into her hands the moneys held by him belonging to the estate. The term of the tenancy has expired; all the crops and live stock have been sold, or are in a condition to be divided; there are no debts to be paid, and nothing remains to be done but to make the settlement. The judgment is reversed, with instructions to overrule the demurrers to the complaint, and for further proceedings in accordance with this opinion.

CUNNINGHAM *vs.* CUNNINGHAM *et al.*

[Supreme Court of Minnesota, June 13, 1900; 53 N. W. Rep. 58.]

WILL—EXECUTION—SUFFICIENCY.

C. duly signed an instrument intended to be his last will and testament, two physicians being present at his request to attest as witnesses. C. was then sitting on the side of his bed, the paper lying on a book in front of him, the book being upon a chair. One of the physicians took the paper, and both stepped through a doorway into an adjoining room, and affixed their signatures at a table which stood ten feet from the testator. He could have seen the table by stepping forward two or three feet, but did not do so. The attestation consumed not to exceed two minutes of time. The witnesses returned to the testator; their signatures were pointed out to him; he took the paper into his own hands, looked it over, and pronounced it "all right." *Held,* that Gen. St. 1894, § 4426, which requires that wills must be attested and subscribed by the witnesses in the "presence" of the testator, was sufficiently complied with.

(Syllabus by the court.)

APPEAL from District Court, Olmstead county; ARTHUR SNOW, Judge.

Application of Emery H. Cunningham for probate of the last will of Robert E. Cunningham, deceased. From a judgment admitting it to probate, Ripley L. Cunningham and others appeal. Affirmed.

Thos. Fraser and *Geo. W. Somerville,* for appellants.

Chas. C. Wilson, for respondent.

COLLINS, J.—Gen. St. 1894, § 4426, provides: " No will, except such nuncupative wills as are hereinafter mentioned, shall be effectual to pass any estate, real or personal, or to change, or in any way effect the same, unless it is in writing, and signed at the end thereof, by the testator, or by some person in his presence, and by his express direction, and attested and subscribed in his presence, by two or more competent witnesses." And the only question in issue on this appeal is whether the alleged will was attested and subscribed in the presence of the testator, Cunningham, by the two persons whose names were attached as witnesses. The testator had been confined to his room for some time. It was a small bedroom with a doorway which led into a large room upon the north, the head of his bed being near the partition between the two. There was no door, but a curtain had been hung in the doorway, which was drawn to the west side at the time in question. Three days before the signing the testator sent for his attending physician, Dr. Adams, to come to his house, and draw his will. At the same time he sent for Dr. Dugan to be present as a witness. The draft of a will made by Dr. Adams as dictated by Cunningham was unsatisfactory, and both of the physicians went away. They were again summoned November 12, 1899, and went to the house in the forenoon. Dr. Adams drew a new will as instructed by Cunningham, the latter remaining in his bed. When the document was fully written, both men stepped to the bedside, and Dr. Adams read it to the sick man. Having heard it read through, Cunningham pronounced it satisfactory, and then signed it. When so signing he sat on the edge of the bed, and used as a place for the paper a large book which was lying upon a chair. Drs. Adams and Dugan were then requested to sign as witnesses. For this purpose they stepped to a table in the sitting room, which stood about ten feet from where Cunningham sat, and there affixed their signatures. The time occupied in so signing did not exceed two minutes, and immediately thereafter Dr. Adams returned to the bedside with the paper. Dr. Dugan stepped to the doorway, about three feet from Cunningham, and then Adams showed the signatures of the witnesses to him as he sat on the edge of the bed. Cunningham took the paper, looked it over, and said, in effect, that it was all right. From where he sat he could not see the table which was used by the witnesses when signing. He could have seen it by moving two or three feet. While they were signing he leaned forward, and inquired if the instrument needed a revenue stamp, to which Dr. Adams replied that he did not know, the reply being audible to Cunningham. These are the salient and controlling facts found by the court below, on which it based an ultimate finding that the instrument so witnessed was attested and subscribed in the presence of the testator, and then affirmed the order of the Probate Court admitting it to probate as the last will and testament of the deceased.

The appellants (contestants below) insist that the attestation and subscription by the witnesses was insufficient, because Mr. Cunningham did not and could not see the witnesses subscribe their names from where he sat, and their contention has an abundance of authority in support of it from jurisdictions in which statutes copied from the English law on the subject, and exactly like our own, are in force. The rule laid down in these authorities is that the attesting and subscribing by the witnesses must take place within the testator's range of vision, so that he may see the act of subscribing, if he wishes, without a material change of his position; and that he must be mentally observant of the act while in progress. Lord ELLENBOROUGH thus stated it in *Doe v. Manifold* (1 Maule & S. 294): "In favor of attestation it is presumed that, if the testator might see, he did see; but I am afraid if we went beyond the rule which requires that the witness should be actually within reach of the organs of sight, we shall be giving effect to an attestation out of the devisor's presence, as to which the rule is that, where the devisor cannot, by possibility, see the act doing, that is an act out of his presence." Construing the same words in the Illinois statute, it was recently held: "The act of attestation consists in the subscription of the names of the witnesses to the attestation clause as a declaration that the signature was made or acknowledged in their presence. It is this act of attestation by subscribing their names to the will as witnesses thereto which the statute requires to be in the presence of the testator. The object of the law, as frequently declared, is to prevent fraud or imposition upon the testator, or the substitution of a surreptitious will; and to effectuate that object it is necessary that the testator shall be able to see and know that the witnesses subscribed their names to the paper which he has executed or acknowledged as his will. The purpose of the statute is not attained by mere ability to see the witnesses, or some part of them, but the act of attestation is the thing which must be in the presence of the testator. * * * It would not be an attestation in the presence of the testator, if he could not see the attestation, but merely understood from the surrounding circumstances that the act was taking place." (*Drury* v. *Connell,* 177 Ill. 43; 52 N. E. 368.) In brief, the courts have almost without exception, construed a statute requiring an attestation of a will to be in the " presence " of the testator to mean that there must not only be a consciousness on the part of the latter as to the act of the witnesses while it is being performed, but a contiguity of persons, with an opportunity for the testator to see the actual subscribing of the names of the witnesses, if he chooses, without any material change of position on his part. And yet an examination of the decided cases wherein the ever-varying circumstances and conditions have been considered, and this rule applied, will convince the reader that the task of application has not been an easy one, and has led to surprising results at times. Some years ago a large number of American and English cases were collected in a note appended to *Manderville* v. *Parker* (31 N. J. Eq. 242), and an examination thereof will show the absurd and inconsistent positions in which the courts have frequently placed themselves. As will be seen from the facts surrounding the cases mentioned in this note, or cited in the text-books in support of this rule, it has been held almost universally that an attestation in the same room with the testator is good, without regard to intervening objects which might or did intercept the view; and also that an attestation outside the room or place where the testator sat or lay is valid if actually within his range of vision. And no court seems to have doubted that a man unable to see at all could properly make a will under the statute, if the witnesses attested within his "conscious" presence, whatever that means. Exactly why or how an exception in the case of one temporarily or permanently blind can be injected into this statute has not been attempted by any court or writer, so far as we know. Nor has there been any success in the effort to show why one kind of an intervening object—a partition wall, for instance—is better calculated to afford an opportunity for the perpetration of a fraud upon the testator than is another kind, say, the closed curtains of an old-fashioned bed, or the head or foot board of a bedstead, or any other article of furniture which happens to be an obstruction to the sight. Again, it is difficult to see what sound distinction can be made, when applying the rule, between a case where the testator can see the witnesses attest, if he chooses to lean his body forward a few inches, and the case where the act can be seen if he steps forward the same distance. Or, take a case where a testator has been injured, and is compelled to lie on his back with his eyes fixed on the ceiling. Must the witnesses affix their signatures from an elevation in order to sign in his presence? No case has gone that far, and yet what difference would it make with such a testator in fact or in sound reason if the will was attested ten feet distant, on a table in an adjoining room, or on a table the same distance from the bed, but in the same room? Take the case at bar. The testator sat on the edge of his bed when the witnesses signed at the table in the adjoining room, a few feet distant, and within easy sound of his voice. If he could have seen them by leaning forward, the authorities in favor of upholding the will are abundant. Physically he was capable of stepping two or three feet forward, and from this point the witnesses could have been within his range of vision. It is extremely difficult to distinguish between the two cases, and yet it has been done again and again in applying the rule. We might continue these suggestions and queries, as has been done quite frequently by courts which have not been entirely satisfied with a very rigid construction of the statute, and have not hesitated to say so; but it seems unnecessary, for there is one feature in these findings of fact which is sufficient, in our judgment, to warrant an affirmance, although there are many decisions to the contrary. As before stated, the court found that the witnessing of the will consumed not more than two minutes, and that immediately thereafter Dr. Adams returned to the testator while Dr. Dugan came to the doorway, not over five feet distant, whereupon the former " showed the signatures of the witnesses to the testator. The latter took the will, looked it over, and said in effect that it was all right." To say that this was not a sufficient attestation within a statute which requires such attestation to be in the " presence " of the testator, simply because the witnesses actually signed a few feet out of the range of his vision, is to be extremely technical without the slightest reason for being so. The signing was within the sound of the testator's voice; he knew what was being done; the act occupied not more than two minutes; the witnesses returned at once to the testator; their signatures were pointed out to him; he took the instrument into his own hands, looked it over, and pronounced it satisfactory. The whole affair, from the time he signed the will himself, down to and including his expression of approval, was a single and entire transaction; and no narrow construction of this statute, even if it has met the approval of the courts, should be allowed to stand in the way of right and justice, or be permitted to defeat a testator's disposition of his own property. In *Cook* v. *Winchester* (81 Mich. 581; 46 N. W. 106; 8 L. R. A. 822), it was said: " In the definition of the phrase ' in the presence of,' due regard must be had to the circumstances of each particular case, as it is well settled by all the authorities that the statute does not require absolutely that the witnessing must be done in the actual sight of the testator, nor yet within the same room with him. If, as before shown, they sign within his hearing, knowledge and understanding, and so near as not to be substantially away from him, they are considered to be in his presence." But, as was said, in substance, in the same case, we agree that this will was validly executed expressly on the ground that the whole transaction was an entirety in fact, and that, immediately after the witnesses had attested, the instrument was returned by them to the hands of the testator, his attention was called to their signatures, and he expressed his satisfaction and approval of what had been done. This view, which does no violence to the spirit and intent of the statute, is not without precedent and authority aside from the Michigan case, although it may, as said by the court below, run contrary to a majority of the decisions. See *Sturdivant* v. *Birchett* (10 Grat. 67), and *Riggs* v. *Riggs* (135 Mass. 238).

Judgment affirmed.

RUTHERFORD LAND & IMPROVEMENT CO. *vs.* SANNTROCK.

[Court of Errors and Appeals of New Jersey, June 18, 1900; 46 Atl. Rep. 648.]

WILLS—CONSTRUCTION—EXECUTORS—POWER TO MORTGAGE.

1. A testator, after ordering debts paid and bequeathing his household furniture, gave the income of his estate to his wife during widowhood, and, in case of her remarriage, devoted such income, above her dower right, to the maintenance and education of his children, who were also made his residuary beneficiaries. He appointed executors, and then provided as follows, viz.: " My real estate, wherever found, I give to my executor and executrix in trust for my estate; giving them full power and authority to dispose of the same at any time, if deemed for the benefit of my estate." *Held*, that the will gave no power to the executors to mortgage the lands of the testator.
2. Otherwise the rulings of the Court of Chancery in 44 Atl. 938, are approved.

(Syllabus by the court.)

APPEAL from Court of Chancery.

Bill by the Rutherford Land & Improvement Company against Frederick Sanntrock. Decree advised for plaintiff (44 Atl. 938), and defendant appeals.

Affirmed.

John I. Weller, for appellant.

Albert I. Drayton and *Joseph F. Randolph*, for respondent.

COLLINS, J.—In affirming this decree, we must disclaim concurrence in the opinion of the learned vice-chancellor that if the . mortgage to the Mutual Life Insurance Company, on which respondent's title rests, had been given directly by Mrs. Mohn, the surviving executrix and trustee of Arnold Mohn, instead of by her grantee, the infirmity of whose title was unknown to the company, it would have been perfectly good. This dictum of an experienced judge should not be passed *sub silentio*. It is based upon the idea that a general power to " dispose of " lands includes a power to mortgage. I find no decision to that effect. In the United States Supreme Court a majority of the judges were of opinion that, in the phrase " sold or disposed of," the disjunctive words ought not be considered as merely superfluous, and therefore that lands mortgaged had been " disposed of," but Mr. Justice BRADLEY, for himself and other judges, vigorously dissented; and the very ground of decision excludes the idea of the vice-chancellor, if the words stand alone. A dictum in a Pennsylvania case has a like basis. (*Gordon* v. *Preston*, 1 Watts, 385.) But in that state there still obtained the early English rule, long since modified, that a general power of sale includes a power to mortgage. (*Lancaster* v. *Dolan*, 1 Rawle, 141.) If there are other adjudged cases on the subject, they will be found to be peculiar in their circumstances, and dependent on the context of the words construed. To " dispose of " imports finality, and only where a power to sell would include a power to mortgage would those words, unmodified or undefined, imply such a power. In this state a general power of sale does not authorize a mortgage. (*Ferry* v. *Laible*, 31 N. J. Eq. 566.) The modification by this court of the decree advised by Vice-Chancellor VAN FLEET in that case was not upon that point. (Id., 32 N. J. Eq. 791.) A power to sell may include a power to mortgage, but only because of some exceptional reason,—generally, where there is a particular charge to which the devise is subject, and it is proper to raise money to meet it. (*Ferry* v. *Laible, ubi supra.*) An illustrative case is *Loebenthal* v. *Raleigh* (36 N. J. Eq. 169), where Chancellor RUNYON authorized a mortgage. The power construed was in these words: " If it should seem necessary at any time to dispose of a portion of my real estate for the payment of my debts, I hereby give my executors power so to do, at either public or private sale." The rule controlling the subject has been well stated as follows: "A power for trustees to sell will authorize a mortgage by them, which is a conditional sale, wherever the objects of the trust will be answered by a mortgage,—as, for instance, where the trust is to pay debts or raise portions. But, where the trusts declared of the purchase money show that the settlor contemplates an absolute conversion of the estate, a mortgage will be an improper execution of the power." (Hill, Trustees, 475.) The scheme of the will of Arnold Mohn is very simple. The testator, after ordering paid his debts and funeral expenses, and bequeathing to his wife his household furniture, devises to his wife, during widowhood, in lieu of dower, the net income of all his estate, with remainder to his children. Should his widow remarry, she is to receive only her dower right, and the rest of the income is to be used for the maintenance and education of his children, who are also made his residuary beneficiaries. He appoints his wife and a friend his executors, and then provides as follows: " My real estate, wheresoever found, I give to my executor and executrix in trust for my estate; giving them full power and authority to dispose of the same at any time if deemed by them for the benefit of my estate." Under such a will there is no reason, and therefore no power, for the trustees to give a mortgage.

GREENE vs. HUNTINGTON et al.

[Supreme Court of Errors of Connecticut, July 13, 1900; 46 Atl. Rep. 883.]

WILLS—CONSTRUCTION—DECISION OF EXECUTORS—LEGAL REPRESENTATIVES—DOWER—EQUITABLE REMAINDER IN FEE—APPORTIONMENT—SAVINGS-BANK DIVIDENDS.

1. Where a testator in his will declared that all questions as to the construction of his will should be determined by the executors appointed by him, their decision thereon is binding, unless in reaching it there is clear abuse of power.

2. A codicil gave a portion of the residuary estate in real property to trustees, to pay the income and profits to one for life, and on her death to convey the trust fund to her legal representatives. A section of the will gave pecuniary legacies to different persons, and, in case of their death before testator, to be given to the legal representatives

of such deceased legatees. *Held,* that as "legal representatives," in the latter case, clearly mean, not executors or administrators, but those who would take for their own benefit, the words in the former case should be construed in the same way, especially in view of the fact that to them the land was to be conveyed in fee.

3. A testator devised one-fourth of a certain portion of his property to his nephew J. in fee, after the determination of the life estate of testator's wife. Of the other three-fourths, he gave a life estate to J.'s brother, and upon his death to be conveyed in fee to J., if living, and, if dead, to his legal representatives. *Held,* that these two provisions should be construed in the same way with respect to the disposition of the beneficial title in remainder, and that, as the executors who had been empowered by the will to determine its construction, had construed the first provision to vest the beneficial title in J., at testator's death, the second provision should be construed to vest the beneficial title in J. at his brother's death.

4. Such remainder after the death of J.'s brother became part of his estate, J. having died before the determination of the life estate, and no conveyance by the trustee was necessary to perfect the title.

5. Under Gen. St. § 618, providing that a widow may have dower in lands of which her husband "died possessed in his own right," dower may be assigned in an equitable remainder in fee, though the possession was in the trustee, which dower interest is subject to the paramount title of the trustee for purposes of the trust.

6. A testator devised a portion of his residuary estate in trust for his wife for life, and on her death to convey the trust fund to her legal representatives. Under Gen. St. § 2952, providing that no estate shall be given by will to any persons not in being at the time of the death of the testator, or to their immediate issue or descendants, such a remainder in favor of her legal representatives, to be first ascertained at the time of her death, would be void. *Held,* that the legal representatives intended were those answering to that description at the death of testator.

7. There can be no apportionment, in favor of the estate of one holding a life estate in lands under her husband's will, of savings bank dividends not declared until after her death, since there can be no right to such dividends until they are severed from the general funds of the bank by vote of the directors.

CASE reserved from Superior Court, New London county; JOHN M. THAYER, Judge.

Action by Gardiner Greene, trustee under the will of Jedediah Huntington, against Annie E. Huntington and others, for a construction of said will. Reserved for the advice of this court upon the complaint and answers.

The fourth section of the will gave two-thirds of certain real estate in Norwich, known as the " Central Wharf Property," to the testator's grandnephews, Jedediah and John R. Huntington, in fee simple, and the rents of one-third of it to their mother, Mary Huntington, during her life, and at her decease devised said third to her said two sons in fee simple ; " thus making the said Jedediah and John R., at the decease of their mother, sole owners of said estate." The fifth section gave pecuniary legacies to a number of different persons, and, " in case any of them should die before I do, to the legal representatives of such deceased." The fifteenth, sixteenth, and seventeenth sections were as follows : " Fifteenth. I give, devise, and bequeath all the residue of my estate to the devisees and legatees named in the second, third, fourth, and fifth sections or clauses of this will, and direct the same to be divided between said devisees and legatees in the same proportion as the devises and bequests are made to them in said sections and clauses. Sixteenth. I authorize and empower my executors to sell any portion of my property at public or private sale, at their discretion, in case they shall deem it necessary so to do to better carry into effect the provisions of this will. Seventeenth. Should any informality appear or questions arise as to the meaning or legal construction of this instrument, I hereby direct that the distribution of my estate shall be made to such persons and associations as my executors shall determine to be my intended legatees and devisees, and their construction of my will shall be binding upon all parties interested." A codicil contained the following provision : " Second. The fourth section of said will is hereby revoked, and the following provisions are made in lieu thereof, to wit : (1) I give, devise, and bequeath one undivided third part of all my property on Central Wharf, in the city of Norwich, consisting of one acre of land, with the buildings thereon standing, to Jedediah Huntington, the eldest son of my deceased nephew, his heirs and assigns, forever. (2) I give, devise, and bequeath the other undivided two-thirds of my said property on Central Wharf to John T. Wait and James A. Hovey, and the survivor of them, in fee, upon trust to pay over one-half of the net income, rents, and profits thereof, as they shall accrue, to Mary, the widow of the said John G. Huntington, during her natural life, and to apply the other half of the said net income, rents, and

profits, or such portion thereof as the said trustees shall deem
necessary, to the maintenance and support of the said John R.
Huntington during his natural life, and after the death of the said
Mary to convey one undivided fourth part of the said trust estate,
in fee, to Jedediah Huntington, the eldest son of my deceased
nephew, or to his legal representatives, and to apply the net income, rents, and profits of the remaining undivided three-fourths
of said trust estate, or such portion thereof as they shall deem
necessary, to the maintenance and support of the said John R.
Huntington during his natural life, and upon the death of the
said John R., to convey the said undivided three-fourths of said
trust estate, in fee, to Jedediah Huntington, if living, or, if he is
dead, then to his legal representatives.   Third. Whereas, by my
said will bearing date the 26th day of April, A. D. 1871, I gave
and bequeathed a portion of my residuary estate to the said Mary
Huntington, I now desire to change my will in that respect, so
as to give, and I do hereby give, that portion of said residuary
estate to said John T. Wait and James A. Hovey, and the survivor of them, upon trust to pay the net income and profits of
said portion, as they shall accrue, to the said Mary during her
natural life, and upon her death to convey the trust fund to her
legal representatives."   The testator died in 1872; John R. Huntington, in 1884; and Mary Huntington, in 1898.   Jedediah died in
1885, intestate, leaving a widow and children.   In 1888, at the
request of the latter, the surviving executors undertook to determine a question which had arisen as to the construction of the
codicil, and, by a paper duly signed and recorded in the probate
records, declared the legal meaning of the second clause of the
second section thereof to be that the undivided two-thirds of the
Central Wharf property, devised by said clause to trustees,
" should vest, and that the same did vest, upon the death of the
said John R. Huntington, in Jedediah Huntington, the eldest son
of the said John R. Huntington, subject to the title of the trustees
under the provisions of said clause, and to the trust for the payment of one-half of the net income, rents, and profits of said estate, as they shall accrue, to the said Mary Huntington during
her natural life, as in said clause is expressed."   The plaintiff
holds in trust two-thirds of the Central Wharf property, which
is let at an annual rent of $800, and also deposits in several savings

banks, representing the share of the residue of the estate set to
trustees under the third section of the codicil. All income received up to October 1, 1898, has been duly paid to the proper
beneficiaries. Mary Huntington died October 26, 1898. Since
October 1, 1898, the plaintiff has received a quarter's rent ($200),
to December 31, 1898, and certain dividends from savings banks,
declared for periods of six months ending after October 26, 1898.
Mrs. Mary Huntington died in debt for the expenses of her last
illness, and left no property, apart from her interest, if any, in
said trust estate. The questions as to which the plaintiff sought
a construction of the will were as follows: " (1) Is the aforesaid
construction of the second paragraph of the second section of said
codicil, made by two of said executors, valid and conclusive? (2)
What is the duty of the trustee as to the conveyance by him of said
undivided two-thirds of said wharf property? To what persons
should the same be conveyed, and what interests therein should be
conveyed to such persons, respectively? What should be the form
of such conveyance? (3) As to the trust funds held under said
third section of said codicil, what is the meaning of the expression
' her legal representatives ' ? (4) If the trust funds under said
third section should be paid to the families of the deceased sons
of said Mary, do the widows of said sons take anything? Is the
division between the descendants of said Mary to be *per capita* or
per stirpes? (5) Is the estate of said Mary Huntington entitled
to apportionment of the income of said trust fund, and, if so, to
what payment is her administrator entitled? (6) In case of any
portion of the trust estate being payable to the residuary legatees
under the will, what is the meaning of the expression ' the legal
representatives of such deceased,' in the fifth section of the will?
(7) In case any of the legacies or devises of the will are wholly or
partly void by the law of perpetuities or otherwise, what persons
take the property covered by such legacies or devises, and in what
shares?

Wallace S. Allis, for Annie R. Dahlgren *et al.*

Amos A. Browning, for Lillian Huntington *et al.*

Solomon Lucas, for Annie E. Huntington *et al.*

Charles F. Thayer, for estate of Mary Huntington.

BALDWIN, J. (after stating the facts).—It was determined in a previous action brought for a judicial construction of this will that the proper tribunal to which to resort for determining its meaning was that which the testator had himself created for that purpose. (*Wait* v. *Huntington,* 40 Conn. 9, 11.) The sixteenth section gave the executors a general power of sale, at their discretion. The seventeenth conferred the power now under consideration. The former unquestionably passed, with the office, upon the death of Jedediah Huntington, to the surviving executors. The same rule must apply to the latter. The construction given in 1888 to the second clause of the second section of the codicil by the two executors then surviving must therefore stand as binding upon all parties interested, unless in reaching it there was a clear abuse of power. (*Wait* v. *Huntington, supra; Pray* v. *Belt,* 1 Pet. 670, 680; 7 L. Ed. 309.) The object of the second section of the codicil was to vest the ultimate ownership of the Central Wharf property in Jedediah Huntington or those who should represent him. The trustees were, after the death of his mother, " to convey one undivided fourth part of the said trust estate in fee to Jedediah Huntington, the eldest son of my deceased nephew, or to his legal representatives." There are no direct words of gift, as respects the fee of this land except that of the legal estate to the trustees. As they, however, took a legal estate only, the beneficial estate should be construed as vesting as of right, at the testator's decease, in those to whom it was to be ultimately conveyed, if the words of the testator may reasonably bear such an interpretation. A devise to A. or his heirs is, in legal effect, a devise to A. if he be living at the decease of the testator, but, if he be not then living, to those who then may be his heirs. The term " legal representatives " had been previously used in the fifth section of the will, in the provision against the lapse of any of the pecuniary legacies therein given. It is plain that, as thus used, it meant, not executors or administrators, who might under certain circumstances represent only creditors, but those who would take for their own benefit. The term " *prima facie* " should receive the same interpretation when repeated in the codicil, and this presumption is strengthened from the fact that it is to these legal representatives that the land is to be conveyed in fee. To direct such a conveyance to an executor or administrator would be unusual, and, under most circumstances, inappropriate. If, therefore, this provision of the codicil stood alone, Jedediah would have taken at the testator's decease an equitable fee in a fourth of the wharf property, subject to the life interest in favor of his mother. As to the conveyance of the other three-fourths, the direction is somewhat different. It is, upon the death of his brother John, to be conveyed in fee " to Jedediah Huntington, if living, or, if he is dead, then to his legal representatives." Taken by themselves alone, these words would point strongly to the conclusion that, unless he should survive John, his representatives were to be the grantees, and so the ultimate beneficiaries in remainder. But it is highly improbable that the testator contemplated a division of the property, by which upon his decease one-fourth should go to Jedediah, and at a later period the other three-fourths to his representatives. To avoid such a result, each of these provisions must be construed in the same way. The executors so construed them as to make the former control, as respects the nature of the beneficial title in remainder after the death of John R. Huntington. If it became vested in Jedediah at the testator's decease, it was certainly vested in him at the decease of his brother. To read the devise to him as absolute in case he survived the testator was, to say the least, not an inadmissible construction of it, and the determination of the executors (which may fairly be rested upon this position) therefore bound all parties in interest. Upon the death of Jedediah this remainder became part of his estate, and no conveyance by the trustee was or is necessary to perfect the title, but there would be no impropriety in his executing release deeds in favor of those who have succeeded to the interest of the decedent. His widow, under our statute, had right of dower in one-third part of the real estate of which he " died possessed in his own right." (Gen. St. § 618.) He was, when he died, the owner of an equitable remainder in fee in the wharf property, in his own right. A reversioner in fee, subject to an estate for life, is said to be seized of the reversion of the tenements as of fee and right. (2 Washb. Real Prop. *391.) He who owns a vested remainder in fee holds equally in his own right. The remainder vested in Jedediah Huntington was only an equitable one, and the land was in the possession of the legal owner. But this possession was for the purpose of protecting and managing the property for the ultimate benefit of the remainder-man, as well as for the present benefit of the life tenant. Dower is an estate favored by the law. The common law of England favored it by establishing the right of the widow in lands held by her husband as a trustee. A different rule was adopted in Connecticut, by allowing her to resort only to lands held by the husband "in his own right." (*Fish* v. *Fish,* 1 Conn. 559; *Goddard* v. *Prentice,* 17 id. 546, 555.) The same considerations which led us to construe the statute as embracing equities of redemption require that it should be read as including equitable remainders in fee, although the possession may be held in trust. The land in such a case is substantially the husband's, and the possession may fairly be deemed to be held for him. (1 Perry, Trusts, § 324; *Hemingway* v. *Hemingway,* 22 Conn. 462, 472.) The term "possessed," in our statute, is more comprehensive that the word "seized," which is employed in those of some other states, the courts of which have felt bound to exclude dower in equitable estates. (*Reed* v. *Whitney,* 7 Gray, 533, 536; *Todd* v. *Oviatt,* 58 Conn. 174, 190; 20 Atl. 440; 7 L. R. A. 693.) The widow of Jedediah Huntington therefore was entitled to dower in the wharf property, subject to the paramount title of the trustee for the purposes of the trust.

The term "legal representatives," in the third section of the codicil, must receive the same meaning already attributed to it when previously used by the testator, in so far as to take it as descriptive of those who would upon Mary Huntington's decease succeed by law, as her next of kin, to the beneficial interest in her intestate estate. We think that it may also be properly held to refer to those answering this description, not at the time of her death, but at that of the testator. This conclusion is supported by the rule that the law favors vested estates, coupled with the fact that there are here no direct words of gift, and by the principle that the testator is not to be presumed to have intended an illegal disposition of his property. Under the statute against perpetuities, which was in force when he died (Gen. St. § 2952), the remainder in favor of Mrs. Huntington's legal representatives would have been void, had he intended those coming under that designation to be first ascertained at the time of her death. (*Tingier* v. *Chamberlin,* 71 Conn. 466; 42 Atl. 718.) If he meant only those who were her next of kin at the date of his own death, his legacy in their favor is valid. That construction is therefore to be adopted. (*St. John* v. *Dann,* 66 Conn. 401, 405; 34 Atl. 110.)

There can be no apportionment in favor of the estate of Mrs. Huntington of the income of the trust received since her decease. Rent is never apportionable, nor are dividends from savings banks. While it may be customary for these banks to make such dividends semi-annually, and at a fixed rate, the sums divided upon the plaintiff's deposits were nevertheless a part of the capital of the trust fund, until severed from it by the vote of the directors. The borrower of money on interest payable semi-annually is under an absolute contractual liability, by virtue of which the interest is deemed, in favor of a life tenant, to accrue from day to day, and so to be apportionable in case of the death of the latter during any half year. Savings banks, on the contrary, are mere agencies for investing the funds of depositors, and their only obligation to them, as to any resulting income, is to pay or credit such dividends from it as the directors may from time to time declare in the exercise of a sound discretion. The moneys thus divided upon the plaintiff's deposits may have been wholly earned since the death of Mrs. Huntington, or they may come from a surplus accumulated years before. Her estate has no interest in anything that was not actually severed from the general funds of the bank during her life. (*Spooner* v. *Phillips,* 62 Conn. 62, 70; 24 Atl. 524; 16 L. R. A. 461.)

The Superior Court is advised that the first question stated in the complaint should be answered in the affirmative, and the fifth in the negative; that the trustee is under no duty to make any conveyance of any interest in the wharf property; that the expression "her legal representatives," in the third section of the codicil, refers to Jedediah and John R. Huntington only; that, upon the death of each of these, his half of the remainder in the trust fund created by said codicil became part of his estate; that no part of said trust estate passes under the residuary clause of the will; and that no part of the dispositions affecting said trust estate offended the statute of perpetuities. No costs will be taxed in this court.

The other judges concurred.

HUDSON *et al. vs.* BARRATT.

[Supreme Court of Kansas, July 7, 1900; 61 Pac. Rep. 737.]

PARTIES — SUBSTITUTION — EXECUTOR — RESIGNATION — SET-
TLEMENT—ACTION ON BOND.

1. The real parties in interest may be substituted as plaintiffs in an action previously brought in the name of the state upon an executor's bond.
2. The Probate Court has the power, and it is its duty, to require a full and final accounting, and to make a settlement with an executor who has resigned, been removed, or whose letters have been revoked, and to order him to deliver the personal effects and assets of the estate to his successor.
3. Where the estate of a deceased person is in process of settlement in the Probate Court, and an accounting has not been had with a former executor therein, and there has been no refusal by such executor to make a full and final accounting, and where a full settlement may be required and an adequate remedy had in that court, no occasion exists . to invoke the equitable jurisdiction of the District Court, or for interference by that court with the settlement in the Probate Court; and in such a case an action cannot be maintained on the executor's bond until an accounting has been had in the proper tribunal, a liability ascertained, and an opportunity afforded the former executor to discharge it.

(Syllabus by the court.)

ERROR from District Court, Atchison county; W. T. BLAND, Judge.

Action by the state against B. F. Hudson and others. Thereafter Norman Barratt, administrator, was substituted as plaintiff. Judgment for plaintiff. Defendants bring error.

Reversed.

B. F. Hudson, C. D. Walker and *J. L. Berry,* for plaintiffs in error.

W. W. & W. F. Guthrie, for defendant in error.

JOHNSTON, J.—Susan Grimes died testate February 6, 1890. The will was at once probated, and B. F. Hudson, who had been designated in the will as executor, was granted letters testamentary. He gave bond in the sum of $120,000, and entered upon the

discharge of his duties.   On May 3' 1890, some of the heirs instituted an action to contest the will, and it was adjudged invalid by
the District Court, July 2, 1891.   Proceedings in error were begun
in this court by the executor on July 13, 1891, when an order was
made staying the execution of the judgment of the District Court
and all proceedings in the case in that court, and later the order
was modified so that the executor might proceed to preserve and
protect the property of the estate, but forbidding any further distribution of the same until the decision of the merits in the Supreme Court.   On December 7, 1895, the Supreme Court affirmed
the judgment of the District Court. (*Hudson* v. *Hughan,* 56
Kan. 152; 42 Pac. 701.)   On January 18, 1896, the Probate Court
made an order appointing Norman Barratt as administrator of the
estate, and from this order an appeal was taken to the District
Court, where it remained pending until April 16, 1897, when the
order of appointment was confirmed.   He at once qualified, and
entered upon the discharge of his duties as administrator *de bonis
non* of the estate.   The will, which was probated, and subsequently set aside, provided for the disposition of the property by
private or public sale, and directed how the proceeds should be
distributed.   While the executor was in control he collected from
the personal estate more than $18,000, and also a considerable
sum from the rentals of real estate.   On February 11, 1891, he
filed his first annual report in the Probate Court, and continued to
administer the estate as executor, under the direction of the
Probate Court, until the will was set aside.   Under the order of
the Supreme Court staying the judgment and proceedings in the
District Court he continued to act as executor of the estate, with
no authority except to preserve and protect the property of the
estate until the final decision of the cause in the Supreme Court.
In September, 1891, after the judgment had been rendered setting
aside the will, the executor divided the moneys in his hands belonging to the estate among the five noncontesting heirs, but gave
nothing to those who were attacking the will.   After the appointment of the administrator, Hudson presented to the Probate Court
what was termed a final settlement of his executorship, and asked
to have the same considered and approved by the Probate Court.
He tendered in court and to his successor any balance of moneys
that might be found due or any property in his possession belong-

ing to the estate, and asked that compensation, expenses, and attorney's fees might be allowed. The noncontesting heirs protested against the acceptance of the report, and the Probate Court refused to accept the report of Hudson as acting executor of the estate, and decided that it would only recognize and deal with the newly-appointed administrator. Barratt, as administrator, made a demand upon Hudson to turn over the property and funds which had come into his hands as executor, and, no accounting having been had, Hudson refused the demand. An action was then brought in the name of the state against Hudson and his sureties upon the bond given by Hudson as executor, and judgment was claimed upon the bond for the sum of $21,039. After the action was instituted, the court, upon the application of the administrator, allowed an amendment of the petition, and the substitution of the administrator as' plaintiff. At the trial elaborate findings of fact were made by the court, and based thereon the court gave judgment against the defendants for $6,758.05, and also directed the delivery to the administrator of a certain promissory note for $1,000, which had been in the possession of the executor.

The defendants complain of the judgment, and the first error assigned is the ruling of the court permitting the amendment of the petition and the substitution of a new plaintiff. The amendment did not change substantially the cause of action stated in the original petition. Both petitions counted upon the executor's bond, and asked for a recovery of the property and moneys of the estate which the executor had failed to account for or turn over to the administrator upon his demand. The amended petition was more elaborate, and set up some additional items and claims upon which there was an alleged liability. No limitation had run in the meantime upon the new matters or added claims of liability, and the defendants were given abundant time for answer and preparation. No error can be predicated on the substitution of the administrator for the state of Kansas as plaintiff. While the bond ran to the state, it was for the benefit of all parties interested in the estate, and, as the administrator was the real party in interest, it was not improper to substitute him as plaintiff. (*City of Atchison* v. *Twine*, 9 Kan. 350; *Hanlin* v. *Baxter*, 20 id. 134; *Commissioners* v. *Munger*, 24 id. 205; *Paola Town Co.* v. *Krutz*, 22 id. 725; Civ. Code, § 139.)

A more serious objection is the bringing of an action against the executor before the Probate Court wherein the settlement of the estate was pending had an accounting with the executor, or had determined that there was a liability upon the bond. The Probate Court has primary and complete jurisdiction over the estates of deceased persons. Jurisdiction had been acquired by the Probate Court of Atchison county over the Grimes estate, the settlement of which is still open and undetermined. That court had probated the will, and from it Hudson had received his credentials as executor. To it he had accounted, and his first annual report had been received and filed. Under the supervision of that court, the estate had been partially administered by Hudson, and his continuance in office and the rightfulness of his possession of the estate while the will case was pending was recognized by this court by the orders of stay. No final accounting had been had with Hudson in the Probate Court, and he had not refused to make such accounting. Why should the Probate Court surrender or be devested of its jurisdiction over the unsettled estate and of the accounting of the personal representatives which had been appointed? What reasons exist for the interference of the District Court, or for the arrest of proceedings already commenced in a court of competent jurisdiction? The Probate Court, as we have seen, has at least primary and complete jurisdiction of the unsettled estate, and, even if the District Court may be regarded as having concurrent jurisdiction in such matters, the universal rule is that where two courts have equal jurisdiction over a subject-matter of dispute, and the parties to it, the one which first obtained jurisdiction is entitled to continue in its exercise to the end. In *Stratton* v. *McCandless* (27 Kan. 296), it was said that " in cases of this kind, where the administrator is still acting and the estate is not settled, and the Probate Court has complete and ample jurisdiction over the administrator and over the estate, actions in other jurisdictions against the administrator and his sureties on the administrator's bond should not be encouraged." The present action, like the one in the case cited, " attempts to take a matter which properly and legitimately belongs to the jurisdiction of the Probate Court, and a matter which ought to be settled and determined in that court, and to place it within a jurisdiction which has no general control over the affairs of the estate." It is true that the jurisdiction of the Probate Court in respect to estates is not absolutely exclusive, but the cases which may be wrested from the jurisdiction of the Probate Court and tried in the District Court are special and limited. " The jurisdiction of the District Court in such matters is an equitable one, and in its exercise the court will be governed by the rules of equity, one of which is that as ·a general rule it will only take jurisdiction where the plaintiff has no other adequate remedy by ordinary legal proceedings in the tribunal especially provided by statute." (*Carter* v. *Christie,* 57 Kan. 492; 46 Pac. 949. See, also, *Proctor* v. *Dicklow,* 57 Kan. 119; 45 Pac. 86.) Is there no adequate remedy in the Probate Court? So far as an accounting and settlement with an executor or administrator is concerned, there appears to be no inadequacy of remedy, nor necessity for appealing to an exceptional jurisdiction. The statute provides for an accounting in the Probate Court annually, and at other times, and as often as that court may require, until the final settlement is made. (Ex'rs & Adm'rs' Act, § 147.)

The obligation of the bond which the executor gave required an accounting in that tribunal, and the statute makes specific provisions as to how an executor or administrator may be compelled to render his account, and it also provides for a final discharge of the executor after the accounting and settlement, which shall exonerate him and his sureties from liability. (Ex'rs & Adm'rs' Act, §§ 149, 151, 175.) It is argued that the court had no authority to require an accounting by Hudson because he was no longer an executor; and, further, that the statute does not provide for an accounting by a removed executor, or that the Probate Court may order him to turn over the assets of the estate to his successor. Hudson, we think, is to be treated as a removed executor. He held his position and administered the estate under the sanction and supervision of the Probate Court, but the final adjudication that the will was invalid necessarily terminated his authority, and removed him from the position of executor. The statute provides that in such cases the sales lawfully made in good faith and other lawful acts done by the executor shall remain valid and effectual. (Ex'rs & Adm'rs' Act, § 27.) The court had jurisdiction of the estate notwithstanding the removal, and we think it also had jurisdiction of a present or former executor

until a final accounting and settlement of the estate was had with
him.   We find nothing in the statute or in the theory of the law
excepting a removed executor from the general requirements of
the act as to an accounting.   The fact that he has been removed
does not close his relations with the estate, nor take the estate or
the property belonging to it out of the jurisdiction of the court.
As indicating that the power of the court is not limited to executors or administrators, or persons holding *quasi* official relations
with the estate, it may be noted that the statute gives the Probate Court authority to cite even strangers before it who have possession of the assets of the estate, or who are suspected of having
concealed, embezzled, or conveyed away any money or assets of
the estate, and to compel a delivery thereof to the executor or administrator entitled to receive the same.   (Ex'rs & Adm'rs' Act,
§§ 196-200.)   The general trend of the authorities is that the
revocation of letters or the resignation or removal of an executor
does not affect the authority of the Probate Court to require an
accounting.   So it has been held that where an executor or administrator resigns before the settlement of his accounts, and his resignation is accepted, the court does not thereby lose jurisdiction over
his person nor the settlement of his accounts, and may proceed
with the settlement in the same manner as if he had continued in
the execution of his trust.   (*Slagle* v. *Entrekin*, 44 Ohio St. 637;
10 N. E. 675.   See, also, *Casoni* v. *Jerome*, 58 N. Y. 315; *Nevitt*
v. *Woodburn*, 160 Ill. 203; 43 N. E. 385; *In re Hood*, 104 N. Y.
103; 10 N. E. 35; *In re Radovich*, 74 Cal. 536; 16 Pac. 321.)
In 1 Woerner, Adm'rs. 589, it is said that, "after revocation, removal, or resignation, the former executor or administrator cannot complete a sale which he has been negotiating on behalf of the
estate, nor collect assets, but the court has jurisdiction to settle
his accounts as though he were still in office."   In Schoulder,
Ex'rs & Adm'rs, § 520, it is said that "the American rule of the
present day is therefore, with few exceptions, that the Court of
Chancery usually has neither jurisdiction nor occasion to interfere
in the settlement of the estate, and to order an accounting by an
executor or administrator; and, even as to one who has resigned
or been discharged from his trust, our law inclines to treat him
as one whose accounts should be closed under probate direction, as
in the case of one who has died in office."   It is true that some of

the decisions cited are based on statutes which expressly authorize an accounting with a former executor or administrator, but the implication of our statute, as well as the power intrusted to our Probate Court, justifies the view which we have taken.

Reference has been made in the argument to the cases of *Ingraham* v. *Maynard* (6 Tex. 130) and *Francis* v. *Northcote* (id. 185), which seem to hold to a contrary view, based apparently upon the provisions of the constitution and statutes of Texas, constituting the court as an inferior tribunal, with jurisdiction limited to certain enumerated subjects. In matters of probate our court is not an inferior tribunal, and we have no doubt that it is the duty and within the power of the Probate Court to settle the accounts of a former executor, determine what shall be allowed him as compensation for his services and for expenses, and then to direct the turning over and delivery of the residue of the estate to his successor. It is not for the successor to decide what allowance shall be made to Hudson for the partial execution of the trust, or for expenses incurred while he acted in that capacity. The orderly and legal course is that a full accounting and settlement shall be made by the former executor in the court having jurisdiction and control of the estate, and that the transfer of the assets and funds remaining in his possession shall be made to the successor, under the direction and supervision of that court. The taking of the matter from the jurisdiction of the Probate Court cannot be sustained on the ground of circumlocution or a multiplicity of suits.

There is full power in the Probate Court to determine whether the estate has been faithfully administered, whether moneys have been improperly paid out or an improper distribution made, and what amount of money and assets should be in Hudson's hands, and for which he is accountable, after allowance has been made for services and expenses. Section 26 of the executors and administrators' act provides, it is true, that an administrator appointed in place of a removed executor is entitled to the possession of the estate, and may maintain an action against the former executor and his sureties on the bond, but nothing in the provision indicates that an accounting and settlement with the former executor may be dispensed with. No good reason can be seen why the sureties upon the executor's bond should be required to answer in court, and be harrassed with litigation, until default has been made by the executor, or why there is any liability upon the bond by the tribunal specially provided to make such determination. If an accounting is had in the Probate Court, and the executor makes a complete and satisfactory settlement, and turns over to his successor all the property and assets of the estate in his hands and for which he is accountable, there will be no necessity for litigation with the sureties upon the bond, and hence there would be no ground for invoking the equitable jurisdiction of the District Court. (*Weihe* v. *Stathan*, 67 Cal. 84; 7 Pac. 143.)

We conclude that there was no occasion to interfere in the settlement of the estate in the Probate Court, and that until the settlement was had by the tribunal appointed for that purpose an action upon the executor's bond could not be maintained. The judgment of the District Court will therefore be reversed and cause remanded for further proceedings. All the justices concurring.

SNIDER *vs.* SNIDER.

[Court of Appeals of New York, October 3, 1899; 160 N. Y. 151; 54 N. E. Rep. 676.]

WILLS—BEQUEST OF LIFE ESTATE—CONSTRUCTIVE APPEAL.

1. A bequest was of a sum to the legatee for life, and at his death to his heirs, if he have any, but, should he die without issue, remainder over to his brother. *Held,* that "heirs" meant "heirs of the body."

2. In an action against the administrator of a deceased legatee of a life estate in money, it appeared that the money had gone into a farm, which the legatee had devised to others; but such devisees were not joined, nor the necessity of their being made parties suggested, but defendant tried the case on the theory that the matter had been adjusted. *Held* that, on appeal, defendant could not first insist that the judgment for the remainder of the legacy should have been charged against the farm.

APPEAL from Supreme Court, Appellate Division, Second Department.

Action by Abraham Snider, individually and as executor of the will of Michael Snider, deceased, against C. Louise Snider, as executor of the will of Michael G. Snider, deceased, and another. From a judgment for plaintiff, affirmed by the Appellate Division (42 N. Y. Supp. 613), defendant C. Louise Snider appeals. Affirmed.

Lewis Hasbrouck and *A. H. Seeger,* for appellant.

George R. Brewster, for respondent.

PARKER, C. J.—This action was brought by Abraham Snider, individually and as executor of the last will and testament of his father, Michael Snider, to recover of the estate of his brother, Michael G. Snider, the sum of $2,500 received by the latter under and by virtue of a provision of the will of Michael Snider reading as follows: " I give and bequeath the sum of two thousand five hundred dollars to my son Michael G. Snider, to be paid to him by the executors of this, my will, and to be held, used, and enjoyed by him, my said son, during his life, and at his death to his heir or heirs, should he have any. Should he die without issue, I give and bequeath said sum of two thousand five hundred dollars to my son Abraham." We agree with the learned Appellate Division that the gift to Michael was only of a life estate, the principal to go to Abraham upon the death of Michael without descendants, the term, " his heir or heirs," in the connection in which it is used, meaning " heirs of his body," and we should have affirmed upon the opinion of that court but for the contention of the appellant that the amount of the legacy should have been charged in the first instance by the judgment upon the farm devised by Michael G. Snider to two of the sons of the plaintiff, resort being had to the rest of the estate for the collection only of such portion of the judgment as the proceeds of a sale of the farm should fail to satisfy. It does appear that Michael G. Snider invested the $2,500 in the farm referred to, which was of the value of between $10,000 and $13,000, but, notwithstanding these facts, the record does not permit this court to pass upon the question suggested. The persons to whom Michael G. Snider devised the farm were not made parties to the action at the time of the commencement, nor were they subsequently brought in, as they might have been. It is true, as the appellant urges, that they might have been made parties upon the application of the plaintiff, and it is also true that it was within the power of the trial court, upon its own motion, to bring them in by its order; and had the defendant directed the attention of the court to the matter, and it had then neglected or refused to bring them in, an exception taken thereto would have presented the question whether it was the defendant's right, under the evidence, to have them brought in, to the end that the rights of all the parties might be determined. A careful examination of the record fails to disclose, in the voluminous and carefully prepared answer, in the objections taken, or in the statements addressed by counsel to the court, that it was then his claim that the farm should first be devoted to the payment of the amount of the legacy, and that in order to accomplish that result, it was necessary that the devisees of the farm should be made parties. On the contrary, when the defendant's counsel introduced the evidence relating to the farm and its value, objection was made to its introduction, and, the court inquiring the purpose of it, counsel answered: " It is a defense; we say in our answer that there was an arrangement by which this matter was adjusted afterwards." Thereupon the objection was overruled and the answer permitted. Objections to other questions were interposed, and the court in overruling one of the objections said: " I will only permit it on the same line that there is to be some proof connecting it." Thus we see that the case was not tried upon the theory that the legacy should be charged upon the real estate in the improvement of wh'ch it was expended, and hence the case is well within the rule that on appeal a party must be held to the theory of his trial. *(People* v. *Dalton,* 159 N. Y. 235; 53 N. E. 1113; *Drucker* v. *Railway Co.,* 106 N. Y. 157; 12 N. E. 568; *Baird* v. *Mayor, etc.,* 96 N. Y. 567, 603; *Stapenhorst* v. *Wolff,* 65 id. 596; *Home Ins. Co.* v. *Western Transp. Co.,* 51 id. 93.) This court is not, therefore, at liberty to pass upon the question pressed upon its attention, whether in equity the farm, in the improvement of which the legacy was invested, is primarily liable for its payment. The judgment should be affirmed with costs. All concur.

Judgment affirmed.

In re Steinmetz's Estate.

Appeal of Provident Life and Trust Co.

[Supreme Court of Pennsylvania, February 12, 1900; 194 Pa. St. 611; 45 Atl. Rep. 663.]

Wills—Beneficiaries—" Children."

The will, by the first item, gave the homestead in trust for the use of testator's wife and his four children, naming them, authorized a sale on the request of a majority of them, or of the survivors of them, provided that the proceeds should go to the wife and four children absolutely, share and share alike; but, if the wife or any of said children should be deceased at his death, or when the sale was made, the share of such one should go to the survivors. The third item gave all the personal estate to the wife and four children, share and share alike. The fourth item gave the income of one-fifth of the real estate, other than the homestead to his wife for life, and from her death gave the one-fifth part to be divided equally between his four children; gave the income of another one-fifth part to his daughter for life, and, from her death, then, as to said one-fifth part, to the children which she might leave; and to each of the three sons it gave one-fifth of the real estate in the same language and for the same uses in which the gift was made to the daughter. The fifth item provided, in case of the death of his said sons or his daughter, or either of them, without surviving issue, he gave the share given to his child so dying to " my surviving child or children " in equal shares. *Held*, that the word " children " did not include testator's grandchildren, and that, where one of his children died, leaving issue, and thereafter the mother died without issue, the children of the one dying first did not participate in the share of the one dying thereafter.

Appeal from Orphans' Court, Montgomery County.

In the matter of the estate of Jacob Steinmetz, deceased. The Provident Life & Trust Company, guardian of Jacob Steinmetz Bailey, a minor, petitioned for citation against the surviving executors of deceased to show cause why a decree of distribution should not be entered awarding certain money to petitioner. From a decree denying the application, petitioner appeals. Affirmed.

Jacob Steinmetz, the testator, made his will in 1878. At this time he was living with his wife and four children, at the home farm. He died in 1881, his wife and four children surviving him. The family was still living together at the home farm, the children being all of full age, and unmarried. The testator left an estate consisting of the home farm, disposed of under the second item of the will, a considerable personal estate passing under the third item, and his residuary real estate passing under the fourth and fifth items. The widow died in 1888, in the lifetime of all the children. Three of the children married,—George H., who has issue; Susan, who had issue (Jacob Steinmetz Bailey, the appellant), and died in 1890; and Jacob R., who died in 1898, without leaving issue. John B. is still a bachelor. The question at issue concerns the trust fund formerly held for Jacob R. Steinmetz, and which passes over, under the fifth item, on his death without issue, and consists of the principal and income of one-third of the residuary real estate disposed of under the fourth item, being the Jacob R. Steinmetz part and its accretion, on the death of the widow.

The opinion of the court below is as follows:

" This application was heard on petition and answer. The rights of the claimant must be determined by the interpretation of the will of Jacob Steinmetz. The testator devised his homestead to the executors, in trust for the use of his wife and children, naming them. This farm, he declares, shall be a home to them ' as long as they can remain together, and desire so to do.' A majority, or majority of the survivors, may request a sale of the farm, and the proceeds he gives to the wife and four children absolutely, share and share alike. If, however, the wife, or any of his said children should be deceased at the time of his death, or at the time of the sale of the farm, then the share of the one so deceased shall go to the survivors in equal shares. All his personal estate he gives to his wife and four children, share and share alike. All the real estate other than the homestead aforesaid he gives, devises, and bequeaths as follows: ' Item 4th. I give, devise, and bequeath the use, improvement, rents, interest, and income arising from one-fifth part thereof unto my beloved wife, Christina T., for and during all the term of her natural life, and from and immediately after her death I give and devise the said one-fifth part or share, to be equally divided, share and share alike, between my four children above named; the part or share in this bequest or devise of my said children to be held, however, by them in the same manner and for the same uses as are hereinafter set forth and declared of and concerning the parts or shares of my said real estate in this item mentioned, bequeathed and devised for the use of my said children. The use, improvement, rents, interest and income arising from one other fifth part thereof I give, devise, and bequeath unto my daughter, Susan Rebecca, for and during all the term of her natural life, and from and immediately after her death, then, as to the said one-fifth part of my said real estate, ground rents, etc., to and for the only proper use and benefit of all and every the child and children which she, my said daughter, may leave, and the lawful issue of any of them who may then be deceased having left such issue, to be equally divided between them, share and share alike, such issue of any deceased child or children of my said daughter taking, however, only such part or share thereof as his or her or their deceased parent or parents would have had and taken had she or they been living.' To each of the three sons he gives and devises one-fifth of his real estate, in the same language and for the same uses in which the bequest is made to the daughter, except that the share of Jacob R. is to be free, clear, and discharged from any claim of his creditors. In Item 5 he provides: ' In case of the decease of my said sons, Jacob R., John B., George H., or my daughter, Susan Rebecca, or either of them, without leaving lawful issue surviving them, then, and in such case, I give, devise, and bequeath the said part or share hereinbefore given, devised, and bequeathed to the child or children of my child so dying, and the use, improvement, rents, interest, and income thereof hereinbefore given for life to my child so dying, in item 4th, unto my surviving child or children, in equal shares and proportions, in the same manner, for the same uses, intents, and purposes as are hereinbefore set forth and declared of and concerning the parts or shares of my said real estate hereinbefore in item 4th given, devised, and bequeathed for the use, benefit, and behoof of my said children respectively.' We cited such parts of the will of Jacob Steinmetz as are pertinent to the issues now pending before us. The wife and four children survived the testator. The widow died in 1888. Susan Rebecca died in 1890, leaving to survive her a husband, Samuel A. Bailey, now deceased, and one child, Jacob Steinmetz Bailey, the petitioner in this case. Jacob R. died in 1897, without leaving lawful issue to survive him. The executors of Jacob Steinmetz, the elder, filed their account showing a balance of real estate in their hands amounting to $91,692.08, and income on the same, accrued after the death of the son Jacob L., amounting to $1,555.62. This said principal fund constitutes three-fourths of that part of testator's estate designated in his will as all the rest, residue, and remainder of his real estate, including ground rents, passing under the fourth and fifth items of the will, and is held by the executors as trustees. The remaining one-fourth of said principal fund was, upon the death of Susan Rebecca, paid to the guardian of Jacob Steinmetz Bailey, who was the only lawful issue of the said Susan.

" The petitioner contends that upon the death of the son Jacob R., without issue, one-third of this principal fund became distributable in equal share to John B., George H., and the minor, Jacob Steinmetz Bailey,—or one-ninth thereof to each. The executors and trustees contend that the income of said principal fund belongs to the said John B. and George H. as the surviving children of the testator, and that the principal fund must remain intact, and be held by the trustees for the benefit of said two surviving children. This controversy arises over the interpretation to be given to the fifth item of testator's will. The other portions of the instrument are important only so far as they may throw light upon the testator's intent and meaning in his use of the language found in the fifth item. This fifth item provides for the disposition of an interest in the real estate in case a son or daughter should die without leaving lawful issue surviving him or her. To what period does the time of survivorship refer? Clearly, not to the death of the testator, but to the death of the son or daughter. It is true that the period of survivorship is to be taken as the death of the testator, unless a contrary intent is apparent. The will gives a life estate in this realty to the sons and daughter. The primary and controlling gift is to the sons and daughter for life, and, upon the death of any one leaving issue, the remainder is to pass to such issue, but, in case of death without leaving issue, then certain interests pass to the surviving children. The words ' Immediately after the death of my son, then, as to the said one-fifth part of my said real estate, to and for the only proper use and benefit of all and every the child and children which my said son may leave,' clearly fix the time when the issue can take, to wit, the death of the son; and the devise to surviving children must refer to the same period, for then only can the contingency, on which alone they are to take, be determined. (*Woelpper's Appeal,* 126 Pa. St. 562; 17 Atl. 870.) The four children and their issue were the principal objects of the testator's bounty, and the time he had in mind when the shares should possibly go to any one else was the death of his children, respectively, and it was with reference to that time that he designated the surviving children. Who are included in the words ' unto my surviving child or children,' in the fifth item of the will? Under a bequest to children, grandchildren and other remote issue are excluded, unless it be the apparent intention of the testator, declared by his will, to provide for the children of a deceased child. But such construction can only arise from a clear intention or necessary implication; as where there are not other children than grandchildren, or when the term ' children ' is further explained by a limitation over in default of issue. The word ' children ' does not ordinarily and properly speaking, comprehend grandchildren, or issue generally. Their being included in that term is only permitted in two cases, viz., from utter necessity, which occurs when the will would remain inoperative unless the sense of the word ' children ' were extended beyond its natural import, and where the testator has clearly shown by other words that he did not intend to use the term ' children ' in the proper, actual meaning, but in a more extended sense. (*In re Hunt's Estate,* 133 Pa. St. 260; 19 Atl. 548; *Barnitz's Appeal,* 5 Pa. St. 264; *Horwitz* v. *Norris,* 49 id. 213; *Castner's Appeal,* 88 id. 478.) The petitioner fails to bring his case within either exception to the general rule of construction. There is no necessity to give the extended meaning to the word. There are children living now, and all the children were living when the testator died and the will went into effect. Nor has the testator clearly shown by other words that he uses the word ' children ' in its most extensive sense. Throughout the whole will, when he uses the word ' children,' there are modifications and explanatory words, which clearly show that by the use of the word he means to designate his three sons and daughter. He speaks of them in the second item as ' my four children,' ' my wife and children, or a majority of them,' ' my said children.'

In the third item, as well as in the fourth, he repeats the words, 'my four children' and 'my said children.' Again, in the fourth item, when he wishes to designate grandchildren, he uses the word 'children' in its restricted or general meaning, by calling them the children of his daughter. When in the fifth item, he uses the words 'my surviving child or children,' we see no justification for giving the word a more extensive meaning than the testator has given to it throughout every other part of his will. Again, the words, 'hereinbefore given for life to my child so dying,' necessarily refer to one of his four children, and the words immediately following, 'unto my surviving child or children,' must be confined to the same class. If the words 'my child,' in the antecedent clause, mean 'son' or 'daughter'—as they clearly do,—how can we give to the words 'my surviving children,' in the subsequent clause, a wider signification? It is said that, unless the word 'children' is held to include grandchildren, a partial intestacy may follow. This is true, but a testator may fail to contemplate and provide for every contingency that can arise under this scheme of distribution. This fact is no justification for giving words a signification that does not belong to them, in order to avoid intestacy. It is also contended that our interpretation of the will works out inequality as to the grandchildren, but inequality as to this class is evinced in the very first disposition the testator makes of any part of his property. The homestead is given to the longest liver of the four children and his issue, to the exclusion of other grandchildren should their parents die before the testator, or before a sale of the property. The inequality in the disposition of the residue of the real estate is entirely consistent with the preference given to a surviving son or daughter in the disposition of the homestead. The fourth and fifth items secure for the grandchildren, if any, the full share set apart for the parent; but when the testator contemplates the death of a son or the daughter without issue, and a further disposition of the share so set apart becomes necessary, his mind and thought turn to the first objects of his bounty,—the survivors of his four children. It may be questioned whether his thought passed beyond the survivors of his four children, for, to our mind, it is not clear that the testator disposed of the *corpus* of a share where the son dies without leaving issue. The survivors of his four children are to have the income of such share just as they receive the income of the one-fifth set apart to them respectively, but what becomes of it upon the death of the last survivor? It is, however, unnecessary to pass upon this last inquiry, and we do not wish to express an opinion upon the subject, for we are satisfied that for the present the principal fund of $91,692.08 must remain intact in the hands of the executors and trustees to pay the rents, income, and interest thereof to the two surviving sons. And now, May 29, 1899, the application for distribution of the principal fund and its accrued interest to the guardian of the minor, Jacob Steinmetz Bailey, is refused, and the application is dismissed."

Charles C. Townsend, Henry Freedley, and *B. Percy Chain,* for appellant.

Montgomery Evans, James B. Holland, and *John M. Detra,* for appellee.

PER CURIAM. The decree in this case is affirmed on the opinion of the learned court below.

BANNING *vs.* GOTSHALL.

[Supreme Court of Ohio, March 6, 1900; 62 Ohio St. 210; 56 N. E. Rep. 1030.]

ACTION BETWEEN EXECUTORS OR ADMINISTRATORS OF DIFFERENT ESTATES—PREDECESSOR OF ONE OF THE PARTIES—WITNESS— DEATH OF INTESTATE LEGATEE—PAYMENT OF LEGACY—FOR- EIGN GUARDIAN OF FOREIGN WARD—PAYMENT BY EXECUTOR TO WRONG PARTY.

1. In an action between executors or administrators of different estates, a person who has been the predecessor of one of the parties is not on that account incompetent as a witness against the adverse party, to testify to facts which occurred before the death of the latter's testator or

.ntestate. Such a case is not within the reason or spirit of the provision of section 5241 of the Revised Statutes, which excludes the testimony of an assignor of a claim in certain cases.

2. Upon the death of a legatee, intestate, before payment of the legacy, the right to receive payment belongs to his personal representative, unless a different disposition is made by the will, and the liability of the executor therefor to the personal representative is not discharged by payment to the heir.

3. Compliance by a foreign guardian with the provisions of section 6279 of the Revised Statutes is necessary, to entitle him to demand or receive money belonging to his ward in the hands of an executor or administrator in this state; and the Probate Court may, in its discretion, refuse to make an order for the payment of the money to the guardian, if satisfied it will be detrimental to the interest of the ward. Payment without such order is unauthorized, and affords no protection to the persons making the payment.

4. The settlement of the final account of an executor or administrator, showing the payment of money to a person not entitled thereto, is no bar to a subsequent action against him for the recovery of the money by one who is legally entitled to the same.

(Syllabus by the court.)

ERROR to Circuit Court, Knox county.

The action below was brought by Harry Gotshall, as administrator of the estate of Henry M. Campbell, against Thomas D. Banning, as executor of John D. Thompson's estate, to recover the amount of a legacy alleged to be due the estate of Henry M. Campbell, under his father's will, from the estate of John D. Thompson, who was executor of that will. The plaintiff recovered in the Court of Common Pleas, and, that judgment having been affirmed by the Circuit Court, error is prosecuted here to obtain a reversal of those judgments.

Affirmed.

J. B. Waight and *A. R. McIntyre,* for plaintiff in error.

S. S. Bloom filed a brief in behalf of the children and heirs at law of Anna J. Love, deceased, a legatee.

Critchfield & Graham, S. R. Gotshall, and *Columbus Ewalt,* for defendant in error.

WILLIAMS, J.—By the will of Charles M. Campbell, his executor was directed to sell certain real property of which he died seized, and pay one-fourth of the proceeds to his son, Henry M. Campbell. John D. Thompson qualified as executor of the will in Knox county in 1873, and afterwards sold the property in accordance with the will, and received the proceeds. The share of Henry under the will amounted to something over $14,000, but before its payment he died intestate in Knox county, and the right to receive the money, it is conceded, vested in his personal representative; no other disposition thereof having been made by the will. He left a widow, who received her share of his personal estate, and an infant daughter, Elizabeth, his only heir at law, whose share, amounting to the sum of $9,558.34, was demanded by Samuel R. Gotshall, who had become the administrator of Henry's estate. The widow of Henry married Marcus A. Miller, and they removed from the county of Knox to the state of Tennessee, taking with them the minor child, Elizabeth, where Miller procured his appointment as guardian of her estate. He presented an authenticated transcript of his appointment, together with a copy of his bond as such guardian, to Thompson, who then paid him the last-mentioned amount of the money bequeathed to Henry by his father's will, taking from Miller the following receipt: " Mount Vernon, Ohio, September, 1892. $9,558.34. I, Marcus A. Miller, as the guardian of Elizabeth Campbell, infant daughter of the late Henry M. Campbell, deceased (she being the only child and sole heir at law of said decedent), do hereby acknowledge to have received of John D. Thompson, sole acting executor of the estate of the late Charles M. Campbell, deceased, father of the said Henry M. Campbell, the sum of nine thousand five hundred and fifty-eight and thirty-four one-hundredths dollars; being the full distributive share of my said ward of the legacy and bequest to the said Henry M. Campbell under the will of his father, the said Charles M. Campbell. Marcus A. Miller, Guardian as Above." No application was made to the Probate Court of Knox county for an order authorizing the payment of the money to Miller, nor was any proof of his appointment filed in that court, nor any order obtained for such payment. Thompson, also, about the same time, paid to the administrator of Henry's estate the sum of $50, for which the following receipt was given: " Mt. Vernon, Ohio, Sept. 15, 1892. $50.00. Received of John D. Thompson, executor of the estate of the late Charles

M. Campbell, deceased, the sum of fifty dollars ($50.00), which I agree to, and do, receive in full satisfaction of all claims due or to become due to me, either in my own right, or as administrator of the estate of Henry M. Campbell, deceased, for commissions on funds in the hands of said executor coming to the heirs of said Henry M. Campbell; I having made claim that the whole of said Henry M. Campbell's share in the said Charles M. Campbell's estate should be paid to me as the administrator of said Henry M. Campbell's estate, while the said Thompson, as such executor, claimed, and the heirs of said Henry M. Campbell were insisting upon the right to have the said share paid directly to the said heirs of said Henry M. Campbell, and thus depriving me of all commissions thereon; and now this amount is paid to me, by and with the consent of the widow and heir of said Henry M. Campbell, deceased, as a compromise and in full satisfaction of my said claim. S. R. Gotshall, Administrator of Henry M. Campbell." Thereafter Thompson filed his final account as executor of the will of Charles M. Campbell; including in the account the two receipts above given, and claiming credit for their respective amounts. No exceptions were filed to the account, and it was approved and confirmed by the court after due publication of notice. Some time after that, Thompson died testate, and Thomas D. Banning qualified as his executor; and, the administrator of Henry's estate having resigned, Harry Gotshall was appointed his successor, and brought the action below. These facts are shown by the uncontroverted allegations of the pleadings and the agreements of the parties. Issues were joined upon various allegations of bad faith on the part of Thompson in the payment of the money to Miller, and of deception and misrepresentation in obtaining the receipt from Samuel R. Gotshall. It was claimed by the plaintiff, and denied by the defendant, that the money was paid by Thompson to Miller in pursuance of an agreement between them that the latter should apply a part of the money to the discharge of an individual obligation of his, on which Thompson was bound, a part to the payment of a debt which Miller owed Thompson, and the balance to be used by Miller in business of a speculative character for his own benefit, and that Thompson so made the payment knowing Miller was pecuniarily irresponsible.

On the trial of the action, Samuel R. Gotshall, the predecessor of the plaintiff as administrator, was permitted to testify to various admissions and statements of Thompson concerning the allegations made against him. Objection was made to this testimony on the ground that the witness was incompetent to give testimony in regard to any fact which occurred prior to Thompson's death. The overruling of that objection, and the admission of the testimony, present one of the questions made in this case. The witness was not a party to the action, and by no express provision of the statute was his testimony rendered incompetent. The contention is that it should have been excluded under that clause of section 5242 of the Revised Statutes which provides that when a case is plainly within the reason and spirit of the three preceding sections, " though not within the letter, their principle shall apply; " the claim being that the testimony admitted was plainly within the reason and spirit of that provision of section 5241, which excludes the testimony of an assignor of a chose in action in respect to any matter to which, if a party, he would not be permitted to testify. The reason for excluding the testimony of an assignor, as provided by section 5241, does not seem applicable to a resigned administrator or executor. Before the enactment of that provision, it was not uncommon to make assignments of claims for the purpose of enabling the assignor, by his testimony, to establish the claim for his own benefit, in an action by his assignee against the representative of an estate. Then the assignment of a claim is usually accompanied with a liability of the assignor, in case the proof is insufficient to enable the assignee to recover upon it. So that the assignor in such cases is a party in interest, though not of record, and his testimony is practically in his own behalf. Upon the resignation of the personal representative, the title to the assets of the estate, and all the rights and duties of further administration, devolve upon his successor, by operation of law, and he ceases to have any interest in the estate. For this reason it is quite generally held that, when an administrator has resigned or been removed, he is a competent witness in behalf of his successor, in all respects as if he were a stranger to the estate. In *Burd's Ex'rs* v. *McGregor's Adm'r* (2 Grant, Cas. 353), an attempt was made to bring a discharged administrator within the rule which excludes an assignor of a chose in action from being a witness to support his claim. But the court said that: " The discharge of one administrator and the appointment of another is nothing like an assignment. The discharged administrator has nothing to do with the appointment of his successor in that trust. He makes no transfer of the claims of the decedent. He receives no value for them. He is therefore a competent witness to support them." And in Rapalje on Witnesses that author, on page 112, says that: "The authorities, even at common law, are quite harmonious in conceding the competency of an executor or administrator who has resigned, or has been removed or superseded, to testify in favor of his successor in the trust; and this even if proceedings are pending to reverse the action of the court removing him. He is no longer a party, nor liable for costs."

It is further urged that, as the testimony admitted related in part to a transaction between the witnesses and Thompson, that part was incompetent, and should have been excluded. But as said in *Farley* v. *Lisey* (55 Ohio St. 627-631; 45 N. E. 1103): "The statute has reference to the adverse character which the parties sustain towards each other as parties to the action, and not necessarily to their relation as parties to the transaction which is the subject of the action or defense."

The payment by Thompson to Miller, the Tennessee guardian of the infant heir of Henry M. Campbell, of the money represented by the receipt of Miller, hereinbefore set forth, is relied on as an equitable defense to the action brought by the plaintiff below; and the failure of the court to render judgment thereon, discharging the defendant from liability, is assigned as error here. It is conceded that upon the death of Henry the legacy was payable to his personal representative, and not to his heir; but it is claimed that, since the latter was ultimately entitled to the money, the payment to the guardian should, in equity, be treated as payment to the personal representative, and by the latter to the heir, as by this means, the expense of further administration and circuity of action would be avoided, and all substantial rights preserved. In support of this contention cases are cited which hold that, where there are no debts of an estate, the heirs may resort to a court of equity for division and distribution of the assets, or, when *sui juris*, may make division and distribution among themselves by agreement, without administration. That doctrine has little relevancy here. A foreign guardian is not entitled, merely by virtue of his appointment and qualification, to receive money belonging to his ward in the hands of an executor or administrator in this state. In Story, Confl. Laws (§504a), the rule is stated to be that "no foreign guardian can, *virtute officii,* exercise any rights, powers, or functions over the movable property of his ward situated in a different state or country from that in which he obtained his letters of guardianship." And, since whatever privileges are accorded such guardian in that respect in another state or country, are conferred merely as a matter of comity, it necessarily follows that their existence and enjoyment may be made subject to such regulations and conditions as the state or country in which the property is situated may deem it just and proper to impose. In the absence of any statute on the subject, it seems to have been usual and necessary to resort to ancillary guardianship in the state where the property was situated, or make application to a court having chancery powers for a proper order authorizing the foreign guardian to exercise control over the personal estate of the ward so situated, or remove it from that state; and in such cases the courts have the discretionary power to make such order as should be deemed for the best interest of the ward. In this state that power is appropriately vested in the Court of Probate, which has exclusive jurisdiction of all probate and testamentary matters, and the control of the conduct of executors, administrators, and guardians, and the settlement of their accounts. Section 6279 of the Revised Statutes provides that "in any case in which a guardian, not appointed in this state, and his ward, are both non-residents of this state, and the ward is entitled to money or other property in the lawful custody of any executor, administrator or other person in this state, such guardian may by order of the Probate Court of the proper county, upon filing therein the proof named in the second preceding section, and giving notice to such custodian as therein prescribed, be permitted to demand, receive or recover by suit, such money or other property and remove the same, unless the terms of limitation attending the rights by which the ward owns the same conflicts with such removal." The second preceding section referred to is section 6277, which requires that the foreign guardian making the application for the order therein provided for shall file in the Probate Court "an exemplification from the record of the court making the foreign appointment, containing all the

entries and proceedings in relation to his appointment and his
giving bond, with a copy thereof, and of the letters of guardianship, all authenticated, as required by the act of congress in that
behalf "; and, before such application shall be heard or any action
taken thereon by the court, at least thirty days' written notice shall
be served on the custodian of the money, specifying the object of
the application, and the time when the same will be heard. And
it is further provided that no such order shall be made unless at
the time of the hearing the state or territory in which the guardian
was appointed has made a similar statutory provision, and the
court may in any case deny the application, unless satisfied that it
would be to the interest of the ward to grant the same. Compliance with these provisions by a foreign guardian is necessary in
order to invest him with the right to receive or recover from an
executor or administrator in this state moneys belonging to his
ward, and to remove the same to another state; for it is only by
virtue of the order of the Probate Court that, in the language
of the statute, the foreign guardian is "permitted to receive the
money or other property " of the ward, "and remove the same."
These are just and salutary provisions, designed for the protection,
not only of the executor or administrator, but also of the interests
and estates of infant wards. They plainly show that, however
formal the application may be, the court is not necessarily required
to make the order requested, but is clothed with a large discretion, similar to that formerly exercised by courts of chancery,
and may refuse to grant the order if satisfied it will be detrimental
to the interests of the ward. There was no compliance with these
statutory provisions by Miller, nor any attempt to comply with
them, which was known to Thompson when he paid over the
money; and this gives color to the claim made by the plaintiff that
there was some ulterior purpose in the transaction looking to the
personal advantage of both, to the prejudice of the ward. Miller
being without authority to demand and receive the money, its payment by Thompson was also without authority, and constitutes no
defense to the plaintiff's action. Whether it would be different
if the money had ultimately reached the heir after becoming of
age, or had been expended for her benefit in a lawful manner, is
a question not before us for decision. Assuming that in such a
case Thompson, having paid the money in good faith, would be

entitled in equity, to subrogation to the rights of the heir against the personal representative of her father, or might, as equitable assignee, set up her right in defense of the plaintiff's action, it is clear that case is not before us. Apparently in pursuance of an understanding when the money was paid, a part of it was at once applied in discharge of Thompson's individual liability for Miller, a part in satisfaction of a debt due from Miller to Thompson, and the balance embarked in a disastrous enterprise of Miller, by which in a brief time it was irretrievably lost, and his bondsmen became hopelessly insolvent.

The only other question we deem it necessary to notice is whether the settlement of the final account of Thompson as executor is a bar to this action. The claim is that as the account includes vouchers for the amount paid Samuel R. Gotshall for commission, and the amount paid to Miller, its settlement, so long as it is not opened up or impeached, is conclusive. And it undoubtedly is, so far as the payments represented by the vouchers are concerned, and against those to whom payments were made. But it has been the settled law of this state since *Swearingen* v. *Morris* (14 Ohio St. 424), that such a settlement, showing payment to one not entitled thereto, is no bar to an action by the person who is entitled to the money. The settlement and order of distribution do not have the effect of determining who is the rightful distributee, but is a general order to pay to the person lawfully entitled to receive payment. The conclusive effect of the settlement, as said in the case just cited, is founded on the condition that the executor or administrator has paid or delivered to the person entitled thereto the money or other property in his hands. It may be remarked here, as it was in that case, that " the money was not ordered out of his [the executor's] hands by a court of competent jurisdiction having the parties in interest before it. He voluntarily paid it away, and now relies upon a subsequent approval of what he had done, to turn wrong into right." The final account of Thompson shows no payment to the plaintiff below, and its approval presents no obstacle to the maintenance of his action for the recovery of the money to which he is legally entitled.

A claim is made here, on a cross petition in error, that the plaintiff should have been awarded interest for a longer period than was allowed by the trial court. But, without entering upon a dis-

cussion of the subject, we are not disposed to disturb the judgment in that respect.

Judgment affirmed.

NOTE.—FOREIGN GUARDIAN.

(a) General rules.
(b) At common law remedy in chancery.
(c) Jurisdiction of local courts.
(d) Minor's interest in land.
(e) Capacity to sue.
(f) Custody of minor.
(g) Illustrative cases.

(a) **General rules.**—It is almost invariably held, in the United States,
that the authority of guardians is limited to the jurisdiction which appointed them, so that it does not extend to other states or countries, unless
permitted by the laws thereof. The rights and powers of guardians are
considered as strictly local, says Story, and not as entitling them to exercise any authority over the person or personal property of their wards in
other states, upon the same general reasoning and policy which have cir-
cumscribed the rights and authorities of executors and administrators.
From which it follows that a foreign guardian who desires that his rights
as such, should be recognized, must obtain ancillary appointment, in the
state of the forum, if the laws of such state permit the appointment, unless
the law, in the spirit of comity, point out some other method by which the
authority of a foreign guardian may be respected in the protection of the
interests of a non-resident infant. (Schouler Am. Law Guardianship, § 28;
Hoyt v. Sprague, 103 U. S. 631; Clarke v. Clarke, 178 id. 194; 20 Sup.
Rep. 873; Watts v. Wilson, 93 Ky. 497; 20 S. W. Rep. 505; Leonard v.
Putnam, 51 N. H. 247; Mitchell v. People's Bank, 20 R. I. 500; 40 Atl.
Rep. 502; Morgan v. Potter, 157 U. S. 197; 15 Sup. Rep. 590; West v.
Gunther, 3 Dem. 386; Morrell v. Dickey, 1 Johns. Ch. 153; McLoskey v.
Reid, 4 Bradf. 334; Rogers v. McLean, 31 Barb. 305.)

(The subject is largely governed by statute in the several states, to which
reference should in the first instance be invariably made; as to principles
governing in analogy to executors and administrators see " Note—Rights
and Duties of Executors and Administrators in Foreign or Other States."
3 Prob. Rep. Ann. 42.)

Before permitting property in this state (S. C.) belonging to an infant
to be transferred beyond the limits of the state, the court must be satisfied
(1) that the guardian has been regularly appointed according to the laws
of the state where the ward resides; (2) the fitness of such guardian for the
appointment; and (3) that sufficient security has been given. (Cochran v.
Fillans, 20 S. C. 237.)

Local court will not order any transfer to a foreign guardian, without being satisfied as to security. (Estate of Goldsmith, 13 Phil. 389; and see Estate of Rice, id. 385.)

(This seems to be the effect of a specific statute in Pennsylvania, but it would seem that the same might be an element bearing on exercise of *discretion* where there was no statute.)

By comity only will anything be conceded to the claims of the guardian of the domicile, although it is usual, by comity, to appoint, if due application is made for the purpose, the same person guardian who was appointed by the domiciliary court. (Hoyt v. Sprague, 103 U. S. 613.)

Matter of comity. (Re Nickals, 21 Nev. 462; 34 Pac. Rep. 250; and see Matcalf v. Lowther, 56 Ala. 312, 318.)

(b) **At common law remedy in chancery.**—At common law a foreign guardian could only resort to a Court of Chancery to have the funds of his ward transferred and turned over to him, and whether such transfer should be made, rested in the sound discretion of the chancellor. And under statute conferring such power in a Probate Court, the removal of property is not granted as of strict right, but rests in the discretion of the court. (Re Wilson, 95 Mo. 184, 188; 8 S. W. Rep. 369; and see Grist v. Forehand, 36 Miss. 70; Matter of Fitch, 3 Redf. 458.)

Power discretionary. (Lary v. Craig, 30 Ala. 631; Re Benton, 92 Iowa, 202; 60 N. W. Rep. 614; Marts v. Brown, 56 Ind. 386.)

As to remedy in Court of Chancery. (Taylor v. Nichols, 86 Tenn. 32; Marts v. Brown, *supra;* Ponder v. Foster, 23 Ga. 489.)

(c) **Jurisdiction of local courts.**—Local courts have power to appoint guardians of the estates of minors resident elsewhere and to control their estates. (Neal v. Bartleston, 65 Tex. 478, 485; Davis v. Hudson, 29 Minn. 27; 11 N. W. Rep. 136; Succession of Cass, 42 La. Ann. 384; 7 So. Rep. 617; Maxwell v. Campbell, 45 Ind. 360; Barnsbeck v. Dewey, 13 Ill. App. 581.)

But no jurisdiction to pass upon accounts of a guardian appointed by the court in another state even with consent of guardian and ward, both of whom had removed from such state. (Anderson v. Story, 53 Neb. 259; 73 N. W. Rep. 735.)

It is not necessary that there should be first a general guardian in the state of the domicile of the minor. (West Duluth Land Co. v. Kurtz, 45 Minn. 380; 47 N. W. Rep. 1134.)

Notice to non-resident infant not necessary. (Kurtz v. St. P. & D. R. Co., 48 Minn. 339; 51 N. W. Rep. 221; and see Kurtz v. West Duluth Land Co., 52 Minn. 140; 53 N. W. Rep. 1132; Mitchell v. People's Bank, 20 R. I. 501; 40 Atl. Rep. 502; and as to notice to minor of sale of land see Myers v. McGavock, 39 Neb. 846; 58 N. W. Rep. 522.)

As dependent on legislation. (See Mitchell v. People's Savings Bank, 20 R. I. 500; 40 Atl. Rep. 502.)

(d) **Minor's interest in land.**—Proceeds of sale of land not transferred to a foreign guardian—under the construction of Maryland statutes. (Clay v. Buttingham, 34 Md. 675.)

Ancillary guardian should not be paid money proceeds of real estate, unless expressly authorized by statute. (Matter Public Parks, 89 Hun, 529; 35 N. Y. Supp. 332.)

Proceedings for sale of real estate by local guardian to raise proceeds for the education of a non-resident minor. (Bouldin v. Miller, 87 Tex. 359, 365; 28 S. W. Rep. 940.)

Lands of minor situate in one state, cannot be disposed of by decree of a court of another state, nor by a guardian appointed there acting under its laws. (Musson v. Fall Back Planting Co., 12 So. Rep. 587 [Miss.].)

Courts of a state where real estate is situated have the exclusive right to appoint a guardian of a non-resident minor and vest in such guardian the exclusive control and management of land belonging to such minor, situated within the state. (Clarke v. Clarke, 178 U. S. 193; 20 Sup. Rep. 873.)

(e) **Capacity to sue.**—Capacity of foreign guardian to sue a former local guardian removed for conversion of ward's property. (Shook v. The State, 53 Ind. 403.)

And as to right of a foreign guardian to sue, see also Sims v. Renwick (25 Ga. 58).

But statutory conditions precedent must be complied with. (Watts v. Wilson, 93 Ky. 495; 20 S. W. Rep. 505; McCleary v. Menke, 109 Ill. 301; Vincent v. Starks, 45 Wis. 458.)

The power as dependent upon legislation. (See Mitchell v. People's Bank, 20 R. I. 501; 40 Atl. Rep. 502; Morgan v. Potter, 157 U. S. 195; 15 Sup. Rep. 590; Re Benton, 92 Iowa, 202, 205; 60 N. W. Rep. 614.)

As to duty of guardian in reference to a note which can be collected only in another state, see Potter v. Hiscox (30 Conn. 508).

(f) **Custody of minor.**—As to custody of the child local court has discretionary power to award it to a foreign guardian. (Wordsworth v. Spring, 4 Allen, 321; Wells v. Andrews, 60 Miss. 373; and see Ex Parte Dawson, 3 Bradf. 130, a case where the English Court of Chancery having refused to award the custody of a minor to its American guardian and decreed the transmission of the property to England, the New York Surrogate's Court refused to make an order requiring the American guardian to transmit the funds abroad.)

But see an English case where custody of minor was recognized and enforced as being in a foreign guardian. (Nugent v. Vetzera, L. R. 2 Eq. 704.)

And see where a foreign guardian was refused custody of a child. (Matter of Rice, 42 Mich. 528; 4 N. W. Rep. 284.)

(g) **Illustrative cases.**—Foreign guardian by invoking the aid of a domestic court, subjects himself to its jurisdiction, and becomes bound by its decree, which may be enforced against him wherever found within the jurisdiction of the court. (Clendenning v. Conrad, 91 Va. 410; 21 S. E. Rep. 818.)

No order for a transfer to foreign guardian while subject to amendment during the term at which it was granted will be allowed to protect him as against the claims of domestic creditors or citizens, even where he has removed the property from the state. (Id.)

Transfer from a local guardian to a foreign guardian subsequently appointed in another state to which the infant removed. (Bernard v. Equitable Trust Co., 80 Md. 118; 30 Atl. Rep. 563.)

Payment by a debtor in this state (N. Y.) to a foreign guardian will be good if the guardian by the law of the state from which he derives his appointment is authorized to receive it. (Wuesthoff v. Germania Life Ins. Co., 107 N. Y. 580; 14 N. E. Rep. 811.)

McCHESNEY vs. DE BOWER et al.

[Supreme Court of Wisconsin, March 20, 1900; 82 N. W. Rep. 149.]

GUARDIAN AND WARD—CUSTODY OF CHILDREN—RIGHTS OF SURVIVING PARENT—EVIDENCE—COMPETENCY.

1. Where the father of minor children, after the death of his divorced wife, in whose custody the children had been placed by a divorce six years previous, petitioned to be appointed their guardian, the evidence on which the divorce had been granted was competent to show that he was not a suitable person for the appointment.

2. Where the father of minor children, after the death of his divorced wife, petitioned to be appointed their guardian, and it was shown that prior to the divorce, which had been granted six years previous, he had been guilty of extreme cruelty to the children and their mother, had committed adultery with the servant girl in his family, had made indecent proposals to his wife's mother and other females, and after the separation had refused to visit his little boy in his last sickness, or to attend his funeral, a finding that he was not a suitable person for appointment will not be disturbed on appeal.

3 In a contest between the father of minor children and their maternal grandmother to be appointed the children's guardian, a clause in the will of the mother of the children, who six years prior to her death had been divorced from the husband, appointing the grandmother their testamentary guardian, was properly admitted in evidence to show the propriety of appointing the grandmother, in case the father was found unsuitable for the trust.

APPEAL from Circuit Court, Dane county; R. G. SIEBECKER, Judge.

Petition by Joseph B. McChesney to be appointed guardian of his minor children, Edna Mabel and Viola Blanche McChesney. From an order denying the petition, and appointing Mary De Bower, the grandmother of the children, their guardian, plaintiff appeals.

Affirmed.

Proceedings for the appointment of a guardian of two minor children of Frances McChesney and the petitioner. The marriage took place in 1887. A divorce was granted in 1894. There were two infant girls, Edna Mabel and Viola Blanche, and an infant boy who died subsequent to the divorce, the custody of whom was awarded to the mother, the petitioner being required to pay to her $200 per year during their minority for their support. In 1898 Mrs. McChesney remarried to William Lappley, with whom she resided until March 31, 1899, when she died. Since such death the two girls have resided on a farm with their grandfather and grandmother, Mr. G. De Bower and Mary De Bower. The petitioner remarried in 1896, since which time he has maintained a home on a farm in Dane county, Wis. The matters stated were set forth in the petition, with allegations to the effect that the De Bowers are unsuitable on account of their age to have the custody of the children and that the petitioner has a good home where the children can be suitably provided for, and maintained. The De Bowers were made parties to the proceedings and answered, raising the question of whether the petitioner is a suitable person to have the care and custody of the children, and whether the allegations as to their suitableness for the trust are true and whether it is for the best interests of the children to remain with them. The answer contained a prayer for the appointment of Mrs. De Bower as guardian of the children with the right to the custody of their persons and property during their minority.

The evidence was to the effect, and the court found, that for some years before the divorce the petitioner's conduct towards his wife was exceedingly cruel and inhuman; that he sustained, for a long period of time, immoral relations with a young servant girl in his family, and solicited other females, including his wife's mother, to submit to his adulterous desires, and that when the separation between himself and wife occurred, he expelled her and her children from his house by physical force and compelled them to go, on a cold winter day, to a neighbor's house for protection, and that the circumstances of the occurrence evinced an entire absence on his part of natural parental feeling. The evidence further showed and the court found, that from the time of the divorce to the commencement of these proceedings, McChesney paid but very little attention to his children; that he had been accustomed to meet them on the highway and not speak to or recognize them in any way; that he never showed any desire for their custody and little or no desire for their company or to treat them as his children in any way till these proceedings were commenced; that when his little boy was sick unto death he was notified of the fact by the mother in order that he might see his son before death occurred; and that after the child died he was notified of the funeral, but that he entirely ignored both of such occurrences, paying no attention to the funeral of the boy though he knew of its occurrence and was in the vicinity where he could readily have attended.

The only evidence to palliate McChesney's conduct in regard to his children, as found by the court, was that on one or two occasions during the life of the mother, she indicated that she preferred that he should not have anything to do with the children, and that the De Bowers, on one or two occasions, repelled his advances in regard to recognizing the children in a fatherly way, and indicated displeasure because he noticed them. There was further evidence, and the court found, that the petitioner is a man of considerable property and has a good home. The evidence further showed that the petitioner's conduct, since his second marriage, aside from that towards his children, has been proper; and that he enjoys the confidence and respect of his neighbors. The evidence further showed, and the court found, that for a considerable time before the death of the mother, the children resided with the De Bowers; that it was the mother's desire, as indicated in her last will and testament that her mother, Mrs. De Bower should have the care of the girls during their minority; that by reason of the wish so expressed the children, from the death of their mother have resided with their grandmother and are very much attached to her and to their grandfather also, and that the grandparents are very much attached to the children; that the grandparents have an excellent home and are of sufficient ability in every way to properly care for the children during their minority, and that the children are' desirous of remaining with the grandparents.

On the facts found as indicated and the evidence the court denied the prayer of the petitioner and granted the prayer of the respondents. An order was thereupon entered accordingly appointing Mrs. De Bower guardian of the children to have the custody of their persons and property upon her giving a bond as indicated in the order. The petitioner appealed.

Jones & Stevens, for appellant.

R. M. La Follette and *G. E. Roe,* for respondents.

MARSHALL, J. (after stating the facts).—There are no legal questions that need be discussed on this appeal. It is conceded that the mother, who was awarded the custody of the children in the divorce action, being dead, the petitioner, as the only living parent, is entitled under the statute to be appointed their guardian, if competent to transact his own business and not otherwise unsuitable within the meaning of section 3964, Rev. St. As regards the first requisite there is no question, so the case comes down to the second. Independent of the petitioner's ability to transact his own business, is he a suitable person to be intrusted with the care and custody of the two infant girls, whose guardianship he seeks? That is the question and is purely one of fact. It is conceded that if the findings in that regard are sustained by the evidence the decision of the trial court is right. We have examined the evidence with care and are unable to say that any material finding is contrary to the clear preponderance thereof.

Complaint is made because the court permitted evidence regarding the character of the petitioner at the time of the divorce decree and prior thereto. It is by no means certain that if all such evidence were out of the record the order appealed from could properly be disturbed, but we cannot say error was committed in receiving it. The trial court had broad discretionary power regarding the limits of the inquiry reasonably necessary to a correct determination of the controversy calling for a decision. The history of the petitioner's life from the date of the marriage down to the hearing, had a bearing on that controversy. True, the fact that he, for several years prior to the hearing, so far as morality and integrity are concerned, had lived a correct life, was a strong circumstance in his favor, but it would be going too far to say that it established his character and suitableness for the guardianship of the infant girls so conclusively as to preclude the court from looking into the circumstances that led to the decree devesting him of their custody and placing them with their mother.

It is useless to discuss here at length the circumstances referred to; they appear sufficiently in the findings of the court and are included in substance in the statement preceding this opinion. Suffice it to say that they are of such a character that it is not unreasonable to hold that a probationary period of more than six years would be required to so obliterate their effect upon the petitioner's suitableness to have the care and custody and education of infant girls as to preclude giving any weight to them in determining his character in that regard.

It is said, the court gave undue weight to the expressed wishes of the children to remain with the grandparents. We cannot tell how that is. There is no indication in the record of what significance the court gave to the chidren's wishes. It is not suggested but that it was entirely proper to inquire of the children, as was done, as to their state of mind as regards being taken from their grandparents. We observe in the finding merely a brief statement that "the children, as expressed by them on the trial, are desirous of remaining with their grandparents, to whom they are warmly attached." There is nothing in that to indicate that the children's wishes were regarded as controlling in any sense.

Error is assigned on the admission in evidence of the mother's will attempting to appoint Mrs. De Bower the testamentary guardian of the children: (1) Because the conditions greatly changed after the making of the will. (2) Because the wishes of a deceased parent are of little weight as against the right of the survivor. (3) Because the mother had no right to appoint a testamentary guardian. In answer to all these suggestions it may be said that the evidence was not treated as vital to the case. Answering the propositions in detail we say, as to the first, the will speaks from the death of the testator and must be presumed to express the wishes she entertained at that time; as to the second, that at most it only goes to the weight of the evidence; and as to the last proposition, that the evidence was not received or considered as proof of a rightful legal disposition of the children.

Section 3965, Rev. St. expressly authorizes the father of a child, if living, and in case of his death the mother, by last will to appoint a guardian therefor. That indicates the legislative policy to be that the parent entitled to the custody and care of a child during its minority shall have the right to appoint a testamentary guardian therefor. It is not necessary to say here, that since the decree of divorce removed the children of the petitioner from his control and placed them in the care and custody of the mother, his right as regards appointing a testamentary guardian for them was thereby taken from him and the right of the mother was substituted instead thereof. Such is the effect of some adjudications elsewhere. (Hoch. Inf. § 78; *Wilkinson* v. *Deming*, 80 Ill. 342.)

There can be no question but that the decree of divorce suspended the statutory power of the petitioner to control the custody of his children by his last will and testament, and that the spirit of it is, that the mother, the father being disabled from acting, may appoint a testamentary guardian. But whatever may have been the exact legal status of the mother in that regard, it is considered that, because of the legislative policy that she shall have the right where the father is so circumstanced that he cannot exercise the power of testamentary appointment, it was proper to consider her wishes, expressed in her will, not as warranting a denial of the right of petitioner to the custody of his children, but as bearing on the propriety of granting the prayer of Mrs. De Bower to be appointed guardian of the children in case the petitioner's claim was not sustained because of his unsuitableness for the trust.

A further contention was made, that the court erred in deciding that the appellant is wanting in natural affection for the children. The evidence on that point abundantly supports the finding. Many circumstances bearing on the subject and indisputably established might be mentioned. The occurrences, unexplained and unexplainable, consistent with natural parental feelings and conceptions of duty, of the appellant's neglect to visit his dying infant son, and of permitting the funeral of the boy to be held unnoticed by him and with less concern than one would naturally have for the funeral of a stranger happening in his vicinity, after special pains were taken by the stricken mother to remove all obstacles to his visiting the dying boy and being present at the funeral, are sufficient in themselves, in the absence of some clear explanation of such conduct, to prevent the finding from being disturbed that the appellant has no fatherly love for the children whose custody he seeks. It seems that no man could be so hardened towards his own flesh and blood, where represented by a child so young as to be free from any intelligent bias against him by reason of a hostile environment, as appellant's conduct indicates. The fact that the appellant so conducted himself suggests the probability that the groundless suspicion the evidence shows he had expressed as to the paternity of the children, or some of them, influenced him, which of itself, as has been held, is entitled to weight in determining whether he is a suitable person to have their care and custody. (*Sheers* v. *Stein,* 75 Wis. 44; 43 N. W. 728; 5 L. R. A. 781.)

We will not further discuss the findings or the evidence. The following is the situation, in brief, as appears by the record: The appellant, by his conduct, forfeited the control of his children and the decree to that effect stands undisturbed. He came before the court with a mere claim of legal right to be preferred as the nominee for the guardianship of the children, since circumstances had arisen that rendered the appointment of a guardian necessary. They being under the age of choice it was the duty of the court to make a choice for them, and to do so having regard for their best interests as the primary consideration and the legal right of the appellant to be chosen if suitable for the trust. In determining the propriety of appointing the appellant, since such appointment would take the children away from the home in which they were pleasantly located, and where they were reasonably certain of having proper parental care, and to place them among those who were comparative strangers to them, such facts were entitled to consideration. The appellant has a second wife and family of children, so it is not certain that the two girls could be received there and permanently treated on an equality with the other child members of the household. Though appellant is now an upright man so far as regards morality and integrity, his past life cannot be entirely ignored. It is entitled to some consideration in determining whether he is a suitable person under all the circumstances for the trust he seeks. He does not possess natural love and affection for the children and the circumstances of the situation render it quite probable that fatherhood is not the moving cause of his present desire to control them. The children were placed legally by the court where the mother, by an attempted testamentary disposition of their custody during their minority, placed them. Such testamentary disposition was in accord with the spirit of the statute as regards the right of the mother, and, though not binding upon the court, was entitled to consideration, since thereby the best interests of the children were conserved and there was no legal impediment, clearly, in the way. The grandparents and the children are warmly attached to each other, so that the relations between them are akin to those between parent and child under normal conditions. The ability of the grandparents to care for the children is equal to that of the appellant, and their disposition to do so, independent of all selfish impulses, is manifestly superior to his. In view of all the things stated, and within all the authorities, the court properly decided that the appellant had no legal right to be selected as guardian of the children, that the proper p ace for them was with their grandparents, and the proper person to have their legal guardianship was their grandmother. The cases in our own court so fully cover the subject, so far as the law is concerned, that it is considered that there is no need of going elsewhere for authority. (*In re Goodenough,* 19 Wis. 274; *Sheers* v. *Stein,* 75 id. 44; 43 N. W. 728; 5 L. R. A. 781 ;*Johnston* v. *Johnson,* 89 Wis. 416; 62 N. W. 181; *Markwell* v. *Pereles,* 95 Wis. 406; 69 N. W. 798.)

The order appealed from is affirmed.

MARKHAM vs. HUFFORD et al.

[Supreme Court of Michigan, March 27, 1900; 82 N. W. Rep. 222.]

WILLS—CONDITIONAL LEGACY—VESTED INTEREST—CONDITION
PRECEDENT.

1. The condition that a legacy shall be paid to the legatee two years from
   date of testator's death, provided that the legatee shall be deemed a
   reformed man, in the judgment of the executors, is not void for uncertainty, and constitutes a valid condition precedent.
2. A legacy directed to be paid at the end of two years, provided that the
   legatee shall be deemed to be a reformed man, in the judgment of the
   executors, is conditional, and does not create a vested interest.

ERROR to Circuit Court, Kent county; ALLER C. ADSIT, Judge.

Petition by Almon L. Markham against Silas L. Hufford and
another, as executors, praying for payment of a legacy. From
a judgment for the petitioner, defendants appeal.
Reversed.

Walker & Fitsgerald, for appellants.

Lombard & McAllister, for appellee.

HOOKER, J.—The testatrix, Mary C. Jones, left a will containing the following provisions: " (1) To Almon L. Markham, the
son of my daughter, Julia J. Markham, deceased, I give and bequeath the sum of five hundred dollars ($500.00), to be paid to
him at the expiration of two years from the date of my demise;
provided, that he shall be deemed a reformed man, in the judgment
of the executors of this will. (2) To my granddaughter, Mary
Maud Markham, I give and bequeath the sum of five hundred
dollars ($500.00), not to be paid to her until she has attained the
age of twenty (20) years, unless it be necessary, in the opinion of
the executors, and then not to exceed the sum of one hundred
and fifty dollars ($150.00); the balance to be paid at the time
specified above, if any disbursement is made. (3) In the event of
the demise of either or both of the aforementioned persons before

the time for the payment of the several amounts due them, then I direct that their shares shall revert to the Society of Women's Christian Temperance Union, to be paid to the Union of Unions of the city of Grand Rapids, and to be by them used for the advancement of the temperance work, without reservation." Several other bequests followed, and then the following: "(8) And all the balance of my estate, both personal and real, or which may accrue or of which I may be possessed of at the time of my decease, I do give and bequeath unto my son, William Hoyle Jones. It is my request that the estate be settled up within three (3) years after my demise. I also give the executors the privilege of disposing of any or all of the estate at public or private sale, as they may deem best for the interest of the estate. I hereby appoint Silas L. Hufford, of Walker, and William Hoyle Jones, both of the state of Michigan, executors of this, my will." The will was duly probated, and the persons named as executors accepted the trust and qualified. The inventory of the estate bears date May 20, 1892. In October, 1898, Almon L. Markham filed a petition in the Probate Court, praying an order that the executors pay him his legacy. This was followed by an amended petition. Upon a hearing the Probate Court denied the relief, and the cause was tried in the Circuit Court upon appeal. The findings of fact and law disclose, among other things, that on January 18, 1896, Almon L. Markham filed in Probate Court a petition alleging the will and its admission to probate, and that more than two years had expired, and that he was a reformed man, and was entitled to his legacy. It prayed that the executors be cited to show cause why they had not paid the legacy, and, in case of their failure to do so, that they be discharged from their office, and petitioner be authorized to bring an action upon their bond in the Circuit Court. A hearing was had, and it was held that the petitioner was not entitled to the relief prayed. No appeal was taken, and such order stands unreversed. In the present proceeding the Circuit Court failed to pass upon the question of petitioner's reformation, and in the finding of law held that petitioner took a vested legacy, and that the conditions attached were indefinite, uncertain, and void. It was also found that petitioner was entitled to his legacy, with interest at six per cent. from May 11, 1896, and costs, all to be paid out of the estate by the executors. The defendants have appealed. They claim (1) that the legacy was not a vested one; (2) that, regardless of that question, the condition was a valid condition precedent; (3) that the claim is barred by the former adjudication in the Probate Court.

The intention of the testatrix, if it can be ascertained, must settle the construction to be placed on this bequest. The section, considered by itself, would, in our opinion, impress the average mind as not ambiguous, and would be interpreted to mean that if, at the expiration of two years from the demise of the testatrix, the executors should deem the petitioner a reformed man, they should pay him $500 from the estate; otherwise, not. Very few would understand from this language that, if not deemed to be reformed, he should still receive the bequest at a later date, and that distant but a year. " A conditional legacy is defined to be a bequest whose existence depends upon the happening or not happening of some uncertain event, by which it is either to take place or to be defeated. No precise form of words is necessary in order to create a condition in a will, but, whenever it clearly appears that it was the testator's intention to make a condition, that condition shall be carried into effect. (2 Williams, Ex'rs, 558, and cases cited.) We are satisfied that the intention of the testatrix was that her grandson should not have this money unless within two years after her death he should change his course of conduct, and she selected persons in whom she had confidence to determine the question at the proper time. It was left to their judgment, and the inference is that they knew the petitioner's faults. Unless at that time the executors should determine that he was a reformed man, the provision would be inoperative. It was unnecessary for her to make a record of petitioner's faults. It is a valid condition to require the reform of bad habits. (*Dustan* v. *Dustan*, 1 Paige, 509; *Webster* v. *Morris*, 66 Wis. 366; 28 N. W. 353.) A condition which involves anything in the nature of consideration is, in general, a condition precedent. (Theob. Wills, 263.) In *Finlay* v. *King* (3 Pet. 346; 7 L. Ed. 701), Chief Justice MARSHALL said: " It is certainly well settled that there are no technical appropriate words which always determine whether a devise be on a condition precedent or subsequent. The same words have been determined differently, and the question is always a question of intention. If the language of the particular clause or of the whole will shows that the act on which the estate depends must be performed before the estate can vest, the condition is, of course, precedent; and unless it be performed the devisee can take nothing. If, on the contrary, the act does not necessarily precede the vesting of the estate, but may accompany or follow it,—if this is to be collected from the whole will,—the condition is subsequent. It is in all cases a question of intention, and not of phrase or form." In support of this, see 4 Kent, Comm. 124; Flood, Wills, 283; 2 Redf. Wills, 283; 2 Washb. Real Prop. 8; *Nicoll* v. *Railroad Co.* (12 N. Y. 121); *Barruso* v. *Madan* (2 Johns. 145); *Robbins* v. *Gleason* (47 Me. 259); *Burnett* v. *Strong* (26 Miss. 116); *Ward* v. *Screw Co.* (1 Cliff. 565; Fed. Cas. No. 17,157); *Creswell* v. *Lawson* (7 Gill & J. 240); *Hayden* v. *Inhabitants of Stoughton* (5 Pick. 528); *Jackson* v. *Kip* (8 N. J. Law, 241); *Bowman* v. *Long* (23 Ga. 247). The following have been held precedent conditions: If he lives three years, with limitation over if he dies within that time. (*Buck* v. *Paine*, 75 Me. 582.) If he attains the age of twenty-one years. (*Jones* v. *Leeman*, 69 Me. 489; *Kelso* v. *Cuming*, 1 Redf. 392; *Bowman* v. *Long*, 23 Ga. 247), it being sufficient if he does so before testator's death (*Eisner* v. *Koehler*, 1 Dem. Sur. 277); or although twenty-one, and has in the meantime learned a trade, and is of good moral character, to be determined by executor (*Webster* v. *Morris*, 66 Wis. 366; 28 N. W. 353); or " shall be desirous and capable of entering into business for himself" (*In re Davidson's Estate*, 17 Phila. 424); or if he withdraws from the Roman Catholic priesthood (*Barnum* v. *Mayor, etc.* 62 Md. 275; *Kenyon* v. *See*, 94 N. Y. 563; 29 Hun, 212); or releases testator's note held by him (*Howard* v. *Wheatley*, 15 Lea, 607); or survives testator (*Gibson* v. *Seymour*, 102 Ind. 485; 2 N. E. 305); or if he aid in the defense of a certain suit, to the satisfaction of the executor (*Cannon* v. *Apperson*, 14 Lea, 553); or to A., for her support, " if she shall lose any part of her own property, and need more " for her support (*Ely* v. *Ely*, 20 N. J. Eq. 43); or " when she should be sick and unable to support herself" (*Reynolds* v. *Denman*, 20 N. J. Eq. 218). So, a power to sell " if income be not sufficient for support." (*Minot* v. *Prescott*, 14 Mass. 495.) In Rop. Leg. 762, 763, it is said: " It is said by an old and learned author that: ' A fifth instance of exception must be made out of the positive rule applicable to the

· vesting of legacies, where the gift of the legacy and the time of payment are in terms distinct, when the period for payment is contingent, as upon the marriage or the taking of holy orders of the legatee; for in neither of those instances will the legacy vest before the happening of the contingency, as we have seen it would have done had the time of payment been certain. The distinction is founded upon the following reasoning: It must be inferred that where the time is certain, as when the legatee attains the age of twenty-one, the testator merely postponed the payment of the legacy in consideration of the legatee's unfitness to manage his affairs prior to that period; but, when the event annexed to the payment may or may not happen, it is to be presumed that the expectation of its taking place was the sole motive, and therefore of the essence of the bequest.' " The provision under discussion was, in our opinion, intended as a condition precedent; and it should not be defeated by the failure to specifically provide for the disposition of the fund, or by an inaccurate use of the word " revert " in the third section of the will. We think that the bequest did not constitute a vested interest, and that the condition is not any more uncertain than it would have been had the will required payment of the legacy provided the executors should at a given date deem petitioner unworthy of it. The provision cannot be distinguished in principle from any other bequest depending upon the happening of an uncertain event.

It becomes unnecessary to decide the third question raised, though there is much force in the claim that this proceeding is barred by the former adjudication. The order of the Circuit Court is reversed, and no new trial ordered.

The other justices concurred.

In re Scott's Estate.

[Supreme Court of California, March 13, 1900; 128 Cal. 57; 60 Pac. Rep. 527.]

WILLS—CONTEST—INSANE DELUSIONS—BURDEN OF PROOF—EVIDENCE—APPEAL.

1. Where the finding of the trial court that the testatrix was of sound mind at the time she executed her will is sustained by the evidence, it cannot be reviewed on appeal, though there is evidence to the contrary.

2. Under Code Civ. Proc. § 1312, declaring that in proceedings to contest a will the contestant is plaintiff, and the petitioner is defendant; and section 1981, declaring that the party holding the affirmative must prove it,—the burden is on the contestant to prove the delusions under which he claims the testator executed the will.

3. Testatrix was a woman of very excitable temper, and when excited was violent, both in language and action. She was highly suspicious of nearly every person with whom she had any relation; feared they were taking advantage of her or seeking to injure her. She was a sufferer from dyspepsia and other diseases of the stomach, which finally resulted in her death. She had a constant fear of being poisoned; charged those about her, while a widow, with trying to poison her; and, after her marriage with contestant, made the same charge against him. She also charged him with seeking to put her in an asylum and of unfaithfulness. Contestant had remarked that his wife was insane, and that he would break any will she would make, which remark was repeated to her. They occupied different apartments, and she had seen contestant with another woman, though there was no evidence that he was ever unfaithful to her, or attempted or thought of poisoning her. By her will, made shortly after her marriage with contestant, and also by her codicil executed some years later, and shortly before her death, she gave him two-fiftieths of her estate. *Held,* that the evidence authorized the trial court in finding that testatrix was not fully convinced of the charges she made against her husband, and hence she was not under any delusion in reference thereto, at the time she made the will.

4. Where the physician who had examined testatrix as to her sanity at the time she made the codicil to her will was called as a witness by contestant, the certificate given by him to the testatrix is admissible on his cross-examination.

5. An instrument signed by testatrix, and witnessed, stating that she wished to make a certain party a gift of $500, filed on the trial of the will contest without a petition for its probate being filed, cannot, in the absence of a showing of a testamentary intent, be held to constitute a will.

DEPARTMENT 1. Appeal from Superior Court, city and county of San Francisco.

Proceeding by Emerson R. Scott to contest the probate of the will of Angelia R. Scott, deceased. From an order admitting the will to probate and denying a motion for a new trial, contestant appeals.
Affirmed.

M. M. Estee, A. Everett Ball, and *Chas. A. Shurtleff,* for appellant.

Philip G. Galpin, A. E. Bolton, and *John B. Gartland,* for respondent.

Houghton & Houghton, for respondents certain legatees.

HARRISON, J.—Angelia R. Scott died December 16, 1897, leaving a last will and testament, with two codicils thereto, which were filed for probate December 22d. Her husband filed a contest against their probate, and the issues made by this contest were tried by the court without a jury. Findings were made against the allegations of the contestant, and in favor of the proponents of the will, and an order entered admitting the will to probate. The contestant moved for a new trial, which was denied, and from this order, as well as from the order admitting the will to probate, he has appealed. Various grounds of objection have been presented by the respondents to the right of the appellant to be heard upon his appeal, but, without passing upon the sufficiency of these objections, we are of the opinion that the action of the Superior Court should be affirmed.

The original will offered for probate was executed November 7, 1891. The first codicil thereto was made February 25, 1892, and the second codicil October 22, 1897. By their provisions as modified by the last codicil, the testatrix gave thirty-three-fiftieths of her estate to certain of her own relatives, twelve-fiftieths to certain relatives of her former husband, two-fiftieths to Mr. Scott, one-fiftieth to his three-children in equal shares, and one-fiftieth to each of two charitable organizations. The grounds of opposition which her husband filed are that she was of unsound mind at the time of the execution of the will and codicils, and that their execution was brought about by reason of the undue influence of certain designated relatives, and that at the time of their execution she was under certain insane delusions in reference to him. There does not appear to have been any evidence introduced at the trial in support of his claim that the testatrix acted under undue influence of others in the execution of the will or either of the codicils, nor has any argument in support of this claim been presented by him. The finding of the court that she was not of unsound mind at the time of their execution is fully sustained by evidence in the record, and, although there was testimony to the contrary, yet under well-settled rules this finding cannot be reviewed.

The delusions of the testatrix which the appellant alleges were such as to render the will invalid, and in reference to which evidence was presented to the trial court, are that he was unfaithful to her; that he was attempting to poison her; and that he was conspiring with others to place her in an insane asylum.

Section 1312, Code Civ. Proc. declares: " On the trial the contestant is plaintiff and the petitioner is defendant; " and under the provisions of sections 1981 id., the burden of proof was upon the contestant to establish the existence of these delusions, and it was incumbent upon him to present to the court evidence in their support which would overcome the presumption that the testatrix was sane at the time of making the will. In ordinary language, a person is said to be under a delusion who entertains a false belief or opinion which he has been led to form by reason of some deception or fraud; but it is not every false or unfounded opinion which is in legal phraseology a delusion, nor is every delusion an insane delusion. If the belief or opinion has no basis in reason or probability, and is without any evidence in its support, but exists without any process of reasoning, or is the spontaneous offspring of a perverted imagination, and is adhered to against all evidence and argument, the delusion may be truly called insane; but if there is any evidence, however slight or inconclusive, which might have a tendency to create the belief, it cannot be said to be a delusion. One cannot be said to act under an insane delusion if his condition of mind results from a belief or inference, however irrational or unfounded, drawn from facts which are shown to exist. " An insane delusion is not only one which is error, but one in favor of the truth of which there is no evidence, but the clearest evidence often to the contrary. It must be a delusion of such character that no evidence or argument will have the slightest effect to remove." (*Merrill* v. *Rolston,* 5 Redf. Sur. 252.) " It is only a delusion or conception which springs up spontaneously in the mind of a testator, and is not the result of extrinsic evidence of any kind that can be regarded as furnishing evidence that his mind is diseased or unsound ; in other words, that he is subject to an insane delusion." (*Middleditch* v. *Williams,* 45 N. J. Eq. 734 ; 17 Atl. 829.) " Delusions are conceptions that originate spontaneously in the mind without evidence of any kind to support them, and can be accounted for on no reasonable hypothesis. The mind that is so disordered imagines something to exist, or imputes the existence of an offense which no rational person would believe to exist or to have been committed without some kind of evidence to support it." (*Potter* v. *Jones,* 20 Or. 249 ; 25 Pac. 772 ; 12 L. R. A. 165 ; see, also, *In re Cole's Will,* 49 Wis. 179 ; 5 N. W. 346 ; *Robinson* v. *Adams,* 62 Me. 369 ; *Boardman* v. *Woodman,* 47 N. H. 139 ; *Appeal of Kimberly,* 68 Conn. 428 ; 36 Atl. 847 ; 37 L. R. A. 261 ; *Society* v. *Hopper,* 33 N. Y. 619 ; *Clapp* v. *Fullerton,* 34 id. 190 ; *In re White's Will,* 121 id. 460 ; 24 N. E. 935 ; *Smith* v. *Smith,* 48 N. J. Eq. 566 ; 25 Atl. 11 ; *In re Carpenter's Estate,* 94 Cal. 406 ; 29 Pac. 1101.)

Mrs. Scott was sixty-four years of age at the time of her death. She had been the wife of S. P. Collins, who died in 1885, leaving to her an estate amounting to about $300,000. She was without children, and remained a widow until March 6, 1889, when she married Mr. Scott. He was at that time a widower some years younger than she, with three children, one of whom he had placed in the East, and the other two he took with him to the house of his wife. It does not appear that at that time he was engaged in any business, or possessed of any considerable estate, and he soon assumed the management of a portion of the business of his wife. She was a woman of excitable temper, and easily irritated, and when excited was violent in both language and action. She was also highly suspicious of nearly every person with whom she had any relation,—feared they were taking some advantage of her, or were seeking to do her some injury. She was a constant sufferer from dyspepsia and other diseases of her stomach and digestive organs, was unable to eat any food except of the simplest nature, would frequently complain of distress from what she had eaten, and finally died of ulceration of the stomach. She was constantly troubled with constipation, had at no time a natural passage of her bowels, but was at all times compelled to make use of enemas. These ailments tended to aggravate her irritableness, and caused her to display her violent temper, and to give expression to her suspicions, and to make severe accusations against those with whom she was in friendly relation. She seemed to have a constant fear that she was liable to be poisoned, and charged nearly every one about her with seeking to poison her. This charge was frequently made while she was a widow, and after her marriage with Mr. Scott she was wont to make the same charge, not only against him, but also against other individuals, both generally and specifically, and would often say that " somebody " was trying to poison her. On one occasion she sent a sample of malted milk and a jar of fæces to Dr. Spencer for chemical analysis, and was informed by him that it showed no presence of poison, but that the fæces contained many red blood cells, indicating that some portion of her alimentary canal was slightly bleeding. She was, moreover, of an exceedingly jealous disposition, and entertained a strong suspicion that her husband was unfaithful to her, just as she had entertained a similar suspicion of her former husband. She frequently accused him of undue intimacy with other women, and stated to others as well as to him that he was unfaithful to her. She also expressed dissatisfaction with his management of her property, and even accused him of appropriating some of it to his own use. She had controversy with him about the disposition of her estate, and the mode in which her will should be made, and he had said to her that he could break any will she could make, because he could prove that she was insane. One witness testified that Mr. Scott told him that she was crazy or insane; that she gave him very little money; was very jealous; that she could not make a will but he could break it; that if she did not make a will to suit him he should break it; that he was going to hold on, and that she would die very soon; and he also testified that he repeated this to Mrs. Scott. She had evidently been previously informed that Scott had made these or similar statements, as she had repeated them to others. She also stated to many persons that her husband was trying to put her into an insane asylum. Prior to the making of her last codicil, under the advice of certain friends, she caused an examination of her mental condition to be made by some expert alienists, for the purpose, it may be assumed, of defeating what she believed or suspected might be the intention of her husband to contest the validity of her will.

There is no evidence in the record from which the court could find that the contestant was ever unfaithful to his wife, or that he ever made any attempt or had any thought to poison her, or to cause her to be placed in an insane asylum. But the court was not authorized to hold that she was under an insane delusion in reference to these propositions unless it was satisfied, from the evidence before it, not only that these charges against him were without any foundation in fact, but also that there was no evidence of any facts brought to her knowledge from which she might form a belief, however irrational or inconclusive it might be, in the existence of the acts or purposes with which she charged him, and, in addition thereto, that she did in fact believe that he was guilty thereof. In *Society* v. *Hopper* (*supra*), upon a similar proposition, the court said: " If he did not really believe what he alleged to be their criminal conduct and intentions; if he uttered the injurious imputations by way of personal abuse, in order to gratify a depraved and malicious disposition, or for the purpose of defaming or otherwise injuring them in the estimation of their acquaintances in the community,—any and all of these dispositions and motives, though most unworthy and reprehensible, would fall short of that degree of mental perversion which would enable the courts to pronounce him *non compos mentis* and incapable of disposing of his property by will. On questions of testamentary capacity courts should be careful not to confound perverse opinions and unreasonable prejudices with mental alienation." See, also, *Smith* v. *Smith* (48 N. J. Eq. 587; 25 Atl. 11).

The finding that the testatrix was not under any delusion upon these subjects is equivalent to a finding that all of the elements necessary to create a delusion in respect to either of them did not exist. If the evidence before the court was such as to authorize it to find that she did not in reality believe in the truth of the statements made by her, or that she made them in consequence of evidence of facts in reference thereto that had been brought to her knowledge, its finding must be sustained. The fact of her making the accusations was not conclusive upon the point, as they may have been made with perverse will, or in the heat of passion, or by reason of some unfounded belief, or some feeling of indignation or resentment. The court was required to determine whether upon all the evidence before it there was established such a fixed belief on her part in the existence of the truth of these charges as to constitute delusion. For this purpose it was proper to consider her nature and temperament, the circumstances under which the statements were made, the habits of her life and association with others, and also her conduct towards her husband, and the nature of her intercourse with him during the period within which they were made.

If the contest had been tried before a jury, the court would not have been authorized to direct a verdict in favor of the contestant merely upon the testimony that she had made these accusations or charges, and that they were without foundation in fact, since the weight and credit to be given to this testimony for the purpose of determining whether the statements were the offspring of a delusion, or were a mere false accusation, could be determined only by the jury. (*Townshend* v. *Townshend*, 7 Gill, 32.) Any attempt by the court to control the jury by instruction, or even by suggestion as to the process of reasoning by which they should determine the issue before them, or in reference to the weight or credibility to be given to the evidence, would be an invasion of their province (*In re Carpenter's Estate, supra*); and, although there was no jury in the present case, the action of the court in determining questions of fact is attended with the same incidents and presumptions as that of a jury, and the weight and credibility given by it to the evidence is entitled to the same consideration as if passed upon by a jury under proper instructions. We cannot, as an Appellate Court, determine that the Trial Court did not sufficiently consider the testimony of these witnesses, or give proper weight thereto; nor can we substitute our judgment for that of the Trial Court as to the conclusion which should have been reached thereon. See *Wallace* v. *Sisson* (114 Cal. 42; 45 Pac. 1000).

There was evidence before the court which would have justified it in finding that the testatrix did not in reality believe in the truth of the statements, or that they were utterances for which she had some ground for belief, or, at least, a suspicion of their truth. A suspicion which rests upon evidence cannot be held to be a delusion. A suspicion which has no evidence to support it is only an unsettled condition of the mind indicating doubt or mistrust. It does not constitute a delusion unless it shall develop into a fixed conviction of the existence of the fact suspected. In *Clapp* v. *Fullerton* (*supra*), the testator was charged with a delusion regarding the legitimacy of his daughter, but the court held that it was unsustained for the reason that " it is evident that he did not arrive at a clear and settled conviction that he had been wronged in the conjugal relation, but he was brought to a condition of doubt, suspense, and uncertainty." In *re White's Will* (121 N. Y. 414; 24 N. E. 937), the court said: " If there are facts however insufficient they may in reality be, from which a prejudiced, or a narrow or a bigoted mind might derive a particular idea or belief, it cannot be said that the mind is diseased in that respect. The belief may be illogical or preposterous, but it is not, therefore, evidence of insanity in the person. Persons do not always reason logically or correctly from facts, and that may be because of their prejudices, or of the perversity or peculiar construction of their minds. Wills, however, do not depend for their validity upon the testator's ability to reason logically, or upon his freedom from prejudice."

It was but natural when her husband told her that he could prove that she was insane, and when she was informed by others that he had made similar declarations to them, that she should at least have a suspicion, if not a fear, that he would cause her to be treated as other insane people are treated, and that under her suspicious and excitable nature she would declare to others that he was trying to put her into an insane asylum. But it cannot be said that there was an entire want of foundation for her making these statements, or that they were the offspring of a perverted imagination. Neither were her charges of unfaithfulness entirely without reasons for a suspicion of its existence. Her husband had ceased to have sexual relation with her shortly after their marriage, and they afterwards occupied different apartments in the house. She told one of the witnesses that she had seen her husband in the sitting room with his arm around one of the female servants. It was also shown that he was wont to visit one of her nieces in the daytime, in the absence of her husband, once a week, and sometimes oftener. These facts were not denied by the contestant. Mrs. Scott was informed of these visits by one who, by her own admission, was malevolently inclined towards the niece, and, although the character and position of the niece were such as to forbid any inference of impropriety in these visits, yet to a jealous mind trifles light as air are sufficient to create a confirmation of the truth of a suspicion. In *Potter* v. *Jones* (20 Or. 249; 25 Pac. 772; 12 L. R. A. 165), where a similar charge was made by the testator against his wife, and where the court said that "her known character for chastity, her everyday walk and life, render it impossible that the interviews could have occurred for the foul purposes which he imputes, or otherwise than accidentally and without concert or evil design in thought or deed," it also said: "But these facts, however falsely or unjustly he may have reasoned from them, or however absurd his conclusions as applied to the wife and contestant impugned by them, nevertheless furnished the evidence which inspired his suspicions and the ground upon which his belief was founded," and held that they were sufficient to defeat the charge of a delusion.

Neither can it be said that she was actually convinced that he had tried or desired to poison her. That she labored under a fear that she might be poisoned may be conceded. The nature of her ailments and her physical condition, and the suffering experienced by her from her food, naturally contributed to this fear; but it does not appear that she felt this fear from her husband more than from others by whom she was surrounded, or that she made any more specific accusation against him than she did against others. She made a direct charge of this nature against Mrs. Swale before she was married to Mr. Scott, but with her, as with him, there was nothing to indicate that it was more than an accusation made by reason of a suspicion, or caused by the nature of her physical condition. If she was possessed of the idea that Scott deemed her insane, the thought that he might poison her was not entirely the fruit of a perverted imagination. Of this charge, as well as of the others, it may be said that her conduct towards her husband, and their relations with each other, furnish some evidence that she was not actually convinced of the truth of her charges against him. During all these times she was seeking some evidence of the fact of his infidelity, urging others to prove that it existed, and employing detectives to follow him and ascertain if her suspicions were justified. She continued to occupy the same house with him, and to sit at the same table, and there does not appear to have been any change in their conduct or intercourse with reference to each other. She was accustomed to drive with him in her carriage, and as late as the month of July previous to her death took a pleasure drive with him to the Cliff House. Mr. Scott testified that down to the time of her death she always consulted with him about her business affairs, and that he did whatever she wished to have him do, and tried to help and assist her, and that often when she had been to her attorney's office she would upon her return tell him the subjects and nature of their conversation. The provision made for him in her will could also be considered by the court in determining whether her conduct so varied from her accusations as to lead to the conclusion that she did not actually believe them to be true. By the will, as originally made in 1891, she gave two-fiftieths of her estate to him, and when in October, 1897, after the making of these accusations against him, and when if she was firmly convinced of their truth, it would not have been natural for her to make a provision for him out of her estate, she, by her codicil of that date, not only expressly reaffirmed her former devise of this two-fiftieths of her estate to him, but in addition thereto she gave one-fiftieth of her estate to his children by his former wife. It must be held that the evidence sufficiently authorized the Superior Court to find that Mrs. Scott was not fully convinced of the truth of the charges made by her against her husband, and, consequently, was not under any delusion in reference thereto.

As hereinbefore stated, before making her last codicil Mrs. Scott caused an examination of herself to be made by certain experts in insanity, and at the trial Dr. Mays, who was one of these experts, was called as a witness by the contestant, and upon his cross-examination the certificate which had been given to Mrs. Scott by these experts was shown to him and identified, and was thereupon offered in evidence by the proponents of the will.

The contestant objected thereto on the ground that it was irrelevant and a part of the proponents' case. The objection was overruled, and this ruling is now assigned as error. That the certificate was relevant appears upon its face, and whether it should be admitted at that time, or when the case of the proponents was reached, was in the discretion of the court. It is urged, however, that by its admission the unsworn statement of Dr. Gardner, who had signed it, was brought before the court without any opportunity for his cross-examination. This objection, however, was not made when it was offered in evidence, and consequently is not available to the appellant. The certificate was signed by Dr. Mays, and was admissible upon his cross-examination as a statement made by him at another time. If the contestant had wished to have its effect limited to the statement of the witness, the court, upon his request would have done so. Several other rulings of the court in reference to the admission of testimony are objected to, but none are of such a character as to justify extended comment. We do not find any error in any of them which could have had any effect upon the decision of the issues before the court.

During the trial Mrs. Wormell was called as a witness by the proponents, and while under examination stated that she was a beneficiary under the following instrument: "December 10, 1897. I wish to make Wealthy Wormell a gift of $500. A. R. Scott. Witness: Dr. J. N. Eckel." The witness testified that she saw Mrs. Scott write and sign that paper, and saw Dr. Eckel sign it. "She said she wished to make me a gift; that I had been kind to her. I was at her bedside,—the night that she was taken to bed. She told me what she was going to write. Dr. Eckel was present. She said that I had been kind to her, and she wanted to make me a present. That was all." The appellant contends that the court erred in failing to find whether this was a will. Whether this is a part of the testamentary disposition by Mrs. Scott of her estate was not one of the issues before the court for trial. The amended contest upon the probate of the will was filed January 22, 1898, and the answers thereto filed in the February following. Upon that contest the execution or relevancy of this instrument was not made an issue. The trial of the contest began March 22d, and this instrument was not produced or filed until March 30th. No notice of its filing was given, nor was any petition for its probate ever presented to the court. There is no evidence in the record that the writing was made with any testamentary intent, and its terms are more compatible with an intention to make a gift *inter vivos* than a testamentary disposition. In the absence of a showing of testamentary intent, it cannot be held to constitute a will. (*Clarke* v. *Ransom*, 50 Cal. 595.) The order admitting the will to probate and the order denying a new trial are affirmed.

We concur: GAROUTTE, VAN DYKE, JJ.

HATT *et al. vs.* RICH *et al.*

BACKUS *vs.* HATT.

[Court of Chancery of New Jersey, March 26, 1900; 45 Atl. Rep. 969.]

SPECIFIC PERFORMANCE—SALE OF REALTY—POWER OF SALE—
EXECUTION.

1. Specific performance of a contract for sale will be decreed although the title is claimed to be disputable, where it appears that the doubts suggested relate to steps in the title which are fully presented to the court, the validity of which can readily be determined, and which, when examined, present no obstacle to the making of an efficient deed under the contract, passing a merchantable title in fee simple.

2. A power of sale given to executors which authorizes them to sell and convey all the testator's real estate at their discretion, is efficient to support a sale by the executors, not only of all the territorial extent of the lands whereof the testator died seized, but also of all his title interest therein; and their sale under the power will devest the estate of residuary devisees, and of all those claiming under them.

3. Such a power does not lose its efficiency because the debts and legacies are paid, nor by mere lapse of time, when it may still be used to accomplish purposes which the testator may have had in view, or to carry into effect the conversion, and setting apart a share to be held in trust for one of the testator's children, according to the terms of his will.

4. The right of the executors to execute the power, and thereby to convey
the fee whereof the testator died seized, is superior to the right of partition held by the purchaser of an undivided interest from a residuary
devisee.

(Syllabus by the court.)

Suit by Joel W. Hatt and others, executors of William King,
against Eleazer C. Rich and others and by Edmond P. Backus
against Henrietta S. Hatt. Causes were heard together.

Decree for executors in the first suit and for defendants in the
second suit.

In the first of these suits the executors of William King's will
seek to compel the performance of a contract they made with the
defendant Rich to convey the homestead property of Mr. King,
in East Orange, under a power of sale in his will. This suit is
defended because it is contended that the executor's power of sale
is not efficient to convey a merchantable title. In the second suit,
Backus, the complainant, is the purchaser of an undivided one-
seventh share of the estate of William King, including his homestead property, and seeks to compel a partition or sale. The defense is that the executors must exercise the power to realize the
funds to be invested for Elizabeth Wright's share; that they have
contracted to sell the homestead property under their power,
which is superior to the devise under which Backus has acquired
his title; and that the terms of the will and codicil and the circumstances of the estate require that the power of sale shall be used to
sell all the testator's lands, and that the execution of the power
will devest the estate of Mr. Backus and of the others who claim,
like him, under the devise. These causes both present the question of the validity of the power of sale given in the will of William
King to be exercised at the discretion of his executors, and
were for this reason heard together. William King by his
will, dated March, 1874, gave and devised all his estate to his
wife during her life for the support, etc., of herself and their
unmarried daughters. The third clause of his will is in these
words: "Third. After the decease of my wife, I give the use
of my homestead property on Grove street, in said township
of East Orange, including the lot on which the barn and carriage
house stands, and all my furniture, implements, utensils, and

articles of personal property belonging to and in use in and about my said homestead, to such of my daughters as may then be unmarried, during their lives, and so long as they remain unmarried and continue to occupy my said homestead as a residence. Upon the death or marriage of all of my said unmarried daughters, or upon their ceasing to occupy my said homestead as a residence, I direct that said homestead property, furniture, and articles of personal property referred to in this clause of my will ` shall sink into the residue of my estate, and be disposed of under this clause of my will, except as otherwise hereinafter provided. It is my intention to give my unmarried daughters a home so long as they remain unmarried, but that they shall have no right to lease my homestead, and receive rent therefrom, but, upon their ceasing to occupy the same as a residence, the same shall become part of the residue of my estate, and be disposed of as therein provided." He bequeathed one money legacy of $5,000 to his granddaughter Anna King, payable after the death of his wife, and then follows the residuary clause, in the sixth item of his will, by which he gave and bequeathed in these words: "All the rest and residue of my estate, real and personal, whatsoever and wheresoever, to my seven children, namely, Phoebe J. King, Henrietta S., wife of Joel W. Hatt, Fannie M. King, John J. King, Lenora W. King, Elizabeth King, and to their heirs, executors, and administrators and assigns, forever." The last item appoints the executors, and creates the power of sale, as follows: "I constitute and appoint my said wife, Mary, and my daughter Phoebe J. King, my son, John J. King, and my sons-in-law, Joel W. Hatt and Edward L. Conklin, and the survirors and survivor of them, executors of this, my last will, and hereby authorize and empower my said executors, and the survivors or survivor of them, to sell and convey all my real estate, in their discretion, at public or private sale; the homestead property not to be sold until the same shall sink into the residue of my estate as hereinbefore provided." By a codicil made in 1879, he ratified his will, save as to the share given to his daughter Elizabeth, as to which he, by the codicil, made the following provision: "I now declare that it is my will that, instead of her receiving the share or portion of my estate as therein provided, such share or portion shall be invested by my executors in safe bonds and mortgages on improved real estate having dwelling houses erected thereon; the value of said real estate to be at least double the amount invested, and to be situated in the county of Essex, New Jersey; and the income thereof paid to her, my said daughter Elizabeth King, during her natural life, as the same shall be received. At the death of my said daughter, the share or portion shall vest in her lawful issue, share and share alike: provided, however, that in case my said daughter shall die leaving lawful issue before such issue shall have reached the age of maturity, then it is my will that the income only arising from said share or portion of my estate shall be devoted to the maintenance and support of such issue until they shall severally reach maturity, at which time the share coming to each child shall be then paid to him or her. In case my said daughter Elizabeth King shall die without lawful issue, then it is my will that said share or portion shall be divided equally between my children Phoebe J. King, Henrietta S. Hatt, Fannie M. King, John J. King, Lenora K. Conklin, and Isaac W. King, and the survivors or survivor of them, share and share alike, the issue of any deceased child taking the share to which said child would have been entitled if living. I further declare it to be my will that, in case my said daughter Elizabeth King shall at any time marry, then the income hereinbefore provided to be paid to her shall, under no circumstances, be subject to any claim, demand, influence, or control of her husband, but the same shall be paid to her for her own separate use and benefit. I hereby nominate and appoint as trustees of said share or portion of my estate set apart for the use of my said daughter the executors named in my last will and testament." William King died in 1882, seized in fee of several tracts of land, including his homestead, referred to in the bills of complaint. His will was proven in the same year by all the executors. Mary King, the widow, died on October 28, 1885. The daughters of the testator who were then living and unmarried were Phoebe J. King, Fannie M. King, and Elizabeth Wright, a widow. The homestead was occupied by Mary King, the testator's widow, during her life, and on her death by Phoebe, Fannie and Elizabeth. Phoebe afterwards died, and Fannie married, leaving Elizabeth the sole occupant. She found the homestead property to be too large for her sole use, and voluntarily ceased to occupy it, and expressed her desire to have the homestead sold under the executors' power. With her consent, upon her ceasing to occupy the homestead, the executors, on August 23, 1897, entered into a written agreement for the sale of the house and lot at the southwesterly corner of Grove and New streets (part of the homestead property) for $15,000, to the defendants, Eleazer C. Rich and Helen C., his wife. A copy of the agreement is annexed to the bill. The cash payment under the agreement has been paid. The deed has been executed by the executors to Mrs. Rich, with her assent, by her husband's request. The bond and mortgage securing payment of the purchase money has been made by them. The conveyances have been approved by both parties, a check for the additional cash drawn, and all these papers have been deposited in escrow until the vendors shall satisfy themselves that the deed of the executors conveys a fee-simple estate clear of incumbrances. When that is ascertained, the papers. shall be delivered and recorded. The proposed vendees have been put into possession of the premises pending an investigation of the title. The vendees refuse to accept delivery of the deed, alleging that it does not convey a good merchantable title. The objections are based upon these facts: " Isaac W. King's undivided share under the devise to him has been made the subject of several conveyances, as to which disputes have arisen, finally resulting in a sheriff's sale of his undivided interest in all the King estate, including the homestead property to Edmond P. Backus, the complainant in the above-named partition suit. Phoebe J. King's share is held, since her death, by her devisees. Neither the devisees named in William King's will nor those claiming under them have joined with the executors in the deed under the contract to convey to Rich. That deed purports to convey a fee-simple estate, solely by virtue of the power of sale given to the executors in William King's will. The defendants Rich claim that the power is void, and deny the efficiency of a deed made under it to pass a fee as against the devisees and those claiming under them, upon grounds hereinafter considered. The partition suit is prosecuted by Edmond P. Backus, the purchaser at sheriff's sale of Isaac W. King's undivided one-seventh interest in his father's estate. He alleges that by the terms of the will the only purpose for which the power of sale in William King's will could be exercised was the payment of his debts and legacies, and that these have all been accomplished, and that there remains no object in keeping such power alive. He prays a partition or sale of the premises. The defendants are the King family who have the other undivided six-sevenths of the estate, and the trustees under the William King will and codicil. They contend that the estate of Backus, as owner of Isaac W. King's undivided one-seventh, and the estates of all the other devisees under William King's will, and of those claiming under them, are subject to the power of sale given by him to his executors. They set forth the executors' agreement to convey to Mrs. Rich a part of the homestead property under the power of sale, and the pendency of the above-named suit for specific performance of that agreement. They allege that all the owners of the devised shares, except Backus, are advised and believe that the executors have full power to convey in fee simple to Mrs. Rich. They deny that the power is obsolete, and insist that it is yet in full force.

Philemon Woodruff, for complainant in the bill for specific performance, and for defendants in the partition suit.

De Witt & Provost, for complainant Edmond P. Backus.

Louis Hood, for defendants Rich and wife.

GREY, V. C. (after stating the facts).—The testator, William King, died seized of an estate in fee simple. The effect of his will in disposing of his real estate, was to devise to his wife an estate during her life in the whole of it, for certain prescribed uses; and, upon his wife's death, to such of his daughters as were then unmarried, an estate in his homestead and its equipment during their lives, which was subject to be defeated by their marriage, or their ceasing to occupy the homestead as a residence; and to his seven children a remainder in fee in the whole estate, including the homestead, which, subject to the two succeeding life estates, vested in the devisees immediately upon the death of the testator. This was the devolution of the title. All of these devises were subject to the power of sale given to the executors, to be exercised at their discretion, but postponed as to the period of its exercise upon the homestead property until it should become a part of the residue by the termination or defeat of the unmarried daughter's life estate. The nature of the power is apparent. There is no direction to sell, but there is the fullest authority to do so, at the discretion of the donees. In such cases the land retains its character as land until it is actually sold. (*Cook's Ex'r v. Cook's Adm'r*, 20 N. J. Eq. 377.) Meanwhile, by the testator's residuary devise, the title to the lands vested in his children, subject to be devested by the execution of the power by the executors. The actual operation of the will was that Mr. King's wife outlived him, and enjoyed her life estate under his will. Upon her death, in October, 1885, there were these daughters unmarried,—Elizabeth Wright, a widow, Phoebe J. King, and Fannie M. King. In these daughters, upon their mother's death, an estate for their lives vested, subject to be defeated by the death or marriage of all of them, or by their ceasing to occupy the homestead as a residence. Phoebe died in 1894, unmarried, and testate; Fannie married in 1894, and "ceased to occupy"; and the estate remained dependent on Elizabeth's death, marriage, or "ceasing to occupy" the homestead. There might be some question whether Elizabeth, who had been married after her father's, but previous to her mother's, death, and had at the time of her mother's death become a widow, was at the latter date unmarried, so as to be within the class of devisees prescribed by the testator. In *Maberly v. Strode* (3 Ves. 453), Sir RICHARD PEPPER ARDEN, M. R., declared that legacies given to unmarried daughters would not go to widowed daughters, unless there were other indications of the testator's purpose; that the word "unmarried" meant never having had any husband at all. In *Bell v. Phyn* (7 Ves. 458), Sir WILLIAM GRANT, M. R., was of opinion that the expression "without being married," must be construed, "without having ever been married." All constructions of single words or phrases must, however, be controlled by the evidences of the testator's intent as shown by the whole will. In this will, the testator, upon the death of his wife, devises the homestead "to such of my daughters as may then be unmarried, during their lives, and so long as they remain unmarried, and continue to occupy my said homestead as a residence." The gift here is to daughters who at the time of the death of the wife should be unmarried, no matter what their previous condition might have been. The testator, by his provision as to the residence in the homestead, and the possibility of their subsequent marriage, contemplated all of his daughters whose single condition at the death of his wife might enable them to use his homestead as their family residence, and did not intend to make the fact that any of them, though single then, and living at home, might previously have been married, a ground of exclusion from his gift. In *Doe* v. *Rawding* (2 Barn. & Ald. 452), it was held that the word "unmarried" may be taken to mean "not married at the time," if that construction be necessary to make it operative. The testator seems to have intended the gift to go to any daughters who might marry, for he provides that their subsequent marriage should defeat the estate. This would not exclude a widowed daughter.

This point is of minor significance, as the life estate of Elizabeth, conceding that she took under the devise, has, as both parties admit, been defeated by her "ceasing to occupy" the homestead as her residence, and it therefore does not interfere with the passing of a perfect title to the defendants. If she was not within the class of unmarried daughters, the same result follows. All the unmarried daughters have now died, married, or "ceased to occupy" the homestead, and their life estate has thus been defeated, and has fallen into the residue, as prescribed by the will. The executors now propose to execute the power of sale by selling the homestead property. The defendants in the bill for specific performance of the contract to purchase part of the homestead property deny the executors' right to execute the power upon several grounds. The first, second, third and fifth grounds set up in their answer contend that the power is inefficient to convey a merchantable title as against the estate which vested in the devisees under the residuary clause of William King's will, and which is now in Backus and others, claiming under the devisees. In the partition suit, Messrs. Hatt and Conklin, who are the surviving executors of the will of William King, and are also, under his will, trustees, etc., for his daughter Elizabeth Wright, are made defendants not in terms as executors, but as trustees. The premises of the partition bill, however, set forth the executors' power of sale, their claim of a right to exercise it and the prayer is that a partition or sale may be made, "free, clear, and discharged of the power of sale given under the will of William King, deceased," etc. In

this case the parties are in court, and have submitted themselves
to its jurisdiction.   The matter of the bill clearly relates to a subject touching which they have answered, and the mere omission
to name the special capacity in which they are pleading will not
affect the proceedings.   (*Walton's Ex'r* v. *Herbert*, 4 N. J. Eq.
75; *Evans* v. *Evans*, 23 id. 75; *White* v. *Davis*, 48 id. 24; 21 Atl.
187.) The complainant Backus, in the partition suit, also disputes
the validity of the power of sale, and its superiority to the estate,
which, by the will, came to the residuary devisees, under one of
whom he claims.   In both suits the question is therefore presented,
whether the executors' power of sale may now be exercised to convey a title to the lands passing as residue, which will be superior
to that which vested in the devisees.   That the power of sale is
well expressed, in the will to accomplish that purpose is beyond
dispute. The testator, who devised the estates in remainder in fee
created the power and made it applicable, as he expressed it,
" to all my real estate."   This included the whole of the testator's real estate, not only to the territorial expanse of all his
lands, but also to the extent of all his title interest therein.
(*Barry* v. *Edgeworth*, 2 P. Wms. 524; *Jackson* v. *Merrill*, 6
Johns. 191.) He also authorized the executors to sell and
convey at their discretion; that is, at such prices, on such terms,
and for such estates as they might deem proper. The power
also included the homestead property, but touching the time when
the power might be exercised upon the homestead, the testator
prohibited its execution until that property should " sink into the
residue, as hereinbefore (in his will) provided; " that is, until the
life estate of the unmarried daughters should terminate or be defeated.   This event has now completely happened.

It is claimed that the executors' power has become void, because
the debts and legacies have been paid, and there is no occasion for
its exercise. The opinion of Chancellor WILLIAMSON in *Brearley*
v. *Brearley* (9 N. J. Eq. 24), is brought forward as sustaining
this proposition. It seems to be assumed by the defendants that,
although a testator may have created a power in clearly expressed
terms, which gave to his executors unlimited authority to sell all
his real estate at their discretion, yet they will not be permitted
to exercise the power at their discretion, as authorized by the testator, but only when it is necessary to be used to raise money to

pay debts or legacies. This is not the doctrine of *Brearley* v: *Brearley*. The learned chancellor in that case states explicitly, touching the creation of powers, that it is the will of the testator which must be executed, however unreasonable it may appear to be; that the testator may dispose of his property arbitrarily, " without giving any reasons for the disposition he makes of it; " and that, where no ambiguity of language or phraseology makes doubtful what the testator's intention is, the absence of all motive on the face of the will, or inability to ascribe a motive for the disposition made, because of the circumstances of the testator and his family, are entitled to no consideration. (Page 25.)   He further declares that, as to the question of the testator's intent in creating powers, each case must stand in great measure upon its own, peculiar circumstances.   (Page 32.)   In that case he was of opinion that there was no such clear expression of the testator's intent upon the face of the will as excluded an ascertainment of his purpose from attending facts, and these he held showed that the testator did not intend that the executors should exercise the power of sale, when, if executed, it would, without reason, convert the lands which had descended to heirs into money, against their united opposition. Each of the numerous other cases cited against the exercise of the power stands upon the expressions of the will in the particular case, and, if they were ambiguous, then upon the circumstances of the testator's property and his family, etc., or beneficiaries. They afford but little aid as precedents, because each case varies in essential particulars of its facts from that under consideration. The cases most nearly resembling that under consideration are *Bacot* v. *Wetmore* (17 N. J. Eq. 250), and, on the same will, *Wetmore* v. *Midmer* (21 N. J. Eq. 245). See, also, *Cruikshank* v. *Parker* (52 N. J. Eq. 310; 29 Atl. 682). In the case in hand the donation of the power to the executors is expressed in the plainest terms, without any ambiguity, and the application of the more modern rule that " the courts have decided that powers, although framed in general terms, are limited by the nature of the limitations contained in the * * * will " (*Peters* v. *Railroad Co.* 18 Ch. Div. 433), is needed to justify any further discussion of its extent. This doctrine is entirely acceptable where the will in terms, or by necessary implication, indicates the purposes to which the testator intended the use of the powers to be limited. But where the will creates an unlimited power in un-questionable terms, yet exhibits no objects save a desire for the exercise of the discretion of the donee, there is some danger that, in holding that the powers may not be enforceable, some unex-pressed purpose of the testator may be defeated. The power given to the executors is, by the express terms of Mr. King's will, exer-cisable at their discretion, without limit of time or circumstance, save as to the homestead property. If, despite this fact, there must be, in order to validate the power, some additional indications of the objects for which the testator intended it should be exercised, the will itself and the circumstances of this case are not lacking in the exhibition of such indications.

Taking up the claim that the power cannot be used to convey a merchantable title to the homestead property. That the testator created the power, that he contemplated its exercise by the exec-utors upon the homestead property, that he postponed their action under their discretion, so that they should not sell the homestead until the last of the unmarried daughters had either married, ceased to occupy it, or died, appears in the very words of the will. It is assumed by the defendants that the payment of debts and legacies must have been the only matter for which the testator intended the power to be exercised. The face of the will indicates that, while the testator intended the homestead property to be sold under the power, it is highly improbable that he had any purpose that its proceeds should go to pay either debts or legacies. This is strongly inferable from the fact that, although the power was undoubtedly extended over the homestead property, the testa-tor postponed the time when the executors might exercise it upon that property, to the end of two successive life estates in it. The testator must be presumed to have known the law that all his debts must have been paid long before the sale of the homestead (which he contemplated after two life estates had expired) could have been effected under the power so postponed. As to the legacies, the $5,000 gift to Annie King, the granddaughter, is the only one in the will for which money had to be raised. The testator post-poned the payment of this legacy until the death of his wife, and, as he postponed the sale of the homestead under the power still further,—beyond the life estate given to his unmarried daughters after the death of his wife,—it is evident he did not expect the power to be exercised to raise the legacy. In this aspect of the case, both the debts and the legacy had to be paid before the power could be used to sell the homestead. Yet the very words of the will show that the testator contemplated the use of the power to sell the homestead. How, then, can it be said that the unlimited discretion which the testator gave to sell the homestead must be limited to be used for two purposes only, when, by the expressed terms of his will, it could not have been used for either of those purposes? Must it not be believed that he meant what he said,— that the executors should use the power at their discretion; that is, for any purposes? Considering that the homestead property has now, using the testator's words, " sunk into the residue," is the executors' power of sale yet forceful to convey a title which is merchantable, and which will devest the fee held by the devisees of the residuary estate? The contestants insist that the satisfaction of the debts and legacies has nullified the power. The decisions in cases where a showing of objects for the execution of general powers has been required have not limited the execution of such powers to the payments of debts and legacies. On the contrary, such general powers appear to have been held valid wherever the court has been able to ascribe to a testator any purpose consistent with the circumstances of his estate and his relations to his beneficiaries. An intent to " secure dominion over his estate," and to " limit the expenses incident to conveyance " (Lord ELDON in *Maundrell* v. *Maundrell,* 10 Ves. 265), " convenience of distribution " (Chancellor WILLIAMSON in *Brearley* v. *Brearley,* 9 N. J. Eq. 31), " convenience of division " (*Smith* v. *Claxton,* 4 Madd. 493), have all been referred to as objects which would sustain the validity and exercise of a general power. In Mr. King's case it is not difficult to believe that, with his large family of sons and daughters, to whom he had given a considerable estate in undivided shares, the lands lying in various parcels, the testator might well have anticipated the very situation which has now happened,—that, by reason of some financial misfortune, the undivided share of some one or more of the family might come to the ownership of a stranger, whose interests and feelings would be foreign to those of the family, and, in order to preserve " dominion over the estate," and the power to dispose of the property by the action of those in whose discretion he trusted, rather than at the instance of strangers, he created the power which could be exercised at the will of his executors (also members of his family), who could thus compel a realization at such times, in such manner, at such prices, and on such terms as they might deem most beneficial.

There is, however, a further indication of the testator's intention regarding the exercise of the power, arising out of the provisions of the codicil to his will, which is applicable to the whole of his real estate. The will and the codicil speak as an entirety, and from the time of the testator's death. He made his will in 1874, and his codicil in 1879. By the codicil he ratifies his will, save as to Elizabeth's share. The complainants in the partition bill assume that this was a ratification of the residuary devise under which they claim, but they do not recognize the attendant fact that it was also a ratification of the power in the will which dominated their devise. By the codicil the testator revokes and alters his will so far as it relates to the share devised to Elizabeth, and declares his will to be as follows: "I now declare that it is my will that, instead of her receiving the share or portion of my estate as therein (in the will) provided, such share or portion shall be invested by my executors in safe bonds and mortgages, * * * and the income thereof paid to her, my said daughter Elizabeth King, during her natural life," etc., "with limitation over to issue of Elizabeth, or, on failure of issue, to the survivors of her brothers and sisters, or their issue." The testator, by the codicil, contemplated a conversion of the share devised to Elizabeth. It was to be invested in safe bonds and mortgages. Income therefrom was to be paid. The whole scheme and the phrasing of this codicil show that the testator was dealing with Elizabeth's share as a fund, and not as land. He then appoints as trustees the executors named in the will. His language is, "as trustees of said share or portion of my estate set apart for the use of my said daughter Elizabeth." Elizabeth's share is thus considered by the testator as "set apart;" that is, to be severed from the rest of the estate. The testator, when he made this codicil providing that the devise given in his will to Elizabeth should be revoked, and that her share should be set apart and invested to produce for her an income, had before him the will by which Elizabeth's share was but an undivided interest, intermingled with other shares. He did not himself, by a self-executing codicil, sever her portion. He also had before him that provision in his will whereby the executors, whom he made trustees for Elizabeth, might sell the whole estate, at their discretion, and thus effect a severance of Elizabeth's interest, and its realization into a fund which might be invested for her benefit. The testator plainly left the severance and setting apart of Elizabeth's share to be done by his executors. There is no way by which the trust fund for her could, under the scheme of the will and codicil, be set apart for her out of the undivided interests, save by executing the power of sale. If, therefore, reasons for the exercise of the power of sale for other than payment of debts and legacies must be found to justify its execution (notwithstanding the words of the will disclose a clear intent of the testator to give an unlimited discretion), they are, I think, apparent upon the face of the will and codicil, not only in the purposes which may fairly be ascribed to the testator, but also in those which the scheme of the testamentary dispositions force into recognition.

The exercise of the power by the executors is further challenged because it is claimed to be stale, or to have become void for want of exercise within a reasonable time. So far as this applies to the sale of the homestead property, the power was exercised substantially coincidently with the opportunity to exercise it. The testator postponed its execution until the life estate given to his unmarried daughters should " sink into the residue." This did not happen until they died, married, or " ceased to occupy " the homestead. The defeat of this estate happened by the cessation of the occupation of the homestead, because of Elizabeth's removal therefrom, which occurred within a few weeks before the making of the deed now deposited in escrow. The delay in exercising the power upon the residue of the estate of the testator has not invalidated it. During Mrs. King's life, up to 1885, while she had the right to the whole estate for the benefit of herself and her unmarried daughters, of whom Elizabeth was (for a time) one, it can readily be understood that the executors found no occasion to separate Elizabeth's share. After Mrs. King's death, so long as the undivided interests were held in the ownership of the family, the provision for Elizabeth was a matter of family arrangement. Now, that a necessity for dealing with a stranger has arisen, the executors seek to exercise that dominion over the estate which the testator left to their discretion, and subject to which the stranger bought. The Court of Appeals, in *Morse* v. *Bank* (47 N. J. Eq. 287-290; 20 Atl. 961; 12 L. R. A. 62), discusses the effect of mere delay in the exercise of an unlimited testamentary power of sale, and declares that no case has come under its observation in which a limitation of time has been imposed upon a power in the nature of a trust not limited in terms, unless the rule against perpetuities is involved, or the power is controlled by an inherent quality in the nature of a trust, or by the object for which it is created. It is true that the controversy in this case as to the validity of the power has arisen some twelve years since Mrs. King's death, but there is no showing that the purposes of the testator to set Elizabeth's share apart, and have it invested, have ever been carried out, nor that any fraudulent use of the power is intended, nor that its present exercise is against public policy in that it may offend the rule against perpetuities; nor does any reason appear why the trust reposed by the testator in the discretion of the executors should not be performed by the use of the power. Mr. Backus, the complainant in the partition suit, holds his title under the conveyance of Isaac King's undivided share of the estate. As devisee of an undivided share, Isaac was a mere volunteer, and his estate was subject to the exercise of the superior power created by the testator, who gave him his share. It is quite possible that Mr. Backus, in making his purchase of Isaac King's undivided interest in the estate, subject to the executor's power of sale, discounted the disadvantages to which the share was subject by the lesser price which he paid. However this may be, he certainly bought with full notice of the superiority of the power of sale over the undivided interest which he purchased, and has, therefore, no equity now to complain. That the exercise of the power will cut out the estate which vested by the devise was determined against a subsequent purchaser of such a devised share at a sheriff's sale in *Wetmore* v. *Midmer* (21 N. J. Eq. 243).

There is no room in this case for the doctrine of election, whereby, when the whole of the proceeds in the lands to be sold under a power belong to the persons who held the title, courts of equity will protect the choice of the beneficiary to retain the title to the land, rather than to take the proceeds under the execution of the power. The whole beneficial interest is not in Mr. Backus. All the other beneficiaries join in asking that the power be exercised. To enforce the testator's intent as to Elizabeth's share, it is necessary that the power be exercised. There is a limitation over of her share, which is contingent. Mr. Backus, being the holder of but an undivided share, cannot alone elect to take the property as land, and thus defeat the operation of the power. (*Fluke* v. *Fluke's Ex'rs*, 16 N. J. Eq. 481.)

It is also objected, in the specific performance suit, that the deed in escrow is not executed by John J. King, originally one of the executors, but who has been removed by an order of the Orphans' Court. This criticism was not urged with much insistence. It has been finally settled by the Court of Appeals in *Denton* v. *Clark* (36 N. J. Eq. 538), approving of the more elaborate exposition of the question in *Weimar* v. *Fath* (43 N. J. Law, 1). The law on the point is declared to be " that when a will gives executors in their official capacity a power to sell, without naming individuals who are to be clothed with such capacity, * * * and one of such executors is removed from the office, the power to sell survives, and can be legally exercised by the remaining executors." The conditions stated apply in this case. The power is efficiently exercised without John J. King joining in the making of the deed.

In the specific performance case the complainants have shown that they have power to convey to Mr. Rich, by the deed in escrow, a fee simple estate in that part of the homestead property which is proposed to be granted by that deed, and that the title which will thus pass is not questionable, so that its acceptance would put upon the defendants the risk which might attend upon settling it. (*Lippincott* v. *Wikoff*, 54 N. J. Eq. 109; 33 Atl. 305.) In the partition suit the power of sale under William King's will, which the executors claim the right to exercise, must be held to be superior to the right of partition or sale acquired by Mr. Backus by his purchase of the undivided interest of Isaac King in the devise to the latter under that will. The executors are bound to exercise that power in order to carry into effect the codicil of the testator regarding the share of Elizabeth, which he directed to be invested and set apart by her trustees, and which must be so delivered to the trustees that they may perform their duty in that regard. The power is superior to the estate of the residuary devisees, and of those claiming under them. They have held the fee since the death of the testator, and are entitled to the profits of the lands (except the homestead property) from the time of Mrs. King's death to the time of the execution of the power. (*Morse v. Bank,* 47 N. J. Eq. 283; 20 Atl. 961; 12 L. R. A. 62.) Their fee will be devested by the execution of the power, but this can work no hardship to Mr. Backus, the purchaser of Isaac's share, for he bought Isaac's undivided interest in a devise which came to him by the same will which gave to the executors the superior power to sell the whole estate. The most that Mr. Backus could acquire by his deed was Isaac's place. The several residuary devisees and those claiming under them will, of course, be entitled to their several shares in the purchase money arising from the execution of the power.

Decrees will accordingly be advised for the complainants in the specific performance suit and for the executors and trustees under William King's will in the partition suit.

In re REYNOLDS' ESTATE.

APPEAL OF CARPENTER.

[Supreme Court of Pennsylvania, March 26, 1900; 195 Pa. St. 225; 45 Atl. Rep. 726.]

ORPHANS' COURT—JURISDICTION—EXPENSES OF ADMINISTRATION —RECORD.

1. The Orphans' Court has jurisdiction to decree a sale of decedent's real estate to pay expenses of administration.
2. Expenses of administration are not debts of decedent, and not subject to the limitation of the lien thereof, so that a sale for their payment may be decreed after expiration of the lien of the debts.
3. The record disclosing that the decree of the Orphans' Court for a sale of decedent's real estate was for the payment of a debt due the executor, and his account showing that the balance claimed by him and allowed by the court was for commissions and expenses of administration, they are sufficient to show jurisdiction.

APPEAL from Orphans' Court, Wyoming county.

In the matter of the estate of Philetus H. Reynolds, deceased.
A rule granted Byron Carpenter on Charles Gardner, executor of
deceased, to show cause why a sale of real estate of deceased
should not be set aside, was discharged, and said Carpenter appeals.

Affirmed.

John A. Sittser and *C. O. Dersheimer*, for appellant.

James E. Frear and *Harding & Harding*, for appellee.

FELL, J.—The Orphans' Court has jurisdiction to decree the
sale of the real estate of a decedent to pay the expenses of the administration of his estate. Such expenses are not debts of the decedent, and the law limiting the lien of his debts does not apply
to them, and a sale for their payment may be decreed after the
expiration of the lien of the debts of a decedent. (*Cobaugh's Appeal,* 24 Pa. St. 143; *Demmy's Appeal,* 43 id. 155.) The decree
of the court was conclusive of the fact that there was a balance due
the executor. Indeed, this is not controverted, but it is claimed that
among the items of credit in the final account of the executor was
one that should have been disallowed, and the disallowance of
which would have left a balance in his hands after deducting his
expenses and commissions. The account was confirmed *nisi* before
the order of sale was made, and absolutely seven days after the
date of the order. All parties interested in the distribution and in
the real estate had notice, and no one of them has ever objected to
the account. The credit referred to was not for a debt of the decedent which had been paid by the executor, and as to which he would
have stood in the shoes of a creditor, and with no higher rights.
It was for the payment to the widow of a part of her exemption
in money, when it does not appear from the inventory that any
money came into the executor's hands. Whether, under the notice
of claim given by the widow, she was strictly entitled to receive
this payment, depends upon facts which are not disclosed by the
record, and which cannot be ascertained from it. If her claim was
made after the personal property had been converted into money,
she was entitled to the amount paid to her. (*Finney's Appeal,* 113
Pa. St. 11; 4 Atl. 60.) The record discloses the fact that the decree of sale was for the payment of a debt due the executor, and

his account shows that the balance claimed by him and allowed by the court was for commissions and expenses of administration. This was sufficient to give jurisdiction, and the sale passed a valid title.

The decree is affirmed at the costs of the appellant.

Note.—CREDITORS' REMEDY AS AGAINST LAND.

(a) Rule at common law.
(b) As dependent upon legislation.
(c) Effect of will.
(d) Some illustrative cases.

(a) **Rule at common law.**—By the common law the land of a deceased debtor was not liable for his debts or obligations. A creditor could not follow the realty which consequently passed to the heir or devisee unencumbered by the engagements of the deceased owner. Nor was there any personal responsibility for any such engagements on the part of the heir, unless the ancestor had executed an obligation by which he had specifically bound his heirs, in which event, his descendant was liable to the extent of the value of the lands which had descended to him and which had not been alienated at the time of the commencement of the suit against him. But even the obligations of such specialties did not extend to the devisees of the debtor. The consequence was, that by force of this system the lands of a debtor passed to his devisees discharged from his debts, or, if he died intestate, they went to his heirs similarly exonerated, unless for such debts as he had specially imposed on his heirs by his contracts under seal. Such a system was defensible only on the policy of the feudal law, the tendency of which was to transmit the heritage unburthened, as the basis of its military organization; but it was plainly inconsistent with modern conditions, and the defects have been remedied by legislation. (New Jersey Ins. Co. v. Meeker, 37 N. J. L. 295; and see Whittelsey v. Brohammer, 31 Mo. 108; People v. Brooks, 123 Ill. 248; 14 N. E. Rep. 39.)

At common law an executor could not sell lands for payment of debts, unless expressly charged. (Ticknor v. Harris, 14 N. H. 272; and see further as to rules at common law, Hall v. Martin, 46 N. H. 340.)

(b) **As dependent upon legislation.**—The jurisdiction of a court to decree or order a sale of land is derivable wholly from a statute. (Pettit v. Pettit, 32 Ala. 288; Gannett v. Leonard, 47 Mo. 205, 208; Hays v. Jackson, 6 Mass. 148. The opinion contains an interesting summary of the rules at common law, modification by statute, etc. And see Long v. Long, 142 N. Y. 545, 552; 37 N. E. Rep. 486.)

A special power limited by statute. (Eberstein v. Oswalt, 47 Mich. 254; 10 N. W. Rep. 360.)

Must be strict compliance. (Hogan v. Cavenaugh, 138 N. Y. 417; 34 N. E. Rep. 292; Dunning v. Dunning, 82 Hun, 462; 31 N. Y. Supp. 719; Matter of Meagley, 39 App. Div. 90; 56 N. Y. Supp. 503; Currie v. Stewart, 27 Miss. 52; Platt v. Platt, 105 N. Y. 489; 12 N. E. Rep. 22; Kingsland v. Murray, 133 N. Y. 170; 30 N. E. Rep. 845; Bompart v. Lucas, 21 Mo. 598; Wright v. Edwards, 10 Ore. 298.)

But in Hudson v. Juringan (39 Tex. 580), it was *held* that such statutes should be liberally construed.

Rights of creditors to payment out of the *proceeds* of real estate, in absence of proof of *laches* on their part. may not be denied, because the executor squandered the personal property which came to his hands. (Matter of Bingham, 127 N. Y. 297; 27 N. E. Rep. 1055. But compare Kingsland v. Murray, *supra*, and Matter of Meagley, 39 App. Div. 91; 56 N. Y. Supp. 503, where it is queried in such a case whether a creditor can resort to a sale of real estate. And see also on this subject Rowland v. Swope, 39 Ill. App. 514; Buel's Appeal, 60 Conn. 63; 22 Atl. Rep. 488; Lea v. Beaman, 101 N. C. 294; 7 S. E. Rep. 887; Smith v. Brown, 101 N. C. 347; 7 S. E. Rep. 890; Conger v. Cook, 56 Iowa, 117; 8 N. W. Rep. 782; Van Bibber v. Julian. 81 Mo. 618.)

Rights of creditors. against real estate of deceased persons attaches to the land as a statutory lien immediately upon the death of the owner; their rights cannot be impaired by any conveyance which is delivered or takes effect subsequently. (Rosseau v. Bleau, 131 N. Y. 177, 182; 30 N. E. Rep. 52; Platt v. Platt, *supra;* Little Falls National Bank v. King, 53 App. Div. 544; 65 N. Y. Supp. 1010; and see Flood v. Strong, 108 Mich. 561; 66 N. W. Rep. 473.)

The heirs cannot alien the land to the prejudice of creditors. In fact and in law they have no right to the real estate of their ancestor, except that of possession, until the creditors shall be paid. As regards the question of power in the legislature, no objection is perceived to their subjecting the lands of the deceased to the payment of his debts, to the exclusion of his personal property. The legislature regulates descents, and the conveyance of real estate. To define the rights of debtor and creditor is their common duty. The whole range of remedies lies within their province. (Watkins v. Hohnan, 16 Pet. 26, 63.)

In Bank of Hamilton v. Dudley (2 Pet. 522), the U. S. Supreme Court say: "The lands of an intestate descend not to the administrator but to the heir. They vest in him, liable it is true to the debts of his ancestor, and subject to be sold for those debts. The administrator has no 'estate in the land but a power to sell under the authority of the local court. This is not an independent power, to be exercised at discretion when the exigency in his opinion may require it, but is conferred by the court in a state of things prescribed by the law. The order of the court is a prerequisite indispensable to the very existence of the power; and if the law which authorized the court to make the order be repealed, the power to sell can never come into existence. The repeal of such a law divests no vested estate, but is the exercise of a legislative power which every legislature possesses. The mode of subjecting the property of a debtor to the demands of a creditor, must always depend on the wisdom of the legislature.

(c) **Effect of will.**—Equitable lien created by charging land devised with payment of debts. (3 Pomeroy Eq. § 1244, *et seq.*)

A power of sale in will to pay debts, does not indicate an intention to charge the debts upon the real estate. (Clift v. Moses, 116 N. Y. 144; 22 N. E. Rep. 393.)

Payment of debts will not be charged upon a devise without clear evidence of such intent in the will. (Matter of City of Rochester, 110 N. Y. 159; 17 N. E. Rep. 740.)

That executor having a power of sale not absolutely imperative may be compelled to exercise it at instance of a creditor. (Wood v. Hubbard, 29 App. Div. 166; 51 N. Y. Supp. 526.)

Where lands are devised charged with payment of debts generally, an acceptance of the devise does not create a personal liability to pay, but simply creates a lien in favor of the creditors, enforceable against the lands devised. (Clift v. Moses, *supra;* and see Gridley v. Gridley, 24 N. Y. 130.)

The common-law rule that the personal estate of deceased will be applied to payment of contract debts, to the relief of real estate, is not of universal application and will not be enforced, where it is in apparent hostility to the plain intent of the deceased as expressed in his will. (Rice v. Harbeson, 63 N. Y. 493.)

Where the power to sell in will is imperative the exercise of it may be compelled by a creditor, and as the debtor had thus provided another remedy, that otherwise provided by statute could not be resorted to. (Matter of Gantert, 136 N. Y. 106; 32 N. E. Rep. 551.)

Where debts are not specifically charged upon the land upon expiration of the statutory lien, a purchaser in good faith for value takes title clear of the encumbrance. (Smith v. Soper, 32 Hun, 46.)

When testator charges the payment of his debts upon certain specified real estate, and if that shall prove insufficient then upon his other real estate, as between the legatees and devisees the personal estate is exonerated from the debts. (Youngs v. Youngs, 45 N. Y. 254.)

When a state statute provides an ample remedy for creditors for the collection of their debts out of the real property of a decedent, the implication of a power of sale in executors, from a simple charge of the debt upon the lands is unnecessary and ought not to be indulged. The power of sale cannot be implied from the mere charge of debts upon the land. (Matter of Fox, 52 N. Y. 530, 537.)

The personal estate will not be discharged from the payment of debts, unless it clearly appears by the will that it was so intended. This will not be inferred simply from the fact that authority is given to sell all or some part of the real estate for the payment of debts, especially in a case where no disposition is made of the personalty. (Sweeney v. Warren, 127 N. Y. 426; 28 N. E. Rep. 413.)

(d) **Some illustrative cases.**—Lien enforced against proceeds of land sold in partition. (Hibbard v. Dayton, 32 Hun, 220.)

The lien of creditors extends only to the real estate, and does not attach to that which may be made out of it by the skill, management or labor of the heir or devisees. (Clift v. Moses, 116 N. Y. 144; 22 N. E. Rep. 393.)

A legislature has no power to assume that debts were due and payable and on that assumption authorize an administrator to sell land, the title to which was vested in the heirs. The power to determine the existence of debts is judicial not legislative. (Rozier v. Fagan, 46 Ill. 404.)

A state legislature may pass a private act authorizing a sale by an administrator of land to pay debts, at *private* sale, even though the act does not require notice to heirs or any one, and although there is a general statute providing for the same object. (Florentine v. Barton, 2 Wall. 210.)

An executor who pays debt with own money becomes subrogated to rights of creditor. (Suydam v. Voorhees, 43 Atl. Rep. 4 [N. J.]; Re O'Brien, 39 App. Div. 321; 56 N. Y. Supp. 925.)

Equitable title of deceased to land under an executory contract may be sold under statute in Missouri; although a deed is executed to his heirs after his death. (Howell v. Jump, 140 Mo. 441; 41 S. W. Rep. 976.)

ROSE *vs.* HALE *et al.*

[Supreme Court of Illinois, April 17, 1900; 185 Ill. 378; 56 N. E. Rep. 1073.]

WILLS—CONSTRUCTION—ESTATES CREATED—APPEAL.

1. A will provided: "Second. * * * I give, devise, and bequeath unto my wife, M. C., the farm on which we now reside. * * * Thirdly. All * * * my personal property not otherwise disposed of, whilst she remains my widow." *Held*, that the limitation "whilst she remains my widow" applied to the farm as well as the personal property, since, unless the second and third clauses be read as one sentence, the third clause would be meaningless, and, when read as one sentence, the limitation applied to both.

2. Where a devise is to testator's wife "whilst she remains my widow," the estate created cannot be greater than a life estate.

3. On an appeal by the grantee of a beneficiary under a will from a decree construing the will, the administrator cannot assign as error rulings of the court in relation to a part of the decree dismissing a petition to authorize him to make a sale of lands for the purpose of paying claims, from which he did not perfect an appeal, and which has no relation to the matters involved in the appeal taken.

APPEAL from Circuit Court, Fulton county; JOHN J. GLENN, Judge.

Bill by Lucinda Hale and others against William Rose. From a decree for plaintiffs, defendant appeals.
Affirmed.

John S. Winter and *Harry M. Waggoner,* for appellant.

M. P. Rice, T. C. Robinson, Chiperfield, Grant & Chiperfield, and *Lucien Gray,* for appellees.

BOGGS, J.—This is a bill in chancery filed by Lucinda Hale, Catherine Severns, Phedora Combs, and Mariah Cluney, appellees for the partition of certain real estate, the title whereof formerly rested in one Reason Church, who died January 1, 1880. On the hearing the court construed the will of said Reason Church to invest a life estate only in the land sought to be partitioned, in Mariah Church, wife of the testator, and that the remainder in fee descended to the heirs at law of the said testator. The appellant, by this appeal, questions the correctness of the construction given said will by the court. He insists that the true construction of said will vested in the said Mariah Church the title to the lands in fee simple, subject to the condition she should not marry again, and defeasible on that condition. Said Mariah Church conveyed the land to the appellant, and died without having again remarried. The position of the appellant is that the fee simple title to the said land rests in him.

The will of the deceased reads as follows:

" l, Reason Church, of Isabel, Fulton county, and state of Illinois, do make and declare this my last will and testament, in manner and form, to wit:

".First it is my will that my funeral expenses and all my just debts be fully paid.

" Second after the payment of my funeral expenses and debts I give devise and bequeath unto my beloved wife Mariah Church the farm on which we now reside, situate in said county and known and described as one hundred forty-five acres of the northwest quarter of section number thirty in township four north of range three east of the fourth principal meridian.

" Thirdly all the live stock horses cattle sheep hogs by me now owned and kept thereon also all the household furniture wagons, carriages and all my farming implements and all my personal property not herein enumerated or otherwise disposed of whilst she remains my widow. But if she should marry then it is my will that she divide the farm and give each of my children an equal share after taking her thirds and lastly I hereby constitute and appoint my said wife Mariah Church executor of this my last will and testament."

As to the true construction thereof it is said in the brief of appellant: " Any one who is acquainted with philology and grammatical construction of the English language, by reading said will will perceive its second and third clauses, as written, consist of three sentences. If ' a sentence is the expression of a thought in words,' as it has been defined, then a construction of this will would be: (1) An absolute devise in fee of the farm on which they resided to his wife; (2) a bequest of all his personal property to his wife so long as she remained his widow; and (3) a limitation to the devise in fee of his farm to the wife; if she should marry again, she should divide the farm equally among his children, ' after taking her thirds.' That part of the third clause of said will in which the testator attempts to bequeath his personal property to his wife ' whilst she remains my widow ' is obviously a parenthetical phrase, intervening between the devise in the second clause of the will and the concluding part of the third, limiting that devise to a third of the farm if his wife should marry, the remainder to be divided equally among his children. Certainly that intervening sentence could be omitted without destroying the meaning of the composition in which it is found, which is the usual test as to whether a phrase is parenthetical or not. By such transposition, and thus placing the first and third of said sentences in their apparent natural relation to each other, the intent of the testator in his will becomes clear and obvious,—that he intended to debase the devise of the fee of his farm to his wife from an absolute to a determinable fee, subject, however, to his wife's marrying again. The second clause clearly, in the first instance, was intended as a devise to his wife of an absolute fee to his farm; the first sentence of the third clause, which, by its position, should be taken as parenthetical and considered as intended as a bequest of his personal property to his wife during her widowhood, and wholly disconnected with the devise in the second clause; and the second or concluding sentence of the third clause as intended as a limitation to the devise of the fee to the farm he had made to his wife in said second clause." We agree with counsel for appellant that the unmistakable intention of the testator was to bequeath his live stock, etc., and all his personal property, to his wife, "while she remained his widow." But we gather this intention by reading as one sentence that part of the will beginning with the word "second" and concluding with the word "widow." It will be observed that, unless this part of the will is read as one sentence, there is no gift or bequest of the live stock, etc., and personal property; for, if the phrase relating to such personal property, etc., be regarded, as appellant insists it should, as but parenthetical, and wholly disconnected from that portion of the will which relates to the real estate, then there are no words of gift, bequest, or devise applicable to said personal property. The phrase referred to as but parenthetical has no meaning if transposed from the position it occupies in the will. It must be construed and read as a part of the sentence, as we before indicated, or rejected as meaningless and unintelligible. A clause or expression may be transposed if it is senseless and contradictory as it stands in a will, or if the transposition is necessary to give effect to an intention clearly expressed or indicated by the context. (1 Jarm. Wills [5th Am. ed.], 499, 502.) But here the clause or expression proposed to be transposed may be given meaning if read in its place as we find it in the will, and is rendered meaningless if removed from that position; and the proposed transposition is not only not necessary to give effect to the intention which all agreed animated the testator, namely, to bequeath his personalty to his wife while she remained his widow, but will operate to defeat that intention. Transposition is only to be made when necessary to give effect to a meaning and purpose of the testator which is certain. (*Latham* v. *Latham,* 30 Iowa, 294.) Clearly, there is no warrant for removing the supposed parenthetical clause from the position given it in the will, or for regarding it as a sentence complete within itself. It is inseparably connected with that which precedes it in the will. The words "give, devise, and bequeath," which precede the description of the real estate, refer to both real estate and personalty, as do also the words "whilst she remains my widow," which, as we construe the will, are the closing words of a single sentence in which the testator made known his wishes as to his property, both real and personal. If the word "thirdly" be omitted from the will, all ground on which to base the contention of appellant disappears. The rule is, the intent of the testator, if clearly disclosed by his will, must prevail, even if some words must be rejected to give effect to such intention. (*Huffman* v. *Young*, 170 Ill. 290; 49 N. E. 570; *Whitcomb* v. *Rodman*, 156 Ill. 116; 40 N. E. 553; 28 L. R. A. 149.) In 2 Jarm. Wills (5th Am. ed. 53), it is said: "It is clear that words and passages in a will which are irreconcilable with the general context may be rejected, whatever may be the local position which they happen to occupy, for the rule which gives effect to the posterior of several inconsistent clauses must not be so applied as in any degree to clash or interfere with the doctrine which teaches us to look for the intention of a testator in the general tenor of the instrument, and to sacrifice to the scheme of disposition so disclosed any incongruous words and phrases which have found a place therein." The word "thirdly" was doubtless inserted from the prompting of some vague conception or idea of legal formalities. It has no meaning there, and serves no purpose in connection with the manifest intention of the testator. It may, therefore, be omitted from consideration in arriving at the true construction of the will. Excluding the word, the devise and bequest of all the property, both real and personal, is expressed in a single sentence, and is to Mariah Church "whilst she remains the widow" of the testator. The estate thus created cannot be greater than an estate for life. (*Willis* v. *Watson*, 4 Ill. 64; *Green* v. *Hewitt*, 97 id. 113; *Kaufman* v. *Breckinridge*, 117 id. 305; 7 N. E. 666; *Siddons* v. *Cockrell*, 131 Ill. 653; 23 N. E. 586.)

During the pendency of the cause in the Circuit Court, Henry Phelps, administrator with the will annexed of the estate of the said testator, by leave of the court filed an intervening petition, praying for a decree authorizing him, as such administrator, to make sale of the lands for the purpose of providing a fund wherewith to pay claims which, as the petition alleged, had been duly presented and allowed against said estate in the Probate Court, to discharge which there were no other assets, as the petition alleged. On a hearing the chancellor dismissed the petition. The administrator prayed and obtained an order granting him an appeal to this court, but failed to comply with the terms and conditions of such order. The administrator has assigned in this court alleged erroneous rulings of the chancellor with reference to the questions which arose in the trial court under his petition for a decree authorizing him to sell the land. That part of the decree dismissing the petition of the administrator had no relation to that other part of the decree construing the will of the deceased and declaring the rights and interests of the parties complainant and defendant to the bill for partition. The different parts of the decree were, in effect, distinct and separate decrees, and an appeal prosecuted from one part of the decree had no effect upon the decree in any other respect. The administrator failed to perfect his appeal from that portion of the decree which touched upon his rights and interests, and thereby is deemed to have acquiesced in the disposition of his petition. The appeal perfected to this court by the appellant only brings in review the action of the court on that branch of the case in which the administrator had no interest. (2 Enc. Pl. & Prac. 96.) He cannot, therefore, on this appeal, assign as for error the rulings or findings of the court with relation to matters not involved in the appeal. (*Walker* v. *Pritchard*, 121 Ill. 221; 12 N. E. 336; 2 Enc. Pl. & Prac. 157.) The decree is affirmed.

Decree affirmed.

TAYLOR *vs.* SYME *et al.*

[Court of Appeals of New York, April 17, 1900; 162 N. Y. 513; 57 N. E. Rep. 83.]

WILLS—FOREIGN EXECUTOR—ANCILLARY LETTERS—WHEN AU-
THORIZED—PETITION FOR APPOINTMENT—RECORD OF ORIGINAL
APPOINTMENT—CONTRADICTORY AS TO JURISDICTIONAL FACT—
EFFECT—SUIT BY EXECUTOR—COLLATERAL ATTACK ON AP-
POINTMENT.

1. Code Civ. Proc. § 2695, limits the powers of the surrogate to grant
   ancillary letters on a foreign probate of a will executed by a person at
   the time a nonresident to the case of probate in the state or territory
   where the will was executed, or the testator resided at time of death.
   Held, that where a petition was filed for ancillary letters testamentary
   under section 2695, which stated that the will of which petitioner was
   executor was executed in Louisiana, but the certified copy of the probate in Louisiana showed that testatrix at her death had her domicile
   in Alabama, and that the will was executed in that state, the surrogate
   had no jurisdiction to issue ancillary letters, since, the court being
   bound to give full faith and credit to the judicial proceedings of a
   sister state, the statement of the record as to a jurisdictional fact prevailed over the petition.

2. Rev. Civ. Code La., art. 1668, provides that testaments made in other
   states cannot be carried into effect on property in that state without
   being registered in the court within the jurisdiction of which the
   property is situated. Article 1220 provides that the succession of
   persons domiciled out of the state of Louisiana, leaving property
   therein, shall be administered on as those of citizens of the state, and
   officers appointed to administer as pointed out by law. *Held*, that
   where testatrix was not a resident of Louisiana, and her will was not
   executed there, but she left property therein, the authority of an executor appointed there extended only to property in that state, not
   being a general administration, and hence, together with the rule that
   a foreign executor cannot sue in the courts of New York, such executor could not sue in such state on a note belonging to the estate.

3. Where defendant was sued on a note by one to whom ancillary letters
   testamentary had been issued as foreign executor of the indorsee of
   the note, it was proper to attack in such action the surrogate's jurisdiction to issue the letters, since, the question being jurisdictional, the
   attack could be made collaterally.

APPEAL from Supreme Court, Appellate Division, First Department.

Action by M. Temple Taylor, as executor, etc., of Eliza Kenner, deceased, against Frederick J. Syme and others. From a judgment of the Appellate Division affirming a judgment for plaintiff entered on a verdict directed by the Supreme Court, defendant Syme appeals.
Reversed.

Edward F. Brown, for appellant.

Erastus D. Benedict, for respondent.

LANDON, J.—This action was commenced by Eliza Kenner, September 3, 1890, against the defendant Syme, upon two promissory notes made December 21, 1892, in New Orleans, La., each for $1,500, by Allen & Syme, co-partners, then residents in New Orleans, to their own order (one payable August 1, 1895, and the other September 1, 1885), and indorsed by the makers to Eliza Kenner, who then resided, and continued to reside until her death, in Mobile, Ala. The notes were the last of a series given in payment of the rent of a rice plantation in Louisiana, which Mrs. Kenner, at the time of their date, leased to Allen & Syme for three years, ending December 31, 1885. The lease contained a provision that if the lessees should be deprived of the use of the premises by and through any causes beyond their control, or any fortuitous event, they should be allowed a reduction of the amount *pro tanto.* Allen and Syme entered into possession of the premises, and at the end of two years failed; and their creditors took possession of their movable property on the plantation, with the result that they did not operate the plantation the third year. We agree with the courts below that Allen & Syme must be held to have brought this misfortune upon themselves by their own improvidence, and that it could not be properly called a " fortuitous event," which the Civil Code of Louisiana defines as " that which happens by a cause which we cannot resist." (Article 3556, No. 15.)

Eliza Kenner died in the state of Virginia in July, 1891; but her domicile was in Mobile, in the state of Alabama. This action was revived in the name of the present plaintiff in October, 1896, ancillary letters testamentary having in September, 1896, been issued to him by the surrogate of the county of New York. The defendant, by his answer and upon the trial, challenged the jurisdiction

of the surrogate of the county of New York to issue the ancillary
letters; the ground of the challenge being that such letters were issued upon the record of the probate of Mrs. Kenner's will, and of
the issue of letters testamentary thereon by a court in the state of
Louisiana, where she did not live, where she did not die, and where
her will was not executed, instead of by a court in the state of
Alabama, in which she was domiciled at the time of her death, and
in which she executed her will. Section 2695 of the Code of Civil
Procedure limits the power of the surrogate to grant ancillary
letters upon a foreign probate, in the case of a will of personal
property made by a person who resided in some other state or territory of the Union at the time of the execution thereof or at the
time of his death, to the case of probate in the state or territory
where the will was executed, or the testator resided at the time of
his death. In August, 1896, the present plaintiff, M. Temple Taylor, by his attorney, presented a petition to the surrogate of the
county of New York for ancillary letters testamentary, ostensibly
under section 2695 of the Code of Civil Procedure. The petition
stated correctly the facts, except that it stated that the will was
executed in Louisiana, which was not true. Accompanying the
petition was a duly-certified transcript of the record of the probate
of the will in the court in Louisiana, and of letters testamentary
issued to the plaintiff with a copy of the will, and proofs, including
a statement of the testimony of the subscribing witnesses, substantially as required by sections 2695, 2698, and 2704. From this
transcript it distinctly appeared that the will of Mrs. Kenner was
executed in the state of Alabama, and that she resided in that state
at the time of her death; that is, had her domicile there. It thereby
appeared that the case was not one in which the surrogate had
jurisdiction to issue ancillary letters upon the transcript of the
record of the probate and proceedings produced before him from
the court in Louisiana. The surrogate was probably diverted from
examining the record before him by the statement in the petition
that the will was executed in Louisiana. But the office of the
petition was to institute the proceeding, and bring the Louisiana
record into court for examination by the surrogate. Manifestly,
if the petition contradicted the record upon a jurisdictional fact,
the record would prevail, since one of the purposes of the provisions of the Code of Civil Procedure in this behalf is to give

full faith and credit, in proper cases, to judicial proceedings of a sister state. No mistake in the petition would create the record of a probate in Alabama, or change the facts presented by the Louisiana record,—that the testatrix executed her will in Alabama, and was domiciled there at her death. The record showed that the surrogate had no jurisdiction. (*Riggs* v. *Cragg*, 89 N. Y. 479; *In re Hawley*, 104 id. 250; 10 N. E. 352; *Morrow* v. *Freeman*, 61 N. Y. 515; *In re New York Catholic Protectory*, 77 id. 342.)

It is suggested that, however this may be, the plaintiff was duly appointed executor in Louisiana, and thus became the owner of the assets of the deceased. The position would have more force if Louisiana had been the domicile of the testatrix, since the law of the domicile governs the succession of personal property. The rule still remains that a foreign executor or administrator cannot sue as such in this state, although in cases where there are no creditors of the decedent within the state the reason of the rule has little force. (*Parsons* v. *Lyman*, 20 N. Y. 103; *Peterson* v. *Bank*, 32 id. 21; *Toronto Gen. Trust Co.* v. *Chicago, B. & Q. R. Co.* 123 id. 37; 25 N. E. 189.) The administration in the state of Louisiana, however, was under the Revised Civil Code of that state, as follows:

" Art. 1220. The succession of persons domiciled out of the state of Louisiana and leaving property in this state at their demise, shall be opened and administered upon as are those of citizens of the state, and the judge before whom such succession shall be opened shall proceed to the appointment or confirmation of the officer to administer it under the name and in the manner pointed out by existing laws."

" Art. 1668 (1681). Testaments made in foreign countries and other states of the Union cannot be carried into effect on property in this state without being registered in the court within the jurisdiction of which the property is situated, and the execution thereof ordered by the judge."

Thus, the professed purpose of the administration in Louisiana was that the will of the testatrix might " be carried into effect on property in this (that) state." It did not purport to extend to the property of the testatrix in the state of her domicile or in any other state, or to be a universal administration, but to cover the administration in that state, like the ancillary administration sought in this state; the ancillary being supplemental to the principal administration, and, except as to domestic creditors, subordinate to it. See section 2700, Code Civ. Proc.

It is said that this is a collateral attack, but, as it is a question of the jurisdiction, the attack can be made collaterally. The defendant had no interest in the proceeding, or standing to challenge it, until the plaintiff asserted against him his right to represent Mrs. Kenner. He could do no more than raise the issue at his first opportunity.

The defendant also urges the statute of limitations of Louisiana as a defense. The Appellate Division held that it was not well taken, because the defendant took up his residence in this state before the expiration of five years after the maturity of the note. The question is an interesting one, but it is not necessary for us to decide it.

It follows that the plaintiff did not show his right to maintain this action. The judgment must be reversed, with costs.

New trial granted; costs to abide the event.

PARKER, C. J., and O'BRIEN, BARTLETT, HAIGHT, MARTIN, and VANN, JJ., concur.

Judgment reversed, etc.

STRAUSS *et al. vs.* BENDHEIM *et al.*

[Court of Appeals of New York, April 17, 1900; 162 N. Y. 469; 56 N. E. Rep. 1007.]

WILLS — EXECUTORS — POWER TO SELL — CONTRACT — SPECIFIC PERFORMANCE — JUDICIAL SALE — COURT DEED — TITLE — SPECIAL GUARDIAN SALE — PURCHASE BY WIFE — DISCRETION OF COURT — CONFIRMING SALE — MARKETABLE TITLE — EXECUTOR'S DEEDS.

1. Where executors in a will are imperatively required to sell property with discretion as to terms and conditions, they also have power to contract to sell and to enforce the contract, and in an action to compel specific performance a judgment can be entered decreeing that defend-

ant specifically perform, and, if he refuses to do so, that the property be sold by a referee, and his deed to the purchaser will convey all the title to the premises which the executors could have conveyed under the power.

2. Executors named in a will were required to sell certain property, and contracted to sell to defendant, who made a payment under the contract, and later refused to perform. Specific performance having been decreed against defendant, with a resale ordered to be made by a referee in case defendant refused, the property was resold. The referee's deed to the purchaser recited all the facts in the judgment, with his power to convey, and that it conveyed all the right, title, and interest of the executor and of the defendant. *Held*, that while executors did have an interest in the property under the power in the will, and the defendant an equitable interest under his contract to purchase, yet the deed conveyed the title of the testatrix.

3. Where a court, in 1873, ordered a special guardian of infants to sell their interests in property, and he entered into a contract of sale with his wife, and the sale was concluded by the purchaser giving a mortgage to the infants payable on their arriving at age, the court ordering the sale had power in its discretion to confirm the sale to the wife, and, having done so with full knowledge of the facts, the purchaser of such property at a judicial sale twenty-six years later gets an unquestionabie title as to this transaction.

4. Where executors in a will have power to sell property with discretion as to terms and conditions, and enter into a contract with defendant to purchase the property, and he refuses to perform, and specific performance is decreed, or a judicial sale by a referee in case of a refusal by defendant to complete the purchase, while the referee's deed conveys the title, yet the executors must also execute a deed to the purchaser at the judicial sale.

APPEAL from Supreme Court, Appellate Division, First Department.

Action for specific performance by Rosa Strauss and another, as executors of Yetta Ullmann, deceased, against Henry M. Bendheim and others. From an order of the Appellate Division (60 N. Y. Supp. 398), reversing an order of the Special Term requiring defendants to complete the purchase, plaintiffs appeal.

Reversed, and the order of the Special Term affirmed as modified.

Charles F. Brown, for appellants

Franklin Pierce, for respondent Hutter.

HAIGHT, J.—Yetta Ullmann died in the city of New York on the 17th day of November, 1897, seized of the lands in question, and leaving a last will and testament, which has been duly proved and admitted to probate, in which, after providing for her funeral expenses, tombstone, and a legacy to her brother, she appoints her son and daughter, the plaintiffs in this action, her executor and executrix, and directs that the residue and remainder of her estate be converted into cash, and the proceeds divided into three parts. One part is given to her daughter, the executrix; another part to her son, the executor; and the remaining part to the children of her deceased daughter, Fanny Reinhardt. For this purpose she empowered her executor and executrix, or the survivor of them, to sell and convey, grant, and dispose of any and all of her real estate at any time after her demise as they might see fit, practicable, and expedient, upon such terms and conditions, and in such manner, in their discretion, as they, or the survivor of them, should deem just or proper, and to make, execute, acknowledge, and deliver any and all deeds necessary or proper to give a marketable title. Pursuant to the power so given by the will, the executor and executrix entered into an agreement in writing with the defendant Henry M. Bendheim, on the 18th of March, 1898, in which they agreed to sell and convey, and he to purchase, the premises in question, for the sum of $12,500. On the day named in the contract for the delivery of the deed and the payment of the purchase price, Bendheim objected to the title, and refused to complete the purchase. Thereupon an action was brought to compel specific performance, which resulted in a judgment in favor of the appellants, decreeing specific performance on the part of the defendant, and adjudging that in case he refused to receive the deed and pay the consideration stipulated in the contract, the premises be sold at public auction by a referee named in the judgment, who was directed to deliver to the purchaser a deed of the premises upon his complying with the terms on which the premises should be sold, and, after deducting from the proceeds the referee's fees and the cost of the action, to pay to the plaintiffs the balance of the purchase money, and, if the proceeds of the sale were insufficient to pay the plaintiffs in full, then they were to have judgment for the deficiency against the defendant Bendheim. The defendant Bendheim refused to receive the deed, or to specifically perform the contract, as ɪequired by the judgment, and thereupon the premises were again sold under the judgment, and the respondent Hutter became the purchaser on such sale. The referee, pursuant to the provisions of the judgment, himself executed a deed and tendered it to Hutter, together· with a deed from the executor and executrix, and demanded that he complete the purchase, but he refused to accept the deeds, claiming that they did not give to him a marketable title.

The first question presented for review is whether ·the Supreme Court had the power to authorize a sale of the premises by a referee in the action brought by the executors for specific performance, without making the beneficiaries under the will parties. It is true that under the will of Yetta Ullmann no trust was created, and the title to the lands was not vested in the executors. The will, however, did invest the executors with an imperative power of sale, with the broadest discretion in reference to terms and conditions. Acting under the power so given by the will, they contracted to convey to Bendheim, and this they had the power to do without making the beneficiaries parties to the contract ; and, had Bendheim performed his part of the contract, the executors could have conveyed to him all of the title to the premises that the testatrix had in her lifetime. Blendheim having refused to perform on his part, the executors had the right to bring an action to compel specific performance by him, and the beneficiaries under the will were not necessary parties in such action. The will having given the executors the power to sell, the duty devolved upon them of exercising that power according to their own wisdom and judgment, and their action bound the beneficiaries. With the power to sell of necessity was the power to contract, and with that the power to enforce the contract. Iɴ the action so brought, judgment was entered for specific performance, following the well-known practice of adjudging a resale, with a personal judgment for deficiency in case the defendant refused or failed to specifically perform the contract. (*Clark* v. *Hall,* 7 Paige, 382, 385.) Judicial sales are usually made by a referee designated by the court or the sheriff of the county, either officer named being the instrument of the court to execute its decree, and as such invested with the power of the court to convey all of the title that the court had the power to order transferred. In this case, the executors, who were invested with the power to sell and convey under the will in the action brought by them, appealed to the court to enforce the performance of the contract made by them, thus investing the court with all the powers that they possessed under the will to compel specific performance of the contract. It follows that the referee's deed tendered to the purchaser under the sale made pursuant to the judgment would have conveyed to him, if accepted, all of the title to the premises which the executors, under their power of sale, could have conveyed.

It is further contended that the deed tendered by the referee was defective, for the reason that it recited that it conveyed " all the right, title and interest " of the executors and of the defendant Bendheim " at the time of the entry of said judgment, it being their interest in said premises so sold and conveyed." It is quite true that the executors did not have the title, and the defendant Bendheim, as contractor, had an equitable title only, but each was possessed of a right or interest,—the executors of a power under the will, and the defendant of an interest in the money which he had paid under the contract and through his obligation to complete the purchase. Upon referring to the terms of the deed, we find that it recites all the facts incorporated into the judgment with the authority given to the trustee to convey, from which it clearly appears that the deed purports to convey the title of the testatrix through the power given by her will, as it had been determined by the court.

In 1873 one Charles Landauer died intestate, seized of the premises in question. He left him, surviving, a widow, four children, and seven infant grandchildren, who were children of deceased daughters of the intestate. On the 12th day of August, 1873, the infants—those over fourteen years of age themselves, and those under that age by their father and next friend—petitioned the Court of Common Pleas for the sale of their interests in the premises. Upon such petition the court appointed Lorenze Weiher, the father of some of the infants, special guardian, and referred the matter to a referee to report the necessity for the sale. The referee took the evidence and made his report, which was confirmed by the court, and the guardian was ordered to enter into a contract for the sale of the premises. This he did with Louise

Weiher, his wife. The contract was reported to the court, where it was confirmed, and the sale concluded, the purchaser giving a mortgage for the amount going to the infants, payable upon their arrival at the age of twenty-one years. The final order of confirmation was entered on the 23d day of October, 1873. It is now contended that the title is defective, for the reason that the wife of the special guardian became the purchaser in such proceedings. This question was raised by the defendant Bendheim and received the attention of the court in the trial of that action, but it does not appear to have been considered by the Appellate Division in these proceedings. While the court will look with disfavor upon an attempt of an officer conducting a judicial sale to convey to his wife, still the court doubtless has the power in the exercise of its discretion to permit and approve such a sale. The leading case in this state upon the subject is that of *Davoue* v. *Fanning* (2 Johns. Ch. 252), which was decided before the adoption of the married women's act. In that case the practice was denounced as poisonous in its consequences, and the court refused to approve of the sale; but in the judgment entered the court directed that the premises should be re-exposed for sale by public auction, and, if the premises failed to sell for an amount greater than the amount of the former sale, the former sale should in all respects stand confirmed. It thus appears that the court in that case held that under circumstances similar to those in question it had the power to confirm, which power it would exercise in case it appeared that the premises could not be sold for any greater sum. In the case under consideration the report of the special guardian, made upon oath, to the court, shows that the contract was for the best terms upon which he could sell the property. It clearly appeared in the testimony taken in the proceeding that Louise Weiher was his wife, and that fact was necessarily before the court when it made the order confirming the contract and directing the conveyance. This, as we have seen, the court had the power to do, and inasmuch as it approved of the sale with full knowledge of the facts, we think the title cannot now, after the lapse of twenty-six years, and long after all of the infants have become of age, be questioned.

It appears, as we have seen, that the deed from the executors was tendered to the purchaser in connection with the deed from the referee. This fact is recited in the order of the Special Term, but in directing the purchaser to accept the deed tendered by the referee the order omits to include that of the executors. While we are of the opinion that the referee's deed conveys the full title, there can be no harm in giving the purchaser the benefit of the deed from the executors, which was tendered to him, and made one of the papers upon which the order was issued. The order should be modified in this particular. The order of the Appellate Division should be reversed, and that of the Special Term, as modified, affirmed, with costs.

PARKER, C. J., and O'BRIEN, BARTLETT, MARTIN, VANN, and LANDON, JJ., concur.

Order reversed, etc.

NOTE.—EXECUTION OF A POWER BY THE COURT.

(a) Power of the court.
(b) As dependent upon a trust.
(c) Illustrative cases.

(a) **Power of the court.**—Upon a final decree in a proper case the court may appoint a trustee; or it may direct the trust to be executed by an officer of the court, if a sale of the premises should be decreed. (King v. Donnelly, 5 Paige, 45, 47; and see 1 Perry on Trusts, § 249, *et seq.* [ed. 1899.].)

When direction to sell is imperative but the time of sale is left to the discretion of the executor, his judgment exercised in good faith is conclusive. If the executor fails to exercise his judgment the court may put him in motion or act in his place. (Haight v. Brisbin, 96 N. Y. 132; and see Manice v. Manice, 43 id. 365.)

When a trustee dies or declines to act, the court may supply his place, or if need be take upon itself the execution of the trust. (Rogers v. Rogers, 111 N. Y. 228, 237; 18 N. E. Rep. 636.)

Execution of a power by a Court of Chancery. (Pedrick v. Pedrick, 48 N. J. Eq. 314; 21 Atl. Rep. 946; rev'd 50 N. J. Eq. 479, but not on this point.)

(b) **As dependent upon a trust.**—Execution of a trust devolves upon the Supreme Court. (Dunning v. Ocean National Bank, 6 Lans. 298; aff'd 61 N. Y. 497.)

Power connected with trust. (See Lahey v. Kortright, 132 N. Y. 457; 30 N. E. Rep. 989.)

Power of Supreme Court under statute to appoint its agent to execute a trust. (Wetmore v. Wetmore, 44 App. Div. 53; 60 N. Y. Supp. 437.)

The Supreme Court has inherent power to execute a trust and in absence of a trustee may take upon itself its execution. (Kirk v. Kirk, 137 N. Y. 510; 33 N. E. Rep. 552.)

Power of sale, not being a personal trust or confidence, may be thus executed. (Royce v. Adams, 123 N. Y. 405; 25 N. E. Rep. 386; and see Clark v. Crego, 51 N. Y. 647; Delaney v. McCormick, 25 Hun, 574; aff'd 88 N. Y. 174.)

But see where the inherent power of a court of equity applicable to an executor as *trustee* is not applicable to an executor so far as relates to the duties of his office as such. (Greenland v. Waddell, 116 N. Y. 243; 22 N. E. Rep. 367.)

A power of sale as a power in trust, although discretionary, on death or removal of the executors may be executed under the direction of the court by a trustee appointed for that purpose. (Cooke v. Platt, 98 N. Y. 35, 39.)

Where a power involves a purely personal trust or confidence, and it is apparent that the testator intended that the person appointed should exercise a personal discretion, the power conferred will not pass to a successor appointed by the court; but it is otherwise where the power properly pertains to the office of the executor or trustee. (Freeman v. Prendergast, 94 Ga. 369, 388; 21 S. E. Rep. 837; and see Nugent v. Cloon, 117 Mass. 219.)

Where power of sale is a naked one and purely discretionary it can be exercised only by the executor named. A statute providing for an appointment upon death of a surviving trustee, etc.,—has no application where there is no trust created by the will. (Matter of Bierbaum, 40 Hun, 504, 507.)

Power of sale vested in court when the power was not a mere naked discretionary one but given in connection with the trust estate, and necessary for the proper performance of the trust. (Mulry v. Mulry, 89 Hun, 533; 35 N. Y. Supp. 618; and see Franklin v. Osgood, 14 Johns. 553.)

(c) **Illustrative cases.**—Executors cannot sell by attorney. (Berger v. Duff, 4 Johns. Ch. 368; and see Neal v. Patten, 47 Ga. 73.)

A discretionary power of sale in an executor cannot be enforced and executed by a receiver. (Cooke v. Platt, 98 N. Y. 35.)

Power not a personal trust or confidence. (Royce v. Adams, 123 N. Y. 402; 25 N. E. Rep. 386.)

Cases where a court of equity under statutory power has conveyed land through and by an agent or trustee of its own appointment. (Felch v. Hooper, 119 Mass. 52; and see Matteson v. Scofield, 27 Wis. 671; Rourke v. McLaughlin, 38 Cal. 196.)

Power conferred by will executed by trustee appointed by the court in place of one deceased. (Osborne v. Gordon, 86 Wis. 92; 56 N. W. Rep. 334.)

Executed by the court with consent of all the beneficiaries. (Wooster v. Cooper, 45 Atl. Rep. 381 [N. J.].)

HOOD *vs.* DORER.

[Supreme Court of Wisconsin, April 6, 1900; 82 N. W. Rep. 546.]

WILLS—EQUITABLE CONVERSION—TRUSTS—INDEFINITE BENEFI-
CIARIES—JUDGMENT—RES JUDICATA.

1. A provision in a will that real and personal property be invested in a
   fund for the support and maintenance of a charity is a direction to
   convert such property into money.
2. Where a testator, after a life estate created in his wife, leaves his entire
   property to be invested in a fund for the support and maintenance of
   the superannuated preachers of the church denominated the United
   Brethren in Christ, a valid trust is created, as a trustee, to be appointed
   by the court, can select the beneficiaries from the class named.
3. Testator, after creating a life estate in his wife, directed that on her
   decease the property should be invested in a fund for the support of the
   superannuated preachers of the church denominated the United Brethren in Christ. The widow, in an action to construe the will, named as
   defendants " the superannuated preachers of the church denominated
   the United Brethren in Christ." Such persons were not a corporate
   body, and none of them appeared. Judgment was entered that the
   real estate descended to the wife in fee. *Held,* that such judgment
   was not *res judicata* as to such persons.   .
   CASSODAY, C. J., dissenting.

APPEAL from Circuit Court, Jefferson county; JOHN R. BEN-
NETT, Judge.

Ejectment by A. J. Hood, administrator *de bonis non* with the
will annexed of Thomas Stewart, deceased, against Dominik
Dorer. From a judgment in favor of defendant, plaintiff appeals.
Reversed.

This is an action in ejectment for the recovery of 120 acres of
land in Grant county, Wis., both parties claiming title under one
Thomas Stewart, now deceased, the plaintiff being the administrator *de bonis non* of the estate of said Thomas Stewart. The evidence upon the trial showed that Thomas Stewart owned the
property in question during his lifetime, and that he died September 13, ·1882, leaving a widow, but no descendants; that he left a

will, which was afterwards probated, the material parts of which
are as follows: " First. After the payment of my just debts and
funeral expenses, I give, devise, and bequeath unto my beloved
wife, Mary Ann Stewart, for and during her natural life, provided
she remains single after my decease, the use of and sole control
and right to all my real and personal estate in the state of Wisconsin or elsewhere of which I may die possessed or be entitled
to, and on her decease the said property to be invested in a fund
provided for that purpose for the support and maintenance of the
superannuated preachers of the church denominated the United
Brethren in Christ. I give and bequeath to Solomon Stewart, my
brother, the sum of one dollar; to my brother Abraham Stewart
the sum of one dollar; and to my sister Susan Keys, the sum of
one dollar. I hereby nominate and appoint —— the executor of
this, my last will and testament, and hereby authorize and empower him, the said ——, to compound, compromise, and settle
any claim or demand which may be against or in favor of my
estate." Mary Ann Stewart, the widow, was duly appointed administrator with the will annexed of the estate of Thomas Stewart, and in August, 1883, she brought an action in the Circuit
Court of Grant county for the construction of the will, naming
as defendants in that action " the superannuated preachers of the
church denominated the United Brethren in Christ " and De Witt
C. Wood and William Loney. The summons and complaint in
said action were served upon the defendants Wood and Loney, one
of whom was a preacher in said denomination, and the other a
class leader, but neither of them was a superannuated preacher.
An answer was served in that action by John D. Wilson, who apparently appeared as the attorney for the defendants generally,
which answer was verified by William Loney, and prayed a judgment of the court declaring the bequest for the benefit of the
superannuated preachers a valid one. The action was tried by the
court, and resulted in findings and judgment that the devise in
question was valid, and that the real estate of Thomas Stewart
descended to Mary Ann Stewart in fee. After this judgment
Mary Ann Stewart sold the real estate in issue in this action to the
defendant, who took possession thereof, and was in possession at
the time of the commencement of this action claiming title. Mary
Ann Stewart afterwards married one Haskins, and died before the

commencement of this action. After her death the plaintiff was appointed administrator *de bonis non* with the will annexed of the estate of Thomas Stewart,, and he brings this action as such administrator, claiming that the provisions of the will are valid, and that he is entitled to the possession of the said real estate in order to sell and convert the same into money, and create the fund directed by said will. On the trial of this action it appeared that the United Brethren in Christ are a sect of Protestant Christians organized early in the present century in the state of Maryland, and that at the time of the execution of Thomas Stewart's will they numbered about 150,000 members in the United States and Canada, and that they had a church government and discipline, having colleges and educational institutions, ordained bishops and ministers, and holding conferences. The court held the direction in the will for the benefit of the superannuated preachers void for uncertainty, and the administrator appeals.

Bushnell, Watkins & Moses, for appellant.

Aldro Jenks and *H. W. Brown,* for respondent.

WINSLOW, J. (after stating the facts).—The sole question presented is as to the validity of that provision of the will of Stewart which directs that upon the decease of his wife his entire property is "to be invested in a fund provided for the purpose for the support and maintenance of the superannuated preachers of the church denominated the United Brethren in Christ." There can be no doubt but that this clause amounts to a direction to convert the real estate of which he died possessed into money. In no other way can real property be invested in a fund. Hence the doctrine of equitable conversion applies, and, if a bequest of personal property to be used for the support of the superannuated preachers of a particular sect is valid, then this clause in the will is valid. In disposing of the case the trial judge held the will void on the ground of uncertainty and indefiniteness, relying upon the case of *In re Fuller's Will* (75 Wis. 431; 44 N. W. 304). Where the rule of that case to be followed, it is not easy to see how the conclusion reached by the trial judge could be avoided. In the recent case of *Harrington v. Pier* ([present term], 82 N. W. 345), however, the doctrine of the *Fuller Case* was substantially overruled. In fact in that case nearly or quite all the questions which arise in this case were fully treated by Justice MARSHALL, the result being to sustain such a trust as that before us, so that it would seem unnecessary to enlarge upon the subject here. In that case it was said: " It follows that indefiniteness of beneficiaries who can invoke judicial authority to enforce the trust, want of a trustee, if there be a trust in fact, or indefiniteness in details of the particular purpose declared, the general limits being reasonably ascertainable, or indefiniteness of mode of carrying out the particular purpose, does not militate against the validity of a trust for charitable uses. Given a trust, with or without a trustee, a particular purpose, as education or relief of the poor as distinguished from a bequest to charity generally, and a class, great or small, and without regard to location necessarily, as 'worthy indigent females,' or ' indigent young men studying for the ministry,' or ' resident poor,' or ' indigent children of Rock county,' or ' boys and girls of California' (*People* v. *Cogswell,* 113 Cal. 129; 45 Pac. 270; 35 L. R. A. 269), and we have a good trust for charitable uses. The court, through its strictly judicial power, may fill the office of trustee, if necessary. The trustee can select the immediate benefits or objects with the designated class and scheme. He can determine upon the details necessary to effect the intention of the donor within the general limits of his declared purpose, and execute the trust accordingly; and the proper public agencies, if necessary, can invoke judicial power to enforce such execution." These considerations really dispose of the present case. There are present in this bequest all the essential requirements above enumerated. The provision is essentially a trust provision. No trustee is appointed, but the proper court has power to appoint one, so that the trust may not fail (*Sawtelle* v. *Witham,* 94 Wis. 412; 69 N. W. 72) ; and there is a particular and meritorious charitable purpose, namely, the support and maintenance of the worn-out preachers of a certain religious body. This completes the charitable scheme so that it may be carried out. The trustee appointed by the court can select the beneficiaries with the class named, and can wisely settle the necessary details of administration of the charity within the general limits of the testator's declared intention without serious difficulty. It is not seriously claimed upon the argument that the judgment in the former action brought by the widow for construction of the will in which "the superannuated preachers" of the sect in question were named as defendants, was of any effect, nor is it seen how it could have any effect. The "superannuated preachers" were not a corporate body, and hence not capable of being sued under a general designation. Furthermore, they are necessarily constantly changing, and, even if some of the then members of the class actually appeared and defended, the result, manifestly, could not bind others.

Judgment reversed, and action remanded, with directions to enter judgment for the plaintiff.

CASSODAY, C. J. (dissenting).—I dissented in *Harrington* v. *Pier* ([unreported officially], 82 N. W. 345). The court holds that the decision of this case is ruled by the opinion of the court in that case. The two cases are fairly distinguishable in their facts. I may, therefore, be permitted to respectfully dissent in this case. In doing so, I shall add but very little to what is contained in my dissenting opinion in that case. I fully concur in the findings of Judge CLEMENTSON in the action to construe the will in this case, and which findings are in the record, and also with the findings and opinion of the late Judge BENNETT, in this case, to the effect that the provision of the will in question is too indefinite and uncertain to enable the court to ascertain and carry out the supposed intentions of the testator; "that the beneficiaries are not ascertained, or in law capable of being ascertained, and that the trust attempted to be created by said will is void." If the *cy pres* doctrine under 43 Eliz. ch. 4 (2 St. at Large, 708), mentioned in the dissenting opinion in the other case, were in force in this state, it might be an important question whether the bequest in this case "for the support and maintenance of the superannuated preachers of the church denominated the United Brethren in Christ" came within any of the numerous objects therein mentioned. If any, it would seem to be the first, which is, "for relief of aged, impotent, and poor people." "Superannuated preachers" are, manifestly, such preachers as are impaired or disabled through old age, for such is the definition of the word. (Cent. Dict.) If such "relief" was only intended for those who are "poor," then it would not come within the provisions of that statute, since, in the language of Sir WILLIAM GRANT, "the question is, not whether he (the trustee) may not apply it upon purposes strictly charitable, but whether he is bound so to apply it." (*Morice* v. *Bishop of Durham,* 9 Ves. 406.) While it may be true that most preachers who are impaired or disabled through old age are poor, yet they are not necessarily all poor. But, as I do not understand that the opinion of the court in *Harrington* v. *Pier* (*supra*), or in this case is based upon the *cy pres* doctrine under the statute of Elizabeth, it is unnecessary to consider the question.

SCHNEE *vs.* SCHNEE *et al.*

[Supreme Court of Kansas, April 7, 1900; 61 Kan. 643; 60 Pac. Rep. 738.]

WILL—PROBATE — APPLICATION BY INFANTS — APPEAL — EVIDENCE—ATTESTING WILL—DEPOSITION.

1. Infants desiring to obtain the probate of a will may institute a proceeding therefor by a next friend, and through him may appeal from a decision of the Probate Court rejecting a will.

2. After a proceeding to prove a last will has been appealed to and is pending in the District Court, a deposition taken as the Code provides may be read in evidence, the same as if it had been taken upon a special commission, as provided in the act relating to wills.

3. In such a proceeding the statements and conduct of the testator at and about the time of making a last will, which had been lost, spoliated, or destroyed after his death, as well as his declarations as to its contents, and his purposes in making bequests, are admissible in evidence.

4. In attesting a last will, the name of a witness who is unable to write may be written by another at the request and in the presence of such witness and of the testator. The fact that the witness did not touch the pen or guide the hand when his name was written will not invalidate the attestation.

5. There is sufficient testimony in the record that the last will had been lost, spoliated, or destroyed to warrant the admission of the testimony received, and to sustain the finding that the will established was not the one previously rejected by the Probate Court.

(Syllabus by the court.)

ERROR from District Court, Cowley county; A. M. JACKSON, Judge.

Application by William G. Schnee and others for the probate of the will of Gilbert Schnee. Maggie Ann Schnee filed contest. From an order of the District Court on appeal from the Probate Court admitting the will to probate, contestant brings error. Affirmed.

Jos. O'Hare, for plaintiff in error.

C. L. Swarts, for defendants in error.

JOHNSON, J.—This proceeding was brought to obtain probate of the last will of Gilbert Schnee, who died in Cowley county in 1883, and left, surviving him, his wife, Annie B. Schnee, who has since intermarried with Frank Reed, and two of their minor children, William G. and Louise. Maggie Ann Schnee contests the probate of the will, and claims that she is an heir of Gilbert Schnee. In his early life, Gilbert Schnee married Mary Jane Reed, and a few months after the marriage he procured a divorce from her on the ground that she was unfaithful. Afterwards the divorced woman gave birth to Maggie Ann, and she claims an interest in the estate as the daughter of Gilbert Schnee. In April, 1892, an application for probate was presented to the Probate Court of Cowley county by W. P. Hackney in behalf of and as the next friend of the two minor children of Gilbert and Annie B. Schnee. It was alleged that about two weeks before his death, and while Gilbert Schnee was of sound mind and memory, he executed a will, drawn up for him by P. A. Lorry, which was subscribed by Lorry and Frank Reed as witnesses. It was alleged that he devised and bequeathed to Mamie Morris, a daughter of Annie B. Schnee by a former marriage, the sum of from $300 to $500, the exact amount to be fixed by her mother, and to Maggie Ann, the daughter of Mary J. Reed, the sum of one dollar, and the residue of the property, personal and real, was given to William G. Schnee and Louise Schnee, his minor children, share and share alike. It is averred that in a few days after the execution of the will he sickened and died without revoking the will, and while the same was in full force and effect. After setting out a description of property owned by him at the time of his death, it is alleged that the will sought to be probated had never been probated or offered for probate, and that it had been lost, spoliated, or destroyed subsequent to the death of Gilbert Schnee. Upon proof taken in the Probate Court, it was decided that a paper purporting to be. the last will of Gilbert Schnee had been presented by Annie B. Schnee on June 25, 1883, for probate, and that the court upon a hearing then had decided that the paper presented was not a will, the same not having been written and witnessed as the law requires. The Probate Court held in the present case that the decision of the court rejecting the will in 1883, never having been modified or vacated, is conclusive, and that the will now offered for probate should be rejected. An appeal was taken from the decision of the Probate Court to the District Court, in which, upon a full hearing, the will propounded was found to be the last will and testament of Gilbert Schnee; that it had been lost, spoliated, or destroyed, but that the contents thereof had been substantially proven; and that the same had been duly executed, and was in full force and unrevoked at the death of the testator. It was decreed that it should be admitted to probate, and that it was as effectual to pass property of the testator as though the original will had been admitted and duly recorded in the Probate Court.

It is contended that error was committed in overruling a motion to dismiss the appeal. A ground for dismissal is that Hackney, who appeared for the minors as a next friend, and took the steps necessary to perfect the appeal, was without authority. Being infants, and not considered to have sufficient discretion to conduct a suit, it was proper that they should be represented, and their interest protected by a next friend. It is true, the statute does not specifically provide that infants may take an appeal from the decisions of the Probate Court through a next friend, but express statutory authority is hardly necessary. All courts guard the interests of infants, and that they may, by next friends, institute proceedings in the courts for the enforcement of their rights or the protection of their interests is the universal practice, and one which may be regarded as part of the common law. Section 31 of the Code of Civil Procedure, which provides that the action of an infant must be brought by guardian or next friend, is only declaratory of the general rule, and of itself would seem to furnish express authority for taking an appeal to the District Court. (*Sutton* v. *Nichols*, 20 Kan. 45; *Burdette* v. *Corgan*, 26 id. 105.)

The record shows that due notice of appeal was given, the amount of the appeal bond fixed by the court, and that it was executed, accepted, and approved. The objections made to the notice and bond are immaterial.

Error is assigned on the overruling of a motion to suppress the deposition of Lyman Herrick, It was taken in pursuance of an ordinary notice, such as is provided in the Civil Code for the taking of a deposition. It is contended that testimony for the probating of a will must be taken by a commissioner appointed by the Probate Court in pursuance of sections 14 and 47 of the act relating to wills. While the court might have issued a special commission to some suitable person to take the deposition, it is evident that the one who did take it was deemed to be a suitable person, as the deposition was received and admitted in evidence. When the deposition was taken the case was pending in the District Court, and the provisions of the Code with respect to the taking of testimony of witnesses beyond the jurisdiction of the court was applicable, and therefore the deposition was taken with authority, and properly admitted. (*Case* v. *Huey*, 26 Kan. 556.)

Objection is made to the declarations of the decedent at the time the will was executed, and while it was in his possession, prior to his death. In offering a will for probate it is necessary to show the mental condition of the testator; and his statements and conduct at the time of making the will, as well as his expressions with reference to his intentions in making the bequests, are admissible in evidence. Aside from that, the will had been lost, and the declarations of a testator as to the contents of a will are generally deemed· to be relevant. (7 Am. & Eng. Enc. Law, 72.) The declarations complained of were largely *res gestæ*, and, while some of them were somewhat remote, they were not of a prejudicial character.

It is next contended that the will is void because the name of one of the subscribing witnesses was written by another person. P. A. Lorry, a neighbor of the testator, was the scrivener, and a subscribing witness. The testator signed the will in the presence of Lorry and Frank Reed. Lorry signed his own name as a witness, and Frank Reed, being unable to write, asked Lorry to sign his name. Reed's name was written by Lorry at Reed's request, in the presence of each other, and in the presence of the testator, who had requested Reed to act as a subscribing witness. The statute provides that the will of a party "shall be attested and subscribed in the presence of such party by two or more competent witnesses who saw the testator subscribe or heard him acknowledge the same. (Section 2 of the act relating to wills.) It appears that Reed did not physically participate in signing his name. It is conceded that, if he had made his mark, touched the top of the penholder, or guided the hand of Lorry when the name was written, it would have been a valid attestation. Will the omission of a mere formality or empty ceremony, no trace of which can be found on the will itself, defeat the attestation? We think not. Under the statute the name of the testator, even, may be signed by another, if done at the request of the testator, and by his express direction. The witnessing of a will is surely of no greater importance than the execution of the same by the testator. He had a right to choose his own witnesses, —the ones who would identify the will, and by whom his capacity and condition at the time of its execution might be established. In all business affairs such a signing is deemed to be sufficient, and the most important documents and instruments may be legally signed by a person other than the maker, if done in his presence, and by his express direction. There is nothing in the statute indicating that the ordinary rules governing the subscribing to papers or the signing of instruments shall not apply in the execution of wills, nor that one who causes his name to be written by another must touch the pen or guide the hand that writes it, in order that it may be deemed his personal act. The purpose of attestation is to make certain that the will offered for probate is the one that was actually executed, and also to surround the testator with witnesses capable of judging and testifying as to his capacity to make a will. These purposes can be as well subserved by a witness like Reed, who causes his name to be written by another, in the presence and at the request of the testator, as if he had gone through the empty form of touching the pen while Lorry wrote his name. Some of the courts have given what we deem to be undue importance to the physical participation in the act of signing, and have ruled that witnesses must do some manual act towards making the signature. The more satisfactory authorities as well as reasons sustain the view that the name of an attesting witness who is unable to write may be written by another at his request, in his presence, and in the presence of the testator. As stated in *Lord* v. *Lord* (58 N. H. 7), " To require a person whose name is to be written in a testamentary transaction to hold or touch the pen, or to do anything which the law does not require him to do in other cases of attestation, seems to establish a distinction without a difference." See, also, *Upchurch* v. *Upchurch* (16 B. Mon. 102); *Jesse* v. *Parker's Adm'r* (6 Grat. 57); *In re Strong's Will* ([Sur.] 16 N. Y. Supp. 104); *In re Crawford's Will* ([S. C.] 24 S. E. 69; 32 L. R. A. 77).

The last contention is that the adjudication refusing to probate the will that was introduced in 1883 was a bar to this proceeding. Under the facts of the case the doctrine of *res adjudicata* does not apply, as we cannot say that the will offered for probate and refused was the last will of Gilbert Schnee. The testimony tends to show that the last will, and the one which was then presented for probate, was changed and mutilated after the testator's death, or at least that it is not the instrument which has been established as the last will and testament of Gilbert Schnee in the present action. When this proceeding was instituted by the minor children to obtain probate of the will, no trace of the document could be found; nor has it been seen by any one since about the time that a will was offered for probate in 1883. There was sufficient proof of loss and spoliation to warrant the introduction of testimony as to the contents of the will, and we think its provisions have been substantially proven, and that it was entitled to be admitted to probate, and is as effectual to pass the property of the testator as though the original will had been probated and recorded.

The judgment of the District Court will be affirmed.

All the justices concurring.

LAW GURANTEE AND TRUST CO. *vs.* JONES *et al.*

[Supreme Court of Tennessee, April 10, 1900; 58 S. W. Rep. 219.]

WILLS—POWERS—EXECUTION—TRUST DEEDS—FOREIGN COR-
PORATION—RIGHT TO DO BUSINESS—LOAN—SUBSEQUENT REG-
ISTRATION OF CHARTER.

1. Where a nonresident loan and trust company made a loan, and took a
   trust deed to secure it, before registration of its charter where the
   transaction took place, such transaction was validated by the subsequent
   filing of an abstract of the company's charter at such place; and the
   company was entitled to recover the amount actually loaned, with six
   per cent. interest.
2. Where a will devising land gave the fathers of the devisees, who were
   minors, power to dispose of the land in any way they thought proper
   for the benefit of such devisees, the fathers being sole judges of what
   was best for the devisees, they were vested with full power to borrow
   money and secure the same by deed of trust on the land, and thereby
   charge the estate of the devisees in such land, since by the will the
   fathers were not made trustees for their children, but held a power of
   appointment, which they might exercise at their discretion.
3. Where by a will the fathers of devisees therein were given power to
   dispose of the land of the devisees in any manner they thought best,
   the appropriation of money borrowed by the fathers, and secured by
   deed of trust on the land devised will not invalidate the loan, when the
   lender had no notice that the fund was to be misappropriated.
4. Where by a will the fathers of devisees therein were given power to
   dispose of their children's land as they thought best, a deed of trust of
   such land need not expressly recite that it was executed in pursuance
   of the power given by the will, in order to convey the interests of the
   children in the land, since the trust deed purported to convey the fee,
   which would have been impossible without the exercise of the power.

APPEAL from Chancery Court, Haywood county; JOHN S.
COOPER, Chancellor.

Bill by the Law Guarantee & Trust Company against Hobson
F. Jones and others to foreclose a deed of trust. From a decree
in favor of complainant, defendants appeal.
Affirmed.

J. W. E. Moore, for appellants.

Smith & Trezevant, for appellee.

McALLISTER, J.—Complainant filed this bill in the Chancery Court of Haywood County to foreclose a deed of trust. This instrument was executed on the 1st of October, 1891, by H. F. Jones and wife and J. W. Jones to Samuel M. Jarvis, trustee, conveying certain lands in Haywood county to secure a note for $5,650 and interest, for a loan, that day made by the Jarvis-Conklin Mortgage Trust Company. The note and mortgage were afterwards, to wit, on the 15th of October, 1892, assigned to complainant, a London corporation. The land embraced in the deed of trust had been devised by Mrs. Elizabeth Jones, deceased, under the following will: " Know all men, that I, Elizabeth Jones, being of sound mind, do make this, my last will and testament. My daughter-in-law Ellen Jones having an equitable right to two-fifths of my landed estate, I therefore make her a legal right to the same two-fifths of my land. The other three-fifths I divide between my grandchildren, giving the children of my son J. W. Jones three-tenths, and to children of my son H. F. Jones three-tenths; my two sons J. W. and H. F. Jones, to have the power to sell or convey, by deed or otherwise, or to dispose of the land in any way they see proper, for the benefit of their children; they, my two sons, being the judges of what is best for their children. That is, my son J. W. Jones has the power to dispose of the land I give to his children, and my son H. F. Jones has the power to dispose of the land I give his children. All the personal property I have I give in the same way as I give my real property." It will be observed that the deed of trust was executed by H. F. and J. W. Jones, the fathers of the infant devisees. It is alleged in the bill that the Jarvis-Conklin Mortgage Trust Company is a foreign corporation, with its situs in Kansas City, Mo., and that it filed its charter with the secretary of state at Nashville, Tenn., on March 30, 1892, and that it filed an abstract thereof in the office of the register of Haywood county on August 16, 1895, but it is admitted that at the time the loan was made it had done neither. It is further shown in the bill that the grandchildren of the testatrix at the time of the execution of the deed of trust were minors.

The defendants demurred to the bill, assigning, among others, the following grounds, to wit: First, that under said will an absolute title to three-tenths of said land vested in the children of H. F. Jones, and three-tenths of same vested in the child of J. W. Jones, and that said deed of trust was nugatory and inoperative so far as the same might affect said interests; second, that H. F. and J. W. Jones had no right or power to make the deed of trust as to six-tenths interests of said grandchildren; third, that said deed of trust only undertook to convey the individual interests of said H. F. Jones and wife, Ellen, and J. W. Jones in said land, and did not undertake to convey, and was not intended to convey, the six-tenths interest of the grandchildren. The chancellor overruled the demurrer, but permitted the defendants to rely upon said causes in their answer. Defendants answered the bill. The grandchildren, who were minors, answered through their guardian *ad litem;* averring they knew nothing of such deed of trust, or its alleged assignment to complainant. They relied upon the demurrer theretofore filed, and insisted that, if any power was created by said will in H. F. and J. W. Jones, it was only for the benefit of their children, and that the deed of trust could not have been for the benefit of the children; that it did not recite that it was for the benefit of the children, and that the will is not even referred to; and that, as a matter of fact, the children received no benefit whatever from the deed of trust. It is insisted that, if H. F. and J. W. Jones had any right or power to convey the interests of their children in said lands, it was under said will, and the power should have been recited in the deed of trust. It is alleged that said deed of trust was made by said H. F. and J. W. Jones for their own benefit, and they received the money and used it for their own purposes, and said grandchildren were in no way benefited thereby. Proof was taken, and on the final hearing the chancellor decreed that under said will H. F. and J. W. Jones were vested with full power to borrow money and mortgage said land, and thereby bind and charge the estates of their children in said lands; that said deed of trust was valid and enforceable to collect the amounts actually received by the borrowers, to wit, $5,003.50, and interest at six per cent. And a decree was pronounced in favor of complainant for $6,073.52 and costs, and the land was ordered to be sold for its satisfaction. Defendants appealed, and have assigned errors.

Two questions are presented by the assignments of error: First, that the Jarvis-Conklin Mortgage Trust Company was not a qualified corporation and hence the mortgage is void; second, that there was no power in the grantors under this will to mortgage the interest of the minors.

In respect of the non-registration of the charter, it does appear that when this loan was made, and the mortgage executed, complainant had not complied with the law on this subject. But it appears that afterwards, on the 30th of March, 1892, it filed an abstract of its charter with the register at Brownsville, where this transaction occurred, and on April 4, 1892, at Memphis, where the matter was in part negotiated. The curative act of 1875 validated this transaction to the extent of the money actually loaned, and six per cent interest. The chancellor's decree was only for the amount actually received by the mortgagees, and six per cent. interest. (*Butler* v. *Association*, 97 Tenn. 679; 37 S. W. 385.)

The main question in the case is presented by the demurrer to that part of the bill which sets out the will of Mrs. Jones, whereby a six-tenths interest in the land was devised to the children of her sons, with an unlimited power in their fathers to dispose of same, and the remaining four-tenths to Mrs. Ellen W. Jones. The language of the will is that the fathers of these children shall have the power to sell or convey, by deed or otherwise, or to dispose of the land in any way they see proper, for the benefit of their children, the two sons being the judges of what is best for their children. It is plain, we think, from the terms of the will, that these sons, H. F. Jones and J. W. Jones, were not constituted trustees for their children, but held a mere power of appointment, which they were authorized to exercise at their discretion. "In some cases the donor makes a direct gift to one party, but subjects the gift to the discretion or power of some previous taker or other party." (1 Perry, Trusts, § 250.) "A power of sale may override estates in fee." (18 Am. & Eng. Enc. Law, 907.) "A donee with general power of appointment is practically the owner." (Id. 916. See *Lawrence's Estate*, 136 Pa. St. 367; 20 Atl. 521; 11 L. R. A. 85; *Beck's Appeal*, 116 Pa. St. 547; 9. N. E. 942; *Hoxie* v. *Finney*, 147 Mass. 616; 18 N. E. 593; *Kull* v. *Kull*, 37

Hun, 476.) " It is obvious that every power of appointment is, strictly speaking, a power of revocation; but still there is a striking distinction between estates actually limited in a settlement with a power of revocation, and estates limited in default of the exercise of a preceding power of appointment. In the first case the estates are vested, subject to be revoked or defeated by the exercise of the power."   (Sugd. Powers, 2, 3.)   " The distinction between a power and a trust has been clearly defined by the courts. A mere power is not imperative, but leaves the action of the party receiving it to be exercised at his discretion; that is, the donor or grantor, having full confidence in the judgment, disposition, and integrity of the party, empowers him to act according to the dictates of that judgment and the promptings of his own heart. A trust is imperative, and is made with strict reference to its faithful execution. The trustee is not empowered, but is required to act in accordance with the will of the one creating the trust."   (Tiff. & B. Trusts, 209, 210.)   If there were a trust in this will, a court of equity would enforce it, but it would never enforce this power. It is a mere discretionary power, with the discretion absolute in the sons, they being the sole judges. (See 2 Sugd. Powers, *158), quoting the language of Lord Chief Justice WILMOT, as follows: " Powers are never imperative. They leave the act to be done at the will of the party to whom they are given. Trusts are always imperative, and obligatory upon the conscience of the party intrusted."   (And see 1 Perry, Trusts, §§ 248, 252, 511; Hill, Trustees [4th ed.] 760; 2 Story, Eq. Jur. § 1070.)   " It sometimes happens that a person having property or money to dispose of intrusts the disposition thereof to the judgment and discretion of another; and where the intention of the donor or grantor is to trust entirely to such discretion, because of the confidence he has that such person will do better than he, at the time of making the gift or grant, can dictate, such intention confers a mere power, and equity will not interfere with the execution of it."   (Tiff. & B. Trusts, 209.)

It is insisted that the predominant idea of this will is that the sons should have absolute power over the property, and that an unlimited power of disposition includes unlimited power to charge, as the greater includes the less. (*Webster* v. *Helm,* 93 Tenn. 325; 24 S. W. 488; *Steifel* v. *Clark,* 9 Baxt. 470.)   It is argued,

however, that while this will constitutes the fathers the exclusive judges of what is best for their children, yet the power to
convey must be exercised for the benefit of the children. The
record shows that the money borrowed was appropriated by the
grantors to their own use, and that the children never received
any benefit from it. There is no proof, however, that the trust
company, or its agents who negotiated the loan, had any notice
that the fund was to be misappropriated; nor did they know it was
the intention of the mortgagors to use this fund for their private
purposes or to misappropriate it. In *Bostick v. Winton* (1 Sneed,
524), it was said, viz.: "A power of appointment must be exercised in good faith for the benefit of those who are intended beneficiaries under it. If it appear that it has been exercised collusively
and for the benefit of the party exercising it, such exercise is a
fraud upon the power, and cannot be maintained." In that case,
however, the court found as a fact that the purchaser had full
notice or knowledge of all the circumstances attending the conveyance.

It is insisted, however, that, because the deed of trust does not
recite on its face that it was executed in pursuance of the power
given by the will, it must be construed to convey simply the
grantor's interest. It is now settled by this court that it is not
necessary that the intention to execute a power should appear by
express recital in the deed. (*Young v. Insurance Co.* 47 S. W.
428, decided at Knoxville, September term, 1898.) In that case
this court approved the rules laid down by Mr. Justice STORY in
Blagge v. Miles (1 Story, 426, Fed. Cas. No. 1,479), which are
held to indicate a sufficient intention to execute the power: "First,
that there is some reference in the will or other instrument to the
power; second, a reference to the property which is the subject of
the power; or, third, when the instrument executed would be
ineffectual and a nullity, and could have no operation as an execution of the power." See, also, *Lee v. Simpson* (134 U. S. 572;
10 Sup. Ct. 631; 33 L. Ed. 1038); *Pate v. Pierce* (4 Cold. 113).
If there is a reference to the property which is subject to the
exercise of the power, and the grantors have no right to convey
except under the power, it is sufficient. (2 Washb. Real Prop. [3d
ed.] 618; 2 Perry, Trusts [4th ed.], § 511c.) It is sufficient if the
intention to execute the power appears by act, words, or deeds

demonstrating the intention. (*Pate* v. *Pierce,* 4 Cold. 113.) In this case it is insisted that the act of both donees and the wife of one joining shows the purpose to convey the whole estate. As to four-tenths of this property, it is true, H. F. Jones might have conveyed simply as husband, but as to the other six-tenths he had no right to convey except under this will; and the joinder of J. W. Jones with H. F. Jones shows clearly that they intended to convey under the power given them by the will. If it had been the intention of H. F. Jones to convey only his wife's interest, he would have so expressed it; but he conveys the whole estate, and, as she did not own the whole, his deed would be insensible and a mere absurdity. If the words of the conveyance cannot be satisfied without supposing an intention to execute the power, it will be referred to the power, on the supposition that the party executing it purposed doing an effective act. (*Yates* v. *Clark,* 56 Miss. 216, citing *White* v. *Hicks,* 33 N. Y. 383.) In this case Clark's widow was donee of a power to employ the testator's (her husband's) property in such manner as she might think for the interest and advantage of herself and her children, and she sold and conveyed the fee. CAMPBELL, J., said, " as she was made the sole judge of their mutual advantage, her power to dispose of the property was unlimited. It was not necessary to refer to the power, if the act shows that the donee had in view the subject of the power, and intended to execute it." Id. In this case the deed of trust purported to convey the fee, which would be impossible without the exercise of the power. Again, it is well settled in this state that a *bona fide* purchaser of trust property is not bound to see to the application of the purchase money. (*Young* v. *Insurance Co.* [Tenn. Sup.] 47 S. W. 428; *Williams* v. *Otey,* 8 Humph. 563; *Loughmiller* v. *Harris,* 2 Heisk. 553; *Brown* v. *Foote,* 2 Tenn. Ch. 255, 263; *Harris* v. *Smith,* 98 Tenn. 286; 39 S. W. 343; *Whatley* v. *Oglesby* [Tex. Civ. App.], 44 S. W. 44.) There was nothing on the face of the deed of trust in this case indicating an intention on the part of the sons to misappropriate the money borrowed, and the mortgagee had no actual notice or knowledge of such intention. The purchaser from a trustee is not bound to see to the proper investment of the proceeds of the sale, unless he knows that the trustee intends to defraud the beneficiary, or the instrument itself discloses such intention. The mortgagee must

have been a party to the fraud, or had notice, actual or constructive, of the intended breach of trust.

Affirmed.

———

Note.—DISTINCTION BETWEEN POWER AND TRUST.

Perry in the latest edition of his excellent work on Trusts says: "Property is sometimes given to a person with a power to dispose of it for a
particular purpose, or to a particular class of persons, or to certain persons to be selected by the donee from a particular class. If the donee
executes the power and disposes of the property, or designates or selects
the persons who are to take under the gift, it goes as directed and there
is no great room for doubt or question; but if the donee refuses or neglects
to execute the power, it becomes a grave inquiry whether the persons in
whose favor the power might have been executed have any interest in the
property, or any remedy for the non-exercise of the power, by the first
taker or donee. In dealing with the cases that have arisen upon these
inquiries, courts have distributed powers into mere powers, and powers
coupled with a trust, or powers which imply a trust. *Mere powers* are
purely discretionary with the donee; he may or may not exercise them
at his sole will and pleasure, and no court can compel or control his discretion, or exercise it in his stead and place, if for any reason he leaves the
power unexecuted.

"When the power is coupled with a trust, or the power implies a trust,
the power is so given that it is considered a trust for the benefit of other
parties; and when the form of the gift is such that it can be construed to
be a trust, the power becomes *imperative* and *must* be executed, whether
a power or trust or power coupled with a trust it must be construed according to the intention as gathered from the whole instrument." (1 Perry
on Trusts, § 248 [ed. 1899].)

Underhill in his late work on Wills says: "A mere direction to an executor or trustee to sell land, though the estate is not otherwise disposed
of, does not give him an estate. All that he has is a naked power, without
the right to the possession or to the right to collect or disburse the rents
and profits. The land descends to the testator's heirs subject to the execution of the power of sale. And when testator after directing his executor
or a trustee to sell his land, devises it to others, the former takes no estate
or interest in the land, but a naked power of sale, solely for the purposes
of the will, and the devisee takes title with right of receiving rents and
profits but subject to the power of sale." (2 Underhill Wills, § 782 [ed.
1900]; and see Steinhardt v. Cunningham, 130 N. Y. 292; 29 N. E. Rep.
100.)

A devise to executors may be void as a trust but valid as a power in
trust, for a sale of land and division of the proceeds; in that case the lands
descend to the heirs, subject to execution of the power. (Konvalinka v.
Schlegel, 104 N. Y. 125; 9 N. E. Rep. 868.)

SUCCESSION OF McCLOSKEY.

[Supreme Court of Louisiana, April 2, 1900; 52 La. Ann. 1122; 27 So. Rep. 705.]

WILL—BEQUEST—VALIDITY—CHARITABLE USES.

1. A bequest in a will for the erection of a memorial window to another in a church, left in trust to trustees who are themselves to fix the amount to be so expended,—the will naming no amount to be thus disbursed,—is not a valid testamentary disposition.

2. A bequest of the residue of the testator's estate to trustees, in trust for such charitable uses and purposes in Ireland as they in their discretion might think proper to apply it to, is not a valid testamentary disposition.

3. The institution of heir or other testamentary disposition, committed to the choice of a third person, is null.

4. Impossible conditions, those contrary to the laws, are reputed not written.

(Syllabus by the court.)

APPEAL from Civil District Court, parish of Orleans; THOMAS C. W. ELLIS, Judge.

In the matter of the succession of Alice B. McCloskey. Petition of legal heirs to annul certain clauses of the last will of deceased. From a judgment granting the same, the executors appeal.
Affirmed.

Ernest T. Florance, for appellant.

Leon L. Labatt, for appellees.

BLANCHARD, J.—Alice McCloskey, of the city of Belfast, Ireland, died there in March, 1897, leaving a last will and testament which was admitted to probate in the District Registry of the Probate and Matrimonial Division of the High Court of Justice in Ireland, for the district of Belfast. She made, in the will, numerous bequests of legacies to persons and charitable institutions, none of them exceeding in amount $2,000. The property constituting her estate was located entirely in the city of New Orleans; over two-thirds of the same being real estate, and the remainder

movable property. Alexander Dempsey and William Dempsey, of
Ireland, were named in the will as executors. James A. Donnelly, of New Orleans, was appointed *dative* testamentary executor
by the court here, and as such administers the estate. Certain
nephews and nieces of the deceased, claiming as legal heirs,
brought suit to have declared void and without effect certain
clauses of the will disposing of the residue of the estate left after
payment of debts and legacies. These clauses are as follows:
" And my trustees shall hold the residue of moneys forming portion or arising from the sale, calling in, collection, and conversion
of my American property in trust to apply such an amount as they
shall think fit in the erection of a stained-glass memorial window
in St. Patrick's church, Donegall street, Belfast, in memory of the
late Rev. Michael Cahill, C. C., formerly of St. Patrick's church
aforesaid, and in trust to pay and apply any surplus of said such
residue for such charitable uses and purposes in Ireland as they
in their discretion shall think fit. * * * I devise and bequeath
my plate, jewelry, and all my estate, property, and effects not hereinbefore disposed of, unto my said trustees, upon trust to pay my
funeral and testamentary expenses and debts, if necessary, and
upon trust either to retain the residue in the condition in which
the same shall be at the time of my death, or to convert the same
into money, and to apply such residuary estate, or the proceeds
thereof, for such charitable uses and purposes in Ireland as they
in their discretion shall think fit; and in case any of the charitable
or other legacies hereinbefore bequeathed, or which I shall bequeath by any codicil to this my will, shall be or become void at
law, or shall otherwise lapse or fail to take effect, then I bequeath
all such legacies which shall be or become void unto my said trustees absolutely, and direct that all such legacies as shall lapse or
fail to take effect shall form part of my residuary estate." It is
represented that these portions of the will are, to begin with, uncertain, vague, and meaningless; that they are null and void, because prohibited substitutions and *fidei commissa;* and that the
same are to be reputed as not written. The executors, answering
the attack upon the will, after pleading the general issue, represent
that a large portion of the assets of the succession consisted of
movables; that the testamentary disposition of the movables is
governed by the law of Great Britain, in which country the de-

ceased had her domicile, where she died, and where the will was confected; and that under the law of Great Britain the testamentary disposition in the manner and form and to the effect as in the will provided is valid and effective. They urge that, should the dispositions attacked be decreed invalid so far as the real estate is concerned, the expenses and debts of the succession should be settled primarily out of the proceeds of the real estate, or at least prorated between the proceeds of the real estate and the movable property. The court *a qua* decreed the nullity of the dispositions attacked in so far as the same affects the real estate situated in the state of Louisiana, but sustained the same in so far as the personal estate of the testatrix is concerned, subject, however, to the condition that the personal estate in Louisiana must contribute its proper portion to the payment of the costs and expenses of the succession and the debts due by the deceased, in the ratio of the value of said personal property to the value of the real estate. The executors appeal.

The legal heirs (appellees) pray in this court that the judgment be so amended as to decree that the burden of the costs and expenses of the succession and of the debts of the deceased be borne by the movable property, and that the movables be exhausted before the real property is called upon to contribute to the satisfaction of any part of the same. It will be observed that no specified sum of money is bequeathed by the testatrix for the purpose of the erection of a memorial window in St. Patrick's church in Belfast. The residue (after payment of the debts and legacies) of funds arising from the sale, collection, and conversion of her property in America is left in trust to trustees named, " to apply such an amount as they shall think fit "to the accomplishment of the object named. It is obvious that this is not a legal testamentary disposition under the law of Louisiana. After applying as much of the residue as they please to the memorial window, whatever is left of the residue is bequeathed to the trustees in trust for such charitable uses and purposes in Ireland as they in their discretion might see proper to apply the same to. It is equally obvious that this is not a valid disposition by will under our law. The institution of heir or other testamentary disposition, committed to the choice of a third person, is null by the express language of the law. (Civ. Code, art. 1573; *Succession of Burke,* 51 L. Ann. 543; 25

South. 387.) The objectionable clause in *Succession of Burke* reads as follows: " Now, after the bequests have been paid, the remainder of my estate I desire my executors to use for any charitable institution they may select or think of benefiting, to perpetuate my memory." In the instant case it read thus: " And in trust to pay and apply any surplus of the said such residue for such charitable uses and purposes in Ireland as they in their discretion shall think fit." They are practically identical. The one in the Burke Case was annulled. So must the one here be annulled.

The clauses of the will do not fall under and are not saved by the provisions of Act No. 124 of 1882, for the reasons assigned in *Succession of Burke (supra)*, and *Succession of Meunier* (52 La. Ann. 80; 26 South. 776). They are to be judged by the codal provisions of the law, and by these are probated. Being void, they must be considered as having no existence. Impossible conditions, those contrary to the laws or to morals, are reputed not written. (Civ. Code, art. 1519.) If they were not written and had no existence, then the subsequent clause, wherein it is declared that in case any of the charitable or other legacies bequeathed " shall be or become void at law, or shall otherwise lapse or fail to take effect, then I bequeath all such legacies which shall be or become void unto my said trustees absolutely, and direct all such legacies as shall lapse or fail to take effect shall form part of my residuary estate," does not apply. The same is, besides, too uncertain and vague to enable any one to take under the terms thereof. The bequest therein is not to the parties named as trustees in their individual capacity, but to them as trustees. It cannot be said with certainty that the testatrix intended the parties named as trustees to take as individuals. It is clearer that she meant for them to take in their capacity as trustees. If the latter was her intention, then must she be considered as vesting her trustees with title to the residuum, in order to carry out her thereinbefore mentioned purpose, viz., its application to such charitable uses in Ireland as they might determine; and to this end and in furtherance of this purpose the concluding words of the clause under consideration contain the direction that the legacies which lapsed or failed to take effect were to form part of her residuary estate. Now, it was this residuary estate, or the proceeds thereof, which was to be applied to charitable uses in Ireland. It was willed to certain persons as trustees who had previously in the will been given directions as to how it was expected they were to apply it. It is the same thing as bequeathing it to them in trust for the purpose. It comes within the prohibitions of the law, and is void. Had the bequest been made to the parties named as trustees in their individual capacity, a different rule might apply.

Counsel for the executors (appellants) say in their brief that the question which the case presents may be briefly stated to be: Are the dispositions of the will governed by the principles laid down in *Succession of Burke* (51 La. Am. 538; 25 South. 387), or those that controlled the decision in *Succession of Meunier* (52 La. Ann. 79; 26 South. 776) ? And they contend that the dispositions attacked are legacies for pious uses, and therefore not affected by the words of trusteeship contained in the will. It is clear that the case is too dissimilar in its facts, in the dispositions made, to bring it within the rule of the Meunier Succession Case. There the legacy was definite in amount, and was made to the commune of Carouge for pious uses. Here no legatee is named, the amount is left uncertain, and the disposition is to trustees, who are directed to apply it to charitable purposes as they in their discretion may think fit. It is a disposition committed to the choice of third persons, and the case is so similar in this respect to that of *Succession of Burke* that it must be considered controlled by the rule there announced.

We have given consideration to the prayer of the appellees for an amendment of the judgment in respect to the apportioning of the costs and expenses, but do not consider this a case where Civ. Code, arts. 1668-1670, in respect to selling property to pay debts, apply.

Judgment affirmed.

ADAMS *et al. vs.* COWEN *et al.*

[United States Supreme Court, April 16, 1900; 177 U. S. 471; 20 Sup.
Rep. 668.]

WILLS—CONSTRUCTION OF—ADVANCEMENT AS A GIFT—RECEIPT
FOR LEGACY WITHOUT CONSIDERATION.

1. Moneys advanced by testator to a son during his lifetime and after the
   will was made, whatever the amount, and whether charged on his
   books or not, cannot be deducted from the share of such son under a
   will reciting that he has made advances to children, which are charged
   to them on his books, and may make further advances which may be
   charged on his books to their respective accounts, and that he desires
   that equal provision made for each shall be in addition to the "advances made or that may hereafter be made," and that " said advances
   made and that may hereafter be made be treated, not as advances, but
   as gifts, not in any manner to be accounted for."

2. A receipt acknowledging payment of a legacy which is not paid, except
   by the cancellation of an alleged debt of the legatee to the testator for
   advances which, by the will, were to be treated as a gift to the son,
   will not be upheld when it was obtained by the representatives of the
   estate, who were in a fiduciary relation to the legatee, and who insisted
   that he was morally, if not legally, bound to execute the release, thereby
   securing it from him, when he was by business reverses broken in
   spirit and wavering in his purposes.

REARGUED January 10, 11, 1900. Decided April 19, 1900.

On writ of certiorari to the United States Circuit Court of Appeals for the Sixth Circuit to review a decision reversing a decree
of the Circuit Court dismissing a bill aginst administrators.
Affirmed.

See same case below (47 U. S. App. 676; 80 Fed. Rep. 448; 25
C. C. A. 547).

Statement by Mr. Justice BREWER.—On November 16, 1891,
the respondents, trustees for the wife and children of William
Means, filed their bill in the Circuit Court of the United States
for the district of Kentucky against the petitioners as administrators (with the will annexed) of Thomas W. Means, deceased,

and John Means, a son of said Thomas W. Means. The case passed to hearing in that court upon pleadings and proofs, and resulted in a decree, on July 31, 1895, in favor of the defendants, dismissing the bill. From such dismissal the plaintiffs appealed to the Circuit Court of Appeals for the Sixth Circuit, which court, on February 8, 1897, reversed the decree of dismissal, and entered a decree in favor of the plaintiffs. (47 U. S. App. 439; 78 Fed. Rep. 536; 24 C. C. A. 198; 47 U. S. App. 676; 80 Fed. Rep. 448; 25 C. C. A. 547.) On May 24, 1897, a petition was filed in this court for a *certiorari,* which was allowed, and on December 6, 1897, the *certiorari* and return were duly filed. At the October term, 1898, of this court, after argument and on May 22, 1899, the decree of the Circuit Court of Appeals was affirmed by a divided court. Thereafter, upon petition, a rehearing was ordered, and the case was argued at the present term before a full bench.

The facts are these: Thomas W. Means, a resident of Ashland, Kentucky, died there on June 8, 1890, leaving an estate consisting chiefly of personal property, which was appraised (including the notes of his son, William Means, for $136,035.75) at $752,302.44. He left four children, John Means, William Means, Margaret Means, and Mary A. Adams and one grandson, Thomas M. Culbertson, the only child of a deceased daughter. Some ten years prior to his death, and on July 20, 1880, he made a will, in which, after provisions for the payment of his debts, funeral expenses, and expenses of administration, were these two items:

" Item 4. I give, devise, and bequeath all the residue and remainder of my estate, personal, real, and mixed, wherever situated or located, of which I shall die possessed, to be equally divided among my four children, John Means, William Means, Mary A. Adams, and Margaret A. Means, and my grandson, Thomas M. Culbertson (son and sole heir of my deceased daughter, Sarah Jane Culbertson), who shall be living at the time of my decease, and the issue of any child now living, and of said grandson, who may then have deceased, such issue taking the share to which such child or grandson would be entitled if living. But said share given, devised, and bequeathed to said grandson or his issue is to be held in trust as hereinafter provided, and to be subject to the provisions hereinafter contained as to said grandson's share.

" Item 5. I have made advances to my said children which are charged to them respectively on my books, and I may make further advances to them respectively, or to some of them, and to my said grandson, which may be charged on my books to their respective accounts. I desire the equal provision, herein made for said children, and the provision for said grandson, to be a provision for them respectively, in addition to said advances made and that may hereafter be made, and that in the division, distribution, and settlement of my said estate said advances made and that may hereafter be made, be treated, not as advancements, but as gifts not in any manner to be accounted for by my said children and grandson, or any of them, or the issue of any of them."

Thomas W. Means was a prosperous iron manufacturer, who had, as stated, accumulated in his lifetime a large estate. For many years he had been in the habit of letting his children have money. This he had been doing for at least twenty-five years before the making of the will. This money was not given to them in equal sums at regular or irregular intervals. In other words, he was not making a partial and equal distribution of his estate in advance of his death, but the money was paid to or for one or another of his children as occasion seemed to call for it. Accounts were entered with each of these children in his books, and the money thus paid to or for them was charged against them in these accounts, so that upon the face of the books they stood as debtors to him for the amounts so charged. The amounts thus charged were sometimes large. The accounts were often reduced by money or property returned to the father. So the father dealt separately with each child, letting him or her have money whenever in his judgment the interest of the child called for it. He was helping them in their business, paying their debts, and otherwise using his large properties for their benefit. At the same time the accounts were kept in his books in such a way as to indicate that he retained a claim against each child for the balance shown on such account. He made memoranda on his books, such as this at the head of John's account: " This account and the accounts of William Means and Mary A. Adams are not to be charged with interest when final settlement is made, or at any time. Thomas W. Means." With that as the relation between himself and children, Thomas W. Means made the will containing the two items above quoted. He was then seventy-seven years old. At the date of the will the accounts showed the following debtor balances:

John	$79,214 36
William	58,409 54
Mrs. Adams	51,207 48
Margaret	39,120 78
Mrs. Culbertson	29,609 82

In 1888 a bank in Cincinnati, of which William was president, failed, a failure which brought financial ruin to William. To relieve him from the embarrassment and dangers which threatened by reason of such failure, a large sum of money was paid out by Thomas W. Means for William's benefit. The question presented in this case is whether the money thus paid out is to be held a part of William's share of his father's estate, or whether it is to be deducted from the estate and the division made of the balance between the five legatees.

Mr. Lawrence Maxwell, Jr., for petitioners.

Messrs. Judson Harmon, J. J. Glidden and *H. P. Whitaker,* for respondents.

Mr. Justice BREWER delivered the opinion of the court.—The primary question is upon the construction of the fifth item of the will of Thomas W. Means. If there had been no such item of course all sums due from the children and grandchild to the father and grandfather would be part of the property of his estate and to be counted in determining the sum to be divided among the five in accordance with item 4. But item 5 evidently contemplated that some amounts were to be deducted from the gross sum of the decedent's property before a division was to be made. What were those deductions? What did the testator intend should be deducted? For, in the absence of some absolute and controlling rule of law to the contrary, the intentions of a testator, as deduced from the language of the will, construed in the light of the circumstances surrounding him at the date of its execution, always control as to the disposition of the estate. Without entering into any discussion we make these quotations from prior decisions of this court. In *Smith* v. *Bell,* (6 Pet. 68; 8 L. ed. 322), it was said by Chief Justice MARSHALL:

" The first and great rule in this exposition of wills, to which all other rules must bend, is that the intention of the testator expressed in his will shall prevail, provided it be consistent with the rules of law. (*Davie* v. *Stephens,* 1 Dougl. 322; *Perrin* v. *Blake,* 1 W. Bl. 672.) This principle is generally asserted in the construction of every testamentary disposition. It is emphatically the will of the person who makes it, and is defined to be ' the legal declaration of a man's intentions which he wills to be performed after his death.' (2 Bl. Com. 499) These intentions are to be collected from his words and ought to be carried into effect if they be consistent with law. In the construction of ambiguous expressions, the situation of the parties may properly be taken into view. The ties which connect the testator with his legatees, the affection subsisting between them, the motives which may reasonably be supposed to operate with him and to influence him in the disposition of his property, are all entitled to consideration in expounding doubtful words and ascertaining the meaning in which the testator used them. * * * No rule is better settled than that the whole will is taken together, and is to be so construed as to give effect, if it be possible, to the whole. * * * Notwithstanding the reasonableness and good sense of this general rule, that the intention shall prevail, it has been sometimes disregarded. If the testator attempts to effect that which the law forbids, his will must yield to the rules of law. But courts have sometimes gone farther. The construction put upon words in one will has been supposed to furnish a rule for construing the same words in other wills; and thereby to furnish some settled and fixed rules of construction which ought to be respected. We cannot say that this principle ought to be totally disregarded; but it should never be carried so far as to defeat the plain intent, if that intent may be carried into execution without violating the rules of law. It has been said truly (*Gulliver* v. *Payntz,* 3 Wills. 141), ' that cases on wills may guide us to general rules of construction; but unless a case cited be in every respect directly in point, and agree in every circumstance, it will have little or no weight with the court, who always look upon the intention of the testator as the polar star to direct them in the construction of wills.' "

And in *Blake* v. *Hawkins* (98 U. S. 315, 324; 25 L. ed. 139, 141), Mr. Justice STRONG used these words:

"It is a common remark, that, when interpreting a will, the attending circumstances of the testator, such as the condition of his family, and the amount and character of his property, may and ought to be taken into consideration. The interpreter may place himself in the position occupied by the testator when he made the will, and from that standpoint discover what was intended."

See, also, *Clarke* v. *Boorman* (18 Wall. 493; 21 L. ed. 904); *Colton* v. *Colton* (127 U. S. 300; 32 L. ed. 138; 8 Sup. Ct. Rep. 1164); *Lee* v. *Simpson* (134 U. S. 572; 33 L. ed. 1038; 10 Sup. Ct. Rep. 631).

In the light of these decisions we turn to inquire, What was the intention of the testator? Suppose that on the next day after making this will he had died, upon what basis would the distribution of his estate have been made? Obviously by first canceling all the gifts and advances made to his children, and then distributing the balance equally between the five. For he declares that the equal provision made by item 4 shall be in addition to his advances, "and that in the division, distribution, and settlement of my said estate said advances * * * be treated, not as advancements, but as gifts not in any manner to be accounted for by my said children and grandson, or any of them, or the issue of any of them." Language could not be more clear. Nothing could express the intent of the testator more forcibly than these words. Whatever he had done in the way of letting his children and grandson have money was to be taken as a matter of gift, for which none of the recipients was to account, and only his estate, less such gifts and advances, was to be equally distributed between the legatees named. And this intent, which is so clearly disclosed in respect to what he had already done, is equally clear in respect to what he might do thereafter. He says that he "may make further advances to them respectively, or to some of them," and declares that in the division, distribution, and settlement of his estate "said advances * * * that may hereafter be made, be treated, not as advancements, but as gifts." In other words, as he had used some of his property in the past again and again to help his children, he saw that it was likely in the future he might do the same thing, and declared, not only that every dollar he had let them have in the past, but also every dollar that he might let them have in the future, should be taken, " not as advancements, but as gifts." Not only that, but that such gifts should not be accounted for in any manner by any of the recipients, and that only the balance of his estate, after all these personal gifts were canceled, should be distributed equally among the legatees. As in the past he had freely used his estate. for the benefit of his children, so he announced his intention to deal as freely with it in the future, and to use any part of it in any way that he might deem best for the interests of any one of his children, and declared that such help given, or that might be given in the future, should not be made the basis of any accounting between his legatees. He knew he had a large estate, and that, whatever he might do with a fraction of it, there would be an abundance left for each of them—enough to place them beyond the reach of want. He had the large and generous paternal feeling; that feeling which prompts the parent to care as best he can during his lifetime for each of his children according to their respective wants, and he did not mean that anything he did for one child should be challenged by another. He doubtless recalled, as every parent does, that during infancy and childhood one child had called for more attention and care, more hours of toil and watch, than another. He realized that as they had grown to manhood and womanhood, and entered into their various places in life, there had been different calls for pecuniary assistance, and that doubtless there would be differences in the future. He knew that he had responded to every need of each child in its early days, was trying in the latter days of manhood and womanhood to make like responses, and felt that while life should be prolonged to him he would be under the same pressure of affection to each. He believed that after he had done in his lifetime what in his judgment they severally required there would be an abundance of his estate left for distribution, and intended that all dealings between himself and each of his children should be wiped out—there should be a *tabula rasa*—and that what was left (and it would be a large estate) after having discharged to each one his paternal obligation, the untouched estate, should be distributed equally. We do not see how that purpose and thought of his could be expressed more clearly and forcibly than it was done in the fifth item of the will, and it would be a sad commentary on the wisdom of the law if that purpose was not recognized and enforced.

It is said that there is an expressed limitation on this generous purpose in that he describes the advances already made as "charged to them respectively on my books," and that as to further advances they "may be charged on my books to their respective accounts," and that in order that any subsequent advances should come within the scope of this provision they should be formally charged on his books "to their respective accounts." We cannot believe that the generous purposes of the father were intended to be limited by the action of a bookkeeper. In the full possession of his faculties and watchful over his books he knew what entries had been made, and that they told the full story of his advances to his children, and so, not unnaturally, he referred to those books as evidence of those advances, but as to future advances he says only that they "may be charged on my books," and surely he did not make the possibilities of such entries the measure of his generosity. He was seventy-seven years of age when this will was made. He could not foresee the length of days which might be allotted to him nor the possible failure of any of his faculties—and indeed before his death there was a failure of eyesight, and possibly, towards the last, of his mental powers. Of course, when he made this will he knew the possibility of these things, and it is inconsistent with the whole spirit of the will to suppose that he meant that his generosity should be determined and measured by the fidelity or forgetfulness of a mere clerk. No man acting in a spirit of generous affection ever contemplates that a stranger shall measure the scope and reach of such affection. It is a matter personal to himself, the beginning and ending of which, the scope and limits of which, he and he only is to determine.

With this understanding of the scope and purpose of this clause in the will, we pass to a consideration of what took place in respect to the advances for the benefit of his son William. At that time the father was feeling the weaknesses of old age, his eyesight was failing, and he had called his son John to act as his agent in the care of his estate. News of the disaster to the bank and the effect of its failure on the welfare of his son William came to the father, and John went to Cincinnati to investigate, came back and reported the situation as he found it; told his father of the personal loans made to William by the bank, and that they were secured by collateral. We quote his testimony as to the conversation with his father:

Q. What communication did you have with your father upon your return to Ashland?

A. I told him of William's debt to the bank—individual debt—and what it would probably amount to, and that friends here advised it was for William's interest that that debt, individual debt, should be paid. I told him that the securities which William had turned over to the bank as security on the debt would some of them probably be sacrificed at a sale here—that I thought we had better pay the debt.

Q. What did he say?

A. He said that he was satisfied to do whatever I thought was best.

Q. What else did he say about the matter other than to say to you that he was satisfied to do whatever you thought was best?

A. Well, I think I have answered it. I cannot repeat the conversation between us any more than the general result of it.

On the faith of this conversation John returned to Cincinnati, and having raised the needed money, paid off William's obligations to the bank and took up the collateral, whose face value was largely in excess of the indebtedness. That the collateral when properly utilized, as it apparently was, did not pay the amount of William's indebtedness to the bank, is immaterial, nor is it material that William gave a note for the amount of this advance, as well as other notes afterwards for like advances, and that such notes were entered on the books of the father in the account of "bills receivable." It appears that this payment was not made at the request of William, but made upon consultation between the father and his son and agent, John, and made probably with the expectation that the collateral, if properly used, would pay the amount of the indebtedness.

And here it becomes important to consider the relations of John Means to his father. As the father grew old and his faculties began to fail he naturally called his oldest son John into his service, and John acted during the last years of his father's life as his agent, and it was really at John's suggestion that the money was advanced for the benefit of William. But in calling John to his service as agent and caretaker of his property there is nothing to indicate that the father meant that the son should do anything to prevent the full carrying out of the purpose expressed in his will. He had no express authority, and indeed no implied authority, to alter that instrument in which had long been recorded the settled determination of the father. So that whatever he may have done in caring for the property as the agent of his father during his lifetime is not to be taken, unless there are other circumstances to indicate the fact, as showing an intent on the part of the father to change in any way the scope and effect of the will.

And indeed it is but simple justice to John Means to say that from the evidence we are satisfied that there was no thought or intent on his part to change or limit his father's will. He did not intend by any strategy or device to thwart his father's purpose of kindness to any of his children, nor did he pursue the course he did in respect to this advance with the idea that he could satisfy his father's desire to help William and at the same time place the act of help outside the reach of item 5 of the will, and thus advance the pecuniary interest of himself and the other legatees not thus helped by his father. Very likely he was uncertain as to the construction which would be placed upon item 5; possibly thought that even if it meant exactly that which we are clear it does mean, there might be an impropriety at his father's age and feebleness in his advancing so much money for the benefit of a single child, and in order that the transaction, in case of his death before that of his father, might be clearly disclosed, took nots from William and entered them on his father's books under the head of " bills receivable." It appears from some of the testimony that there was also a thought of protecting William's share in the estate which by the death of the father might soon come to him, from attacks of creditors, and it may also be that partly on that account William executed the notes which were received for these moneys. At any rate, the correspondence between the brothers at the time of these transactions indicates that they were friendly, and that John was willingly doing that which he thought the father desired in using a portion of the father's estate in helping William out of his troubles. But whatever John or William may have purposed or thought, the evidence does not indicate that the father intended that this help extended to William should stand in any different attitude to that which he had theretofore extended to others of his children, or meant that this advance should not come within the scope of the provisions in item 5; and that is the fundamental question in the case. It is the father's estate which is being distributed, and it is the duty of the courts to see that it is distributed according to his expressed intention.

The testimony in this case is voluminous, and there are many facts and circumstances disclosed in it throwing light on the questions which we have considered. We have deemed it unnecessary to refer to them in view of the very full and satisfactory opinion filed by the Circuit Court of Appeals, in which these facts and circumstances are recited and considered at length, and which in the main meets our approval.

One further question remains for consideration: The father died June 8, 1890. The will was duly probated, and administrators with the will annexed were appointed and qualified. On October 16, 1890, William Means executed and delivered to these administrators the following receipt:

ASHLAND, KY., October 16, 1890:

Received of Thomas M. Adams and E. C. Means, administrators with the will annexed of the estate of Thomas W. Means, deceased, the sum of one hundred and thirty-six thousand and thirty-five and 75-100 dollars, being a part of my distributable share as legatee under said will applied by them as ordered by me upon the following notes and claims owed by me to the estate of said decedent, and payable to his order."

(Here follows description of ten notes, with balance due on each, aggregating $136,035. 75.)

This receipt is given in pursuance of settlement made October 6, 1890.   WILLIAM MEANS.

Attest: JOHN F. HAGER.
          A. E. LAMPTON.

The validity of this receipt or release was challenged by the respondents (plaintiffs in the Circuit Court), who claimed title to that portion of the estate of Thomas W. Means passing under the will to William Means by virtue of the following proceedings: At the May term, 1891, of the Common Pleas Court of the county of Greene, state of Ohio, a decree was entered in a cause then pending in said court between William Means on the one side and on the other Martha E. C. Means, his wife, and their children, Gertrude E. Means and Pearl E. Means and Patti Means, a minor, by her next friend, her mother, which after finding that in the lifetime of Thomas W. Means, for a good and valuable consideration, William Means made an agreement with his wife and children whereby he settled upon them, through trustees, for their maintenance and support, his interest in expectancy in the estate of his father Thomas W. Means, transferred all such interest to the plaintiffs as trustees. This decree having been entered after personal service upon William Means, of course binds him both by its findings and order. How far the findings in such decree as to the agreement and the time at which it was made may affect the action of the administrators is a matter discussed in the briefs, but which we deem it unnecessary to consider.

Neither do we stop to consider the charge of fraudulent conduct on the part of the administrators, for, independently of those considerations, we are of opinion that equity will not enforce this receipt or release. It was a surrender by William Means, without any consideration, of practically his whole interest in his father's estate, amounting to between $100,000 and $200,000. The administrators were acting in a fiduciary capacity. Their obligations to each of the beneficiaries were equal. Their duty was to dispose of the property placed in their hands according to the expressed will of the testator, and they were not at liberty to act in the interests of one legatee as against those of another. If they were doubtful as to the meaning of any clause in the will they should have applied to the court for its construction and direction. If they chose to act upon their own interpretation of its meaning they should have so acted, and not sought to conclude any of the legatees by a contract binding him to accept their interpretation. As shown by papers introduced in evidence signed by William Means, they proceeded with more than promptness and with great activity and energy to secure this and other releases. Obviously William Means was in such a condition as to require that they who were in fact trustees of his interests should seek to protect instead of destroying them. We think the evidence justifies that which was said by the Court of Appeals in its opinion:

"William had lost all his property, and was in very straitened circumstances. Since his downfall he has been broken in spirit and wavering in his purposes. He seems at times to have been impressed that the administrators had a moral, if not a legal, claim upon him, that he should yield up his legacy to the estate, and this claim was pressed and insisted upon by the administrators. That they had no such legal claim upon him we have already determined. His brother and sisters all being in affluent circumstances, and his own family in needy circumstances, that he should have voluntarily given up the whole of this large sum, with no mistake in regard to what his legal rights were, it is difficult to believe. It amounted simply to a gift to the administrators for the benefit of the other legatees, whose only claim rested on the bounty of the testator. Courts of equity view such transactions with distrust, and, if the circumstances indicate that the trustee has dealt with the beneficiary unjustly, will not hesitate to set them aside. The absence of any adequate consideration in itself raises a presumtion of unfairness which the trustee is bound to repel." (47 U. S. App. 467; 78 Fed. Rep. 552; 24 C. C. A. 214.)

While a man in the full possession of his faculties and under no duress may give away his property, and equity will not recall the gift, yet it looks with careful scrutiny upon all transactions between trustee and beneficiary, and if it appears that the trustee has taken any advantage of the situation of the beneficiary, and has obtained from him, even for only the benefit of other beneficiaries, large property without consideration, it will refuse to uphold the transaction thus accomplished. (*Taylor* v. *Taylor*, 8 How. 183; 12 L. Ed. 1040; *Comstock* v. *Herron*, 6 U. S. App. 626-637; 55 Fed. Rep. 803; 5 C. C. A. 266, and cases cited; 1 Story, Eq. Jur. §§ 307, 308; 2 Pomeroy, Eq. Jur. §§ 951, 958, 1088.) So, without considering the debatable questions presented in respect to this receipt or release, we are of opinion that the Circuit Court of Appeals was right in refusing to uphold it.

There is nothing else in the case that seems to us to call for consideration. We find no error in the conclusions of the Circuit Court of Appeals, and its decree is affirmed.

Dissenting: Mr. Justice HARLAN, Mr. Justice GRAY, Mr. Justice BROWN, and Mr. Justice WHITE.

NOTE.—TRANSACTIONS BETWEEN TRUSTEE AND CESTUI QUE TRUST.

(a) General principles.
(b) When relation exists.
(c) Acquiescence or ratification.
(d) Effect of release or settlement.
(e) When trustee may purchase from *cestui que trust.*
(f) Purchase by trustee of trust property.
(g) Application of rule forbidding purchase.
(h) Purchase not void but voidable.
(i) When trustee may purchase.
(j) Confirmation or ratification of purchase.
(k) Some illustrative cases.

(a) **General principles.**—All agreements or contracts between trustee and *cestui que trust* are looked upon with suspicion by the court, and are closely scrutinized; therefore in order that the release, confirmation, waiver, or acquiescence may have any effect, the *cestui que trust* must have full knowledge of all the facts and circumstances of the case; he must also know the law, and what his rights are, and how they would be dealt with by the court. He must not execute the release, or do the acts relied upon as a waiver, confirmation, or acquiescence, under undue influence or fear of the trustee. The *cestui que trust* must be *sui juris,* as an infant cannot be bound by a release or other act; and if the *cestui que trust* has just come of age he ought to have proper legal advice. (2 Perry on Trusts, § 851 [ed. 1899].)

(b) **When relation exists.**—Situation of trust and confidence may embrace wives, partners and clerks. (Taylor v. Klein, 47 App. Div. 346; 62 N. Y. Supp. 4.)

Confidential relations. (Darlington's Estate, 147 Pa. St. 631; 23 Atl. Rep. 1046.)

Attorney and client same as trustee and *cestui que trust.* (Yonge v. Hooper 73 Ala. 119; Hawley v. Cramer, 4 Cow. 718; Bulkely v. Wilford, 2 Cl. & F. 102; Hindson v. Weatherill, 5 De G., M. & G. 301; Waters v. Thorn, 22 Beav. 547.)

(c) **Acquiescence or ratification.**—A trustee who would excuse himself for breach of trust on the ground of acquiescence by the *cestui que trust,* has the burden of showing, by full and satisfactory proof, that the *cestui que trust,* at the time of such acquiescence, was under no disability, and that he acted with a full knowledge of the facts, freely, deliberately and advisedly, with the intention of confirming a transaction which at the time he knew he had the right to impeach. (White v. Sherman, 168 Ill. 589; 48 N. E. Rep. 128.)

To sustain ratification by *cestui que trust* it must be shown that he was not only aware of the facts, but was apprised of his legal rights. (Smith v. Howlett, 29 App. Div. 182, 190; 51 N. Y. Supp. 910.)

(d) **Effect of release or settlement.**—A release by *cestui que trust* is not binding unless he is first made fully acquainted with his rights, and the nature and full extent of the liabilities of the trustee. Any concealment, misrepresentation or other fraudulent conduct on part of the trustee, will vitiate such a release. The burden of proof rests upon the trustee to show that the transaction was perfectly fair and reasonable in every respect. (Jones v. Lloyd, 117 Ill. 597; 7 N. E. Rep. 119.)

When trustee relies on sustaining a release from the *cestui que trust* that latter acted on advice of an independent solicitor, the burden rests upon the former to show that the *cestui que trust* did in fact authorize an independent solicitor to act for them. (Lloyd v. Atwood, 3 De G. & J. 614.)

Releases given to an executor without full knowledge of all the circumstances, where such information has been withheld by the executor, and menaces and promises thrown out to prevent inquiry, are not binding. (Michoud v. Girod, 4 How. 503.)

When trustee induced his *cestui que trust* to accept securities in lieu of sum of money due, at their face value, when they proved to be worth only fifty cents on the dollar. (Smith v. Howlett, 29 App. Div. 182; 51 N. Y. Supp. 910.)

Taking worthless securities and see Lloyd v. Atwood (3 De G. & J. 614),

A receipt, by *cestuis que trust*, in "full discharge of all claims," means of all those which were known. (Eaves v. Hickson, 30 Beav. 142.)

But such a receipt given with knowledge is binding. (Aveline v. Melhuish, 2 De G. J., & S. 288.)

Burden rests on trustee to satisfy as to *release*. (Lloyd v. Atwood, 3 De G. & J. 614.)

Not bound by a receipt obtained by his wilful misrepresentation. (Berryhill's Appeal, 35 Pa. St. 245.)

Trustee must put his *cestui que trust* in possession of a full and true state of his affairs, before any settlement is binding. (Diller v. Brubaker, 52 Pa. St. 498; Danforth v. Moore, 55 N. J. Eq. 127; 35 Atl. Rep. 410.)

Releases from *cestuis que trust* to their trustees without settlement of the account, are looked upon with suspicion, although this is not enough to set them aside. (Shartel's Appeal. 64 Pa. St. 25.)

(e) **When trustee may purchase from cestui que trust.**—Trustee may buy from the *cestui que trust*, but there is a presumption against its validity, and the burden of sustaining the transaction rests upon the trustee in proving everything to have been fair and honest. (Cole v. Stokes, 113 N. C. 270; 18 S. E. Rep. 321 [the opinion contains an interesting review of the principle and cases]; and see Bryan v. Duncan, 11 Ga. 67;

Brown v. Cowell, 116 Mass. 465; Miggett's Appeal, 109 Pa. St. 520;
Ford's Estate, 185 id. 420; 39 Atl. Rep. 1106; Golson v. Dunlap, 73 Cal.
157; 14 Pac. Rep. 576; Leach v. Leach, 65 Wis. 284; 26 N. W. Rep. 754;
Stuart v. Kissam, 2 Barb. 494; Graves v. Waterman, 63 N. Y. 657; Randall v. Errington, 10 Ves. Jr. 423; Morse v. Royal, 12 id. 372, 373.)

To support a purchase by a trustee of the trust estate from the *cestui
que trust*, it must appear that the trustee has thoroughly divested himself
of that character in the transaction, and entered into a new and distinct
contract with the *cestui que trust*, that person having the fullest information on every subject. There must be no fraud, no concealment, no advantage taken by the trustee of information acquired by him in that character. (Smith v. Tounshend, 27 Md. 369.)

A trustee or executor who purchases the estate from the *cestui que trust*
or heir must pay therefor a full, fair and adequate consideration, and if
there be any concealment as to the real value of the property, or a false
or fraudulent representation as to value thereof, the sale will be set aside.
(Hickman v. Stewart, 69 Tex. 255; 5 S. W. Rep. 833.)

(f) **Purchase by trustee of trust property.**—(See also Note " Purchase by Executors or Administrators," 4 Prob. Rep. Ann. 654.) Where the
trustee has conveyed property to himself, the conveyance may be avoided
by a part only of the *cestuis que trust*. If latter represent the whole beneficial interest, they can insist upon a re-conveyance from the purchasing
trustee, or from any person who purchased from him with notice or knowledge that he has purchased from himself; but the purchase money must be
repaid with interest, and, where there has been no actual fraud, permanent
improvements must be paid for; and the purchaser must account for
rents, profits, and waste. If the *cestuis que trust* do not wish a re-conveyance, the property can be put up for sale either absolutely or at a minimum
price. If the purchasing trustee has sold the property, he can be held to
account as trustee for the price he has received; or if the property remains
unsold in his hands, the *cestuis que trust* if they so elect, can compel him
to account for its actual value, at the time of the purchase. The first two
remedies can only be given by a court of equity, when the title to the
property has passed out of the trustee; the last two can also be given by a
court of probate if the accounts are settled in that court. Morse v. Hill,
136 Mass. 60, 64; and see Renew v. Butler, 30 Ga. 954; Marshall v. Carson, 38 N. J. Eq. 250; Gibson v. Barbour, 100 N. C. 192; 6 S. E. Rep. 766;
Thompson v. Hartline, 105 Ala. 263; 16 So. Rep. 711; French v. Woodruff, 25 Col. 339; 54 Pac. Rep. 1015.)

A trustee cannot purchase the trust property save with consent of all
parties interested. (European & N. A. R. Co. v. Poor, 59 Me. 277; Darling
v. Potts, 118 Mo. 507; 24 S. W. Rep. 461; Wright v. Smith, 23 N. J. Eq.
106; North Baltimore Building Assoc. v. Caldwell, 25 Md. 423; Stephen
v. Beall, 22 Wall. 329, 341; Everett v. Henry, 67 Tex. 402; 3 S. W. Rep.
566; Freeman v. Harwood, 49 Me. 195; Patterson's Appeal, 118 Pa. St.
571; 12 Atl. Rep. 679; Shelton v. Homer, 46 Mass. 462; Farnam v.
Brooks, 9 Pick. 213; Boynton v. Brastow, 53 Me. 362.)

Cannot take a conveyance in name of trustee's wife, through a third party. (McGaughey v. Brown, 46 Ark. 25; and see Clarke v. Lee, 14 Iowa, 425; Hamilton v. Dooly, 15 Utah, 280; 49 Pac. Rep. 769.)

(g) **Application of rule forbidding purchase.**—The rule forbidding purchase by trustee extends to all cases in which confidence has been reposed and applies as strongly to those who have gratuitously or officiously undertaken the management of another's property, as to those who are engaged for that purpose and paid for it. (Wright v. Smith, 23 N. J. Eq. 106; and see King v. Remington, 36 Minn. 25; 29 N. W. Rep. 352; Michoud v. Girod, 4 How. 503.)

Embraces all persons acting in representative capacity. (Porter v. Woodruff, 36 N. J. Eq. 181.) Or where one party is so situated as to exercise a controlling influence over the will and conduct and interests of another. (Sears v. Shafer, 6 N. Y. 272.) Or where he has a duty to perform in relation to the property, which is inconsistent with the character of a purchaser on his own account and for his individual use and benefit. (Van Epps v. Harrison, 9 Paige, 238.)

Rule forbidding purchase by trustee extends to all who have duty to perform in relation to the trust property. (Hinman v. Devlin, 31 App. Div. 593; 52 N. Y. Supp. 124.)

(h) **Purchase by trustee not void but voidable.**—While purchase by trustee is not absolutely void, it is discountenanced by courts of equity; presumption is against the validity and is never upheld unless free from all taint of unfairness. (Pain v. Vickery, 37 Md. 468.)

Voidable not void. (Gardner v. Dembrinsky, 52 App. Div. 476; 65 N. Y. Supp. 183; Merrick v. Waters, 51 App. Div. 86; 64 N. Y. Supp. 542; Dodge v. Stevens, 94 N. Y. 209; and see People v. Board of Brokers, 92 id. 98; Kahn v. Chapin, 152 id. 305; 46 N. E. Rep. 489; Rice v. Cleghorn, 21 Ind. 81; Buell v. Buckingham, 16 Iowa, 284; McGaughey v. Brown, 46 Ark. 25; Gibson v. Barbour, 100 N. C. 192; 6 S. E. Rep. 766.)

The burden of establishing fairness and consideration rests upon the trustee. (Wistar's Appeal, 54 Pa. St. 60; Pain v. Vickery, 37 Md. 468.)

(i) **When trustee may purchase.**—Purchase under a trust for payment of debts by a trustee as agent of his father, both creditors in partnership, sustained. (Coles v. Trecothick, 9 Ves. Jr. 234. [There is a *note* to this case.])

Trustee may purchase at a judicial sale brought about by a third party, which he had taken no part in procuring, and over which he could not have had control. (Allen v. Gillette, 127 U. S. 589; 8 Sup. Rep. 1331. Compare Jewett v. Miller, 10 N. Y. 402; Atkins v. Judson, 33 App. Div. 48; 53 N. Y. Supp. 504.)

A trustee who has himself an individual interest in the subject of the sale, may purchase in protection of that interest. (Julian v. Reynolds, 8 Ala. 680; Appeal of Lusk, 108 Pa. St. 152.)

Purchase in protection of individual interest. (De Caters v. De Chaumont, 3 Paige, 177.)

But must have permission of court to bid. (Scholle v. Scholle, 101

N. Y. 167, 172; 4 N. E. Rep. 334.) And this has been declared to be the only exception to the rule forbidding a trustee to purchase the trust property. (Taylor v. Klein, 47 App. Div. 346; 62 N. Y. Supp. 4; and see Boswell v. Cooks, 23 Ch. Div. 302, 310.)

Under special circumstances trustee may purchase at own sale under order of court. (Markle's Estate, 182 Pa. St. 378; 38 Atl. Rep. 612.)

A permission to bid at a sale does not allow the trustee to speculate on the trust. (Cadwalader's Appeal, 64 Pa. St. 293.)

After trustee has made sale in good faith to a third person, he may afterwards purchase from him and acquire a good title. (Creveling v. Fritts, 34 N. J. Eq. 134; and see Welch v. McGrath, 59 Iowa, 520; 10 N. W. Rep. 810; 13 id. 638; Stephen v. Beall, 22 Wall. 329.)

The court has power in its discretion to permit and approve purchase by trustee. (Strauss v. Bendheim, 162 N. Y. 476; 56 N. E. Rep. 1007; this volume, p. 540.)

(j) **Confirmation or ratification of purchase by trustee.**—*Cestuis que trust* may ratify and affirm a purchase by trustee, either directly or by acquiescence and silent approval; in such a case, if they have ample notice of the facts, or sufficient to put them on further inquiry, and then wait until they can see whether the transaction is likely to prove a profitable speculation, they are guilty of *laches,* amounting to ratification and approval. (Hoyt v. Latham, 143 U. S. 553; 12 Sup. Rep. 568; and see Hammond v. Hopkins, 143 U. S. 224; 12 Sup. Rep. 418.)

Title in trustee may be confirmed by acquiescence and lapse of time as well as by express act of the *cestui que trust.* (Kahn v. Chapin, 152 N. Y. 305; 46 N. E. Rep. 489; Harrington v. Erie County Bank, 101 N. Y. 257; 4 N. E. Rep. 346.)

May be avoided by *cestuis que trust* within reasonable time by a direct proceeding for that purpose; but avoidance cannot be had at suit of third person. (Rice v. Cleghorn, 21 Ind. 81.)

Confirmation of a sale by the trustee to himself must be with full knowledge and after a deliberate examination by the *cestuis que trust.* (Campbell v. McLain, 51 Pa. St. 200.)

(k) **Some illustrative cases.**—A trustee will not be permitted to derive any profit from the use of trust funds in his hands. (Staats v. Bergen, 17 N. J. Eq. 554.)

Transaction by voluntary conveyance of daughter on arriving at full age to her mother, set aside. (Chambers v. Crabbe, 34 Beav. 457.)

And see a case where the young lady signed a note as surety for her step-father. (Espey v. Lake, 10 Hare, 260.)

Provision for counsel in deed of trust drawn by him for his services as trustee is void unless the grantor knew of the particular clause, and acted without influence of those interested. If there is any doubt the provision for compensation is invalid. (Greenfield's Estate, 14 Pa. St. 490.)

A trustee dealing with the property of a *cestui que trust* cannot divert to purposes foreign to the trust or agency without the utmost openness and frankness with the party beneficially interested. (Persch v. Quiggle, 57 Pa. St. 248.)

The law always presumes that a trustee when acting in reference to the subject of the trust, acts in the character of trustee, and not for his individual benefit; and this rule is applicable to executors. (Johnson v. Blackman, 11 Conn. 342.)

There is no illegality in a *cestui que trust* authorizing an act which would otherwise be a breach of trust towards himself, or in his releasing or agreeing to hold harmless his trustee for such an act after it is done. (Pope v. Farnsworth, 146 Mass. 339; 16 N. E. Rep. 262.)

But not when he acts on false representations of the trustee. (Nichols' appellant, 157 Mass. 23; 31 N. E. Rep. 683.)

Settlement between trustee and *cestui que trust* not sustained in absence of proof of absolute good faith. (Newman v. Newman, 152 Mo. 398; 54 S. W. Rep. 19.)

But sustained when there is evidence of understanding of agreement, and no misinformation. (Bromfield's Estate, 193 Pa. St. 151; 44 Atl. Rep. 246; and see Hathaway v. Hynson, 89 Md. 305; 43 Atl. Rep. 306.)

MOORE *vs.* MOORE *et al.*

[Supreme Court of Indiana, May 15, 1900; 57 N. E. Rep. 242.]

EXECUTORS AND ADMINISTRATORS—REAL ESTATE—APPLICATION TO PAY DEBTS—CONTRACT FOR SALE—CONSENT OF ADMINISTRATOR—ESTOPPEL.

1. In an action by an administrator to sell real estate to pay debts, a cross complaint alleging that under an agreement of sale with the administrator and the heirs defendant took possession of the real estate, and made valuable improvements thereon, and asking that she be given a first lien on the proceeds of such sale for the present value of the improvements, does not state a cause of action. as, the heirs taking the estate subject to debts of the deceased, a purchaser from them acquires their rights only, subject to the application of the property to payment of debts.

2. That an administrator. before settlement of the estate. consented to the sale of land by the heirs, did not divest a creditor of his right to have the debt made out of the land, nor estop the administrator from procuring an order of sale, for the payment of such creditor's debt.

APPEAL from Circuit Court, Boone county; B. S. HIGGINS, Judge.

Action by Jonathan J. Moore, administrator of the estate of Willis E. Moore, deceased, to sell real estate to pay debts, against Jonathan J. Moore and others. Ada Fox filed a cross complaint asking that she be reimbursed for improvements made on such real estate. From a judgment in favor of defendants, plaintiff appeals.

Reversed.

Ira M. Sharp, for appellant.

Greenlee & Call and *A. J. Shelby*, for appellees.

MONKS, J.—Appellant commenced this proceeding to sell the real estate of his intestate described in the petition to pay debts. Charles J. and Ada Fox were made defendants to said petition, to answer as to their interest, if any, in said real estate. Ada Fox filed a cross complaint, asking that she be reimbursed for valuable and lasting improvements made by her on said real estate, and for other relief. After issues were joined, the cause was tried by the court, and, over appellant's motion for a new trial, said real estate was ordered sold, and that, after applying a part of the proceeds of the sale to the payment of the debts of said decedent, said Ada Fox be paid the sum of $800 to reimburse her for the improvements made by her on said real estate, and the remainder to be accounted for by said administrator. The assignment of errors calls in question the sufficiency of the cross complaint of Ada Fox. The allegations of the cross complaint of Ada Fox are substantially as follows: That Willis E. Moore died intestate in September, 1896, the owner of the real estate described in the petition, leaving as his only heirs his sons, Jonathan J., David A., and Willis C. Moore; the said Jonathan J. was duly appointed administrator of his estate; that in 1897 the cross complainant entered into an oral agreement with said Johnathan J. Moore, administrator, and the other heirs, that said administrator was to obtain an order of court to sell said real estate at private sale, and convey the same to this cross complainant, for which she was to pay $1,200; that under said agreement she took possession of said real estate, and while in possession thereof she made lasting and valuable improvements thereon in rebuilding the dwelling house and outhouses and fences to the value of $1,050; that said real estate, by reason of said improvements, has been greatly enhanced in value, and is now worth $2,500, and without them would not be worth over $1,200; that this cross complainant took possession of said real estate and made said lasting improvements thereon relying upon the statement made and the agreement entered into with said parties as herein set forth; that said parties and said administrator at the time of making said agreement represented to this cross complainant that said estate was solvent, and that said real estate would not be needed by said administrator to pay the liabilities of said estate; that said administrator and said parties have failed and refused to carry out their part of said agreement, or any part thereof. Prayer that the court " order said administrator to sell said real estate and the improvements thereon, and that the cross complainant be given a first lien on the proceeds of said sale for $1,400, the present value of said improvements," etc.

The devisee or heir of real estate takes the same subject to the indebtedness of the deceased. (*Baker* v. *Griffitt*, 83 Ind. 411, 416; *Moncrief* v. *Moncrief*, 73 id. 587; *Weakley* v. *Conradt*, 56 id. 430.) In this state the real and personal estate of a decedent are equally chargeable with the payment of his debts, it being provided, however, that the real estate can only be sold when the personal estate has been exhausted, or is insufficient for the payment of debts. (*Fiscus* v. *Moore*, 121 Ind. 547, 552, 553; 23 N. E. 362; 7 L. R. A. 235.) Under our statutes the real estate is as completely subject to the debts of the intestate as the personal estate; and when the personal estate is sufficient to pay the debts of the intestate, yet, if it is wasted by the administrator, the real estate may be sold for the payment of debts of the intestate, even though the heirs have sold and conveyed the same to third parties. (Id.; *Nettleton* v. *Dixon*, 2 Ind. 446; Henry Prob. Law, § 188.) It is evident, therefore, that a purchaser from the heirs acquires precisely the same right and interest the heirs have, and no more, and he is bound to know that, until the estate is finally settled, the sale of the real estate may become necessary for the payment of debts. (Henry, Prob. Law, §§ 189, 195; *Chaplin* v. *Sullivan*, 128 Ind. 50; 27 N. E. 425.) It is clear, therefore, that the right or interest in said real estate, if any, acquired by appelleee Ada Fox, from the heirs of said decedent under the alleged oral agreement are subject to the debts of said deceased, and she is entitled to no relief or protection in this proceeding on account of any such right or interests acquired from the heirs. (*Fiscus* v. *Moore, supra.*) The consent of an administrator to a sale of the land by the heirs does not devest the creditor of his right to have his debt made out of the land, nor estop the administrator from procuring an order of sale to pay such creditor. (*Moncrief* v. *Moncrief,* 73 Ind. 587, 591 ; *Baker* v. *Griffitt,* 83 id. 411, 415.) An administrator has no right to the possession of the real estate of his decedent, but the title to the same, with the right of possession, rests at the instant of the death of the intestate in his heirs, subject to the debts of the intestate ; and they take and retain such title with all the rights and incidents belonging thereto, subject to the right of the administrator to procure an order to sell the same to pay said debts. An executor or administrator has no authority to sell the real estate of his decedent except by order of court, in the absence of a testamentary provision authorizing such sale. (*Duncan* v. *Gainey,* 108 Ind. 579, 584; 9 N. E. 470; *Edwards* v. *Haverstick,* 47 Ind. 138; *Hankins* v. *Kimball,* 57 id. 42; *Kidwell* v. *Kidwell,* 84 id. 224.) An estate is not liable for false representations or other torts of an administrator. (*Riley* v. *Kepler,* 94 Ind. 308, 311, and cases cited.) It is clear that the administrator had no authority to make the contract alleged in the cross complaint, and that the appellee Ada Fox acquired no right, title, or interest whatever in or to said real estate from said administrator under said contract. She was bound to know that said administrator had no authority to make such contract, and that she acquired no right thereunder from him or against said estate. She made the improvements alleged with full knowledge of such want of authority, and her rights are no greater than they would have been if the administrator had not joined in said oral contract, and had never made any agreement or representation as such. It is clear that said cross complaint did not state facts sufficient to constitute a cause of action. So far as the judgment orders $800 of the proceeds of the sale of real estate paid to Ada Fox, and adjudges costs in her favor, the same is reversed, with instructions for further proceedings in accordance with this opinion.

ANDREWS *vs.* ANDREWS.

[Supreme Judicial Court of Massachusetts, May 16, 1900; 57 N. E. Rep. 333.]

FOREIGN DIVORCE—VALIDITY—DOMICILE OF PLAINTIFF—CONDUCT OF WIFE—ADMINISTRATION—WIFE'S RIGHT.

1. Under Comp. Laws Dak., § 2578 (Laws S. D. 1890, ch. 105, § 1), requiring a plaintiff in a divorce suit to have been a resident of the territory ninety days before the commencement of the action, the residence of a citizen of another state in the territory for such time for the sole purpose of obtaining a divorce will not sustain a divorce granted in a suit instituted by him, when attacked by his wife in the state of his domicile.

2. Under Pub. St. ch. 146, § 41, declaring that a divorce granted a citizen of Massachusetts, who goes into another state to obtain such divorce for a cause arising in Massachusetts, or a cause not authorized by its laws, shall be of no validity, a divorce so granted in South Dakota in a suit by a citizen of Massachusetts who obtained a domicile in South Dakota without a *bona fide* intention of remaining there, and only for the purpose of obtaining the divorce, was void, regardless of the fact that the wife appeared and denied plaintiff's residence, which defense was afterwards withdrawn on payment of a sum of money.

3. The right of such wife to be appointed administratrix of the estate of the husband was superior to the right of one who married the husband after the divorce was granted.

APPEAL from Supreme Judicial Court, Suffolk county; JOHN W. HAMMOND, Judge.

Petition of Annie Andrews to be appointed administratrix of the estate of Charles S. Andrews. From a decree appointing her as administratrix, Kate H. Andrews appeals.

Affirmed.

Alfred Hemenway and *Frank D. Allen,* for appellant.

C. W. Bartlett, E. R. Anderson, E. B. Hale, and *Jabez Fox,* for appellee.

HOLMES, C. J.—This is an appeal from the decree of the Probate Court appointing Annie Andrews administratrix of the estate of Charles S. Andrews. The appellant is the first wife of the deceased. The appellee married him later, in good faith, after he had obtained a decree of divorce in South Dakota. The questions are whether the divorce is valid in this state, or whether, if it is invalid, the appellant, on the ground of connivance and acquiescence, is estopped to deny its validity. Charles S. Andrews went to South Dakota for the purpose of getting the divorce, and intended to return to Massachusetts as soon as he had done so. Subject to this intention, it is found that he intended to become a resident of South Dakota for the purpose of getting a divorce, and to do all that was needful to make him such a resident. The statute of South Dakota forbids a divorce " unless the plaintiff has in good faith been a resident of the territory ninety days next preceding the commencement of the action." (Comp. Laws, Dak. § 2578; Laws S. D. 1890, ch. 105, § 1.) Andrews lived in South Dakota ninety days, and the Dakota court found in favor of its own jurisdiction, substantially in the words of the section just quoted, and granted the divorce for a cause which would not authorize a divorce by the laws of this commonwealth.

The consensus of English-speaking courts founds jurisdiction of divorce on domicile. It may be that a state might substitute for domicile by statute, if it choose, simple bodily presence within its borders for a certain number of days. It may be (at least, under the constitution of the United States) that a divorce granted under such a statute between parties, both of whom were before the court, would be entitled to respect here, notwithstanding Pub. St. ch. 146, § 41. But compare *People* v. *Dawell* (25 Mich. 247, 264); *Dolphin* v. *Robins* (7 H. L. Cas. 390, 414). But no such question arises in this case, because the language of the South Dakota statute must be taken to require, not merely bodily presence, but domicile. In the light of the decisions upon similar acts, and the generally accepted rule making domicile the foundation, the words " resident of the territory " mean domiciled in the territory, whether they also mean personally present or not. (*Graham* v. *Graham* [N. D.] 81 N. W. 44; *Dickinson* v. *Dickinson,* 167 Mass. 474, 475; 45 N. E. 1091; *Reed* v. *Reed,* 52 Mich. 117, 122; 17 N. W. 720; *Leith* v. *Leith,* 39 N. H. 20, 41; *Van Fossen* v. *State,* 37 Ohio St. 317, 319.)

The finding of the single justice clearly means that the deceased did not get a domicile in South Dakota. He meant to stay there ninety days, and such further time, perhaps, as was necessary to get his divorce, and then he meant to come back to Massachusetts. It is true that he meant to do all that was needful to get a divorce, but he meant it because he was mistaken as to what was needful. In other words, he meant only to do what he supposed to be needful, and that was not enough. Whether, if he had known what was needful, he would have meant that and would have done it, is a speculation. In fact, he did not mean or do it, on the facts so far stated. It is clear that the finding of the South Dakota court in favor of its own jurisdiction upon an *ex parte* hearing would not be conclusive, but that the facts would be open to examination here. (*Adams* v. *Adams*, 154 Mass. 290, 294; 28 N. E. 260; 13 L. R. A. 275, and cases cited; *Inhabitants of Hanover* v. *Turner*, 14 Mass. 227, 230, 231; *Thompson* v. *Whitman*, 18 Wall. 457; 21 L. Ed. 897; *Hoffman* v. *Hoffman*, 46 N. Y. 30; *Gregory* v. *Gregory*, 78 Me. 187; 3 Atl. 280; *Watkins* v. *Watkins*, 125 Ind. 163; 25 N. E. 175.)

But the appellant appeared in the divorce suit and denied the alleged residence of the deceased, although afterwards, upon receiving a certain sum of money, she directed her counsel to withdraw. There is a plain difference between a case in which a respondent has not submitted herself to the power of the court, and one in which she has done so. In the former, a foreign state within whose territory she is domiciled may decline to allow her rights to be affected by the decree, whatever the record may allege. In the latter, there is stronger ground for saying that if the libel alleges residence, and any other facts necessary to give jurisdiction, the libellee no more can dispute the validity of the decree on the ground that the court was mistaken as to residence, than she could upon the ground that it went wrong on the merits. Notwithstanding the language of some decisions which do not distinguish in terms between judgments where there has been no service and those where there has been no appearance (*Sewall* v. *Sewall*, 122 Mass. 156, 161), the decisions in some states where the question has been raised is in favor of the distinction. (*Kinnier* v. *Kinnier*, 45 N. Y. 535, 540, 541; *Cross* v. *Cross*, 108 id. 628, 630; 15 N. E. 333; *Fairchild* v. *Fairchild*, 53 N. J. Eq. 678; 34 Atl. 10; *Waldo* v. *Waldo*, 52 Mich. 94, 99; 17 N. W. 710;

In re Ellis' Estate, 55 Minn. 401, 411; 56 N. W. 1056; 23 L. R. A.
287; *Van Fleet*, Coll. Attack, § 389, p. 377; id. 648. See *Loud* v.
Loud, 129 Mass. 14, 18; *Thompson* v. *Whitman*, 18 Wall, 457; 21
L. Ed. 897; *Bigelow*, Estop [5th ed.], 296.)

Supposing the state decisions just mentioned to be correct as to
the effect of the decree between the parties, the general consequence
would be that it was effective as to the rest of the world. As a
general rule, it would be inconvenient to admit that parties who
were divorced as between themselves were not divorced as against
others. (*Kinnier* v. *Kinnier*, and *Waldo* v. *Waldo, ubi supra;
Adams* v. *Adams*, 154 Mass. 290, 295; 28 N. E. 260; 13 L. R. A.
275.) But a further distinction is taken. The world at large has
no interest in the divorce, and therefore may be bound by it, but
it is suggested that the state of the domicile has an interest, and
that it cannot be concluded by a mere false recital in the record,
because the foreign court did not even pretend to jurisdiction
over that state. (*People* v. *Dawell*, 25 Mich. 247, 257.) In
People v. *Dawell* this proposition was applied in favor of the state
of the domicile as a prosecutor, and at an earlier date it was applied by this court in favor of the state as a legislator. (*Chase* v.
Chase, 6 Gray, 157, 161.)

It will be borne in mind that on the facts before us, the case
is not one in which the legislature of South Dakota has undertaken to allow the grant of a divorce. It is one in which the court
of that state has been deceived, and in which it would have refused
to act, and would have had no right to act, had it known the facts.
In such a case as this, the state of the domicile, if it sees fit, may
decline to be bound by recitals in a record to which it is not a
party. It may say, as Massachusetts has said by Pub. St. ch 146,
§ 41, that it will be governed by the fact, not by a possibly col-
lusive record, and therefore that the fact must be ascertained, tried,
and found here. Whether or not the statute goes further than the
law would go without it, we are of opinion, in accordance with
the decision in *Chase* v. *Chase*, that as applied to this case, it does
not go beyond the constitutional powers of the state. In *Hardy*
v. *Smith* (136 Mass. 328, 331), it would seem, from the papers
in the case, that there was an appearance for the respondent in the
Utah court. The validity of the statute has been affirmed in a
general way more than once (*Sewall* v. *Sewall*, 122 Mass. 156,

161; *Smith* v. *Smith*, 13 Gray, 209; *Dickinson* v. *Dickinson*, 167 Mass. 174; 45 N. E. 1091); and confined, as it should be, to persons retaining their Massachusetts domicile (*Clark* v. *Clark*, 8 Cush. 385, 387), it seems to be mainly declaratory of the law (*Lyon* v. *Lyon*, 2 Gray, 367, 368), unless in cases like the present, where, perhaps, apart from it, the parties (both having appeared) could not dispute the foreign adjudication of jurisdiction disclosed by the record. A further question might arise, as we have suggested, if the state granting the divorce had established a test of jurisdiction other than domicile, but that has not happened, and is not likely to happen.

The commonwealth having intervened by legislation, the appellant gets the benefit of it, irrespective of any merits of her own. The possibility of a distinction such as was sanctioned by *In re Ellis' Estate* (55 Minn. 401; 56 N. W. 1056; 23 L. R. A. 287), upholding the divorce as between the parties, and so far as concerns property rights, but treating it as void as against the state, and for the purposes of the criminal law, is done away with by the act. It is settled that in a case within the statute the divorce is to be treated here as void for all purposes. (*Chase* v. *Chase*, 6 Gray, 157, 160.) It is settled that there is no estoppel, even as against the party instituting the foreign proceedings. (*Smith* v. *Smith*, 13 Gray, 209, 210.) If the appellant's conduct amounted to connivance, as found, so that she could not have maintained a libel for adultery on the ground of the second marriage, that does not go far enough to constitute an estoppel. (*Loud* v. *Loud*, 129 Mass. 14, 19.) All that she did was to withdraw her active opposition to the divorce, in consideration of a payment of money, and thereafter to remain silent. We are compelled to overrule the exception.

Exception overruled.

STEINWAY *vs.* STEINWAY *et al.*

[Court of Appeals of New York, May 15, 1900; 163 N. Y. 183; 57 N. E. Rep. 312.]

APPEAL—AFFIRMANCE—WILL—CONSTRUCTION.

1. Where there is evidence to support a finding of fact by the Appellate Division which justifies a reversal by that court, it must be affirmed.
2. A testator devised shares of stock to be paid to the legatee on a future date, or, in case of his death prior to that date, to his children " or their heirs in equal proportions, to have and to hold to him, her, or them, his, her, or their heirs or assigns, forever." *Held,* that the absolute ownership thereof vested in the children within the period measured by less than two designated lives in being at the testator's death; the words " or their heirs " being words of limitation, and not of substitution.
3. A devise of shares of corporate stock and the income thereof to several legatees, each of whom is to take both income and principal in equal proportions, creates a tenancy in common.
4. The rule that payment to the legatee of the whole income of a legacy pending delay in payment of principal is essential to the immediate vesting of the legacy is not violated where the excess over a certain per cent. of the income is devised to executors as compensation for the management of the legacy.

APPEAL from Supreme Court, Appellate Division, First Department.

Action by Henry W. T. Steinway against Charles H. Steinway and others, as executors, to declare void a certain clause in the will of C. F. T. Steinway, deceased. From a judgment of the Appellate Division, First Department (48 N. Y. Supp. 1046), reversing a judgment for plaintiff both on the facts and the law, and directing a final judgment against him, he appeals.

Affirmed.

Wheeler H. Peckham, for appellant.

Geo. W. Cotterill and *John Delahunty,* for respondents.

LANDON, J.—The trial court decided that the thirty-third clause of the last will and testament of Christian Frederick Theodore

Steinway, and all other provisions of said will relating to the execution of the alleged trust provided for in said clause, were null and void, and that the 4,000 shares of the capital stock of the Steinway & Sons Corporation, attempted to be disposed of in the thirty-third clause of the will, passed under the thirty-fourth clause to the plaintiff and the other residuary legatees therein named, and directed judgment accordingly. If the thirty-third clause is valid, the plaintiff's ultimate share in said capital stock would not exceed one-twelfth. If it is invalid, and the whole of said capital stock fell into the residuary estate, then his present share thereof is one-ninth. In the latter case, under the judgment of the trial court, one-half of said capital stock is vested in persons other than those to whom the testator intended to bequeath it by the thirty-third clause of his will.

The Appellate Division reversed the judgment of the special term both upon the law and the facts. As our review is limited by the constitution to questions of law, we must affirm the judgment, unless we find that the reversal upon the facts was an error of law. If there is evidence tending to support a finding of fact by the Appellate Division which would justify the reversal by that court, then it was not error of law to reverse upon the facts, and we must affirm. (*Livingston* v. *City of Albany,* 161 N. Y. 602; 56 N. E. 148.)

The Appellate Division seems to have found, and the defendants contend it might have found within the evidence, that before the commencement of this action the plaintiff, with full knowledge of all the facts, and presumably with full knowledge of his legal rights, or, at least, with knowledge that it was doubtful whether any part of the said capital stock fell into the residuary estate, and intending to waive any claim to more, and faithfully to observe the terms of the will, received from the executors upward of $33,000 of the assets of the estate, other than from said stock, in full satisfaction of his interest under the residuary clause, and thereupon released, under his hand and seal, all claim for more; and, in addition to this, that the plaintiff's acts in support of the will, and in taking benefits under it, and inducing the other beneficiaries to act with him in its support, make it so inequitable for him to maintain this action that a court of equity should refuse to assist him.

There is no conflict in the evidence. The plaintiff, however, contends that none of it tends to support the reversal upon the facts; that, in the language of this court in the case cited, "there are neither facts nor inferences deductible from conceded facts in opposition to the decision of the trial court." We must determine whether this is so. The testator died March 26, 1889, possessed of the 4,000 shares of capital stock in question, of an estimated value of about $1,000,000, and of real estate and other personal property of an estimated value of about $500,000. He was a widower, and never had any children. His parents were dead. His next of kin were his brother William, his sister Dorette Ziegler, and the children of a deceased sister, Wilhelmine Candidus, and of his deceased brothers, Henry, Henry Albert, and Charles. By thirty-two clauses of his will he disposed of the half-million of his estate absolutely and immediately among his brothers, sisters, nephews, and nieces, naming them all, and a few other legatees and devisees. The terms of his will in this respect have been fully observed, and this portion of his estate has been settled and closed. The thirty-third clause of his will is as follows: "Thirty-third. I give and bequeath all my shares in the corporation of Steinway & Sons, of the city of New York, to my executors and trustees hereinafter named, in trust to be managed by them until the first day of January, in the year 1904, as follows: (a) One-fourth part of such shares in the Steinway & Sons Corporation to and for the benefit of the five children of my sister Wilhelmine Candidus, late of the city of New York, deceased, viz. Louise Deppermann, wife of Gustav Deppermann, of Hamburg, Germany; Albertine S. Ziegler, wife of Henry Ziegler, of New York; and Harry Candidus, Johanne Candidus, and Gustav Candidus; and to pay to them in equal proportions an annual sum representing an income of five per centum on and from such shares, and on the first day of January, 1904, to pay over in equal proportions to the said five children of Wilhelmine Candidus, deceased, or their heirs, the said shares in the Steinway & Sons Corporation, or the proceeds thereof; to have and to hold to him, her, or them, his, her, or their heirs and assigns, forever. The excess of the annual income of such shares in the Steinway & Sons Corporation, New York, over and above said five per centum, shall be retained by my executors and trustees hereinafter named, as their compensation for the management of such shares, and such excess annually shall be divided *pro rata* among them or their successors until January 1, 1904." Subdivisions " b " and " c " are in the same words, except that in subdivision " b " the four children of his living sister, Dorette Ziegler, naming them, are the beneficiaries of the so called trust, and in subdivision " c " the three sons of his deceased brother Charles, naming them, of whom the plaintiff is one, are the beneficiaries. Subdivision " d " is in these words: " (d) One-fourth part of my shares in the said Steinway & Sons Corporation to and for the benefit of my brother William Steinway, or, in case of his death prior to January 1, 1904, to and for his son George A. Steinway, his daughter, Paula Th. Steinway, and his children by his second wife, Elizabeth C. Steinway, *nee* Ranft, and to pay to him, or in case of his death, to his said children, an annual sum representing an income of five per centum on and from such shares, and on the first day of January, 1904, to pay over to my said brother William Steinway, or, in case of his death prior to that date, to his said children, as mentioned in this section of this my last will and testament, or their heirs, in equal proportions, the said shares in the Steinway & Sons Corporation, or the proceeds thereof; to have and to hold, to him, her, or them, his, her, or their heirs or assigns, forever." To which is added the same provision in the same words as to the excess of the annual income as set forth in subdivision " a," " b," and " c." The residuary clause of the will is in these words: " Thirty-fourth. All the rest, residue, and remainder of my estate, real and personal, of whatever nature and wherever situated, I give and bequeath as follows: (a) One-third part thereof to my sister Dorette Ziegler, wife of Jacob Ziegler, of the city of New York, to have and to hold unto her, her heirs and assigns, forever; (b) one-third part thereof to my brother William Steinway, of the city of New York, to have and to hold unto him, his heirs and assigns, forever; (c) one-third part thereof to my nephews Henry W. T. Steinway (the plaintiff), Charles H. Steinway, and Frederick Th. Steinway, in equal proportions, to have and to hold unto them, their heirs and assigns, forever."

There was a considerable amount in the half-million portion of property to be divided under this residuary clause. Respecting this property, the plaintiff and the other residuary legatees, in-

cluding the defendant William Steinway, a brother of the testator
and also a devisee, and a legatee, general, specific, and residuary,
under his will, and one of the four executors and trustees named
therein, executed an instrument bearing date April 6, 1891, which,
after specifying some of the items, and mentioning others as " un-
realized assets and articles," proceeds: " Whereas, it is very desirable that the said estate of C. F. Theodore Steinway should
be closed up, and final assets distributed and paid over to the heirs
at law according to the terms of the deceased's last will and testament: Now, it is hereby agreed that all unsettled assets above
referred to be hereby placed in the hands of Mr. William Steinway, one of the deceased's heirs at law, to dispose of, collect, compromise according to his best judgment, with full authority from
us to exercise his own discretion, * * * and pay over to us the
net proceeds, as follows,"—specifying the proportional share of
each residuary legatee as provided in the will, thus: " One-ninth
thereof to Henry W. T. Steinway (plaintiff), deceased's nephew,"
—and continuing: " And we, the undersigned, heirs at law of Mr.
C. F. Theodore Steinway, deceased, hereby consent and authorize
the executors of the said estate to close up same, and make the
final distribution to the heirs at law, as directed in deceased's will,
and we hereby separately bind ourselves to give a final receipt in
duplicate to such executors, on receiving from them such share
as provided in said will."

William Steinway executed the trust thus confided to him, and
on October 6, 1891, distributed the net proceeds of the residuary
estate among the said residuary legatees, the plaintiff receiving, in
addition to $23,000 previously paid him thereon, the sum of $10,-
743.09, and eleven shares of capital stock in the Matthias Gray
Company, the value of which is not stated; the total making the
one-ninth part due him under the residuary clause of the will,
upon the half-million portion of the estate. He thereupon gave
the executors a release under seal, describing himself therein as
" one of said testator's testamentary heirs at law inheriting one-
ninth part of all the rest, residue, and remainder of said estate,"
specifying the amounts of money and the eleven shares of stock
received my him, and thus continuing: " In full payment of the
principal amount of my inheritance as such heir at law bequeathed
to me in and by said last will and testament, and I hereby quit-

claim to and forever release said executors and said estate from any further claim whatsoever of and by myself, my heirs, executors, or administrators, as such heir at law." This release recited that the executors had " kindly relinquished their commissions " in plaintiff's favor. Up to this time the plaintiff had co-operated with the executors, legatees, and devisees in settling the estate according to the terms of the will. He had accepted the income allotted to him by the thirty-third clause.

The executors and trustees were authorized by the thirty-sixth clause of the will " in their discretion to assent to or oppose any reduction or increase of the capital stock of said Steinway & Sons Corporation." In April, 1891, the trustees of the corporation decided to increase its capital stock by the addition of 5,000 shares, at $100 each, to be subscribed for by the shareholders in proportion to the stock each one held. The plaintiff subscribed and paid for 111 shares of the additional stock as the owner of 333 shares under the thirty-third clause of the testator's will that being the one-twelfth part of the 4,000 shares of which he was therein named as beneficiary or legatee. He thus assumed that the 111 shares were vested in him. He induced several of the other beneficiaries under the thirty-third clause to subscribe in like manner for their proportions, and thus conceded that their proportions were in like manner vested. The plaintiff has since received dividends of ten per centum per annum upon the additional stock thus allotted to him.

The thirty-fifth clause of the will provides: " In case any one of the legatees named in this my last will and testament shall not be living at the time of my death, his or her share or legacy shall form part of and pass into the bulk of my estate. This, however, shall not affect in any way the distribution of my shares in the Steinway & Sons Corporation, of New York, as provided for in the thirty-third section of this my last will and testament."

The defendants contend that the thirty-fifth clause affords evidence that the intent of the testator was that no part of the Steinway & Sons capital stock should fall into the residuary estate, and that, in case an invalid suspension of absolute ownership results from one part of the testator's scheme, that part is separable from his main scheme, and that the capital stock must be distributed among the beneficiaries named in the thirty-third clause, or, failing that, as in case of intestacy. Whether any of these questions of construction were present to the mind of the plaintiff when he accepted the $33,000 and upward which were paid him in satisfaction of his interest under the residuary clause, and he gave his release in full therefor, the evidence does not inform us. His learned counsel now contends that they were not, and that the release was given, and all his acts and declarations showing his own support of the will and encouragement of other beneficiaries to observe its terms were the natural result of his ignorance of his rights under it. Thus, the learned counsel deduces an inference of fact. Under all the circumstances, we think it was competent for the Appellate Division to draw the opposite inference. That court might have found within the evidence that his release covered all his claim, present and prospective, to the residuary estate, and that he so intended it; that it was not without valuable consideration, and that there were family considerations as well as a sequence of his acts in support of the will tending to uphold it, making his present claim to a further residuary interest, if successful, most unjust and disastrous to such of his kindred as would thereby be disinherited; who, under the decree of the trial court, are adjudged to have received for years, without legal right, five per centum of the income upon the shares of stock allotted to them by the testator, and the executors are granted a recovery against each one of them for the sum he or she has thus severally received. And the executors are adjudged to pay into the residuary estate the amount of the dividends they have severally received upon the stock under the terms of the will in excess of the five per centum, less their commissions and reasonable charges. And yet the plaintiff assented for about four years to such disposition of the income.

This leads to an affirmance of the judgment of reversal, but, as upon a new trial the plaintiff might make a different case upon the equities, it is doubtful whether the Appellate Division should have directed final judgment against him. We therefore proceed to the question of the validity of the thirty-third clause.

We may test its validity by examining the provision by which the testator gives and bequeathed the 4,000 shares of corporate stock "to his executors and trustees in trust, to be managed by them until January 1, 1904, as follows," and the following subdivisions ("a," "b," "c," and "d"), in which he severally directs the management of the one-fourth part thereof "to and for the benefit" of the several beneficiaries designated in each sub-division, with directions for the disposition of the income and ulti-mate payment of the *corpus* of the fund. There are no difficulties in subdivisions "a," "b," and "c" which are not present in sub-division "d," and we therefore examine that subdivision.

The question is whether the testator has thus provided that the absolute ownership of the 1,000 shares, disposed of in subdivision "d," shall be suspended until January 1, 1904, and thus for a period not measurable by two designated or ascertainable lives in being at the death of the testator. The Revised Statutes prohibit the suspension of the absolute ownership of personal property for a longer period than during the continuance and until the termi-nation of not more than two lives in being at the death of the tes-tator. (1 Rev. St. 773, § 1.) In other respects limitations of future or contingent interests in personal property are subject to the rules prescribed in the first chapter of the second part of the Revised Statutes. (Id. § 2.) If it must be held that the testator has so provided for a suspension thus prohibited, then the thirty-third clause is void. If it may be held consistently with all the terms of the will that he has not so provided, but that the suspen-sion of absolute ownership does not and cannot extend beyond the life of William Steinway, but provides that, upon his death before 1904 (an event which has occurred since the trial of this action), each of the equal proportions of the 1,000 shares become vested severally and absolutely in each of his children named and desig-nated at the death of the testator, then, because the law favors the vesting of estates, and such permissible construction as will save and not destroy the will, it should be so held. It is settled law that the absolute ownership is suspended in one of two ways,—either by the creation of future estates vesting upon the occurrence of some future and contingent event, or by the creation of a trust which vests the estate in trustees. (*Smith* v. *Edwards,* 88 N. Y. 93; *Everitt* v. *Everitt,* 29 id. 71.)

Passing for the present the question of a trust estate, and as-suming a direct bequest to each legatee, we may concede that the absolute ownership of the 1,000 shares mentioned in subdivision "d" was suspended during the life of William Steinway, and since at the death of the testator it was uncertain whether William would die before 1904 that the future estates given to William's children were contingent. Following the rule as to future estates in land, as we must (1 Rev. St. 773, § 2), these future estates would remain contingent, "whilst the person to whom or the event upon which they are limited to take effect remains uncertain" (1 Rev. St. 723, § 13); but no longer. When the contingency happened the precedent estate was determined, and the estate hitherto contingent became vested in his children "in equal proportions." (Id. §§ 10, 13.) If any children were born to William Steinway after the death of his testator, the vesting in them of their shares was only postponed during the life of their father, —that is, a single, designated life. (*Smith* v. *Edwards*, 88 N. Y. 92; *In re Brown*, 154 id. 313; 48 N. E. 537; *Campbell* v. *Stokes*, 142 N. Y. 23; 36 N. E. 811.) Such after-born children would be let in. Was this corporate stock, or, rather, each of these "equal proportions" of it, vested in each child in absolute ownership? Withholding of payments seems to be withholding of possession and control, and thus of absolute ownership, and that seemed to be the view in *Converse* v. *Kellogg* (7 Barb. 596), and was shared by the learned trial judge; but it was said in *Bliven* v. *Seymour* (88 N. Y. 478), that whatever was said in *Converse* v. *Kellogg* in support of such an inference has no sanction in the decisions of this court.

It is contended by the plaintiff that, if any of William's children should die before 1904, his or her share would not vest in his or her executors or administrators, but in his or her heirs, because the direction to the trustees is to pay on the first day of January, 1904, in case of the prior death of William "to his said children * * * or their heirs, in equal proportions, the said shares or the proceeds thereof, to have and to hold to him, her, or them, his, her, or their heirs or assigns, forever." The words "or their heirs" are usually words of limitation, and not of substitution, and must be so construed, unless the will clearly imports their use in a substitutionary sense. As we must as to future estates in personal property follow the rules as to future estates in land, we may deny to the word "heirs" any more substitutionary force than it has in devises of estates in land. That would here give the word the meaning of "next of kin." (*Tillman* v. *Davis*, 95 N. Y. 17.) This will negatives the idea that these words were

used in a substitutionary sense, but supports the conclusion that
they were used as words of limitation, and especially with the
purpose to vest the absolute ownership of the legacy in each child
of William Steinway in case of the latter's death before 1904,
irrespective of the child's living at that date.   Thus the devises
and bequests to eighteen different devisees and legatees named in
eighteen several clauses of the will previous to the thirty-third
clause are severally made in case " he (or she) survive me," and
the thirty-fifth clause provides: " In case any one of the legatees
* * * shall not be living at the time of my death, his or her
share or legacy shall form part of and pass into the bulk of my
estate.   This, however, shall not affect in any way the distribution
of my shares in the Steinway & Sons Corporation, of New York,
as provided for in the thirty-third clause of this my last will and
testament."   Following out the purpose thus expressed as to the
shares disposed of in the thirty-third clause, the testator, manifestly *ex industria,* meant by his first use of the words " or their
heirs "—an obscure expression, taken collectively,—and then by
repeating them distributively with the addition " or assigns, forever," to emphasize the absoluteness of his final gift to the children of William Steinway, and to exclude all doubt of its being
to them " forever."   Thus the absolute ownership was not suspended beyond two lives in being at the testator's death, but only
for one life.

   We have thus far assumed that the contingent estates were
given to the children of William Steinway as tenants in common,
and not as joint tenants.   Tenancy in common in such cases is the
statutory rule, unless the will expressly declares a joint tenancy.
(1 Rev. St. 727, § 44.)   Here it does not so declare, but the import of the words employed is that each one of William's children
is to take both income and principal in equal proportions, and by
that the testator meant that each one should take what he intended
to give him, separately and solely for himself or herself.   No survivorship or accumulation is mentioned.   This court has steadily
refused to infer a joint tenancy, in the absence of words expressly
intended to declare it.   (*Stevenson* v. *Lesley,* 70 N. Y. 512.)   For
the purposes of management only, the whole fund is treated as a
single fund; for the purposes of his several gifts to the several
legatees, each " equal proportional part " is treated as separate

and distinct from every other. To the mind of the testator the shares of capital stock were tangible things, as separable in their nature as if each were an ingot of gold of like value. The corporation, and not the trustees under the will, would make the income, and there would be no occasion to touch the certificates representing the corporate stock until 1904. By directing its division, the testator substantially accomplished it. (*Wells* v. *Wells*, 88 N. Y. 323; *Savage* v. *Burnham*, 17 id. 571.) If the several legacies were given to each legatee in severalty at the death of the testator, the time of payment alone being postponed until 1904, and the whole income accruing upon each legacy also given to each legatee to be paid to him annually in the meantime, then each legatee became, at the death of the testator, the absolute owner of the *corpus* of his or her legacy and of its full beneficial use, and thus of the whole of it, except as suspended for the life of William Steinway,—a suspension permitted by the statute. (*Dodge* v. *Pond*, 23 N. Y. 69; *Woodgate* v. *Fleet*, 64 id. 566.)

Did the testator intend to postpone the vesting of the legacies until 1904, or simply the payment of the *corpus* of them? If the foregoing views are correct, then the case is substantially brought to the same conditions as exist in the leading case of *Warner* v. *Durant* (76 N. Y. 133), greatly relied upon by the plaintiff. There the bequest was in form to the executors of an invested fund of $250,000, which the testator directed his executors to keep invested, and to pay, for five years from the first of January after his death, interest at the rate of seven per centum per annum upon various specified amounts thereof to various persons named, among whom was Oliver Blush, to whom he directed such payment of interest upon $15,000, and that sum to him at the end of said five years. Blush died before the day of payment arrived, and the question was whether the legacy vested in him at the testator's death. If not, it lapsed. The court held that it was vested. To do this the court had to find in the will itself, notwithstanding the formal gift to the executors to hold the fund in trust for five years, and the absence of any words of gift to Blush, except the direction to pay him the fund at the end of five years, and the seven per centum per annum thereon in the meantime, that the testator intended the gift to be absolute, and the time of payment only postponed; thus making the gift as of the time of the testator's death, but deferring its payment for five years.

The court found the intention to make the gift absolute as of the time of the testator's death, because (1) the gift was by the will itself at once severed from the general estate for the benefit of the legatee. That circumstance exists in the will before us. (2) During the five years in which the payment of the legacy was deferred, the interest upon it was to be paid to the legatee, and therefore, since the testator intended that the legatee should have the whole fund and all its income, he actually gave him at the outset the whole of it, notwithstanding that he interposed the trustees as intermediate and final paymasters. Thus, the payment of the whole interest or income of the legacy pending the delay in payment of the principal is essential to the immediate vesting of the legacy. The learned counsel for the plaintiff insists that the will before us fails to direct such payment, and that, therefore, the legacies were not immediately vested. We concede that the question is a vital one. It is said in *Smith* v. *Edwards* (88 N. Y. 92), that, if any part of the interest is diverted to purposes other than the benefit of the legatees, that is treating the principal as not belonging to them, and *Warner* v. *Durant* is to the same effect. See, also, *Delafield* v. *Shipman* (103 N. Y. 463; 9 N. E. 184).

The direction in each of the four subdivisions of the thirty-third clause is that the executors pay to the legatees, " in equal proportions, an annual sum representing an annual income of five per centum on and from such shares (of corporate stock). * * * The excess of the annual income of such shares over and above said five per centum shall be retained by my executors and trustees as their compensation for the management of such shares." What this annual income would be was, of course, unknown to the testator. It subsequently proved to be from eighteen to twenty per centum per annum, until about the time this action was commenced. But, whatever it might prove to be, it was " on and from such shares," and the excess over five per centum was not given by the testator to his trustees as a legacy or in diminution of the several legacies to the named legatees, nor retained in or for the benefit of the estate, but " as their compensation for the management of such shares " of capital stock. We must treat it as the

testator did, as compensation for their management, for the benefit of the legatees, and therefore not diverted to other purposes.
So treated, the five per centum per annum was the whole net income of the *corpus* of the legacies. The objection is insisted upon
that the five per centum is not income, but a sum representing it,
and that, unless it is paid as income *eo nomine,* it does not meet
the requirements of the rule. In *Warner* v. *Durant* the direction
was to pay the legatees seven per centum interest, not expressed as
the exact or the whole interest that the fund produced. The circumstance did not escape notice. The court held that the payment
of " an amount equal to all which it is capable of yielding, or may
be expected in legal methods to yield," would suffice. In *Smith*
v. *Edwards* some expressions of the learned judge who delivered
the opinion of the court seem to imply that payment of the interest or income should be directed *eo nomine,* following the rule
stated in *Watson* v. *Hayes* (5 Mylne & C. 125) ; but in *Smith* v.
Edwards the testator directed the application of the income to
various purposes other than payment to the legatees, and thus
failed to direct the payment of the whole *eo nomine* or otherwise.
We are not constrained by authority to sacrifice substance to form.

The plaintiff invokes the rule that where there is no gift, but by
a direction to executors or trustees to pay or divide, and to pay at
a future time, the vesting in the beneficiary will not take place
until that time arrives. (*Warner* v. *Durant, supra; Smith* v. *Edwards, supra; Delafield* v. *Shipman, supra; Goebel* v. *Wolf,* 113
N. Y. 405; 21 N. E. 388.) But these and other cases show how
rare it is that there is no other expression in the will indicating
the time when the gift is to vest. If there are other expressions,
all must be considered. (*In re Brown, supra.*) The rule is to
aid in ascertaining the testator's intention, not in defeating it.
(*Campbell* v. *Stokes, supra.*) It was said in *Smith* v. *Edwards*
that the rule is a flexible one, and the way is open to explore the
other terms and conditions of the will to ascertain whether they do
import a present gift irrespective of the direction for payment.
This we have already done.

What we have said practically disposes of any title in the trustees. The testator gave the management which he specially
pointed out and limited to his trustees, but the property to be
managed to his legatees. Everything the trustees are directed to

do, they can do under a power as well as if they had absolute title in themselves. Where neither the statute nor the terms of the will require it, the trustees take nothing more than is necessary to accomplish the purposes of the testator. No statute requires the trustees to take title, even to support the contingent bequests to the children of William Steinway. (1 Rev. St. 723, § 10.) It may be conceded that they have an administrative title, such as executors usually have to the personal property of their testator, for the purposes of administration, good against all the world except the beneficiaries, but as to them a mere aid and instrument to pass it forward to them in the due course of administration, as the law and the will appoints, free and clear of further needs or liens of the estate. In such cases the courts, for the purpose of sustaining the will, construe an authority and duty conferred or imposed upon executors, where it is possible to do so, as a mere power in trust, although the duty imposed, or the authority conferred, may require that the executors shall have control, possession, and actual management of the estate. (*Robert* v. *Corning*, 89 N. Y. 237; *Downing* v. *Marshall*, 23 id. 366; *Post* v. *Hover*, 33 id. 593; *Tucker* v. *Tucker*, 5 id. 408.) We think these trustees took no title, but only a power in trust, and that the several legacies vested severally in the several legatees in absolute ownership within the period measurable by less than two designated lives in being at the death of the testator. The judgment should be affirmed, with costs to the respondents payable out of the income of the fund.

PARKER, C. J., and GRAY, O'BRIEN, HAIGHT, CULLEN, and WERNER, JJ., concur.

Judgment affirmed.

MARSHALL vs. MASON.

[Supreme Judicial Court of Massachusetts, May 18, 1900; 57 N. E. Rep. 340.]

WILLS—WITNESSES SIGNING BEFORE TESTATOR.

Where the witnesses to a will signed before the testator, and immediately thereafter the latter signed the instrument in their presence, it was not a sufficient attestation, and the will was of no validity.

REPORT from Supreme Judicial Court, Middlesex county; JAMES M. BARKER, Judge.

Proceedings in probate by one Marshall against one Mason. Decree declaring a will invalid.

Affirmed.

Geo. R. Pulsifer, for appellant.

John M. Marshall and *H. W. Brown*, for appellee.

HOLMES, C. J.—The only question with which we need to deal upon this report is whether an instrument is duly executed as a will under our statutes if the witnesses sign first in the presence of the testator, and the testator signs immediately afterwards in their presence, the whole transaction being as completely one as it can be with that order of events. The question has been answered so fully by Chief Justice GRAY in delivering the judgment of this court in *Chase* v. *Kittredge* (11 Allen, 49, 56, 63, 64), that we think discussion unnecessary. The manifest intention of the statute is that: First, the will should be put in writing, and signed by the testator; second, his will so written be attested by the witnesses; and, third, the witnesses subscribe in his presence in evidence of their attestation to his written will." It is true that in that case the witness in question signed in the absence of the testator, and some time before him. But the chief justice does not confine his reasoning to that case, and evidently meant, with the concurrence of his brethren, to establish a general rule in the words which we have quoted. We regard that rule as founded on good sense and the plain meaning of the words of the statute. Many of the cases cited at the present argument are cited in the opinion. Others in accord with it are *Jackson* v. *Jackson* (39 N. Y. 153, 162); *Sisters of Charity of St. Vincent de Paul* v. *Kelly* (67 N. Y. 409, 413); *Brooks* v. *Woodson* (87 Ga. 379; 13 S. E. 712; 14 L. R. A. 160). See also *Mendell* v. *Dunbar* (169 Mass. 74, 76; 47 N. E. 402).

Decree of Probate Court affirmed.

NOTE.—WITNESSES TO WILL.

(a) Value of attestation clause.
(b) Must see testator sign or signature.
(c) Request to witness.
(d) Order of signing.
(e) Presence of testator.
(f) Presence of other witnesses.
(g) Signing by another.
(h) By mark.
(i) Some illustrative cases.

(a) **Value of attestation clause.**—The attestation clause raises a presumption of the truth of the facts certified, and mere failure of witnesses to recollect the facts certified not alone sufficient to overcome such presumption and justify denial of probate. (Will of Meurer, 44 Wis. 392; McCurdy v. Neall, 42 N. J. Eq. 334; 7 Atl. Rep. 566; Mundy v. Mundy, 15 N. J. Eq. 290; Hobart v. Hobart, 154 Ill. 610; 39 N. E. Rep. 581; Will of O'Hagan, 73 Wis. 78; 40 N. W. Rep. 649; Will of Kellum, 52 N. Y. 517; Peck v. Cary, 27 id. 9; and see Stewart v. Stewart, 56 N. J. Eq. 761; 40 Atl. Rep. 438; Re Lewis' Will, 51 Wis. 113; 7 N. W. Rep. 829; Barnes v. Barnes, 66 Me. 286; Abbott v. Abbott, 41 Mich. 540; 2 N. W. Rep. 810; Ayres v. Ayres, 43 N. J. Eq. 569; 12 Atl. Rep. 621; Farley v. Farley, 50 N. J. Eq. 454; 26 Atl. Rep. 178; Matter of Nelson, 141 N. Y. 152; 36 N. E. Rep. 3; Brown v. Clark, 77 N. Y. 369; Will of Pepoon, 91 id. 256; Rolla v. Wright, 2 Dem. 482; Rugg v. Rugg, 83 N. Y. 592; Walsh v. Walsh, 4 Redf. 165; Weir v. Fitzgerald, 2 Bradf. 42, 73; Matter of Schweigert, 17 Misc. 186; 40 N. Y. Supp. 979.)

An attestation clause is not necessary at common law; sufficient if the witnesses subscribe their names opposite the word witnesses or attest. (Berberet v. Berberet, 131 Mo. 399, 408; 33 S. W. Rep. 61; Olerick v. Ross, 146 Ind. 282; 45 N. E. Rep. 192; Robinson v. Brewster, 140 Ill. 649; 30 N. E. Rep. 683.)

The attestation clause while not essential is valuable as presumptive evidence in case of death of witnesses, or failure of recollection. (Chaffee v. Baptist Convention, 10 Paige, 85; Jackson v. Jackson, 39 N. Y. 153; Taylor v. Brodhead, 5 Redf. 624.)

Where attestation clause is full and complete court may find due publication, although only one of the witnesses testifies to the essential facts and the other denies them. (Matter of Bernsee, 141 N. Y. 389; 36 N. E. Rep. 314; aff'g 71 Hun, 27; 24 N. Y. Supp. 504; and see Rogers v. Diamond, 13 Ark. 476; Harp v. Parr, 168 Ill. 460; 48 N. E. Rep. 113.)

An attestation clause corroborated by other competent evidence, will prevail against positive evidence of the subscribing witnesses to the contrary. (Will of Cottrell, 95 N. Y. 330, 335.)

Will not defeated by failure of memory of witness. Statutory requirements may be established by other competent testimony, though witness did not subscribe to the will. (Gillis v. Gillis, 96 Ga. 15; 23 S. E. Rep. 107.)

The fact that witnesses have signed above instead of below the words designating the attestation does not affect the validity of the attestation when it is clearly manifest that they signed for the purpose of attestation. (Moale v. Cutting, 59 Md. 510; Potts v. Felton, 70 Ind. 166.)

Or where they sign in the attestation clause and not after it. (Franks v. Chapman, 64 Tex. 161; and see as to importance of place of signatures of witnesses in determining the question of purpose, Goods of Wilson, L. R. 1 P. & D. 269; Goods of Streatley [1891], Prob. 172.)

Distinction between attestation and subscription. (Swift v. Wiley, 1 B. Mon. 117; Sloan v. Sloan, 184 Ill. 583; 56 N. E. Rep. 952; Goods of Maddock, L. R. 3 P. & D. 169.)

Must sign at end of will. (Matter of Case, 4 Dem. 124; and see Matter of Conway, 124 N. Y. 455; 26 N. E. Rep. 1028; Will of Hewitt, 91 N. Y. 261.)

(b) **Must see testator sign or signature.**—Witness must either see the testator sign, or see the signature when or before he subscribes as witness. (Matter of Mackay, 110 N. Y. 611; 18 N. E. Rep. 433; Matter of McDougall, 87 Hun, 349; 34 N. Y. Supp. 302; Matter of Losee, 13 Misc. 298; 34 N. Y. Supp. 1120; Matter of Bernsee, 141 N. Y. 392; 36 N. E. Rep. 314; and see Matter of Abercrombie, 24 App. Div. 408; 48 N. Y. Supp. 414; Matter of De Haas, 9 App. Div. 568; 41 N. Y. Supp. 696; Ludwig's Estate, 81 N. W .Rep. 758; this volume, p. 409; Purdy's Will, 46 App. Div. 33; 61 N. Y. Supp. 430; aff'g 25 Misc. 458; 55 N. Y. Supp. 644.)

Does not depend on their recollection. (Gwillum v. Gwillum, 3 Sw. & T. 200; and see Goods of Huckvale, L. R. 1 P. & D. 375.)

(c) **Request to witness.**—Testator's request to witnesses may be express or implied. (Higgins v. Carlton, 28 Md. 117; Will of Meurer, 44 Wis. 392; Coffin v. Coffin, 23 N. Y. 9; Lane v. Lane, 95 id. 494; Hutchings v. Cochrane, 2 Bradf. 295; Inglesant v. Inglesant, L. R. 3 P. & D. 172.)

May be inferred from signs or gestures as well as words. (Rogers v. Diamond, 13 Ark. 476; and see Allen's Will, 25 Minn. 39.)

By testator handing pen to the witnesses. (Allison v. Allison, 46 Ill. 61.)

May be request by a third party in testator's presence. (Bundy v. Mc-Knight, 48 Ind. 502; Dyer v. Dyer, 87 id. 13; Cheatham v. Hatcher, 30 Gratt. 56; Harp v. Parr, 168 Ill. 460; 48 N. E. Rep. 113; Gilbert v. Knox, 52 N. Y. 125; Matter of Nelson, 141 id. 152; 36 N. E. Rep. 3; Matter of McGraw, 9 App. Div. 372; 41 N. Y. Supp. 481; Burney v. Allen, 125 N. C. 314; 34 S. E. Rep. 500; this volume, p. 281.)

But when testator is in a dying condition proof must be clear. (Heath v. Cole, 15 Hun, 100.)

(d) **Order of signing.**—Witnesses must subscribe their names as such after will is signed by testator. It makes no difference that each is part of the same transaction. (Brooks v. Woodson, 87 Ga. 379; 13 S. E. Rep. 712. And see note to this case, p. 381, where the cases are collected and conflict pointed out, where all sign on same occasion. And see Jackson v. Jackson, 39 N. Y. 153, 162; Sisters of Charity v. Kelly, 67 id. 413; Hindmarsh v. Charlton, 8 H. L. Cas. 160; Chase v. Kittredge, 93 Mass. 49.)

Order of signing not material where all done at same time. (O'Brien v. Galagher, 25 Conn. 229; Swift v. Wiley, 1 B. Mon. 117.)

Acknowledgment of execution by testator may be made to a witness after latter has signed. (Lyman v. Phillips, 3 Dem. 459, opinion reviews the cases; and see Herrick v. Snyder, 27 Misc. 462; 50 N. Y. Supp. 229.)

(e) **Presence of testator.**—Will is not signed by witnesses in presence of testator, when signed by them in another room no part of which was visible from any part of the room where the testator was, even though their signatures are subsequently shown to the testator. (Mendell v. Dunbar, 169 Mass. 74; 47 N. E. Rep. 402; and see Downie's Will, 42 Wis. 66; Chase v. Kittredge, 93 Mass. 49. The opinion contains an interesting and valuable review of the English and American cases.)

Nor is it in presence of testator where the witnesses sign in an adjoining room, with the door open, but where the testator could not see them, without getting out of bed. (Mandeville v. Parker, 31 N. J. Eq. 242. To this case is added a valuable note or collection of cases bearing upon signing in presence of testator.)

Otherwise when he could see them without materially changing his position. (Will of Meurer, 44 Wis. 392; and see Witt v. Gardiner, 158 Ill. 176; 41 N. E. Rep. 781; Lamb v. Girtman, 33 Ga. 289.)

Must be so circumstanced that he can see them if he chose to do so. (Ambre v. Weishaar, 74 Ill. 109; Hill v. Barge, 12 Ala. 687; Campbell v. McGuiggan, 34 Atl. Rep. 383 [no offi. rep.]; Maynard v. Vinton, 59 Mich. 149; 26 N. W. Rep. 401; Hopkins v. Wheeler, 45 Atl. Rep. 551 [R. I.]; Burney v. Allen, 125 N. C. 314; 34 S. E. Rep. 500; this volume, p. 281.)

But testator's ailment may so operate as to prevent the physical movement to enable him to see, and in that event will is not signed in his presence. (Maynard v. Vinton, *supra*. Compare Riggs v. Riggs, 135 Mass.

238, where the will was held to have been witnessed in testator's presence, where the witnesses signed in an adjoining room about nine feet from where testator was lying in bed, unable to move and able to look upward only.)

As dependent upon physical ability to change position so as to see. (Walker v. Walker, 67 Miss. 529; 7 So. Rep. 491.)

That testator actually saw the witnesses sign need not be shown if done in his immediate and conscious presence, so that he could have seen had he felt so disposed. (Allen's Will, 25 Minn. 39.)

To be in testator's presence the witnesses must sign within the uninterrupted range of the testator's vision. (Drury v. Connell, 177 Ill. 43; 52 N. E. Rep. 368.)

It is proper to instruct a jury that the subscribing witness must have attested the will in the "personal and actual" presence of the testator. (Greene v. Greene, 145 Ill. 266; 33 N. E. Rep. 941.)

If witnesses sign within hearing, knowledge, and understanding. and so near as not to be substantially away from him, they are considered to be in testator's presence. Cases reviewed and narrow construction of the word "presence" criticized. (Cook v. Winchester, 81 Mich. 581; 46 N. W. Rep. 106.)

The opinion in this case also considered the fact of a subsequent acknowledgment of their signatures by the witnesses to the testator as a circumstance of great weight. But this seems to be denied in Mendell v. Dunbar (169 Mass. 74; 47 N. E. Rep. 402); Hindmarsh v. Charlton (8 H. L. Cas. 160).

Presence of subscribing witnesses means a presence of which the testator is conscious. (Chappel v. Trent, 90 Va. 850; 19 S. E. Rep. 314.)

In presence of testator when he lay in bed with high footboard, beyond which in same room stood a bureau upon which the witnesses signed. (Ayres v. Ayres, 43 N. J. Eq. 570; 12 Atl. Rep. 621.)

(f) **Presence of other witnesses.**—Not necessary that a witness should see the testator sign the will, nor that he should subscribe in the presence of the other witnesses. (Simmons v. Leonard, 91 Tenn. 186; 18 S. W. Rep. 280.)

Not necessary that witnesses should sign in presence of each other. (Cravens v. Faulconer, 28 Mo. 19; Hoffman v. Hoffman, 26 Ala. 535; Flinn v. Owen, 58 Ill. 112; Will of Smith, 52 Wis. 543; 8 N. W. Rep. 616; 9 id. 665; Hoysradt v. Kingman, 22 N. Y. 372; Willes v. Mott, 36 id. 486; Gaylor's Appeal, 43 Conn. 82.)

Where statute requires attestation by witnesses in presence of the testator *and of each other*, if the witnesses are in same room and *might* have seen the attestation of one another, that is sufficient. (Blanchard v. Blanchard, 32 Vt. 62.)

(g) **Signing for another.**—Witnesses unable to write or with difficulty may request another subscribing witness to write his name as a witness for him. (Smythe v. Irick, 46 S. C. 299; *sub nom.* Re Crawford's Will, 24 S. E. Rep. 69; Lord v. Lord, 58 N. H. 7; Strong's Will, 2 Conolly, 574; 16 N. Y. Supp. 104.)

But see *contra,* where it is held that such signing is not of itself sufficient without the witness making a mark or touching or guiding the pen. (McFarland v. Buck, 94 Tenn. 538; 29 S. W. Rep. 899.)

(h) **By mark.**—Where statute requires that a witness shall *sign his name,* another name or wrong name inadvertently signed, is not sufficient even as a mark. (Re Walker, 110 Cal. 387; 42 Pac. Rep. 815. The opinion contains an interesting review of the cases on signing of wills.)

Witnesses signing by mark. (Re Walker, *supra;* Smythe v. Irick, 46 S. C. 312; Campbell v. Logan, 2 Bradf. 96; Meehan v. Rourke, id. 385; Morris v. Kniffin, 37 Barb. 336; Chase v. Kittredge, 93 Mass. 59; Davis v. Semmes, 51 Ark. 48; 9 S. W. Rep. 434; Gillis v. Gillis, 96 Ga. 5; 23 S. E. Rep. 107; Hindmarsh v. Charlton, 8 H. L. Cas. 160; and see Note " Signing by Mark," 3 Prob. Rep. Ann. 258.)

(i) **Some illustrative cases.**—When testator was deaf and dumb (Matter of Perego, 65 Hun, 478; 20 N. Y. Supp. 394.)

Witness may sign " servant to Mr. Sperling," without any name. (Goods of Sperling, 3 Sw. & T. 272.)

May sign testator's name by his express direction, and also his own name as one of the witnesses. (Ex parte Leonard, 39 S. C. 518; 18 S. E. Rep. 216; Herbert v. Berrier, 81 Ind. 1.)

The fact that witness to a will adds a superfluous certificate, for instance that of a justice of the peace in his official capacity, does not affect the validity of the signing as a witness. (Payne v. Payne, 54 Ark. 415; 16 S. W. Rep. 1; Murray v. Murphy, 39 Miss. 215.)

A defective subscription by a witness, cannot be made subsequently effective by correction of error in writing his name, his acknowledgment of it, or adding a date to it. (Hindmarsh v. Charlton, 8 H. L. Cas. 160.)

ADAMS *vs.* JONES.

[Supreme Court of Massachusetts, May 18, 1900; 57 N. E. Rep. 362.]

WILLS—INTERPRETATION—WORDS OF LIMITATION—CONVERSION.

1. Testator bequeathed one moiety of his estate, both real and personal, after payment of all just claims against his estate, to his " brothers and sisters and their heirs," subject to the life estate of the testator's wife. When the will was executed testator had brothers and sisters living, and nephews and nieces, the issue of deceased brothers and sisters. *Held,* that the words, "and their heirs," were words of limitation,

applying only to heirs of brothers and sisters living on testator's death, and hence that the nephews and nieces are not entitled to take under the will.

2. Where words have an ascertained meaning, and admit of a rational interpretation, and there is nothing in other portions of the will indicating that they were not used in their ordinary sense, such sense will not be departed from for the purpose of giving effect to what it may be guessed was the intention of the testator, though it would result in a more fair distribution of the estate.

3. Since Pub. St. ch. 142, § 9, provides that, in every sale of the real estate of a decedent by an executor or administrator, the proceeds remaining on the final settlement of the accounts shall be considered as real estate, and be disposed of as such, the unexpended balance of the proceeds of the sale of real estate of a testator sold to pay debts is to be treated as real estate, and should be paid over by the administrator to those entitled thereto.

REPORT from Supreme Judicial Court, Middlesex county; MARCUS P. KNOWLTON, Judge.

Petition by the executor of the will of Oliver Bacon, deceased, for instructions as to the disposition of a surplus of the proceeds of real estate sold to pay debts. Heard by single justice, and reported to full bench. Decree ordered.

John M. Raymond, for petitioner.

James W. Grimes, for defendant.

LORING, J.—Oliver Bacon died, leaving a will containing two bequests. The first was a bequest of " all my estate, both real and personal, wherever it may be situated, after all just claims against me or my estate are satisfied," to his wife for life, and " whatever remain at her decease shall be.divided into two equal parts to be inherited and divided, the one moiety by my brothers and sisters and their heirs, and the other moiety by my said wife's brother and sisters and their heirs." The will was made in 1858, on the day on which the testator died, and his widow died twenty-nine years later, in 1887. When the will was made he had four sisters and two brothers, and several nephews and nieces, the issue of two sisters and one brother who had previously died; and there were also issue of one brother who had disappeared about 1840,—that is, about eighteen years before the will was made, and has not since been heard from. For the purposes of this discussion, we will treat that brother as having been dead at that time. The children of these deceased brothers and sisters claim that the class to whom the remainder was given consisted of the brothers and sisters living at the date of the will, the day of the testator's death, and of the heirs then living of brothers and sisters who had previously died; and they rely on the case of *Huntress* v. *Place* (137 Mass. 409), in support of this contention. The bequest in *Huntress* v. *Place* was practically the same as the bequest in the case at bar, but the circumstances under which the will was made were different. In that case there was but one sister of the testator alive when he made his will, and it was held that, under those circumstances, the words, "and their heirs," were not words of limitation, but were words of purchase, used to describe the members of the class which were to take in remainder subject to the life estate in the testator's widow. This result was reached on the ground that some meaning had to be given to the use of the word " sisters " in the plural, in the place of " sister " in the singular, and, on the authority of *Gowling* v. *Thompson* (L. R. 11 Eq. 366, and note). The testator's bequest in *Gowling* v. *Thompson* was to " his 'brothers and sisters or their issue ' in equal shares as tenants in common, ' and to their respective heirs, executors, administrators, and assigns ' "; and it was held that the children of a deceased sister took under the words, " or their issue " ; that those words would be construed to be part of the description of the class, and not a substitutional gift, in case one of the class previously described died; that since the testator had but one sister, and he gave a bequest to his sisters or their issue, the word " sisters " must have been used in the plural in place of the singular to indicate the *stirps,* and the words " or their issue " were a part of the description of the class; and for that reason the case did not come within *Christopherson* v. *Naylor* (1 Mer. 320), which has been much relied upon by counsel for the surviving brothers and sisters in this case. But the question which arose in *Huntress* v. *Place,* and which arises in this case, is not the question which arose in *Christopherson* v. *Naylor* and *Gowling* v. *Thompson.* In those cases, the question was whether the words, which were confessedly words of purchase, constituted a substitutional gift, or were words enlarging the description of the class. In this case, as in *Huntress* v. *Place,* the question is whether the words are words of purchase or words of limitation. We are of opinion that in the case at bar the words, " and their heirs," are words of limitation, and that the gift cannot be construed to be a gift to the brothers and sisters of the testator then living, and to the heirs of brothers and sisters who had previously died. The gift is a gift, in the first place, to " my brothers and sisters." The claimants were not brothers and sisters of the testator, but nephews and nieces, and therefore are not within the class described by those words. In the second place, the rest of the gift is contained in the words " and their heirs." Grammatically, this means, " and the heirs of the testator's brothers and sisters already mentioned."

But apart from the conclusion to be reached by a strict grammatical construction of the words used, it is settled in this commonwealth that, in the case of a gift to A. B. and his heirs, the words, " and his heirs," are words of limitation, and not of purchase, even though the gift is a gift of personal property alone; that such a gift of personal property is a gift to A. B. absolutely, and is not a gift to A. B. if living, and to his heirs if he is dead. (*Wood* v. *Seaver,* 158 Mass. 411; 33 N. E. 587. See, also *Bryson* v. *Holbrook,* 159 Mass. 281; 34 N. E. 270; *Horton* v. *Earle,* 162 Mass. 448; 38 N. E. 1135.)

No reasonable distinction can be made between the construction of the words, " and his heirs," added to a gift of personalty to a person by name, and the construction of those words when added to a gift to a class such as brothers and sisters. If, in the first of these two cases, the words are not construed to have been inserted to prevent the legacy lapsing in case the person named dies after the will is made, in the second place they cannot be construed to have been introduced to include the heirs of brothers and sisters who had previously died. Furthermore, it would be inconsistent with the rule of construction adopted in *Wood* v. *Seaver* (158 Mass. 411; 33 N. E. 587), to hold that the words, " and his heirs," in the case at bar are words of purchase. In *Wood* v. *Seaver,* the subject of the gift was personal property and personal property only. In such a case " and his heirs " are not properly words of limitation at all. They add nothing to the gift which is contained in the words, " to A. B." In spite of that, they were held in *Wood* v. *Seaver* to be words of limitation. But in the case at bar the words " to my brothers and sisters and their heirs," operated on real estate alone, though the gift in terms applied to " both real estate and personal " estate. In such a case, the adoption of the words, " and their heirs," is most proper to indicate that the persons described were to take a fee, though it is now provided by statute that the insertion of those words is not indispensable. (Pub. St. 127, § 24.) It is to be noted that the words used by the testator are the words, " and their heirs." Had the words been, " or their heirs," and the only property been personal property, there would have been more ground for the contention of these defendants. (See *In re Potter's Trust*, 4 Kay & J. 188.)

Counsel for these defendants have urged upon us very strenuously the opinion of Sir GEORGE JESSEL, M. R., in *Re Smith's Trusts* (5 Ch. Div. 497, 498, and note), in which he said: " The question is whether I am to attribute to this testatrix the capricious intention that if a brother died before her will his children should not take, but if a brother died after her will his children should take." That was perhaps a fair question to be considered in construing the words used in that case, which, taken in connection with other provisions of the will, were susceptible of two meanings. But when words have an ascertained meaning, and admit of a rational interpretation, and there is nothing in other portions of the will indicating that they were not used in their ordinary sense, a court cannot depart from that ordinary sense for the purpose of giving effect to what it may be guessed was the intention of the testator, because it would result in a fair distribution of the estate. If, in such a case, the testator did in fact intend to make an equal distribution he has failed to express that intention in using the words he did use, and the power of the court goes no further than to ascertain the true meaning of the words used by him as he used them. The only case in support of the claimant's contention which has come to our attention is that of ¯*Brothers* v. *Cartwright* (53 N. C. 113) ; but no reasons are given in the opinion in that case for adopting that conclusion. *Bond's Appeal* (31 Conn. 183), does not support the contention of these defendants. It was held that the heirs of deceased children were included in the gift to " my children and their heirs " in that case, because of the addition of the words, " respectively to be divided in equal shares between them."

The question whether William Bacon, who disappeared about 1840, or about eighteen years before the death of the testator, is to be treated as alive at the death of the testator or not, is not raised in this bill, though it has been discussed in one of the briefs, and we express no opinion upon that point.

We are of opinion that the administrator *de bonis non* with the will annexed is the person to make the distribution of the $1,631.75, with any interest which may have accrued thereon in his hands, being " the unexpended balance of the proceeds of the sale of real estate of said Oliver Bacon sold to pay debts, with interest thereon." That fund is, by virtue of Pub. St. ch. 142, § 9, to be treated as real estate, and should be paid over by the administrator to those entitled thereto. We are of opinion that if William Bacon should be treated as dead when the will was made, the fee in an undivided sixth part of one moiety of the residue of the testator's estate (which estate appears to have been real estate only), vested on the death of the testator in each of the testator's two brothers and four sisters who survived him, subject to the widow's rights therein during her life.

The conclusion to which we have come disposes of the other questions which were started in the bill. A decree must be entered by a single justice in accordance with this opinion.

So ordered.

McCarn *vs.* Rundall *et al.*

[Supreme Court of Iowa, May 16, 1900; 82 N. W. Rep. 924.]

Will—Revocation—Intention—Witnesses—Proof of
CONTENTS.

1. A general finding that a will, objected to on the grounds of mental incapacity, undue influence, and fraud and duress, was not a valid will,
   does not show that there was lack of mental capacity, so as to invalidate
   revocation of a prior will, destroyed on the same day that the second
   was executed.
2. Intention to revoke a will is shown by testimony of witness that testatrix
   called for it, and wanted it destroyed and done away with, and that he
   tore it up by her direction.
3. Code, § 3274, requiring two witnesses to subscribe a will, is not satisfied
   by one witness subscribing it and others being present.
4. That a paper offered as a copy of a destroyed will is such is not satisfactorily proved by witness saying, when it was read over to him on the
   trial, " That is right, as near as I can recollect."

APPEAL from District Court, Jones county; H. M. REMLEY,
Judge.

This is an action in equity to probate a destroyed will. There
was a trial to the court, and the will was admitted to probate. The
defendants appeal.

Reversed.

Jamison & Smyth, for appellants.

D. McCarn, for appellee.

SHERWIN, J.—Ella Foos departed this life September 14, 1897.
On or about the 17th day of June, 1897, she executed an instrument in writing purporting to be her will. On the 31st day of
July, 1897, this instrument was destroyed by her direction, and the
fragments thereof burned in her presence. On the same day,
and as a part of the same transaction, a new will was executed by
her. This last will was offered for probate after her death, and

objections were made thereto on the grounds of mental incapacity, undue influence, and fraud and duress. Upon the issue thus made there was a trial to a jury, which resulted in the general finding that the instrument offered was not the valid will of Ella Foos, and its probate was denied. After the termination of that trial, this action was brought in equity, setting up the facts as above stated, and a purported copy of the instrument of June 17, 1897, and praying that the same be admitted to probate as the last will and testament of Ella Foos. The defendants are the heirs of Ella Foos, and objected to the probate of the instrument of June 17th for the reasons following: First, because the will under which plaintiff claims was revoked, as provided by law; and, second, because the setting aside of the second will did not operate to revive the destroyed will. The plaintiff herein was named as a legatee in both wills. Section 3276 of the Code provides that " wills can only be revoked, in whole or in part, by being canceled or destroyed by the act or direction of the testator, with the intention of so revoking them." The plaintiff admits the destruction of the instrument executed June 17, 1897, but contends that said destruction did not work a revocation thereof, because it does not appear that such was the intention of the testator, and for the further reason that, the jury having found the second will invalid, the testator did not have the mental capacity to revoke the former will. The fallacy of this position is apparent for two reasons: First, because the jury did not indicate in its verdict that it was based upon the lack of mental capacity in the testator, and there is no evidence before us tending even in the remotest degree to sustain such conclusion; and, second, because the only witness who testified upon the trial of this cause was called by the plaintiff, and upon his cross-examination testified that in his opinion Ella Foos was of sound mind when she directed him to destroy the first will, " and intelligently and deliberately directed him to destroy and do away with it." The witness says: " She called for the June will, and wanted it destroyed and done away with; and I tore it up by her directions, and the pieces were put in the stove and burned." This evidence clearly and unmistakably proves the intention of the testator to revoke the first will entirely, and that she had the mental capacity so to do. There is nothing in the record to indicate that its revocation was dependent upon the validity of the subsequent will, and, the revocation being complete under the statute, the will cannot be revived by parol. (*Carey v. Baughn*, 36 Iowa, 540; 29 Am. & Eng. Enc. Law, 333; *Stewart v. Mulholland*, 88 Ky. 38; 10 S. W. 125; 21 Am. St. Rep. 320.) There is, if possible, a still stronger reason why the will of June 17, 1897, should not have been admitted to probate. The statute requires that two witnesses must subscribe the will to make it valid. (Code, § 3274; *In re Boyeus' Will*, 23 Iowa, 354.) The evidence before us only shows that one witness signed the will. It is true the testimony shows that other witnesses were present, but this is not sufficient. It must be proven that the will was executed with the formality required by the statute. The testamentary right to dispose of property is regulated by the statute, which requires the will to be witnessed in a certain way, and we are not at liberty to presume that it was signed by others who were present when it was executed. And, as said in *Re Walker's Estate* (110 Cal. 387; 42 Pac. 815; 52 Am. St. Rep. 104): "It is not for the courts to say that these requirements, or any of them, are mere formalities, which may be waived without impairing the status of the instrument. It is not for courts to say that a mode of execution or authentication other than that prescribed by law subserves the same purpose, and is equally efficient to validate the instrument." Nor is the evidence satisfactory that the paper offered as a copy of the destroyed will is such. The only witness heard on that subject did not claim that he had ever read the will of June, 1897. He did not read the purported copy. When it was read over to him on the trial he said, "That is right, as near as I can recollect." The proof of the contents of a destroyed will ought to be of the clearest and most satisfactory character. (2 Greenl. Ev. [15th ed.] 668; *Newell v. Homer*, 120 Mass. 277; *Dudley v. Wardner's Ex'rs*, 41 Vt. 59; *In re Johnson's Will*, 40 Conn. 587.) This burden rested upon the plaintiff. (*Newell v. Homer, supra.*) She has failed to sustain it. (See *Clark v. Turner* [Neb.], 69 N. W. 843.) Plaintiff's authorities on the question of revocation under undue influence are not in point, because there is no evidence upon which to base them. Even if it were proven that the subsequent will was the product of undue influence, it would not follow as a natural sequence that such influence inhered also in the revocation of the former will. The will of June 17, 1897, should nòt have been probated, and the judgment of the District Court is reversed.

ELLIS *vs.* SOPER.

[Supreme Court of Iowa, May 24, 1900; 82 N. W. Rep. 1024.]

PLEADING—REPLY—GUARDIAN AND WARD—ACCOUNTING—RE-
LEASE—DISCHARGE—CONCLUSIVENESS—PARENT AND CHILD—
SUPPORT.

1. Allegations setting up a new cause of action or matters already in issue are not permissible in a reply.

2. A ward is not concluded by a release acknowledging final and satisfactory settlement with the guardian, where it is given without any accounting or settlement in fact on the mistaken assurance of the guardian that nothing is due, though no fraud or undue influence is practiced in obtaining it.

3. An order discharging a guardian pursuant to a release acknowledging final settlement, given without any settlement in fact on the mistaken assurance of the guardian that nothing was due, is not an adjudication on an accounting, and hence is not a bar to an action by the ward for an accounting.

4. A guardian's final account should cover the entire period of guardianship, where the intermediate reports filed are incomplete.

5. In the absence of an order allowing a widow who is guardian of her children's estate to use the same for their support, a court of equity, on final accounting, will allow her credit for past support, where it is shown that her own estate was insufficient to support them properly.

6. A widow having an estate worth $11,500 and an annual income of $1,100 for the support of herself and children, for whom she is guardian, should be allowed only the income of their estate towards their support and education when the estate of each is worth only $1,800, since she is primarily liable for their support during minority.

APPEAL from District Court, Jones county; WILLIAM G. THOMPSON, Judge.

Plaintiff brings this action in equity against the defendant, formerly her guardian, to set aside an order in probate approving the final report of said guardian, and discharging her, and for an accounting and judgment in the sum of $1,800. Plaintiff alleges as grounds for such relief that there is $1,800 due to her; that her receipt to and release of said guardian upon which said order was based was obtained from plaintiff by fraud, deceit and undue influence. The defendant answered, in effect, denying that there is anything due to plaintiff, alleging a complete settlement with plaintiff, after she became of age by marriage; that said release was given upon such settlement, and denying said allegations of fraud. The defendant sets up a counterclaim and asks judgment thereon, but the record does not support this demand, and, as the lower court found against her thereon, and she has not appealed, the counterclaim requires no further notice. The plaintiff, in reply, alleged that her guardian failed to protect her interest in the division of the land; that she never obtained any order of the court authorizing her to lease plaintiff's land; that she allowed the land to run down, and converted the rents thereof to her own use. These allegations were stricken out on motion as setting up a new cause of action for negligence or malfeasance. A further allegation was made in the reply of matters already in issue, which will be hereafter considered. In the reply the plaintiff, for want of knowledge or information, denied defendant's allegation as to the amount of taxes paid. Upon these issues decree was rendered dismissing the plaintiff's petition, from which she appeals.

Reversed.

C. M. Brown and *J. W. Doxsee,* for appellant.

E. B. Soper and *Ellison, Ercanbrack & Lawrence,* for appellee.

GIVEN, J.—1. There was no error in sustaining the defendant's motion to strike from the reply. The first paragraph stricken presents a new cause of action, and this is not permissible in a reply. The second presents issues already joined, issues involved in the accounting asked, and therefore was properly stricken.

2. The facts necessary to be noticed are, in substance, these: George Soper died intestate on the 28th day of October, 1886, leaving the defendant, his widow, and their thirteen children, of

whom the plaintiff is one, surviving him. Five of said children (including the plaintiff) were then minors, plaintiff being seven years old, and for these five children the defendant was appointed guardian. On distribution of the personal estate, there was paid to the defendant, as guardian of .the plaintiff, $469.88, and on partition of the real estate there was set off to the plaintiff fifty-two acres of land valued at $1,315. There was set off to the defendant as widow a farm valued at $7,233, and personal property, including her temporary allowance and exempt property, of the value of $4,430.98. The plaintiff and said other minor children continued to reside with and to be supported by their mother from the time of their father's death until they became of age by marriage or lapse of time. Plaintiff married one John W. Ellis in 1897, when nearly seventeen years of age. The defendant, with her children, resided on the farm set apart to her until a few years prior to 1897, when she removed to town for the purpose of securing better school facilities for the children. The plaintiff was kept in school about nine months of each year, and received instruction in music, the expenses of which the defendant paid. On the 31st day of August, 1889, the defendant filed a report charging herself with rent of plaintiff's land, and interest thereon, taking credit for the taxes of 1887-88, a small amount in attorney's fees, and showing a balance due the plaintiff at that time of $691.27. On the 25th day of March, 1897, after the marriage of the plaintiff, the defendant filed a final report showing that plaintiff had become of age by marriage on the 19th day of February, 1897, and stating that since then defendant had a final and complete settlement with her, as shown by the following voucher: " I, the undersigned, Dessie D. Ellis, née Soper, hereby acknowledge that I became of lawful age on the 28th day of January, 1897, by marriage with Jno. W. Ellis, and I was seventeen years of age on February 19th, 1897, and that I examined the report of my guardian, Margery A. Soper, filed in this court, as her first report, and on this 23d day of March, 1897, after being made acquainted with the business pertaining to my guardian's management during my minority, have made a full, final, and satisfactory settlement with my said guardian. And I also waive notice on me of the hearing of the final report, and I ask that the same be approved, and she be discharged and released from her bonds, so far as I am concerned. Dated March 23d, 1897. Dessie D. Soper Ellis." No statement of account accompanied this report, but by virtue of said release the defendant was discharged as guardian.

3. We first inquire whether the plaintiff should be concluded by said receipt and release of March 23, 1897. Appellant cites many authorities to show that in receiving that release the defendant is held to the exercise of the utmost good faith. This rule is undisputed, and, in view of the facts of this case, should be applied in all its force. We are satisfied that in giving and receiving that release both parties acted upon the assumption that the plaintiff's estate had been consumed in her support, and that no fraud was intended, nor deceit or undue influence practiced, by the defendant in obtaining that voucher. If it be true that the plaintiff had not received all that was due to her, but acted on the mistaken assurances of her mother that she had been fully paid when she gave that release, then the release operated as a fraud upon her, and she is entitled to an accounting. The defendant never did render a full account of this guardianship, and, while there was some talk of settlement, there was in fact no accounting to or settlement with the plaintiff when this release was taken. It was taken upon a mere guess as to the true state of the account, and therefore we conclude that the plaintiff is entitled in equity to an accounting. It is insisted by defendant that the order discharging her was an adjudication, and therefore she cannot be held to an accounting. It was not an adjudication upon an accounting, but upon the release alone, and, if that release is fraudulent, the order does not prevent the court of equity from ascertaining the true state of the account between these parties. Plaintiff insists that in this accounting the balance of $691.27, as shown by the first order, should be taken as the basis of a further accounting, while defendant now presents her account covering the entire period of the guardianship. That first report was evidently incomplete. It was never approved nor disapproved. Therefore we conclude that an accounting should now be made covering the entire period. The defendant, in her answer, states the account as follows: " To maintenance of plaintiff by defendant for ten years, at $1.50 per week, $780.00; to clothing, music lessons, school books, etc., for the years 1887,

1888, and 1889, at $35 per year, $105; to taxes paid on the real property belonging to plaintiff for the years 1887 to '96, inclusive, $635.76; to cash expended for or paid over to the plaintiff at her request, as per Exhibit B hereof, $22.89,—making the total amount of the charges of this defendant against the plaintiff the sum of $1,682.69. That against the same the plaintiff should be credited with the following: By rental of real property for ten years at the rate of $85.00 per year, $850.00; by cash from administrator of estate of George Soper as per inventory, $469.88,—making the total amount for which this plaintiff should be credited, $1,319.88." The credit of $22.89 is for cash and clothing given to the plaintiff after she became of age by marriage, and is not proper to be considered in this accounting.

4. There is no dispute but that defendant furnished to plaintiff and paid for all items charged in her account, and that the amounts charged are reasonable. The plaintiff assigns two reasons why defendant should not be credited therewith, namely: First, that, being the mother of the plaintiff, the defendant was legally bound to support her during minority, and that without an order of court so authorizing she will not be permitted to encroach upon the estate of the ward for her support. Schouler, in his work on Domestic Relations (5th ed.; A. D. 1895), in the chapter treating of duties of parents, says: " Sec. 239. The mother, after the death of the father, remains the head of the family. * * * And since the tendency of the day is to give the mother a more equal share in the parental rights, it follows that she should assume more of the parental burdens. It is nevertheless clear that the courts show special favor to the mother, as they should; and, if a child has property and means of its own, they will rather, in any case, charge the expenses of its education and maintenance upon such property than force her to contribute." A court of chancery will not readily make the support and education of infant children a charge upon the property of their widowed mother while their own means are ample. " Sec. 240. Courts of chancery, following the well-known principle, largely restrict a child's maintenance to the income of his property; but where the property is small, and the income insufficient for his support, the court will sometimes allow the capital to be broken, though rarely for the purpose of the child's past maintenance, when his future

education and support will be left thereby unprovided for." In 17 Am. & Eng. Enc. Law, under the title " Parent and Child," on page 358, we find in regard to the duty of parents, as regards the maintenance of their children, the following: " The principle is clearly established that a father must maintain and educate his minor children if he has the ability, and he has at common law no right to reimbursement for any expenditures for this purpose, and no allowance can be made to him out of the property of the children while his own means are sufficient; but when the father is not of sufficient ability to support them the court will order so much of their income to be applied to that purpose as is necessary. The child's fortune and the circumstances of the father will be considered in deciding what, if any, allowance should be made. The welfare of the child requires that he should be educated and maintained in accordance with the social position which his means will enable him to enjoy, and the whole or any part of the expense thereof will be charged upon his estate, according as the circumstances of the father require. A parent should properly, before applying his child's income to its support, procure the sanction of the court, but the expense of past maintenance may be allowed on proper cause shown. The father, even if not needy, may maintain the child from any fund vested in him for that purpose. Although modern tendency is to hold that the mother is bound to support her child after the death of the father, yet the courts show special favor to the mother, and, if the child has property, they will charge the expense of its education and maintenance on said property, rather than force her to contribute,"— citing cases. " The court, in allowing maintenance, will generally restrict it to the income from the child's property; but where the property is small, and the income is not sufficient for his support, the capital may be broken into, although rarely to allow for past maintenance, when his future support will be thereby rendered doubtful,"—citing cases. *In re Besondy* (32 Minn. 385; 20 N. W. 366), in delivering the opinion, the court says: " The law shows special favor to the mother, and her application for past maintenance will be granted in cases where that of the father would not be listened to. This, we apprehend, grows out of her naturally dependent position, and of the consequent reluctance of the courts to encroach upon her estate. We do not, however,

undertake to say that her affirmative application for past maintenance will in all cases be granted when the child has property of
his own, though his support was not intended to be a gratuity.
The circumstances of the case might be such as to render it altogether inequitable. * * * The courts are not, ordinarily,
careful to require of a mother who remains unmarried, as in the
case of a father, that a special case be made showing the inadequacy of her own means, and the necessity of an allowance for
that reason." (See, also, *Pierce* v. *Pierce*, 64 Wis. 73; 24 N. W.
498; *Voessing* v. *Voessing*, 4 Redf. Sur. 360; *Perkins* v. *Westcoat*
[Colo. App.], 33 Pac. 139; *Melanefy* v. *O'Driscoll*, 164 Mass.
422; 41 N. E. 654; Herrick & D. Prob. Law [2d ed.], 618; *Welch*
v. *Burris*, 29 Iowa, 186; *Minor Heirs of Bradford* v. *Bodfish*, 39
id. 681; *Gerdes* v. *Weiser*, 54 id. 591; 7 N. W. 42.) There
can be no doubt from these authorities that upon a proper showing
the defendant might have had an order of court allowing her to
use the principal of the plaintiff's estate for her support. That,
in the absence of such an order, a court of equity may, upon an accounting and proper showing, allow for past support, is well established by the authorities already cited. Parents are alike liable
for the support of their minor children, and the authorities we
have cited only apply when there is question as to the ability of
either to furnish support. The favor shown to the mother is not
because she is less liable than the father, but for the reason that
usually she is less able to earn the support.

5. We have cited the authorities most favorable to the defendant that have come to our notice, and it is clear from them that
the defendant was primarily bound for the support of the plaintiff,
and that she would not be allowed to encroach upon plaintiff's
estate, especially the principal thereof, unless her own circumstances were such as to render her unable to furnish the support.
We have seen that the plaintiff's estate consisted of the $469.88
derived from the distribution of the personal property and fifty-
two acres of farm land, and the defendant's of the farm, valued at
$7,233, and personal property valued at $4,430.98. This was
quite a competency to the defendant, and, well managed, should
have brought her an income of about $1,100 a year,—quite a sum
with which to support the family,—yet all of it appears to have
been consumed. Courts are more ready to allow the income to

be used for support than the principal.   We think, in view of the number of minor children, the manner in which they were supported and educated, and the amount of defendant's income, that she should be allowed the income of the plaintiff's estate towards her support and education.   Assuming, as we may, that the income of the other four children was the same as the plaintiff's, this gave the defendant an income of about $1,600 a year for the support of herself and family.   Surely, the defendant, with this income, and an estate worth over $11,500, should not be allowed to charge the principal of the plaintiff's estate for her support and education.   We conclude that the plaintiff should have judgment against the defendant for the $469.88 cash received from the administratrix, with six per cent. per annum interest thereon from the 19th day of February, 1897, the date at which plaintiff became of age by marriage, and entitled to the money.   The judgment of the District Court is reversed, and the case remanded for judgment in harmony with this opinion.

Reversed.

DEEMER, J.—I agree to the conclusion, but not to some of the statements of law announced in the opinion.

NOTE.—TRANSACTIONS BETWEEN GUARDIAN AND WARD.

(a) General principles.
(b) Burden of proof.
(c) Settlement may be binding.
(d) Purchase by guardian.
(e) *Laches*, acquiescence, ratification.
(f) Illustrative cases.

(a) **General principles.**—Courts of equity look with a jealous and scrutinizing eye upon settlements made between a guardian and his ward, especially where the latter has just arrived at full age. Where there has been no accounting, that fact alone is sufficient to cast suspicion upon a settlement, which will not be sanctioned until it is first shown to be fair and just by the guardian. (Briers v. Hackney, 6 Ga. 422; Smith v. Davis, 49 Md. 489; Hawkins' Appeal, 32 Pa. St. 263; Roth's Estate, 150 id. 261; 24 Atl. Rep. 685; Gaylord v. Goodell, 173 Mass. 140; 53 N. E. Rep. 275; and see Note, this vol. p. 585, "Transactions Between Trustee and *Cestui que Trust;* 1 Perry on Trusts, § 200 [ed. 1899].)

Ward's receipt in full or release is not conclusive, and settlement will be re-opened on his application. (Say v. Barnes, 4 Serg. & R. 112; Wade v. Lobdell, 58 Mass. 510; Stark v. Gamble, 43 N. H. 465, 467; Harris v. Carstaphen, 69 N. C. 419; Line v. Lawder, 122 Ind. 548; 23 N. E. Rep. 758; Voltz v. Voltz, 75 Ala. 555; Beedle v. Small, 62 Ind. 27; Bennett v. Hanifin, 87 Ill. 31; McConkey v. Cockey, 69 Md. 286; 14 Atl. Rep. 465; Powell v. Powell, 52 Mich. 432; 18 N. W. Rep. 203.)

But may be conclusive on an accounting in the Probate Court, that court having no jurisdiction to set aside or try validity of settlements. (Downing v. Smith, 4 Redf. 310; and see Hatch v. Hatch, 9 Ves. 292, and *note.*)

From the confidential relation between a guardian and his ward it will be presumed that the ward acts under the influence of the guardian, and all transactions and dealings between them, prejudicially affecting the interests of the ward will be held to be constructively fraudulent. This presumption continues even after the guardianship has ended, when the matters between the guardian and ward have not yet been fully settled; and transactions between them, during the presumed influence which are injurious to the ward, will be set aside, unless shown to have been the deliberate act of the ward, after full knowledge of his rights. In all such cases the burden rests upon the guardian to prove the circumstances of knowledge and full consent on the part of the ward, good faith and absence of influence, which alone can overcome this presumption. (Gillett v. Wiley, 126 Ill. 310; 18 N. E. Rep. 287; Carter v. Tice, 120 Ill. 277; 11 N. E. Rep. 529; Harris v. Carstaphen, 69 N. C. 416; Meek v. Perry, 36 Miss. 190; Mulholland's Estate, 154 Pa. St. 491; 26 Atl. Rep. 612; Voltz v. Voltz, 75 Ala. 555; Berkmeyer v. Kelleman, 32 Ohio St. 240; McConkey v. Cockey, *supra;* Webb v. Branner, 59 Kans. 190; 52 Pac. Rep. 429; Gale v. Wells, 12 Barb. 84, 97; Wood v. Downes, 18 Ves. 120.)

In Hylton v. Hylton (2 Ves. Sr. 547), Lord HARDWICKE says: "Where a man acts as guardian, or trustee in nature of a guardian for an infant, the court is extremely watchful to prevent that person's taking any advantage, immediately upon the ward's coming of age, and at the time of settling accounts or delivering up the trust, because an undue advantage may be taken. It would give an opportunity either by flattery or force, by good usage unfairly meant, or by bad usage imposed, to take such an advantage.

(b) **Burden of proof.**—Burden of proof rests upon the wife of a guardian to whom the ward a few days after attaining her majority conveyed real estate for an inadequate compensation to show good faith, absence of influence, knowledge of ward, etc. (McFarland v. Larkin, 155 Ill. 84; 39 N. E. Rep. 609.)

Practice in equity was to allow the ward a year's time to investigate the guardian's accounts; on the ground that when he first comes of age, he is still too much under the guardian's influence to protect himself. (Douglass v. Low, 36 Hun, 499.)

Four years and more acquiescence by ward in final settlement and receipts in full, shifts the burden of proof from the guardian to the ward, who must show fraud or other good and lawful reason in avoiding same, (Steadhim v. Sims, 68 Ga. 741.)

So where a settlement is made three years after ward attains majority, the undue influence is not then presumed to exist and burden rests on the ward or his legal representatives to impeach the settlement. (Kittredge v. Betton, 14 N. H. 401.)

·A guardian who makes an informal settlement with and obtains a release from his ward, assumes the burden of making it clearly appear that he fully and fairly disclosed the condition of the ward's estate at the time of the settlement,. and that he paid over the amount due either in money or in such securities as had been taken in pursuance of the order of the court, or in the exercise of such diligence and prudence as men display in the conduct of their own affairs. (Line v. Lawder, 122 Ind. 548; 23 N. E. Rep. 758.)

Where ward has for several years been emancipated from the influence and control of his former guardian, and where owing to lapse of time, the vouchers and papers furnishing the elements that enter into the settlement have been lost or mislaid, and where the settlement appears to have been carefully made, and understood by the ward, and no objection was made thereto, but the guardian was voluntarily released by the ward, it would be inequitable to require the guardian to recast the account and show that the settlement was in all respects free from error. (Smith v. Davis, 49 Md. 472.)

(c) **Settlement may be binding.**—If ward of full age acts understandingly, with full knowledge of all the facts, in making settlement with guardian, and releases him he will be concluded thereby, there being no bad faith or fraud. (Adams v. Reviere, 59 Ga. 793; Ela v. Ela, 84 Me. 423; 24 Atl. Rep. 893; Lewis v. Browning, 111 Pa. St. 493; 4 Atl. Rep. 842; Davis v. Hagler, 40 Kans. 187; 19 Pac. Rep. 628; Fielder v. Harbison, 93 Ky. 482; 20 S. W. Rep. 508; Kittredge v. Betton, 14 N. H. 401; Alexander's Estate, 156 Pa. St. 368; 27 Atl. Rep. 18; Kirby v. Taylor, 6 Johns. Ch. 242.)

Ward must have acted with deliberation and with full knowledge of all material facts. (Gillett v. Wiley, 126 Ill. 310; 19 N. E. Rep. 287; Sullivan v. Blackwell, 28 Miss. 737.) And without influence springing out of the relation. (Ferguson v. Lowery, 54 Ala. 510.)

Such a settlement is binding upon personal representatives of the ward after her decease. (Hawkin's Appeal, 32 Pa. St. 263.)

And especially is such a settlement binding where the estate is small, consisting of only a few hundred dollars, and the guardian is dead. (Roth's Estate, 150 Pa. St. 261; 24 Atl. Rep. 685.)

The presumption or fact of influence is not alone a fatal objection. (McClellan v. Kennedy, 8 Md. 230.)

A ward may settle with guardian without an accounting by latter in Probate Court. (Davenport v. Olmstead, 43 Conn. 67.)

Release held binding where executed by a female ward after her marriage, three years after her arrival at maturity, on solicitation of her husband, and without any fraud on part of the guardian or influence by him. (Satterfield v. John, 53 Ala. 127.)

But see where a married ward was *held* not bound by a settlement which her husband negotiated, the guardian having without their knowledge taken credit for depreciated Confederate money. (State v. Fenner, 73 N. C. 566.)

In Hatch v. Hatch (9 Ves. 298), Lord Chancellor ELDON said in a similar case " an unrighteous transaction cannot be made holy by the circumstance of coverture."

Where after settlement and release by ward, he joins with the guardian in obtaining a decree discharging the guardian and his sureties, such decree cannot afterwards be vacated without proof of some specific act of fraud and of injury occasioned by it. (Marr's Appeal, 78 Pa. St. 66; and see State v. Parsons, 147 Ind. 579; 47 N. E. Rep. 17.)

(d) **Purchase by guardian.**—Purchase by guardian not void, but voidable; where instead of repudiating it the ward waits until eighteen years after he became of age, during which time the title had passed into hands of innocent parties, it was *held* that he had waived the objection and affirmed the sale. (Bostwick v. Atkins, 3 N. Y. 53; Gallatin v. Cunningham, 8 Cow. 361.)

But see as to effect of a specific statute forbidding such purchase and declaring void. (O'Donoghue v. Boies, 159 N. Y. 101; 53 N. E. Rep. 537; and see Note "Transactions Between Trustee and *Cestui que Trust*," this vol. p. 585; Note "Purchase by Executor or Administrator," 4 Prob. Rep. Ann. 654.)

(e) **Laches, acquiescence, ratification.**—Six years' *laches* held fatal. (Kelly v. McQuinn, 42 W. Va. 774; 26 S. E. Rep. 517.)

Four years' *laches held* fatal to right of recovery against a surety. (Aaron v. Mendel, 78 Ky. 427.)

Ratification by settlement and acceptance of the proceeds of sale made by guardian. (Seward v. Didier, 16 Neb. 59; 20 N. W. Rep. 12.)

Five years *held* an unreasonable delay in objecting to settlement. (Hardin v. Taylor, 78 Ky. 594.)

Seven years' acquiescence or failure to object to settlement and release binds the ward, in absence of fraud. (Ela v. Ela, 84 Me. 423; 24 Atl. Rep. 893.)

Ratification by ward must be with knowledge of all the facts, and of their legal bearing upon his rights. (Long v. Long, 142 N. Y. 547; 37 N. E. Rep. 486.)

When bill was filed nearly ten years after settlement and after death of guardian, dismissed on ground of *laches*. (Jackson v. Harris, 66 Ala. 565.)

No *laches* where bill filed by ward two years after settlement and release where filed promptly to set same aside on discovering the facts. (McConkey v. Cockey, 69 Md. 286; 14 Atl. Rep. 465.)

Where there is no fraud in a settlement ward is bound thereby, both upon principle of acquiescence in lapse of time and by a statute of limitations. (Chorpenning's Appeal, 32 Pa. St. 315; and see as to limitation, Seward v. Didier, *supra.*)

Time as bearing on *laches* or acquiescence does not run against ward when continuing to live with guardian and under his influence and control. (Carter v. Tice, 120 Ill. 277; 11 N. E. Rep. 529.)

Presumption of knowledge of law does not apply to a ward; his ignorance of the legal effect of a settlement and conveyance is a complete answer to a guardian's claim of acquiescence and *laches* of five years in delay before seeking to set aside settlement and release. (Voltz v. Voltz, 75 Ala. 555.)

So long as a ward does not make a binding agreement for extension of time for guardian to account, and does not preclude himself in any way from instituting the proper proceedings against the guardian, mere delay will not affect the obligation of sureties on the guardian's bond, providing the right to proceed is not barred by the statute of limitations. (Douglass v. Ferris, 138 N. Y. 192, 206; 33 N. E. Rep. 1041; and see Note " *Laches*," this vol. p. 307.)

(f) **Illustrative cases.**—Ward is bound by records filed in Probate Court; concealment cannot be predicated on facts therein disclosed. (Robert v. Morrin, 27 Mich. 306.)

Ward while thus bound is not limited to a remedy by appeal, but may maintain a direct proceeding in proper time to set same aside. (Doan v. Dow, 8 Ind. App. 324; 35 N. E. Rep. 709.)

Guardian may purchase his ward's real estate when sold by sheriff under a judgment against the personal representative of the ward's ancestor. (Chorpenning's Appeal, 32 Pa. St. 315.)

Where influence by guardian continues after majority of the ward, conveyance by latter of real estate to former set aside. (Tucke v. Bucholz, 43 Iowa, 415.)

A guardian is never allowed to make any money out of his ward; if he does it must be accounted for. (Eberts v. Eberts, 55 Pa. St. 110.)

Any dealing by which he derives a benefit must be fair and just to the ward, and burden rests upon the guardian to establish it. (Goodrick v. Harrison, 130 Mo. 263; 32 S. W. Rep. 661.)

The legal presumption of undue influence by guardian over ward extends to a will made by the ward, in favor of his guardian. (Meek v. Perry, 36 Miss. 190; Garvin v. Williams, 44 Mo. 465; and see Morris v. Stokes, 21 Ga. 552; Breed v. Pratt, 18 Pick. 115.)

Settlement about time female ward became of age, she being in poor health, uneducated, of weak mind, and under the influence of her guardian, cannot stand. (Condon v. Churchman, 32 Ill. App. 317.)

Contracts between guardian and ward as to former's compensation, if fair and just, and do not appear to tend unduly to the benefit of the guardian, may be upheld. (Huff v. Wolfe, 48 Ill. App. 589.)

Ward cannot have a settlement set aside, where he obtained it upon a false representation as to his age; where the guardian is the deceived and injured party. (Hayes v. Parker, 41 N. J. Eq. 630.) But *it seems* that a guardian is not thereby relieved from his obligation to file an account if demanded within reasonable time. (Maulfair's Appeal, 110 Pa. St. 402; 2 Atl. Rep. 530.)

In re BARRETT'S WILL.

[Supreme Court of Iowa, May 22, 1900; 82 N. W. Rep. 998.]

WILLS—CONSTRUCTION—LANDS—INTEREST DEVISED.

Where testator gave all his property to his wife, to use, enjoy, and manage as she, in her judgment, saw fit, the wife took a fee, and not simply a life estate.

APPEAL from District Court, Linn county; WILLIAM G. THOMPSON, Judge,

Proceedings for the construction of the will of Philip Barrett, deceased. The Trial Court held that Eleanor S. Barrett, widow, took but a life estate, and she appeals. Reversed.

J. C. Davis and *Smith & Smith*, for appellant.

Giffen & Voris, for appellee.

DEEMER, J.—The provision of the will we are asked to construe reads as follows: " I give and bequeath to my beloved wife, Eleanor S. Barrett, all of my property, real and personal, of every description, to use, enjoy, and manage as she, in her judgment, sees fit." Does this devise a fee or life estate? The Trial Court held that it created but a life estate. If that which follows the word " description," in the will, were eliminated, there would be no doubt that an absolute estate was devised to the widow; for the words " give and bequeath " are the equivalent of " devise." (*In re Burbank's Will*, 69 Iowa, 378; 28 N. W. 648.) Is the estate limited to a life interest by reason of the use of the words, " to use and enjoy and manage as she, in her judgment, sees fit "? Conditions or limitations imposed on an absolute devise are strictly construed, and will not be allowed to defeat the estate unless it clearly appears that the testator intended to devise but a qualified estate. (Schouler, Wills, § 475; *Allen* v. *White*, 97 Mass. 504.) In *Bulfer* v. *Willigrod* (71 Iowa, 620; 33 N. W. 136), the will read as follows: " I give and bequeath to my beloved wife all my property, both real and personal and mixed, and of every kind, manner, and nature, to use, to her own use and benefit, as she shall deem best for herself and our beloved daughter, Anna M. Kline." Judge REED, speaking for the court, said: " The present bequest is a devise of all of the property. Under it she took the title to the property, coupled with the power to make absolute disposition of it. Under the settled rule, it must be regarded as an absolute bequest to her." If the words, " use to her own use and benefit," give power of absolute disposition, surely the words, " to use, enjoy it, and manage, as long as she, in her judgment, sees fit," do no less. A devise of property to one, to use and enjoy, is not confined to personal use, unless the context clearly calls for the more limited construction. Such words, as a rule, carry the beneficial estate to the devisee. (*Hance* v. *West*, 32 N. J. Law, 233; *Stone* v. *North*, 41 Me. 265.) There is nothing to indicate that the testator intended to devise but a life estate to his wife. He does not undertake to dispose of the remainder, and there is every reason to think that he supposed he was disposing of the whole of his property to his wife. Technical construction corresponds, then, with the testator's intention, and both give the widow an estate in fee. The case is clearly ruled by *Bulfer* v. *Willigrod* (*supra.*) There should be a decree finding that Eleanor S. Barrett took an estate in fee, and the cause is remanded for that purpose.

Reversed.

In re MORRISON's ESTATE.

[Supreme Court of Pennsylvania, May 14, 1900; 196 Pa. St. 80; 46 Atl. Rep. 257.]

EXECUTORS AND ADMINISTRATORS—ACCOUNTING—SERVICES— TRUSTEE FOR HEIRS—MANAGEMENT OF REALTY—ACCOUNTS— AUDIT—COSTS—APPORTIONMENT.

1. An administrator, on the audit of his accounts, can have an allowance only for his services as administrator; and he having, in addition to services performed as administrator, performed services in his own in-

terest as heir, as trustee for some of the other heirs, and as agent for others, must recover therefor in another proceeding.

2. Though an administrator assume to act in his representative capacity in the management of the real estate and the collection of the income thereof, he is merely the agent of the heirs.

3. Costs of the audit of an administrator's accounts are properly apportioned, his failure to keep proper accounts making a reference necessary, and the audit being needlessly prolonged by the beneficiaries of the estate.

APPEAL from Orphans' Court, Warren county.

Judicial accounting by B. G. Morrison, administrator of the estate of Stephen R. Morrison, deceased. From a decree sustaining exceptions to the account, the administrator appeals. Affirmed.

W. J. Knupp and *D. I. Ball,* for appellant.

D. U. Arird, for appellees.

FELL, J.—The main contention at the audit related to the accountant's claim for compensation for services and for the allowance of expenses incurred in the management of the real estate of the decedent. All questions relating to these subjects were carefully considered and properly decided by the learned judge of the Orphans' Court specially presiding The services of the accountant were of an unusual character, and of great value to the estate, but they were not performed by him entirely in his capacity as administrator. He was acting in his own interest as an heir, as a trustee for some of the other heirs, possibly as an agent for others, and as administrator. The allowance made is in excess of the usual amount, being five per cent. of the total fund, a large part of which was realized from the sale of real estate. This is all he was entitled to. Whatever claim for compensation and for expenses incurred he may have against the other heirs may be adjusted in another proceeding, but it cannot be considered in this. While in this state lands are assets for the payment of debts, they are not assets in the hands of an administrator, and without an order of the Orphans' Court he has nothing to do with them. In case of intestacy they descend to the heirs, and, if needed for the payment of debts, there is a mode pointed out by the act of assembly which the administrator is bound to pursue, " for the real fund is not absolutely, but *sub modo,* assets in his hands." (*McCoy* v. *Scott,* 2 Rawle, 221; *Bakes* v. *Reese,* 150 Pa. St. 44; 24 Atl. 634.) Although the administrator may assume to act in his representative capacity in the management of the real estate and the collection of the income thereof, he is merely the agent of the heir. (*Appeals of Fross and Loomis,* 105 Pa. St. 258; *Appeal of Walker,* 116 id. 419; 9 Atl. 654.) This rule has been strictly adhered to. The refusal of the court to apply it in *Appeal of Hoffman* (185 Pa. St. 315; 39 Atl. 954), was on the ground of estoppel, the administrator having collected the rents under an agreement with the heirs, and included them in his account, and by his conduct having induced them not to resort to another tribunal until the statute of limitations had interposed a bar to a recovery against him. In this case the court finds that there was no agreement, and that there were no facts to warrant an inference of the knowledge and assent of the other heirs. The disposition of the costs of the audit is entirely just. A part of them were charged to the accountant, as his failure to keep proper accounts had made the reference to an auditor necessary, and the balance were placed upon the estate for the reason that the audit had been needlessly prolonged by the appellees.

The decree is affirmed, at the cost of the appellant.

ANGUS vs. NOBLE et al.

[Supreme Court of Errors of Connecticut, May 22, 1900; 46 Atl. Rep. 278.]

WILLS — ANNUITIES — TRUSTS — VALIDITY — DURATION —
REMAINDERS — WHEN VESTED — NATURE OF REMAINDER —
DISTRIBUTION OF SURPLUS — DISTRIBUTION OF REMAINDER —
DUTIES OF TRUSTEE — EXPRESSION OF TESTATOR'S DESIRES —
SPECIFIC LEGACIES.

1. A will provided for the payment of specific legacies in the form of annuities, payable every three months. In another provision it was declared that the rents of the estate should be paid every month, and
kept three months, and all debts paid out of them, and the balance kept
to the end of the year, and divided among the heirs. The will required the payment of all testator's debts before such fund came into
existence. *Held*, that the specific legacies were not inconsistent with
the provision requiring the rents to be divided among the heirs, as the
testator intended by the use of the word "debt" to include the quarterly payments to the legatees.

2. Where, by the terms of a will, an executor is given the functions of a
trustee, he is entitled to qualify as such after completing the settlement
of the estate, regardless of the fact that the name of trustee was not
conferred by the will.

3. Where, by a will, certain annuities to be paid by a trustee to certain
persons are to go on their death to testator's heirs, or to some designated person and then to testator's heirs, or to the heirs of such annuitants, the trust will continue till the death of the annuitants.

4. When a will provides for certain remainders after the determination
of prior life estates, the remainder is vested at the death of testator.

5. Where a will imports an intention of the testator to dispose of her entire estate, and life estates in the income are created, and remainders
created thereafter are also expressed as being in the income, but no
limit is placed on the enjoyment, such remainder-men acquire a legal
title to the property.

6. Where a testator provides specific legacies, in the form of annuities, for
all his heirs, which differs in proportion from the rule provided by the
statute of distribution, and it is provided in the will that any surplus
shall be divided among the heirs, such surplus is to be distributed in
the same proportion as the sum distributed in annuities.

7. Where a clause in a will provides an annuity to certain persons, stated
by the will to have no children, remainder to other heirs, the remainder
is to the other heirs of the testator.

8. Where a will provides a life estate in a trust fund to a certain person, remainder to his heirs, the children of such person acquire an equitable interest in remainder in the fund at the death of testator, subject to open and let in a child thereafter born.

9. Where a will creating annuities, not distributed according to the statute of distributions, provides for remainders to the other heirs on the death of a certain annuitant, such remainders will be distributed according to the statute of distribution.

10. When a testator prefers certain heirs in his will, but provides that on their death the property shall pass to testator's other heirs, such persons are excluded from taking an interest in remainder in property devised to testator's heirs.

11. When a will provides for various annuities for life, to be distributed by a trustee, remainder over to testator's heirs, it is the duty of the trustee, after the expiration of any life estate, to divide the interest therefrom quarterly among those entitled to the remainder, till the expiration of the trust.

12. Where a will provided that a trustee should collect the rents and income of testator, and distribute the fund thereby created to certain annuitants, an alien annuitant is entitled to receive his share, as such fund is personal property, which an alien may take by inheritance.

13. A will creating a trust, requiring that the estate be kept up and that graves be kept clean, is binding on the trustee.

14. A provision in a will creating a trust that flowers be placed on graves " once in a while " is void for uncertainty.

15. A clause in a will, that the testator would like his estate kept in a certain place, and as it was at his death, is but the expression of a desire, and does not impose any duty to respect it.

16. When a testator devised a sum due on a mortgage to certain persons, the right of such legatees will not be impaired by the fact that the income of the rest of the estate is insufficient to pay annuities given by the will.

CASE reserved from Superior Court, Hartford county; SILAS A. ROBINSON, Judge.

Suit by Hattie Angus, as executrix of the estate of Susan Mansley, against George Noble and others, for the construction of a will. Case reserved on special finding.

The will was drawn by the testatrix herself in 1897, and was as follows: " I, Susan Mansley, of Enfield, Hartford county, state of Connecticut, of sound mind and memory, do make my last will and testament, revoking all wills heretofore made by me void. After the payment of my just debts, obligations, expenses of last sickness, funeral, and expenses of settling my estate, I do give, be-

queath, and devise my estate as follows: (1) I give to my niece,
Hattie Angus, one hundred dollars every three months while she
lives, and at her death to be divided among the other heirs. ·
(2) I leave to my brother George Noble forty dollars every three
months, and at his death to go to his children. (3) I leave to my
brother William Noble forty dollars every three months, and at
his death to go to his wife, and at her death to go to the other
heirs. They have no children. (4) I leave to my nephew John
Noble twenty-five dollars every three months, and at his death
to go to his children. (5) I leave to my nephew William Noble
twenty-five dollars every three months, and at his death to go
to Annie Noble, his daughter, and at her death to go back to the
Nobles, if she has no children. (6) I leave to my nephew,
Walter Maude, England, fifteen dollars every three months, and
at his death to go to his children. (7) I leave to John W. Maude
fifteen dollars every three months, and at his death to go back ·
to the heirs. (8) The rents to be paid every month, and kept
for three months, and all debts to be paid out of them; the balance
to be kept until the end of the year, and then to be divided among
the heirs. The estate to be kept up in good repair, and our graves
to be kept clean, and flowers once in a while, to show that you
have not forgotten us. (9) I would like my estate to be in
Thompsonville, for I have lived here so long, and I would like
the estate kept as it is. (10) To the First Presbyterian Society
on Church street, in Thompsonville, Conn., I give the sum of
five hundred dollars, to be kept as a separate fund, and the income
thereof to be paid over to the home missions with which the said
church is connected. This can be taken from the mortgage of
Frederick and Emma Gliesman, of North Main street, Thompsonville, and the other six hundred that is due on the mortgage
to go to the children of Mr. and W. H. Whitney, one for each,
and one for Clark Hamilton, that will take up the mortgage, or, if
all parties wish, they can take the interest thereof, and keep the
mortgage. I appoint my niece, Hattie Angus, executrix of this
will, no bonds being required of her; and, if she shall be unable or
unwilling to act as executor of this will, then I appoint Lilla
Noble. They will have to collect all rents and pay all debts.
Divide balance, if any, and if you go short, take out of each one
share." She died in 1899, leaving real and personal property.

When she made her will her estate was yielding an income nearly or quite sufficient to pay the annuities therein given, but before she died she gave away part of it, and the income of what she left was not sufficient for that purpose. The gross rental of her real estate is $95 a month. Walter Maude is dead. The other facts found are sufficiently stated in the opinion.

Charles H. Briscoe, for plaintiff.

Charles E. Perkins, for defendants William Noble and wife.

William H. Leete, for defendants the children of George and John Noble and the children of Walter Maude.

BALDWIN, J. (after stating the facts).—The heirs of the testatrix were two brothers; Hattie Angus; John Noble and William V. Noble, the children of a deceased brother; and John W. Maude and Walter Maude, the children of a deceased sister. In her will she makes provision for each of them, by name, and in a way which shows that she did not intend to be governed by the principles of the statute of distributions. The bequests of specified sums to be paid every three months to Hattie Angus, George Noble, William Noble (her brother), John Noble, William Noble (her nephew), Walter Maude, and John W. Maude, are each valid. It is argued in behalf of the heirs at law that these three provisions are inconsistent with that in the eighth clause of the will, which is that the rents are to be paid (by which is obviously meant that they are to be collected) " every month, and kept for three months, and all debts to be paid out of them; the balance to be kept until the end of the year, and then to be divided among the heirs." It is apparent that the term " debts " was here used as including the quarterly payments to the legatees. The fund out of which they were to come was, by the opening words of her will, to come into existence only after the payment of all her debts and obligations, the expenses of her last sickness and funeral, and those of settling her estate. She evidently thought there might be a surplus of rents after satisfying all payments which she had directed, but, as the collections might be better in one quarter than another, it would be wiser not to divide such surplus oftener than once a year. This construction is confirmed by the statement with which the will concludes,—that the executrix would "have to collect all rents and pay all debts. Divide balance, if any, and, if you go short, take out of each one share." To "go short," in the mind of the testatrix, evidently meant to be unable, from the net income available for the purpose, to pay the full amount of the quarterly legacies every three months, since the remedy she provides in that case is a corresponding deduction from the share of each. If these legacies were not considered as coming under the term "debts," that word must have been used to signify either debts due at her decease from her estate, or those subsequently contracted by the executrix. That it did not mean those due at her decease is proved by the express provision for their payment before any legacies. That it did not mean only those subsequently contracted by the executrix is shown by the provision for deducting whatever is necessary to meet them from the shares of the annuitants. This presupposes that there will be something left to go to the legatees, whereas there could be nothing left if the entire income were wanted to meet the proper charges of administration. The phrase "each one share" should read "each one's share." This is justified by the rule of *idem sonans.* She intended that each legatee should receive his full annuity if the income proved adequate, but, if not, that his appointed share should be proportionately reduced.

The executrix was given the functions of a trustee, and is entitled to qualify as such, after completing the settlement of the estate. It is unimportant that the name of trustee was not conferred upon her in terms. (*Hayden* v. *Connecticut Hospital*, 64 Conn. 320, 323; 30 Atl. 50.) The trust will continue until the decease of Hattie Angus, George Noble, William Noble, Sarah J. Noble (the present wife of William Noble), John Noble, William V. Noble, Annie Noble, and John W. Maude, subject to the power of the Court of Probate to direct a partial distribution of the estate from time to time, if it be deemed expedient, and can be done without prejudice to the interest of the annuitants then surviving. The ultimate remainders to take effect in enjoyment after the determination of these life estates became vested at the death of the testatrix.

The introductory part of the will concludes thus: "I do give, bequeath, and devise my estate as follows." These words import an intention to dispose of the whole of it. Only $1,100, how-ever, is afterwards made the subject of an absolute gift, in express terms. This is preceded by other bequests which will exhaust the income annually accruing from the residue of the estate during the lives of certain persons particularly described. The ultimate remainders over are also interests in the income, but these are not limited in terms to the lives of the remainder-men. A devise of the rents of a parcel of real estate is, in law, a devise of the parcel itself. (*Stewart* v. *Garnett*, 3 Sim. 398.) It is such because the value of land lies in its rents and profits, and he who is given that value is in effect given the thing which produces it. The same rule applies to a gift of the income of an estate or of the produce of a fund, without limit as to time. (*Mannox* v. *Greener*, L. R. 14 Eq. 456; *Gulick's Ex'rs* v. *Gulick*, 25 N. J. Eq. 324; *Bristol* v. *Bristol*, 53 Conn. 242, 259; 5 Atl. 687.)

Under these principles of construction, effect may properly be given to the general intent of the testatrix in creating the various remainders over in favor of certain classes of her kindred. She established a trust which was to endure, at least, during a number of lives. It was her wish that throughout this period her estate should be kept as it was. The reference to adorning the graves with "flowers once in a while, to show that you have not forgotten us," indicates something to be done by those who, like the executors she named, had been personally acquainted with her, and so that she did not look forward to a perpetual trust, to be administered by and for those to whom she would be unknown except by name. The total amount of the quarterly payments to be made to the various legatees is $260. After satisfying these and the charges of administration, and expenses for repairs and keeping the graves clean, if there should remain at the end of any year, during the continuance of the trust, a balance in the hands of the trustee, it is, by clause eight, " to be divided among the heirs." In the clauses immediately preceding, all of her heirs had been named, and a specified sum out of the income of the estate assigned to each. She had given her brothers much less than was to go to a niece, and to two of her nephews much more than to two others. In this way one of the four collateral stocks of descent, between which her estate, had she left no will, would have been equally divided, is annually to receive more than the other three put together. This general intention must control the effect of the provision in clause eight for a division among the heirs. Taking, not as heirs, but as purchasers, and having been treated as purchasers unequally in the previous clauses of the will · by which the bulk of her property was distributed among them, it must have been her intention that the annual surplus, if any there was, should be divided in similar proportions; and we think, taking the whole will together, that this intention is sufficiently expressed. Of the $260 a quarter, which is the subject of the various life estates, Hattie Angus is, by clause one of the will, to receive $100. If the income in any year be insufficient to satisfy all the bequests, she must suffer an abatement; if it be more than sufficient, she will share in the surplus; and in either event she will receive annually a $\frac{100}{260}$ part of whatever is to be distributed. This is " at her death to be divided among the other heirs," and they were thereby invested,· upon the decease of the testatrix, with an absolute equitable interest in remainder in an undivided $\frac{100}{260}$ part of the entire trust fund, including both real and personal estate. The words "to be divided" import a gift, and the gift dates from the day when the will speaks; its enjoyment only being deferred for the benefit of Hattie Angus. (*Johnson* v. *Webber*, 65 Conn. 501, 513; 33 Atl. 506.) The term "the other heirs" is used twice in describing those who are to take in remainder,—once here, and once in clause three. In the latter it is obvious that it refers to the other heirs of the testatrix; that is, those other than William Noble. He had no children who could inherit his share, and she therefore wished that it should ultimately belong to the rest of her nearest kindred. A similar meaning *prima facie* attaches to these words as used in clause one, and there is nothing to rebut the presumption that such was the intent of the testatrix. Upon her decease, therefore, it was her heirs at law, other than Hattie Angus, who became invested with this estate in remainder in an undivided $\frac{100}{260}$ part of the trust fund. It must remain in the hands of the trustee, and undivided, until the expiration of the last of the life estates specifically created in the quarterly income, unless a partial distribution should be previously ordered by the Court of Probate. It follows from these principles of construction that by clause two the children of George

Noble, as a class, were invested at the decease of the testatrix with a like absolute equitable interest in remainder in an undivided ₁₆ part of the entire trust fund. This class would open to let in any child who might be thereafter born. (*Johnson* v. *Webber*, 65 Conn. 501, 514; 33 Atl. 506.) Sarah J. Noble, who was at the decease of the testatrix the wife of William Noble, took, upon that event, a life estate in remainder, which will entitle her to receive after his death $40 every three months, or a ₁₆ part of the annual net income from the trust fund. The use of the term "wife," instead of "widow," imports that this life estate will not inure to the benefit of his widow unless she be the person who was his wife at the decease of the testatrix. (2 Redf. Wills, *28.) Subject to these life estates, and to the duty of the trustee, unless otherwise ordered by the Court of Probate, to retain the whole fund in her hands until the expiration of all the other life estates, those, other than William Noble, who were the heirs of the testatrix at the time of her decease, became thereupon invested with an absolute equitable estate in remainder in an undivided ₁₆ part of the entire trust fund. Clause four is to be construed in the same manner, *mutatis mutandis,* as clause two. Should Annie Noble marry and have a child, an absolute equitable estate, by way of executory devise, in an undivided ₁₆ part of the entire trust fund, would thereupon arise in favor of such child, subject to its opening to let in afterborn children on an equal footing; and this estate would not be devested should such child or children die before her. Meanwhile, upon the decease of the testatrix, subject to being hereafter devested by the birth of a child to Annie Noble, an absolute equitable estate in remainder in this same undivided ₁₆ part of the trust fund became invested in those whom the testatrix described in clause five as "the Nobles." It was "to go back" to them. This indicates that it was to go back in the line through which it came down, namely, the line of James Noble. His stock was that to which the testatrix had already showed especial favor; for, of the legacies left by way of life estates, his children had received considerably more than half. This remainder, therefore, upon the decease of the testatrix, became vested in the three children of James Noble. The construction of clause six follows that of clause two, *mutatis mutandis.* The remainder which was created subject to the life estate in favor of John W. Maude was at his death "to go back to the heirs." This expression can only refer to the heirs of the testatrix. It excludes any descent to his heirs or to his mother's heirs, because there had been no preceding estate in their favor; John W. Maude having taken as an immediate purchaser. At the decease of the testatrix, therefore, an absolute equitable remainder in an undivided $\frac{1}{14}$ part of the entire trust fund became vested in her heirs at law.

The heirs who take in remainder under clauses one, three, and seven, take *per stirpes,* and not in the proportions which regulate the distribution of the income during the existence of the life estates. The exclusion of Hattie Angus under clause one, and of William Noble under clause three, shows that the testatrix did not contemplate an ultimate division for the benefit of the same persons whom she sought to prefer during their lives. In testamentary gifts to be divided among heirs at law, the rule of the statute of distributions is pursued unless a contrary intention be apparent. (*Lyon* v. *Acker,* 33 Conn. 222.) So long as the trust continues, the income accruing upon each undivided share, after the expiration of any life estate which may be charged upon it, should be paid quarterly to those entitled in remainder. That their actual possession of the property may be postponed for the security of the surviving annuitants should not operate to deprive them of the enjoyment of its fruits.

Walter Maude is described in the will as of England, and in the writ both he and his brother are named as belonging to that country. If at the decease of the testatrix they were aliens, they could not take any interest in remainder in fee in real estate in this state. Nor, if the children of Walter Maude were aliens at the decease of the testatrix, could they take any remainder in fee in real estate in this state under clause six. The provisions in favor of the Maudes, so far as they relate to the remainder interests in personal estate, or to the quarterly payments from the net income of the trust fund during the continuance of the trust, are valid. (*Cosgrove* v. *Cosgrove,* 69 Conn, 416, 423; 38 Atl. 219.) The rents lose their quality of real estate when mingled with the general fund. The children of Walter Maude, so long as the *corpus* of the trust estate remains undivided, will therefore be entitled to the quarterly payments which would have been

enjoyed by their father, were he living. Whether any equity
would arise in their favor, upon its final division, to have their
share of the *corpus* set out in personal property, were that found
to be practicable, is a question which requires no present answer,
and the facts bearing upon it are not fully presented upon the
record.

The provisions for repairs and for keeping the graves clean, in
clause eight, are obligatory upon the trustee during the continuance of the trust, but upon its final termination cease to be of any
further effect. That for placing flowers on the graves is so uncertain in its terms as not even to amount to a precatory trust, and
imposes no obligation whatever. Clause nine expresses a desire,
but not in such a way as to impose any duty to respect it. Clause
ten creates a demonstrative legacy to the First Presbyterian Society, which, subject to the rights of all the legatees under this
clause to demand a transfer to them of the Gliesman mortgage
(as respects the principal sum due thereon), is to be paid in full
if the mortgage suffices for that purpose. Any balance collectible
on the principal of this mortgage is specifically bequeathed to the
six persons described. No deficiency of assets to meet the charges
upon the income of the trust fund will impair the rights of the
legatees under clause ten. (2 Redf. Wills, *137 to *143.)

The Superior Court is advised that the first nine clauses or
sections of the will are valid and fully operative, except so far as
it is otherwise above stated with regard to clause nine; that no part
of the estate of the testatrix is intestate, unless there be an incapacity, from alienage, to take in remainder, on the final division
of the *corpus* of the trust estate, on the part of some of the devisees; that under clause ten the First Presbyterian Society takes a
demonstrative, which, by agreement of the parties in interest, may
be made a specific legacy, and the Whitney children and Clark
Hamilton specific legacies; and that a decree be passed conform-
ably to the construction given to the will in the foregoing opinion.
Costs in this court will be taxed in favor of the plaintiff, and of
George Noble, and of the children of Walter Maude, against the
estate of the testatrix.

The other judges concur.

MULLER *et al. vs.* MULLER *et al.*[1]

[Court of Appeals of Kentucky, May 18, 1900; 56 S. W. Rep. 802.]

REVOCATION OF WILL—LOSS OF SUBSEQUENT WILL—BURDEN OF
PROOF ON CONTESTANTS TO SHOW INCONSISTENCY.

1. Under Ky. St. § 4833, providing that, "no will or codicil, or any part
thereof, shall be revoked unless by the marriage of the testator, or by a
subsequent will or codicil or by some writing declaring an intention
to revoke the same executed in the manner in which a will is required
to be executed," where a will is contested on the ground that it was
revoked by a subsequent will, which has been lost, the burden is on the
contestants to show the due and proper execution of the subsequent
will, and also that it expressly revoked the will in contest, or was substantially inconsistent therewith.
2. After proof that the subsequent will is lost, its contents may be established by parol testimony, and the declarations of the testator are
competent to show that it was inconsistent with the will in contest.
GUFFY, J., dissenting.

APPEAL from Circuit Court, McCracken county.

" To be officially reported."
Contest by John P. Muller and others of the will of Barbara
Muller, deceased. Judgment for contestants, and William H.
Muller and others, the propounders, appeal.
Reversed.

R. T. Lightfoot and *T. L. Crice,* for appellants.

J. W. Bloomfield, for appellees.

BURNAM, J.—Appellants, without notice to appellees, caused a
paper dated July 22, 1893, to be probated in the McCracken
County Court on the 12th day of May, 1897, as the last will and
testament of Barbara Muller, deceased. Appellees appealed to
the Circuit Court, and on the trial the jury found the paper not

---

[1] Reported by Edward W. Hines, Esq., of the Frankfort bar and formerly
State reporter.

to be the last will of Barbara Muller, and judgment was rendered in accordance therewith. This paper devised to appellants property of the value of several thousand dollars, and excluded appellees, with the exception of a bequest of five dollars to each of them.

The grounds relied upon by appellees for setting aside the will probated by the County Court were: First, that testatrix had subsequent to its execution, in 1895, executed another will, in which she made an entirely different disposition of her property, and in which she provided for appellees equally with appellants, and which had either been mislaid or destroyed subsequently; second, that the will of 1893 was procured by reason of the undue influence of William Muller and others over testatrix. Appellants denied, in substance, that the will of 1893 was revoked by testatrix by the execution of any subsequent paper, or that she was induced to execute it by undue influence. There seems to have been little or no testimony offered to support the charge of undue influence, and the real point relied upon by appellees to invalidate the will of 1893 was that the execution of the will of 1895, in due form of law, *ipso facto* revoked all previous wills executed by testatrix, while on the other hand it was the contention of appellants that the mere proof of the execution of the paper of 1895 did not necessarily revoke the will of 1893, and that the burden was upon appellees to have shown either that it contained a clause expressly revoking the earlier will, which existed uncanceled, or that testatrix by the execution of the last paper made a disposition of her property which was entirely inconsistent with the will of 1893, and that it was intended by her to take the place of the former paper.

Section 4832 of the Kentucky statutes provides that " the will of a testator will be revoked by his subsequent marriage," with certain exceptions pointed out in the statute. Section 4833 provides that " no will or codicil, or any part thereof, shall be revoked unless by the marriage of the testator, or by a subsequent will or codicil or by some writing declaring an intention to revoke the same executed in the manner in which a will is required to be executed." The statute does not say that the mere execution by testator of a subsequent testamentary paper, or paper purporting to be a subsequent will, shall *ipso facto* revoke all previous wills. On the contrary, it provides that a will duly executed shall not be revoked except by the marriage of testator, or by a subsequent will or codicil or writing, declaring an intention to revoke, executed in the same manner in which a will is required to be executed. If the mere execution of a subsequent testamentary paper without regard to its intent or contents, necessarily revokes *in toto* all former wills, it would follow that the execution of a codicil, without regard to its contents, would also have the same effect to revoke a prior will *in toto,* as the statute uses the term " subsequent will or codicil " in exactly the same sense. The law is well settled that a subsequent will does not revoke a former one unless it contains a clause of revocation, or is substantially inconsistent with it. Where it is inconsistent with the former will only in some of its provisions, it is only a revocation *pro tanto.* See *Nelson* v. *McGiffert* (3 Barb. Ch. 158) ; *Brant* v. *Wilson* (8 Cow. 56), and *Minor* v. *Guthrie* ([Ky.] 4 S. W. 179). Schouler, Wills, § 407, says : " The latter will, though well executed, does not revoke the earlier one, as such, and without express words of revocation, except by being inconsistent with it. And by the extent of such inconsistency must be measured the extent of the revocation. To operate a total revocation in such a case, the two dispositions must be so plainly inconsistent as to be incapable of standing together. Only a revocation *pro tanto* results where the effect is that of a partial inconsistency. It is like making a will, and then adding a codicil ; the final disposition reading by the light of both instruments together, as a correct whole. For any number of testamentary instruments, executed at different times, may constitute one's ' last will,' in legal effect. * * * The governing principle in all such cases is the testator's intention. And one's intention in making a new will may have been to dispose of other property or make new provisions perfectly consistent with the former, or else thereby to revoke *pro tanto* by amendment. It does not follow that a full revocation was intended." And the same author, in section 412, says : " The execution of a subsequent will of different tenor operates to revoke a former one, notwithstanding the latter will be lost or mislaid, or at least cannot be found at testator's death. * * * But where a will which cannot be produced is relied upon, as revoking by implication a former one, its contents should be thoroughly established. And the mere fact that a later will was made by no means justifies the inference that it revokes in effect, without proof of its actual contents." Williams, Ex'rs, § 162, says: "A subsequent will revokes only so much of a former will as is inconsistent with the last instrument. If, therefore, the latter or latest will dispose of the whole of the testator's estate, all former wills are thereby revoked; but if, in the absence of an expressed revocation, a partial disposition of the estate is thereby made, consistent with the dispositions made in the prior will or wills, or with a portion of them, they may both or all stand as the last will of the testator, to the extent to which the latter do not exclude the former. It is clear that it is the duty of the court to give effect to every part of every will of the testator, if the several dispositions can be reconciled; the rule of construction being substantially the same where there are several wills to be harmonized, as where there are several clauses in the same will or in a will and codicil. Subsequent wills, indeed, perform the office of codicils. It is held that the revocation of a will may be proved by proving the execution of a subsequent will by the testator, which is lost, and has not been, therefore, admitted to probate. This rule is necessarily confined to cases where the subsequent will either expressly revokes the former, or contains a different disposition of the whole estate, as by appointment of an executor and residuary legatee; and the evidence to establish its execution, as well as its inconsistency with the former will, should be clear and satisfactory. There can be no revocation by a later will, of which the contents are unknown."

The testimony in this case shows conclusively the execution by the testatrix in 1895 of a testamentary paper. Graves, one of the attesting witnesses, says that decedent came to the office of Mr. Lightfoot and himself, accompanied by his son, for the purpose of having a will prepared; that he wrote the will at the dictation of Mr. Lightfoot; that each clause was read and explained to testatrix; that it was duly signed and executed by her, and attested by himself and Mr. Winchester; that she took the will away with her; and that he had never seen it afterwards. The testimony of Winchester is to the same effect.

Contestants offered to prove by the witness Graves that the paper prepared by him was a lengthy document, purporting to dispose of the whole estate of testatrix, and that it was his recollection that it gave to contestant John P. Muller a house and lot in Paducah, Ky. This testimony was objected to, and the objection sustained, and we think erroneously. After proof that this paper was lost and could not be found, it was competent to establish its contents by parol testimony, and to show either that it contained a clause revoking all former wills, or that it made a disposition of her property which was inconsistent with the bequests of the former will; and the declaration of the testatrix as to the contents of the will itself were competent, as secondary evidence, to show its provisions, and to establish the fact that they were inconsistent with those of the former paper, as the burden of proof was on contestants not only to show a due and proper execution of the last instrument, but also that the disposition of the property of testatrix therein made was substantially different from that made in the will offered for probate, and inconsistent therewith.

In all of the instructions given to the jury on the trial, they were told, in substance, that the mere execution of a subsequent will was of itself sufficient 'o authorize them to find that the prior will had thereby been revoked, and all testimony offered by contestants conducing to establish the contents of the last will, and to show its inconsistency with the former will, was excluded upon the ground that it was immaterial. We think the court erred in the instruction given to the jury and in the rejection of this testimony, and. for these reasons the judgment is reversed, and the cause remanded for a new trial consistent with this opinion.

GUFFY, J., dissents.

KOSTER *vs.* GELLEN.

[Supreme Court of Michigan, May 15, 1900; 82 N. W. Rep. 823.]

WILLS—ELECTION BY WIDOW—HOMESTEAD—ESTOPPEL TO CLAIM.

1. Under Comp. Laws 1897, §§ 8935, 8936, providing that when a widow shall be entitled to elect whether to take under the will or be endowed of the lands of her husband she shall be deemed to have elected to take under the will, unless within one year after the husband's death she

shall commence proceedings for assignment of dower, a widow, by failing to commence such proceedings within one year after her husband's death, and by petitioning the Probate Court to proceed under the will, and allow her a reasonable sum instead of her dower, waives her right to dower.

2. Where a widow, without children, elects to take under the will which provides for a sale of the premises, and a payment to her in cash in lieu of dower, and petitions the court to proceed under the will, which is done, she is not estopped from setting up the homestead interest granted by Const., art. 16, § 4, providing that, if the owner of a homestead die, leaving a widow, but no children, the same shall be exempt, and the rents and profits shall accrue to her benefit during widowhood, unless she be the owner of a homestead in her own right.

CASE made from Circuit Court, Kent county; ALLEN C. ADSIT, Judge.

Ejectment by Anna Koster against Catherine Gellen. There was a judgment for defendant, and plaintiff brings error. Affirmed.

Smedley & Corwin, for appellant.

Stuart & Barker, for appellee.

LONG, J.—This is an action of ejectment. The premises in controversy belonged to John Gellen in his lifetime, and were occupied as a homestead by him and his ·vife, the defendant. He died in October, 1895, leaving a last will and testament, which was duly probated. By the will Peter Braun was appointed executor of the estate. The will directed that the executor should sell and dispose of all the real estate of the deceased, and that the executor should pay out of the estate all the debts of the deceased, and should also pay the widow of the deceased such sum or amount as might be agreed upon between the executor and the widow in lieu of her dower interest, " and, in case of disagreement, such sum or amount as the court may direct." It appears that the executor and the widow could not agree upon the amount the widow should receive in lieu of her dower interest, and thereupon the executor filed a petition in the Probate Court, asking the court to fix the amount he should pay said widow in lieu of her dower right, according to the terms of said will. At the same time the widow petitioned the Probate Court for the same purpose. The prayer of her petition reads as follows: "Your petitioner therefore asks the court to proceed under the provisions of the will above cited, and allow your petitioner a reasonable sum out of said estate, instead of her dower interest, but to be in lieu thereof." The Probate Court heard both petitions as one, and made a decree which provides that " said Catherine Gellen be allowed the sum of one hundred and ninety-six and forty-three hundredths dollars in lieu of her dower interest in the real estate of said deceased, and that the executor pay the same to her accordingly." The executor tendered her the amount fixed by the decree, which she refused to accept, claiming that it was not enough for her dower interest. No appeal, however, was taken from this decree. The executor, after advertising, according to law, sold the premises in controversy here at public sale by virtue of the power given him by the will, and the plaintiff became the purchaser thereof, and received the executor's deed therefor. Written demand was served by the plaintiff upon defendant for possession of the premises before suit was commenced. The defendant has occupied the premises ever since the death of her husband as her homestead, and still occupies and claims them as such, and avers that she has no other homestead. December 14, 1896, plaintiff commenced proceedings against defendant before a Circuit Court Commissioner, under section 8295, How. Ann. St., for the purpose of obtaining possession of these premises and other lands. The defendant, in her plea before the commissioner, claimed the premises as her homestead. The commissioner decided that the plaintiff was entitled to that part of the premises not occupied by defendant as a homestead, but was not entitled to a judgment for that part which was occupied by defendant as her homestead. No appeal was taken by either party from this judgment. The widow took no proceeding for the assignment or recovery of her dower, as provided by How. Ann. St. (*supra*), and Comp. Laws 1897 (§§ 8935, 8936). On these facts the court below found as a conclusion of law that the defendant was entitled to the premises as and for a homestead so long as she remained the widow of John Gellen. Plaintiff brings error.

It is now contended by counsel for plaintiff:

1. That the defendant, by failing to commence proceedings for

the assignment or recovery of her dower within one year after the death of her husband, as provided by statute, and by petitioning the Probate Court to proceed under the provisions of the will, and allow her a reasonable sum out of the estate, instead of her dower interest, in lieu thereof, has waived her right to dower under the statute, and has elected to take under the will. In this, we think, counsel for plaintiff is correct. (*In re Smith,* 60 Mich. 142; 27 N. W. 80; *In re Bloss' Estate,* 114 Mich. 204; 72 N. W. 148.) The statute provides: " If any lands be devised to a woman, or other provision be made for her in the will of her husband, she shall make her election whether she will take the lands so devised, or the provision so made, or whether she will be endowed of the lands of her husband; but she shall not be entitled to both unless it plainly appears by the will to have been so intended by the testator." (Comp. Laws 1897, § 8935.) " When a widow shall be entitled to an election under either of the two last preceding sections, she shall be deemed to have elected to take such jointure, devise or other provision unless within one year after the death of her husband she shall commence proceedings for the assignment or recovery of her dower." (Id. § 8936.)

2. It is contended that, the estate being solvent, no homestead right attached in favor of the widow in this piece of land. The argument of counsel is that the widow has elected to take under the will, and the will provides for a sale of the premises, and a payment to her in cash in lieu of her dower; that the executor has proceeded under the power of sale contained in the will, and sold the premises, and the purchaser is seeking to obtain possession of the property in an action of ejectment under the executor's deed; that the estate was solvent, and all the debts paid before the executor sold the land; that the executor did not sell the land in order to pay debts, but sold it in pursuance of the provisions of the will, which directed him to sell and dispose of all the real estate of said deceased; that defendant now seeks to hold possession of the house and lot in question as a homestead. It is the contention that, under such circumstances, no homestead right attaches in favor of the widow in the piece of land. Counsel cite in support of this contention: *Zoellner* v. *Zoellner* (53 Mich. 624; 19 N. W. 556); *Patterson* v. *Patterson* (49 Mich. 176; 13 N. W. 504);

Robinson v. *Baker* (47 Mich. 619; 11 N. W. 410). The constitutional provisions relative to homestead rights are as follows:

"Sec. 2. Every homestead of not exceeding forty acres of land and the dwelling house thereon, and the appurtenances to be selected by the owner thereof, and not included in any town plat, city or village; or instead thereof, at the option of the owner, any lot in any city, village or recorded town plat, or such parts of lots as shall be equal thereto, and the dwelling house thereon, and its appurtenances, owned and occupied by any resident of the state, not exceeding in value fifteen hundred dollars, shall be exempt from forced sale on execution, or any other final process from a court, for any debt contracted after the adoption of this constitution. Such exemption shall not extend to any mortgage thereon lawfully obtained; but such mortgage or other alienation of such land by the owner thereof, if a married man, shall not be valid without the signature of his wife to the same.

"Sec. 3. The homestead of a family, after the death of the owner thereof, shall be exempt from the payment of his debts contracted after the adoption of this constitution, in all cases during the minority of his children.

"Sec. 4. If the owner of a homestead die, leaving a widow, but no children, the same shall be exempt, and the rents and profits thereof shall accrue to her benefit during the time of her widowhood, unless she be the owner of a homestead in her own right."

Const. art. 16, §§ 2-4.

In each of the above cases cited by counsel for plaintiff there were children having interests in the property in controversy. In *Robinson* v. *Baker* (*supra*), a bill was filed for partition by one who had purchased the interest of one of the children. The deceased owner of the land left a widow and three children surviving him. The land in question consisted of a quarter section and two village lots. One of the village lots was occupied by the deceased as a homestead prior to his death, and the widow continued to occupy it as a homestead. It was held that the statutes and constitutional provision did not preclude proceedings for partition as between the heirs at law and their assigns; that, in making such partition, where there is a homestead, and also other lands, if there is a widow with a right of dower she shall have her dower and homestead right saved to her in the homestead land

whenever it can be done consistently with justice. In *Patterson*
v. *Patterson* (*supra*), it appeared that Patterson died, leaving surviving him two adult children and three infant children, besides
his widow, who was the mother of two of the infant children.
The widow was occupying the dwelling house upon the farm, and
claimed a homestead in the dwelling house and forty acres of
land, of which she was in possession with her children. It appeared that one of the adult children had harvested and carried
off the crop from this land claimed as a homestead. The widow
sued in trespass. It was held that the constitutional provisions
which protect homestead rights in Michigan are strictly exemptions, and give the right only as against the creditor, and that the
statutes have not enlarged it. It was also held that adult heirs
residing away from home cannot disturb an existing possession in the widow while the estate is in process of settlement; that
the heirs can claim no distinct part until partition actually made.
In *Zoellner* v. *Zoellner* (*supra*), the bill was filed by one of the
two minor children for partition. It was said: "The case presents some novel questions. Unless there are creditors at the time
the owner of the homestead dies, and the estate, aside from such
homestead is insolvent, no homestead right attaches in favor of
the widow or children, and the premises pass at once to the heirs,
subject to the widow's right of dower. Here the widow claims a
homestead. She is the only creditor. Were it not for her claim
as a creditor of the estate, it would descend immediately to the
heirs of the deceased." It will be seen that none of these cases
comes within the provisions of section 4, art. 16, of the constitution, above quoted. In that section provision is made for the
widow when no children are left surviving the deceased. Our
statutes in case of intestacy have also made better provisions for
the widow in such cases than where children are left surviving.
In case no children are living at the death of the intestate, then
of the lands the widow takes one-half in fee in lieu of dower. As
we have seen, the widow has elected to take under the will, and
therefore the question of her dower interest is disposed of; but
she also had a homestead interest in this property, which is described as the N. ½ of the E. ½ of lots 5 and 7, Jefferson street,
Scribner's addition to the city of Grand Rapids, being 66 feet wide
and 66 feet deep, with dwelling house thereon. The widow had a

dower interest in these premises as above described. She also had a homestead interest in them, which was in no manner affected by the disposition made of her dower interest. Under section 4, art. 16, of the constitution, she is entitled to this homestead interest so long as she remains the widow of the testator, as it appears that she has no other homestead. The petition for the sale of the dower interest cannot estop her from setting up a claim to the homestead interest. In *Showers* v. *Robinson* (43 Mich. 502; 5 N. W. 988), it was held that a widow is not estopped from claiming a homestead in lands by the fact that she desired its sale for the payment of debts, and requested a party to buy the land, and received from the proceeds the amount of a claim allowed in her favor; that it must be presumed that the sale the widow desired was a sale subject to the homestead. We think, in the present case, neither the widow, nor any one else connected with the property, expected her homestead interest was to be sold; nor is it claimed that it was sold, but the claim is that, under the circumstances, she is estopped from setting it up. We think not. The property was valued at $1,400, and it was sold by the executor for $975, yet all the widow received from it was $196.43. Under the statute she was entitled to one-half of it in fee, aside from her homestead interest in the whole. The court found from these facts that the plaintiff was not entitled to recover. The other questions need not be considered. The judgment must be affirmed.

The other justices concurred.

Note.—ELECTION BY WIDOW.

(a) General principles and rule at common law.
(b) Rule as modified or changed by statute.
(c) What law governs.
(d) A personal right.
(e) Gift to wife through a trustee.
(f) Effect of devise of life estate to wife.
(g) As to property not disposed of by the will.
(h) As affected by debts of husband.
(i) Election requires knowledge of rights.
(j) Acceptance may be implied.
(k) Time or manner of election.

(l) Effect of election.

(m) Illustrative cases as to election.

(n) Community property.

(o) Homestead.

(a) **General principles and rule at common law.**—The right of dower is regarded with great favor both in law and in equity. The widow should, and usually does, receive the utmost consideration from the court. The presumption is, in the absence of a clearly contrary intention, that the testator, in devising property to her in his will, intends it as a bounty, and not as a substitute for what she is entitled to of right. So it is a general rule in equity, as regards the widow's dower, that the court will not compel her to elect between her dower or other statutory right and interest which she may have in the estate of the testator, and a provision made for her in the will, unless, first, it shall appear in express terms that the bequest or devise was given in lieu or satisfaction of her dower; or second, unless it appear by clear and manifest implication from the circumstances of the case that the testator intended her to elect. She will not be compelled to elect unless her claim of dower is plainly inconsistent with the will of the testator and so repugnant to it that both her claim of dower and the devises in the will cannot consistently be upheld. She has a right to take both, despite the fact that the benefit given by the will may be much greater in fact than her dower. (2 Underhill Wills, § 744 [ed. 1900].)

The correct rule in respect to testamentary dispositions in favor of a wife is, that she will be put to her election when it clearly appears from the will that the provision made for her therein was intended to take the place of that which the law makes; and the intention need not be declared in words, but may be deduced from clear and manifest implication, if the claim under the law would be plainly inconsistent with the will. Whenever it is reasonably clear that the provisions of the will were intended to be in lieu of the provision made for the widow by law, if she accepts the former she thereby waives the latter. (Hurley v. McIver, 119 Ind. 54; 21 N. E. Rep. 325.)

It is a settled rule in the construction of wills that where there is no express declaration in the will barring the dower of the wife, the intention that it shall be barred must be deduced by clear and manifest implication from the instrument, founded on the fact that the claim of dower would be inconsistent with the will or so repugnant to some of its dispositions as to disturb and defeat them. (Metteer v. Wiley, 34 Iowa, 214; and see Baldwin v. Hill, 97 id. 586, 590; 66 N. W. Rep. 889; Estate of Franke, 97 Iowa, 704; 66 N. W. Rep. 918; Daugherty v. Daugherty, 69 Iowa, 679; 29 N. W. Rep. 778; Sutherland v. Sutherland, 102 Iowa, 535; 71 N. W. Rep. 424.)

Whether a widow is put to her election between her dower at law, and the provisions of the will, depends on the intention of the testator in making such provision as to whether it was in lieu of dower or not. Such intent may be found in the whole will and circumstances of the estate.

(Griggs v. Veghte, 47 N. J. Eq. 179; 19 Atl. Rep. 867; and see Stokes v. Norwood, 44 S. C. 424; 22 S. E. Rep. 417.)

Such intent may be implied when the taking of dower would destroy the equality among the devisees plainly intended. (Helme v. Strater, 52 N. J. Eq. 591; 30 Atl. Rep. 333; compare Closs v. Eldert, 30 App. Div. 338; 51 N. Y. Supp. 881; rev'g 16 Misc. 104; 37 N. Y. Supp. 353; Horstman v. Flege, 32 Misc. 665; 66 N. Y. Supp. 446.) And that it may be implied. (Bennett v. Packer, 70 Conn. 357; 39 Atl. Rep. 739.)

The intent to substitute the provision in the will for dower must be unequivocally expressed; it cannot be so construed by implication. (Hasenritter v. Hasenritter, 77 Mo. 162; and see Martian v. Norris, 91 Mo. 465; 3 S. W. Rep. 849.)

But such intention will be implied where the claim of dower would be clearly inconsistent with the will. (Stewart v. Stewart, 31 N. J. Eq. 398; and see Hiers v. Gooding, 43 S. C. 428; 21 S. E. Rep. 310; Cooper v. Cooper, 56 N. J. Eq. 48; 38 Atl. Rep. 198.)

The rule is that a wife is not put to her election between dower and a testamentary disposition in her favor unless it clearly appear from the will that the provision made for her was intended as a substitute for that to which she is entitled by law. The intention need not be declared in express words. It may be implied, if the claim of dower would be plainly inconsistent with the will or so repugnant thereto, that they cannot stand together. (Savage v. Burnham, 17 N. Y. 561, 577; Tobias v. Ketchum, 32 id. 319, 325.)

To put the widow to her election there must be a clear incompatibility arising on the face of the will, between a claim of dower and a claim to the benefit given by the will. (Konvalinka v. Schlegel, 104 N. Y. 125, 129; 9 N. E. Rep. 868; and see Asche v. Asche, 113 N. Y. 232; 21 N. E. Rep. 70; Closs v. Eldert, 30 App. Div. 338; 51 N. Y. Supp. 881; Horstman v. Flege, 32 Misc. 665; 66 N. Y. Supp. 446; Kimbel v. Kimbel, 14 App. Div. 570; 43 N. Y. Supp. 900; Sanford v. Jackson, 10 Paige, 269; Adsit v. Adsit, 2 Johns. Ch. 448; Fuller v. Yates, 8 Paige, 325; Mills v. Mills, 28 Barb. 454; Church v. Bull, 2 Denio, 430; Lewis v. Smith, 9 N. Y. 502; Matter of Hayden, 54 Hun, 198; 7 N. Y. Supp. 313; Starr v. Starr, 54 Hun, 300; 7 N. Y. Supp. 580; Grotrian's Estate, 30 Misc. 23; 62 N. Y. Supp. 996.)

Widow should never be excluded from dower by a provision in the will except by express words or by necessary implication; she should not be put to an election, unless it is clear to a demonstration that the testator intended that she should elect. (Gray v. Gray, 5 App. Div. 132; 39 N. Y. Supp. 57.)

At common law where there was a provision in the will for the widow the presumption was that the testator intended it to be in addition to dower, there being no express words putting the widow to her election, nor any incompatibility arising on the face of the will between the two claims. (Corry v. Lamb, 45 Ohio St. 207; 12 N. E. Rep. 660; Sanders v. Wallace, 118 Ala. 418; 24 So. Rep. 354; Hilliard v. Binford, 10 Ala. 977; Schorr

v. Etling, 124 Mo. 42; 27 S. W. Rep. 395; Huhlein v. Huhlein, 87 Ky. 247; 8 S. W. Rep. 260; and see *note* to Wake v. Wake, 1 Ves. Jr. 337.)

Where the widow accepts land devised, and the will discloses an intention that she shall not have dower in his other lands not devised to her, the rule at common law is that such other lands will be released from dower. (Hall v. Smith, 103 Mo. 289; 15 S. W. Rep. 621.)

Any statute in derogation of the common law rights of the widow should be liberally construed in her favor; such statutes are designed as rules of construction in determining intention, where none is expressed. (Thompson v. Egbert, 17 N. J. L. 460.)

A devise in the will which in substance amounts to what the widow would have received under the statute is in lieu of dower, and the widow takes same not as a beneficiary, but as a purchaser. A provision in will in lieu of dower is in fact and legal effect a mere offer by the testator to purchase out the dower interest for benefit of the estate. (Carper v. Crowl, 149 Ill. 465, 479; 36 N. E. Rep. 1040; Dunning v. Dunning, 82 Hun, 462; 31 N. Y. Supp. 719; affirmed on opinion below 147 N. Y. 686; 42 N. E. Rep. 722.)

(b) **Rule as modified or changed by statute.**—Under the peculiar terms of the Illinois statute the provision in the will is declared to be a bar (to dower) unless the intention that it shall not be bar is expressed in the will. The statute makes the silence of the testator the conclusive index to his intention; and it also makes the failure to renounce within a specified time conclusive evidence that the wife has elected to take under the will. (Warren v. Warren, 148 Ill. 641, 649; 36 N. E. Rep. 611.)

And that widow is not entitled to both, unless such an intent appears in the will, see the following cases where the state indicates the existence of a statute changing or reversing the rule at common law. (Like v. Cooper, 132 Ind. 391; 31 N. E. Rep. 1118; Adams v. Adams, 5 Metc. 278; and see Reed v. Dickermann, 12 Pick. 149; Melms v. Pabst Brewing Co., 93 Wis. 146; 66 N. W. Rep. 244; Corry v. Lamb, 45 Ohio St. 203, 207; 12 N. E. Rep. 660; Bolling v. Bolling, 88 Va. 524; 14 S. E. Rep. 67; Spalding v. Hershfield, 15 Mont. 259; 39 Pac. Rep. 88; Sanders v. Wallace, 118 Ala. 418; 24 So. Rep. 354; Dow v. Dow, 36 Me. 215; Schorr v. Etling, 124 Mo. 42; 27 S. W. Rep. 395; Huhlein v. Huhlein, 87 Ky. 247; 8 S. W. Rep. 260.)

A statute providing that widow shall not have both dower and gift by will, unless such appears in the will to have been the intention, has no application to lands outside of the state. (Staigg v. Atkinson, 144 Mass. 564; 12 N. E. Rep. 354.)

Where will devised part of the real estate to the wife in fee, bequeathed to her all the personal property and then provided " the other part of my real estate is to be disposed of as the law directs." *Held*, that an intent that the wife should have both dower and the property under the will, could not be made out from words quoted. (Adams v. Adams, *supra.*)

(c) **What law governs.**—Where testator domiciled in New York, bequeathed personal property to his wife, but made no disposition of his real estate in Virginia, and there is no incompatibility between the claim for dower and her claim to the bequest, the testator's intentions must be construed according to the laws of New York, which requires an expression of *intent* in the *will*, that the widow shall not take both dower and bequest. (Citing Konvalinka v. Schlegel, 104 N. Y. 125; 9 N. E. Rep. 868; Bolling v. Bolling, 88 Va. 524; 14 S. E. Rep. 67.) As to real estate. (Staigg v. Atkinson, 144 Mass. 564; 12 N. E. Rep. 354; and see Note "What Law Governs," this volume, p. 206.)

(d) **A personal right.**—The right of election must be exercised by the widow in person before her death. (Milliken v. Welliver, 37 Ohio St. 460; Fosher v. Guilliams, 120 Ind. 172; 22 N. E. Rep. 118; Page v. Eldridge Library, 45 Atl. Rep. 411 [N. H.].)

But her written election when executed by her, may be filed after her death within the period prescribed by statute. (McGrath v. McGrath, 38 Ala. 246.)

Widow may exercise her right of election and formally waive provision under the will, before it is in fact admitted to probate; and if she dies before that time her interest in the personal estate is such a vested right as to pass to her representatives. (Atherton v. Corliss, 101 Mass. 40, 47.)

If incompetent, election by court or guardian. (State v. Urland, 30 Minn. 277; 15 N. W. Rep. 245.)

(e) **Gift to wife through a trustee.**—Creation by the will of a trust estate is not inconsistent with right of dower in the subject of a trust. (Gray v. Gray, 5 App. Div. 132; 39 N. Y. Supp. 57.)

A provision made for the widow through a trustee may be so inconsistent with dower, as to put her to election. (Savage v. Burnham, 17 N. Y. 562, 577.)

Devise may be to a third party in trust for the wife, and not to her directly, and when will shows an intent that it shall be in lieu of dower, she is put to her election. (Hill v. Hill, 62 N. J. L. 442; 41 Atl. Rep. 943; and see under Illinois statute, Warren v. Warren, 148 Ill. 641, 650; 36 N. E. Rep. 611.)

But she is not put to her election when the devise is to a trustee to pay the widow the income. (Colgate v. Colgate, 23 N. J. Eq. 372.)

The fact that the wife through a trustee is given the income of all the estate sustains the implication that the testator did not intend that she should also have dower. (Asche v. Asche, 113 N. Y. 232; 21 N. E. Rep. 70.)

If the purposes of a trust as declared in the will, require that the entire title, free from the dower interest of the widow, should be vested in the trustee in order to effectuate the intent of the testator in creating it, a clear case for an election is presented. But the mere creation of a trust for the sale of real property and its distribution is not inconsistent with the existence of a dower interest in the same property. (Konvalinka v. Schlegel, 104 N. Y. 125, 130; 9 N. E. Rep. 868.) But compare Vernon v. Vernon (53 N. Y. 352), where it was *held* that authority given to executors to sell real estate, not devised to the wife, at a price fixed, was inconsistent with a claim of dower; and that the wife was put to her election, and was barred by her acceptance of the testamentary provision; and see Kimbel v. Kimbel (14 App. Div. 570; 43 N. Y. Supp. 900), where it was *held* that a power of sale given to executors was not inconsistent with a claim of dower; although it might be otherwise if the will had directed a sale, free from incumbrances.

(f) **Effect of devise of life estate to wife.**—Widow may take one-third of the estate under claim of dower, and the residue as devised under the will. (Lewis v. Smith, 9 N. Y. 502.)

Where will devised life estate to widow and then specifically devised the residue " absolutely and in fee," the widow is put to her election. (Cooper v. Cooper, 56 N. J. Eq. 48; 38 Atl. Rep. 198.)

While a simple devise of all the testator's real estate to his wife, during life, is not inconsistent with the claim of dower, and does not put her to an election, the rule is otherwise where the devise is upon *conditions* which cannot have full force and effect unless dower is excluded. (Matter of Zahrt, 94 N. Y. 605, 609; distinguishing Lewis v. Smith, 9 id. 502.)

Devise to a widow of a life estate, does not put her to an election, where the will does not indicate an intent that such devise was in lieu of dower. (Estate of Proctor, 103 Iowa, 232; 72 N. W. Rep. 516; McGuire v. Brown, 41 Iowa, 650; Metteer v. Wiley, 34 id. 216; but see Anthony v. Anthony, 55 Conn. 256; 11 Atl. Rep. 45, where it was held that a devise of use of nearly one-half the real estate, excluded dower as such, although there was nothing in the will to the effect that it was in lieu of dower.)

And so where the devise is substantially an estate for life to the widow. (Cooper v. Cooper, 56 N. J. Eq. 48; 38 Atl. Rep. 198; and see Carper v. Crowl, 149 Ill. 465, 479; 36 N. E. Rep. 1040; Dunning v. Dunning, 82 Hun, 462; 31 N. Y. Supp. 719; aff'd on opinion below 147 N. Y. 686; 42 N. E. Rep. 722.)

(g) **As to property not disposed of by the will.**—Where the only bequest is in lieu of dower, and while the widow may take or not take that at her pleasure, she cannot take the bequest and claim anything else which is not bequeathed as for instance a share in the personal estate as by intestacy. (Estate of Smith, 60 Mich. 136, 142; 27 N. W. Rep. 80.)

But *it seems* to be held otherwise. (Nelson v. Pomeroy, 64 Conn. 257; 29 Atl. Rep. 534; and see Re Kempton, 23 Pick. 163; Bennett v. Packer, 70 Conn. 357; 39 Atl. Rep. 739.)

And so in case of intestacy as to real estate under the Illinois statute. (Sutton v. Read, 176 Ill. 69; 51 N. E. Rep. 801.)

A gift to the wife in lieu of dower and accepted by her has no effect on her right under any statute or any other source, to the personal property not bequeathed by the will, as to which the testator died intestate. (Hatch v. Bassett, 52 N. Y. 359; Lefevre v. Lefevre, 59 id. 434.)

But *held* otherwise as to lapsed legacies where the will provided that the gift to the wife was " in full satisfaction and recompense of and for her dower *or* thirds which she may or can in *anywise* claim or demand." (Matter of Hodgman, 140 N. Y. 421, 427; 35 N. E. Rep. 660.) And so where as to a portion of lands devised, the testator died intestate, owing to illegality of the devise, acceptance by the widow of the provision in the will in legal effect operates as a consent to all the terms and conditions annexed to it, and she yields every right inconsistent therewith. Bequest in this case was * * * "to be in lieu, substitution and satisfaction of her dower, thirds, *and all other* interest in my estate, real and personal and mixed." (Lee v. Tower, 124 N. Y. 370; 26 N. E. Rep. 943.)

Husband's right to bequeath personal property absolute. (Jochem v. Dutcher, 104 Wis. 611; 80 N. W. Rep. 949.)

(h) **As affected by debts of husband.**—A bequest in lieu of dower, accepted by the widow, is substantially a purchase, and it should not bear any portion of the debts of the testator. (Dunning v. Dunning, 82 Hun, 462; 31 N. Y. Supp. 719; affirmed on opinion below 147 N. Y. 686; 42 N. E. Rep. 722; and see Carper v. Crowl, 149 Ill. 465; 36 N. E. Rep. 1040.) But compare Beekman v. Vandeveer (3 Dem. 619), where it was held that the debts of the husband must be satisfied before any property of his estate can be lawfully applied to the discharge of the wife's legacy given to her and accepted in lieu of dower. (Citing and following Isenhart v. Brown, 1 Edw. Ch. 411; Babcock v. Stoddard, 3 T. & C. 207; Sanford v. Sanford, 4 Hun, 753.)

A devise or legacy given to the widow in lieu of dower, is not to be required to contribute with other legacies to the payment of debts due from the estate. (Lord v. Lord, 23 Conn. 330.)

Widow in accepting a devise in lieu of dower, where there is a mortgage thereon at time of testator's death, takes subject to the same. This by express terms of the New York statute. (Meyer v. Cahen, 111 N. Y. 270, 273; 18 N. E. Rep. 852.)

Liability of land devised to widow in lieu of dower, for debts of testator. (See Bray v. Neill, 21 N. J. Eq. 344; Harrison v. Taylor, 51 S. W. Rep. 193 [Ky.]; no off. rep.)

(i) **Election requires knowledge of rights.**—A widow may have relief in equity where she did not make her election fairly and understandingly; she may have rescission on restoring property received by her or upon other equitable terms, provided it is without prejudice to acquired rights of others. (Hill v. Hill, 62 N. J. L. 442; 41 Atl. Rep. 943; and see Warren v. Warren, 148 Ill. 641; 36 N. E. Rep. 611; Collins v. Woods, 63 Ill. 285.)

Acts claimed to constitute an election must be plain and unequivocal, and be done with a full knowledge of her rights and the condition of the estate. Mere acquiescence, without a deliberate and intelligent choice, will not be an election. (Sill v. Sill, 31 Kans. 248; 1 Pac. Rep. 556.)

Election must be exercised by the widow with full knowledge of her rights; otherwise not binding. (Hindley v. Hindley, 29 Hun, 318.)

But where she is given a year to elect, she cannot repudiate her election on the ground of ignorance, when she made no inquiry, and no effort to become informed. (Akin v. Kellogg, 48 Hun, 459; 1 N. Y. Supp. 846;

aff'd 119 N. Y. 441; 23 N. E. Rep. 1046; and see a prior decision on a demurrer, id. 39 Hun, 252.)

And that election requires knowledge of rights. (See Carper v. Crowl, 149 Ill. 465, 480; 36 N. E. Rep. 1040; Stokes v. Norwood, 44 S. C. 424, 427; 22 S. E. Rep. 417; Beem v. Kimberly, 72 Wis. 343, 365; 39 N. W. Rep. 542; Milliken v. Welliver, 37 Ohio St. 461; Reville v. Dubach, 60 Kans. 572; 57 Pac. Rep. 522.)

(j) **Acceptance may be implied.**—Acceptance of devise may be presumed. (Reed v. Dickerman, 12 Pick. 145.)

Election may be implied from acts indicating choice. (Gullett v. Farley, 164 Ill. 566; 45 N. E. Rep. 972.)

Election may be made by acts *in pais.* (Craig v. Walthall, 14 Gratt. 518, 525; Reville v. Dubach, 60 Kans. 572; 57 Pac. Rep. 522; and see Hill v. Hill, 62 N. J. L. 442; 41 Atl. Rep. 943; Collins v. Woods, 63 Ill. 285; Estate of Franke, 97 Iowa, 704; 66 N. W. Rep. 918; Milliken v. Welliver, 37 Ohio St. 461; Brokaw v. Brokaw, 41 N. J. Eq. 304; 7 Atl. Rep. 414.)

But they have no such effect where all her acts were done as executrix and there is nothing to indicate that they were done in any other capacity. (Estate of Proctor, 103 Iowa, 232; 72 N. W. Rep. 516.)

Acceptance and acquiescence may prevent subsequent claim of dower on theory of an equitable estoppel. (Jones v. Powell, 6 Johns. Ch. 194.)

Where widow dies a few days after the testator without having made any election, the presumption is that she took under the will. (Jackson's Appeal, 126 Pa. St. 108; 17 Atl. Rep. 535; and see Fosher v. Guilliams, 120 Ind. 172; 22 N. E. Rep. 118.)

(k) **Time or manner of election.**—Time of election may be governed by an expression of intent in regard thereto in the will. (Gale v. Gale, 48 Ill. 471, 474.)

Acceptance of a sum of money from the executor for her support, does not estop the widow from exercising her right of election during the period of time prescribed by statute. (Beem v. Kimberly, 72 Wis. 343, 365; 39 N. W. Rep. 542.)

Failure to comply with a statute requiring evidence of election to take under the law and not under the will, is the equivalent of acceptance of provision in the will. (Archibald v. Long, 144 Ind. 452, 455; 43 N. E. Rep. 439; and see Hastings v. Clifford, 32 Me. 132; Dougherty v. Barnes, 64 Mo. 159; Gough v. Manning, 26 Md. 348; Draper v. Morris, 137 Ind. 169; 36 N. E. Rep. 714.)

The time prescribed by statute for making such election is not extended by a stay of proceedings during pendency of an appeal from a decree refusing to admit will to probate. (Albright v. Albright, 70 Wis. 528; 36 N. W. Rep. 254; and see Pindell v. Pindell, 40 Md. 537; Church of Acquackenonk v. Ackerman, 1 N. J. Eq. 40; Price v. Woodford, 43 Mo. 247.)

Election when prescribed by statute, must be in substantial compliance therewith, otherwise measure of widow's interest must be found in the will. Draper v. Morris, 137 Ind. 169, 173; 36 N. E. Rep. 714; and see Fosher

v. Guilliams, 120 Ind. 172; 22 N. E. Rep. 118; Price v. Woodford, 43 Mo. 247; Sanders v. Wallace, 118 Ala. 418; 24 So. Rep. 354; Jones' Estate, 75 Minn. 53; 77 N. W. Rep. 551.)

(1) **Effect of election.**—Where widow by her election to take under the statute terminates her life estate created by the will, the residuary legatees are entitled to take immediately. (Schultz's Estate, 113 Mich. 592; 71 N. W. Rep. 1079.)

Such election is equivalent to her death and accelerates rights of second taker or residuary legatee. (Randall v. Randall, 85 Md. 430; 37 Atl. Rep. 209; and see Vance's Estate, 141 Pa. St. 201; 21 Atl. Rep. 643; Ferguson's Estate, 138 Pa. St. 208; 20 Atl. Rep. 945; Sherman v. Baker, 20 R. I. 218, 613; 40 Atl. Rep. 765; Slocum v. Hagaman, 176 Ill. 533; 52 N. E. Rep. 332.)

But the rule is otherwise where the result produced would contravene the intention of the testator. (Hinkley v. House of Refuge, 40 Md. 461, 469.)

And the law is different where there are other trusts in the will besides those for the widow; then the intention of the testator with reference to these is as far as possible to be carried out and performed. (Portuondo's Estate, 185 Pa. St. 473; 39 Atl. Rep. 1105.)

Election by widow to take under statute does not render the will inoperative any further than as between her and others claiming portions of the estate. (Allen v. Hannum, 15 Kans. 625.)

A widow having enjoyed provisions of will for ten years, is estopped from making an election. (Bennett v. Parker, 70 Conn. 357; 39 Atl. Rep. 739.)

When widow declined to renounce provision in the will, expressed herself satisfied with its provision, took possession of the property and held it for four years, until she married, *held,* that she had elected to take under the will and could not claim dower. (Craig v. Walthall, 14 Gratt. 518.)

Receipt by widow of one-third of the rent of real estate, in lieu of dower, for several years after death of her husband, does not constitute an assignment of dower or bar her action therefor. (Aikman v. Harsell, 98 N. Y. 186.)

An acceptance under the will of that which belongs to the widow by law, does not constitute an election; such acceptance is an idle ceremony which does not preclude her from claiming her rights under the law. (O'Harrow v. Whitney, 85 Ind. 140, 143.)

Acceptance of pecuniary provision from her husband during his lifetime in lieu of dower, bars widow from claiming dower after his death, having retained such provision and never offered to return it; she will be deemed to have elected to keep it in lieu of dower. (Jones v. Flemming, 104 N. Y. 418; 10 N. E. Rep. 693.)

Where devise is to wife during widowhood, and she elects to accept same, her estate is limited accordingly; such election precludes her from claiming under the law after she ceases to be a widow. (O'Harrow v. Whitney, *supra.*)

But it may be otherwise where the will provides that on the marriage of

the widow the land was "to take course designated by existing laws."
(McGuire v. Brown, 41 Iowa, 650.)

By widow's election to take under the will she relinquishes her right to
dower, not only in lands of which her husband died seized, but as to all
land, conveyed by him in his lifetime without her joining in the conveyance. (Spalding v. Hershfield, 15 Mont. 253; 39 Pac. Rep. 88; Corry v.
Lamb, 45 Ohio St. 203; 12 N. E. Rep. 660; and see Buffington v. Fall
River Bank, 113 Mass. 246; Fairchild v. Marshall, 42 Minn. 14; 43 N. W.
Rep. 563; Stokes v. Norwood, 44 S. C. 424, 430; 22 S. E. Rep. 417; Gibbon v. Gibbon, 40 Ga. 562; Palmer v. Voorhis, 35 Barb. 479.) But compare Hall v. Smith (103 Mo. 289; 15 S. W. Rep. 621), where under the
statute the duty of election is confined to lands of which the husband died
seized.

In Nelson v. Brown (144 N. Y. 384; 39 N. E. Rep. 355), the devise to
the wife was * * * "enjoyed, accepted and received by her in lieu of
dower, and in addition to what she would have as doweress if this devise
was not so made to her." *Held*, that the last clause was explanatory
rather than limiting or controlling what preceded, and that therefore the
wife was barred of dower by her acceptance of the provision in the will.

And see as to effect of taking land in payment of a debt, on a claim of
dower, Mannan v. Mannan (55 N. E. Rep. 855).

(m) **Illustrative cases as to election.**—A charge in the will upon real
estate for "a comfortable support and maintenance" of the widow, is not
inconsistent with a claim of dower, and she is not put to any election.
(Smith v. Kniskern, 4 Johns. Ch. 9; compare Worthen v. Pearson, 33 Ga.
385.)

A devise equally to widow, son and daughter "share and share alike," is
consistent with dower, and does not put the widow to her election; the
court holding that there should be read into the clause by construction "excluding the dower right to the wife." (Closs v. Eldert, 30 App. Div. 338;
51 N. Y. Supp. 881.)

Expression in will "in lieu of dower," is conclusive as to intention.
(Knighton v. Young, 22 Md. 360; and see as to gift "in lieu of dower,"
Gibbon v. Gibbon, 40 Ga. 562; Nelson v. Pomeroy, 19 Atl. Rep. 534;
Hubbard v. Hubbard, 47 Mass. 50; Clayton v. Aikin, 38 Ga. 320.)

If the provisions of the will are inconsistent with the dower of the wife
in the real estate, the provision for her in the will shall be held as intended
in lieu of dower, and she shall be put to her election. (Colgate v. Colgate,
23 N. J. Eq. 372, 378. The opinion reviews the cases both English and
American. Cooper v. Cooper, 56 id. 48; 38 Atl. Rep. 198; Brokaw v. Brokaw, 41 N. J. Eq. 304; 7 Atl. Rep. 414; Fairchild v. Marshall, 42 Minn.
14; 43 N. W. Rep. 563.)

A power to executors to sell and convey giving a "good and sufficient
deed," implies a conveyance free of dower, so that where there is provision
in the will for the widow, she is put to her election. (Cooper v. Cooper, 56
N. J. Eq. 48; 38 Atl. Rep. 198.)

Where will shows a clear intent that as to one part of the property devised it should not be subject to a claim of dower, the widow is put to her election; a charge of an annuity upon land or "a support and home" for her is sufficient for that purpose. (Worthern v. Pearson, 33 Ga. 385; but see Smith v. Kniskern, 4 Johns. Ch. 9.)

(n) **Community property.**—In several of the states, such as Texas, Louisiana, California, and a few others where the law of community property is applied by statute, and where there is no dower right, the general subject is regulated by the local statute and decisions thereunder to which reference is made. (And see Gilmore's Estate, 81 Cal. 240; 22 Pac. Rep. 655; Smith v. Butler, 85 Tex. 126; 19 S. W. Rep. 1083; Rogers v. Trevathan, 67 Tex. 406; 3 S. W. Rep. 569; Eyes' Estate, 7 Wash. 291; 34 Pac. Rep. 831; Estate of Stewart, 74 Cal. 98; 15 Pac. Rep. 445; Lee v. McFarland, 19 Tex. Civ. App. 292; 46 S. W. Rep. 281; Smith's Estate, 108 Cal. 115; 38 Pac. Rep. 950.)

(o) **Homestead.**—Election as to homestead. (See Helm v. Leggett, 66 Ark. 23; 48 S. W. Rep. 675; Schorr v. Etling, 124 Mo. 42; 27 S. W. Rep. 395; Lewis v. Smith, 9 N. Y. 502; Well's Estate v. Congregational Church, 63 Vt. 116; 21 Atl. Rep. 270; Carr v. Carr, 177 Ill. 454; 52 N. E. Rep. 732; Fry v. Morrison, 159 Ill. 244, 252; 42 N. E. Rep. 774; Kincaid v. Wilson, 40 S. W. Rep. 333 [Ky.].)

KOPPELMANN *et al. vs.* KOPPELMANN *et al.*

[Supreme Court of Texas, June 18, 1900; 57 S. W. Rep. 570.]

ADMINISTRATOR'S PROPERTY—INVENTORY—ESTOPPEL—GUARD-IAN—DEED—DELIVERY—PLACING OF RECORD—FRADULENT CONVEYANCE—GRANTEE.

1. Where a surviving husband, as administrator of his deceased wife, included in the inventory his separate real estate, designating the same as community property, he was not thereby estopped from claiming that the inventory was incorrect, or divested of title to the land; no rights having supervened in reliance thereon.

2. Where a father, as guardian of his children, included in the inventory of his wards' estate real estate which belonged to himself, he was not thereby estopped from asserting title to such realty, or divested of the title thereof.

3 Where a father made a deed of real estate to his children, which he did not deliver to them, but placed the same of record, with no intention

that the same should operate as a conveyance of the title, he was not estopped thereby to assert that the deed conveyed nothing; nor did such deed divest him of title.

4. Where a father, to prevent his wife from recovering a share of his property in a divorce suit, made a deed of realty to his children by a former marriage, without intending that title should pass to them, and making no delivery thereof, he was not estopped, in a suit by the children based on such deed, to assert that it passed no title; and the fact that it was made to defraud a third person gave the children no better right.

CERTIFIED question from Court of Civil Appeals of Fourth Supreme Judicial District.

Action by Herman Koppelmann and others against Adolph Koppelmann and others to recover real estate and personal property. On certified question from Court of Civil Appeals.

J. L. Story and *J. D. Guinn*, for appellants.

F. J. Maier and *L. H. Blevins*, for appellees.

WILLIAMS, J.—The Court of Civil Appeals of the Fourth District have stated facts, and propounded the question arising upon them, as follows:

"This suit was brought by appellants against the appellee, Adolph Koppelmann, and the sureties on his bond as the surviving husband of appellants' mother, to recover the value of their interest in the community property of their mother, and also to recover of Koppelmann certain lands which appellants claim by virtue of deeds from him. After an exception to appellants' petition upon the ground of misjoinder of actions was sustained by the Trial Court, the objection was waived, and the title to the land was tried, as well as appellants' right to recover upon the bond. The appellants are the children of Herman Koppelmann and Lisette Koppelmann, who married on the 21st of April, 1866. Lisette died on the 18th day of November, 1877. On the 21st day of August, 1880, Herman Koppelmann filed in the County Court of Comal county an inventory and appraisement of the community property of himself and his deceased wife, which inventory includes three tracts of land. It was sworn to by Kop-

pelmann, and was on the 17th day of November, 1880, approved
by the county judge of Comal county. On the same day, Koppelmann gave bond, as required by statute, conditioned that he
would faithfully administer the community estate, and pay one-
half of the surplus thereof, after the payment of the debts with
which the whole of the property was chargeable, to such persons
as should be entitled to so receive the same. At the same time he
made affidavit that he would faithfully administer the community
property of himself and his deceased wife, Lisette, and on the
next day said bond was approved by the county judge. On the
16th day of November, 1882, Adolph Koppelmann executed and
acknowledged an instrument in the form of a deed conveying to
the children of his marriage with Lisette (among whom are appellants) the three tracts of land which were inventoried, as above
stated, as the community property of himself and said deceased
wife. The consideration expressed in the deed was the natural
love and affection of the grantor for the grantees. On the same
day, this deed was filed for record in the office of the county
clerk of Comal county, in which county the land is situated, and
was on the 1st day of December, 1882, duly recorded. The deed
was handed to the county clerk for record by Koppelmann himself, and when recorded was returned by the clerk to him in person, and remained in the possession and in the control of Koppelmann from that time until this case was tried in the court
below, when he was required by the trial court to produce said
deed in evidence.   The grantees, including appellants, were
minors ; the oldest being about fifteen, and the youngest five, years
of age when the deed was executed. At the August term, A. D.
1884, of the County Court of Comal county, Adolph Koppelmann
applied to said court for letters of guardianship of the estate of
his minor children, of whom are the appellants in this case, stating
in his application that said minors were possessed of certain real
estate situated in Comal county, of the probable value of $3,000;
and on the 4th day of August, 1894, he gave bond and qualified
as guardian of the estate of the said minor children. The only
property inventoried and appraised as the estate of said minors
was the three tracts of land described in the inventory of the
community estate, and conveyed by his deed of November 16,
1882. After Adolph Koppelmann qualified, as surviving hus-

band, to administer the community estate of himself and deceased wife, Lisette, and before he made the deed of November 16, 1882, he married again. He now claims, in defense of appellants' action, that one of the tracts of land described in the inventory of the community estate of himself and deceased wife was not in fact community property, but was the separate property of himself, and that the deed made by him to appellants, and the letters of guardianship procured on their estate, were made and procured solely for the purpose of defeating the suit which his wife was then about to bring against him for divorce and for a large amount of his property, and that the deed was not in fact delivered, and no title passed thereby to the grantees.

"Question: Under the facts stated, is the appellee estopped from proving as a defense that his deed of November 16, 1882, was never in fact delivered, and from showing that it was made only for the purpose of defeating the suit which he alleges his wife was about to bring against him for a large amount of his property?"

In answering the question, it must be assumed that the truth is, as the appellee contends, that the property had belonged to him, and that he never delivered the deed nor did any of the acts stated with reference to it for the purpose of giving effect to it; and the question then is, do the acts stated, or some of them, have the legal effect of precluding him from showing the truth? Those acts are: First, the making of the inventory of the property as belonging to the community estate of himself and his deceased wife; second, the inclusion of it in the inventory of the property of his wards as belonging to them; and, third, the signing and recording of the deed for the purpose stated. That neither of the inventories was conclusive of the question, or had the effect of estopping Koppelmann from showing that the property did not in fact belong to his children, but was his own, we believe to be conclusively settled by'the decisions of this court. (*Dunham* v. *Chatham*, 21 Tex. 248; *White* v. *Shepperd*, 16 id. 166, 167; *Little* v. *Birdwell*, 21 id. 607; *Carroll* v. *Carroll*, 20 id. 732.) As in the cases cited, there had been nothing done in this by any third person upon the faith of the statements in the inventories. In order for a deed to pass title, there must be a delivery of it, either actual or constructive. (*Steffian* v. *Bank*, 69

Tex. 517, 518; 6 S. W. 823; *McCartney* v. *McCartney* [Tex. Sup.], 55 S. W. 310.) The depositing of a deed for record by or at the instance of the grantor had often been held to be sufficient evidence of delivery, but it is not conclusive; and where the deed is not actually delivered, but possession of it is retained by the maker, he is not estopped from showing that the registration was not intended to take the place of delivery or to give effect to the conveyance. From. this it results as we have heretofore held, *McCartney* v. *McCartney* (*supra*), that the question as to the effect of a deed thus recorded, but continuing in the possession of the signer of it, is open for investigation, and its decision depends upon the intent with which the acts relied on as taking the place of actual delivery were done, and, if they were not done for the purpose of completing the conveyance of title, the deed is inoperative. Where the execution of the deed is not thus completed, the purpose of the party to deceive and defraud cannot take the place of execution. A bad intent cannot operate to pass title without the execution of the deed. When the deed has been delivered, its effect is to pass the title as between the grantor and grantee, and the former will not be allowed to defeat it by showing that it was made without consideration for the purpose of defrauding creditors, nor to enforce an agreement on the part of the grantee to reconvey or to hold in trust, because out of such a fraudulent transaction no cause of action can arise. The courts in such cases leave the parties where they find them. In all the cases relied on by appellant, the deed had been delivered. But when, for want of the execution of the deed, the title has not passed out of the grantor, he is in no need of a decree restoring it. He protects himself, without the aid of the fraudulent agreement, by simply showing that he has not parted with his property. The party relying on a deed must prove its execution, which includes its delivery, and his adversary may disprove or rebut the circumstances relied on as showing such execution. Since no one of the facts stated in itself constitutes an estoppel, it follows that collectively they cannot have that effect. They are merely evidence upon the issues as to the original ownership of the property and the execution of the deed.

SHEPARD *et al. vs.* HANSON.

[Supreme Court of North Dakota, May 2, 1900; 83 N. W. Rep. 20.]

ACTION ON NOTE—DIRECTING VERDICT—POWERS OF GUARDIAN.

1. The mere possession of a negotiable promissory note, which is not payable to bearer and is unindorsed, by another than the payee, is not
   prima facie evidence of the ownership of such note. Accordingly it
   was error for the trial court to direct a verdict for the amount of the
   note in suit; there being no other evidence of title; and plaintiff's
   ownership being denied by the answer.
2. A guardian, in making contracts relating to the estates of his wards,
   can bind himself only, and can bind neither his wards personally nor
   their estates.
   (Syllabus by the court.)

APPEAL from District Court, Cass county; CHARLES A. POL-
LOCK, Judge.

Action by Ralph W. Shepard and another, by W. C. Resser,
guardian, against Ole K. Hanson. Judgment for plaintiffs, and
defendant appeals.
Reversed.

Hildreth & Ingwaldson, for appellant.

Turner & Lee, for respondents.

YOUNG, J.—This action was originally commenced by Frank
W. Herline, as guardian of the estate of Ralph W. Shepard and
Frank L. Shepard, minors, to recover for his wards the amount
due upon a certain promissory note executed by the defendant,
which it is alleged is the property of these minors, and is wholly
unpaid. After the issues in the case were joined, and some time
prior to the trial of the action, Herline resigned as guardian; and
the County Court of Cass county, which had appointed him, appointed in his place W. C. Resser, who, by stipulation of counsel,
was substituted as plaintiff. At the close of the case, the District

Court, upon motion of plaintiffs' counsel, directed a verdict in plaintiffs' favor for the full amount claimed, and judgment was ordered and entered on the verdict. Defendant's appeal is from the judgment, and, in a settled statement, he presents for review numerous alleged errors of law. Among these, the only one we shall have occasion to notice is the order directing a verdict for the plaintiffs. The defendant's answer admits the execution of the note, but specifically denies that it is or ever was the property of the plaintiff's wards, and alleges that the note ever was and is the individual property of Frank W. Herline, the payee named in the note, and that any transfer or indorsement thereof by him was without consideration and in bad faith. For a further defense the defendant then set up three several counterclaims as existing in his favor and against Herline, as guardian, and his two wards, arising out of work, labor, and services alleged to have been done and furnished for them at their request. The amount of these claims exceeds the amount of the note sued upon. The following is the note in full: " Mapleton, North Dakota, July 1st, 1892. Ninety days after date I promise to pay to the order of F. W. Herline one hundred and fifty-four dollars, at Red River Valley National Bank of Fargo, value received, with interest, at the rate of 12 per cent. per annum. I hereby agree to pay the further sum $—— as attorney's fees, should the collection of this note be enforced by law. Ole K. Hanson." The following indorsement appears upon the back: " Pay to the guardian of Ralph W. and Fred L. Shepard, F. W. Herline, without recourse." The motion for a directed verdict was based upon the ground "that defendant had failed to show any defense by way of nonownership of the note by plaintiffs, or counterclaim or payment." This motion was granted, and, we hold, improperly granted. The ownership of the note by plaintiff's wards was specifically controverted by the answer. It was therefore incumbent on the plaintiff to establish by evidence the ownership and title to the notes in his wards, as a basis for recovery: The present guardian testified that it had been turned over to him by his predecessor, Mr. Herline, and that he had it in his possession. The note was then received in evidence. This is all the evidence offered to establish title to the note in the wards. This was insufficient. It is true that the possession of a negotiable instrument payable to bearer or payable to order, and indorsed in blank or indorsed to the holder, is *prima facie* evidence of ownership, and that the holder acquired it *bona fide* for full value, in the usual course of business, before maturity, and without notice of any circumstance impeaching its validity. See Daniel, Neg. Inst. § 812. But it is equally true that the possession by one not the payee of such an instrument, which is not indorsed and is not payable to bearer, is not *prima facie* evidence of ownership by the party having possession, where the ownership is controverted. In *Van Eman* v. *Stanchfield* (10 Minn. 255 [Gil. 197]), the court said: " Where a negotiable note, payable to order, is transferred without indorsement, the holder takes it as a mere chose in action; and, while he may maintain an action upon it in his own name, he must prove the transfer to himself, and mere possession is not *prima facie* evidence of the fact." See, also, in support of the doctrine that the possession of an unindorsed promissory note by one not the payee is no evidence of the ownership of the holder, *Cavitt* v. *Tharp* (30 Mo. App. 131); *Dorn* v. *Parsons* (56 Mo. 601); *Merlin* v. *Manning* (2 Tex. 351); *Ross v. Smith* (19 id. 171); 4 Am. & Eng. Enc. Law (2d. ed.) 319; Daniel, Neg. Inst. (§ 812); Rand. Com. Paper (§ 792). The note, it will be seen, is payable to order, and not bearer; and it is not indorsed by the payee, either generally in blank, or specially to any person by name. The words on the back of the note, " Pay to the guardian of Ralph W. and Fred L. Shepard," are not a direction to pay either to the wards themselves or to their estate. If the language used has any effect, it is as an indorsement to some person, not by name, but by description. The person described was F. W. Herline, the payee in the note, so that no new feature was added to the note by these words. It was already payable to himself, and was at best no more than a direction to pay to himself. As to the effect of words *descriptio personæ*, see *Thornton* v. *Rankin* (19 Mo. 194); *Jeffries* v. *McLean* (12 id. 355); *Mellen* v. *Moore* (68 Me. 390); *Shaw* v. *Smith* ([Mass.], 22 N. E. 887; 6 L. R. A. 348).

There being no evidence of ownership of the note in suit by plaintiff's wards, it was therefore error to direct a verdict in his favor, and the judgment must accordingly be reversed. But, inasmuch as a new trial must be had, we wish to refer to the counterclaims set up by defendant. Counsel for the respective parties have spent considerable time discussing the evidence, to determine whether or not there is any evidence that the contracts with the defendant which are the basis of the counterclaims were made by Herline as guardian, and for and on behalf of his wards. It is the contention of plaintiff's counsel that he acted individually. It may be conceded that defendant's contention is true, and that Herline acted as guardian and that the services were for him as guardian, yet it is entirely immaterial. It was still Herline's personal contract, for the law is well settled that the guardian of an estate of minors cannot as such make a contract which will bind the wards personally or their estate. He is bound personally. (*Rollins* v. *Marsh,* 128 Mass. 116; *Hospital* v. *Fairbanks,* 132 id. 414; *Sperry* v. *Fanning,* 80 Ill. 371; *Adams* v. *Jones,* 8 Mo. App. 602; *Dalton* v. *Jones,* 51 Miss. 585; *Tenney* v. *Evans,* 14 N. H. 343; *Phelps* v. *Worcester,* 11 N. H. 51.) In *Reading* v. *Wilson* (38 N. J. Eq. 446), the court said: " A guardian has no authority whatever to bind either the person or the estate of his ward by contract. It is his duty to see that his ward is maintained and educated in a manner suitable to his means, and if, in the performance of this duty, it becomes necessary for him to enter into contracts, such contracts impose no duty on the ward, and do not bind his estate, but bind the guardian personally and alone. For any reasonable expenditure made by a guardian, out of his own means, for the benefit of his ward, he is, of course, entitled to be reimbursed out of the ward's estate; but this is the limit of the ward's liability, whether measured by rules of law or rules of equity. A guardian is without the least capacity or authority to impose contract obligations on his ward." Whatever causes of action the defendant has, then, arising out of his alleged services to Herline as guardian of those wards, exist against Herline individually. The District Court is directed to enter an order reversing its judgment and granting a new trial.

All concur.

PETITION FOR REHEARING.

(June 2, 1900.)

Counsel for plaintiff have filed a petition for a rehearing. in which it is urged that the court was mistaken in asserting that there is no evidence in the record showing that plaintiff's wards are the owners of the note in suit. They contend that there is other evidence than that sought to be derived from the possession of the instrument, and refer us to a certain written account or report made by Herline at the close of his guardianship, and filed and recorded in the County Court on March 21, 1899. This document, which was received in evidence against defendant's objection, purports to be an account of Herline's guardianship from January 12, 1892, up to the time it was filed in the County Court. Under the heading of "Receipts" there appears this entry: "July 1st, 1892. Ole K. Hanson paid on $168 note $14.00, interest on said note $19.02." Under the heading of "New Notes" the following entry appears: "(Stock) Ole K. Hanson, dated April 1st, 1892, due 90 days, 12 per cent. par, ren $168." This abbreviation evidently means that the last described note is a part renewal of the former note, and doubtless refers to the note in suit. On the margin of the report, and opposite the description of the note involved in this action, and certain other notes, these words appear: "These notes are not assets of the guardianship." It would seem that this entry conclusively negatives the idea that the note in question belongs to plaintiff's wards. However, it is unimportant what is meant by these entries; for, conceding that they tend to show that Herline purchased the note, and from the funds of these wards, yet that fact utterly fails to establish title of the note in the wards. At best, the note can be no more than an investment of the wards' funds made by the guardian, for it was not a part of the original assets. The law requires investments to be made in a particular manner, and a guardian in this state may not either sell his ward's property, or make investments of his ward's funds, save on an order of the County Court. The office of a guardian is highly fiduciary in its nature, and has been made the subject of careful regulation by statutory provisions. A guardian may pay the just debts of his ward, and demand and sue for debts due to his ward. He may apply the income and profits of the estate to the comfortable and suitable maintenance and support of the ward. In these matters considerable latitude is given to his discretion. See sections 6553, 6554, 6556, Rev. Codes. But the power to sell the estate of the wards, or any portion of it, does not rest in the guardian individually. Neither has he authority to invest the funds of the estate in any kind of securities, except upon application to, and an order of, the County Court. The legal authority for both sales and investments emanates from the County Court, and that court alone. See sections 6561, to 6574 id., both inclusive. The requirement as to the method to be pursued to make sales of property and to invest funds belonging to wards is specific and requires that it shall be in pursuance of an order or decree therefor. It was held by the Supreme Court of Iowa, in construing a statute which required guardians to manage estates under the direction of the court, that such requirement implied an inhibition upon the doing of these acts without the direction of the court. See *Bates* v. *Dunham* (58 Iowa, 308; 12 N. W. 309). And the court in that case also held that a direction to loan the funds of the ward must precede the act of loaning. In the very recent case of *Easton* v. *Somerville* ([Iowa], 82 N. W. 475), the court said: " A guardian cannot, as at common law, loan his ward's money, or invest it in securities, without an order of court. His powers are conferred by statute, and he may loan their money, and in all other respects manage their affairs, under .proper orders of the court, or a judge thereof. (Code, § 3200.) Under this section it has been held that a guardian cannot loan the money of his ward, lease his land or invest his funds without an order of court. * * * Such transactions, made without the order or direction of the Probate Court, are invalid, or voidable, at least, until approved by the proper court." See, also, *McReynolds* v. *Anderson* (69 Iowa, 208; 28 N. W. 558); *Slusher* v. *Hammond* (94 Iowa, 512; 63 N. W. 185); *Reed* v. *Lane* (96 Iowa, 454; 65 N. W. 380); *Garner* v. *Hendry* (95 Iowa, 44; 63 N. W. 359); *Alexander* v. *Buffington* (66 Iowa, 360; 23 N. W. 754); *Dohms* v. *Mann* (76 Iowa, 724; 39 N. W. 823). The County Court of Cass county has exclusive jurisdiction over this estate, and it does not lie within the jurisdiction of any other court to usurp its authority by fastening the title of a guardian's void investments upon his wards by independent evidence. It is patent, then, that where the issue is whether the wards own certain property, which is the fruit of an investment made by the guardian, we must look to the order or decree of the County Court authorizing or directing it, and not to the guardian's report, for the latter is binding only upon himself. In this case plaintiffs have offered no evidence to show that Herline was authorized by the County

Court to purchase the note in suit, or that such purchase was approved by the County Court. Neither was the report of the guardian filed in the County Court, and above referred to, approved and allowed. When the plaintiff's wards obtain their majority they may demand the original estate, or its value, reduced only by lawful expenditures and such bad investments as have been authorized by the County Court. They are not at the mercy either of the improvident judgment of their former guardian, or his unlawful diversion of their funds. The bond required to be executed under section 6544, Rev. Codes, stands in lieu of the original estate until it is fully accounted for under the statutes regulating the powers and duties of guardians. It is not necessary to consider whether the written report of Herline was admissible for any other purpose. It is sufficient to say that it has no probative weight on the question of the title of the note, for the reasons already stated. If it affirmatively appeared that no order was in fact made either authorizing or approving the investment of the funds of the wards in the note in suit, it would clearly be our duty to direct a dismissal of the action. As the. case stands, however, the record is simply silent on that point. For that reason the order reversing the judgment and directing a new trial, which will afford an opportunity to produce competent evidence of ownership in the wards if it exists, will stand.

The petition for a rehearing is denied.

Note.—CONTRACTS OF GUARDIAN.

(a) Guardian personally bound.
(b) How protected. ·
(c) Mechanics' lien.
(d) Remedy—In accounting.
(e) Remedy—In equity.

(a) **Guardian personally bound.**—That guardian is personally bound by his contracts. (See also, in addition to cases cited in preceding opinion, Brown v. Eggleston, 53 Conn. 111; 2 Atl. Rep. 321; Rice v. Paschal, 59 Ga. 637; Ray v. McGinnis, 81 Ind. 451; Elson v. Spraker, 100 id. 374; Young v. Smith, 22 Tex. 345; Reading v. Wilson, 38 N. J. Eq. 446; Meyers v. Cohn, 4 Misc. 185; 23 N. Y. Supp. 996.)

The addition of the words "as guardian" in the contract, does not relieve the guardian from personal liability. (Sperry v. Fanning, 80 Ill. 371.)

(b) **How protected.**—Guardian may protect himself from individual liability by special contract that credit is given solely to estate of ward in his hands. (Salem Female Academy v. Phillips, 68 N. C. 491; Sperry v. Fanning, *supra;* Bradner Smith & Co. v. Williams, 178 Ill. 427; 53 N. E. Rep. 358.)

(c) **Mechanic's lien.**—Guardian cannot by his contract for repair of his ward's building subject same to a mechanic's lien, without first obtaining an order of the court authorizing the making of the contract. (Fish v. McCarthy, 96 Cal. 484; 31 Pac. Rep. 529; and see Rice v. Paschal, 59 Ga. 637; Ray v. McGinnis, 81 Ind. 451; Robinson v. Hersey, 60 Me. 225; Sperry v. Fanning, 80 Ill. 371; Copley v. Harlow, 57 Barb. 299; Kent v. West, 33 App. Div. 112, 117; 53 N. Y. Supp. 244; note to James v. Lane, 33 N. J. Eq. 31.)

A court of competent jurisdiction may authorize guardian to contract so as to bind the estate of the ward. (Reading v. Wilson, 38 N. J. Eq. 446; Dalton v. Jones, 51 Miss. 585; and see Kent v. West, 33 App. Div. 117; 53 N. Y. Supp. 244.)

(d) **Remedy—In accounting.**—While guardian cannot contract so as to bind the ward or the estate, and is personally liable, he may be reimbursed out of the trust estate. (St. Joseph's Academy v. Augustini, 55 Ala. 493.)

Guardian's remedy in reimbursement by taking credit on his accounting. (Brent v. Grace, 30 Mo. 253; and see Matter of Wood, 71 id. 623; Merkel's Estate, 154 Pa. St. 294; 26 Atl. Rep. 428.)

An attorney may have remedy as against the ward's estate for services rendered at the guardian's request, upon an accounting by latter. (Price's Appeal, 116 Pa. St. 410; 9 Atl. Rep. 856. The opinion in this case is exceptionally interesting and valuable as limiting the doctrine of the personal liability of a guardian on his contracts for benefit of his ward's estate. Woodward's Appeal, 38 Pa. St. 322. And see as to remedy in equity where the guardian gave the creditor a power of attorney to collect rents as security of the debt contracted for benefit of the ward's Estate. James v. Lane, 33 N. J. Eq. 30.)

A guardian who has paid debt of his ward under his contract for which he was personally liable, may lawfully indemnify himself out of the ward's estate, or if he be discharged from his guardianship, he may have an action against the ward for money paid for his use. (Sperry v. Fanning, 80 Ill. 371.)

(e) **Remedy—In equity.**—There may be remedy in equity as against the ward and his estate, when the guardian is insolvent. (Owens v. Mitchell, 38 Tex. 588.) Or where third parties support and educate the child, without guardian's contract. (Barnum v. Frost, 17 Gratt. 398.)

In this case the court says: "At common law the contract of the guardian is deemed personal; but where there is no ground to assert or imply a personal contract of the guardian, and where the credit and reliance rest

exclusively on the ward's estate, there is no reason or policy of the law
that would forbid the asserting in a court of equity of such a claim upon
the ward's estate in a course of administration and settlement in such a
forum." (Id. 405.) And see this case considered at length and denied
as authority. (Reading v. Wilson, 38 N. J. Eq. 449.)

A creditor who has boarded and educated ward under a contract with
guardian, has no remedy in equity to charge real estate of the ward, where
the guardian wasted all the personal assets and he and his sureties are insolvent. (St. Joseph's Academy v. Augustini, 55 Ala. 493.)

A guardian having right to possession of real estate of his ward has right
to contract with an attorney to bring ejectment and for his compensation
upon the basis of one-third contingent fee; if such a contract is a fair,
reasonable and proper one, under the circumstances, specific performance
of same may be adjudged. (Matter of Hynes, 105 N. Y. 560; 12 N. E.
Rep. 60; and see as to specific performance against a guardian, Sherman
v. Wright, 49 N. Y. 228.)

No remedy in equity where no benefit received by the ward or his estate.
(Noble v. Runyan, 85 Ill. 618.)

As to remedy in equity, see also, Reading v. Wilson (38 N. J. Eq. 446).

CHAMBERLIN vs. GLEASON et al.

[Court of Appeals of New York, June 5, 1900; 163 N. Y. 214; 57 N. E.
Rep. 487.)

MUNICIPAL CORPORATIONS—PAVING ASSESSMENT—LIFE TENANT
—NOTICE — EFFECT — REMAINDER-MEN — APPORTIONMENT
INJUNCTION—WILLS—TAXES—AMBIGUITY IN JUDGMENT—
PRESUMPTION ON APPEAL—HARMLESS ERROR.

1. Olean City Charter, § 88, requires publication of a notice of paving
assessments, and a day for their correction, and provides that, after
correction and confirmation, they shall become liens. Section 113 provides that notice to one tenant in common shall be notice to all. A
paving assessment was levied against plaintiff, who was a life tenant
of property abutting on the paved street. Held, that notice to plaintiff
was not notice to the remainder-men, since a life tenant is not a
tenant in common with remainder-men, and hence the assessment was
levied against plaintiff personally, and not against the remainder-men.

2. Where expenses of repairing a pavement are to be paid by general taxation, so that the improvement is permanent in its nature, and the whole
of the paving assessment is levied against a life tenant of property

abutting the paved street, the life tenant's remedy to secure a proper apportionment of liability between herself and the remainder-men is by injunction against the city to prevent collection of the assessment except in such proportion as shall be adjudged.

3. A paving assessment for an improvement which is to be permanent, levied against abutting property, is properly apportioned so that the life tenant pays the interest on the assessment during her life, and the remainder-men pay the principal of the assessment as it falls due.

4. A husband's will devising real estate to his wife for life, remainder over, provided that the wife should pay all taxes assessed against the property during her lifetime, and also all premiums for insurance, not only for her interest as life tenant but also as mortgagee, the remainder-men being required to mortgage the property to her to secure her an allowance out of the estate. *Held,* that a paving assessment for a permanent improvement was not included in the word "taxes," used in the will, and hence that the remainder-men, and not the widow, were liable therefor.

5. Where a judgment below apportions a paving assessment payable in ten successive annual installments, with interest, between the life tenant and remainder-men, so that the life tenant pays the interest thereon becoming due during her life, and the remainder-men pay the principal, and also adjudges that the remainder-men are liable for the assessment except whatever interest becomes due during the tenant's lifetime, according to the condition of bonds issued for the payment of the assessment, and the record fails to show the condition of the bonds as to whether interest is payable on the entire assessment annually, or is postponed as to each installment until it becomes due, it will be assumed, on appeal, that the life tenant is to pay the interest accruing on the entire assessment during her life.

6. Where a paving assessment amounts to $459, and a life tenant of the property against which it is levied is sixty-nine years old at the time of a trial to apportion the assessment between herself and the remainder-men, and it does not appear that the item of interest on the assessment during her life was of sufficient importance to be brought to the notice of the court below, an ambiguity in a judgment apportioning the interest accruing during the tenant's life to her, and the balance of the assessment to the remainder-men, will not warrant a reversal of the judgment.

APPEAL from Supreme Court, Appellate Division, Fourth Department.

Suit by Seraph M. Chamberlin against the city of Olean, Ella V. Gleason, Clara N. Pancoast, and others. From a judgment in favor of plaintiff, defendants Gleason and Pancoast appealed to the Appellate Division, where the judgment was affirmed (46 N. Y. Supp. 1090). From this affirmance of the judgment they again appeal.

Affirmed.

Appeal from a judgment of the Appellate Division, Fourth Department (46 N. Y. Supp. 1090), affirming unanimously the judgment in favor of the plaintiff entered upon the decision of the trial court, apportioning an assessment for paving, authorizing the city to collect it as apportioned, and enjoining the city from collecting of the plaintiff except as apportioned. The proper authorities of the city of Olean, pursuant to the provisions of its charter, in 1893 caused Barry street to be paved. The plaintiff then was, and since has been, the occupant, as tenant for life, under the will of her deceased husband, of a lot abutting upon Barry street. Each of the appellants Gleason and Pancoast is, under the same will, the owner in remainder of one undivided third of the same lot. The defendants, the owners in remainder of the other one-third, do not appeal. The plaintiff's name appeared upon the general assessment roll as the owner of the lot, and the names of the remainder-men did not appear. The charter of the city (Laws 1893, ch. 478, § 98) provides that the expense of such paving " shall be assessed to and be paid by the owners of property lying along and adjoining such street on each side thereof. The assessment shall be made by the assessors of said city and they shall proceed in the same manner as is prescribed in this act for making sewer assessments, except as hereinafter modified [in respect of street railroads]. Each lineal foot of property shall pay its proportion of the total cost, and one lineal foot shall not be assessed a greater or less amount than another." Section 88 relates to sewer assessments, and provides as follows: " It shall be the duty of the assessors to proceed forthwith and assess said amount upon the land and real property lying upon or adjoining that portion of said street or alley along which said sewer or drain has been constructed." The section also provides for the publication of a notice and a day for correction, and that after such correction and confirmation such assessment shall be a lien and charge upon the property so assessed. The entire assessment chargeable to the lot in question was levied against the plaintiff. It was made payable in ten equal annual installments, with interest. Section 110 of the charter provides that "all taxes and assessments charged upon real estate, including those for local improvements, shall be a lien upon the same from the time of completing the tax roll therefor, and such lien shall be prior and superior to all other liens and incumbrances." The defendant the city clerk, pursuant to the charter and the direction of the common council, was proceeding to enforce by sale of the lot the payment of the first installment and interest thereon when the plaintiff brought this action, and procured judgment upon the trial at Special Term, adjudging that the plaintiff pay "whatever interest becomes due and payable upon said assessment, or any portion thereof, during her lifetime," and that the appellants each pay one-third of "whatever sum or sums, installment or installments, which become due and payable during the lifetime of the plaintiff," and the defendants, the owners of the other undivided one-third, pay the other third thereof, and also that the assessment was a lien upon the premises, and said remainder-men were liable therefor, "except whatever interest may become due and payable during the lifetime of the plaintiff." Whether the interest is payable annually or upon each installment when the principal thereof falls due is not clear from the record, the provision of the judgment being, "accordingly with the provisions and conditions of the bonds or other obligations issued by the city of Olean for the payment of said assessment." The record shows the due issue of such bonds, but not when they promise payment of interest. Section 113 of said charter provides that "whenever any real estate in said city is owned by two or more persons jointly, or as tenants in common, a notice served on one of such persons shall be sufficient notice to all, and for any and all purposes requiring a notice under this act."

J. H. Waring, for appellants.

Henry Donnelly, for individual respondents.

C. S. Cary and *Allen J. Hastings,* for respondent city of Olean.

LANDON, J. (after stating the facts).—The city has not appealed, and we assume that it is content with the judgment. As between the city and the remainder-men, the city did not take the statutory steps to make this assessment against them personally,

and did not assume to levy it against their respective interests in
the lot in question. It assumed the plaintiff to be the owner of
the lot. The tenant for life and the remainder-men are not tenants in common, since the possession of the tenant for life is exclusive of like possession by the remainder-men, and unity of
possession, or promiscuous occupation, or the right to it, is one
essential of tenancy in common. (2 Bl. Comm. 191; 4 Kent,
Comm. 367; *Sullivan* v. *Sullivan,* 66 N. Y. 37; *Cromwell* v. *Hull,*
97 id. 209; *Hughes* v. *Hughes,* 30 Hun, 349.)

But the city did regularly make the assessment against the
plaintiff personally, and the charter makes the assessment a lien
upon her interest in the lot, and provides for the sale thereof for
a term of years after default in payment of any installment, and
this sale the city was proceeding to make. It is not urged that
the plaintiff has any ground upon which to vacate the assessment
or prevent the sale, except by payment.

The remainder-men do not complain that the plaintiff has failed
in her duty to them in not bringing their respective interests to
the notice of the assessors. They were willing that the whole burden should fall upon her, and but for the interposition of equity,
which takes cognizance of the facts which the assessment record
does not disclose, it would so fall. In equity, between herself and
them, she was only liable with them ratably according to their
several interests and several benefits from the paving, the proper
share of each one's liability being dependent upon the unknown
duration of the plaintiff's life and the life of the improvement.

The plaintiff can have no relief at law. The charter provides
that the expense of the repairs of the pavement shall be paid by
general taxation, and thus the improvement becomes permanent in
its nature. The general rule is that municipal assessments for
permanent improvements are apportionable between the life
tenant and the remainder-men according to the circumstances of
the case and their respective interests in the property. (*Thomas*
v. *Evans,* 105 N. Y. 601; 12 N. E. 571; *Peck* v. *Sherwood,* 56 N.
Y. 615.) Unless the creator of the several estates has otherwise
provided, the life tenant should pay the usual current charges,
such as ordinary taxes, interest, and repairs, and the remainder-
men the unavoidable charges for permanent improvements. (*In
re Albertson* 113 N. Y. 434; 21 N. E. 117; *Stevens* v. *Melcher,*

152 N. Y. 551; 46 N. E. 965.) In equity, the remainder-men's share of the burden should not rest upon the plaintiff in the first instance, but upon them, and they should discharge it, lest the whole burden prove greater than the plaintiff can bear without irreparable injury to her life estate.

The will of the testator, under which the life tenant and remainder-men derive title, provides: " My wife [the plaintiff] shall pay all taxes assessed against said house and lot during her lifetime, and also all premiums for insurance of said house, not only for her interest as a life tenant, but also her interest as mortgagee." The testator also provided that the plaintiff be paid twelve dollars per week out of his estate, the same to be secured by a mortgage to be given by the remainder-men upon the house and lot in question. We think the testator did not intend to include assessments for permanent improvements in the word " taxes " as used by him in the will. (*Peck* v. *Sherwood, supra.*) It is not clear from the judgment whether the interest payable upon each installment is deferred until the principal shall become due, as the record does not show what is the promise of the bonds issued by the city to pay for the improvement as to the time of the payment of interest. We assume that the effect of the judgment is that the plaintiff must pay or provide for the payment of the interest which accrues during her life while the principal of the installment is maturing.

The appellants urge that the plaintiff ought to be charged, in favor of the remainder-men, with the interest upon the entire assessment during her life, since she is in the enjoyment of the property. (*Cogswell* v. *Cogswell,* 2 Edw. Ch. 231; *Bates* v. *Underhill,* 3 Redf. Sur. 365; *Cairns* v. *Chabert,* 3 Edw. Ch. 312.) The whole assessment is $459.37. The plaintiff was sixty-nine years of age at the time of the trial, and it does not appear that the item of interest during her life, after payment of the principal, was deemed of sufficient importance to be brought to the notice of the court. The judgment should be affirmed, with costs to the plaintiff against the appellants.

PARKER, C. J., and O'BRIEN, BARTLETT, HAIGHT, MARTIN, and VANN, JJ., concur.

Judgment affirmed.

NOTE.—EXPENSE AS BETWEEN LIFE TENANT AND REMAIN-
DER-MEN.

(a) General rules and principles.
(b) A distinction noted.
(c) Taxes.
(d) Interest.
(e) Repairs.
(f) Insurance.
(g) Costs of litigation.
(h) Apportionment.
(i) Illustrative cases.

(a) **General rules and principles.**—Expenses of administration
chargeable to *corpus*. (Matter of Bartlett, 163 Mass. 511, 522; 40 N. E.
Rep. 899.)

Life tenant must bear taxes, insurance and repairs. (Matter of Redding
[1897], 1 Ch. 876, 879.)

Repairs, taxes and insurance, are properly chargeable to life tenant.
(Amory v. Lowell, 104 Mass. 266; Greene v. Greene, 19 R. I. 620; 35
Atl. Rep. 1042; Williams v. Herrick, 18 R. I. 123; 25 Atl. Rep. 1099;
Bridge v. Bridge, 146 Mass. 373; 15 N. E. Rep. 899.)

The expense of administering a particular trust fund is chargeable to
income. (Butterbaugh's Appeal, 98 Pa. St. 351.)

But general expenses of administration incurred for the benefit of the
whole estate are chargeable to capital, and not to income. (Bridge v.
Bridge, 146 Mass. 373; 15 N. E. Rep. 899.)

Ordinary expense of the care and management of the principal, are
properly chargeable to life estate, and payable out of income. (Pierce v.
Burroughs, 58 N. H. 302.)

Life tenant is liable for all current expenses attending the enjoyment of
the property; such expenses are not properly chargeable to the *corpus*.
(Jones v. Dawson, 19 Ala. 672.)

The rule as to taxes and repairs being chargeable to the life tenant has
no application when the will shows an intent otherwise. (Griffin v. Flem-
ing, 72 Ga. 697, 703; and see where will contained clause as to their payment, Fischer, Petitioner, 19 R. I. 53; 31 Atl. Rep. 557; Greene v. Greene,
19 R. I. 620; 35 Atl. Rep. 1042; Hopkins v. Keazer, 89 Me. 347; 36 Atl.
Rep. 615; or a clause giving to executor or trustee discretionary power to
"charge property," etc., Sohier v. Eldredge, 103 Mass. 345; and the expense of administration is not chargeable to income when will shows intent
otherwise. Wethered v. Safe Deposit Co., 79 Md. 153; 28 Atl. Rep. 812.
And see where power to mortgage the *corpus* or real estate to raise money
to make repairs was upheld under clause in will "the trustees are to make
out of the income *or capital*" any outlay which they may consider proper,
Matter of Bellinger [1898], 2 Ch. Div. 534.)

But it was *held* that the interest on the moneys thus raised should be paid out of income. (Id. 538.)

The general rule applicable to the relation of life tenants and remainder-men, does not authorize the former to charge the latter with the cost and expense of permanent improvements put upon the property by him during the life tenancy. (Thomas v. Evans, 105 N. Y. 601, 611; 12 N. E. Rep. 571.)

To sustain construction of a will, whereby the capital of a trust fund may be impaired by using it in payment of taxes and of interest on mortgages and in maintaining the realty used by the life tenant, it must contain words of the most unmistakable import pointing unequivocally in that direction. (Matter of Albertson, 113 N. Y. 435; 21 N. E. Rep. 117.)

Charges and expenses properly incurred by a trustee in execution of the trusts of a will and for the benefit of the whole estate, are properly chargeable to capital and not income. (Matter of Bennett [1896], 1 Ch. Div. 778; and see Matter of Leslie, L. R. 2 Ch. Div. 185, 190; Fountaine v. Pellet, 1 Ves. Jr. 337, *note.*)

A tenant for life is bound out of the rents and profits to keep down all incidental charges upon the land, which accrue during the continuance of the life estate as for repairs, taxes, and the like. Special assessments for paving and sewerage, as well as taxes and repairs, may be included within such incidental charges. (Warren v. Warren, 148 Ill. 642; 36 N. E. Rep. 611.)

As to powers and duties of trustees as between tenant for life and re-mainder-men. (2 Perry on Trusts, § 539. *et seq.* [ed. 1899].)

(b) **A distinction noted.**—Where will gives property to trustees to "hold, invest and manage" during the life of a certain person, to collect the income and pay the same to such person and on the latter's death to divide the estate among specified remainder-men, the life beneficiary does not occupy the position of life tenant but that of *cestui que trust.* (Stevens v. Melcher, 152 N. Y. 551; 46 N. E. Rep. 965; modifying 80 Hun, 514; 30 N. Y. Supp. 625.) The opinion in this case considers the duties of a life tenant and the items properly chargeable to that interest, and points out the above distinction. (And see Cass v. Cass, 15 App. Div. 235; 44 N. Y. Supp. 186.)

(c) **Taxes.**—Ordinary taxes are paid by the tenant for life. (Plympton v. Boston Dispensary, 106 Mass. 547; Pierce v. Burroughs, 58 N. H. 302; and see Matter of Shipman, 82 Hun, 109; Williams v. Herrick, 18 R. I. 123; 25 Atl. Rep. 1099.)

Cost of paving a street in front of property chargeable to life tenant. (Warren v. Warren, 148 Ill. 642; 36 N. E. Rep. 611.)

Distinction between tax and special assessment. (Id.)

Under special terms of the will duty of remainder-men to pay taxes. (Clarke v. Clarke, 145 N. Y. 476; 40 N. E. Rep. 220; and see opinion at Special Term, 8 Misc. 339; 29 N. Y. Supp. 338, upon which it was affirmed at General Term, 75 Hun, 612; 29 N. Y. Supp. 1142, and in terms approved by the Court of Appeals, p. 482.)

Taxes assessed prior to death of testator constitute a debt of the estate and should be paid from principal and not from income. (Matter of Young, 17 Misc. 681; 41 N. Y. Supp. 539; on appeal, 15 App. Div. 285; 44 N. Y. Supp. 585.)

Where trustee foreclosed a mortgage, and afterwards sold the land, but before doing so was under the necessity of paying taxes for two years, which the mortgagor ought to have paid, the investment having yielded no income, it was *held* that those taxes should be charged to the principal. (Stone v. Littlefield, 151 Mass. 485; 24 N. E. Rep. 592. And as to liability for taxes, see also, Patrick v. Sherwood, 4 Blatch. 112; Varney v. Stevens, 22 Me. 331; Cairns v. Chabert, 3 Edw. Ch. 312; Thomas v. Evans, 105 N. Y. 601, 612; 12 N. E. Rep. 571.)

(d) **Interest.**—Interest on a mortgage chargeable to income or life tenant or interest. (Bridge v. Bridge, 146 Mass. 373; 15 N. E. Rep. 899; Ivory v. Klein, 54 N. J. Eq. 379; 35 Atl. Rep. 346.)

And so is the interest on debts of testator ascertained to be a charge. (Marshall v. Crowther, L. R. 2 Ch. Div. 199.)

Life tenant is chargeable with interest on mortgage, even after payment by the executor out of the estate. (Cogswell v. Cogswell, 2 Edw. Ch. 231; and see North American Coal Co. v. Dygett, 7 Paige, 9, 16.)

The obligation of a life tenant of an estate subject to incumbrances to keep down the interest on same, exists only as between him and the remainder-man, and not as between him and the encumbrancers. (Re Morley, L. R. 8 Eq. 594.)

In case of a mortgage the tenant for life is bound to keep down the interest, but not to pay the principal; and upon the discharge of the mortgage by the remainder-man, a strict adherence to the rule would require the tenant for life to pay interest on the amount during his life; although tor the convenience of all parties, the value of such an annuity is usually estimated, and paid at once in gross. (Plympton v. Boston Dispensary, 106 Mass. 547.)

(e) **Repairs.**—Necessary repairs are properly chargeable to life tenant. (Thurston v. Thurston, 6 R. I. 296; and see Matter of Hotchkyss, 32 Ch. Div. 408, 417; Matter of Braunsdorf, 2 App. Div. 73; 37 N. Y. Supp. 229; Matter of Jones, 103 N. Y. 621; 9 N. E. Rep. 493.)

In Matter of De Teissier ([1893], 1 Ch. 153), the court refused to charge interest of an infant tenant for life in remainder with repairs necessary for the preservation of a house.

Where property is in bad state of repair at the death of the testator, the life tenant cannot be required to do more than keep in same state of repair; there is no obligation on the tenant for life to put in such state of repair as to comply with terms of a lease. (Matter of Courtier, 34 Ch. Div. 136; but see this case commented upon in Matter of Redding [1897], 1 Ch. 876, 879.)

(f) **Insurance.**—Life tenant receiving full value of property insured, holds same as trustee for the remainder-men. (Welsh v. London Assur Co., 151 Pa. St. 608; 25 Atl. Rep. 142.)

Proceeds of insurance in such a case should be used in rebuilding or should go to the remainder-men, reserving the interest of the life tenant. (Green v. Green, 50 S. C. 514; 27 S. E. Rep. 953.)

But these two preceding cases are considered and distinguished in Spalding v. Miller (Not Off. Rep; 45 S. W. Rep. 462), and it is there held that where the life tenant insures to full value, or in excess of his own interest, paying the premium, and without any intention of doing so for benefit of the remainder-men, there is no trust resulting in behalf of the remainder-men, and the excess could not be applied to rebuilding.

And as to duty of life tenant as to insurance, see Hopkins v. Keazer (89 Me. 347; 36 Atl. Rep. 616).

(g) **Costs of litigation.**—Costs of litigation or legal proceedings, in good faith, from a conviction of duty, chargeable to *corpus*. (Sanders v. Miller, 25 Beav. 154; Matter Earl De La Warr, 16 Ch. Div. 587; Stott v. Milne, 25 id. 710; Whitton's Trusts, 8 Eq. Cas. 352; and see *note* to Fountaine v. Pellet, 1 Ves. Jr. 337.)

Costs caused by a due and proper administration of the *corpus* of a trust estate, should not be imposed on a life interest, but should be thrown upon the *corpus*. (Powys v. Blagrave, 4 De G., M. & G. 448, 459; and see Matter of Bennett [1896], 1 Ch. Div. 778.)

Costs of petition or legal proceedings by life tenant in his own interest are payable out of income. (Marner's Trusts, L. R. 3 Eq. Cas. 432; Evan's Trusts, 7 Ch. App. Cas. 609; overruling in effect Matter of Turnley, 1 id. 152; and see also Smith's Trusts, 9 Eq. Cas. 374; Whitton's Trusts, 8 id. 353; Matter Berkeley's Will, 10 Ch. App. 56; Matter of T., 15 Ch. Div. 78.)

But *it seems* it may be ordered paid out of the *corpus* where the fund deposited in court, is directed by the will to be invested in land. (Scrivener v. Smith, 8 Eq. Cas. 310; and Whitton's Trusts, *supra*.)

(h) **Apportionment.**—Expense of insurance on buildings and lightning rods, should be apportioned between tenant for life and remainder-men. (Peck v. Sherwood, 56 N. Y. 615.)

Adjustment of equitable rights as between life tenant and remainder-men in case of a mortgage. (Bell v. Mayor, 10 Paige, 50, 70.)

Municipal assessments for permanent improvements upon land, are apportioned between the life tenant and remainder-men according to circumstances and their respective interests. (Thomas v. Evans, 105 N. Y. 601, 611; 12 N. E. Rep. 571; Peck v. Sherwood, 56 N. Y. 615.)

Where the whole estate is subject to and benefited by a public improvement equity will apportion the assessment ratably between the life tenant and remainder-man, the former bearing the interest during his life in the amount paid and the latter on death of the life tenant the charge of the principal. (Plympton v. Boston Dispensary, 106 Mass. 544.)

And see where taxes paid under a special arrangement were charged equally between income and principal. (Barger's Appeal, 100 Pa. St 240.) And a case where one-quarter of executor's compensation was charged to principal and balance to income. (Gorden v. West, 8 N. H. 444.)

While a life tenant has no right to compel the executor to improve vacant lots, *it seems* that under special circumstances a court of equity may direct the improvement at expense of the residuary estate, making an equitable adjustment as between the parties. (Cogswell v. Cogswell, 2 Edw. Ch. 231.)

(i) **Illustrative cases.**—Expense of contest over probate chargeable to *corpus*. (Matter of Bartlett, 163 Mass. 511, 522; 40 N. E. Rep. 899.)

A tenant for life who puts improvements upon the land is not as a general rule entitled to compensation from the remainder-men. (5 Rich. Eq. 301 [S. C.]; Martin's Appeal, 23 Pa. St. 439.)

Under terms of a will cost of improvement or building was chargeable to income. (Matter of Nesmith, 71 Hun, 139; 24 N. Y. Supp. 527.)

Tenant for life can insist upon executor paying balance due under a contract for purchase of the land devised. (Cogswell v. Cogswell, 2 Edw. Ch. 231.)

Under peculiar language of the will, expenses and debts incurred in continuing testator's business were chargeable to income or life tenant. (Matter of Jones, 103 N. Y. 621; 9 N. E. Rep. 493.)

The question as to whether the depreciation through approaching maturity of the premium on government bonds should be borne by the life tenant or remainder-men is to be determined not by any arbitrary rule, but by ascertaining the meaning and intention in the will, from the relation of the parties to each other, and all the surrounding facts and circumstances of the case. (McLouth v. Hunt, 154 N. Y. 179; 48 N. E. Rep. 548; Matter of Hoyt, 27 App. Div. 285; 50 N. Y. Supp. 623; rev'd 160 N. Y. 607; 55 N. E. Rep. 282.) But not on above proposition which was re-affirmed; but the Court of Appeals differed with the Appellate Division upon a question of construction as to the intent of the testator. (P. 617.)

The expenses to be paid or deducted out of income by a trustee are limited to such as he may lawfully incur in the management of the property. He cannot diminish the income by charging to it an amount payable to him under a special agreement as compensation for his services as executor and trustee. (Matter of Young, 15 App. Div. 285; 44 N. Y. Supp. 585; aff'd 160 N. Y. 705, without opinion.)

DUDLEY *vs.* GATES *et al.*

[Supreme Court of Michigan, June 5, 1900; 83 N. W. Rep. 97.]

PROBATE COURTS—JURISDICTION—WILLS—REVOCATION—EXPERT
EVIDENCE.

1. Courts of Probate are not empowered to construe wills when presented
for probate.
2. A will, expressly revoking former wills, is held effective as a revocation,
although the principal bequest of the later one is void.
3. Where the opinion of a medical expert is based upon a hypothetical question, it is proper to instruct the jury that if the assumed facts, or any
of them, are not true, the opinion must be rejected by the jury.
(Syllabus by the court.)

ERROR to Circuit Court, Wayne county; GEORGE S. HOSMER,
Judge.

In the matter of the estate of Helen E. Gibson, in probate on
presentation by Sarah M. Dudley, Jasper G. Gates and Lulu F.
Gates, contestants, appeal.
Affirmed.

This is a contest over the probate of the will of Helen E. Gibson, deceased, executed July 16, 1898. The contestants are legatees under a prior will executed by the deceased March 1, 1895.
The last will revokes all former wills, provides for the defraying
of the expenses of the interment of the testatrix, and then bequeaths all her estate, real and personal, to the proponent, Sarah
M. Dudley, "to be used as she may deem prudent and proper, for
starting up, if enough remains, a little home for aged men and
women who are deemed worthy, and should there not be sufficient
remaining for above purpose as stated, they then to become the
property of the said Mrs. Sarah Marie Dudley." Mrs. Gibson
died January 19, 1899. The contestants attack the will upon three
grounds: (1) That it is void because of the indefiniteness of its
provisions; (2) that the testatrix was mentally incompetent to
execute it; and (3) that it was obtained by fraud and undue influ-

ence. Upon appeal to the Circuit Court the jury sustained the validity of the will.

T. E. Tarsney and *W. G. Fitzpatrick,* for appellants.

George F. Robison, Walter Barlow, and *James A. Robison,* for appellee.

GRANT, J. (after stating the facts).—L Courts of Probate have only such jurisdiction as is conferred by statute. (Const. art. 6, sec. 13.) They are not empowered to construe wills when presented for probate. The sole question, then, is, did the testatrix execute the will? Parties in interest may appear and contest it on the ground that it was not properly executed, or was obtained through undue influence, or was forged, or that the testatrix was incompetent. If it is admitted to probate, its construction is a matter for after consideration. If its provisions are of doubtful meaning, either the executor, legatee, or heir should apply to a court of chancery for their construction. (*Byrne* v. *Hume,* 84 Mich. 185, 191 ; 47 N. W. 679.) This has been the universal practice in this state, and is also the rule in other courts. (1 *Woerner Adm'n,* § 222 ; *Hawes* v. *Humphrey,* 9 Pick. 350, 361 ; *In re John's Will,* 30 Or. 494; 47 Pac. 341; 50 id. 226; 36 L. R. A. 242; *Hegarty's Appeal,* 75 Pa. St. 503.) After the estate is settled and is before the Probate Court for distribution, it must be distributed according to the terms of the will, which is the sole guide for the court in its order of distribution. The Probate Court then has jurisdiction to interpret the various provisions of the will, but not otherwise. (*Glover* v. *Reid,* 80 Mich. 228; 45 N. W. 91; *Byrne* v. *Hume, supra.*) The construction of this will was not, therefore, before the court. Two of its provisions were certainly valid, viz., the payment of the expenses of her interment, and the revocation of the former will. It was also lawful for her to devise her property to Mrs. Dudley without condition, or upon the condition that it was insufficient for the charitable bequest. After the will is probated, the executrix, or the heirs, if any, or the state, if there be no heirs, can enter the proper suit to construe the will. All the important questions now raised will then be before the court for determination.

2. Should the charitable bequest be held void for indefiniteness or other reason, still the will, being properly executed by a competent person, must be held to revoke the former will by its express provision to that effect. Powell thus states the rule: " If the latter· will contained an express revocation of the former, it is immaterial whether the latter be or be not inconsistent with the former, or whether it operate as a will at all or not." (Pow. Dev. 116.) This is cited with approval in *Smith* v. *McChesney* (15 N. J. Eq. 359.) The question is discussed at some length in *Pickens* v. *Davis* (134 Mass. 252), in which the court say: " Since the enactment of the English statute of wills (St. 7 Wm. IV. and 1 Vict. ch. 26, § 22), the decisions in all the courts have been uniform that after the execution of a subsequent will which contained an express revocation, or which, by reason of inconsistent provisions, amounted to an implied revocation, of a former will, such former will would not be revived by the cancellation or destruction of the later one." Where a will was lost or destroyed, and its contents (other than the revocatory clause) could not be proved so that it could be allowed and executed as a will, held to be effectual as a revocation of the former will. (*In re Cunningham*, 38 Minn. 169; 36 N. W. 269.) It is there said: " Such a revocation is generally effectual, although the will cannot otherwise be executed." The same rule was held in *Wallis* v. *Wallis* (114 Mass. 510). Where a codicil revoked valid bequests, and bequeathed them to a void charity, held, that the revocation took effect. (*Tupper* v. *Tupper*, 1 Kay & J. 665; *Baker* v. *Story* [N. S.], 31 Law T. 631.) In *Scott* v. *Fink* (45 Mich. 241; 7 N. W. 799), it was held that a will is not revived by the destruction of a subsequent will when the latter will had contained a clause revoking the former will. In *Stevens* v. *Hope* (52 Mich. 65; 17 N. W. 698), it was held that, when a will has once been expressly revoked by a later one, nothing can be claimed under it, though the later has been destroyed. See, also, *Cheever* v. *North* (106 Mich. 390; 64 N. W. 455; 37 L. R. A. 561). Counsel for contestants cite *Laughton* v. *Atkins* (1 Pick. 542); *Reid* v. *Borland* (14 Mass. 208); *Rudy* v. *Ulrich* (69 Pa. St. 177); and *In re Goods of Fraser* ([N. S.], 21 Law T. 680), in support of their contention. In *Laughton* v. *Atkins,* and in *Rudy* v. *Ulrich* the wills were denied probate because obtained through undue influence. In *Reid* v. *Borland* the instrument pre-

sented as a will was held void because not executed in accordance with the statute. The instruments in these cases were held void *in toto*, and therefore not admissible for any purpose. Incompetency or undue influence vitiates the revocatory clause as well as the other provisions. They have no application to cases like the present, where there was no undue influence. The testatrix was competent, and the intention to divert her property from the devisees by a former will is plain. Those cases would apply if the present will were held void for incompetency or undue influence, or because not lawfully executed, and the other will were before the court for probate, and a contestant should offer this one as evidence of a revocation of the other. In *Re Goods of Fraser,* the testator had written across the will, " This will was canceled this day in the presence of Dr. Robert Fraser, Esq., physician, and Margaret Rielly, nurse," and was witnessed by them. The motion before the court was that this memorandum be included in the grant of administration to the widow. The opinion cites the English statute as to revocation of wills, and then says: " The statute draws a distinction between ' wills and codicils ' and ' some writing.' I am clearly of the opinion that this is some writing declaring an intention to revoke a previous will, and, being only a writing of that character, it cannot be called a will. It disposes of nothing; it throws no light on the testamentary intentions of the deceased; it does not declare an intestacy. It simply revokes one particular paper. The application, therefore, must be refused." The opinion cites *In re Goods of Hicks* (38 Law J. Prob. 65), in which a similar memorandum was written upon a will. In that case Lord PENZANCE said: " The language of the statute therefore, implies that a will may be revoked either by a subsequent will, or by a codicil executed as a will, or by something which is neither a will nor a codicil, namely, ' some writing declaring an intention to revoke ' the will. I had serious doubts whether this paper ought not to be looked upon merely as ' some writing,' and consequently neither a will nor a codicil, so as properly to be made the subject of a probate or administration with the will annexed." He then cites the case of *Brenchley* v. *Still* (2 Rob. Ecc. 162), and stated the proper course was "to allow the grant to go with the paper annexed." Counsel in *Re Goods of Fraser* also cited *In re Goods of Hubbard* (35 Law J. Prob. 27).

In that case, at the foot of a deed was written, "I do add unto my will this codicil, hereby revoking any other codicil or codicils heretofore made by me. I constitute and appoint said son A. G. [a trustee under the deed] my sole and only trustee and administrator under my said will." It was held (1) that the deed was not entitled to probate as a will; (2) that, as there was no will, A. G. was not executor; (3) that, as the codicil revoked other codicils, administration with it annexed should be granted to the next of kin. I am unable to see that these cases support the contestants' claim.

3. The testimony as to competency and undue influence was in sharp conflict, and both questions were properly submitted to the jury. In reply to special questions, the jury found that Mrs. Gibson executed the will; that she had sufficient mental capacity; and that she was not under the undue influence, restraint, or duress of any one.

It remains to consider whether there was error committed upon the trial. Two expert witnesses were placed upon the stand by the contestants, and a hypothetical question put to each of them, covering seven pages of the record, and containing a statement of the facts as claimed by the contestants. Based upon these facts, the witnesses testified that, in their opinion, she was incompetent to comprehend the will. Each of the witnesses stated that his opinion was based upon the assumption that the statements made in the question were facts. The court instructed the jury upon this testimony as follows: "In order to make their opinions as to the mental incapacity of the testatrix to make such will competent evidence in the case, all the facts assumed and stated in the hypothetical questions put to them must be proved as true, and if the facts assumed as stated in such questions, or any portion of them, are not proven to be true, then the opinions of those two expert witnesses as to the mental incapacity of the testatrix to make the will in question are of no value as evidence in this case, and must be rejected by the jury. I think, gentlemen of the jury, that that is a proper request. You will remember that Dr. Emerson and Dr. Inglis were not eye witnesses as to the condition of Mrs. Gibson in the month of July, 1898. Now, if you believe that the several facts which are embodied in those hypothetical questions are true, then I think you are justified in giving importance to the testimony of the physicians; but, of course, if you do not find that those facts are true, or that any of those facts are untrue, then, inasmuch as the testimony of those witnesses is confessedly based upon the facts which are assumed in the question at least, then, under those circumstances, of course, their evidence would become valueless; but it is for you to say, of course, being the judges of what the actual facts were, what credit should be given to their testimony, if you find the facts to be true." The opinions of the experts were evidently based upon the supposed facts set forth in the question, and the instruction limited the jury to the opinions based upon the question. If counsel desired their opinion upon a portion of those facts, they should have propounded a question which included them and excluded the others. We think the instruction was correct. (*Rice* v. *Rice*, 50 Mich. 454; 15 N. W. 545; *Kempsey* v. *McGinniss*, 21 Mich. 123.) We find nothing in the remarks of counsel to justify a reversal of the case. We find no error upon the record. The judgment is affirmed.

The other justices concurred.

NOTE.—JURISDICTION TO CONSTRUE WILLS.

(a) Of a Court of Probate.
(b) Of a court of equity depends upon a trust.
(c) Who may maintain suit for construction.
(d) Jurisdiction limited.

(a) **Of a Court of Probate.**—It is often necessary for a Probate Court to construe the terms of a will in order to determine who are entitled to the estate, and to ascertain the interest to which they are entitled. Sometimes the court makes the distribution in the language of the will, but where there is any doubt as to the persons entitled, or as to the extent or nature of the estate or interest given by the terms of the will, the Probate Court not only may, but should, construe the will and define the interest given. to such devisee. (Goldtree v. Allison, 119 Cal. 344, 346; 51 Pac. Rep. 561; Crew v. Pratt, 119 Cal. 139, 150; 51 Pac. Rep. 38; and see Hudgins v. Leggett, 84 Tex. 207; 19 S. W. Rep. 387; Brown v. Stark, 47 Mo. App. 370; State v. Weland, 30 Minn. 277; 15 N. W. Rep. 245; Glover v. Reid, 80 Mich. 228; 45 N. W. Rep. 91; Blasini v. Blasini, 30 La. Ann. 1388; Appeal of Schaeffner, 41 Wis. 260; Covert v. Sebern, 73 Iowa, 564; 35 N. W. Rep. 636; Johnson v. Longmire, 39 Ala. 143; May v. May, 28 id. 141; Webster v. Seattle Trust Co., 7 Wash. 642; 33 Pac. Rep. 970; 35 id. 1082; Ward v.

Congregational Church, 66 Vt. 490; 29 Atl. Rep. 770; Hill v. Bloom, 41
N. J. Eq. 276; 7 Atl. Rep. 438.)

Surrogate has power to construe and determine the meaning and validity
of provisions in a will, when necessary in order to make his decree of dis-
tribution. (Garlock v. Vandevort, 128 N. Y. 374; 28 N. E. Rep. 599.) Or
when necessary to enable him to perform a duty imposed upon him by law.
(Washbon v. Cope, 144 N. Y. 287; 39 N. E. Rep. 388; and see Danser v.
Jeremiah, 3 Redf. 130; Tappen v. M. E. Church, 3 Dem. 187; Matter of
Perkins, 75 Hun, 129; 26 N. Y. Supp. 958; aff'd 145 N. Y. 599; 40 N. E.
Rep. 165.)

Surrogate has jurisdiction to construe a will so far as is necessary to
determine to whom legacies shall be paid. (Matter of Verplanck, 91 N. Y.
439; Riggs v. Cragg, 89 N. Y. 480; and see Du Bois v. Brown, 1 Dem.
317.)

Incidentally to hear and determine meaning and validity of dispositions
in the will. (Danser v. Jeremiah, 3 Redf. 130; Garlock v. Vandevort, 128
N. Y. 374; 28 N. E. Rep. 599; Brown v. Wheeler, 53 App. Div. 8; 65
N. Y. Supp. 436; Matter of Ullman, 137 N. Y. 408; 33 N. E. Rep. 480;
Borrowe v. Corbin, 31 App. Div. 179; 52 N. Y. Supp. 741.)

Jurisdiction of surrogate limited and statutory. (Bevan v. Cooper, 72
N. Y. 317; Riggs v. Cragg, 89 id. 480; Matter of Shrader, 63 Hun, 36;
17 N. Y. Supp. 273; Chadwick v. Chadwick, 6 Mont. 566; 13 Pac. Rep.
385; First Baptist Church v. Robberson, 71 Mo. 327.)

Limited to disposition of personal property, and there is no jurisdiction
unless provision in will in regard thereto is independent and separable from
the disposition of the real estate. (Matter of Shrader, supra; and see
Matter of Walker, 136 N. Y. 20; 32 N. E. Rep. 633; Matter of Merriam,
136 N. Y. 58; 32 N. E. Rep. 621.)

But jurisdiction does not extend to trusts created by wills, nor to litigation between the cestui que trust and the executor as trustee. (Harrison v.
Harrison, 9 Ala. 470.)

Cannot declare trusts in the estate distributed or impose conditions upon
its use and disposition. (Bramell v. Cole, 136 Mo. 201; 37 S. W. Rep.
924.)

Nor adjudicate question of title dependent upon the operation and effect
of the will, nor decide upon the right of disposition. (Schull v. Murray,
32 Md. 9; Ramsey v. Welby, 63 id. 584; and see Williams v. Herrick, 18
R. I. 120; 25 Atl. Rep. 1099. And see as to jurisdiction of Probate or
Surrogate Court. Matter of Randall, 152 N. Y. 508; 46 N. E. Rep. 945;
Kager v. Brenneman, 47 App. Div. 67; 62 N. Y. Supp. 339; Hegarty's
Appeal, 75 Pa. St. 503; Hanscom v. Marston, 82 Me. 288, 295; 19 Atl. Rep.
460; Denegre v. Denegre, 33 La. Ann. 689, 692; Crew v. Pratt, 119 Cal.
139, 150; 51 Pac. Rep. 38; Hull v. Hull, 81 N. W. Rep. 89.)

(b) Of a court of equity depends upon a trust.—Jurisdiction of
equity over trusts gives it authority to construe wills whenever necessary
to guide the action of a trustee. (Wager v. Wager, 89 N. Y. 161.)

Jurisdiction may be conferred by statute allowing an executor to petition for instructions as to construction of the will. Swasey v. Jaques, 144 Mass. 135; 10 N. E. Rep. 758; Green v. Hogan, 153 Mass. 462; 27 N. E. Rep. 413.)

A plaintiff for purpose of giving a court jurisdiction cannot allege a trust and in the same breath deny the legal existence of the same trust, and claim legal rights inconsistent therewith. (Chipman v. Montgomery, 63 N. Y. 221. But see this case distinguished or modified by Read v. Williams, 125 N. Y. 560; 26 N. E. Rep. 730.)

Jurisdiction of a court of equity rests upon the ground that the plaintiff is a trustee under a will affecting large interests, the construction of which is open to serious question, and that he cannot safely discharge the duties of his office as trustee, without the advice and protection of a Court of Chancery. (Belfield v. Booth, 63 Conn. 299, 309; 27 Atl. Rep. 585; and see Little v. Thorne, 93 N. C. 69; Dill v. Wisner, 88 N. Y. 160.)

Where Surrogate's Court has jurisdiction to give complete relief, a court of equity may in its discretion decline to entertain an action for an accounting or other relief against executors; but where jurisdiction retained it has power to adjust the whole controversy. (Wager v. Wager, 89 N. Y. 161.)

But the refusal to entertain jurisdiction is not authorized unless the jurisdiction of the surrogate has already been invoked. (Ludwig v. Bungart, 48 App. Div. 616; 63 N. Y. Supp. 91.)

The right of an administrator with the will annexed to ask for instructions is confined to matters of difficulty in his own administration. As to those in which the trustee and his *cestui que trust* alone are interested, the administrator has no right to the opinion of the court, and it would not be proper for the court to give it; and so as to construction of devises in the will, as to which and the trusts he has nothing to do. (Casperson v. Dunn, 42 N. J. Eq. 87; 6 Atl. Rep. 488; and see Muldoon v. Muldoon, 133 Mass. 111; Wilbur v. Maxam, 133 id. 541. And as to jurisdiction of courts of equity to construe wills, see also, 1 Underhill Wills, § 455, *et seq.* [ed. 1900]; Williams v. Williams, 73 Cal. 99; 14 Pac. Rep. 394; Mechanics and Traders' Bank v. Harrison, 68 Ga. 463; Eldred v. Meek, 183 Ill. 26; 55 N. E. Rep. 53; this vol. p. 128.)

(c) **Who may maintain suit for construction.**—The next of kin of a testator may bring an equitable action for the construction of a will where the disposition made therein of personal property is claimed to be invalid or inoperative for any cause. Although in such a case the next of kin claim in hostility to the will, the executors in case it is invalid or cannot take effect, hold the personalty upon a resulting trust for those entitled under the statute of distribution, and jurisdiction attaches as incident to the jurisdiction of equity over trusts. This independent of statute, which in New York extended the remedy so as to include suits for construction of devises in behalf of heirs, claiming adversely to the will. (Read v. Williams, 125 N. Y. 560; 26 N. E. Rep. 730; distinguishing Chipman v. Montgomery, 63 N. Y. 221; and Horton v. Cantwell, 108 N. Y. 255; 15 N. E. Rep. 546.)

There need be no express trust created by the will as to the personal estate. (Wager v. Wager, 89 N. Y. 161.)

But one who claims as a purchaser cannot maintain action for construction of will. (Mellen v. Mellen, 139 N. Y. 210; 34 N. E. Rep. 925.)

An heir at law or devisee who claims a mere legal estate in the real property, where there is no trust, cannot maintain a suit in equity merely for purpose of obtaining a judicial construction of the provisions of the will. The decision of such legal questions belongs exclusively to courts of law, except where they arise incidentally in this court in the exercise of its legitimate powers; or where the court has obtained jurisdiction of the case for some other purpose. (Bowers v. Smith, 10 Paige, 193, 200; and see Mellen v. Mellen, 139 N. Y. 210, 217; 34 N. E. Rep. 925; Bailey v. Briggs, 56 N. Y. 407, 413; Wager v. Wager, 89 id. 161; Chipman v. Montgomery, 63 id. 221; and this case distinguished in Read v. Williams, 125 id. 560; 26 N. E. Rep. 730; Torrey v. Torrey, 55 N. J. Eq. 410; 36 Atl. Rep. 1084; Kalish v. Kalish, 45 App. Div. 530; 61 N. Y. Supp. 448.)

A suit for construction of a will can be properly brought only by the executor or trustee. Heirs and legatees have no right thus to create a controversy, and ask the interposition of the courts to prevent anticipated disputes which may never arise. Their place in such a proceeding is that of defendants only. (Belfield v. Booth, 63 Conn. 299, 309; 27 Atl. Rep. 585; Little v. Thorne, 93 N. C. 69, 73; and see Bowen v. Bowen, 38 Ohio St. 429; Sprague v. West, 127 Mass. 471; Tyson v. Tyson, 100 N. C. 360; 6 S. E. Rep. 707; Woodlief v. Merritt, 96 N. C. 226; 2 S. E. Rep. 350.)

But see where suit maintained for construction, account, and partition by a tenant in common. (Nash v. Simpson, 78 Me. 143; 3 Atl. Rep. 53; and compare Minkler v. Simons, 172 Ill. 323, 326; 50 N. E. Rep. 176, where it is *held* that if a *trust* exist or be established, any one interested in its distribution has the right to invoke the aid of a court of equity to obtain a construction of the will and enforce the trust.)

Where there is a trust created by a will, a suit for construction may be maintained in a court of equity by any parties interested. (Simmons v. Burrell, 8 Misc. 388; 28 N. Y. Supp. 625.)

But this may depend upon statute and is limited. (Horton v. Cantwell, 108 N. Y. 255; 15 N. E. Rep. 546.) And independent of any statute the jurisdiction in equity is limited to cases of trust. (Bowers v. Smith, 10 Paige, 193.)

Where trust involved court of equity may be moved by executor, trustee, or *cestui que trust.* (Bailey v. Briggs, 56 N. Y. 407; Wager v. Wager, 89 id. 161.)

As to jurisdiction of action brought by heir, next of kin, legatee, or devisee, see also, Kalish v. Kalish (45 App. Div. 530; 61 N. Y. Supp. 448); Peverly v. Peverly (173 Mass. 203; 53 N. E. Rep. 395).

(d) **Jurisdiction limited.**—The construction or advice of a court of equity is given only upon an existing state of facts requiring it in execution of a trust; the jurisdiction will never be exercised merely to obtain an abstract opinion as to future conduct or future rights or duties. (Little v. Thorne, 93 N. C. 69, 72; Bullard v. Chandler, 149 Mass. 532; 21 N. E. Rep. 951; Morse v. Lyman, 64 Vt. 167; 24 Atl. Rep. 763; Bowen v. Bowen, 38 Ohio St. 429; Rexroad v. Wells, 13 W. Va. 812; Gafney v. Kenison, 64 N. H. 354; 10 Atl. Rep. 706; Greeley v. Nashua, 62 N. H. 166; Goddard v. Brown, 12 R. I. 31; Tyson v. Tyson, 100 N. C. 360; 6 S. E. Rep. 707; Collins v. Collins, 19 Ohio St. 468; Crosby v. Mason, 32 Conn. 482; Edgar v. Edgar, 26 Ore. 65; 37 Pac. Rep. 73; Miller v. Dane, 100 Wis. 1; 75 N. W. Rep. 413; Bullard v. Attorney-General, 153 Mass. 249; 26 N. E. Rep. 691.)

Existence of a trust not essential in Texas. (Crosson v. Dwyer, 9 Tex. Civ. App. 482; 30 S. W. Rep. 929.)

The court should be called upon to decide and direct, not to counsel and advise. (Griggs v. Veghte, 47 N. J. Eq. 179; 19 Atl. Rep. 867; and see Clay v. Gurley, 62 Ala. 14, 19.)

Instructions cannot be asked upon a question relating to *past* administration of the trust. (Sohier v. Burr, 127 Mass. 221; and see Miles v. Strong, 60 Conn. 393; 22 Atl. Rep. 959; nor merely for purpose of declaring legal titles. (Minkler v. Simons, 172 Illl. 323, 326; 50 N. E. Rep. 176; Harrison v. Owsley, 172 Ill. 629; 50 N. E. Rep. 227; Siddall v. Harrison, 73 Cal. 560; 15 Pac. Rep. 130; but compare Wintermute v. Heinly, 81 Iowa, 169; 47 N. W. Rep. 66.)

Cannot instruct as to *future* duties. (White v. Massachusetts Institute, 171 Mass. 85; 50 N. E. Rep. 512.)

ELMORE *vs.* ELMORE.

[Supreme Court of South Carolina, July 26, 1900; 36 S. E. Rep. 656.]

EXECUTORS AND ADMINISTRATORS—CLAIM AND DELIVERY—PERSONAL PROPERTY—ACTIONS.

An action of claim and delivery cannot be maintained against an executor of an estate to recover possession of personal property unlawfully withheld by him. (By divided court.)

APPEAL from Common Pleas Circuit Court of Laurens county; R. C. WATTS, Judge.

Action of claim and delivery by L. C. Elmore against J. T. Elmore, executor of the last will and testament of George Elmore, deceased. From a judgment in favor of defendant, plaintiff appeals.

Affirmed.

W. R. Richey, for appellant.

J. L. M. Irby, for respondent.

GARY, A. J.—The record contains the following statement of facts: "On the 21st day of November, 1898, appellant, L. C. Elmore, named above, commenced this action in Magistrate J. M. HUDGENS' court, in Laurens county, against J. T. Elmore, as executor of the last will and testament of George Elmore, deceased, the defendant (respondent) above named, to recover possession of a mule alleged to be of value of seventy-five dollars. On the trial of the case, Magistrate HUDGENS dismissed plaintiff's complaint upon the grounds' that the action was prematurely brought, and that the plaintiff had not given any undertaking. The plaintiff appealed to the Circuit Court of Common Pleas for Laurens county, alleging error on the part of the magistrate. The appeal was heard at February, 1899, term of court, by Judge GEORGE W. GAGE, who reversed the judgment of the magistrate, and remanded the case to the court of J. M. HUDGENS, magistrate, or his successor in office, for trial. There was no appeal from Judge GAGE's order. On the 8th day of July, 1899, the case was tried before J. W. PETERSON, magistrate, who had succeeded J. M. Hudgens as magistrate, at Laurens, S. C. Before the plaintiff closed the testimony, and before he concluded the examination of his first witness, Magistrate PETERSON granted a nonsuit. The plaintiff again appealed to the Circuit Court of Common Pleas for Laurens county, upon various grounds. The second appeal was heard at October, 1899, term of court by Judge R. C. WATTS, who did not consider plaintiff's grounds of appeal, but dismissed plaintiff's appeal and confirmed the judgment of the magistrate on the ground that no action of claim and delivery of personal property could be sustained against a party, as executor, for an unlawful possession. The plaintiff appeals to this court, alleging error on the part of Judge WATTS."

The practical question raised by the exceptions is whether there was error in the ruling of the circuit judge that " no action of claim and delivery of personal property could be sustained against a party, as executor, for an unlawful possession." There can be no question as to the manner in which the defendant came into possession of the property, for in his answer he alleges, as a fact which the plaintiff does not deny, that he came into possession of the mule as the executor of the will of George Elmore, deceased. In 7 Am. & Eng. Enc. Law ([1st ed.], 332), the doctrine is thus laid down: " At common law no action founded upon a tort committed by the deceased, for which damages only could be recovered as satisfaction, such as trespass, trover, false imprisonment, assault and battery, slander, deceit, * * * and the like, where the declaration imputed a tort to person or property, and the plea must be ' Not guilty,' lay against his executor or administrator. But if by reason of the tort the estate has derived pecuniary advantage, the representative could be compelled to account to the injured party, in another form of action, for the benefit so obtained. Thus, if goods wrongfully taken away by the deceased remain in specie in the hands of the executor or administrator, the rightful owner might maintain replevin or *detinue* against such executor or administrator to recover them back; or trover, laying the conversion to have been by the representative; or, if sold, an action for money had and received to recover their value." In 3 *Williams, Ex'rs* (1602), it is said: " In some, however, of the cases above mentioned, a remedy may be had against the executor or administrator in another form. Thus, although at the common law an action of trover upon a conversion of the testator dies with him, yet if the goods, etc., taken away continue still in specie in the hands of the executor or administrator of the wrongdoer, replevin or *detinue* will lie against such executor or administrator to recover them back; or trover, laying the conversion to have been by the executor; or, in case they are sold, an action for money had and received, to recover their value." The following cases throw light upon this question: (*Jenkins* v. *Bennett*, 40 S. C. 393; 18 id. 929; *Huff* v. *Watkins*, 20 id. 477; *Chaplin* v. *Barrett*, 12 Rich. Law, 284; *Ford* v. *Caldwell*, 3 Hill, 248; *Middleton's Ex'rs* v. *Robinson*, 1 Bay, 58.) If the testator had sold the mule, the plaintiff could have sued the executor for the value thereof, and we see no reason why he should not be allowed to recover the specific property, if he can show that it belongs to him. Since there is no question that the mule came into the possession of the defendant as executor of the testator's will, I think the judgment of this court should be that the judgment of the Circuit Court be reversed, and the case remanded for a new trial, but as two members of this court are of the contrary opinion, the judgment of the Circuit Court must stand affirmed.

Pope, J. (concurring).—I am conscious that an example is to be set, but I am ready to assist in setting such example. I cannot conceive that a man who takes my mule, and then dies, having named an executor, which executor takes possession of my mule as assets of his testator's estate, to be by him administered, and upon my demand for my mule declines to surrender the mule to me, and, when I sue him to recover my mule in a magistrate's court, his reply is, " You cannot sue in claim and delivery," will be protected by law. If the executor surrenders the mule on my demand, without suit, will not he have to account for such surrender to the legatees of his testator? If the executor refuses to surrender, must I stand by and take no steps to recover my mule? If the executor had been the original tort feasor, I admit that he could plead that his taking of the mule was his personal act, and in no manner connected with his testator's estate. But the testator took my mule, and died with said mule in his possession (which last, we have heard it said, was nine points out of a possible ten in the law). His executor succeeds to the testator's possession, in his representative character. When I demand my mule, and I am refused possession of him by such executor on the ground that the mule belonged to the estate of his testator, of course I must sue him as executor. I concur in the opinion of Justice GARY and the judgment of reversal.

McIver, C. J.—Being unable to concur in the conclusion reached by Mr. Justice GARY in the opinion which he has prepared in this case, I propose to state the grounds of my dissent. The appeal turns upon the single question whether the circuit judge erred in holding that an action of claim and delivery of personal property brought against the defendant as executor of the will of the testator, George Elmore, under the allegations that he, as such executor, is in the unlawful possession of such property, cannot be maintained, but that such action should have been brought against the defendant individually, and not as executor. This is an important question, far-reaching in its results, and, it is claimed, has never heretofore been distinctly decided in this state. It is not a mere question of pleading or of the proper parties to an action, but its decision vitally affects the interests of those who may be interested in the estates of decedents; for if this case is allowed to proceed in its present form, and the plaintiff shall succeed in establishing his right to the possession of the mule sued for, or damages in lieu thereof, then it is clear that a liability will be fastened upon the estate of the testator, not by reason of any act of his own (for it is distinctly declared that " no wrong is imputed to defendant's testator "), but solely because of a tort committed by the defendant, who has been appointed executor of the testator's will. So that it seems to me that the practical inquiry is whether one who has been intrusted by a decedent with the execution of his will can by any act or omission of his own fasten a legal liability upon the estate of his testator, in the absence of any provision in the will investing him with authority so to do; and it is not pretended that there is any such provision in the will in the case.

The doctrine is well settled that neither an executor, in the absence of authority in the will so to do, nor an administrator, can, by contract, either express or implied, impose any new debt upon the estate of the testator or intestate, as the case may be. (*McBeth* v. *Smith*, 2 Tread. Const. 676 [reported, also, in 3 Brev. 511]; *Nehbe* v. *Price*, 2 Nott & McC. 328), where Mr. Justice Huger, in delivering the opinion of the court, said that the point had been repeatedly decided; (*O'Neal* v. *Abney*, 2 Baily, 317; *Wilson* v. *Huggins*, 11 Rich. Law, 410; *Cook* v. *Cook*, 24 S. C. 204.) This rule is also recognized in the court of equity, as may be seen by reference to the case of *Boggs* v. *Reid*, which, though an equity case, is reported in the appendix to 3 Rich. Law, at page 450. So, also, it seems to be the well settled rule elsewhere; for it is said in 11 Am. & Eng. Enc. Law (2d ed.), at page 932 of that very valuable work: " The rule is well settled that an executory contract of an executor or administrator, if made on a new and independent consideration, moving between the promisee and the executor or administrator as promisor, is his personal contract, and does not, in the absence of authority given by statute or by the will of the decedent, bind the estate, though the consideration moving from the promisee is such that the executor or administrator could properly have paid from the assets, and been allowed for on the settlement of his accounts. So inflexible is the rule denying to personal representatives the power to bind by any original contract the estates committed to their charge, that its application is not affected by the fact that the contract was made or the debt incurred for the benefit of the estate,"—citing quite an array of authorities. I may add, however, that notwithstanding this well-settled rule a court of equity, in a proper case, where an executor has paid an obligation contracted by him for the benefit of the estate, will allow him credit for the amount so paid, although no action could be maintained against him as executor to enforce the payment of such obligation, though this is scarcely pertinent to the present inquiry.

Now, if an executor or administrator has no power to fasten upon the estate which he represents any liability by contract, either express or implied, even though such contract may be entered into for the benefit of the estate, how much stronger is the reason for holding that an executor has no power to fix upon the estate placed in his charge any liability for any tort that he may commit, and hence that no action based upon a tort committed by him can be maintained against him as executor, for that would be imposing upon the estate a liability for his own wrongful act. This view is supported by authority. See 11 Am. & Eng. Enc. Law (2d ed.), at page 492, where it is said: " Executors and administrators can create no liability against the estates represented by them by any tortious or wrongful act. Their torts are their individual acts, for which the only remedy of the person injured is against them individually, and the rule is the same whether the injury results from intentional wrong or negligence." On the next page of the same volume, under subdivision 17, treating of the liability of an executor or administrator for taking property of third persons, I find the following language: " If an .executor or administrator, as such, receives money, or takes possession of property to which the estate has no right, he is liable to an action by the real owner for its recovery. The authorities are uniform in holding this, and they generally hold that he incurs personal liability; but there is some diversity as to whether his liability is only personal, or whether he also becomes liable in his representative capacity. The English courts, adhering to the principle that an executor or administrator has no power to create any new liability on the estate, hold that he becomes liable in his individual capacity alone, though the money or property is applied to the purposes of the estate; and some of the decisions in the United States are to the same effect,"—citing cases from the states of Alabama, Arkansas, Iowa, Massachusetts, Mississippi, New Jersey, Pennsylvania, and Virginia. The writer of the article in the Encyclopædia then proceeds to say: " But other authorities have adopted a more equitable rule, and hold that, if an executor or administrator has applied to the use of the estate money or proceeds of property belonging to third persons, he is liable in his represent- ative capacity, and that the person injured may elect whether he will hold the executor or administrator liable personally or in his representative capacity." The cases of *Ford* v. *Caldwell* (3 Hill, 248), and *Huff* v. *Watkins* (20 S. C. 477), seem to indicate that the courts of this state are disposed to hold what the writer in the Encyclopædia calls the " more equitable doctrine,"—that, where the estate of a decedent has received benefit from the use of money or property not rightfully belonging to it, an action *ex contractu*, but not an action *ex delicto,* may be maintained against the execu- tor or administrator, as the case may be, in his representative capacity, for the recovery of the amount to which the estate has thus been benefited. This, it seems to me, is the true and logical doctrine, but that in no case can an action *ex delicto* be maintained against executor or administrator in his representative character. If the tort upon which such an action is founded was committed by the decedent, then it dies with him. (*Chaplin* v. *Barrett*, 12 Rich. Law, 284; *Huff* v. *Watkins*, 20 S. C. 477.) But, if the tort was committed by the executor or administrator, then the action can only be brought against him in his individual, and not in his representative, capacity; for, as is said in the foregoing quotation from the Encyclopædia, " their torts are their individual acts, for which the only remedy of the person injured is against them individually." In this connection it may be noted that the case of *Rose* v. *Cash* (58 Ind. 278), relied upon by the appellant, is one of the many cases from Indiana cited to sustain the doctrine laid down in the Encyclopædia, cited above, from which I infer that the action in that case was brought against the defendant in his individual, and not in his representative, capacity, and that what the court really held was that he would be liable, " whether he claim as owner, agent, administrator, trustee, custodian, or in any other capacity," if he tortiously withheld the possession of the property sued for from the real owner. But as I have not, at present, access to that case, this is a mere inference from the fact that I find it cited in the Encyclopædia to sustain a doctrine contrary to that for which it is cited in the argument of the counsel for appellant. The case of *Middleton's Ex'rs* v. *Robinson* (1 Bay, 58), likewise cited by appellant's counsel, has no application to this case. That was a special action on the case, brought by the executors, for the value of certain cattle taken from the plantation of testator in his lifetime. There was also a count in the declaration for money had and received. The court sustained the action upon two grounds: First, because, by the terms of the statute of 4 Edw. III. ch. 7, executors were expressly allowed to sue for trespass in taking away the property of a testator in his lifetime; second, because the tort might be waived, and the action proceed in assumpsit, under the count for money had and received. But it will be observed that the statute of 4 Edw., now incorporated in Rev. St. 1893, as section 2319, only gives the right to executors to sue trespassers, but does not give any right to third persons to sue executors for trespasses or other torts, and we know of no statute which confers any such right. As to the second ground it only proceeds upon the well-settled doctrine that there are cases in which the tort may be waived, and the action proceed, upon proper allegations, as an action *ex contractu*, as was properly allowed in that case, under the count in the declaration for money had and received which rests upon an implied assumpsit. But in the case now under consideration the action is not brought by an executor against an alleged trespasser upon the property of his testator (which is the only case provided for by the statute of Edward), but the action is brought against an executor for an alleged tort committed by him, and there is no pretense that the tort has been waived. It is plain, therefore, that the case cited

by appellant has no application to the present case. It seems to
me that it would not only be anomalous, but illogical to hold that
while an administrator or executor cannot be sued in his representative capacity on a contract made by him, and not by his intestate or testator, as the case may be, whereby a new debt or liability may be fastened upon the estate which he represents, yet
he may be sued in his representative capacity for a tort committed
by him, with which his testator or intestate had nothing whatever
to do and is in no way responsible for, and thus a new liability
may be fixed upon the estate which he represents. Such a doctrine would not only be anomalous and illogical, but would tend
to prejudice, perhaps to destroy, the interests of those beneficially
interested—oftentimes minors—in the estates of decedents.

In the present case no wrong whatever is imputed to defendant's
testator, and, on the contrary, appellant, in his argument, distinctly repudiates any intention to make such an imputation. The
action is based upon a tort committed by the defendant since the
death of his testator, in wrongfully withholding the possession of
the chattel sued for from the alleged rightful owner; and for that
he can only be held liable in his individual, and not in his representative capacity. It is not difficult to conceive of a case in
which no wrong could be imputed to the testator in taking and
retaining the possession of the chattel in dispute, and yet the person
who may unlawfully withhold the possession of such chattel from
the rightful owner would be guilty of a wrong in so doing. For
example, if the testator was entitled to a life interest in the
chattel, with remainder over to the plaintiff, there could be no
possible wrong on the part of the testator in taking and retaining
the possession of such chattel during his lifetime. But if after
his death any person, be he executor or administrator or a third
person, should unlawfully withhold the possession of the chattel
from the person entitled in remainder, then the wrong done is that
of such person, for which he would be liable in his individual,
and not in his representative, capacity. If it should be said that
it would be a hard case upon the executor if he should be held
individually responsible in a case like the one supposed, the answer is obvious. The Court of Equity would, in a proper case,
and upon a proper showing that the executor had acted in good
faith, allow him credit for whatever he had been required to pay

in an honest effort to protect the interests of the estate committed to his charge. It is everyday practice to allow an executor, upon his accounting, credits for amounts paid out by him for counsel fees and other proper expenses incurred by him in the management of the estate, upon contracts for which he is responsible in his individual, and not in his representative, capacity, whenever the court is satisfied that such obligations have been incurred in good faith for the benefit of the estate. I think, therefore, that there was no error upon the part of the Circuit Court in holding that this action could not be maintained against the defendant in his representative capacity, but that the action should have been brought against the defendant individually. This view being conclusive of the case, there was no error in holding that it was not necessary to pass upon appellant's exceptions.

Note.—REPLEVIN AS AGAINST EXECUTOR.

In Matter of Van Slooten v. Dodge (145 N. Y. 327; 39 N. E. Rep. 950), which originated in a proceeding against the executor to recover a ring, the New York Court of Appeals uses the following language: "an executor cannot subject the estate in his hands for administration to some new liability, either by his contract or by his wrongful act. Whatever claim the claimant had because of the taking of the ring by the executor, was against him individually, and in no sense against him in his executorial capacity." It being suggested that the claim might be regarded as limited to a question of possession, and not as founded on a contract, nor a claim for damages, and that therefore it could be regarded as without the ordinary rule, the court further said: "We fail to see any force in the suggestion; the result has been to impose costs on the estate, and to that extent to unlawfully diminish the assets of the estate."

The opinion seems to recognize, however, the fact that liability as executor or administrator may exist, where there was a transaction to which deceased was a party, and where his estate had become chargeable with a liability which he was under, or would have been under, *if he had lived.*

And see *Note* "Liability for torts of executor or administrator," 4 Prob. Rep. Ann. 578.

In re HENNES' ESTATE.

HENNES *vs.* HUSTON.

[Supreme Court of Minnesota, July 30, 1900; 63 N. W. Rep. 439.]

WILL—EXECUTION—EVIDENCE.

1. Where the execution of a will is proved by a subscribing witness, who knows that such instrument was declared by testatrix to be her will, but, from haste and inattention to details, cannot state whether he saw her sign the same or acknowledge her signature thereto, the proper statutory formalities of execution may be presumed, in the absence of any evidence to the contrary, or that would excite suspicion of fraud and concealment.
2. Evidence of the proof of execution of the will in this case considered, and held to support the findings of the trial court that the same was properly subscribed and attested.
3. The case of *In re Ludwig's Estate* ([Minn.] 81 N. W. 758), considered and distinguished.
(Syllabus by the court.)

APPEAL from District Court, Hennepin county; ALEXANDER M. HARRISON, Judge.

Nicholas Hennes presented the will of Maria Hennes for probate. From an order admitting the same to probate, Annie Huston (formerly Annie Hennes) appeals to the District Court, where the judgment was affirmed, and she again appeals.
Affirmed.

A. C. Middlestadt, for appellant.

S. M. Finch, for respondent.

LOVELY, J.—The will of Maria Hennes was admitted to probate against the objection of contestant, an heir at law. The objections filed to the probate of the will were numerous, but upon this appeal are resolved into the one question whether the same was legally executed under the laws of this state. On an appeal from the order of the Probate Court there was a hearing upon this issue, solely, in the District Court of Hennepin county, wherein the order of the Probate Court was affirmed, and judgment thereon duly entered, from which this appeal is prosecuted.

The will was actually written, signed, and witnessed on the 21st day of April, 1883. When presented for probate, fifteen years later, it appeared to have been executed with the formalities required in such cases. The testatrix having signed her name and affixed her seal at the bottom of the will, an acknowledgment of the witnesses in due form follows, signed by M. L. Cummings and August Kegel. It was probated on the 20th day of August, 1898. At the trial in the District Court, Kegel was not to be found. Cummings was produced to support the will, and stated that he was called from his place of business, in a room adjoining that of the testatrix; that he went to her room, she being present; that the will lay upon the table before her; that it was by her declared to be her will; and that he affixed his name thereto as a witness. His recollection of details in other respects is quite dim and uncertain. He is unable to state positively that she signed her name in his presence, or that her signature was actually attached to the will before he signed it as a witness, but says that there was nothing unusual or peculiar about the circumstances attending the matter to attract his attention, and that there was no concealment of any fact or detail of the business; his uncertainty arising merely from lapse of time and neglect on his part to pay particular attention to the details of the transaction. The signature of the testatrix was proved and undisputed. The signature of the absent witness, Kegel, was also proved. We are of the opinion that the evidence was sufficient to sustain the finding of the trial court, who was warranted in inferring from this evidence, and the manner in which the making of the will was concluded, that the same had been legally executed. It is true that the subscribing witness who was produced was unable to state that he saw the testatrix sign her name, or even that he saw her signature; but he said that she called him to witness her will, and that he signed as a witness. It was an open transaction in the presence of third parties; and in the absence of any evidence that the legal, regular, and ordinary course in such cases was not pursued, it must be presumed that it was without any concealment of fact. The apparent order in which the signatures to the will were affixed—first by the testatrix, followed by an acknowledgment, then by the witnesses—authorizes the reasonable inference which the trial court adopted, namely, that the formalities of the statute had been complied with. This view is supported by the authority of *Allen* v. *Griffen* (69 Wis. 530; 35 N. W. 21), in which the reasoning of that court, in accordance with this view, seems to us unanswerable. This case is clearly distinguishable from the recent decision of this court in *Re Ludwig's Estate* (81 N. W. 758). A reference to the latter case will disclose the fact that the testatrix did not acknowledge at the time that the witnesses signed the paper purporting to be her will that it was a will, or that she had signed the same, and they were unable to state that it was in fact a will or had been signed by her, for the reason that every portion of the instrument preceding their own signatures was purposely covered and concealed. Upon this evidence the trial court in the *Ludwig Case* found that the will was not executed as required by law, and this court held that the finding of the lower court in that case was not against the evidence. We think that the cases are clearly distinguishable from each other, and that the judgment appealed from must be affirmed.

Judgment affirmed.

O'REILLY *vs.* KELLY.

[Supreme Court of Rhode Island, June 6, 1900; 46 Atl. Rep. 681.]

DECEDENT'S ESTATE—CLAIMS—FLOWERS FOR FUNERAL.

Where deceased left an estate of $6,000, and no widow or child, flowers to the value of $15, ordered by his housekeeper, who was his sister-in-law, for his funeral, were necessary, and hence his estate was liable therefor.

EXCEPTIONS from Court of Common Pleas, Providence county.

Action by Frank O'Reilly against Charles J. Kelly, administrator of the estate of James Monaghan. From a judgment in favor of defendant, plaintiff brings exceptions.

Sustained.

Hugh J. Carroll, for plaintiff.

Joseph Osfield, Jr., for defendant.

TILLINGHAST, J.—This is assumpsit for flowers furnished for the funeral of James Monaghan, the defendant's intestate, upon the order of Charlotte Campbell, who was a sister-in-law of the intestate, and who had lived with him as his housekeeper for eighteen years previous to his death. The case shows that the deceased left no widow or children, and that he left real estate valued at about $4,000, and life insurance of the value of $2,000. It does not appear that he left any debts. The value of the flowers furnished for the funeral was fifteen dollars. At the trial of the case in the District Court of the Tenth Judicial District the plaintiff was nonsuited on the ground that as matter of law the estate could not be held to pay for the flowers which were furnished, as they were not necessary. The plaintiff excepted to the ruling, and has brought the case here on a bill of exceptions to have said ruling reviewed. We think the ruling was erroneous. As the deceased left no widow or children, and, so far as appears, no relatives who were disposed to take upon themselves the duty of making the necessary arrangements for the funeral, it became the duty of the sister-in-law, as housekeeper for the deceased, and the only person left in charge of the body, to make such arrangements, and see to it that the deceased was decently interred. What expense may properly be incurred in such circumstances depends largely upon the custom of people of like rank and condition in society, and the condition of the estate left by the deceased. (2 Woerner, §§ 357, 358; 7 Am. & Eng. Enc. Law, 301; note 3.) The demands of common propriety and decency should always be observed in connection with the burial of the dead, and the law pledges the credit of the estate for the payment of such expenses as are reasonably incurred for this purpose after the death, and before the appointment of an administrator. (*Phillips* v. *Phillips*, 87 Me. 324; 32 Atl. 963; *Fogg* v. *Holbrook*, 88 Me. 169; 33 Atl. 792; 3 Williams, Ex'rs, *1789.) The custom of having flowers at funerals is now well-nigh universal in this country; and, when not abused by extravagance or unseemly ostentation, it is certainly to be commended as giving appropriate expression to our feelings of respect and love for the departed. It is true that, strictly speaking, flowers are not a necessity on such occasions; but, like many other things of which the same might be said they are certainly appropriate, and in harmony with the better feelings and sentiments of our common humanity. And we think it is clear that in the case at bar the housekeeper of the intestate, in the circumstances above mentioned, was warranted in obtaining, upon the credit of the estate, the flowers in question. Mr. Woerner, in his valuable work on the American Law of Administration (vol. 2, p. 759), says: " It is the duty of the executor or administrator to bury the deceased in a manner suitable to the estate he leaves behind him; and if this duty, in the absence or neglect of the executor, is performed by another,—not officiously, but under the necessity of the case,—the law implies a promise to reimburse him for the reasonable expenses incurred and paid." So careful is the law to provide for necessary funeral expenses that liabilities incurred therefor invariably take the first rank as debts against the estate, and in this state they are made a preferred claim even in cases of insolvency. (Gen. Laws, ch. 215, § 16; and also ch. 274, § 27.) The estate, real and personal, of every deceased person, is also expressly made chargeable with such expenses by Gen. Laws, ch. 218, § 1. See *Buxton* v. *Barrett* (14 R. I. 40).

It is common knowledge that an administrator is almost never appointed until after the burial of the intestate. Somebody other than he, therefore, must necessarily make the arrangements for the funeral, and in connection therewith incur, either personally, or as informally representing the estate, the necessary indebtedness therefor. And such acts do not make the person performing them an *executor de son tort*. (Williams, Ex'rs, 261 ; Younge & J. 37, note a.) If an undertaker is employed, somebody must employ him, and, if it is understood that the person employing him is thereby to be rendered personally liable for the services to be rendered, it might sometimes happen that the funeral would be unduly delayed, and the divine injunction " to let the dead bury their dead " be literally heeded. In *Samuel* v. *Thomas' Estate* (51 Wis. 552; 8 N. W. 361), the question to be determined was what expenses incurred intermediate the death of an intestate and the granting of letters of administration were legally chargeable to the estate, and the answer of the court was as follows: " We think that only such necessary expenditures as from the nature of the circumstances cannot properly be postponed until an administrator shall be appointed are so chargeable. This rule will, of course, entitle an heir, a legatee, widow, or guardian, or even a stranger, who has paid reasonable burial expenses, necessarily incurred before administration could be granted, to be reimbursed from the estate. But, as we understand the law, the rule goes no further. Every expenditure which can decently and reasonably be postponed until an administrator is appointed should be so postponed, and one who, before such appointment, voluntarily incurs an expense for which there is no immediate necessity, does so in his own wrong, and cannot compel the administrator, when appointed, to reimburse him."

In *Tugwell* v. *Heyman* (3 Camp. 298), the defendants were sued as executors for the funeral expenses of the testator, who left considerable property. The reasonableness of the plaintiff's bill was not denied, but it appeared that the defendants had given no orders whatever respecting the funeral. The question therefore arose whether, under these circumstances, they were liable upon an implied promise to the plaintiff. Lord ELLENBOROUGH said: "I think the defendants are liable in this action. It is allowed that the funeral was conducted in a manner suitable to the testator's degree and circumstances, and that the plaintiff's charge is fair and reasonable. The defendants do not deny that they have assets. Then will not the law imply a promise on their part to satisfy this demand? It was their duty to see that the deceased was decently buried, and the law allows them to defray the reasonable expense of doing so before all other debts and charges. It is not pretended that they ordered any one else to furnish the funeral, and the dead body could not remain on the surface of the earth. It became necessary that some one should see it consigned to the grave, and I think, the executors, having sufficient assets, are liable for the expense thus incurred."

In *Rogers* v. *Price* (3 Younge & J. 27), it was held that an executor who has assets sufficient for that purpose is liable upon an implied promise to pay for a funeral suitable to the degree of his testator, furnished by the direction of a third person. In delivering his opinion in the case, GARROW, B., used the following forcible illustration in support of his position: "Suppose a person to be killed by accident at a distance from his home; what, in such a case, ought to be done? The common principles of decency and humanity, the common impulses of our nature, would direct every one, as a preliminary step, to provide a decent funeral, at the expense of the estate, and to do that which is immediately necessary upon the subject, in order to avoid what, if not provided against, may become an inconvenience to the public. Is it necessary in that or any other case to wait until it can be ascertained whether the deceased has left a will or appointed an executor; or, even if the executor be known, can it, where the distance is great, be necessary to have communication with that executor before any step is taken in the performance of those last offices which require immediate attention?" He then added: "It is admitted here that the funeral was suitable to the degree of the deceased, and upon this record it must be taken that the defendant is executor with assets sufficient to defray this demand. I therefore think that, if the case had gone to the jury, they would have found for the plaintiff, and that therefore this rule should be made absolute."

In *Luscomb* v. *Ballard* (5 Gray, 403), which was cited by DURFEE, C. J., in support of the position taken by this court in *Tucker* v. *Whaley,* which will be referred to later on, the court held that for the funeral expenses of the deceased the executor was chargeable in his representative character, and that judgment therefor should be rendered *de bonis testatoris.*

Sweeney v. *Muldoon* (139 Mass. 304; 31 N. E. 720), was a case where the plaintiff, at the request of the widow and the remaining relatives of the deceased, purchased a burial lot for the deceased at a cost of $125, and also incurred other expenses, as follows: Digging grave, $3; use of chapel for service and for funeral ceremony, $12; curtains, $10; flowers, $6; underwear and clothing, $3.40; monument, carting, and setting, and fixing lot, $113. These items were all allowed as proper funeral expenses, excepting the last named; FIELD, J., saying that "the law raises a promise on the part of the administrator, so far as he has assets, to pay the reasonable funeral expenses of burying the deceased, although they are incurred before his appointment."

In *Hapgood* v. *Houghton* (10 Pick. 154), PUTNAM, J., said: "The estate in the hands of the executor is bound by law for the payment of the expenses of the decent interment of the deceased.

den, 6 N. H. 201; Campfield v. Ely, 13 N. J. L. 150; Matter of Miller, 4 Redf. 302; Patterson v. Patterson, 59 N. Y. 574, 582; Shaffer v. Bacon, 35 App. Div. 252; 54 N. Y. Supp. 796.)

Public administrator held liable. (Rappelyea v. Russell, 1 Daly, 214.)

(b) **Husband's liability.**—Husband may recover his wife's funeral expenses from her executor. (Constantinides v. Walsh, 146 Mass. 281; 15 N. E. Rep. 631; Morrissey v. Mulhern, 168 Mass. 412; 47 N. E. Rep. 407.)

Husband insolvent, third person who has paid expense of burial of his wife may recover from her estate. (Gould v. Moulahan, 53 N. J. Eq. 341; 33 Atl. Rep. 483.)

Duty of husband to bury his wife, and he has no right to charge same against her estate. (Staples' Appeal, 52 Conn. 425; Re Weringer, 100 Cal. 345; 34 Pac. Rep. 825; Sears v. Giddey, 41 Mich. 590; 2 N. W. Rep. 917; Galoway v. McPherson, 67 Mich. 546; 35 N. W. Rep. 114; but compare McClellan v. Filson, 44 Ohio St. 184, 188; 5 N. E. Rep. 861 [under Ohio statute]. There is an interesting discussion of the subject in the opinion, with review of the cases.)

A husband who is administrator for his wife's estate is properly allowed her funeral expenses. (Moulton v. Smith, 16 R. I. 126; 12 Atl. Rep. 891; McCue v. Garvey, 14 Hun, 562; Freeman v. Coit, 27 Hun, 447.)

And it is his duty to pay expenses incurred for medical services or other expenses in his wife's last illness. (Re Weringer, *supra;* Waesch's Estate, 166 Pa. St. 204; 30 Atl. Rep. 1124.) And same are not properly chargeable against her estate. (Freeman v. Coit, *supra.*)

As to right of husband to be reimbursed out of wife's estate, for her funeral expenses, cases do not agree. (See Gould v. Moulahan, 53 N. J. Eq. 343; 33 Atl. Rep. 483.)

(c) **Tombstone or monument.**—Tombstone or monument. (Spire v. Lorell, 17 Ill. App. 559; Crapo v. Armstrong, 61 Iowa, 697; 17 N. W. Rep. 41; Estate of Barclay, 11 Phil. 123; Durkin v. Langley, 167 Mass. 577; 46 N. E. Rep. 119; Pistorius' Appeal, 53 Mich. 350; 19 N. W. Rep. 31; Donald v. McWhorter, 44 Miss. 124; Lund v. Lund, 41 N. H. 355, 362; Fairman's Appeal, 30 Conn. 205; Webb's Estate, 165 Pa. St. 330; 30 Atl. Rep. 827; Lutz v. Gates, 62 Iowa, 513; 17 N. W. Rep. 747; Van Emon v. Superior Court, 76 Cal. 589; 18 Pac. Rep. 877; Bell v. Briggs, 63 N. H. 592; 4 Atl. Rep. 702; Re Weringer, 100 Cal. 345; 34 Pac. Rep. 825; Campbell v. Purdy, 5 Redf. 434; Matter of Erlacher, 3 id. 9.)

Widow may be liable on her contract. (Foley v. Bushway, 71 Ill. 386.)

Estate not liable for a *family* monument. Morgan v. Morgan, 83 Ill. 196.)

Administrator personally liable on his order for tombstone or monument. (Ferrin v. Myrick, 41 N. Y. 315.)

But expense of same may be properly allowed to an executrix, on her accounting as part of the funeral expenses. (Matter of Shipman, 82 Hun, 109; 31 N. Y. Supp. 571.)

(d) **Illustrative cases.**—As a preferred claim. (Sullivan v. Horner, 41 N. J. Eq. 299; 7 Atl. Rep. 411; Booth v. Radford, 57 Mich. 357; 24 N. W. Rep. 102; and see Ball v. Ball, 45 S. W. Rep. 605 [Tex.].)

Extravagant funeral expenses not allowed. (Estate of Bi
87.)

Expense of removal of body not allowed. (Watkins v.
Ind. 378; 7 N. E. Rep. 193.)

Fencing private burial place not allowed. (Tuttle v. Robii
104.)

Not limited to shroud, coffin and grave. (Donald v. M
Miss. 124.)

But in Hewett v. Bronson (5 Daly, 2), it was *held* that the
to what is necessary in connection with the funeral and inte
not extend to advertising, procuring clergyman, and use of

In Hasler v. Hasler (1 Bradf. 248), an expense of $12
special messenger to Philadelphia to relatives informing then
deceased, and a charge of $10 for accompanying the body
were allowed.

Transportation of body from distant place to home or res
considered as part of funeral expenses. (Sullivan v. Horne)
299; 7 Atl. Rep. 411; and see Estate of Millenovich, 5 Ne

Dinner and horse feed for persons attending funeral not pi
expenses. (Schaffer v. Schaffer, 54 Md. 680; Santre's E
142 [Pa.].)

Mourning apparel may be properly allowed to administr
counting as part of funeral expenses. (Allen v. Allen, 3 Dem

Mourning rings allowed to executor when he has discretio
(Paice v. Archbishop, 14 Ves. 364.)

Mourning apparel not necessarily a funeral expense. (Gris
dler, 5 N. H. 492; Succession of Holbert, 3 La. Ann. 436.)

When funeral expenses paid by a benevolent society, it is t
that amount which can be charged to the estate. (Estate of
Phil. 135.)

Expense carriages, hearse, and caring for body of dece
Osburn's Estate, 36 Ore. 8; 58 Pac. Rep. 521; this vol. p. 1.

Expense of burial plat allowed. (Chalker v. Chalker, 5 R
see Matter of Erlacher, 3 id. 9.)

An undertaker may be allowed a reasonable sum for fui
when suitable to apparent circumstances of deceased, even
proves to be insolvent. (Matter of Rooney, 3 Redf. 15.)

7. Where executors have distributed to an insolvent legatee indebted to their testator, his share under the will, without deducting therefrom his indebtedness to the estate, and the share thus distributed has been sold by the legatee's trustees in insolvency to third parties for value, and without notice, the executors should not be allowed to restate their account, in order to enable them to make a claim against the purchasers. *Hoffman* v. *Armstrong,* 241

8. That trustees of an insolvent legatee did not object to an order allowing executors tó restate their account does not affect their right to object to the account as restated. *Id.*

9. Under Code, art. 93, § 224, providing that "the bare naming an executor in a will shall not operate to extinguish any just claim which the deceased had against him," it was error for the Orphans' Court, in an order allowing executors to restate an account, to provide that they should not retain any of the distribution to which one of the executors might be entitled on account of any alleged indebtedness from him to the estate, where such executor was indebted to the estate as a surviving partner of the deceased. *Id.*

10. Where the failure of executors to collect an amount due their testator from a distributee was due to their negligence, they should be charged with the amount. *Id.*

11. Under Code, § 219, providing that executors may be allowed such commissions on receipts and disbursements by them as may appear to the Probate Court a fair compensation for their trouble, risk and responsibility, not to exceed two and one-half per cent. on the receipts and the same percentage on disbursements, the discretion of the court has but two limitations,—the allowance must be a fair compensation, and must not exceed said percentage. *Noble* v. *Jackson,* 345

12. Executors who institute a suit in good faith and on reasonable grounds are entitled to reimbursement of costs and expenses of litigation, though unsuccessful. So, too, they are entitled to reimbursement for a reasonable amount paid by them to an attorney to represent them in a proceeding to require them to give a bond, or for their removal, they having in good faith, and on reasonable grounds, defended against it. *Id.*

13. Where an agreement is made by executors with the residuary legatee, the only other person interested, that they pay themselves $2,400 as commissions, subject to their right to have the amount increased and the legatee's right to have it reduced, the executors, on the amount being reduced to $1,800, should not be charged interest thereon. *Id.*

14. Executors who do not distribute the assets at the end of eighteen months after grant of letters, will be charged interest on all the amount in their hands, except such as they might reasonably have retained to meet the claims against the estate which were disputed, and on which suits were threatened. *Id.*

ADMINISTRATOR.

See EXECUTORS AND ADMINISTRATORS.

ADMINISTRATOR WITH WILL ANNEXED.

1. The duties and powers imposed on an executor as a trustee, being in
   the nature of a personal trust or confidence reposed in him by the
   testator, do not devolve on the administrator with the will annexed.
   Penn v. *Fogler,*   95

2. A decree giving generally to an administrator with the will annexed
   "all the powers, rights, duties, and authority that an executor
   could or might have, if named and mentioned in said will," limits
   such administrator to duties belonging properly to the office of
   executor, and does not clothe him with power to execute a trust
   created by the will. *Id.*

3. Where an administrator with the will annexed executes, without
   authority, a trust created by the will, he becomes a constructive
   trustee or a trustee *de son tort. Id.*

4. An administrator with the will annexed, holding stock of a national
   bank in trust, has no power or authority to invest it in a private
   banking partnership. *Id.*

   **See Editorial Note, "Powers of Administrator with
   Will Annexed,"**   119

ADOPTED CHILDREN.

See WORDS AND PHRASES.

ADVANCEMENT.

1. Where a testator, in his will, makes advancements to his children, and
   directs that they shall be charged interest thereon, it is proper to
   charge such interest in making distribution of his estate. *Hays* v.
   Freshwater,   329

2. Moneys advanced by testator to a son during his lifetime and after
   the will was made, whatever the amount, and whether charged on
   his books or not, cannot be deducted from the share of such son
   under a will reciting that he has made advances to children, which
   are charged to them on his books, and may make further advances
   which may be charged on his books to their respective accounts,
   and that he desires that equal provision made for each shall be in
   addition to the "advances made or that may hereafter be made,"
   and that "said advances made and that may hereafter be made be
   treated, not as advances, but as gifts, not in any manner to be
   accounted for." *Adams* v. *Cowen,*   572

3. A receipt acknowledging payment of a legacy which is not paid, except by the cancellation of an alleged debt of the legatee to the
   testator for advances which, by the will, were to be treated as a gift
   to the son will not be upheld when it was obtained by the representatives of the estate, who were in a fiduciary relation to the
   legatee, and who insisted that he was morally, if not legally, bound

to execute the release, thereby securing it from 1
by business reverses broken in spirit and waverin,
Id.

ANCILLARY LETTERS.

See JURISDICTION.

ANNUITIES.

1. Where a testator provides specific legacies, in the f
for all his heirs, which differs in proportion from
by the statute of distribution, and it is provided in
surplus shall be divided among the heirs, such
distributed in the same proportion as the sum d
nuities. *Angus* v. *Noble,*
2. Where a will provided that a trustee should colle
income of testator, and distribute the fund thereb
tain annuitants, an alien annuitant is entitled to 1
as such fund is personal property, which an ali
inheritance. *Id.*

See LEGACY; REMAINDERS; TRUSTS AND TRUS:

APPEAL.

1. Where the record does not clearly state the grou
questions and answers were excluded, nor upon '
objected to, and the Appellate Court cannot say wi
the rulings were erroneous, the trial court will be a
of *Turner,*
2. Stating reasons of appeal to be that the court erred
the jury as to burden of proof, and as to amount c
of evidence necessary to establish a will, is not in
Prac. Book, 258, rule 14, § 1, requiring the precise
to be set forth. *Id.*
3. Where, in a will contest, objections are sustained to
tions as to undue influence and mental incapacity,
reversed, although no offer of proof or showing is
what the rejected evidence is, or how it is material,
Civ. Proc. § 2545, provides that a decree upon a
shall not be reversed for error in admitting or rej
unless it appears that appellant was necessarily pre;
In re Potter's will,
4. A finding of a referee on a question as to the domicil
unanimously affirmed below, is conclusive on appe
Life Ins. and T. Co. v. *Viele,*
5. Where plaintiff, as special administratrix, was served
to dismiss the action, she has the right to appeal :
ment against her on such motion, although her spe:
been revoked prior to taking the appeal. *Peck* v.

18. Where there is evidence to support a finding of fact by the Appellate
Division which justifies a reversal by that court, it must be affirmed.
See PLEADING AND PRACTICE.

APPORTIONMENT.

1. There can be no apportionment, in favor of the estate of one holding
a life estate in lands under her husband's will, of savings bank
dividends not declared until after her death, since there can be
no right to such dividends until they are severed from the general
funds of the bank by vote of the directors. *Greene* v. *Huntington,*   448

ASSETS.

1. The *prima facie* presumption of D.'s ownership of a note given
by R. to him as a payee, and of a certificate of deposit to his own
order, arising from his possession thereof at the death of his
mother, is overcome by evidence that the money for which they
were given belonged to the mother, constituted nearly her whole
personal estate, and had been loaned by her agent A.; that she
complained to him of the irregularity of the payment of the interest,
directed him to collect the principal, and told him that, as her
health was poor, she would send D. to see about the collections
from time to time; that A. disposed of most of the money in the
bank to her order, and shortly afterwards she gave a check therefor
to D., who, in a few days, loaned the money to R., taking the note
in question; and that, on A. giving a check for the balance of the
collection, D. deposited it, taking therefor the said certificate of
deposit. *Adams* v. *Adams,*   59
    See EXECUTORS AND ADMINISTRATORS.

ATTORNEY.

    See ACCOUNTING; EVIDENCE.
    **See Editorial Note, "Employment of Attorney by Ex-
    ecutor or Administrator,"**   354

CHARITABLE BEQUESTS.

1. A bequest in a will for the erection of a memorial window to another in a church, left in trust to trustees who are themselves to
fix the amount to be so expended,—the will naming no amount to
be thus disbursed,—is not a valid testamentary disposition. *Succession of McCloskey,*   567
2. A bequest of the residue of the testator's estate to trustees, in trust
for such charitable uses and purposes in Ireland as they in their
discretion might think proper to apply it to, is not a valid testamentary disposition. *Id.*
3. The institution of heir or other testamentary disposition, committed
to the choice of a third person, is null. *Id.*

receipt in full settlement of his claim against the estate is not a valid tender, as the administrator has no right to require such a receipt. *Id.*

8. In an action by an administrator to sell real estate to pay debts, a cross complaint alleging that under an agreement of sale with the administrator and the heirs defendant took possession of the real estate, and made valuable improvements thereon, and asking that she be given a first lien on the proceeds of such sale for the present value of the improvements, does not state a cause of action, as, the heirs taking the estate subject to debts of the deceased, a purchaser from them acquires their rights only, subject to the application of the property to payment of debts. *Moore* v. *Moore,* 590

9. That an administrator, before settlement of the estate, consented to the sale of land by the heirs, did not divest a creditor of his right to have the debt made out of the land, nor estop the administrator from procuring an order of sale, for the payment of such creditor's debt. *Id.*

10. Where deceased left an estate of $6,000, and no widow or child, flowers to the value of $15, ordered by his housekeeper, who was his sister-in-law, for his funeral, were necessary, and hence his estate was liable therefor. *O'Reilly* v. *Kelly,* 718

See EVIDENCE; EXECUTORS AND ADMINISTRATORS; PLEADING AND PRACTICE; SALE.

See Editorial Note, " Creditor's Remedy as against Land," 527

COMMISSIONS.

See ACCOUNTING.

CONDITIONAL LEGACY.

See LEGACY.

CONSTRUCTION OF WILLS.

1. The cardinal rule for the construction of a will is to ascertain the intent of the testator from the entire instrument. *Hays* v. *Freshwater,* 329

See PLEADING AND PRACTICE; WILLS.

DEATH.

See EVIDENCE; WIDOW.

DELUSION.

1. Testator's son, who had been educated at his father's expense, became intemperate and improvident, and took his mother's part in divorce proceedings, consulted with an attorney who was his father's bitter foe and wrote a letter to an uncle in which he abused his father, and spoke of him as being fit for the penitentiary. After the divorce he lived with his mother, and never again saw or com-

municated with his father, who died fourteen years later. The father had, without reason, while in anger, called the son a bastard, but doubtless as a countercharge to his wife, who had accused him of adultery. Five years before his death testator conveyed property to a college, and later made a holographic will, leaving the bulk of his estate to the college. To this a codicil was added, slightly changing the conditions, and before his death he made another will to the same effect. He was a man of extraordinary intellectual vigor, managed his estate until his death with ability, and his letters to the college trustees showed a purpose, formed several years before his death, so to dispose of his property, *Held*, not to show a mental delusion, with respect to the son's character and habits, sufficient to justify submission of the testator's capacity to make a will to the jury. *Dobie* v. *Armstrong*, 170

2. There may be an insane delusion although the belief entertained is not, in the nature of things, a physical impossibility; but, if such belief is, entertained against all evidence and probability, and after argument to the contrary, it affords grounds for inferring that the person entertaining it labors under an insane delusion. *Medill* v. *Snyder*, 216

3. Under Code Civ. Proc. § 1312, declaring that in proceedings to contest a will the contestant is plaintiff, and the petitioner is defendant; and section 1981, declaring that the party holding the affirmative must prove it,—the burden is on the contestant to prove the delusions under which he claims the testator executed the will. *In re Scott's Estate*, 498

4. Testatrix was a woman of very excitable temper, and when excited was violent, both in language and action. She was highly suspicious of nearly every person with whom she had any relation; feared they were taking advantage of her and seeking to injure her. She was a sufferer from dyspepsia and other diseases of the stomach, which finally resulted in her death. She had a constant fear of being poisoned and charged those about her, while a widow, with trying to poison her, and, after her marriage with contestant, made the same charge against him. She also charged him with seeking to put her in an asylum and of unfaithfulness. Contestant had remarked that his wife was insane, and that he would break any will she would make, which remark was repeated to her. They occupied different apartments, and she had seen contestant with another woman, though there was no evidence that he was ever unfaithful to her, or attempted or thought of poisoning her. By her will, made shortly after her marriage with contestant, and also by her codicil executed some years later, and shortly before her death, she gave him two-fiftieths of her estate. *Held*, that the evidence authorized the trial court in finding that testatrix was not fully convinced of the charges she made against her husband, and

hence she was not under any delusion in reference thereto. at the time she made the will. *Id.*

See Evidence; Testamentary Capacity.

See Editorial Note, "Delusions," 224

DIVORCE.

See Executors and administrators.

DOWER.

1. Under Gen. St. § 618, providing that a widow may have dower in lands of which her husband "died possessed in his own right," dower may be assigned in an equitable remainder in fee, though the possession was in the trustee, which dower interest is subject to the paramount title of the trustee for purposes of the trust. *Greene* v. *Huntington,* 448

See Election.

ELECTION.

1. Under Comp. Laws 1897, §§ 8935, 8936, providing that when a widow shall be entitled to elect whether to take under the will or be endowed of the lands of her husband she shall be deemed to have elected to take under the will, unless within one year after the husband's death she shall commence proceedings for assignment of dower, a widow, by failing to commence such proceedings within one year after her husband's death, and by petitioning the Probate Court to proceed under the will, and allow her a reasonable sum instead of her dower, waives her right to dower. *Koster* v. *Gellen,* 657

2. Where a widow, without children, elects to take under the will, which provides for a sale of the premises, and a payment to her in cash in lieu of dower, and petitions the court to proceed under the will, which is done, she is not estopped from setting up the homestead interest granted by Const., art. 16, § 4, providing that, if the owner of a homestead die, leaving a widow, but no children, the same shall be exempt, and the rents and profits shall accrue to her benefit during widowhood, unless she be the owner of a homestead in her own right. *Id.*

See Estates.

See Editorial Note, "Election by Widow," 663

EQUITABLE CONVERSION.

1. A provision in a will that real and personal property be invested in a fund for the support and maintenance of a charity is a direction to convert such property into money. *Hood* v. *Dorer,* 548

ESTATES.

1. A child of a devisee of a life estate with remainder to his children has a vested remainder, if he is *in esse* when testator dies, and, if other children are born afterwards, the estate will open for their benefit. *Field* v. *Peeples,* 1

of testator's wife. Of the other three-fourths, he gave a life estate to J.'s brother, and upon his death to be conveyed in fee to J., if living, and if dead, to his legal representatives. *Held*, that these two provisions should be construed in the same way with respect to the disposition of the beneficial title in remainder, and that, as the executors who had been empowered by the will to determine its construction, had construed the first provision to vest the beneficial title in J., at testator's death, the second provision should be construed to vest the beneficial title in J. at his brother's death. *Greene* v. *Huntington,* 448

9. Such remainder after the death of J.'s brother became part of his estate, J. having died before the determination of the life estate, and no conveyance by the trustee was necessary to perfect the title. *Id.*

10. A will provided: " Second.* * * I give, devise, and bequeath unto my wife, M. C., the farm on which we now reside. * * * Thirdly. All * * * my personal property not otherwise disposed of, whilst she remains my widow." *Held,* that the limitation " whilst she remains my widow " applied to the farm as well as the personal property, since, unless the second and third clauses be read as one sentence, the third clause would be meaningless, and, when read as one sentence, the limitation applied to both. *Rose* v. *Hale,* 530

11. Where a devise is to testator's wife " whilst she remains my widow," the estate created cannot be greater than a life estate. *Id.*

12. Where testator gave all his property to his wife, to use, enjoy, and manage as she, in her judgment, saw fit, the wife took a fee, and not simply a life estate. *In re Barrett's Will,* 639

See POWERS; SPECIFIC PERFORMANCE; TRUSTS AND TRUSTEES.

ESTOPPEL.

1. Where a surviving husband, as administrator of his deceased wife, included in the inventory his separate real estate, designating the same as community property, he was not thereby estopped from claiming that the inventory was incorrect, or divested of title to the land; no rights having supervened in reliance thereon. *Koppelmann* v. *Koppelmann,* 673

2. Where a father, as guardian of his children, included in the inventory of his wards' estate real estate which belonged to himself, he was not thereby estopped from asserting title to such realty, or divested of the title thereof. *Id.*

3. Where a father made a deed of real estate to his children, which he did not deliver to them, but placed the same of record, with no intention that the same should operate as a conveyance of the title, he was not estopped thereby to assert that the deed conveyed nothing; nor did such deed divest him of title. *Id.*

4. Where a father, to prevent his wife from recovering a share of his

property in a divorce suit, made a deed of realty to his children
by a former marriage, without intending that title should pass
to them, and making no delivery thereof, he was not estopped, in
a suit by the children based on such deed, to assert that it passed
no title; and the fact that it was made to defraud a third person
gave the children no better right. *Id.*

    See CLAIMS AGAINST DECEDENT'S ESTATE; EXECUTORS AND AD-
      MINISTRATORS; SALE; WILL.

EVIDENCE.
  1. Prior declarations and statements of a testator, whether oral or con-
     tained in previous wills, are admissible, where in harmony with
     the provisions of the last will, to rebut the claim of undue influ-
     ence. *Kaenders* v. *Montague,*   11
  2. Declarations of testator, made before or after the execution of will,
     are admissible to show his mental condition at the time the will
     was executed. *Nieman* v. *Schnitker,*   121
  3. In a contest over the validity of a will on the ground of want of
     testamentary capacity, a previous will, made when the soundness
     of testator's mind was unquestioned, and which disposed of property
     approximately the same as the contested will, is admissible in
     evidence as tending to show soundness of mind when the con-
     tested will was executed. *Id.*
  4. Where previous wills, made by a testator, are in evidence as showing
     mental soundness at the time a contested will was made, proof
     of the mental soundness of testator when such previous wills were
     executed is admissible. *Id.*
  5. In a contest over the validity of a will on the ground of want of
     testamentary capacity, the jury were instructed that the opinions of
     subscribing witnesses to a will as to testator's mental soundness
     are not entitled to greater weight than opinions of other witnesses,
     equally credible, who had better opportunities of observing testa-
     tor. There was no evidence that other witnesses were present when
     the will was executed, nor that there were others who had better
     opportunities for observing deceased. *Held,* that the instruction
     was erroneous, as suggesting that other witnesses had better op-
     portunities of observing deceased than the subscribing witnesses.
     Id.
  6. A witness testifying to certain facts on direct examination cannot
     be asked on cross-examination if at a former trial he was not
     present when another testified to different facts, and he did not
     correct such testimony. *Appeal of Turner,*   155
  7. When witnesses' answers, material to the case, are stricken out be-
     cause they are not responsive to questions, there is no error when
     such witnesses, under proper questions, are afterwards allowed to
     testify to the same matters so stricken out. *Id.*
  8. In a will contest the opinion of a nonexpert witness as to the mental

condition of the testator is not receivable until the witness is shown to have had sufficient knowledge and opportunities of personal observation to form a correct conclusion as to the testator's mental condition, or until he has testified to sufficient particular facts upon which to base such opinion. *Id.*

9. In a will contest a qualified witness may be asked whether, in his opinion, the testator possessed sufficient understanding to transact ordinary business matters incident to the management of his household affairs and property. *Id.*

10. Where testamentary capacity was involved, a lawyer testified that he knew the testatrix for many years, and had frequent opportunities of observing her, and frequent conversations with her. When asked to detail the conversations, objection was made on the ground that they were confidential communications, but no evidence was offered to show that they were of a professional nature. The objection being overruled, witness detailed conversations concerning the settlement of an estate, and stated that she inquired about her interests therein, seeking information as to facts, and that subsequently she strenuously objected to a charge for fees against said estate, and that he appeared for her and contested the same, but it did not appear that he was being consulted professionally in the prior conversation. *Held,* that admitting said testimony was not error. *Id.*

11. The rule forbidding an attorney disclosing as a witness matters communicated in professional confidence should be strictly construed, as tending to prevent a full disclosure of the truth in court. *Id.*

12. Code Civ. Proc. § 829, declaring that no person interested in a suit shall be examined in his own behalf or interest, against the survivor of a deceased person, concerning a personal transaction or communication between the witness and the deceased, does not render the testimony of legatees inadmissible on the part of contestants in a proceeding to set aside the will. *In re Potter's Will,*   178

13. In a will contest, the contestants may prove entire conversations between deceased and the legatees, which tend to show undue influence and mental incapacity of the testator, and it is error to restrict such evidence to what the legatees said, and exclude what deceased said. *Id.*

14. Where, in an action by a housekeeper for services, a witness who stated that she had kept house for her father for fourteen years, and had had experience in housekeeping and hiring domestics, had testified to services rendered by plaintiff, she was competent to testify as to what they were worth. *Sprague* v. *Sea,*   264

15. An attorney who drew decedent's will, and was a subscribing witness thereto, is qualified to testify as to its contents in an action between decedent's heirs and his devisees, though Burns' Rev. St.

mony received, and to sustain the finding that the will established
was not the one previously rejected by the Probate Court. *Id.*

    See APPEAL; ASSETS; CLAIMS AGAINST DECEDENT'S ESTATE;
        GUARDIAN AND WARD; PLEADING AND PRACTICE; UNDUE
        INFLUENCE.

    See Editorial Note, " Declarations of Testator as Evi-
    dence,"   18

    See Editorial Note, " Evidence of Transactions with
    Deceased,"   182

EXECUTORS AND ADMINISTRATORS.

1. Where an administrator files a final account, showing he has administered the estate, he is estopped to deny his representative character, or liability to account. *In re Osburn's Estate.*   148

2. Under Hill's Ann. Laws, § 1144, authorizing the court to order an
administrator to sell at private sale, it may order him to sell a
stock of goods, and close it out in the regular course of business,
and for this purpose to incur the necessary expense of lighting,
clerk hire, etc. *Id.*

3. But the court has no authority to authorize the administrator to replenish the stock by the purchase of other goods. *Id.*

4. An administrator appointed in this State cannot sue to redeem from
a mortgage on land of his intestate in another State by setting off
against the mortgage debt waste committed thereon by the mortgagee in possession after the death of the intestate, nor to recover
for damages to or trespass committed on the land, since he is not
entitled to the possession thereof, and it is not assets in his hands
for the payment of debts. *Price* v. *Ward,*   249

5. Failure of an administrator to comply with Hill's Ann. Laws, § 1131,
making it his duty, immediately after appointment, to publish notice
to present claims within six months, and § 1112, requiring him to
file an inventory within one month after appointment, is sufficient
ground, in the discretion of the court, for his removal, under
§§ 1094, 1100, providing that he may be removed for unfaithfulness
or neglect of his trust, to the probable loss of persons interested
in the estate. *Barnes* v. *Rockey,*   323

6. In an action by an executor to set aside a conveyance of eighty acres
of land by his testator, and for a decree that the land be sold to
pay testator's debts, defendant's cross complaint alleged that the
eighty acres was part of 241 acres owned by the testator, which
testator conveyed in different parcels, at the same time and without consideration, to several beneficiaries, of which defendant was
one. *Held,* sufficient to entitle defendant to a decree that the testator's indebtedness was chargeable ratably, according to value,
against all parcels conveyed. *Kaufman* v. *Elder,*   388

7. A will creating a trust for the maintenance of testator's children, and
empowering the executor to sell and reinvest the property when

deemed by him expedient, confers no authority to continue a mercantile business of the testator, or to purchase goods for that purpose. *Eufaula Nat. Bank* v. *Manasses*, 393

8. Where an executor, without authority to carry on a business of his testator, purchases goods for that purpose, the title to such goods vests in him individually, and they are subject to an execution against him. *Id.*

9. An agreement whereby an owner of land contracts with another to occupy and cultivate it, each to furnish a certain proportion of the seeds, implements, and stock, and to share at the end of the term equally in the products, does not create a partnership between the parties. *Shrum* v. *Simpson*, 435

10. A complaint disclosing defendant's possession of money and property of the estate of a decedent, to which complainant is entitled as administratrix, and his refusal to settle, entitles complainant to an accounting. *Id.*

11. The Probate Court has the power, and it is its duty, to require a full and final accounting, and to make a settlement with an executor who has resigned, been removed, or whose letters have been revoked, and to order him to deliver the personal effects and assets of the estate to his successor. *Hudson* v. *Barratt*, 457

12. Where the estate of a deceased person is in process of settlement in the Probate Court, and an accounting has not been had with a former executor therein, and there has been no refusal by such executor to make a full and final accounting, and where a full settlement may be required and an adequate remedy had in that court, no occasion exists to invoke the equitable jurisdiction of the District Court, or for interference by that court with the settlement in the Probate Court; and in such a case an action cannot be maintained on the executor's bond until an accounting has been had in the proper tribunal, a liability ascertained, and an opportunity afforded the former executor to discharge it. *Id.*

13. Under Comp. Laws Dak., § 2578 (Laws S. D. 1890, ch. 105, § 1), requiring a plaintiff in a divorce suit to have been a resident of the territory ninety days before the commencement of the action, the residence of a citizen of another State in the territory for such time for the sole purpose of obtaining a divorce will not sustain a divorce granted in a suit instituted by him, when attacked by his wife in the State of his domicile. *Andrews* v. *Andrews*, 594

14. Under Pub. St. ch. 146, § 41, declaring that a divorce granted a citizen of Massachusetts, who goes into another State to obtain such divorce for a cause arising in Massachusetts, or a cause not authori _d by its laws, shall be of no validity, a divorce so granted in South Dakota, in a suit by a citizen of Massachusetts, who obtained a domicile in South Dakota without a *bona fide* intention of remaining there, and only for the purpose of obtaining the divorce, was void, regardless of the fact that the wife appeared and denied

plaintiff's residence, which defense was afterwards withdrawn on payment of a sum of money. *Id.*

15. The right of such wife to be appointed administratrix of the estate of the husband was superior to the right of one who married the husband after the divorce was granted. *Id.*

16. Since Pub. St. ch. 142, § 9, provides that, in every sale of the real estate of a decedent by an executor or administrator, the proceeds remaining on the final settlement of the accounts shall be considered as real estate, and be disposed of as such, the unexpended balance of the proceeds of the sale of real estate of a testator sold to pay debts is to be treated as real estate, and should be paid over by the administrator to those entitled thereto. *Adams* v. *Jones,* 618

17. Though an administrator assume to act in his representative capacity in the management of the real estate and the collection of the income thereof, he is merely the agent of the heirs. *In re Morrison's Estate,* 640

18. An action of claim and delivery cannot be maintained against an executor of an estate to recover possession of personal property unlawfully withheld by him. (By divided court.) *Elmore* v. *Elmore,* 706

FOREIGN WILL.

FRAUD.

FUNERAL EXPENSES.

1. Where an estate is appraised at $2,400, an order approving an expense of $31 for carriages, hearse, and caring for the body of deceased will not be disturbed. *In re Osburn's Estate,* 148

GUARDIAN AND WARD.

1. A widow married a second husband, and he, with a child by his former marriage, and she and her minor children by her former marriage all resided on her homestead as one family. He was appointed guardian of her children, and for ten years thereafter cultivated the farm, consisting of said homestead and other land belonging to her and her children, and still other land conveyed to him, but purchased with the money of her children. He apparently treated the crops of all of this land as his own, never kept any separate account of the crops or profits of any part of it, but the crops were mingled together, and the family were supported out of the common mass. There was no evidence as to what arrangement he had with his wife as to the cultivation of her part of the land, and he never made any arrangement with her as to who should support her children, or what funds should be applied for that purpose. In a proceeding to settle the guardian's account, *held*, he was the head of the family, and a finding that the wife's children boarded with her and that she supported them during the ten years is not sustained by the evidence. *In re Dahlmier,* 297

2. Compliance by a foreign guardian with the provisions of § 6279, of the Revised Statutes, is necessary, to entitle him to demand or receive money belonging to his ward in the hands of an executor or administrator in this State; and the Probate Court may, in its discretion, refuse to make an order for the payment of the money to the guardian, if satisfied it will be detrimental to the interests of the ward. Payment without such order is unauthorized, and affords no protection to the persons making the payment. *Banning* v. *Gotshall,* 473

3. Where the father of minor children, after the death of his divorced wife, in whose custody the children had been placed by a divorce six years previous, petitioned to be appointed their guardian, the evidence on which the divorce had been granted was competent to show that he was not a suitable person for the appointment. *McChesney* v. *De Bower,* 485

4. Where the father of minor children, after the death of his divorced wife, petitioned to be appointed their guardian, and it was shown that prior to the divorce, which had been granted six years previous, he had been guilty of extreme cruelty to the children and their mother, had committed adultery with the servant girl in his family, had made indecent proposals to his wife's mother and other females, and after the separation had refused to visit his little boy in his last sickness, or to attend his funeral, a finding that he was not a suitable person for appointment will not be disturbed on appeal. *Id.*

5. In a contest between the father of minor children and their maternal grandmother, to be appointed the children's guardian, a clause in the will of the mother of the children, who six years prior to her

death had been divorced from her husband, appointing the grand-mother their testamentary guardian, was properly admitted in evi-dence to show the propriety of appointing the grandmother, in case the father was found unsuitable for the trust. *Id.*

6. A ward is not concluded by a release acknowledging final and satis-factory settlement with the guardian, where it is given without any accounting or settlement in fact on the mistaken assurance of the guardian that nothing is due, though no fraud or undue influence is practiced in obtaining it. *Ellis* v. *Soper,* 627

7. An order discharging a guardian pursuant to a release acknowledging final settlement, given without any settlement in fact on the mis-taken assurance of the guardian that nothing was due, is not an adjudication on an accounting, and hence is not a bar to an action by the ward for an accounting. *Id.*

8. A guardian's final account should cover the entire period of guardian-ship, where the intermediate reports filed are incomplete. *Id.*

9. In the absence of an order allowing a widow who is guardian of her children's estate to use the same for their support, a court of equity, on final accounting, will allow her credit for past support, where it is shown that her own estate was insufficient to support them properly. *Id.*

10. A widow having an estate worth $11,500 and an annual income of $1,100, for the support of herself and children, for whom she is guardian, should be allowed only the income of their estate towards their support and education, when the estate of each is worth only $1,800, since she is primarily liable for their support during minority. *Id.*

11. A guardian, in making contracts relating to the estates of his wards, can bind himself only, and can bind neither his wards personally nor their estates. *Shepard* v. *Hanson,* 678

12. The mere possession of a negotiable promissory note, which is not payable to bearer, and is unindorsed, by another than the payee, is not *prima facie* evidence of the ownership of such note. Accord-ingly it was error for the trial court to direct a verdict for the amount of the note in suit; there being no other evidence of title, and plaintiff's ownership being denied by the answer. *Id.*

See ESTOPPEL; SALE.

HEIRS.

See WORDS AND PHRASES.

HUSBAND AND WIFE.

See ESTATES; EXECUTORS AND ADMINISTRATORS; TRUSTS AND TRUSTEES; WILL.

INTEREST.
>*See* ACCOUNTING; ADVANCEMENT.

INVENTORY.
>*See* ESTOPPEL; EXECUTORS AND ADMINISTRATORS.

JURISDICTION.
1. On a collateral attack of a decree of the County Court ordering a sale of a minor's land, jurisdiction to make the decree will be presumed, where the record does not show a want of it. *Field* v. *Peeples,*   1
2. A decree of the County Court, ordering a sale of a minor's land will be sustained when collaterally assailed, though the petition has been destroyed and the decree does not show that the land was to be sold for the minor's support or education, or for investment in other land, and such facts were essential to give jurisdiction under the statute in force when the decree was made. *Id.*
3. Where, in an action, no summons is served, and part of the defendants appear by demurrer, the court has no jurisdiction, under § 581, Code Civ. Proc., providing that, if appearance has been made by defendants within three years, such action may be prosecuted as if summons had been issued and served, to dismiss such action, on motion of defendants, as to those defendants who demurred. *Peck* v. *Agnew,*   213
4. This court, sitting in equity, cannot establish an unprobated will. *Cousens* v. *Advent Church,*   312
5. If, after the probate of a will, a later will, which revokes the first, is found, it should be presented for probate to the Probate Court. From the decree of that court an appeal lies to the Supreme Court of Probate. *Id.*
6. The prior probate of the earlier will does not preclude the probate of the later will. If the later will revokes the former, upon its probate the court authorized to admit wills to probate has authority to revise or revoke the former decree so far as to give effect to the last will. *Id.*
7. The Orphans' Court has jurisdiction to decree a sale of decedent's real estate to pay expenses of administration. *In re Reynold's Estate,*   525
8. The record disclosing that the decree of the Orphans' Court for a sale of decedent's real estate was for the payment of a debt due the executor, and his account showing that the balance claimed by him and allowed by the court, was for commissions and expenses of administration, they are sufficient to show jurisdiction. *Id.*
9. Code Civ. Proc., § 2695, limits the powers of the surrogate to grant ancillary letters on a foreign probate of a will executed by a person at the time a non-resident to the case of probate in the State or Territory where the will was executed, or the testator resided at time of death. *Held,* that where a petition was filed for ancil-

lary letters testamentary under § 2695, which stated that the will of which petitioner was executor was executed in Louisiana, but the certified copy of the probate in Louisiana, showed that testatrix at her death, had her domicile in Alabama, and that the will was executed in that State, the surrogate had no jurisdiction to issue ancillary letters, since, the court being bound to give full faith and credit to the judicial proceedings of a sister State, the statement of the record as to a jurisdictional fact prevailed over the petition. *Taylor* v. *Syme,* 536

10. Rev. Civ. Code La., art. 1668, provides that testaments made in other States cannot be carried into effect on property in that State without being registered in the court within the jurisdiction of which the property is situated. Article 1220 provides that the succession of persons domiciled out of the State of Louisiana, leaving property therein, shall be administered on as those of citizens of the State, and officers appointed to administer as pointed out by law. *Held,* that where testatrix was not a resident of Louisiana, and her will was not executed there, but she left property therein, the authority of an executor appointed there extended only to property in that State, not being a general administration, and hence, together with the rule that a foreign executor cannot sue in the courts of New York, such executor could not sue in such State on a note belonging to the estate. *Id.*

11. Where defendant was sued on a note by one to whom ancillary letters testamentary had been issued as foreign executor of the indorsee of the note, it was proper to attack in such action, the surrogate's jurisdiction to issue the letters, since, the question being jurisdictional, the attack could be made collaterally, *Id.*

12. Courts of Probate are not empowered to construe wills when presented for probate. *Dudley* v. *Gates,* 697

See CLAIMS AGAINST DECEDENT'S ESTATE; EXECUTORS AND ADMINISTRATORS; TRUSTS AND TRUSTEES.

See Editorial Note, "Jurisdiction to Construe Wills,"
702

LACHES.

1. Where a cause of action arises from a fraud, the bar created by *laches* does not apply in equity until the fraud is discovered by the exercise of reasonable diligence. *Penn* v. *Fogler,* 95

2. The failure to use diligence in discovering fraud is excused where there is a relation of trust and confidence which renders it the duty of the party committing the fraud to disclose the truth to the other. *Id.*

3. Where an heir permitted his stepmother to continue in possession of land which she held in trust for him and other heirs, and to appropriate its rents and profits for the necessary support of herself and such other heirs, without demanding or suing for his interest therein until eight or nine years after he became of age, he is not

the period measured by less than two designated lives in being at the testator's death; the words "or their heirs" being words of limitation, and not of substitution. *Steinway v. Steinway,* 599

7. A devise of shares of corporate stock and the income thereof to several legatees, each of whom is to take both income and principal in equal proportions, creates a tenancy in common. *Id.*

8. The rule that payment to the legatee of the whole income of a legacy pending delay in payment of principal is essential to the immediate vesting of the legacy is not violated where the excess over a certain per cent. of the income is devised to executors as compensation for the management of the legacy. *Id.*

9. A will provided for the payment of specific legacies in the form of annuities, payable every three months. In another provision it was declared that the rents of the estate should be paid every month, and kept three months, and all debts paid out of them, and the balance kept to the end of the year, and divided among the heirs. The will required the payment of all testator's debts before such fund came into existence. *Held,* that the specific legacies were not inconsistent with the provision requiring the rents to be divided among the heirs, as the testator intended by the use of the word "debt" to include the quarterly payments to the legatees. *Angus v. Noble,* 643

10. When a testator devised a sum due on a mortgage to certain persons, the right of such legatees will not be impaired by the fact that the income of the rest of the estate is insufficient to pay annuities given by the will. *Id.*

See ADVANCEMENT; TRUSTS AND TRUSTEES; WILL.

LEGAL REPRESENTATIVES.

1. A codicil gave a portion of the residuary estate in real property to trustees, to pay the income and profits to one for life, and on her death to convey the trust fund to her legal representatives. A section of the will gave pecuniary legacies to different persons, and, in case of their death before testator, to be given to the legal representatives of such deceased legatees. *Held,* that as "legal representatives," in the latter case, clearly mean, not executors or administrators, but those who would take for their own benefit, the words in the former case should be construed in the same way, especially in view of the fact that to them the land was to be conveyed in fee. *Greene v. Huntington,* 448

2. A testator devised a portion of his residuary estate in trust for his wife for life, and on her death to convey the trust fund to her legal representatives. Under Gen. St., § 2952, providing that no estate shall be given by will to any persons not in being at the time of the death of the testator, or to their immediate issue or descendants, such a remainder in favor of her legal representatives,

to be first ascertained at the time of her death, would be void. *Held,* that the legal representatives intended were those answering to that description at the death of testator. *Id.*

LIFE ESTATE.
See APPORTIONMENT.

LIFE TENANT.
See TAXES AND ASSESSMENTS.

See Editorial Note, "Expense as Between Life Tenant and Remainder-man,"   692

LIMITATION.
See CLAIMS AGAINST DECEDENT'S ESTATE; PLEADING AND PRACTICE; TRUSTS AND TRUSTEES.

MARRIAGE—EFFECT OF ON WILL.
See WILL.

PARTNERSHIP.
See EXECUTORS AND ADMINISTRATORS; TRUSTS AND TRUSTEES.

PERPETUITIES.
1. Where certain provisions of a will constitute a general scheme for the disposition of testator's property to a class of beneficiaries, and one is void as a perpetuity, such provision invalidates the others connected with it, though, standing alone, they would be valid. *Eldred* v. *Meek,*   128
2. A will directed a trustee to transfer a portion of testator's estate to grandchildren on their arrival at twenty-five years of age, and declared that, if one or more of such grandchildren should die without issue before arriving at twenty-five, his or their interest should be paid to the survivors, and, if any should die under twenty-five leaving issue, the interest of such a one should go to his issue on arrival at twenty-five. *Held,* that, since the grandchildren's interest was a contingent remainder, the clause providing for the disposition of the interest of one who should die before twenty-five leaving issue would postpone the vesting of such interest longer than a life or lives in being and twenty-one years, and hence such provision was void as a perpetuity. *Id.*

PLEADING AND PRACTICE.
1. The approval by the court of a report of a sale of a minor's land, indorsed on the report, is valid, though the better practice would be to require an order of the court to be duly entered on the records of the court, approving the sale. *Field* v. *Peeples,*   2
2. Where a demurrer to a declaration is sustained because the remedy is in equity, the action is defeated by a defect of form, within Pub.

St., ch. 136, § 12, providing that, if an action commenced against an executor or administrator before the expiration of two years from the time of his giving bond be defeated by a defect in the form of the writ or a mistake in the form of the proceeding, plaintiff may commence a new action for the same cause within one year thereafter. *Taft* v. *Snow*, 24

3. On a bill by a beneficiary against the executor of a trustee for an accounting, the beneficiary is entitled to an execution as at common law against the estate of the trustee in the hands of the executor for the principal sum found due, and another execution for costs against the executor personally. *Id.*

4. A bill is not objectionable as multifarious where the construction of a will is the primary matter in controversy, around which all the matters in issue revolve, and on which all the relief sought depends, and all the complainants are immediately interested in the various clauses to be construed and in all the questions involved, and defendant is concerned in them all, and will be affected by their decision. *Dillard* v. *Dillard*, 52

5. A decree dismissing a suit by one for construction of a will and for an interest claimed thereunder, on the ground that he took nothing under the will, is not *res judicata*, against persons joined with the executor as defendants in such suit, where they bring a suit for construction of the will, not claiming in the same right as the plaintiff in the former motion, but asserting rights separate, distinct, and antagonistic to those asserted by him, and they not being in privity with him. *Id.*

6. Pleading the lien by the judgment creditor, in an action brought by the personal representative to sell the land for the payment of debts, is not the commencement of an action, within the purview of the statute limiting the time within which actions may be commenced against executors and administrators. *Ambrose* v. *Byrne*, 89

7. A bill need not charge all the circumstances which may conduce to prove the general charge, as these are matters of evidence. *Penn* v. *Fogler*, 95

8. Relief which is consistent with the allegations and proof is properly granted, though it may be different from that specifically prayed for. *Id.*

9. Where a bill makes a case for account, evidence which discloses other facts in addition to those charged should be considered, when the facts disclosed strengthen the right claimed, and merely expand the measure of accounting. *Id.*

10. The filing of an account by an administrator makes the inventory on which it is predicated a part of the record, and it is properly included in the transcript on appeal, though not offered in evidence. *In re Osburn's Estate*, 148

11. The petition for letters, order appointing administrator, his bond, and the order of distribution, not being necessary parts of the ad-

25. An instruction that a person who signs as a witness to a will impliedly certifies to the testator's testamentary capacity, and that, while the law will subsequently permit him to testify to the contrary, yet the jury may consider the fact of such implied contradiction in weighing his testimony, is a correct statement of the law, and does not usurp the province of the jury. *Id.*

26. Since the statutory cause for which a new trial may be demanded is that the verdict is not sustained by sufficient evidence, it is not necessary, in addition thereto, to separately assign that the verdict was contrary to the evidence. *Id.*

27. The trial court's refusal to grant a new trial on account of the alleged insufficiency of the evidence will not be disturbed. *Id.*

28. In an action to set aside a conveyance by a testator, and for a sale of the property for payment of debts, evidence that other property conveyed by testator was equally bound with defendant's was not admissible under the general denial, where the grantees, other than defendant, were not made parties to the action. *Kaufman* v. *Elder,*   388

29. In an action to set aside a conveyance by a testator, and for a sale of the property necessary to pay debts, an answer alleging that other property conveyed by testator was equally liable with that conveyed to defendant was insufficient. *Id.*

30. The real parties in interest may be substituted as plaintiffs in an action previously brought in the name of the state upon an executor's bond. *Hudson* v. *Barratt,*   457

31. In an action against the administrator of a deceased legatee of a life estate in money, it appeared that the money had gone into a farm, which the legatee had devised to others; but such devisees were not joined, nor the necessity of their being made parties suggested, but defendant tried the case on the theory that the matter had been adjusted. *Held* that, on appeal, defendant could not first insist that the judgment for the remainder of the legacy should have been charged against the farm. *Snider* v. *Snider,* 464

32. Testator, after creating a life estate in his wife, directed that on her decease the property should be invested in a fund for the support of the superannuated preachers of the church denominated the United Brethren in Christ. The widow, in an action to construe the will, named as defendants "the superannuated preachers of the church denominated the United Brethren in Christ." Such persons were not a corporate body, and none of them appeared. Judgment was entered that the real estate descended to the wife in fee. *Held,* that such judgment was not *res judicata* as to such persons. *Hood* v. *Dorer,*   548

33. Infants desiring to obtain the probate of a will may institute a proceeding therefor by a next friend, and through him may appeal from a decision of the Probate Court rejecting a will. *Schnee* v. *Schnee,*   553

POWERS.

best, the appropriation of money borrowed by the fathers, and secured by deed of trust on the land devised will not invalidate the loan, when the lender had no notice that the fund was to be misappropriated. *Id.*

13. Where by a will the fathers of devisees therein were given power to dispose of their children's land as they thought best, a deed of trust of such land need not expressly recite that it was executed in pursuance of the power given by the will, in order to convey the interests of the children in the land, since the trust deed purported to convey the fee, which would have been impossible without the exercise of the power. *Id.*

See TRUSTS AND TRUSTEES.

See Editorial Note, " Termination of Power of. Sale," 64

See Editorial Note, " Execution of Power by the Court," 546

See Editorial Note, " Distinction Between Power and Trusts," 566

PRECATORY TRUSTS.

See ESTATES.

See Editorial Note, " Precatory Trusts," 144

REMAINDERS.

1. When a will provides for certain remainders after the determination of prior life estates, the remainder is vested at the death of testator. *Angus* v. *Noble,* 643

2. Where a will imports an intention of the testator to dispose of her entire estate, and life estates in the income are created, and remainders created thereafter are also expressed as being in the income, but no limit is placed on the enjoyment, such remaindermen acquire a legal title to the property. *Id.*

3. Where a clause in a will provides an annuity to certain persons, stated by the will to have no children, remainder to other heirs, the remainder is to the other heirs of the testator. *Id.*

4. Where a will provides a life estate in a trust fund to a certain person, remainder to his heirs, the children of such person acquire an equitable interest in remainder in the fund at the death of testator, subject to open and let in a child thereafter born. *Id.*

5. Where a will creating annuities, not distributed according to the statute of distributions, provides for remainders to the other heirs on the death of a certain annuitant, such remainders will be distributed according to the statute of distribution. *Id.*

6. When a testator prefers certain heirs in his will, but provides that on their death the property shall pass to testator's other heirs, such persons are excluded from taking an interest in remainder in property devised to testator's heirs. *Id.*

7. When a will provides for various annuities for life, to be distributed by a trustee, remainder over to testator's heirs, it is the duty of the trustee, after the expiration of any life estate, to divide the interest therefrom quarterly among those entitled to the remainder, till the expiration of the trust. *Id.*

 See ESTATES; PERPETUITIES; TAXES AND ASSESSMENTS; TRUSTS AND TRUSTEES; WORDS AND PHRASES.

 See Editorial Note, "Expense as Between Life Tenant and Remainder-man,"   692

REPLEVIN.

 See EXECUTORS AND ADMINISTRATORS.

REVOCATION.

1. A general finding that a will, objected to on the grounds of mental incapacity, undue influence, and fraud and duress, was not a valid will, does not show that there was lack of mental capacity, so as to invalidate revocation of a prior will, destroyed on the same day that the second was executed. *McCarn v. Rundall,* 624

2. Intention to revoke a will is shown by testimony of witness that testatrix called for it, and wanted it destroyed and done away with, and that he tore it up by her direction. *Id.*

3. A will, expressly revoking former wills, is held effective as a revocation, although the principal bequest of the later one is void. *Dudley v. Gates,*   697

 See JURISDICTION; PLEADING AND PRACTICE; WILL.

SALE.

1. An auctioneer at an administrator's sale, being interested in having the property bring its full value, by fictitious bidding ran the bids up to about the full value, and then knocked it off to one who had made no bid whereupon the administrator, who had had no intention of buying, but who had advertised the sale thoroughly, and thereupon acted in good faith, publicly assumed the bid, took possession at once, and made valuable improvements. The heirs were all of age, and lived near, and complainant made no objection to the court's approval of the sale a month later; exceptions being first taken to the administrator's account charging himself with the amount bid. The account was approved, and no bill to set aside the sale was filed for over a year, during which time complainant saw the administrator making improvements of a substantial character. *Held,* that complainant was estopped to claim that the sale was invalid, or have it vacated. *Voorhes v. Bailey,*   228

2. A vendor's right to a forfeiture for the purchaser's default in the payment of an installment on an executory contract for a sale of land was waived by his subsequent acceptance of payment, and the execution of a deed. *Zunkel v. Colson,*   303

3. Expenses of administration are not debts of decedent, and not subject to the limitation of the lien thereof, so that a sale for their payment may be decreed after expiration of the lien of the debts. *In re Reynold's Estates,* 525

4. Where a court, in 1873, ordered a special guardian of infants to sell their interests in property, and he entered into a contract of sale with his wife, and the sale was concluded by the purchaser giving a mortgage to the infants payable on their arriving at age, the court ordering the sale had power in its discretion to confirm the sale to the wife, and having done so with full knowledge of the facts, the purchaser of such property at a judicial sale twenty-six years later gets an unquestionable title as to this transaction. *Strauss* v. *Bendheim,* 540

5. Where executors in a will have power to sell property with discretion as to terms and conditions, and enter into a contract with defendant to purchase the property, and he refuses to perform, and specific performance is decreed, or a judicial sale by a referee in case of a refusal by defendant to complete the purchase, while the referee's deed conveys the title, yet the executors must also execute a deed to the purchaser at the judicial sale. *Id.*

See CLAIMS AGAINST DECEDENT'S ESTATE; EXECUTORS AND ADMINISTRATORS; JURISDICTION; POWERS; SPECIFIC PERFORMANCE.

SPECIFIC PERFORMANCE.

1. Where executors in a will are imperatively required to sell property with discretion as to terms and conditions, they also have power to contract to sell and to enforce the contract, and in an action to compel specific performance a judgment can be entered decreeing that defendant specifically perform, and, if he refuses to do so, that the property be sold by a referee, and his deed to the purchaser will convey all the title to the premises which the executors could have conveyed under the power. *Strauss* v. *Bendheim,* 540

2. Executors named in a will were required to sell certain property, and contracted to sell to defendant, who made a payment under the contract, and later refused to perform. Specific performance having been decreed against defendant, with a resale ordered to be made by a referee in case defendant refused, the property was resold. The referee's deed to the purchaser recited all the facts in the judgment, with his power to convey, and that it conveyed all the right, title, and interest of the executor and of the defendant. *Held,* that while executors did have an interest in the property under the power in the will and the defendant an equitable interest under his contract to purchase yet the deed conveyed the title of the testatrix. *Id.*

See POWERS.

STATUTE OF LIMITATION.
  See CLAIMS AGAINST DECEDENT'S ESTATE; PLEADING AND PRAC-
  TICE; TRUSTS AND TRUSTEES.

TAXES AND ASSESSMENTS.
 1. Olean City Charter, § 88, requires publication of a notice of paving
  assessments, and a day for their correction, and provides that, after
  correction and confirmation, they shall become liens. Section 113
  provides that notice to one tenant in common shall be notice to
  all. A paving assessment was levied against plaintiff, who was
  a life tenant of property abutting on the paved street. *Held,* that
  notice to plaintiff was not notice to the remainder-men, since a
  life tenant is not a tenant in common with remainder-men, and
  hence the assessment was levied against plaintiff personally, and
  not against the remainder-men. *Chamberlin* v. *Gleason,* 686
 2. Where expenses of repairing a pavement are to be paid by general
  taxation, so that the improvement is permanent in its nature, and
  the whole of the paving assessment is levied against a life tenant
  of property abutting the paved street, the life tenant's remedy to
  secure a proper apportionment of liability between herself and the
  remainder-men is by injunction against the city to prevent collection of the assessment except in such proportion as shall be adjudged. *Id.*
 3. A paving assessment for an improvement which is to be permanent,
  levied against abutting property, is properly apportioned so that
  the life tenant pays the interest on the assessment during her
  life, and the remainder-men pay the principal of the assessment
  as it falls due. *Id.*
 4. A husband's will devising real estate to his wife for life, remainder
  over, provided that the wife should pay all taxes assessed against
  the property during her lifetime, and also all premiums for insurance, not only for her interest as life tenant but also as mortgagee,
  the remainder-men being required to mortgage the property to her
  to secure her an allowance out of the estate. *Held,* that a paving
  assessment for a permanent improvement was not included in the
  word "taxes," used in the will, and hence that the remainder-
  men, and not the widow, were liable therefor. *Id.*
 5. Where a judgment below apportions a paving assessment payable in
  ten successive annual installments, with interest, between the life
  tenant and remainder-men, so that the life tenant pays the interest
  thereon becoming due during her life, and the remainder-men pay
  the principal, and also adjudges that the remainder-men are liable
  for the assessment except whatever interest becomes due during
  the tenant's lifetime, according to the condition of bonds issued
  for the payment of the assessment, and the record fails to show
  the condition of the bonds as to whether interest is payable on
  the entire assessment annually, or is postponed as to each install-

ment until it becomes due, it will be assumed, on appeal, that the life tenant is to pay the interest accruing on the entire assessment during her life. *Id.*

6. Where a paving assessment amounts to $459, and a life tenant of the property against which it is levied is sixty-nine years old at the time of a trial to apportion the assessment between herself and the remainder-men, and it does not appear that the item of interest on the assessment during her life was of sufficient importance to be brought to the notice of the court below, an ambiguity in a judgment apportioning the interest accruing during the tenant's life to her, and the balance of the assessment to the remainder-men, will not warrant a reversal of the judgment. *Id.*

    See TRUSTS AND TRUSTEES.

TENANCY IN COMMON.
    See LEGACY.

TESTAMENTARY CAPACITY.

1. The reasonableness of the provisions of a will may be considered by the jury only as a circumstance tending to show unsoundness of mind or undue influence, in connection with all the other facts and circumstances in the case. *Kaenders* v. *Montague,* 11

2. In a contest over the validity of a will on the ground of want of testamentary capacity, it is error to instruct the jury that "unsoundness of mind embraces every species of mental incapacity from raging mania to delicate and extreme feebleness of mind," because a testator's mind might be in a partial sense unsound, and yet not incapacitate him from making a will. *Nieman* v. *Schnitker,* 121

3. In a contest over the validity of a will on the ground of want of testamentary capacity, it is error to give an instruction that, "if the will was made under the influence of partial insanity, and is the product of it, it is invalid," when there is no evidence that the testator was laboring under any delusion or mania. *Id.*

4. In a contest over the validity of a will on the ground of want of testamentary capacity, it is not within the province of the jury to determine whether the will is a reasonable and proper distribution of the testator's property, and an instruction giving the jury such an understanding is ground for reversal. *Id.*

5. One may make a valid will, if he understands the nature and elements of such a transaction, although he is mentally incapable of transacting business generally. *Appeal of Turner,* 155

6. The fact that the testator was, at the time of the making of his will, suffering great pain, would not of itself take away his testamentary capacity. *Stevens* v. *Leonard,* 369

    See DELUSIONS; EVIDENCE; PLEADING AND PRACTICE.

TITLE.

TRUSTS AND TRUSTEES.

1. Where money is received to be invested and held in trust, and after
investment the trustee withdraws the money without the beneficiary's knowledge, and mingles it with his own funds, an accounting is necessary to enforce the beneficiary's rights, and, since a
trust is involved, it can be obtained only in equity. *Taft* v.
Snow, 24

2. The beneficiary cannot sue at law as for money had and received,
nor has he any remedy at law that is plain and adequate. *Id.*

3. Where one conveys property in trust, to be held for the benefit of such
"charitable corporations" as he may appoint by will, a testamentary direction to his executor, an individual, to expend a
certain sum in providing free excursions for poor children is valid,
and the executor may give the money to a charitable corporation
to be so expended. *Loring* v. *Wilson,* 31

4. Where one conveys property in trust, to be held for the benefit of
such persons sustaining a specified relation to him as he may appoint by will, a testamentary appointment of a person not within
the class is invalid. *Id.*

5. Where one conveys property to be held in trust for the benefit of
such persons as he may appoint by will, and he dies seized of
general assets, and in disposing of the latter he makes a legacy,
the trust estate is not liable therefor. *Id.*

6. Testator's mother created a trust in his favor, giving him a general
power of appointment by will. He conveyed other property in
trust, reserving a power of appointment by will, and died, seized
of general assets. His will first purported to dispose of the property
included in the trust created by his mother, and his own property,
giving a pecuniary legacy, and bequeathing the "residue" to another legatee. It then purported to dispose of the estate conveyed by testator in trust, and in doing so enumerated certain
chattels that had always been used in connection therewith, but
which, in fact, were included in the trust created by the mother.
Held, that said chattels passed by the latter clause, and not to the
residuary legatee named in the former. *Id.*

7. The latter devise, including the gift of the chattels, having been
charged with certain pecuniary legacies, the legatees waived all
right to have their legacies paid out of any real estate or chattels
included in the trust created by the testator's conveyance. *Held,*
that the chattels included in the trust created by the mother, and
given by the latter clause of the will, were not thereby exempted.
Id.

8. Testator's debts were payable, first out of his own property, and
then out of that included in the trust created by his mother of

which he disposed in the former clause of the will, and then out of the chattels which were included in the trust created by the mother, but which were disposed of in the latter clause of the will. *Id.*

9. Property conveyed in trust to pay the income to the grantor during her life, and the principal on her death to be transferred to such persons as she should appoint by her will, when such will has been executed and has taken effect by her death, and the appointees are within the terms of St. 1891, ch. 425, is subject to the collateral inheritance tax imposed thereby, as property passing "by deed, grant, sale or gift made or intended to take effect in possession or enjoyment after the death of the grantor;" the will in such case being referred to the instrument creating the power of disposition and being regarded as a disposition made by the donor of such power, whether such donor is the testatrix or another. *Crocker* v. *Shaw,*   41

10. The fact that the instrument creating the trust and the power of appointment was executed prior to the passage of the statute is immaterial; the transfer having been thereby made to take effect in possession and enjoyment only on the grantor's death, which took place after the statute became effective. *Id.*

11. The discretionary power jointly confided to three trustees by name, to give all or any part of the fund to a certain person, though coupled with an interest, cannot, after death of one of them, be executed by the survivors; Code, § 3419, as amended by Acts 1889-90, p. 41, and Acts 1897-98, p. 687, not referring to a trust involving such power. *Dillard* v. *Dillard,*   52

12. Where discretionary power is jointly given to three trustees, by name, to give all or any part of the fund to D., and they are also directed, whenever and on such terms as they think proper, to sell the property belonging to the fund and remaining unappropriated, and divide the proceeds equally between three certain persons, one of the trustees having died without any of the property having been given by them to D., their only other discretion (determination of time and terms of sale) then ceases, and the sale and division among the three persons must be made in a reasonable time. *Id.*

13. Where a partner, who is a trustee, improperly employs trust funds in the partnership business, or in the payment of partnership debts, the *cestui que trust* is entitled to reimbursement by the firm, if the other partners had knowledge of the nature of the fund at the time of the misapplication. *Penn* v. *Fogler,*   95

14. Where an incoming partner, at the time of entering the firm, has knowledge that trust funds have been improperly invested in the business and are being used by the firm, he becomes liable for such misapplication thereof as occurs after he becomes a member. *Id.*

15. Where an outgoing partner knew that trust funds were improperly employed in the firm business, he is liable therefor to the extent of his interest which he afterwards sold. *Id.*

16. A beneficiary of a trust, whose interest does not accrue under the will until after the death of the last survivor of life annuitants, being a mere remainder, cannot acquiesce in the management of the property until his interest comes into possession. *Id.*

17. Where a will directs that a trustee shall transfer parts of testator's estate to beneficiaries on the happening of certain contingencies, and in the meantime keep the lands rented and the personalty invested, pay taxes, repair and rebuild buildings, etc., and apply the balance of the income to the maintenance and education of such beneficiaries, it creates an active trust, and not a naked power only, and the Circuit Court has jurisdiction to construe it. *Eldred* v. *Meek,* 128

18. Where a widow collected money from her deceased husband's estate, and paid the balance due on land which he had bought and partially paid for, and took the deed in her own name, she holds the land in trust for his heirs. *Zunkel* v. *Colson,* 303

19. The execution of a mortgage by one holding the legal title to land in trust will not be regarded as a repudiation of the trust, and an act of adverse possession, where it was intended to benefit the estate, and was soon after satisfied by the trustee. *Id.*

20. The act of a trustee in giving a third person an option, unavailed of, to buy minerals underlying land constituting the trust estate, was not an act of adverse possession, as against the beneficiary. The statute of limitations does not begin to run in favor of one holding land in trust, as against the beneficiary, until the former has clearly notified the latter that he claims the land adversely. *Id.*

21. A devise by a testatrix of a farm to her executors, to invest the proceeds in bonds and mortgages, or in such other ways as they should deem advisable, the income to be paid equally to her two sons as long as they should live, and on the death of either to pay one-half of such proceeds to his heirs, devisees, or legatees, created an active trust; and the fact that the trustees had allowed the *cestuis que trustent* to occupy and enjoy the property did not deprive other beneficiaries of their contingent interest in the property. *Hunt* v. *Hunt,* 419

22. Under Comp. Laws 1897, § 8867, providing that, when a general and beneficial power to devise the inheritance shall be given to the tenant for life, such tenant shall be deemed to possess an absolute power of disposition, a devise of a farm to executors, to invest the proceeds and pay the interest to the *cestuis que trustent,* and on the death of either of them to pay one-half of the same to his heirs, devisees, or legatees, did not vest the title in fee to the trust property in the *cestuis que trustent,* since they were not life

tenants, because the will vested the absolute title in the trustees. *Id.*

23. Under Comp. Laws 1897, § 8810, providing that when a remainder shall be limited to the heirs of the body, to whom a life estate in the same premises shall be given, the persons who, on the termination of the life estate, shall be heirs or heirs of the body of such tenant for life shall be entitled to take as purchasers, where a devise was made to executors to pay the income of the devised property to the sons of the testatrix during their lifetime, and on the death of either to pay one-half to his heirs, devisees, or legatees, the words "heirs, devisees, or legatees," as used in such devise, are words of purchase, and an order terminating the trust on the petition of one of the sons, after the death of the other, was erroneous, since the surviving son had no interest in the property other than the enforcement of the trust. *Id.*

24. Where testatrix devised property to her executors in trust, the income to be paid to her two sons equally, and, on the death of either, one-half of the property to be paid to his heirs, devisees, or legatees, on the death of one son the heirs of the surviving son are entitled to institute proceedings to protect the trust fund. *Id.*

25. Where the absolute title to real estate was vested in trustees, with power to the *cestuis que trustent* to dispose of the same by will, the fact that after the death of one of the *cestuis que trustent* the other executed a will did not confer on him the power to terminate the trust, since he possessed no interest in the property other than the faithful enforcement of the trust. *Id.*

26. Where a testator, after a life estate created in his wife, leaves his entire property to be invested in a fund for the support and maintenance of the superannuated preachers of the church denominated the United Brethren in Christ, a valid trust is created, as a trustee, to be appointed by the court, can select the beneficiaries from the class named. *Hood* v. *Dorer,* 548

27. Where a nonresident loan and trust company made a loan, and took as a trust deed to secure it, before registration of its charter where the transaction took place, such transaction was validated by the subsequent filing of an abstract of the company's charter at such place; and the company was entitled to recover the amount actually loaned, with six per cent. interest. *Law Guarantee and Trust Co.* v. *Jones,* 559

28. Where, by the terms of a will, an executor is given the functions of a trustee, he is entitled to qualify as such after completing the settlement of the estate, regardless of the fact that the name of trustee was not conferred by the will. *Angus* v. *Noble,* 643

29. Where, by a will, certain annuities to be paid by a trustee to certain persons are to go on their death to testator's heirs, or to some designated person and then to testator's heirs, or to the heirs of

such annuitants, the trust will continue till the death of the annuitants. *Id.*

30. A will creating a trust, requiring that the estate be kept up and that graves be kept clean, is binding on the trustee. *Id.*

31. A provision in a will creating a trust that flowers be placed on graves "once in a while" is void for uncertainty. *Id.*

32. A clause in a will, that the testator would like his estate kept in a certain place, and as it was at his death, is but the expression of a desire, and does not impose any duty to respect it. *Id.*

> See ACCOUNTING; ADMINISTRATOR WITH WILL ANNEXED; ANNUITIES; CHARITABLE BEQUESTS; DOWER; ESTATES; EXECUTORS AND ADMINISTRATORS; LACHES; LEGACY; PLEADING AND PRACTICE; POWERS; REMAINDERS; WIDOW; WORDS AND PHRASES.
>
> **See Editorial Note, "Transactions Between Trustee and Cestui que Trust,"** 585

UNDUE INFLUENCE.

1. To establish undue influence, the testator's free agency and independence must be overcome, and some domination or control exercised over his mind must have constrained him to do, contrary to his will, what he was unable to refuse, or too weak to resist. *Appeal of Turner,* 155

2. Neither mere kindness of treatment by a legatee towards a testator, nor moderate and reasonable solicitation, amount to undue influence, when yielded to intelligently, from a sense of duty, and without restraint. *Id.*

3. Suggestion of confidential relations between testator and M. and his wife,—the latter a sister of testator,—should not be made in instructions to the jury on the question of undue influence, the evidence being that testator had no confidential relations with any one; that he was exceptionally self-willed down to and including the time he made his will; that he did his own thinking, and on the occasion of making the will expressed fully the reasons for his conduct; that he had lived alone for many years, except a short period of unsatisfactory association with two of his children; that he was at the house of M. when the will was made, without solicitation or influence on their part; that he was taken sick while on an ordinary visit to his sister, where it was more natural to go than elsewhere, as she lived on their father's old homestead, where she had been his associate more recently than any other member of their family; and that shortly after being taken sick he sent M. to get B. to draw some papers for him, and instructed him (B.) as to drawing the will. *Fox v. Martin,* 185

4. It is no evidence that the testator's sister prejudiced his mind against his daughter, that she advised him to send the daughter away

if he could not get along with her, and that she did not encourage
the daughter's presence when he was sick; he having endeavored
to live with his daughter and her children, and being so annoyed
by them that he had to send them away; and the daughter having
never afterwards visited him, though living in the neighborhood,
till he was on his death-bed; and the sister not having told the
daughter that testator was not in condition to see her till she had
communicated with him, and he not having afterwards inquired
for her; and he having, after providing for one of his children,
said that it made little difference what he gave the others, as they
would not be satisfied till it was all wasted. *Id.*

5. Secrecy in the making of a will does not raise an inference of undue
influence, testator's mind not being weak or susceptible to undue
influence. *Id.*

6. The fact that some of the relatives of the testator were needy is
of itself entitled to little weight in determining whether undue
influence was exercised over the testator, where he had ignored
them in his will. *Stevens* v. *Leonard,* 369

See EVIDENCE; PLEADING AND PRACTICE; TESTAMENTARY CA-
PACITY.

VESTING.

1. Under a will giving money in trust to pay the income to a niece for
life, and on her death to pay and divide the principal to and
among her children " and to their lawful representatives, forever," the issue of any child then dead to take his parent's share,
the gift to the children will not vest if they die before their mother,
leaving no issue. *Clark* v. *Cammann,* 72

See LEGACY; PERPETUITIES; REMAINDER.
See **Editorial Note, "Vesting,"** 79

WAIVER.
See WIDOW.

WIDOW.

1. Where the widow fails, until discharged as administratrix, to apply
under the statute for a necessary allowance out of the estate for
support during twelve months after her husband's death, she waives
all claim thereto. *Zunkel* v. *Colson,* 303

2. A widow's claim to an allowance for support pending administration abates with her death. *Id.*

3. The fact that testator's widow, entitled to the income of his estate
for life, failed to claim the income during administration, until
after approval of the executor's accounts, including such income
as turned over to the trustees under the will, did not constitute
a waiver of her right thereto, since the order approving the account merely found that a certain sum had been paid over to the
trustees. *Dickinson* v. *Henderson,* 359

4. Where a widow was entitled to the income from her husband's estate

for life, and the income arising during administration was paid over to the trustee by the executors, the trustee was authorized to pay such income to the widow. *Id.*

5. Though no formal order was made on the hearing of a widow's petition for an allowance for support, yet where the executor's final account, approved by the probate judge, showed that a certain sum had been paid therefor, such sum constituted a payment from testator's estate, and not from the widow's estate under the will. *Id.*

6. Under a will giving testator's wife the income of his estate for life, subject to certain trusts, and appointing trustees to collect the income of the estate and to pay to the widow all net income collected, keeping the principal, etc., invested during the widow's life, she was only entitled to the income after payment of necessary expenses incurred in caring for the estate. *Id.*

See ELECTION; ESTATES; GUARDIAN AND WARD; TRUSTS AND TRUSTEES.

WILLS.

1. Under statute of wills, requiring a will to be attested in the presence of the testator by two witnesses, who are present and see the testator sign the will, or to whom he acknowledges it to be his will, it is not essential that the testator sign first, if the signature and attestation be parts of the same transaction. *Gibson* v. *Nelson,* 67

2. Where a testatrix resided in New York, but was temporarily settled in Saxony when she executed her will, it will be interpreted according to the laws of New York, her domicile. *New York Life Ins. and T. Co.* v. *Viele,* 197

3. The general rule is that one who receives and retains property and benefits under a will thereby recognizes its validity, and is estopped to deny or contest it; but this rule does not apply where such person acted in ignorance of the facts showing invalidity, and of her rights in the premises. *Medill* v. *Snyder,* 216

4. In such case if, when a legatee learns the facts of invalidity as to her rights, she returns or offers to return what has been received under the will, she may institute a proceeding to set the will aside, and assert her rights in the estate under the law. *Id.*

5. A testator must actually have seen, or been in a position to see, not only the witnesses, but the paper writing itself, at the time the witnesses signed it. *Burney* v. *Allen,* 281

6. In the execution of a will, it is not necessary, in the absence of statutory requirement, for the testator to request the witnesses to sign. Such request may be made by any person, so long as the testator acquiesces or approves it, or by his conduct such acquiescence or approval can be implied. *Id.*

7. A will executed by a single woman is revoked by her subsequent marriage, at least to the extent it would operate to exclude her husband from his right as tenant by curtesy in any lands of which

that it was revoked by a subsequent will, which has been lost, the burden is on the contestants to show the due and proper execution of the subsequent will, and also that it expressly revoked the will in contest, or was substantially inconsistent therewith. *Muller* v. *Muller*, 653

24. After proof that the subsequent will is lost, its contents may be established by parol testimony, and the declarations of the testator are competent to show that it was inconsistent with the will in contest. *Id.*

25. Where the execution of a will is proved by a subscribing witness, who knows that such instrument was declared by testatrix to be her will, but, from haste and inattention to details, cannot state whether he saw her sign the same or acknowledge her signature thereto, the proper statutory formalities of execution may be presumed, in the absence of any evidence to the contrary, or that would excite suspicion of fraud and concealment. *In re Henne's Estate*, 716

26. Evidence of the proof of execution of the will in this case considered, and held to support the findings of the trial court that the same was properly subscribed and attested. *Id.*

27. The case of *In re Ludwig's Estate* ([Minn.] 81 N. W. 758), considered and distinguished. *Id.*

WITNESS.

See APPEAL; EVIDENCE.

WORDS AND PHRASES.

1. In a will creating a remainder in case a life tenant "dies without issue" the words "dies without issue" mean if the life tenant dies without having had issue. *Field* v. *Peeples*, 1

2. The term "money," in a gift to testatrix's husband for life, and thereafter over to another, of "all the money that may be in the hands of my said husband as trustee for me at my decease," includes a debt to him as trustee for money of the trust fund which he has loaned out. *Dillard* v. *Dillard*, 52

3. Testatrix, whose domicile was in New York, in 1855, went to live with married daughter in Saxony, where she executed her will in 1878, bequeathing a portion of her estate on her daughter's death to her daughter's "then living lawful issue," if any; otherwise, to testatrix's grandchildren. No reference was otherwise made to an adopted child of her daughter, who was then forty years of age, and had no living issue. This child had been legally adopted in

1873, by the daughter and her husband, under the laws of Saxony, and after her mother's death claimed under the will as "lawful issue." *Held*, that such term referred alone to her daughter's off-spring, and hence did not include children by adoption. *New York Life Ins. and T. Co.* v. *Viele*, 197

4. A bequest was of a sum to the legatee for life, and at his death to his heirs, if he have any, but, should he die without issue, remainder over to his brother. *Held*, that "heirs" meant "heirs of the body." *Snider* v. *Snider*, 464

5. The will, by the first item, gave the homestead in trust for the use of testator's wife and his four children, naming them, authorized a sale on the request of a majority of them, or of the survivors of them, provided that the proceeds should go to the wife and four children absolutely, share and share alike; but, if the wife or any of said children should be deceased at his death, or when the sale was made, the share of such one should go to the survivors. The third item gave all the personal estate to the wife and four children, share and share alike. The fourth item gave the income of one-fifth of the real estate, other than the homestead, to his wife for life, and from her death gave the one-fifth part to be divided equally between his four children; gave the income of another one-fifth part to his daughter for life, and, from her death, then, as to said one-fifth part, to the children which she might leave; and to each of the three sons it gave one-fifth of the real estate in the same language and for the same uses in which the gift was made to the daughter. The fifth item provided, in case of the death of his said sons or his daughter, or either of them, without surviving issue, he gave the share given to his child so dying to "my surviving child or children" in equal shares. *Held*, that the word "children" did not include testator's grandchildren, and that, where one of his children died, leaving issue, and thereafter the mother died without issue, the children of the one dying first did not participate in the share of the one dying thereafter. *In re Steinmetz's Estate*, 467

6. Testator bequeathed one moiety of his estate, both real and personal, after payment of all just claims against his estate, to his "brothers and sisters and their heirs," subject to the life estate of the testator's wife. When the will was executed testator had brothers and sisters living, and nephews and nieces, the issue of deceased brothers and sisters. *Held*, that the words "and their heirs," were words of limitation, applying only to heirs of brothers and sisters living on testator's death, and hence that the nephews and nieces are not entitled to take under the will. *Adams* v. *Jones*, 618

7. "Whilst she remains my widow," 530

See VESTING.

Lightning Source UK Ltd.
Milton Keynes UK
UKHW010319120219
337137UK00004B/404/P